ROGER STEVENSON
NOVEMBER, 1996

A TREASURY OF NORTH AMERICAN FICTION

A TREASURY OF
NORTH AMERICAN FICTION

A COLLECTION FROM
HARPER'S MAGAZINE

GALLERY BOOKS
An Imprint of W. H. Smith Publishers Inc.
112 Madison Avenue
New York City 10016

This volume first published in 1991 by
Reed International Books Limited
Michelin House, 81 Fulham Road, London SW3 6RB

This edition published in 1991 by Gallery Books
an imprint of W. H. Smith Publishers Inc.
112 Madison Avenue, New York 10016

ISBN 0 - 8317 - 4259 - 3

Printed in Great Britain by The Bath Press, Avon.

CONTENTS

THE MAN WHO CORRUPTED HADLEYBURG
  by Mark Twain 7

FAME'S LITTLE DAY *by Sarah Orne Jewett* 33

LOUISA PALLANT *by Henry James* 39

TOP FLOOR BACK *by Zona Gale* 59

PROSPER'S OLD MOTHER *by Bret Harte* 68

LOVE-LETTERS OF FALSTAFF *by James Branch Cabell* 78

THE MONSTER *by Stephen Crane* 84

CRAPY CORNELIA *by Henry James* 118

THE RECKONING *by Edith Wharton* 133

LA TINAJA BONITA *by Owen Wister* 147

THE CHINAGO *by Jack London* 168

A SILHOUETTE *by Rebecca Harding Davis* 176

MRS NOAH'S ARK *by Gelett Burgess* 185

MY COUSIN THE COLONEL *by Thomas Bailey Aldrich* 196

TOM SAWYER, DETECTIVE (PART 1)
  (As told by Huck Finn) by Mark Twain 216

TOM SAWYER, DETECTIVE (PART 2)
  (As told by Huck Finn) by Mark Twain 234

TWO COUNTRIES *by Henry James* 253

OLE 'STRACTED *by Tomas Nelson Page* 287

SISTER PEACHAMS TURN *by Sarah Orne Jewett* 295

THE GREAT MEDICINE-HORSE *by Frederic Remington* 300

A FABLE FOR YOUTHS *by Alice Duer* 306

THE COCK LANE GHOST *by Howard Pyle*...............................308

THE SPORT OF FORTUNE *by Melville Davisson Post*............320

THE MOVING FINGER by Edith Wharton...............................329

THE FROG THAT PLAYED THE TROMBONE
    by Brander Matthews................................339

JESSEKIAH BROWN'S COURTSHIP
    by Ruth McEnry Stuart...........................346

SILENCE *by Mary E. Wilkins*...............................355

THE PROMISED LAND *by Owen Wister*...............................373

THE RECOVERY *by Edith Wharton*...............................389

A THANKSGIVING BREAKFAST
    by Harriet Prescott Spofford...............................399

A DESERTION *by Stephen Crane*...............................410

THE BEDQUILT *by Dorothy Canfield*...............................412

A PAIR OF PATIENT LOVERS *by W.D. Howells*.........419

HOPSON'S CHOICE *by Rose Terry Cooke*...............................439

FLUTE AND VIOLIN *by James Lane Allen*...............................449

THE LITTLE MAID AT THE DOOR *by Mary E. Wilkins*.........471

GIFTS OF OBLIVION *by Dorothy Canfield*...............................482

TALKING OF PRESENTIMENTS *by W.D. Howells*...............................492

JULIA BRIDE (PART 1) *by Henry James*...............................498

JULIA BRIDE (PART 2) *by Henry James*...............................512

LITTLE BIG HORN MEDICINE *by Owen Wister*...............................521

THE HOUSEWIFE *by James Branch Cabell*...............................536

THE MAN WHO CORRUPTED HADLEYBURG

by Mark Twain

I.

IT was many years ago. Hadleyburg was the most honest and upright town in all the region round about. It had kept that reputation unsmirched during three generations, and was prouder of it than of any other of its possessions. It was so proud of it, and so anxious to insure its perpetuation, that it began to teach the principles of honest dealing to its babies in the cradle, and made the like teachings the staple of their culture thenceforward through all the years devoted to their education. Also, throughout the formative years temptations were kept out of the way of the young people, so that their honesty could have every chance to harden and solidify, and become a part of their very bone. The neighboring towns were jealous of this honorable supremacy, and affected to sneer at Hadleyburg's pride in it and call it vanity; but all the same they were obliged to acknowledge that Hadleyburg was in reality an incorruptible town; and if pressed they would also acknowledge that the mere fact that a young man hailed from Hadleyburg was all the recommendation he needed when he went forth from his natal town to seek for responsible employment.

But at last, in the drift of time, Hadleyburg had the ill luck to offend a passing stranger—possibly without knowing it, certainly without caring, for Hadleyburg was sufficient unto itself, and cared not a rap for strangers or their opinions. Still, it would have been well to make an exception in this one's case, for he was a bitter man and revengeful. All through his wanderings during a whole year he kept his injury in mind, and gave all his leisure moments to trying to invent a compensating satisfaction for it. He contrived many plans, and all of them were good, but none of them was quite sweeping enough; the poorest of them would hurt a great many individuals, but what he wanted was a plan which would comprehend the entire town, and not let so much as one person escape unhurt. At last he had a fortunate idea, and when it fell into his brain it lit up his whole head with an evil joy. He began to form a plan at once, saying to himself, "That is the thing to do—I will corrupt the town."

Six months later he went to Hadleyburg, and arrived in a buggy at the house of the old cashier of the bank about ten at night. He got a sack out of the buggy, shouldered it, and staggered with it through the cottage yard, and knocked at the door. A woman's voice said "Come in," and he entered, and set his sack behind the stove in the parlor, saying politely to the old lady who sat reading the *Missionary Herald* by the lamp:

"Pray keep your seat, madam, I will not disturb you. There—now it is pretty well concealed; one would hardly know it was there. Can I see your husband a moment, madam?"

No, he was gone to Brixton, and might not return before morning.

"Very well, madam, it is no matter. I merely wanted to leave that sack in his care, to be delivered to the rightful owner when he shall be found. I am a stranger; he does not know me; I am merely passing through the town tonight to discharge a matter which has been long in my mind. My errand is now completed, and I go pleased and a little proud, and you will never see me again. There is a paper attached to the sack which will explain everything. Good-night, madam."

The old lady was afraid of the mysterious big stranger, and was glad to see him go. But her curiosity was roused, and she went straight to the sack and brought away the paper. It began as follows:

"To be Published; or, the right man sought out by private inquiry — either will answer. This sack contains gold coin weighing a hundred and sixty pounds four ounces—"

"Mercy on us, and the door not locked!"

Mrs. Richards flew to it all in a tremble and locked it, then pulled down the window-shades and stood frightened, worried, and wondering if there was anything else she could do toward making herself and the money more safe. She listened awhile for burglars, then surrendered to curiosity and went back to the lamp and finished reading the paper:

"I am a foreigner, and am presently going back to my own country, to remain there permanently. I am grateful to America for what I have received at her hands during my long stay under her flag; and to one of her citizens—a citizen of Hadleyburg—I am especially grateful for a great kindness done me a year or two ago. Two great kindnesses, in fact. I will explain. I was a gambler. I say I *was*. I was a ruined gambler. I arrived in this village at night, hungry and without a penny. I asked for help—in the dark; I was ashamed to beg in the light. I begged of the right man. He gave me twenty dollars—that is to say, he gave me life, as I considered it. He also gave me fortune; for out of that money I have made myself rich at the gaming-table. And finally, a remark which he made to me has remained with me to this day, and has at last conquered me; and in conquering has saved the remnant of my morals: I shall gamble no more. Now I have no idea who that man was, but I want him found, and I want him to have this money, to give away, throw away, or keep, as he pleases. It is merely my way of testifying my gratitude to him. If I could stay, I would find him myself; but no matter, he will be found. This is an honest town, an incorruptible town, and I know I can trust it without fear. This man can be identified by the remark which he made to me; I feel persuaded that he will remember it.

"And now my plan is this:

"IT LIT UP HIS WHOLE HEAD WITH AN EVIL JOY."

If you prefer to conduct the inquiry privately, do so. Tell the contents of this present writing to any one who is likely to be the right man. If he shall answer, 'I am the man; the remark I made was so-and-so,' apply the test — to wit: open the sack, and in it you will find a sealed envelope containing that remark. If the remark mentioned by the candidate tallies with it, give him the money, and ask no further questions, for he is certainly the right man.

"But if you shall prefer a public inquiry, then publish this present writing in the local paper—with these instructions added, to wit: Thirty days from now, let the candidate appear at the town-hall at eight in the evening (Friday), and hand his remark, in a sealed envelope, to the Rev. Mr. Burgess (if he will be kind enough to act); and let Mr. Burgess there and then destroy the seals of the sack, open it, and see if the remark is correct; if correct, let the money be delivered, with my sincere gratitude, to my benefactor thus identified."

Mrs. Richards sat down, gently quivering with excitement, and was soon lost in thinkings—after this pattern: "What a strange thing it is!.... And what a fortune for that kind man who set his bread afloat upon the waters!.... If it had only been my husband that did it!—for we are so poor, so old and poor!.... " Then, with a sigh —"But it was not my Edward; no, it was not he that gave a stranger twenty dollars. It is a pity too; I see it now...." Then, with a shudder—"But it is *gambler's*

"BUT IT WAS NOT MY EDWARD."

money! the wages of sin; we couldn't take it; we couldn't touch it. I don't like to be near it; it seems a defilement." She moved to a farther chair.... "I wish Edward would come, and take it to the bank; a burglar might come at any moment; it is dreadful to be here all alone with it."

At eleven Mr. Richards arrived, and

while his wife was saying, "I am *so* glad you've come!" he was saying, "I'm so tired—tired clear out; it is dreadful to be poor, and have to make these dismal journeys at my time of life. Always at the grind, grind, grind, on a salary—another man's slave, and he sitting at home in his slippers, rich and comfortable."

"I am so sorry for you, Edward, you know that; but be comforted; we have our livelihood; we have our good name—"

"Yes, Mary, and that is everything. Don't mind my talk—it's just a moment's irritation and doesn't mean anything. Kiss me—there, it's all gone now, and I am not complaining any more. What have you been getting? What's in the sack?"

Then his wife told him the great secret. It dazed him for a moment; then he said: "It weighs a hundred and sixty pounds? Why, Mary, it's for-ty thou-sand dollars —think of it—a whole fortune! Not ten men in this village are worth that much. Give me the paper."

He skimmed through it and said:

"Isn't it an adventure! Why, it's a romance; it's like the impossible things one reads about in books, and never sees in life." He was well stirred up now; cheerful, even gleeful. He tapped his old wife on the cheek, and said, humorously, "Why, we're rich, Mary, rich; all we've got to do is to bury the money and burn the papers. If the gambler ever comes to inquire, we'll merely look coldly upon him and say: 'What is this nonsense you are talking? We have never heard of you and your sack of gold before;' and then he would look foolish, and—"

"And in the mean time, while you are running on with your jokes, the money is still here, and it is fast getting along toward burglar-time."

"True. Very well, what shall we do— make the inquiry private? No, not that; it would spoil the romance. The public method is better. Think what a noise it will make! And it will make all the other towns jealous; for no stranger would trust such a thing to any town but Hadleyburg, and they know it. It's a great card for us. I must get to the printing-office now, or I shall be too late."

"But stop—stop—don't leave me here alone with it, Edward!"

But he was gone. For only a little while, however. Not far from his own house he met the editor-proprietor of the paper, and gave him the document, and said, "Here is a good thing for you, Cox —put it in."

"It may be too late, Mr. Richards, but I'll see."

At home again he and his wife sat down to talk the charming mystery over; they were in no condition for sleep. The first question was, Who could the citizen have been who gave the stranger the twenty dollars? It seemed a simple one; both answered it in the same breath—

"Barclay Goodson."

"Yes," said Richards, "he could have done it, and it would have been like him, but there's not another in the town."

"Everybody will grant that, Edward —grant it privately, anyway. For six months, now, the village has been its own proper self once more—honest, narrow, self-righteous, and stingy."

"It is what he always called it, to the day of his death—said it right out publicly, too."

"Yes, and he was hated for it."

"Oh, of course; but he didn't care. I reckon he was the best-hated man among us, except the Reverend Burgess."

"Well, Burgess deserves it—he will never get another congregation here. Mean as the town is, it knows how to estimate *him*. Edward, doesn't it seem odd that the stranger should appoint Burgess to deliver the money?"

"Well, yes—it does. That is—that is—"

"Why so much that-*is*-ing? Would *you* select him?"

"Mary, maybe the stranger knows him better than this village does."

"Much *that* would help Burgess!"

The husband seemed perplexed for an answer; the wife kept a steady eye upon him, and waited. Finally Richards said, with the hesitancy of one who is making a statement which is likely to encounter doubt,

"Mary, Burgess is not a bad man."

His wife was certainly surprised.

"Nonsense!" she exclaimed.

"He is not a bad man. I know. The whole of his unpopularity had its foundation in that one thing—the thing that made so much noise."

"That 'one thing,' indeed! As if that 'one thing' wasn't enough, all by itself."

"Plenty. Plenty. Only he wasn't guilty of it."

"GOODSON LOOKED HIM OVER."

"How you talk!. Not guilty of it! Everybody knows he *was* guilty."

"Mary, I give you my word—he was innocent."

"I can't believe it, and I don't. How do you know?"

"It is a confession. I am ashamed, but I will make it. I was the only man who knew he was innocent. I could have saved him, and—and—well, you know how the town was wrought up—I hadn't the pluck to do it. It would have turned everybody against me. I felt mean, ever so mean; but I didn't dare; I hadn't the manliness to face that."

Mary looked troubled, and for a while was silent. Then she said, stammeringly:

"I—I don't think it would have done for you to—to— One mustn't—er—public opinion—one has to be so careful— so—" It was a difficult road, and she got mired; but after a little she got started again. "It was a great pity, but— Why, we couldn't afford it, Edward—we couldn't indeed. Oh, I wouldn't have had you do it for anything!"

"It would have lost us the good-will of so many people, Mary; and then—and then—"

"What troubles me now is, what *he* thinks of us, Edward."

"He? *He* doesn't suspect that I could have saved him."

"Oh," exclaimed the wife, in a tone of relief, "I am glad of that. As long as he doesn't know that you could have saved him, he he—well, that makes it a great deal better. Why, I might have known he didn't know, because he is always trying to be friendly with us, as little encouragement as we give him. More

than once people have twitted me with
it. There's the Wilsons, and the Wil-
coxes, and the Harknesses, they take a
mean pleasure in saying, ' *Your friend*
Burgess,' because they know it pesters
me. I wish he wouldn't persist in liking
us so; I can't think why he keeps it up."

"I can explain it. It's another confession. When the thing was new and hot,
and the town made a plan to ride him on
a rail, my conscience hurt me so that I
couldn't stand it, and I went privately
and gave him notice, and he got out of
the town and staid out till it was safe
to come back."

"Edward! If the town had found it
out—"

"*Don't!* It scares me yet, to think of
it. I repented of it the minute it was
done; and I was even afraid to tell you,
lest your face might betray it to somebody.
I didn't sleep any that night, for worrying. But after a few days I saw that no
one was going to suspect me, and after
that I got to feeling glad I did it. And I
feel glad yet, Mary—glad through and
through."

"So do I, now, for it would have been
a dreadful way to treat him. Yes, I'm
glad; for really you did owe him that,
you know. But, Edward, suppose it
should come out yet, some day!"

"It won't."

"Why?"

"Because everybody thinks it was
Goodson."

"Of course they would!"

"Certainly. And of course *he* didn't
care. They persuaded poor old Sawlsberry to go and charge it on him, and he
went blustering over there and did it.
Goodson looked him over, like as if he
was hunting for a place on him that he
could despise the most, then he says, ' So
you are the Committee of Inquiry, are
you?' Sawlsberry said that was about
what he was. ' Hm. Do they require
particulars, or do you reckon a kind of a
general answer will do?' ' If they require particulars, I will come back, Mr.
Goodson; I will take the general answer
first.' ' Very well, then, tell them to go
to hell — I reckon that's general enough.
And I'll give you some advice, Sawlsberry: when you come back for the particulars, fetch a basket to carry the relics
of yourself home in.' "

"Just like Goodson; it's got all the
marks. He had only one vanity ; he

thought he could give advice better than
any other person."

"It settled the business, and saved us,
Mary. The subject was dropped."

"Bless you, I'm not doubting *that*."

Then they took up the gold-sack mystery again, with strong interest. Soon the
conversation began to suffer breaks—in-
terruptions caused by absorbed thinkings.
The breaks grew more and more frequent.
At last Richards lost himself wholly in
thought. He sat long, gazing vacantly
at the floor, and by-and-by he began to
punctuate his thoughts with little nervous
movements of his hands that seemed to
indicate vexation. Meantime his wife too
had relapsed into a thoughtful silence,
and her movements were beginning to
show a troubled discomfort. Finally
Richards got up and strode aimlessly
about the room, ploughing his hands
through his hair, much as a somnambu-
list might do who was having a bad dream.
Then he seemed to arrive at a definite
purpose; and without a word he put on
his hat and passed quickly out of the
house. His wife sat brooding, with a
drawn face, and did not seem to be aware
that she was alone. Now and then she
murmured, "Lead us not into t.... but
—but—we are so poor, so poor!.... Lead
us not into.... Ah, who would be hurt by
it?—and no one would ever know....
Lead us...." The voice died out in mum-
blings. After a little she glanced up and
muttered in a half-frightened, half-glad
way—

"He is gone! But, oh dear, he may be
too late—too late.... Maybe not—maybe
there is still time." She rose and stood
thinking, nervously clasping and unclasping her hands. A slight shudder
shook her frame, and she said, out of a
dry throat, "God forgive me—it's awful
to think such things — but. . . . Lord,
how we are made—how strangely we are
made!"

She turned the light low, and slipped
stealthily over and kneeled down by the
sack and felt of its ridgy sides with her
hands, and fondled them lovingly; and
there was a gloating light in her poor
old eyes. She fell into fits of absence;
and came half out of them at times to
mutter, "If we had only waited!—oh, if
we had only waited a little, and not been
in such a hurry!"

Meantime Cox had gone home from
his office and told his wife all about the

strange thing that had happened, and they had talked it over eagerly, and guessed that the late Goodson was the only man in the town who could have helped a suffering stranger with so noble a sum as twenty dollars. Then there was a pause, and the two became thoughtful and silent. And by-and-by nervous and fidgety. At last the wife said, as if to herself,

"Nobody knows this secret but the Richardses....and us....nobody."

The husband came out of his thinkings with a slight start, and gazed wistfully at his wife, whose face was become very pale; then he hesitatingly rose, and glanced furtively at his hat, then at his wife—a sort of mute inquiry. Mrs. Cox swallowed once or twice, with her hand at her throat, then in place of speech she nodded her head. In a moment she was alone, and mumbling to herself.

And now Richards and Cox were hurrying through the deserted streets, from opposite directions. They met, panting, at the foot of the printing-office stairs; by the night-light there they read each other's face. Cox whispered,

"Nobody knows about this but us?"

The whispered answer was,

"Not a soul—on honor, not a soul!"

"If it isn't too late to—"

The men were starting up stairs; at this moment they were overtaken by a boy, and Cox asked,

"Is that you, Johnny?"

"Yes, sir."

"You needn't ship the early mail—nor *any* mail; wait till I tell you."

"It's already gone, sir."

"*Gone?*" It had the sound of an unspeakable disappointment in it.

"Yes, sir. Time-table for Brixton and all the towns beyond changed to-day, sir —had to get the papers in twenty minutes earlier than common. I had to rush; if I had been two minutes later—"

The men turned and walked slowly away, not waiting to hear the rest. Neither of them spoke during ten minutes; then Cox said, in a vexed tone,

"What possessed you to be in such a hurry, *I* can't make out."

The answer was humble enough:

"I see it now, but somehow I never thought, you know, until it was too late. But the next time—"

"Next time be hanged! It won't come in a thousand years."

Then the friends separated without a good-night, and dragged themselves home with the gait of mortally stricken men. At their homes their wives sprang up with an eager "Well?"—then saw the answer with their eyes and sank down sorrowing, without waiting for it to come in words. In both houses a discussion followed of a heated sort—a new thing; there had been discussions before, but not heated ones, not ungentle ones. The discussions to-night were a sort of seeming plagiarisms of each other. Mrs. Richards said,

"If you had only waited, Edward—if you had only stopped to think; but no, you must run straight to the printing-office and spread it all over the world."

"It *said* publish it."

"That is nothing; it also said do it privately, if you liked. There, now—is that true, or not?"

"Why, yes—yes, it is true; but when I thought what a stir it would make, and what a compliment it was to Hadleyburg that a stranger should trust it so—"

"Oh, certainly, I know all that; but if you had only stopped to think, you would have seen that you *couldn't* find the right man, because he is in his grave, and hasn't left chick nor child nor relation behind him; and as long as the money went to somebody that awfully needed it, and nobody would be hurt by it, and—and—"

She broke down, crying. Her husband tried to think of some comforting thing to say, and presently came out with this:

"But after all, Mary, it must be for the best—it *must* be; we know that. And we must remember that it was so ordered—"

"Ordered! Oh, everything's *ordered*, when a person has to find some way out when he has been stupid. Just the same, it was *ordered* that the money should come to us in this special way, and it was you that must take it on yourself to go meddling with the designs of Providence —and who gave you the right? It was wicked, that is what it was—just blasphemous presumption, and no more becoming to a meek and humble professor of—"

"But, Mary, you know how we have been trained all our lives long, like the whole village, till it is absolutely second nature to us to stop not a single moment to think when there's an honest thing to be done—"

"Oh, I know it, I know it—it's been one everlasting training and training and training in honesty—honesty shielded, from the very cradle, against every possible temptation, and so it's *artificial* honesty, and weak as water when temptation comes, as we have seen this night. God knows I never had shade nor shadow of a doubt of my petrified and indestructible honesty until now—and now, under the very first big and real temptation, I— Edward, it is my belief that this town's honesty is as rotten as mine is; as rotten as yours is. It is a mean town, a hard, stingy town, and hasn't a virtue in the world but this honesty it is so celebrated for and so conceited about; and so help me, I do believe that if ever the day comes that its honesty falls under great temptation, its grand reputation will go to ruin like a house of cards. There, now, I've made confession, and I feel better; I am a humbug, and I've been one all my life, without knowing it. Let no man call me honest again—I will not have it."

"I— Well, Mary, I feel a good deal as you do; I certainly do. It seems strange, too, so strange. I never could have believed it—never."

A long silence followed; both were sunk in thought. At last the wife looked up and said,

"I know what you are thinking, Edward."

Richards had the embarrassed look of a person who is caught.

"I am ashamed to confess it, Mary, but—"

"It's no matter, Edward, I was thinking the same question myself."

"I hope so. State it."

"You were thinking, if a body could only guess out *what the remark was* that Goodson made to the stranger."

"It's perfectly true. I feel guilty and ashamed. And you?"

"I'm past it. Let us make a pallet here; we've got to stand watch till the bank vault opens in the morning and admits the sack.... Oh, dear, oh, dear— if we hadn't made the mistake!"

The pallet was made, and Mary said:

"The open sesame—what could it have been? I do wonder what that remark could have been? But come; we will get to bed now."

"And sleep?"

"No; think."

"Yes, think."

By this time the Coxes too had completed their spat and their reconciliation, and were turning in—to think, to think, and toss, and fret, and worry over what the remark could possibly have been which Goodson made to the stranded derelict: that golden remark; that remark worth forty thousand dollars, cash.

The reason that the village telegraph-office was open later than usual that night was this: The foreman of Cox's paper was the local representative of the Associated Press. One might say its honorary representative, for it wasn't four times a year that he could furnish thirty words that would be accepted. But this time it was different. His despatch stating what he had caught got an instant answer:

"*Send the whole thing—all the details —twelve hundred words.*"

A colossal order! The foreman filled the bill; and he was the proudest man in the State. By breakfast-time the next morning the name of Hadleyburg the Incorruptible was on every lip in America, from Montreal to the Gulf, from the glaciers of Alaska to the orange-groves of Florida; and millions and millions of people were discussing the stranger and his money-sack, and wondering if the right man would be found, and hoping some more news about the matter would come soon—right away.

II.

Hadleyburg village woke up world-celebrated — astonished — happy — vain. Vain beyond imagination. Its nineteen principal citizens and their wives went about shaking hands with each other, and beaming, and smiling, and congratulating, and saying *this* thing adds a new word to the dictionary — Hadleyburg, synonym for *incorruptible*— destined to live in dictionaries forever! And the minor and unimportant citizens and their wives went around acting in much the same way. Everybody ran to the bank to see the gold-sack ; and before noon grieved and envious crowds began to flock in from Brixton and all neighboring towns; and that afternoon and next day reporters began to arrive from everywhere to verify the sack and its history and write the whole thing up anew, and make dashing free-hand pictures of the sack, and of Richards's house, and the bank, and the Presbyterian church, and the Baptist church, and the public square, and the town-hall where the test would be applied and the money delivered; and damnable portraits of the Richardses, and Pinkerton the banker, and Cox, and the foreman, and Reverend Burgess, and the postmaster—and even of Jack Halliday, who was the loafing, good-natured, no-account, irreverent fisherman, hunter, boys' friend, stray-dogs' friend, typical "Sam Lawson" of the town. The little mean, smirking, oily Pinkerton showed the sack to all comers, and rubbed his sleek palms together pleasantly, and enlarged upon the town's fine old reputation for honesty and upon this wonderful endorsement of it, and hoped and believed that the example would now spread far and wide over the American world, and be epoch-making in the matter of moral regeneration. And so on, and so on.

By the end of a week things had quieted down again; the wild intoxication of pride and joy had sobered to a soft, sweet, silent delight—a sort of deep, nameless, unutterable content. All faces bore a look of peaceful, holy happiness.

Then a change came. It was a gradual change: so gradual that its beginnings were hardly noticed; maybe were not noticed at all, except by Jack Halliday, who always noticed everything; and always made fun of it, too, no matter what it was. He began to throw out chaffing remarks about people not looking quite so happy as they did a day or two ago; and next he claimed that the new aspect was deepening to positive sadness; next, that it was taking on a sick look; and finally he said that everybody was become so moody, thoughtful, and absent-minded that he could rob the meanest man in town of a cent out of the bottom of his breeches pocket and not disturb his revery.

At this stage—or at about this stage —a saying like this was dropped at bedtime—with a sigh, usually—by the head of each of the nineteen principal households:

"Ah, what *could* have been the remark that Goodson made!"

And straightway—with a shudder—came this, from the man's wife:

"Oh, *don't!* What horrible thing are you mulling in your mind? Put it away from you, for God's sake!"

But that question was wrung from those men again the next night—and got the same retort. But weaker.

And the third night the men uttered the question yet again—with anguish, and absently. This time—and the following night—the wives fidgeted feebly, and tried to say something. But didn't.

And the night after that they found their tongues and responded—longingly,

"Oh, if we *could* only guess!"

Halliday's comments grew daily more and, more sparklingly disagreeable and disparaging. He went diligently about, laughing at the town, individually and in mass. But his laugh was the only one left in the village: it fell upon a hollow and mournful vacancy and emptiness. Not even a smile was findable anywhere. Halliday carried a cigar-box around on a tripod, playing that it was a camera, and halted all passers and aimed the thing and said, "Ready!—now look pleasant, please." but not even this capital joke could surprise the dreary faces into any softening.

So three weeks passed—one week was left. It was Saturday evening—after supper. Instead of the aforetime Saturday-evening flutter and bustle and shopping and larking, the streets were empty and desolate. Richards and his old wife sat apart in their little parlor—miserable and thinking. This was become their evening habit now: the life-long habit which had preceded it, of reading, knitting, and contented chat, or receiving or paying neighborly calls, was dead and gone and forgotten, ages ago—two or three weeks ago; nobody talked now, nobody read, nobody visited—the whole village sat at home, sighing, worrying, silent. Trying to guess out that remark.

The postman left a letter. Richards glanced listlessly at the superscription and the post-mark—unfamiliar, both—and tossed the letter on the table and resumed his might-have-beens and his hopeless dull miseries where he had left them off. Two or three hours later his wife got wearily up and was going away to bed without a good-night—custom now—but she stopped near the letter and eyed it awhile with a dead interest, then broke it open, and began to skim it over. Richards, sitting there with his chair tilted back against the wall and his chin between his knees, heard something fall. It was his wife. He sprang to her side, but she cried out:

"Leave me alone, I am too happy. Read the letter—read it!"

He did. He devoured it, his brain

"READY!—NOW LOOK PLEASANT, PLEASE."

reeling. The letter was from a distant State, and it said:

"I am a stranger to you, but no matter: I have something to tell. I have just arrived home from Mexico, and learned about that episode. Of course you do not know who made that remark, but I know, and I am the only person living who does know. It was *Goodson*. I knew him well, many years ago. I passed through your village that very night, and was his guest till the midnight train came along. I overheard him make that remark to the stranger in the dark—it was in Hale Alley. He and I talked of it the rest of the way home, and while smoking in his house. He mentioned many of your villagers in the course of his talk—most of them in a very uncomplimentary way, but two or three favorably: among these latter yourself. I say 'favorably'—nothing stronger. I remember his saying he did not actually *like* any person in the town—not one; but that you—I *think* he said you—am almost sure—had done him a very great

service once, possibly without knowing the full value of it, and he wished he had a fortune, he would leave it to you when he died, and a curse apiece for the rest of the citizens. Now, then, if it was you that did him that service, you are his legitimate heir, and entitled to the sack of gold. I know that I can trust to your honor and honesty, for in a citizen of Hadleyburg these virtues are an unfailing inheritance, and so I am going to reveal to you the remark, well satisfied that if you are not the right man you will seek and find the right one and see that poor Goodson's debt of gratitude for the service referred to is paid. This is the remark: '*You are far from being a bad man: go, and reform.*'
HOWARD L. STEPHENSON."

"Oh, Edward, the money is ours, and I am so grateful, *oh*, so grateful—kiss me, dear, it's forever since we kissed—and we needed it so—the money—and now you are free of Pinkerton and his bank, and nobody's slave any more; it seems to me I could fly for joy."

It was a happy half-hour that the couple spent there on the settee caressing each other; it was the old days come again—days that had begun with their courtship and lasted without a break till the stranger brought the deadly money. By-and-by the wife said:

"Oh, Edward, how lucky it was you did him that grand service, poor Goodson! I never liked him, but I love him now. And it was fine and beautiful of you never to mention it or brag about it." Then, with a touch of reproach, "But you ought to have told me, Edward, you ought to have told your wife, you know."

"Well, I—er—well, Mary, you see—"

"Now stop hemming and hawing, and tell me about it, Edward. I always loved you, and now I'm proud of you. Everybody believes there was only one good generous soul in this village, and now it turns out that you— Edward, why don't you tell me?"

"Well—er—er— Why, Mary, I can't!"

"You can't? Why can't you?"

"You see, he—well, he—he made me promise I wouldn't."

The wife looked him over, and said, very slowly,

"Made—you—promise? Edward, what do you tell me that for?"

"Mary, do you think I would lie?"

She was troubled and silent for a moment, then she laid her hand within his and said:

"No....no. We have wandered far enough from our bearings—God spare us that! In all your life you have never uttered a lie. But now—now that the foundations of things seem to be crumbling from under us, we—we—" She lost her voice for a moment, then said, brokenly, "Lead us not into temptation.... I think you made the promise, Edward. Let it rest so. Let us keep away from that ground. Now—that is all gone by; let us be happy again; it is no time for clouds."

Edward found it something of an effort to comply, for his mind kept wandering—trying to remember what the service was that he had done Goodson.

The couple lay awake the most of the night, Mary happy and busy, Edward busy, but not so happy. Mary was planning what she would do with the money. Edward was trying to recall that service. At first his conscience was sore on account of the lie he had told Mary—if it was a lie. After much reflection—suppose it *was* a lie? What then? Was it such a great matter? Aren't we always *acting* lies? Then why not *tell* them? Look at Mary—look what she had done. While he was hurrying off on his honest errand, what was she doing? Lamenting because the papers hadn't been destroyed and the money kept! Is theft better than lying?

That point lost its sting—the lie dropped into the background and left comfort behind it. The next point came to the front: *had* he rendered that service? Well, here was Goodson's own evidence as reported in Stephenson's letter; there could be no better evidence than that—it was even *proof* that he had rendered it. Of course. So that point was settled.... No, not quite. He recalled with a wince that this unknown Mr. Stephenson was just a trifle unsure as to whether the performer of it was Richards or some other —and, oh dear, he had put Richards on his honor! He must himself decide whither that money must go—and Mr. Stephenson was not doubting that if he was the wrong man he would go honorably and find the right one. Oh, it was odious to put a man in such a situation—ah, why couldn't Stephenson have left out that doubt! What did he want to intrude that for?

Further reflection. How did it happen that *Richards's* name remained in Stephenson's mind as indicating the right man, and not some other man's name? That looked good. Yes, that looked very good. In fact, it went on looking better and better, straight along—until by-and-by it grew into positive *proof*. And then Richards put the matter at once out of his mind, for he had a private instinct that a proof once established is better left so.

He was feeling reasonably comfortable now, but there was still one other detail that kept pushing itself on his notice: of course he had done that service — that was settled: but what *was* that service? He must recall it—he would not go to sleep till he had recalled it; it would make his peace of mind perfect. And so he thought and thought. He thought of a dozen things — possible services, even probable services—but none of them seemed adequate, none of them seemed large enough, none of them seemed worth the money—worth the fortune Goodson had wished he could leave in his will. And besides, he couldn't remember having done them, anyway. Now, then—now, then—what *kind* of a service would it be that would make a man so inordinately grateful? Ah—the saving of his soul! That must be it. Yes, he could remember, now, how he once set himself the task of converting Goodson, and labored at it as much as—he was going to say three months; but upon closer examination it shrunk to a month, then to a week, then to a day, then to nothing. Yes, he remembered, now, and with unwelcome vividness, that Goodson had told him to go to thunder and mind his own business —*he* wasn't hankering to follow Hadleyburg to heaven!

So that solution was a failure—he hadn't saved Goodson's soul. Richards was discouraged. Then after a little came another idea: had he saved Goodson's property? No, that wouldn't do— he hadn't any. His life? That is it! Of course. Why, he might have thought of it before. This time he was on the right track, sure. His imagination-mill was hard at work in a minute, now.

Thereafter during a stretch of two exhausting hours he was busy saving Goodson's life. He saved it in all kinds of difficult and perilous ways. In every case he got it saved satisfactorily up to a certain point; then, just as he was beginning to get well persuaded that it had really happened, a troublesome detail would turn up which made the whole thing impossible. As in the matter of drowning, for instance. In that case he had swum out and tugged Goodson ashore in an unconscious state with a great crowd looking on and applauding, but when he had got it all thought out and was just beginning to remember all about it a whole swarm of disqualifying details arrived on the ground: the town would have known of the circumstance, Mary would have known of it, it would glare like a limelight in his own memory instead of being an inconspicuous service which he had possibly rendered "without knowing its full value." And at this point he remembered that he couldn't swim, anyway.

Ah—*there* was a point which he had been overlooking from the start: it had to be a service which he had rendered "possibly without knowing the full value of it." Why, really, that ought to be an easy hunt—much easier than those others. And sure enough, by-and-by he found it. Goodson, years and years ago, came near marrying a very sweet and pretty girl, named Nancy Hewitt, but in some way or other the match had been broken off; the girl died, Goodson remained a bachelor, and by-and-by became a soured one and a frank despiser of the human species. Soon after the girl's death the village found out, or thought it had found out, that she carried a spoonful of negro blood in her veins. Richards worked at these details a good while, and in the end he thought he remembered things concerning them which must have gotten mislaid in his memory through long neglect. He seemed to dimly remember that it was *he* that found out about the negro blood; that it was he that told the village; that the village told Goodson where they got it; that he thus saved Goodson from marrying the tainted girl; that he had done him this great service "without knowing the full value of it," in fact without knowing that he *was* doing it; but that Goodson knew the value of it, and what a narrow escape he had had, and so went to his grave grateful to his benefactor and wishing he had a fortune to leave him. It was all clear and simple now, and the more he went over it the more luminous and certain it grew; and at last, when he nestled to sleep satisfied and happy, he remembered the whole thing just as if it had been yesterday. In fact, he dimly remembered Goodson's *telling* him his gratitude once. Meantime Mary had spent six thousand dollars on a new house for herself and a pair of slippers for her pastor, and then had fallen peacefully to rest.

That same Saturday evening the postman had delivered a letter to each of the other principal citizens—nineteen letters in all. No two of the envelopes were alike, and no two of the superscriptions were in the same hand, but the letters inside were just like each other in every detail but one. They were exact copies of the letter received by Richards—handwriting and all—and were all signed by Stephenson, but in place of Richards's name each receiver's own name appeared.

All night long eighteen principal citizens did what their caste-brother Richards was doing at the same time—they put in their energies trying to remember what notable service it was that they had unconsciously done Barclay Goodson. In no case was it a holiday job; still they succeeded.

And while they were at this work, which was difficult, their wives put in the night spending the money, which was easy. During that one night the nineteen wives spent an average of seven thousand dollars each out of the forty thousand in the sack—a hundred and thirty-three thousand altogether.

Next day there was a surprise for Jack Halliday. He noticed that the faces of the nineteen chief citizens and their wives bore that expression of peaceful and holy happiness again. He could not understand it, neither was he able to invent any remarks about it that could damage it or disturb it. And so it was his turn to be dissatisfied with life. His private guesses at the reasons for the happiness failed in all instances, upon examination. When he met Mrs. Wilcox and noticed the placid ecstasy in her face, he said to himself, "Her cat has had kittens"—and went and asked the cook; it was not so; the cook had detected the happiness, but did not know the cause. When Halliday found the duplicate ecstasy in the face of "Shadbelly" Billson (village nickname), he was sure some neighbor of Billson's had broken his leg, but inquiry showed that this had not happened. The subdued ecstasy in Gregory Yates's face could mean but one thing—he was a mother-in-law short; it was another mistake. "And Pinkerton—Pinkerton—he has collected ten cents that he thought he was going to lose." And so on, and so on. In some cases the guesses had to remain in doubt, in the others they proved distinct errors. In the end Halliday said to himself, "Anyway it foots up that there's nineteen Hadleyburg families temporarily in heaven; I don't know how it happened; I only know Providence is off duty to-day."

An architect and builder from the next State had lately ventured to set up a small business in this unpromising village, and his sign had now been hanging out a week. Not a customer yet; he was a discouraged man, and sorry he had come. But his weather changed suddenly now. First one and then another chief citizen's wife said to him privately: "Come to my house Monday week—but say nothing about it for the present. We think of building."

He got eleven invitations that day. That night he wrote his daughter and broke off her match with her student. He said she could marry a mile higher than that.

Pinkerton the banker and two or three other well-to-do men planned country-seats—but waited. That kind don't count their chickens until they are hatched.

The Wilsons devised a grand new thing —a fancy-dress ball. They made no actual promises, but told all their acquaintanceship in confidence that they were thinking the matter over and thought they should give it—"and if we do, you will be invited, of course." People were surprised, and said, one to another, "Why, they are crazy, those poor Wilsons, they can't afford it." Several among the nineteen said privately to their husbands, "It is a good idea; we will keep still till their cheap thing is over, then we will give one that will make it sick."

The days drifted along, and the bill of future squanderings rose higher and higher, wilder and wilder, more and more foolish and reckless. It began to look as if every member of the nineteen would not only spend his whole forty thousand dollars before receiving-day, but be actually in debt by the time he got the money. In some cases light-headed people did not stop with planning to spend, they really spent—on credit. They bought land, mortgages, farms, speculative stocks, fine clothes, horses, and various other things, paid down the bonus, and made themselves liable for the rest—at ten days. Presently the sober second thought came, and Halliday noticed that a ghastly anxiety was beginning to show up in a good many faces. Again he was puzzled, and didn't know what to make of it. "The Wilcox kittens aren't dead, for they weren't born; nobody's broken a leg; there's no shrinkage in mother-in-laws; nothing has happened—it is an insolvable mystery."

There was another puzzled man, too— the Rev. Mr. Burgess. For days, wherever he went, people seemed to follow him or to be watching out for him; and if he ever found himself in a retired spot, a member of the nineteen would be sure to appear, thrust an envelope privately into his hand, whisper "To be opened at the town-hall Friday evening," then vanish away like a guilty thing. He was expecting that there might be one claimant for the sack—doubtful, however, Goodson being dead—but it never occurred to him that all this crowd might be claimants. When the great Friday came at last, he found that he had nineteen envelopes.

III.

The town-hall had never looked finer. The platform at the end of it was backed by a showy draping of flags; at intervals along the walls were festoons of flags; the gallery fronts were clothed in flags; the supporting columns were swathed in flags; all this was to impress the stranger, for he would be there in considerable force, and in a large degree he would be connected with the press. The house was full. The 412 fixed seats were occupied; also the 68 extra chairs which had been packed into the aisles; the steps of the platform were occupied; some distinguished strangers were given seats on the platform; at the horseshoe of tables which fenced the front and sides of the platform sat a strong force of special correspondents who had come from everywhere. It was the best-dressed house the town had ever produced. There were some tolerably expensive toilets there, and in several cases the ladies who wore them had the look of being unfamiliar with that kind of clothes. At least the town thought they had that look, but the notion could have arisen from the town's knowledge of the fact that these ladies had never inhabited such clothes before.

The gold-sack stood on a little table at the front of the platform where all the house could see it. The bulk of the house gazed at it with a burning interest, a mouth-watering interest, a wistful and pathetic interest; a minority of nineteen couples gazed at it tenderly, lovingly, proprietarily, and the male half of this minority kept saying over to themselves the moving little impromptu speeches of thankfulness for the audience's applause and congratulations which they were presently going to get up and deliver. Every now and then one of these got a piece of paper out of his vest pocket and privately glanced at it to refresh his memory.

Of course there was a buzz of conversation going on—there always is; but at last when the Rev. Mr. Burgess rose and laid his hand on the sack he could hear his microbes gnaw, the place was so still. He related the curious history of the sack, then went on to speak in warm terms of Hadleyburg's old and well-earned reputation for spotless honesty, and of the town's just pride in this reputation. He said that this reputation was a treasure of priceless value; that under Providence its value had now become inestimably enhanced, for the recent episode had spread this fame far and wide, and thus had focussed the eyes of the American world upon this village, and made its name for all time, as he hoped and believed, a synonym for commercial incorruptibility. (*Applause.*) "And who is to be the guardian of this noble treasure—the community as a whole? No! The responsibility is individual, not communal. From this day forth each and every one of you is in his own person its special guardian, and individually responsible that no harm shall come to it. Do you—does each of you—accept this great trust? [*Tumultuous assent.*] Then all is well. Transmit it to your children and to your children's children. To-day your purity is beyond reproach—see to it that it shall remain so. To-day there is not a person in your community who could be beguiled to touch a penny not his own—see to it that you abide in this grace. [*"We will! we will!"*] This is not the place to make comparisons between ourselves and other communities—some of them ungracious toward us; they have their ways, we have ours; let us be content. [*Applause.*] I am done. Under my hand, my friends, rests a stranger's eloquent recognition of what we are; through him the world will always henceforth know what we are. We do not know who he is, but in your name I utter your gratitude, and ask you to raise your voices in indorsement."

The house rose in a body and made the walls quake with the thunders of its thankfulness for the space of a long minute. Then it sat down, and Mr. Burgess took an envelope out of his pocket. The house held its breath while he slit the envelope open and took from it a slip of paper. He read its contents—slowly and impressively—the audience listening with tranced attention to this magic document, each of whose words stood for an ingot of gold:

"'*The remark which I made to the distressed stranger was this:* "*You are very far from being a bad man; go, and re-*

form.'' Then he continued: "We shall know in a moment now whether the remark here quoted corresponds with the one concealed in the sack; and if that shall prove to be so—and it undoubtedly will—this sack of gold belongs to a fellow-citizen who will henceforth stand before the nation as the symbol of the special virtue which has made our town famous throughout the land—Mr. Billson!"

The house had gotten itself all ready to burst into the proper tornado of applause; but instead of doing it, it seemed stricken with a paralysis; there was a deep hush for a moment or two, then a wave of whispered murmurs swept the place—of about this tenor: "*Billson!* oh, come, this is *too* thin! Twenty dollars to a stranger—or *anybody—Billson!* Tell it to the marines!" And now at this point the house caught its breath all of a sudden in a new access of astonishment, for it discovered that whereas in one part of the hall Deacon Billson was standing up with his head meekly bowed, in another part of it Lawyer Wilson was doing the same. There was a wondering silence now for a while. Everybody was puzzled, and nineteen couples were surprised and indignant.

Billson and Wilson turned and stared at each other. Billson asked, bitingly,

"Why do *you* rise, Mr. Wilson?"

"Because I have a right to. Perhaps you will be good enough to explain to the house why *you* rise?"

"With great pleasure. Because I wrote that paper."

"It is an impudent falsity! I wrote it myself."

It was Burgess's turn to be paralyzed. He stood looking vacantly at first one of the men and then the other, and did not seem to know what to do. The house was stupefied. Lawyer Wilson spoke up, now, and said,

"I ask the Chair to read the name signed to that paper."

That brought the Chair to itself, and it read out the name,

"'John Wharton *Billson.*'"

"There!" shouted Billson, "what have you got to say for yourself, now? And what kind of apology are you going to make to me and to this insulted house for the imposture which you have attempted to play here?"

"No apologies are due, sir; and as for the rest of it, I publicly charge you with pilfering my note from Mr. Burgess and substituting a copy of it signed with your own name. There is no other way by which you could have gotten hold of the test-remark; I alone, of living men, possessed the secret of its wording."

There was likely to be a scandalous state of things if this went on; everybody noticed with distress that the shorthand scribes were scribbling like mad; many people were crying "Chair, Chair! Order! order!" Burgess rapped with his gavel, and said:

"Let us not forget the proprieties due. There has evidently been a mistake somewhere, but surely that is all. If Mr. Wilson gave me an envelope—and I remember now that he did—I still have it."

He took one out of his pocket, opened it, glanced at it, looked surprised and worried, and stood silent a few moments. Then he waved his hand in a wandering and mechanical way, and made an effort or two to say something, then gave it up, despondently. Several voices cried out:

"Read it! read it! What is it?"

So he began in a dazed and sleep-walker fashion:

"'*The remark which I made to the unhappy stranger was this:* "*You are far from being a bad man.* [The house gazed at him, marvelling.] *Go, and reform.*'" [*Murmurs:* "Amazing! what can this mean?"] This one," said the Chair, "is signed Thurlow G. Wilson."

"There!" cried Wilson, "I reckon that settles it! I knew perfectly well my note was purloined."

"Purloined!" retorted Billson. "I'll let you know that neither you nor any man of your kidney must venture to—"

The Chair. "Order, gentlemen, order! Take your seats, both of you, please."

They obeyed, shaking their heads and grumbling angrily. The house was profoundly puzzled; it did not know what to do with this curious emergency. Presently Thompson got up. Thompson was the hatter. He would have liked to be a Nineteener; but such was not for him; his stock of hats was not considerable enough for the position. He said:

"Mr. Chairman, if I may be permitted to make a suggestion, can both of these gentlemen be right? I put it to you, sir, can both have happened to say the very same words to the stranger? It seems to me—"

The tanner got up and interrupted him. The tanner was a disgruntled man; he

believed himself entitled to be a Nineteener, but he couldn't get recognition. It
made him a little unpleasant in his ways
and speech. Said he:

"Sho, *that's* not the point! *That* could
happen—twice in a hundred years—but
not the other thing. *Neither* of them
gave the twenty dollars!" (*A ripple of
applause.*)

Billson. "*I* did!"

Wilson. "*I* did!"

Then each accused the other of pilfering.

The Chair. "Order! Sit down, if you
please—both of you. Neither of the
notes has been out of my possession at
any moment."

A Voice. "Good—that settles *that!*"

The Tanner. "Mr. Chairman, one thing
is now plain: one of these men has been
eavesdropping under the other one's bed,
and filching family secrets. If it is not
unparliamentary to suggest it, I will remark that both are equal to it. [*The
Chair.* "Order! order!"] I withdraw the
remark, sir, and will confine myself to
suggesting that *if* one of them has overheard the other reveal the test-remark to
his wife, we shall catch him now."

A Voice. "How?"

The Tanner. "Easily. The two have
not quoted the remark in exactly the same
words. You would have noticed that, if
there hadn't been a considerable stretch of
time and an exciting quarrel inserted between the two readings."

A Voice. "Name the difference."

The Tanner. "The word *very* is in
Billson's note, and not in the other."

Many Voices. "That's so—he's right!"

The Tanner. "And so, if the Chair
will examine the test-remark in the sack,
we shall know which of these two frauds
—[*The Chair.* "Order!"]—which of these
two adventurers—[*The Chair.* "Order!
order!"]—which of these two gentlemen—[*laughter and applause*]—is entitled to wear the belt as being the first
dishonest blatherskite ever bred in this
town—which he has dishonored, and
which will be a sultry place for him
from now out!" (*Vigorous applause.*)

Many Voices. "Open it!—open the
sack!"

Mr. Burgess made a slit in the sack,
slid his hand in and brought out an envelope. In it were a couple of folded
notes. He said:

"One of these is marked, 'Not to be

examined until all written communications which have been addressed to the
Chair—if any—shall have been read.'
The other is marked '*The Test*.' Allow
me. It is worded—to wit:

"'I do not require that the first half
of the remark which was made to me by
my benefactor shall be quoted with exactness, for it was not striking, and could
be forgotten; but its closing fifteen words
are quite striking, and I think easily re-
memberable; unless *these* shall be accu-
rately reproduced, let the applicant be regarded as an impostor. My benefactor
began by saying he seldom gave advice
to any one, but that it always bore the
hall-mark of high value when he did
give it. Then he said this—and it has
never faded from my memory: "*You are
far from being a bad man—*"'"

Fifty Voices. "That settles it—the
money's Wilson's! Wilson! Wilson!
Speech! Speech!"

People jumped up and crowded around
Wilson, wringing his hand and congratulating fervently—meantime the Chair
was hammering with the gavel and
shouting:

"Order, gentlemen! Order! Order!
Let me finish reading, please." When
quiet was restored, the reading was resumed—as follows:

"'"*Go, and reform—or, mark my
words—some day, for your sins, you
will die and go to hell or Hadleyburg—
TRY AND MAKE IT THE FORMER.*"'"

A ghastly silence followed. First an
angry cloud began to settle darkly upon
the faces of the citizenship; after a pause
the cloud began to rise, and a tickled expression tried to take its place; tried so
hard that it was only kept under with great
and painful difficulty; the reporters, the
Brixtonites, and other strangers bent their
heads down and shielded their faces with
their hands, and managed to hold in by
main strength and heroic courtesy. At
this most inopportune time burst upon
the stillness the roar of a solitary voice—
Jack Halliday's:

"*That's* got the hall-mark on it!"

Then the house let go, strangers and
all. Even Mr. Burgess's gravity broke
down presently, then the audience considered itself officially absolved from all
restraint, and it made the most of its
privilege. It was a good long laugh, and
a tempestuously whole-hearted one, but
it ceased at last—long enough for Mr.

Burgess to try to resume, and for the people to get their eyes partially wiped; then it broke out again; and afterward yet again; then at last Burgess was able to get out these serious words:

"It is useless to try to disguise the fact—we find ourselves in the presence of a matter of grave import. It involves the honor of your town, it strikes at the town's good name. The difference of a single word between the test-remarks offered by Mr. Wilson and Mr. Billson was itself a serious thing, since it indicated that one or the other of these gentlemen had committed a theft—"

The two men were sitting limp, nerveless, crushed; but at these words both were electrified into movement, and started to get up—

"Sit down!" said the Chair, sharply, and they obeyed. "That, as I have said, was a serious thing. And it was—but for only one of them. But the matter has become graver; for the honor of *both* is now in formidable peril. Shall I go even further, and say in inextricable peril? *Both* left out the crucial fifteen words." He paused. During several moments he allowed the pervading stillness to gather and deepen its impressive effects, then added: "There would seem to be but one way whereby this could happen. I ask these gentlemen—Was there *collusion?—agreement?*"

A low murmur sifted through the house; its import was, "He's got them both."

Billson was not used to emergencies; he sat in a helpless collapse. But Wilson was a lawyer. He struggled to his feet, pale and worried, and said:

"I ask the indulgence of the house while I explain this most painful matter. I am sorry to say what I am about to say, since it must inflict irreparable injury upon Mr. Billson, whom I have always esteemed and respected until now, and in whose invulnerability to temptation I entirely believed—as did you all. But for the preservation of my own honor I must speak—and with frankness. I confess with shame—and I now beseech your pardon for it—that I said to the ruined stranger all of the words contained in the test-remark, including the disparaging fifteen. [*Sensation.*] When the late publication was made I recalled them, and I resolved to claim the sack of coin, for by every right I was entitled

to it. Now I will ask you to consider this point, and weigh it well: that stranger's gratitude to me that night knew no bounds; he said himself that he could find no words for it that were adequate, and that if he should ever be able he would repay me a thousandfold. Now, then, I ask you this: could I expect—could I believe—could I even remotely imagine—that, feeling as he did, he would do so ungrateful a thing as to add those quite unnecessary fifteen words to his test?—set a trap for me?—expose me as a slanderer of my own town before my own people assembled in a public hall? It was preposterous; it was impossible. His test would contain only the kindly opening clause of my remark. Of that I had no shadow of doubt. You would have thought as I did. You would not have expected a base betrayal from one whom you had befriended and against whom you had committed no offence. And so, with perfect confidence, perfect trust, I wrote on a piece of paper the opening words—ending with 'Go, and reform,'—and signed it. When I was about to put it in an envelope I was called into my back office, and without thinking I left the paper lying open on my desk." He stopped, turned his head slowly toward Billson, waited a moment, then added: "I ask you to note this: when I returned, a little later, Mr. Billson was retiring by my street door." (*Sensation.*)

In a moment Billson was on his feet and shouting:

"It's a lie! It's an infamous lie!"

The Chair. "Be seated, sir! Mr. Wilson has the floor."

Billson's friends pulled him into his seat and quieted him, and Wilson went on:

"Those are the simple facts. My note was now lying in a different place on the table from where I had left it. I noticed that, but attached no importance to it, thinking a draught had blown it there. That Mr. Billson would read a private paper was a thing which could not occur to me; he was an honorable man, and he would be above that. If you will allow me to say it, I think his extra word '*very*' stands explained; it is attributable to a defect of memory. I was the only man in the world who could furnish here any detail of the test-mark—by *honorable* means. I have finished."

There is nothing in the world like a

persuasive speech to fuddle the mental
apparatus and upset the convictions and
debauch the emotions of an audience not
practised in the tricks and delusions of
oratory. Wilson sat down victorious.
The house submerged him in tides of approving applause; friends swarmed to
him and shook him by the hand and
congratulated him, and Billson was shouted down and not allowed to say a word.
The Chair hammered and hammered with
its gavel, and kept shouting,

"But let us proceed, gentlemen, let us
proceed!"

At last there was a measurable degree
of quiet, and the hatter said,

"But what is there to proceed with,
sir, but to deliver the money?"

Voices. "That's it! That's it! Come
forward, Wilson!"

The Hatter. "I move three cheers for
Mr. Wilson, Symbol of the special virtue
which—"

The cheers burst forth before he could
finish; and in the midst of them—and in
the midst of the clamor of the gavel also
—some enthusiasts mounted Wilson on a
big friend's shoulder and were going to
fetch him in triumph to the platform.
The Chair's voice now rose above the
noise—

"Order! To your places! You forget that there is still a document to be
read." When quiet had been restored he
took up the document, and was going to
read it, but laid it down again, saying,
"I forgot; this is not to be read until all
written communications received by me
have first been read." He took an envelope out of his pocket, removed its enclosure, glanced at it—seemed astonished
—held it out and gazed at it—stared at
it.

Twenty or thirty voices cried out:

"What is it? Read it! read it!"

And he did—slowly, and wondering:

"'The remark which I made to the
stranger—[*Voices.* "Hello! how's this?"]
—was this: "You are far from being a
bad man. [*Voices.* "Great Scott!"] Go,
and reform."' [*Voice.* "Oh, saw my leg
off!"] Signed by Mr. Pinkerton the
banker."

The pandemonium of delight which
turned itself loose now was of a sort to
make the judicious weep. Those whose
withers were unwrung laughed till the
tears ran down; the reporters, in throes
of laughter, set down disordered pot-

hooks which would never in the world
be decipherable; and a sleeping dog
jumped up, scared out of its wits, and
barked itself crazy at the turmoil. All
manner of cries were scattered through
the din: "We're getting rich—*two* Symbols of Incorruptibility!—without counting Billson!" "*Three!*—count Shadbelly
in—we can't have too many!" "All
right—Billson's elected!" "Alas, poor
Wilson—victim of *two* thieves!"

A Powerful Voice. "Silence! The
Chair's fished up something more out of
its pocket."

Voices. "Hurrah! Is it something
fresh? Read it! read! read!"

The Chair (reading). "'The remark
which I made,' etc. 'You are far from
being a bad man. Go,' etc. Signed,
'Gregory Yates.'"

Tornado of Voices. "Four Symbols!"
"'Rah for Yates!" "Fish again!"

The house was in a roaring humor
now, and ready to get all the fun out of
the occasion that might be in it. Several
Nineteeners, looking pale and distressed,
got up and began to work their way
toward the aisles, but a score of shouts
went up:

"The doors, the doors—close the doors;
no Incorruptible shall leave this place!
Sit down, everybody!"

The mandate was obeyed.

"Fish again! Read! read!"

The Chair fished again, and once more
the familiar words began to fall from its
lips—"'You are far from being a bad
man—'"

"Name! name! What's his name?"

"' L. Ingoldsby Sargent.'"

"Five elected! Pile up the Symbols!
Go on, go on!"

"'You are far from being a bad—'"

"Name! name!"

"'Nicholas Whitworth.'"

"Hooray! hooray! it's a symbolical
day!"

Somebody wailed in, and began to sing
this rhyme (leaving out "it's") to the
lovely *Mikado* tune of "When a man's
afraid of a beautiful maid"; the audience
joined in, with joy; then, just in time,
somebody contributed another line—

"And don't you this forget—"

The house roared it out. A third line
was at once furnished—

"Corruptibles far from Hadleyburg are—"

The house roared that one too. As

the last note died, Jack Halliday's voice rose high and clear, freighted with a final line—

"But the Symbols are here, you bet!"

That was sung, with booming enthusiasm. Then the happy house started in at the beginning and sang the four lines through twice, with immense swing and dash, and finished up with a crashing three-times-three and a tiger for "Hadleyburg the Incorruptible and all Symbols of it which we shall find worthy to receive the hall-mark to-night."

Then the shoutings at the Chair began again, all over the place:

"Go on! go on! Read! read some more! Read all you've got!"

"That's it—go on! We are winning eternal celebrity!"

A dozen men got up now and began to protest. They said that this farce was the work of some abandoned joker, and was an insult to the whole community. Without a doubt these signatures were all forgeries—

"Sit down! sit down! Shut up! You are confessing. We'll find *your* names in the lot."

"Mr. Chairman, how many of those envelopes have you got?"

The Chair counted.

"Together with those that have been already examined, there are nineteen."

A storm of derisive applause broke out.

"Perhaps they all contain the secret. I move that you open them all and read every signature that is attached to a note of that sort—and read also the first eight words of the note."

"Second the motion!"

It was put and carried—uproariously. Then poor old Richards got up, and his wife rose and stood at his side. Her head was bent down, so that none might see that she was crying. Her husband gave her his arm, and so supporting her, he began to speak in a quavering voice:

"My friends, you have known us two —Mary and me—all our lives, and I think you have liked us and respected us—"

The Chair interrupted him:

"Allow me. It is quite true—that which you are saying, Mr. Richards; this town *does* know you two; it *does* like you; it *does* respect you; more—it honors you and *loves* you—"

Halliday's voice rang out:

"That's the hall-marked truth, too!

If the Chair is right, let the house speak up and say it. Rise! Now, then—hip! hip! hip!—all together!"

The house rose in mass, faced toward the old couple eagerly, filled the air with a snow-storm of waving handkerchiefs, and delivered the cheers with all its affectionate heart.

The Chair then continued:

"What I was going to say is this: We know your good heart, Mr. Richards, but this is not a time for the exercise of charity toward offenders. [Shouts of "Right! right!"] I see your generous purpose in your face, but I cannot allow you to plead for these men—"

"But I was going to—"

"Please take your seat, Mr. Richards. We must examine the rest of these notes —simple fairness to the men who have already been exposed requires this. As soon as that has been done—I give you my word for this—you shall be heard."

Many Voices. "Right!—the Chair is right—no interruption can be permitted at this stage! Go on!—the names! the names!—according to the terms of the motion!"

The old couple sat reluctantly down, and the husband whispered to the wife, "It is pitifully hard to have to wait; the shame will be greater than ever when they find we were only going to plead for *ourselves.*"

Straightway the jollity broke loose again with the reading of the names.

"'You are far from being a bad man —' Signature, 'Robert J. Titmarsh.'"

"'You are far from being a bad man —' Signature, 'Eliphalet Weeks.'"

"'You are far from being a bad man —' Signature, 'Oscar B. Wilder.'"

At this point the house lit upon the idea of taking the eight words out of the Chairman's hands. He was not unthankful for that. Thenceforward he held up each note in its turn, and waited. The house droned out the eight words in a massed and measured and musical deep volume of sound (with a daringly close resemblance to a well-known church chant)—"'You are f a-r from being a b-a-a-d man.'" Then the Chair said, "Signature, 'Archibald Wilcox.'" And so on, and so on, name after name, and everybody had an increasingly and gloriously good time except the wretched Nineteen. Now and then, when a particularly shining name was called, the house made the Chair wait while it chanted the whole of the test-remark from the beginning to the closing words, "And go to hell or Hadleyburg—try and make it the for-or-m-e-r!" and in these special cases they added a grand and agonized and imposing "A-a-a-men!"

The list dwindled, dwindled, dwindled, poor old Richards keeping tally of the count, wincing when a name resembling his own was pronounced, and waiting in miserable suspense for the time to come when it would be his humiliating privilege to rise with Mary and finish his plea, which he was intending to word thus: ". . . for until now we have never done any wrong thing, but have gone our humble way unreproached. We are very poor, we are old, and have no chick nor child to help us; we were sorely tempted, and we fell. It was my purpose when I got up before to make confession and beg that my name might not be read out in this public place, for it seemed to us that we could not bear it; but I was prevented. It was just; it was our place to suffer with the rest. It has been hard for us. It is the first time we have ever heard our name fall from any one's lips—sullied. Be merciful—for the sake of the better days; make our shame as light to bear as in your charity you can." At this point in his revery Mary nudged him, perceiving that his mind was absent. The house was chanting, " You are f-a-r," etc.

" Be ready," Mary whispered. "Your name comes now; he has read eighteen."

The chant ended.

"Next! next! next!" came volleying from all over the house.

Burgess put his hand into his pocket. The old couple, trembling, began to rise. Burgess fumbled a moment, then said, " I find I have read them all."

Faint with joy and surprise, the couple sank into their seats, and Mary whispered, " Oh, bless God, we are saved!—he has lost ours—I wouldn't give this for a hundred of those sacks!"

The house burst out with its *Mikado* travesty, and sang it three times with ever-increasing enthusiasm, rising to its feet when it reached for the third time the closing line—

" But the Symbols are here, you bet!"

and finishing up with cheers and a tiger for " Hadleyburg purity and our eighteen immortal representatives of it."

Then Wingate, the saddler, got up and proposed cheers " for the cleanest man in town, the one solitary important citizen in it who didn't try to steal that money— Edward Richards."

They were given with great and moving heartiness; then somebody proposed that Richards be elected sole Guardian and Symbol of the now Sacred Hadleyburg Tradition, with power and right to stand up and look the whole sarcastic world in the face."

Passed, by acclamation; then they sang the *Mikado* again, and ended it with,

" And there's *one* Symbol left, you bet!"

There was a pause; then—

A Voice. " Now, then, who's to get the sack?"

The Tanner (with bitter sarcasm). "That's easy. The money has to be divided among the eighteen Incorruptibles. They gave the suffering stranger twenty dollars apiece—and that remark—each in his turn—it took twenty-two minutes for the procession to move past. Staked the stranger—total contribution, $360. All they want is just the loan back—and interest—forty thousand dollars altogether."

Many Voices (derisively). " That's it! Divvy! divvy! Be kind to the poor— don't keep them waiting!"

The Chair. "Order! I now offer the stranger's remaining document. It says: ' If no claimant shall appear [*grand chorus of groans*], I desire that you open the sack and count out the money to the principal citizens of your town, they to take it in trust [*Cries of "Oh! Oh! Oh!"*], and use it in such ways as to them shall seem best for the propagation and preservation of your community's noble reputation for incorruptible honesty [*more cries*]—a reputation to which their names and their efforts will add a new and far-reaching lustre.' [*Enthusiastic outburst of sarcastic applause.*] That seems to be all. No—here is a postscript:

" ' P. S.—CITIZENS OF HADLEYBURG: There *is* no test-remark—nobody made one. [*Great sensation.*] There wasn't any pauper stranger, nor any twenty-dollar contribution, nor any accompanying benediction and compliment—these are all inventions. [*General buzz and hum of astonishment and delight.*] Allow me to tell my story—it will take but a word or two. I passed through your town at a certain time, and received a deep offence which I had not earned. Any other man would have been content to kill one or two of you and call it square, but to me that would have been a trivial revenge, and inadequate; for the dead do not *suffer*. Besides, I could not kill you all—and, anyway, made as I am, even that would not have satisfied me. I wanted to damage every man in the place, and every woman—and not in their bodies or in their estate, but in their vanity—the place where feeble and foolish people are most vulnerable. So I disguised myself, and came back and studied you. You were easy game. You had an old and lofty reputation for honesty, and naturally you were proud of it—it was your treasure of treasures, the very apple of your eye. As soon as I found out that you carefully and vigilantly kept yourselves and your children *out of temptation*, I knew how to proceed. Why, you simple creatures, the weakest of all weak things is a virtue which has not been tested in the fire. I laid a plan, and gathered a list of names. My project was to corrupt Hadleyburg the Incorruptible. My idea was to make liars and thieves of nearly half a hundred smirchless men and women who had never in their lives uttered a lie or stolen a penny. I was afraid of Goodson. He was neither born nor reared in Hadleyburg. I was afraid that if I started to operate my scheme by getting my letter laid before you, you would say to yourselves, "Goodson is the only man among us who would give away twenty dollars to a poor devil" —and then you might not bite at my bait. But Heaven took Goodson; then I knew I was safe, and I set my trap and baited it. It may be that I shall not catch all the men to whom I mailed the pretended test secret, but I shall catch the most of them, if I know Hadleyburg nature. [*Voices.* "Right—he got every last one of them."] I believe they will even steal ostensible *gamble*-money, rather than miss, poor, tempted, and mistrained fellows. I am hoping to eternally and everlastingly squelch your vanity and give Hadleyburg a new renown—one that will *stick*—and spread far. If I have succeeded, open the sack and summon the Committee on Propagation and Preservation of the Hadleyburg Reputation.'"

A Cyclone of Voices. "Open it! Open

it! The Eighteen to the front! Committee on Propagation of the Tradition! Forward—the Incorruptibles!"

The Chair ripped the sack wide, and gathered up a handful of bright, broad, yellow coins, shook them together, then examined them—

"Friends, they are only gilded disks of lead!"

There was a crashing outbreak of delight over this news, and when the noise had subsided, the tanner called out:

"By right of apparent seniority in this business, Mr. Wilson is Chairman of the Committee on Propagation of the Tradition. I suggest that he step forward on behalf of his pals, and receive in trust the money."

A Hundred Voices. "Wilson! Wilson! Wilson! Speech! Speech!"

Wilson (in a voice trembling with anger). "You will allow me to say, and without apologies for my language, *damn* the money!"

A Voice. "Oh, and him a Baptist!"

A Voice. "Seventeen Symbols left! Step up, gentlemen, and assume your trust!"

There was a pause—no response.

The Saddler. "Mr. Chairman, we've got *one* clean man left, anyway, out of the late aristocracy; and he needs money, and deserves it. I move that you appoint Jack Halliday to get up there and auction off that sack of gilt twenty-dollar pieces, and give the result to the right man—the man whom Hadleyburg delights to honor—Edward Richards."

This was received with great enthusiasm, the dog taking a hand again; the saddler started the bids at a dollar, the Brixton folk and Barnum's representative fought hard for it, the people cheered every jump that the bids made, the excitement climbed moment by moment higher and higher, the bidders got on their mettle and grew steadily more and more daring, more and more determined, the jumps went from a dollar up to five, then to ten, then to twenty, then fifty, then to a hundred, then—

At the beginning of the auction Richards whispered in distress to his wife: "Oh, Mary, can we allow it? It—it— you see, it is an honor-reward, a testimonial to purity of character, and—and— can we allow it? Hadn't I better get up and— Oh, Mary, what ought we to do? —what do you think we—" (*Halliday's voice.* "*Fifteen I'm bid!—fifteen for the sack!—twenty!—ah, thanks!—thirty— thanks again! Thirty, thirty, thirty!— do I hear forty?—forty it is! Keep the ball rolling, gentlemen, keep it rolling! —fifty!—thanks, noble Roman!—going at fifty, fifty, fifty!—seventy!—ninety! —splendid!—a hundred!—pile it up, pile it up!—hundred and twenty—forty!— just in time!—hundred and fifty!—TWO hundred!—superb! Do I hear two h— thanks!—two hundred and fifty!—*")

"It is another temptation, Edward—I'm all in a tremble—but, oh, we've escaped *one* temptation, and that ought to warn us, to—   [" *Six did I hear?—thanks!—six fifty, six f—*SEVEN *hundred!*"] And yet, Edward, when you think—nobody susp— [" *Eight hundred dollars!—hurrah!— make it nine!—Mr. Parsons, did I hear you say—thanks!—nine!—this noble sack of virgin lead going at only nine hundred dollars, gilding and all—come! do I hear — a thousand! — gratefully yours!—did some one say eleven?—a sack which is going to be the most celebrated in the whole Uni—*"]   Oh, Edward" (beginning to sob), "we are *so* poor!—but— but—do as you think best—do as you think best."

Edward fell—that is, he sat still; sat with a conscience which was not satisfied, but which was overpowered by circumstances.

Meantime a stranger, who looked like an amateur detective gotten up as an impossible English earl, had been watching the evening's proceedings with manifest interest, and with a contented expression in his face; and he had been privately commenting to himself. He was now soliloquizing somewhat like this: "None of the Eighteen are bidding; that is not satisfactory; I must change that—the dramatic unities require it; they must buy the sack they tried to steal; they must pay a heavy price, too—some of them are rich. And another thing, when I make a mistake in Hadleyburg nature the man that puts that error upon me is entitled to a high honorarium, and some one must pay it. This poor old Richards has brought my judgment to shame; he is an honest man:—I don't understand it, but I acknowledge it. Yes, he saw my deuces-*and* with a straight flush, and by rights the pot is his. And it shall be a jack-pot, too, if I can manage it. He disappointed me, but let that pass."

He was watching the bidding. At a thousand, the market broke; the prices tumbled swiftly. He waited—and still watched. One competitor dropped out; then another, and another. He put in a bid or two, now. When the bids had sunk to ten dollars, he added a five; some one raised him a three; he waited a moment, then flung in a fifty-dollar jump, and the sack was his—at $1282. The house broke out in cheers—then stopped; for he was on his feet, and had lifted his hand. He began to speak.

"I desire to say a word, and ask a favor. I am a speculator in rarities, and I have dealings with persons interested in numismatics all over the world. I can make a profit on this purchase, just as it stands; but there is a way, if I can get your approval, whereby I can make every one of these leaden twenty-dollar pieces worth its face in gold, and perhaps more. Grant me that approval, and I will give part of my gains to your Mr. Richards, whose invulnerable probity you have so justly and so cordially recognized to-night; his share shall be ten thousand dollars, and I will hand him the money to-morrow. [*Great applause from the house.* But the "invulnerable probity" made the Richardses blush prettily; however, it went for modesty, and did no harm.] If you will pass my proposition by a good majority—I would like a two-thirds vote—I will regard that as the town's consent, and that is all I ask. Rarities are always helped by any device which will rouse curiosity and compel remark. Now if I may have your permission to stamp upon the faces of each of these ostensible coins the names of the eighteen gentlemen who—"

Nine-tenths of the audience were on their feet in a moment—dog and all—and the proposition was carried with a whirlwind of approving applause and laughter.

They sat down, and all the Symbols except "Dr." Clay Harkness got up, violently protesting against the proposed outrage, and threatening to—

"I beg you not to threaten me," said the stranger, calmly. "I know my legal rights, and am not accustomed to being frightened at bluster." (*Applause.*) He sat down. "Dr." Harkness saw an opportunity here. He was one of the two very rich men of the place, and Pinkerton was the other. Harkness was proprietor of a mint; that is to say, a popular patent medicine. He was running for the Legislature on one ticket, and Pinkerton on the other. It was a close race and a hot one, and getting hotter every day. Both had strong appetites for money; each had bought a great tract of land, with a purpose: there was going to be a new railway, and each wanted to be in the Legislature and help locate the route to his own advantage; a single vote might make the decision, and with it two or three fortunes. The stake was large, and Harkness was a daring speculator. He was sitting close to the stranger. He leaned over while one or another of the other Symbols was entertaining the house with protests and appeals, and asked, in a whisper,

"What is your price for the sack?"

"Forty thousand dollars."

"I'll give you twenty."

"No."

"Twenty-five."

"No."

"Say thirty."

"The price is forty thousand dollars; not a penny less."

"All right, I'll give it. I will come to the hotel at ten in the morning. I don't want it known; will see you privately."

"Very good." Then the stranger got up and said to the house:

"I find it late. The speeches of these gentlemen are not without merit, not without interest, not without grace; yet if I may be excused I will take my leave. I thank you for the great favor which you have shown me in granting my petition. I ask the Chair to keep the sack for me until to-morrow, and to hand these three five-hundred dollar notes to Mr. Richards." They were passed up to the Chair. "At nine I will call for the sack, and at eleven will deliver the rest of the ten thousand to Mr. Richards in person, at his home. Good-night."

Then he slipped out, and left the audience making a vast noise, which was composed of a mixture of cheers, the *Mikado* song, dog-disapproval, and the chant, "You are f-a-r from being a b-a-a-d man —a-a-a-a-men!"

IV.

At home the Richardses had to endure congratulations and compliments until midnight. Then they were left to themselves. They looked a little sad, and they sat silent and thinking. Finally Mary sighed and said,

"Do you think we are to blame, Edward—*much* to blame?" and her eyes wandered to the accusing triplet of big bank-notes lying on the table, where the congratulators had been gloating over them and reverently fingering them. Edward did not answer at once; then he brought out a sigh and said, hesitatingly:

"We—we couldn't help it, Mary. It —well, it was ordered. *All* things are."

Mary glanced up and looked at him steadily, but he didn't return the look. Presently she said:

"I thought congratulations and praises always tasted good. But—it seems to me, now— Edward?"

"Well?"

"Are you going to stay in the bank?"

"N-no."

"Resign?"

"In the morning—by note."

"It does seem best."

Richards bowed his head in his hands and muttered:

"Before, I was not afraid to let oceans of people's money pour through my hands, but— Mary, I am so tired, so tired—"

"We will go to bed."

At nine in the morning the stranger called for the sack and took it to the hotel in a cab. At ten Harkness had a talk with him privately. The stranger asked for and got five checks on a metropolitan bank—drawn to "Bearer,"—four for $1500 each, and one for $34,000. He put one of the former in his pocket-book, and the remainder, representing $38,500, he put in an envelope, and with these he added a note, which he wrote after Harkness was gone. At eleven he called at the Richards house and knocked. Mrs. Richards peeped through the shutters, then went and received the envelope, and the stranger disappeared without a word. She came back flushed and a little unsteady on her legs, and gasped out:

"I am sure I recognized him! Last night it seemed to me that maybe I had seen him somewhere before."

"He is the man that brought the sack here?"

"I am almost sure of it."

"Then he is the ostensible Stephenson too, and sold every important citizen in this town with his bogus secret. Now if he has sent checks instead of money, we are sold too, after we thought we had escaped. I was beginning to feel fairly comfortable once more, after my night's rest, but the look of that envelope makes me sick. It isn't fat enough; $8500 in even the largest bank-notes makes more bulk than that."

"Edward, why do you object to checks?"

"Checks signed by Stephenson! I am resigned to take the $8500 if it could come in bank-notes—for it does seem that it was so ordered, Mary—but I have never had much courage, and I have not the pluck to try to market a check signed with that disastrous name. It would be a trap. That man tried to catch me; we escaped somehow or other; and now he is trying a new way. If it is checks—"

"Oh, Edward, it is too bad!" and she held up the checks and began to cry.

"Put them in the fire! quick! we mustn't be tempted. It is a trick to make the world laugh at us, along with the rest, and— Give them to me, since you can't do it!" He snatched them and tried to hold his grip till he could get to the stove; but he was human, he was a cashier, and he stopped a moment to make sure of the signature. Then he came near to fainting.

"Fan me, Mary, fan me! They are the same as gold!"

"Oh, how lovely, Edward! Why?"

"Signed by Harkness. What can the mystery of that be, Mary?"

"Edward, do you think—"

"Look here—look at this! Fifteen—fifteen — fifteen — thirty - four. Thirty-eight thousand five hundred! Mary, the sack isn't worth twelve dollars, and Harkness — apparently — has paid about par for it."

"And does it all come to us, do you think—instead of the ten thousand?"

"Why, it looks like it. And the checks are made to 'Bearer,' too."

"Is that good, Edward? What is it for?"

"A hint to collect them at some distant bank, I reckon. Perhaps Harkness doesn't want the matter known. What is that—a note?"

"Yes. It was with the checks."

It was in the "Stephenson" handwriting, but there was no signature. It said:

"I am a disappointed man. Your honesty is beyond the reach of temptation. I had a different idea about it, but I wronged you in that, and I beg pardon, and do it sincerely. I honor you—and that is sincere, too. This town is not worthy to kiss the hem of your garment. Dear sir, I made a square bet with myself that there were nineteen debauchable men in your self-righteous community. I have lost. Take the whole pot, you are entitled to it."

Richards drew a deep sigh, and said:

"It seems written with fire—it burns so. Mary—I am miserable again."

"I, too. Ah, dear, I wish—"

"To think, Mary—he believes in me."

"Oh, don't, Edward—I can't bear it."

"If those beautiful words were deserved, Mary—and God knows I believed I deserved them once—I think I could give the forty thousand dollars for them. And I would put that paper away, as representing more than gold and jewels, and keep it always. But now— We could not live in the shadow of its accusing presence, Mary."

He put it in the fire.

A messenger arrived and delivered an envelope. Richards took from it a note and read it; it was from Burgess.

"You saved me, in a difficult time. I saved you last night. It was at cost of a lie, but I made the sacrifice freely, and out of a grateful heart. None in this village knows so well as I know how brave and good and noble you are. At bottom you cannot respect me, knowing as you do of that matter of which I am accused, and by the general voice condemned; but I beg that you will at least believe that I am a grateful man; it will help me to bear my burden.

|Signed| BURGESS."

"Saved, once more. And on such terms!" He put the note in the fire. "I —I wish I were dead, Mary, I wish I were out of it all."

"Oh, these are bitter, bitter days, Edward. The stabs, through their very generosity, are so deep—and they come so fast!"

Three days before the election each of two thousand voters suddenly found himself in possession of a prized memento—one of the renowned bogus double-eagles. Around one of its faces was stamped these words: "THE REMARK I MADE TO THE POOR STRANGER WAS—" Around the other face was stamped these: "GO, AND REFORM. (SIGNED) PINKERTON." Thus the entire remaining refuse of the renowned joke was emptied upon a single head, and with calamitous effect. It revived the recent vast laugh and concentrated it upon Pinkerton; and Harkness's election was a walk-over.

Within twenty-four hours after the Richardses had received their checks their consciences were quieting down, discouraged; the old couple were learning to reconcile themselves to the sin which they had committed. But they were to learn, now, that a sin takes on new and real terrors when there seems a chance that it is going to be found out. This gives it a fresh and most substantial and important aspect. At church the morning sermon was of the usual pattern; it was the same old things said in the same old way; they had heard them a thousand times and found them innocuous, next to meaningless, and easy to sleep under; but now it was different: the sermon seemed to bristle with accusations; it seemed aimed straight and specially at people who were concealing deadly sins. After church they got away from the mob of congratulators as soon as they could, and hurried homeward, chilled to the bone at they did not know what—vague, shadowy, indefinite fears. And by chance they caught a glimpse of Mr. Burgess as he turned a corner. He paid no attention to their nod of recognition! He hadn't seen it; but they did not know that. What could his conduct mean? It might mean—it might mean —oh, a dozen dreadful things. Was it possible that he knew that Richards could have cleared him of guilt in that bygone time, and had been silently waiting for a chance to even up accounts? At home, in their distress they got to imagining that their servant might have been in the next room listening when Richards revealed the secret to his wife that he knew of Burgess's innocence; next, Richards began to imagine that he had heard the swish of a gown in there at that time; next, he was sure he had heard it. They would call Sarah in, on a pretext, and watch her face: if she had been betraying them to Mr. Burgess, it would show in her manner. They asked her some questions—questions which were so random and incoherent and seemingly purposeless that the girl felt sure that the

old people's minds had been affected by their sudden good fortune; the sharp and watchful gaze which they bent upon her frightened her, and that completed the business. She blushed, she became nervous and confused, and to the old people these were plain signs of guilt—guilt of some fearful sort or other—without doubt she was a spy and a traitor. When they were alone again they began to piece many unrelated things together and get horrible results out of the combination. When things had got about to the worst, Richards was delivered of a sudden gasp, and his wife asked,

"Oh, what is it?—what is it?"

"The note—Burgess's note! Its language was sarcastic, I see it now." He quoted: "'At bottom you cannot respect me, *knowing*, as you do, of *that matter* of which I am accused'—oh, it is perfectly plain, now, God help me! He knows that I know! You see the ingenuity of the phrasing. It was a trap—and like a fool, I walked into it. And Mary—?"

"Oh, it is dreadful—I know what you are going to say—he didn't return your transcript of the pretended test-remark."

"No — kept it to destroy us with. Mary, he has exposed us to some already. I know it—I know it well. I saw it in a dozen faces after church. Ah, he wouldn't answer our nod of recognition—*he* knew what he had been doing!"

In the night the doctor was called. The news went around in the morning that the old couple were rather seriously ill—prostrated by the exhausting excitement growing out of their great windfall, the congratulations, and the late hours, the doctor said. The town was sincerely distressed; for these old people were about all it had left to be proud of, now.

Two days later the news was worse. The old couple were delirious, and were doing strange things. By witness of the nurses, Richards had exhibited checks— for $8500? No—for an amazing sum— $38,500! What could be the explanation of this gigantic piece of luck?

The following day the nurses had more news—and wonderful. They had concluded to hide the checks, lest harm come to them; but when they searched they were gone from under the patient's pillow—vanished away. The patient said:

"Let the pillow alone; what do you want?"

"We thought it best that the checks—"

"You will never see them again—they are destroyed. They came from Satan. I saw the hell-brand on them, and I knew they were sent to betray me to sin." Then he fell to gabbling strange and dreadful things which were not clearly understandable, and which the doctor admonished them to keep to themselves.

Richards was right; the checks were never seen again.

A nurse must have talked in her sleep, for within two days the forbidden gabblings were the property of the town; and they were of a surprising sort. They seemed to indicate that Richards had been a claimant for the sack himself, and that Burgess had concealed that fact and then maliciously betrayed it.

Burgess was taxed with this and stoutly denied it. And he said it was not fair to attach weight to the chatter of a sick old man who was out of his mind. Still, suspicion was in the air, and there was much talk.

After a day or two it was reported that Mrs. Richards's delirious deliveries were getting to be duplicates of her husband's. Suspicion flamed up into conviction, now, and the town's pride in the purity of its one undiscredited important citizen began to dim down and flicker toward extinction.

Six days passed, then came more news. The old couple were dying. Richards's mind cleared in his latest hour, and he sent for Burgess. Burgess said:

"Let the room be cleared. I think he wishes to say something in privacy."

"No!" said Richards; "I want witnesses. I want you all to hear my confession, so that I may die a man, and not a dog. I was clean—artificially—like the rest; and like the rest I fell when temptation came. I signed a lie, and claimed the miserable sack. Mr. Burgess remembered that I had done him a service, and in gratitude (and ignorance) he suppressed my claim and saved me. You know the thing that was charged against Burgess years ago. My testimony, and mine alone, could have cleared him, and I was a coward, and left him to suffer disgrace—"

"No—no—Mr. Richards, you—"

"My servant betrayed my secret to him—"

"No one has betrayed anything to me—"

—"and then he did a natural and justifiable thing; he repented of the saving kindness which he had done me, and he *exposed* me—as I deserved—"

"Never!—I make oath—"

"Out of my heart I forgive him."

Burgess's impassioned protestations fell upon deaf ears; the dying man passed away without knowing that once more he had done poor Burgess a wrong. The old wife died that night.

The last of the sacred Nineteen had fallen a prey to the fiendish sack; the town was stripped of the last rag of its ancient glory. Its mourning was not showy, but it was deep.

By act of the Legislature—upon prayer and petition—Hadleyburg was allowed to change its name to (never mind what—I will not give it away), and leave one word out of the motto that for many generations had graced the town's official seal.

It is an honest town once more, and the man will have to rise early that catches it napping again.

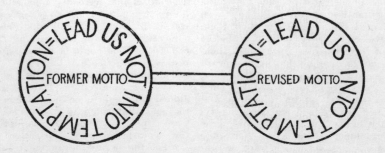

FAME'S LITTLE DAY
by Sarah Orne Jewett

I.

NOBODY ever knew, except himself, what made a foolish young newspaper reporter, who happened into a small old-fashioned hotel in New York, notice Mr. Abel Pinkham with deep interest, listen to his talk, ask a question or two of the clerk, and then go away and make up an effective personal paragraph for one of the morning papers. He must have had a heart full of fun, this young reporter, and something honestly rustic and pleasing must have struck him in the guest's demeanor, for there was a flavor in the few lines he wrote that made some of his fellows seize upon the little paragraph, and copy it, and add to it, and keep it moving. Nobody knows what starts such a thing in journalism, or keeps it alive after it is started, but on a certain Thursday morning the fact was made known to the world that among the notabilities then in the city, Abel Pinkham, Esq., a distinguished citizen of Wetherford, Vermont, was visiting New York on important affairs connected with the maple-sugar industry of his native State. Mr. Pinkham had expected to keep his visit unannounced, but it was likely to occasion much interest in business and civic circles. This was something like the way that the paragraph started, but here and there a kindred spirit of the original journalist caught it up and added discreet lines about Mr. Pinkham's probable stay in town, his occupation of an apartment on the fourth floor of the Ethan Allen Hotel, and other circumstances so uninteresting to the reading public in general that presently, in the next evening edition, one city editor after another threw out the item, and the young journalists, having had their day of pleasure, passed on to other things.

Mr. and Mrs. Pinkham had set forth from home with many forebodings, in spite of having talked all winter about taking this journey as soon as the spring opened. They would have caught at any reasonable excuse for giving it up altogether, because when the time arrived it seemed so much easier to stay at home. Mrs. Abel Pinkham had never seen New York; her husband himself had not been to the city for a great many years; in fact, his reminiscences of the former visit were not altogether pleasant, since he had foolishly fallen into many snares, and been much gulled in his character of honest young countryman. There was a tarnished and worthless counterfeit of a large gold watch still concealed between the outer boarding and inner lath and plaster of the lean-to bedroom which Mr. Abel Pinkham had occupied as a bachelor; it was not the only witness of his being taken in by city sharpers, and he had winced ever since at the thought of their wiles. But he was now a man of sixty, well-to-do, and of authority in town affairs; his children were all well married and settled in homes of their own, except a widowed daughter, who lived at home with her young son, and was her mother's lieutenant in household affairs.

The boy was almost grown, and at this season, when the maple sugar was all made and shipped, and it was still too early for spring work on the land, Mr. Pinkham could leave home as well as not, and here he was in New York, feeling himself to be a stranger and foreigner to city ways. If it had not been for that desire to appear well in his wife's eyes, which had buoyed him over the bar of many difficulties, he could have found it in his heart to take the next train back to Wetherford, Vermont, to be there rid of his best clothes and the stiff rim of his heavy felt hat. He could not let his wife discover that the noise and confusion of Broadway had the least power to make him flinch: he cared no more for it than for the woods in snow-time. He was as good as anybody, and she was better. They owed nobody a cent; and they had come on purpose to see the city of New York.

They were sitting at the breakfast table in the Ethan Allen Hotel, having arrived at nightfall the day before. Mrs. Pinkham looked a little pale about the mouth. She had been kept awake nearly all night by the noise, and had enjoyed but little the evening she had spent in the stuffy parlor of the hotel, looking down out of the window at what seemed to her but garish scenes, and keeping a reproachful and suspicious eye upon some unpleasantly noisy young women of forward behavior who were her only companions. Abel himself was by no means so poorly entertained in the hotel office and smoking-room. He felt much more at home

the business of serving them; and Mrs. Abel Pinkham, whose cooking was the triumph of parish festivals at home, had her own opinion about the beefsteak.

"THERE 'TIS, RIGHT BY YOUR THUMB."

than she did, being better used to meeting strange men than she was to strange women, and he found two or three companions who had seen more than he of New York life. It was there, indeed, that the young reporter found him, hearty and country-fed, and loved the appearance of his best clothes, and the way Mr. Abel Pinkham brushed his hair, and loved the way that he spoke in a loud and manful voice the belief and experience of his honest heart.

In the morning at breakfast-time the Pinkhams were depressed. They missed their good bed at home; they were troubled by the roar and noise of the streets, that hardly stopped overnight before it began again in the morning. The waiter did not put what mind he may have had to

She was a woman of imagination, and now that she was fairly here, spectacles and all, it really pained her to find that the New York of her dreams, the metropolis of dignity and distinction, of wealth and elegance, did not seem to exist. These poor streets, these unlovely people, were the end of a great illusion. They did not like to meet each other's eyes, this worthy pair. The man began to put on an unbecoming air of assertion, and Mrs. Pinkham's face was full of lofty protest.

"My gracious me, Mary Ann! I *am* glad I happened to get the *Tribune* this mornin'," said Mr. Pinkham, with sudden excitement. "Just you look here! I'd like well to know how they found out about our comin'!" and he handed the pa-

"LATER THAT DAY THE GUESTS WALKED UP BROADWAY."

knew we was comin' this week: you know I sent word I was comin' to settle with them myself. I suppose they send folks round to the hotels, these newspapers, but I shouldn't thought there'd been time. Anyway, they've thought 'twas worth while to put us in!"

Mrs. Pinkham did not take the trouble to make a mystery out of the unexpected pleasure. "I want to cut it out an' send it right up home to daughter Sarah," she said, beaming with pride, and looking at the printed names as if they were flattering photographs. "I think 'twas most too strong to say we was among the notables. But there! 'tis their business to dress up things, and they have to print somethin' every day. I guess I shall go up and put on my best dress," she added, inconsequently— "this one's kind of dusty; it's the same I rode in."

"Le' me see that paper again," said Mr. Pinkham, jealously. "I didn't more'n half sense it, I was so taken aback. Well, Mary Ann, you didn't expect you was goin' to get into the papers when you come away. 'Abel Pinkham, Esq., o' Wetherford, Vermont.' It looks well, don't it? But you might have knocked me down with a feather when I first caught sight of them words."

"I guess I will put on my other dress," said Mrs. Pinkham, rising, with quite a different air from that with which she had sat down to her morning meal. "This one looks a little out o' style, as Sarah said, but when I got up this mornin' I was so homesick it didn't seem to make any kind o' difference. I expect that saucy girl last night took us to be no-

per to his wife across the table. "There —there 'tis; right by my thumb," he insisted. "Can't you see it?" and he smiled like a boy as she finally brought her large spectacles to bear upon the important paragraph.

"I guess they think somethin' of us, if you don't think much o' them," continued Mr. Pinkham, grandly. "Oh, they know how to keep the run o' folks who are somebody to home! Draper and Fitch bodies. I'd like to leave the paper round where she couldn't help seein' it.''

"Don't take no notice of her," said Abel, in a dignified tone. "If she can't do what you want an' be civil, we'll go somewheres else. I wish I'd done what we talked of at first an' gone to the Astor House, but that young man in the cars told me 'twas remote from the things we should want to see. The Astor House was the top o' everything when I was here last, but I expected to find some changes. I want you to have the best there is," he said, smiling at his wife as if they were just making their wedding journey. "Come, let's be stirrin'; 'tis long past eight o'clock," and he ushered her to the door, newspaper in hand.

II.

Later that day the guests walked up Broadway, holding themselves erect, and feeling as if every eye was upon them. Abel Pinkham had settled with his correspondents for the spring consignments of maple sugar, and a round sum in bankbills was stowed away in his breast pocket. One of the partners had been a Wetherford boy, and when there came a renewal of interest in maple sugar, and the best confectioners were ready to do it honor, and the finest quality was at a large premium, this partner remembered that there never was any sugar made in Wetherford of such melting and delicious flavor as that from the trees on the old Pinkham farm. He had now made a good bit of money for himself on this private venture, and was ready that morning to pay Mr. Abel Pinkham cash down, and to give him a handsome order for the next season for all he could make. Mr. Fitch was also generous in the matter of such details as freight and packing; he was immensely polite and kind to his old friends, and begged them to come out to stay with him and his wife, where they lived now, in a not far distant New Jersey town.

"No, no, sir," said Mr. Pinkham, promptly. "My wife has come to see the city. Our time is short. Your folks 'll be up this summer, won't they? An' we can visit then."

"You must certainly take Mrs. Pinkham up to the Park," said the commission merchant. "I wish I had time to show you round myself. I suppose you've been seeing some things already, haven't you? I noticed your arrival in the *Herald*."

"The *Tribune* it was," said Mr. Pinkham, blushing through a smile and looking round at his wife.

"Oh no; I never read the *Tribune*," said Mr. Fitch. "There was quite an extended notice in my paper. They must have put you and Mrs. Pinkham into the *Herald* too." And so the friends parted, laughing. "I am much pleased to have a call from such distinguished parties," said Mr. Fitch, by way of final farewell, and Mr. Pinkham waved his hand grandly in reply.

"Let's get the *Herald*, then," he said, as they started up the street. "We can go an' sit over in that little square that we passed as we came along, and rest an' talk things over about what we'd better do this afternoon. I'm tired out a-trampin' and standin'. I'd rather have set still while we were there, but he wanted us to see his store. Done very well, Joe Fitch has, but 'tain't a business I should like."

There was a lofty look and sense of behavior about Mr. Pinkham of Wetherford. You might have thought him a great politician as he marched up Broadway, looking neither to right hand nor left. He felt himself to be somebody very particular.

"I begin to feel sort of at home myself," said his wife, who always had a certain touch of simple dignity about her. "When we was comin' yesterday New York seemed to be 'way off, and there wasn't nobody expectin' us. I feel now just as if I'd been here before."

They were now on the edge of the better-looking part of the town; it was still noisy and crowded, but noisy with fine carriages instead of drays, and crowded with well-dressed people. The hours for shopping and visiting were beginning, and more than one person looked with appreciative and friendly eyes at the comfortable pleased-looking elderly man and woman who went their easily beguiled and loitering way. The pavement peddlers detained them, but the cabmen beckoned them in vain; their eyes were busy with the immediate foreground. Mrs. Pinkham was embarrassed with the recurring reflection of herself in the great windows.

"I wish I had seen about a new bonnet before we came," she lamented. "They seem to be havin' on some o' their spring things."

"Don't you worry, Mary Ann. I don't

see anybody that looks any better than you do," said Abel, with boyish and reassuring pride.

Mr. Pinkham had now bought the *Herald*, and also the *Sun*, well recommended by an able newsboy, and presently they crossed over from that corner by the Fifth Avenue Hotel which seems like the very heart of New York, and found a place to sit down on the square — an empty bench, where they could sit side by side and look the papers through, reading over each other's shoulder, and being impatient from page to page. The paragraph was indeed repeated, with trifling additions. Ederton of the *Sun* had followed the *Tribune* man's lead, and fabricated a brief interview, a marvel of art and discretion, but so general in its allusions that it could create no suspicion; it almost deceived Mr. Pinkham himself, so that he found unaffected pleasure in the fictitious occasion, and felt as if he had easily covered himself with glory. Except for the bare fact of the interview's being imaginary, there was no discredit to be cast upon Mr. Abel Pinkham's having said that he thought the country near Wetherford looked well for the time of year, and promised a fair hay crop, and that his income was augmented one-half to three-fifths by his belief in the future of maple sugar. It was likely to be the great coming crop of the Green Mountain State. Ederton suggested that there was talk of Mr. Pinkham's presence in the matter of a great maple-sugar trust, in which much of the capital of Wall Street would be involved.

"How they do hatch up these things, don't they?" said the worthy man at this point. "Well, it all sounds well, Mary Ann."

"It says here that you are a very personable man," smiled his wife, "and have filled some of the most responsible town offices" (this was the turn taken by Goffey of the *Herald*). "Oh, and that you are going to attend the performance at Barnum's this evening, and occupy reserved seats! Why, I didn't know—who have you told about that? who was you talkin' to last night, Abel?"

"I never spoke o' goin' to Barnum's to any livin' soul," insisted Abel, flushing. "I only thought of it two or three times to myself that perhaps I might go an' take you. Now that is singular; perhaps they put that in just to advertise the show."

"Ain't it a kind of a low place for folks like us to be seen in?" suggested Mrs. Pinkham, timidly. "People seem to be payin' us all this attention, an' I don't know 's 'twould be dignified for us to go to one o' them circus places."

"I don't care; we sha'n't live but once. I ain't comin' to New York an' confine myself to evenin' meetin's," answered Abel, throwing away discretion and morality together. "I tell you I'm goin' to spend this sugar-money just as we've a mind to. You've worked hard, an' counted a good while on comin', an' so've I; an' I ain't goin' to mince my steps an' pinch an' screw for nobody. I'm goin' to hire one o' them hacks an' ride up to the Park."

"Joe Fitch said we could go right up in one o' the elevated railroads for five cents, an' return when we was ready," protested Mary Ann, who had a thriftier inclination than her husband; but Mr. Pinkham was not to be let or hindered, and they presently found themselves going up Fifth Avenue in a somewhat battered open landau. The spring sun shone upon them, and the spring breeze fluttered the black ostrich tip on Mrs. Pinkham's durable winter bonnet, and brought the pretty color to her faded cheeks.

"There! this is something like. Such people as we are can't go meechin' round; it ain't expected. Don't it pay for a lot o' hard work?" said Abel; and his wife gave him a pleased look for her only answer. They were both thinking of their gray farm-house on a long western slope, with the afternoon sun full in its face, the old red barn, the pasture, the shaggy woods that stretched far up the higher mountain-side.

"I wish Sarah an' little Abel was here to see us ride by," said Mary Ann Pinkham, presently. "I can't seem to wait to have 'em get that newspaper. I'm so glad we sent it right off before we started this mornin'. If Abel goes to the post-office comin' from school, as he always does, they'll have it to read to-morrow before supper-time."

III.

This happy day in two plain lives ended, as might have been expected, with the great Barnum show. Mr. and Mrs. Pinkham found themselves in possession of countless advertising cards and circulars next morning, and these added somewhat

"IT ALL SOUNDS WELL, MARY ANN."

to their sense of responsibility. Mrs. Pinkham became afraid that the hotel-keeper would charge them double. "We've got to pay for it some way, an' I don't know but I'm more'n willin'," said the good soul. "I never did have such a splendid time in all my life. Findin' you so respected 'way off here is the best of anything; an' then seein' them dear little babies in their splendid carriages, all along the streets and up to the Central Park! I never shall forget them beautiful little creatur's. And then the houses, an' the hosses, an' the store windows, an' all the rest of it! Well, I can't make my country pitcher hold no more, an' I want to get home an' think it over, goin' about my house-work."

They were just entering the door of the Ethan Allen Hotel for the last time, when a young man met them and bowed cordially. He was the original reporter of their arrival, but they did not know it, and the impulse was strong within him to formally invite Mr. Pinkham to make an address before the members of the Produce Exchange on the following morning; but he had been a country boy himself, and their look of seriousness and self-consciousness appealed to him unexpectedly. He wondered what effect this great experience would have upon their after-life. The best fun, after all, would be to send marked copies of his paper and Ederton's to all the weekly newspapers in that part of Vermont. He saw before him the evidence of their happy increase of self-respect, and he would make all their neighborhood agree to do them honor. Such is the dominion of the press.

"Who was that young man?—he kind of bowed to you," asked the lady from Wetherford, after the journalist had meekly passed; but Abel Pinkham, Esq., could only tell her that he looked like a young fellow who was sitting in the office the night that they came to the hotel. The reporter did not seem to these distinguished persons to be a young man of any consequence.

LOUISA PALLANT
by *Henry James*

I.

NEVER say you know the last word about any human heart! I was once treated to a revelation which startled and touched me, in the nature of a person with whom I had been acquainted (well, as I supposed) for years, whose character I had had good reasons, Heaven knows, to appreciate, and in regard to whom I flattered myself that I had nothing more to learn.

It was on the terrace of the Kursaal at Homburg, nearly ten years ago, one lovely night toward the end of July. I had come to the place that day from Frankfort, with vague intentions, and was mainly occupied in waiting for my young nephew, the only son of my sister, who had been intrusted to my care by a very fond mother for the summer (I was expected to show him Europe—only the very best of it), and was on his way from Paris to join me. The excellent band discoursed music not too abstruse, and the air was filled, besides, with the murmur of different languages, the smoke of many cigars, the creak, on the gravel of the gardens, of strolling shoes, and the thick tinkle of beer glasses. There were a hundred people walking about, there were some in clusters at little tables, and many on benches and rows of chairs, watching the others with a kind of solemn dumbness. I was among these last —I sat by myself, smoking my cigar, and thinking of nothing very particular, while families and couples passed and repassed me.

I scarcely know how long I had sat there when I became aware of a recognition which made my meditations definite. It was on my own part, and the object of it was a lady who moved to and fro, unconscious of my observation, with a young girl at her side. I had not seen her for ten years, and what first struck me was the fact, not that she was Mrs. Henry Pallant, but that the girl who was with her was remarkably pretty—or rather, first of all, that every one who passed her turned round to look at her. This led me to look at the young lady myself, and her charming face diverted my attention for some time from that of her companion. The latter, moreover, though it was night, wore a thin light veil, which made her features vague. The couple walked and walked, slowly, but though they were very quiet and graceful, and also very well dressed, they seemed to have no friends. Every one looked at them, but no one spoke; they appeared even to talk very little to each other. Moreover, they bore with extreme composure, and as if they were thoroughly used to it, the attention they excited. I am afraid it occurred to me to take for granted that they were not altogether respectable, and that, if they had been, the elder lady would have covered the younger up a little more from the public stare, and not have been so ashamed to show her own face. Perhaps this question came into my mind too easily just then—in view of my prospective mentorship to my nephew. If I was to show him only the best of Europe, I should have to be very careful about the people he should meet—especially the ladies—and the relations he should form. I suspected him of knowing very little of life, and I was rather uneasy about my responsibilities. Was I completely relieved and reassured when I perceived that I simply had Louisa Pallant before me, and that the girl was her daughter Linda, whom I had known as a child—Linda grown up into a regular beauty?

The question is delicate, and the proof that I was not very sure is perhaps that I didn't speak to the ladies immediately. I watched them awhile—I wondered what they would do. No great harm, assuredly; but I was anxious to see if they were really isolated. Homburg is a great resort of the English—the London season takes up its tale there toward the first of August—and I had an idea that in such a company as that Louisa would naturally know people. It was my impression that she "cultivated" the English, that she had been much in London, and would be likely to have views in regard to a permanent settlement. This supposition was quickened by the sight of Linda's beauty, for I knew there is no country in which a handsome person is more appreciated. You will see that I took time, and I confess that, as I finished my cigar, I thought it all over. There was no good reason, in

"THE COUPLE WALKED AND WALKED, SLOWLY."

fact, why I should have rushed into Mrs. Pallant's arms. She had not treated me well, and we had never really made it up. Somehow, even the circumstance that (after the first soreness) I was glad to have lost her had never put us quite right with each other; nor, for herself, had it made her less ashamed of her heartless behavior that poor Pallant, after all, turned out no great catch. I had forgiven her; I had not felt that it was anything but an escape not to have married a girl who had it in her to take back her given word, and break a fellow's heart, for mere flesh-pots —or the shallow promise, as it pitifully-proved, of flesh-pots; moreover, we had met since then, on the occasion of my former visit to Europe; we had looked each other in the eye, we had pretended to be free friends, and had talked of the wickedness of the world as composedly as if we were the only just, the only pure. I knew then what she had given out—that I had driven her off by my insane jealousy before she ever thought of Henry Pallant, before she had ever seen him. This had not been then, and it could not be to-day, a ground of real reunion, especially if you add to it that she knew perfectly what I thought of her. It is my belief that it doesn't often minister to friendship that your friend shall know your real opinion, for he knows it mainly when it is unfavorable, and this is especially the case when (if the solecism may pass) he is a woman. I had not followed Mrs. Pallant's fortunes;

the years elapsed, for me, in my own country, whereas she led her life, which I vaguely believed to be difficult (after her husband's death, which was virtually that of a bankrupt), in foreign lands. I heard of her from time to time—always as "established" somewhere, but on each occasion in a different place. She drifted from country to country, and if she had been of a hard composition at the beginning, it could never occur to me that her struggle with society (as it might be called) would have softened the paste. Whenever I heard a woman spoken of as "horribly worldly," I thought immediately, somehow, of the object of my early passion. I imagined she had debts, and when I now at last made up my mind to recall myself to her, it was present to me that she might ask me to lend her money. More than anything else, at this time of day, I was sorry for her, and such an idea didn't operate as a deterrent.

She pretended afterward that she had not noticed me—expressing great surprise, and wishing to know where I had dropped from—but I think the corner of her eye had taken me in, and she was waiting to see what I would do. She had ended by sitting down, with her girl, on the same row of chairs with myself, and after a little, on the seat next her becoming vacant, I went and stood before her. She looked up at me a moment, staring, as if she couldn't imagine who I was or what I wanted; then, smiling and extending her hands, she broke out, "Ah, my dear old friend! what a delight!" If she had waited to see what I would do, in order to choose her own line, she at least carried out this line with the utmost grace. She was cordial, friendly, artless, interested, and indeed I am sure she was very glad to see me. I may as well say immediately, however, that she gave neither then nor later any sign of a disposition to borrow money. She had none too much —that I learned—but for the moment she seemed able to pay her way. I took the empty chair, and we remained talking for an hour. After a while she made me sit on the other side of her, next to her daughter, whom she wished to know me— to love me—as one of their oldest friends. "It goes back, back, back, doesn't it?" said Mrs. Pallant; "and of course she remembers you as a child." Linda smiled very sweetly, but vaguely, and I saw she didn't remember me at all. When her

mother intimated that they had often talked about me, she didn't take it up, though she looked extremely nice. Looking nice was her strong point; she was prettier even than her mother had been. She was such a little lady that she made me ashamed of having doubted, however vaguely, and for a moment, of her position in the scale of propriety. Her appearance seemed to say that if she didn't know people, it was because she didn't want to—because there were none there who struck her as attractive; there was not the slightest difficulty about her choosing her friends. Linda Pallant, young as she was, and fresh and fair, and charming and gentle and sufficiently shy, looked somehow exclusive—as if the dust of the common world had never been meant to settle upon her. She was simpler than her mother, and was evidently not a young woman of professions—except in so far as she was committed to an interest in you by her bright, pure, intelligent smile. A girl who had such a lovely way of showing her teeth could never pass for heartless.

As I sat between the pair I felt that I had been taken possession of, and that, for better or worse, my stay at Homburg would be intimately associated with theirs. We gave each other a great deal of news, and expressed unlimited interest in each other's history since our last meeting. I don't know what Mrs. Pallant kept back, but, for myself, I was frank enough. She let me see, at any rate, that her life had been a good deal what I supposed, though the terms she used to describe it were less crude than those of my thought. She confessed that they had drifted, and that they were drifting still. Her narrative rambled and got what is vulgarly called slightly mixed, as I thought Linda perceived, while she sat watching the passers in a manner which betrayed no consciousness of their attention, without coming to her mother's aid. Once or twice Mrs. Pallant made me feel like a cross-questioner, which I had no intention of being. I took it that if the girl didn't put in a word it was because she had perfect confidence in her mother's ability to come out straight. It was suggested to me, I scarcely knew how, that this confidence between the two ladies went to a great length; that their union of thought, their system of reciprocal divination, was remarkable, and that they probably seldom needed to resort to

the clumsy, and in some cases dangerous, expedient of putting their ideas into
words. I suppose I didn't make this reflection all at once—it was not wholly the
result of that first meeting. I was with
them constantly for the next several days,
and my impressions had time to settle.

I do remember, however, that it was on
this first evening that Archie's name came
up. She didn't attribute her own stay at
Homburg to any refined or exalted motive—didn't say that she was there because she always came, or because a high
medical authority had ordered her to
drink the waters; she frankly admitted
that the reason of her visit had been simply that she didn't know where else to
turn. But she appeared to assume that
my behavior rested on higher grounds,
and even that it required explanation, the
place being frivolous and modern—devoid
of that interest of antiquity which I used
to value. "Don't you remember—ever so
long ago—that you wouldn't look at anything in Europe that wasn't a thousand
years old? Well, as we advance in life,
I suppose we don't think that's quite such
a charm." And when I told her that I
had come to Homburg because it was as
good a place as another to wait for my
nephew, she exclaimed: "Your nephew—
what nephew? He must have come up of
late." I answered that he was a youth
named Archer Pringle, and very modern
indeed; he was coming of age in a few
months, and was in Europe for the first
time. My last news of him had been from
Paris, and I was expecting to hear from
him one day to the other. His father was
dead, and though a childless bachelor,
with little of such experience, I was considerably counted on by his mother to see
that he didn't smoke too much or fall off
an Alp.

Mrs. Pallant immediately guessed that
his mother was my sister Charlotte, whom
she spoke of familiarly, though I knew
she had seen her but once or twice. Then
in a moment it came to her which of the
Pringles Charlotte had married; she remembered the family perfectly, in the old
New York days—"that disgustingly rich
lot." She said it was very nice having
the boy come out that way to my care;
to which I replied that it was very nice
for him. She declared that she meant
for me—I ought to have had children;
there was something so parental about
me, and I would have brought them up

so well. She could make an allusion
like that—to all that might have been and
hadn't been—without a gleam of guilt in
her eye; and I foresaw that before I left
the place I should have confided to her
that though I detested her, and was very
glad we had fallen out, yet our old relations had left me no heart for marrying
another woman. If I was a maundering
old bachelor to-day, it was no one's fault
but hers. She asked me what I meant to
do with my nephew, and I said it was
much more a question of what he would
do with me. She inquired whether he
were a nice young man, and if he had
brothers and sisters, and any particular
profession. I told her that I had really
seen but little of him, but believed him to
be six feet high and of tolerable parts. He
was an only son, but there was a little
sister, a poor, delicate child, demanding
all the mother's care, at home.

"So that makes your responsibility
greater, as it were, about the boy, doesn't
it?" said Mrs. Pallant.

"Greater? I'm sure I don't know."

"Why, if the girl's life is uncertain, he
may be, some moment, all the mother has.
So that being in your hands—"

"Oh, I shall keep him alive, I suppose,
if you mean that," I rejoined.

"Well, *we* won't kill him, shall we,
Linda?" Mrs. Pallant went on, with a
laugh.

"I don't know—perhaps we shall!" said
the girl, smiling.

II.

I called on them the next day at their
lodgings, the modesty of which was enhanced by a hundred pretty feminine devices—flowers and photographs and port-
able knick-knacks, and a hired piano, and
morsels of old brocade flung over angular
sofas. I asked them to drive; I met them
again at the Kursaal; I arranged that we
should dine together, after the Homburg
fashion, at the same *table d'hôte;* and during several days this revived familiar intercourse continued, imitating intimacy if
it didn't achieve it. I liked it, for my
companions passed my time for me, and
the conditions of our life were soothing—
the feeling of summer, and shade, and music, and leisure, in the German gardens
and woods, where we strolled and sat and
gossiped; to which may be added a kind
of sociable sense that, among people whose
challenge to the curiosity was mainly not

irresistible, we kept quite to ourselves. We were on the footing of old friends who, with regard to each other, still had discoveries to make. We knew each other's nature, but we didn't know each other's experience; so that when Mrs. Pallant related to me what she had been "up to" (as I called it) for so many years, the former knowledge attached a hundred interpretative foot-notes (as if I had been editing an author who presented difficulties) to the interesting page. There was nothing new to me in the fact that I didn't esteem her, but there was a sort of refreshment in finding that this didn't appear necessary at Homburg, and that I could like her in spite of it. She seemed to me, in the oddest way, both improved and degenerate, as if in her nature the two processes had gone on together. She was battered and world-worn, and, spiritually speaking, vulgarized; something fresh had rubbed off her (it even included the vivacity of her early desire to do the best thing for herself), and something very stale had rubbed on. On the other hand, she betrayed a skepticism, and that was rather becoming, as it quenched the eagerness of her prime, which had taken a form so unfortunate for me. She had grown weary and indifferent; and as she struck me as having seen more of the evil of the world than of the good, that was a gain; in other words, the cynicism that had formed itself in her nature had a softer surface than some of her old ambitions. And then I had to recognize that her devotion to her daughter had been a kind of religion; she had done the very best possible for Linda.

Linda was curious; Linda was interesting. I have seen girls I liked better (charming as she was), but I have never seen one who, for the time I was with her (the impression passed, somehow, when she was out of sight), occupied me more. I can best describe the sort of attention that she excited by saying that she struck one above all things as a final product— just as some plant or fruit does, some orchid, or some perfect peach. More than any girl I ever saw she was the result of a process of calculation; a process patiently educative; a pressure exerted in order that she should reach a high point. This high point had been the star of her mother's heaven (it hung before her so definitely), and had been the source of the only light—in default of a better—

that shone upon the poor lady's path. It stood her in stead of every other inspiration. The very most and the very best— that was what the girl had been led on to achieve; I mean, of course (for no real miracle had been wrought), the most and the best that she was capable of. She was as pretty, as graceful, as intelligent, as well bred, as well informed, as well dressed, as it would have been possible for her to be; her music, her singing, her German, her French, her English, her step, her tone, her glance, her manner, and everything in her person and movement, from the shade and twist of her hair to the way you saw her finger-nails were pink when she raised her hand, had been carried so far that one found one's self accepting them as a kind of standard. I regarded her as a model, and yet it was a part of her perfection that she had none of the stiffness of a pattern. She was like some one's grounds when you say they are well kept up; but just as such a place seems a kind of courtship of nature, so Linda's enthusiasm appeared to have gone all the way with her high culture; she had enjoyed it and made it her own, and was not merely passive and parrot-like. If she held the observation, it was because one wondered where and when she would break down; but she never did, either in her French accent or in her evidently complete amiability.

After Archie had come, the ladies were manifestly a great resource to him, and all the world knows that a party of four is more convenient than a party of three. My nephew kept me waiting a week, with a placidity all his own; but this same placidity was an element of success in our personal relations—so long, that is, as I didn't lose my temper with it. I didn't, for the most part, because my young man's unsurprised acceptance of the most various forms of good fortune had, more than anything else, the effect of amusing me. I had seen little of him for the last three or four years. I didn't know what his impending majority would have made of him (he didn't look himself in the least as if the wind were rising), and I watched him with a solicitude which usually ended in a joke. He was a tall, fresh-colored youth, with a candid, pleasant countenance, and a love of cigarettes, horses, and boats which had not been sacrificed to more transcendent studies. He was refreshingly natural, in a supercivilized

"I HAD BEFORE ME THE DAILY SPECTACLE OF HER MANNER WITH MY NEPHEW."

age, and I soon made up my mind that the formula of his character was a certain simplifying serenity. After that I had time to meditate on the line which divides the serene from the inane, and simplification from death. Archie was not clever—that theory it was not possible to maintain, though Mrs. Pallant tried it once or twice; but, on the other hand, it seemed to me that his plainness was a good defensive weapon. It was not of the sort that would let him in, but of the sort that would keep him out. By which I don't mean that he had short-sighted suspicions, but, on the contrary, that imagination would never be needed to save him, because she would never put him in danger. In short, he was a well-grown, well-washed, muscular young American, whose extreme good nature might have made him pass for conceited. If he looked pleased with himself, it was only because he was pleased with life (as he might be, with the money he was on the point of stepping into), and his big, healthy, independent person was an inevitable part of that. I am bound to add that he was accommodating—for which I was grateful. His own habits were active, but he didn't insist on my adopting them, and he made noteworthy sacrifices for the sake of my society. When I say for the sake of mine, I must, of course, remember that mine and that of Mrs. Pallant and Linda were now very much the same thing. He was willing to sit and smoke for hours under the trees, or, regulating his long legs to the pace of his three companions, stroll through the nearer woods of the charming little hill range of the Taunus to th~~e~~ ~~r~~~~ustic~~ ~~Wi~~ ~~M~~~~achus~~*ten* where coffee might be drunk under a trellis.

Mrs. Pallant took a great interest in him; she talked a great deal about him, and thought him a delightful specimen as a young gentleman of his period and country. She even asked me the sort of figure that his fortune might really amount to, and expressed the most hungry envy when I told her what I supposed it to be. While we talked together, Archie, on his side, could not do less than converse with Linda, nor, to tell the truth, did he manifest the least inclination for any different exercise. They strolled away together while their elders rested; two or three times, in the evening, when the ballroom of the Kursaal was lighted and dance music played, they whirled over the smooth floor in a waltz that made me remember. Whether it had the same effect on Mrs. Pallant I know not, for she didn't speak. We had, on certain occasions, our moments, almost our half-hours, of unembarrassed silence, while our young companions disported themselves. But if, at other times, her inquiries and comments were numerous, on the subject of my ingenuous kinsman, this might very well have passed for a courteous recognition of the frequent admiration that I expressed for Linda—an admiration to which I noticed that she was apt to give but a small direct response. I was struck with

something anomalous in her way of taking my remarks about her daughter—they produced so little of a maternal flutter. Her detachment, her air of having no fatuous illusions, and not being blinded by prejudice, seemed to me at times to amount to an affectation. Either she answered me with a vague, slightly impatient sigh, and changed the subject, or else she said, before doing so: "Oh yes, yes, she's a very brilliant creature. She ought to be; God knows what I have done for her!"

The reader will have perceived that I am fond of looking at the explanations of things, and in regard to this I had my theory that she was disappointed in the girl. What had been her particular disappointment? As she couldn't possibly have wished her prettier or more pleasing, it could only be that Linda had not made a successful use of her gifts. Had she expected her to capture a prince the day after she left the school-room? After all, there was plenty of time for this, as Linda was only two-and-twenty. It didn't occur to me to wonder whether the source of her mother's tepidity was that the young lady had not turned out as conscientious as she had hoped, because in the first place Linda struck me as perfectly innocent, and in the second, I was not paid, as the French say, for thinking that Louisa Pallant would much mind whether she were or not. The last hypothesis I should have resorted to was that of private despair at bad moral symptoms. And in relation to Linda's conscientiousness I had before me the daily spectacle of her manner with my nephew. It was as charming as it could be, without the smallest indication of a desire to lead him on. She was as familiar as a cousin; but as a distant one—a cousin who had been brought up to observe degrees. She was so much cleverer than Archie that she couldn't help laughing at him, but she didn't laugh enough to exclude variety, being well aware, no doubt, that a woman's cleverness most shines in contrast with a man's stupidity when she pretends to take that stupidity for wisdom. Linda Pallant, moreover, was not a chatterbox; as she knew the value of many things, she knew the value of intervals. There were a good many in the conversation of these young persons; my nephew's own speech, to say nothing of his thought, being not exempt from pauses; so that I sometimes wondered how their intercourse was kept at that pitch of friendliness of which it certainly bore the stamp.

It was friendly enough, evidently, when Archie sat near her—near enough for low murmurs, if they had risen to his lips—and watched her with interested eyes, and with liberty not to try too hard to make himself agreeable. She was always doing something—finishing a flower in a piece of tapestry, cutting the leaves of a magazine, sewing a button on her glove (she carried a little work-bag in her pocket, and was a person of the daintiest habits), or plying her pencil in a sketch-book which she rested on her knee. When we were in-doors, at her mother's house, she had always the resource of her piano, of which she was, of course, a perfect mistress. These avocations enabled her to bear such close inspection with composure (I ended by rebuking Archie for it—I told him he stared at the poor girl too much), and she sought further relief in smiling all over the place. When my young man's eyes shone at her, her own addressed themselves brightly to the trees and clouds and other surrounding objects, including her mother and me. Sometimes she broke out into a sudden embarrassed, happy, pointless laugh. When she wandered away from us she looked back at us in a manner which said that it wasn't for long, or that she was with us still in spirit. If I was pleased with her, it was for a good reason: it was a long time since any pretty girl had had the air of taking me so much into account. Sometimes, when they were so far away as not to disturb us, she read aloud a little to Mr. Archie. I don't know where she got her books—I didn't provide them, and certainly he didn't. He was no reader, and I dare say he went to sleep.

III.

I remember well the first time—it was at the end of about ten days of this—that Mrs. Pallant remarked to me: "My dear friend, you are quite amazing! You behave, for all the world, as if you were perfectly ready to accept certain consequences." She nodded in the direction of our young companions, but I nevertheless put her at the pains of saying what consequences she meant. "What consequences?" she repeated. "Why, the consequences that ensued when you and I first became acquainted."

I hesitated a moment, and then, look-ing her in the eyes, I said, "Do you mean that she would throw him over?"

"You are not kind, you are not generous," she replied, coloring quickly. "I am giving you a warning."

"You mean that my boy may fall in love with her?"

"Certainly; it looks even as if the harm might be already done."

"Then your warning is too late," I said, smiling. "But why do you call it a harm?"

"Haven't you any sense of responsibility?" she asked. "Is that what his mother sent him out to you for—that you should procure him a wife—let him put his head into a noose the day after his arrival?"

"Heaven forbid I should do anything of the kind! I know, moreover, that his mother doesn't want him to marry young. She thinks it's a mistake, and that at that age a man never really chooses. He doesn't choose till he has lived awhile—till he has looked about and compared."

"And what do you think yourself?"

"I should like to say I consider that love itself, however young, is a sufficient choice. But my being a bachelor at this time of day would contradict me too much."

"Well, then, you're too primitive. You ought to leave this place to-morrow."

"So as not to see Archie tumble in?"

"You ought to fish him out now, and take him with you."

"Do you think he is in very far?" I inquired.

"If I were his mother I know what I should think. I can put myself in her place—I am not narrow—I know perfectly well how she must regard such a question."

"And don't you know that in America that's not thought important—the way the mother regards it?"

Mrs. Pallant was silent a moment, as if I partly mystified and partly vexed her. "Well, we are not in America; we happen to be here."

"No; my poor sister is up to her neck in New York."

"I am almost capable of writing to her to come out," said Mrs. Pallant.

"You are warning me," I exclaimed, "but I hardly know of what. It seems to me that my responsibility would begin only at the moment when it should appear that your daughter herself was in danger."

"YOU MAKE MY REPARATION—MY EXPIATION—DIFFICULT!"

"Oh, you needn't mind that; I'll take care of her."

"If you think she is in danger already, I'll take him away to-morrow," I went on.

"It would be the best thing you could do."

"I don't know. I should be very sorry to obey a false alarm. I am very well here; I like the place, and the life, and your society. Besides, it doesn't strike me that—on her side—there is anything."

She looked at me with an expression that I had never seen in her face, and if I had puzzled her, she repaid me in kind. "You are very annoying; you don't deserve what I would do for you," she declared.

What she would do for me she didn't tell me that day, but we took up the subject again. I said to her that I didn't really see why we should assume that a girl like Linda—brilliant enough to make one of the greatest matches—should fall into my nephew's arms. Might I inquire whether her mother had won a confession from her—whether she had stammered out her secret? Mrs. Pallant answered that they didn't need to tell each other such things—they hadn't lived together for nothing for twenty years in such intimacy.

To this I rejoined that I had guessed as much, but that there might be an exception for a great occasion like the present. If Linda had shown nothing, it was a sign that, for her, the occasion wasn't great, and I mentioned that Archie had not once spoken to me of the young lady, save to remark, casually and rather patronizingly, after his first encounter with her, that she was a regular little flower. (The little flower was nearly three years older than himself.) Apart from this, he hadn't alluded to her, and had taken up no allusion of mine. Mrs. Pallant informed me again (for which I was prepared) that I was quite too primitive; and then she said: "We needn't to discuss the matter if you don't wish to, but I happen to know —how I obtained my knowledge isn't important—that the moment Mr. Pringle should propose to my daughter she would gobble him down. Surely it's a detail worth mentioning to you."

"Very good. I will sound him. I will look into the matter to-night."

"Don't, don't; you will spoil everything!" she murmured, in a peculiar tone of discouragement. "Take him off—that's the only thing."

I didn't at all like the idea of taking him

off; it seemed too summary and unnecessarily violent, even if presented to him on specious grounds; and, moreover, as I had told Mrs. Pallant, I really didn't wish to move. I didn't consider it a part of my bargain with my sister that, with my middle-aged habits, I should jump and dodge about Europe. So I said: "Should you really object to the boy so much as a son-in-law? After all, he's a good fellow, and a gentleman."

"My poor friend, you are too superficial—too frivolous," Mrs. Pallant rejoined, with a certain bitterness.

There was a hint of contempt in this which nettled me, and I exclaimed, "Possibly; but it seems odd that a lesson in consistency should come from you."

I had no retort from her; but at last she said, quietly: "I think Linda and I had better go away. We have been here a month—that's enough."

"Dear me, that will be a bore!" I ejaculated; and for the rest of the evening, until we separated (our conversation had taken place after dinner, at the Kursaal), she remained almost silent, with a subdued, injured air. This, somehow, didn't soothe me, as it ought to have done, for it was too absurd that Louisa Pallant, of all women, should propose to put me in the wrong. If ever a woman had been in the wrong herself— Archie and I usually attended the ladies back to their own door—they lived in a street of minor accommodation, at a certain distance from the Rooms—and we parted for the night late on the big cobble-stones, in the little sleeping German town, under the closed windows of which, suggesting stuffy interiors, our English farewells sounded gay. On this occasion, however, they were not gay, for the difficulty that had come up (for me) with Mrs. Pallant appeared to have extended, by a mysterious sympathy, to the young couple. They too were rather conscious and dumb.

As I walked back to our hotel with my nephew I passed my hand into his arm and asked him, by no roundabout approach to the question, whether he were in serious peril of love.

"I don't know, I don't know—really, uncle, I don't know!"—this was all the satisfaction I could extract from the youth, who had not the smallest vein of introspection. He might not know, but before we reached the inn (we had a few more words on the subject) it seemed to me that I did. His mind was not made to contain many objects at once, but Linda Pallant, for the moment, certainly constituted its principal furniture. She pervaded his consciousness, she solicited his curiosity, she associated herself, in a manner as yet undefined and unformulated, with his future. I could see that she was the first sharp impression of his life. I didn't betray to him, however, how much I saw, and I slept not particularly well, for thinking that, after all, it had been none of my business to provide him with sharp impressions. To find him a wife was the last thing that his mother had expected of me, or that I had expected of myself. Moreover, it was quite my opinion that he himself was too young to be a judge of wives. Mrs. Pallant was right, and I had been strangely superficial in regarding her, with her beautiful daughter, as a "resource." There were other resources, and one of them would be, most decidedly, to go away. What did I know, after all, about the girl, except that I was very glad to have escaped from marrying her mother? That mother, it was true, was a singular person, and it was strange that her conscience should have begun to fidget before my own did, and that she was more anxious on my nephew's behalf than I was. The ways of women were mysterious, and it was not a novelty to me that one never knew where one would find them. As I have not hesitated, in this narrative, to reveal the irritable side of my own nature, I will confess that I even wondered whether Mrs. Pallant's solicitude had not been a deeper artifice. Was it not possibly a plan of her own for making sure of my young man—though I didn't quite see the logic of it. If she regarded him, as she might, in view of his large fortune, as a great catch, might she not have arranged this little comedy, in their own interest, with the girl?

That possibility, at any rate, only made it a happier thought that I should carry the boy away to visit other cities. There were many, assuredly, much more worthy of his attention than Homburg. In the course of the morning (it was after our early luncheon) I walked round to Mrs. Pallant's, to let her know that this truth had come over me with force, and while I did so I again felt the unlikelihood of the part attributed by my fears, and by the mother's own, if they were real, to

Linda. Certainly, if she was such a girl as these fears represented her, she would fly at higher game. It was with an eye to high game, Mrs. Pallant had frankly admitted to me, that she had been trained, and such an education, to say nothing of such a subject, justified a hope of greater returns. A young American who could give her nothing but pocket-money was a very moderate prize, and if she was prepared to marry for ambition (there was no such hardness in her face or tone, but then there never is), her mark would be at the least an English duke. I was received at Mrs. Pallant's lodgings with the announcement that she had left Homburg, with her daughter, half an hour before. The good woman who had entertained the pair professed to know nothing of their movements beyond the fact that they had gone to Frankfort, where, however, it was her belief that they did not intend to remain. They were evidently travelling beyond. Sudden? Oh yes, tremendously sudden. They must have spent the night in packing, they had so many things, and such pretty ones; and their poor maid all the morning had scarcely had time to swallow her coffee. But they evidently were ladies accustomed to come and go. It didn't matter. With such rooms as hers she never wanted; there was a new family coming in at three o'clock.

IV.

This quick manœuvre left me staring, and I confess it made me rather angry. My only consolation was that Archie, when I told him, looked as blank as myself, and that the trick touched him more nearly, for I was not in love with Louisa. We agreed that we required an explanation, and we pretended to expect one the next day in the shape of a letter satisfactory even to the point of being apologetic. When I say "we" pretended, I mean that I did, for my suspicion that he knew (through an arrangement with Linda) what had become of our friends lasted only a moment. If his resentment was less than my own, his surprise was equally great. I had been willing to bolt, but I felt rather slighted by the facility with which Mrs. Pallant had shown that she could part with us. Archie was not angry, because, in the first place, he was good-natured, and in the second, it was evidently not definite to him that he had been encouraged, having, I think, no very

particular idea of what constituted encouragement. He was fresh from the wonderful country in which, between the ingenuous young, there may be so little question of "intentions." He was but dimly conscious of his own, and would have had no opinion as to whether he had been provoked or jilted. I had no wish to exasperate him, but when, at the end of three days more, we were still without news of our late companions, I remarked that it was very simple; it was plain they were just hiding from us; they thought us dangerous; they wished to avoid entanglements. They had found us too attentive, and didn't wish to raise false hopes. He appeared to accept this explanation, and even had the air (so at least I judged from his asking me no questions) of thinking that the matter might be delicate for myself. The poor youth was altogether much mystified, and I smiled at the image, in his mind, of Mrs. Pallant fleeing from his uncle's importunities.

We decided to leave Homburg, but if we didn't pursue her, it was not simply that I didn't know where she was. I could have found that out, with a little trouble, but I was deterred by the reflection that this would be her own reasoning. She was dishonest, and her departure was a provocation—I am afraid that it was in that stupid conviction that I made out a little independent itinerary with Archie. I even said to myself that we should learn where they were quite soon enough, and that our patience—even my young man's—would be longer than theirs. Therefore I uttered a small private cry of triumph when, three weeks later (we happened to be at Interlaken) he told me that he had received a note from Miss Pallant. His manner of telling me was to inquire whether there were any particular reasons why we should longer delay our projected visit to the Italian lakes; was not the fear of the hot weather, which was, moreover, in summer, our native temperature, at an end, as it was already the middle of September? I answered that we would start on the morrow, if he liked, and then, pleased apparently that I was so easy to deal with, he revealed his little secret. He showed me the letter, which was a graceful, natural document—it covered, with a few flowing strokes, but a single sheet of notepaper—not at all compromising to the young lady. If, however, it was almost the apology I had looked for (save that that should have come from the mother), it was not ostensibly in the least an invitation. It mentioned, casually (the mention was mainly in the date), that they were on the Lago Maggiore, at Baveno; but it consisted mainly of the expression of a regret that they had to leave us at Homburg without the usual forms. She didn't say under what necessity they had found themselves; she only hoped we had not judged them too harshly, and would accept "these few hasty words" as a substitute for the omitted good-by. She also hoped we were passing our time in an interesting manner, and having the same lovely weather that prevailed south of the Alps, and she remained very sincerely, with the kindest remembrances to me.

The note contained no message from her mother, and it was open to me to suppose, as I should judge, either that Mrs. Pallant had not known she was writing, or that they wished to make us think she had not known. The letter might pass as a common civility of the girl's to a person with whom she had been on very familiar terms. It was, however, as something more than this that my nephew took it; at least so I was warranted in inferring from the very distinct nature of his determination to go to Baveno. I saw it was useless to drag him another way; he had money in his own pocket, and was quite capable of giving me the slip. Yet —such are the sweet incongruities of youth —when I asked him if he had been thinking of Linda Pallant ever since they left us in the lurch, he replied, " Oh dear no; why should I ?" This fib was accompanied by an exorbitant blush. Since he must obey the young lady's call, I must also go and see where it would take him, and one splendid morning we started over the Simplon in a post-chaise.

I represented to him, successfully, that it would be in much better taste for us to alight at Stresa, which, as every one knows, is a resort of tourists, also on the shore of the major lake, at about a mile's distance from Baveno. If we staid at the latter place we should have to inhabit the same hotel as our friends, and this would be indiscreet, considering our peculiar relations with them. Nothing would be easier than to go and come between the two points, especially by the water, which would give Archie a chance for unlimited

paddling. His face lighted up at the vision of a pair of oars, he pretended to take my plea for discretion very seriously, and I could see that he immediately began to calculate opportunities for being afloat with Linda. Our post-chaise (I had insisted on easy stages, and we were three days on the way) deposited us at Stresa toward the middle of the afternoon; and it was within an amazingly short time that I found myself in a small boat with my nephew, who pulled us over to Baveno with vigorous strokes. I remember the sweetness of the whole impression (I had had it before, but to my companion it was new, and he thought it as pretty as the opera), the enchanting beauty of the place and hour, the stillness of the air and water, with the romantic, fantastic Borromean Islands in the midst of them. We disembarked at the steps at the garden foot of the hotel, and somehow it seemed a perfectly natural part of the lovely situation that I should immediately become conscious Mrs. Pallant and her daughter were sitting there—on the terrace—quietly watching us. They had all the air of expecting us, and I think we looked for it in them. I had not even asked Archie if he had answered Linda's note; that was between themselves, and in the way of supervision I had done enough in coming with him.

There is no doubt there was something very odd in our meeting with our friends —at least as between Louisa and me. I was too much taken up with that part of it to notice very much what was the manner of the encounter of the young people. I have sufficiently indicated that I couldn't get it out of my head that Mrs. Pallant was " up to" something, and I am afraid she saw in my face that this suspicion had been the motive of my journey. I had come there to find her out. The knowledge of my purpose couldn't help her to make me very welcome, and that is why I say we met in strange conditions. However, on this occasion, we observed all forms, and the admirable scene gave us plenty to talk about. I made no reference, before Linda, to the retreat from Homburg. She looked even prettier than she had done on the eve of that manœuvre, and gave no sign of any awkward consciousness. She struck me so, afresh, as a nice, clever girl that I was puzzled, afresh, to know why we should get —or should have got—into a tangle about her. People had to want to complicate a situation to do it on so simple a pretext as that Linda was magnificent. So she was, and why should not the consequences be equally so? One of them, on the spot, was that at the end of a very short time Archie proposed to her to take a turn with him in his boat, which awaited us at the foot of the steps. She looked at her mother with a smiling "May I, mamma?" and Mrs. Pallant answered, "Certainly, darling, if you are not afraid." At this—I scarcely knew why—I burst out laughing; it seemed so droll to me, somehow, that timidity should be imputed to this young lady. She gave me a quick, slightly sharp look as she turned away with my nephew; it appeared to challenge me a little—to say, "Pray what is the matter with *you*?" It was the first expression of the kind I had ever seen in her face. Mrs. Pallant's eyes, on the other hand, were not turned to mine; after we had been left there together she sat silent, not heeding me, looking at the lake and mountains—at the snowy crests, which wore the flush of evening. She seemed not even to watch our young companions as they got into their boat and pushed off. For some minutes I respected her reverie; I walked slowly up and down the terrace, and lighted a cigar, as she had always permitted me to do at Homburg. I noticed that she had an expression of weariness which I had never seen before; her delicate, agreeable face was pale; I fancied there were new lines of fatigue, almost of age, in it. At last I stopped in front of her and asked her, since she looked so sad, if she had any bad news.

"The only bad news was when I learned—through your nephew's note to Linda—that you were coming to us."

"Ah, then he wrote?" I exclaimed.

"Certainly he wrote."

"You take it all harder than I do," I remarked, sitting down beside her. And then I added, smiling, "Have you written to his mother?"

She slowly turned her face to me and rested her eyes on mine. "Take care, take care, or you'll insult me," she said, with an air of patience before the inevitable.

"Never, never! Unless you think I do so if I ask you if you knew when Linda wrote."

She hesitated a moment. "Yes; she showed me her letter. She wouldn't have done anything else. I let it go because I

didn't know what it was best to do. I am afraid to oppose her, to her face."

"Afraid, my dear friend? with that girl!"

"That girl? Much you know about her! It didn't follow that you would come—I didn't think it need follow."

"I'm like you," I said "I'm afraid of my nephew. I don't venture to oppose him, to his face. The only thing I could do, under the circumstances, was to come with him."

"I'm—and I'm glad you have done it," said Mrs. Pallant, thoughtfully.

"Oh, I was conscientious about that. But I have no authority; I can't order him nor forbid him—I can use no force. Look at the way he is pulling that boat, and see if you can fancy me."

"You could tell him she's a bad, hard girl, who would poison any good man's life!" my companion suddenly broke out, with a kind of passion.

"Dear Mrs. Pallant, what do you mean?" I murmured, staring.

She bent her face into her hands, covering it over with them, and remained so for a minute; then she went on, in a different manner, as if she had not heard my question: "I hoped you were too disgusted with us, after the way we left you planted."

"It was perturbing, assuredly, and it might have served, if Linda hadn't written; that patched it up," I said, laughing. But my laughter was hollow, for I had been exceedingly impressed with her little explosion of a moment before. "Do you really mean she is bad?" I added.

Mrs. Pallant made no immediate answer to this; she only said that it didn't matter, after all, whether the crisis should come a few weeks sooner or a few weeks later, since it was destined to come at the first opening. Linda had marked my young man—and when Linda had marked a thing!

"Bless my soul! how very grim! Do you mean she's in love with him?" I demanded, incredulous.

"It's enough if she makes him think she is—though even that isn't essential."

"If she makes him think so? Dearest lady, what do you mean? I have observed her, I have watched her, and after all, what has she done? She has been nice to him, but it would have been much more marked if she hadn't. She has really shown him nothing but the common friendliness of a bright, good-natured girl. Her note was nothing; he showed it to me."

"I don't think you have heard every word that she has said to him," Mrs. Pallant rejoined, with a persistence that struck me as cold, even unnatural.

"No more have you, I take it!" I exclaimed. She evidently meant more than she said, and this impression chilled me, made me really uncomfortable.

"No, but I know my own daughter. She's a very rare young woman."

"You have a singular tone about her," I remarked—"such a tone as I think I have never heard on a mother's lips. I have observed it before, but never so accentuated."

At this Mrs. Pallant got up; she stood there an instant, looking down at me. "You make my reparation—my expiation—difficult!" And leaving me rather startled, she began to move along the terrace.

I overtook her presently, and repeated her words. "Your reparation—your expiation—what on earth do you mean by that?"

"You know perfectly what I mean—it is too magnanimous of you to pretend you don't."

"Well, at any rate, I don't see what good it does me, or what it makes up to me for, that you should abuse your daughter."

"Oh, I don't care; I shall save him!" she exclaimed, as we went, with a kind of perverse cheerfulness. At the same moment two ladies, apparently English, came toward us (scattered groups had been sitting there, and the inmates of the hotel were moving to and fro), and I observed the immediate charming transition (it seemed to me to show such years of social practice) by which, as they greeted us, she exchanged her excited, almost fevered, expression for an air of recognition and pleasure. They stopped to speak to her, and she asked, with eagerness, whether their mother were better. I strolled on, and she presently rejoined me; after which she said, impatiently, "Come away from this—come down into the garden." We descended into the garden, strolled through it, and paused on the border of the lake.

V.

The charm of the evening had deepened, the stillness was like a solemn expression on a beautiful face, and the whole air of the place divine. In the fading light my nephew's boat was too far out to be perceived. I looked for it a little, and then, as I gave it up, I remarked that from such an excursion as that, on such a lake, at such an hour, a young man and a young woman of ordinary sensibility could only come back doubly pledged to each other. To this observation Mrs. Pallant's answer was, superficially at least, irrelevant: she said, after a pause:

"With you, my dear sir, one has certainly to dot one's 'i's.' Haven't you discovered, and didn't I tell you at Homburg, that we are miserably poor?"

"Isn't 'miserably' rather too much when you are living at an expensive hotel?"

"They take us en pension, for ever so little a day. I have been knocking about Europe long enough to learn there are certain ways of doing things. Besides, don't speak of hotels; we have spent half our life in them, and Linda told me only last night that she hoped never to put her foot into one again. She thinks that when she comes to such a place as this, it's the least that she should find a villa of her own."

"Well, her companion there is perfectly competent to give her one. Don't think I have the least desire to push them into each other's arms; I only ask to wash my hands of them. But I should like to know why you want, as you said just now, to save him. When you speak as if your daughter were a monster, I take it that you are not serious."

She was facing me there in the twilight, and to let me know that she was more serious perhaps than she had ever been in her life, she had only to look at me awhile without protestation. "It's Linda's standard: God knows I myself could get on! She is ambitious, luxurious, determined to have what she wants, more than any one I have ever seen. Of course it's open to you to tell me that it's my fault, that I was so before her, and have made her so. But does that make me like it any better?"

"Dear Mrs. Pallant, you are most extraordinary," I stammered, infinitely surprised and not a little pained.

"Oh yes, you have made up your mind about me; you see me in a certain way, and you don't like to change. But you will have to—if you have any generosity!" Her eyes shone in the summer dusk, and she looked remarkably hand-some.

"Is this a part of the reparation, of the expiation?" I inquired. "I don't see what you ever did to Archie."

"It's enough that he belongs to you. But it isn't for you that I do it; it's for myself," she went on.

"Doubtless you have your own reasons, which I can't penetrate. But can't you sacrifice something else—must you sacrifice your child?"

"She's my punishment, and she's my stigma!" cried Louisa Pallant, with veritable exaltation.

"It seems to me rather that you are hers."

"Hers? What does *she* know of such things?—what can she ever feel? She's cased in steel; she has a heart of marble. It's true! it's true! She appalls me!"

I laid my hand upon the poor lady's; I uttered, with the intention of checking and soothing her, the first incoherent words that came into my head, and I drew her toward a bench which I perceived a few yards away. She dropped upon it; I placed myself near her, and I besought her to consider well what she was saying. She owed me nothing, and I wished no one injured, no one denounced or exposed, for my sake.

"For your sake? Oh, I am not thinking of you!" she answered, and indeed the next moment I thought my words rather fatuous. "It's a satisfaction to my own conscience—for I have one, little as you think I have a right to speak of it. I have been punished by my sin itself. I have been hideously worldly; I have thought only of that; and I have taught her to be so—to do the same. That's the only instruction I have ever given her, and she has learned the lesson so well that, now that I see it printed there in all her nature, I am horrified at my work. For years we have lived that way; we have thought of nothing else. She has learned it so well that she has gone far beyond me. I say I am horrified, because she is horrible."

"My poor extravagant friend," I pleaded, "isn't it still more so to hear a mother say such things?"

"Why so, if they are hideously true? Besides, I don't care what I say, if I save him."

"Do you expect me to repeat to him—"
"Not in the least," she broke in; "I

will do it myself." At this I uttered some strong inarticulate protest, and she went on, with a sort of simplicity, "I was very glad at first, but it would have been better if we hadn't met."

"I don't agree to that, for you interest me immensely."

"I don't care for that, if I can interest him."

"You must remember, then, that your charges are strangely vague, considering how violent they are. Never had a girl a more innocent appearance: you know how I have admired it."

"You know nothing about her. *I* do, for she is the work of my hand!" Mrs. Pallant declared, with a curious, bitter little laugh. "I have watched her for years, and little by little, for the last two or three, it has come over me. There is not a tender spot in her whole composition. To arrive at a brilliant social position, if it were necessary, she would see me drown in this lake without lifting a finger, she would stand there and see it—she would push me in—and never feel a pang. That's my young lady. To climb up to the top, and be splendid and envied there—to do it at any cost, or by any meanness and cruelty, is the only thing she has a heart for. She would lie for it, she would steal for it, she would kill for it!" My companion brought out these words with a tremendous low distinctness, and an air of sincerity that was really solemn. I watched her pale face and glowing eyes; she held me in a kind of stupor, but her strange, almost vindictive earnestness imposed itself. I found myself believing her, pitying her more than I pitied the girl. It was as if she had been bottled up for longer than she could bear, suffering more and more from the fulness of her knowledge. It relieved her to warn and denounce and expose. "God has let me see it in time, in his mercy," she continued; "but his ways are strange, that he has let me see it in my daughter. It is myself that he has let me see, myself as I was for years. But she's worse—she is, I assure you; she's worse than I ever intended or dreamed." Her hands were clasped tightly together in her lap; her low voice quavered, and her breath came short; she looked up at the faint stars with a kind of religious perversity.

"Have you ever spoken to her as you speak to me?" I asked. "Have you ever admonished her, reproached her?"

"Reproached her? How can I? when all she would have to say would be, 'You —*you*—you base one—who made me!'"

"Then why do you want to play her a trick?"

"I'm not bound to tell you, and you wouldn't understand if I did. I should play that boy a far worse trick if I were to hold my tongue."

"If he loves her, he won't believe a word you say."

"Very possibly, but I shall have done my duty."

"And shall you say to him simply what you have said to me?"

"Never mind what I shall say to him. It will be something that will perhaps affect him, if I lose no time."

"If you are so bent on gaining time," I said, "why did you let her go out in the boat with him?"

"Let her? how could I prevent it?"

"But she asked your permission."

"That's a part of all the comedy!"

We were silent a moment, after which I questioned: "Then she doesn't know you hate her?"

"I don't know what she knows. She has depths and depths, and all of them bad. Besides, I don't hate her in the least; I pity her, simply, for what I have made of her. But I pity still more the man who may find himself married to her."

"There's not much danger of there being any such person, at the rate you go on."

"Oh, perfectly; she'll marry some one. She'll marry a title, as well as a fortune."

"It's a pity my nephew hasn't a title," I murmured, smiling.

She hesitated a moment. "I see you think I want that, and that I am acting. God forgive you! Your suspicion is perfectly natural: how can any one tell, with people like us?"

The way she uttered these last words brought tears to my eyes. I laid my hand on her arm, holding her awhile, and we looked at each other through the dusk. "You couldn't do more if he were my son," I said at last.

"Oh, if he had been your son, he would have kept out of it! I like him for himself; he's simple and honest—he needs affection."

"He would have an admirable, a devoted, mother-in-law," I went on.

Mrs. Pallant gave a little impatient sigh, and replied that she was not joking.

We sat there some time longer, while I thought over what she had said to me, and she apparently did the same. I confess that even close at her side, with the echo of her passionate, broken voice still in the air, some queer ideas came into my head. Was the comedy on *her* side, and not on the girl's, and was she posturing as a magnanimous woman at poor Linda's expense? Was she determined, in spite of the young lady's preference, to keep her daughter for a grander personage than a young American whose dollars were not numerous enough (numerous as they were) to make up for his want of high relationships, and had she brought forth these cruel imputations to help her to her end? If she was prepared really to denounce the girl to Archie, she would have to go very far to overcome the suspicion he would be sure to feel at so unnatural a proceeding. Was she prepared to go far enough? The answer to these doubts was simply the way I had been touched—it came back to me the next moment—when she used the words, "people like us." The effect of them was poignant. She made herself humble indeed, and I felt in a manner ashamed, on my own side, that I saw her in the dust. She said to me at last that I must wait no longer; I must go away before the young people came back. They were staying very long, too long; all the more reason that she should deal with Archie that evening. I must drive back to Stresa, or, if I liked, I could go on foot; it wasn't far—for a man. She disposed of me freely, she was so full of her purpose, and after we had quitted the garden and returned to the terrace of the hotel she seemed almost to push me to leave her—I felt her fine hands, quivering a little, on my shoulders. I was ready to do what she liked— she affected me painfully—and I wanted to get away from her. Before I went I asked her why Linda should regard my young man as such a *parti*; it didn't square, after all, with her account of the girl's fierce ambitions. By that picture, it would seem, a reigning prince was the least she would look at.

"Oh, she has reflected well; she has regarded the question in every light," said Mrs. Pallant. "If she has made up her mind, it is because she sees what she can do."

"Do you mean that she has talked it over with you?"

"Lord! for what do you take us? We don't talk over things to-day. We know each other's point of view, and we only have to act. We can take reasons, which are awkward things, for granted."

"But in this case she certainly doesn't know your point of view, poor thing."

"No—that's because I haven't played fair. Of course she couldn't expect I would cheat. There ought to be honor among thieves. But it was open to her to do the same."

"How do you mean, to do the same?"

"She might have fallen in love with a poor man; then I should have been done."

"A rich one is better; he can do more," I replied, with conviction.

"So you would have reason to know if you had led the life that we have. Never to have had really enough—I mean to do just the few simple things we have wanted; never to have had the sinews of war, I suppose you would call them—the funds for a campaign; to have felt every day and every hour the hard, monotonous pinch, and found the question of dollars and cents (and so horridly fond of them) mixed up with every experience, with every impulse—that *does* make one mercenary, it does make money seem a good beyond all others, and it's quite natural it should. That is why Linda is of the opinion that a fortune is always a fortune. She knows all about that of your nephew, how it's invested, how it may be expected to increase, exactly on what sort of footing it would enable her to live. She has decided that it's enough, and enough is as good as a feast. She thinks she could lead him by the nose, and I dare say she could. She will make him live here: she has not the least intention of settling in America. I think she has views upon London, because in England he can hunt and shoot, and that will make him let her alone."

"It strikes me that he would like that very much," I interposed; "that's not at all a bad programme, even from Archie's point of view."

"It's no use of talking about princes," Mrs. Pallant pursued, as if she had not heard me. "Yes, they are most of them more in want of money even than we are. Therefore a title is out of the question, and we recognized that at an early stage. Your nephew is exactly the sort of young man we had constructed in advance—he was made on purpose. Dear Linda was

her mother's own daughter when she recognized him on the spot! It's enough of a title to-day to be an American—with the way they have come up. It does as well as anything, and it's a great simplification. If you don't believe me, go to London and see."

She had come with me out to the road. I had said I would walk back to Stresa, and we stood there in the complete evening. As I took her hand, bidding her good-night, I exclaimed, "Poor Linda! poor Linda!"

"Oh, she'll live to do better," said Mrs. Pallant.

"How can she do better, since you have described this as perfection?"

She hesitated a moment. "I mean better for Mr. Pringle."

I still had her hand—I remained looking at her. "How came it that you could throw me over, such a woman as you?"

"Ah, my friend, if I hadn't, I couldn't do this for you!" And disengaging herself, she turned away quickly and went back to the hotel.

VI.

I don't know whether she blushed as she made this avowal, which was a retraction of a former denial and the real truth, as I permitted myself to believe; but I did, while I took my way to Stresa —it is a walk of half an hour—in the darkness. The new and singular character in which she had appeared to me produced an effect of excitement which would have made it impossible for me to sit still in a carriage. This same agitation kept me up late, after I had reached my hotel; as I knew that I shouldn't sleep, it was useless to go to bed. Long, however, as I deferred this ceremony, Archie had not turned up when the lights in the hotel began to be put out. I felt even slightly nervous about him, and wondered whether he had had an accident on the lake. I reflected that in this case—if he had not brought his companion back to Baveno— Mrs. Pallant would already have sent after me. It was foolish, moreover, to suppose that anything could have happened to him after putting off from Baveno, by water, to rejoin me, for the evening was absolutely windless and more than sufficiently clear, and the lake as calm as glass. Besides, I had unlimited confidence in his power to take care of himself in circumstances much more difficult. I went to my room at last: his own was at some distance, the people of the hotel not having been able—it was the height of the autumn season—to place us together. Before I went to bed I had occasion to ring for a servant, and then I learned, by a chance inquiry, that my nephew had returned an hour before, and had gone straight to his own apartment. I had not supposed he could come in without my seeing him—I was wandering about the saloons and terraces—and it had not occurred to me to knock at his door. I had half a mind to do so then, I had such a curiosity as to how I should find him; but I checked myself, for evidently he had not wished to see me. This didn't diminish my curiosity, and I slept even less than I had expected to. His dodging me that way (for if he hadn't perceived me down-stairs he might have looked for me in my room) was a sign that Mrs. Pallant's interview with him had really come off. What had she said to him?—what strong measures had she taken? The impression of almost morbid eagerness of purpose that she had given me suggested possibilities that I was almost afraid to think of. She had spoken of them, as we parted there, as something she would do for me; but I had made the mental comment, as I walked away from her, that she hadn't done it yet. It wouldn't really be done till Archie had backed out. Perhaps it was done by this time: his avoiding me seemed almost a proof. That was what I thought of most of the night. I spent a considerable part of it at my window, looking out at the sleeping mountains. *Had* he backed out?—was he making up his mind to back out? There was a strange contradiction in it; there were, in fact, more contradictions than ever. I believed what Mrs. Pallant had told me about Linda, and yet that other idea made me ashamed of my nephew. I was sorry for the girl; I regretted her loss, if loss it was to be, of a great chance; and yet I hoped that the manner in which her mother had betrayed her (there was no other word) to her lover had been thorough-going. It would need very radical measures on Mrs. Pallant's part to excuse Archie. For him too I was sorry, if she had made an impression on him—the impression she desired. Once or twice I was on the point of going in to condole with him, in my dressing-gown: I was sure he

too had jumped up from his bed and was looking out of his window at the everlasting hills.

I am bound to say that he showed very little, when we met in the morning and breakfasted together. Youth is strange; it has resources that experience seems only to deprive us of. One of these is simply to do nothing—to say nothing. As we grow older and cleverer we think that is too simple, too crude; we dissimulate more elaborately, but with an effect much less baffling. My young man didn't look in the least as if he had lain awake, or had something on his mind; and when I asked him what he had done after my premature departure (I explained that by saying I had been tired of waiting for him—I was weary with my journey and wanted to go to bed), he replied: "Oh, nothing in particular. I hung about the place: I like it better than this. We had an awfully jolly time on the water. *I* wasn't in the least tired." I didn't worry him with questions: it seemed to me indelicate to try to probe his secret. The only indication he gave was on my saying, after breakfast, that I should go over again to see our friends, and my appearing to take for granted that he would be glad to accompany me. Then he remarked that he would stop at Stresa—he had paid them such a tremendous visit; also he had some letters to write. There was a freshness in his scruples about the length of his visits, and I knew something about his correspondence, which consisted entirely of twenty pages every week from his mother. But he satisfied my curiosity so little that it was really this sentiment that carried me back to Baveno. This time I ordered a conveyance, and as I got into it he stood watching me in the porch of the hotel, with his hands in his pockets. Then it was for the first time that I saw in this young man's face the expression of a person slightly dazed, slightly foolish even, to whom something disagreeable has happened. Our eyes met as I watched him, and I was on the point of saying, "You had really better come with me," when he turned away. He went into the house as if he wished to escape from my call. I said to myself that Mrs. Pallant had warned him off, but that it wouldn't take much to bring him back.

The servant of whom I asked for my friends at Baveno told me that they were in a certain summer-house in the garden, to which he led the way. The place had an empty air; most of the inmates of the hotel were dispersed on the lake, on the hills, in picnics, excursions, visits to the Borromean Islands. My guide was so far right as that Linda was in the summer-house, but she was there alone. On finding this to be the case I stopped short, rather awkwardly, for I had a sudden sense of being an unmasked hypocrite—a conspirator against her security and honor. But there was no awkwardness about Linda Pallant; she looked up, with a little cry of pleasure, from the book she was reading, and she held out her hand with the most engaging frankness. I felt as if I had no right to touch her hand, and I pretended not to see it. But this gave no chill to her pretty manner; she moved a roll of tapestry off the bench, so that I might sit down, and praised the place as a delightful shady corner. She had never been fresher, fairer, kinder; she made her mother's damning talk about her seem a hideous dream. She told me Mrs. Pallant was coming to join her; she had remained in-doors to write a letter. One couldn't write out there, though it was so nice in other respects; the table was too rickety. They too, then, had pretexts between them in the way of letters; I judged this to be a token that the situation was tense. It was the only one, however, that Linda gave; like Archie, she had her youthfulness to relieve her from embarrassment. She had been used to seeing us always together, and she made no comment on my having come over without him. I waited in vain for her to say something about it; this would only be natural—it was almost unfriendly to omit it. At last I observed that my nephew was very unsociable that morning; I had expected him to join me, but he had left me to come alone.

"I am very glad," she answered. "You can tell him that if you like."

"If I tell him that, he will come immediately."

"Then don't tell him: I don't want him to come. He staid too long last night," Linda went on, "and kept me out on the water till the most dreadful hours. That isn't done here, you know, and every one was shocked when we came back—or rather when we didn't come back. I begged him to bring me in, but he wouldn't. When we did return—I al-

most had to take the oars myself—I felt as if every one had been sitting up to time us, to stare at us. It was very embarrassing."

These words made an impression upon me; and as I have treated the reader to most of the reflections—some of them perhaps rather morbid—in which I indulged on the subject of this young lady and her mother, I may as well complete the record, and let him know that I now wondered whether Linda—candid and accomplished maiden—had conceived the fine idea of strengthening her hold of Archie by attempting to prove that he had "compromised" her. "Ah, no doubt that was the reason he had a bad conscience last evening!" I exclaimed. "When he came back to Stresa he sneaked off to his room; he wouldn't look me in the face."

"Mamma was so vexed that she took him apart and gave him a scolding," the girl went on. "And to punish me she sent me straight to bed. She has very old-fashioned ideas—haven't you, mamma?" she added, looking over my head at Mrs. Pallant, who had just come in behind me.

I forget what answer Mrs. Pallant made to Linda's appeal; she stood there with two letters, sealed and addressed, in her hand. She greeted me gayly, and then asked her daughter if she had any postage-stamps. Linda consulted a rather shabby pocket-book, and confessed that she was destitute; whereupon her mother gave her the letters, with the request that she would go into the hotel, buy the proper stamps at the office, carefully affix them, and put the letters into the box. She was to pay for the stamps, not have them put on the bill—a preference for which she gave her reasons. I had bought some at Stresa that morning, and was on the point of offering them to Mrs. Pallant, when, apparently having guessed my intention, she silenced me with a look. Linda told her she had no money, and she fumbled in her pocket for a franc. When she had found it, and the girl had taken it, Linda kissed her before going off with the letters.

"Darling mother, you haven't any too many of them, have you?" she murmured; and she gave me, sidelong, as she left us, the prettiest half comical, half pitiful smile.

"She's amazing—she's amazing," said Mrs. Pallant, as we looked at each other.

"Does she know what you have done?"

"She knows I have done something, and she is making up her mind what it is—or she will in the course of the next twenty-four hours, if your nephew doesn't come back. I think I can promise you he won't."

"And won't she ask you?"

"Never!"

"Shall you not tell her? Can you sit down together in this summer-house this divine day with such a dreadful thing as that between you?"

"Don't you remember what I told you about our relations—that everything was implied between us, and nothing expressed? The ideas we have had in common —our perpetual worldliness, our always looking out for chances—are not the sort of thing that can be expressed gracefully between persons who like to keep up forms, as we both do; so that if we understood each other it was enough. We shall understand each other now, as we have always done, and nothing will be changed, because there has always been something between us that couldn't be talked about."

"Certainly, she is amazing — she is amazing," I repeated; "but so are you." And then I asked her what she had said to my boy.

She seemed surprised. "Hasn't he told you?"

"No; and never will."

"I am glad of that," she said, simply.

"But I am not sure he won't come back. He didn't this morning, but he had already half a mind to."

"That's your imagination," said Mrs. Pallant, decisively. "If you knew what I told him you would be sure."

"And you won't let me know?"

"Never, my dear friend."

"And did he believe you?"

"Time will show; but I think so."

"And how did you make it plausible to him that you should take so unnatural a course?"

For a moment she said nothing, only looking at me. Then at last—"I told him the truth."

"The truth?" I repeated.

"Take him away—take him away!" she broke out. "That's why I got rid of Linda, to tell you that you mustn't stay— you must leave Stresa to-morrow. This time it's you that must do it; I can't fly from you again—it costs too much!" And she smiled strangely.

"Don't be afraid; don't be afraid. We will leave to-morrow; I want to go myself." I took her hand in farewell, and while I held it I said, "The way you put it, about Linda, was very bad."

"It was horrible."

I turned away—I felt indeed that I wanted to leave the neighborhood. She kept me from going to the hotel, as I might meet Linda coming back, which I was far from wishing to do, and showed me another way into the road. Then she turned round to meet her daughter and spend the rest of the morning in the summer-house with her, looking at the bright blue lake and the snowy crests of the Alps. When I reached Stresa again I found that Archie had gone off to Milan (to see the cathedral, the servant said), leaving a message for me to the effect that, as he should not be back for a day or two (though there were numerous trains) he had taken a small portmanteau with him. The next day I got a telegram from him, notifying me that he had determined to go on to Venice, and requesting me to forward the rest of his luggage. "Please don't come after me," this missive added; "I want to be alone; I shall do no harm." That sounded pathetic to me, in the light of what I knew, and I was glad to leave the poor boy to his own devices. He proceeded to Venice, and I recrossed the Alps. For several weeks after this I expected to discover that he had rejoined Mrs. Pallant; but when we met in Paris, in November, I saw that he had nothing to hide from me, except indeed the secret of what that lady had told him. This he concealed from me then, and has concealed ever since. He returned to America before Christmas, and then I felt that the crisis had passed. I have never seen my old friend since. About a year after the time to which my story refers, Linda married, in London, a young Englishman, the possessor of a large fortune, acquired by his father in some useful industry. Mrs. Gimingham's photographs (such is her present name) may be obtained at the principal stationers'. I am convinced her mother was sincere. My nephew has not changed his state yet, and now even my sister is beginning, for the first time, to desire it. I related to her, as soon as I saw her, the substance of the story I have written here, and (such is the inconsequence of women) nothing can exceed her reprobation of Louisa Pallant.

TOP FLOOR BACK
by Zona Gale

"I ONCE knowed a man in New York city," said Peleg Bemus, "that done some sacrificin' that ain't called by that name when it gets into the newspapers." He looked over at us expectantly, and with a manner of pointing at us with his head. "You come from New York," he said; "ain't you ever heard o' Mr. Loneway—Mr. John Loneway?"

We regretted that we might not answer "yes." Instinctively one longed to make his pointed eyes twinkle.

"Him an' I lived in the same buildin' in East Fourteenth Street there," he explained. "That is to say, he lived top floor back an' I was janitor. That was a good many years ago, but whenever I get an introduction to anybody from New York I allus take an interest. I'd like to know what ever become o' him."

Not so much in concern for Mr. John Loneway as in expectation of what the old man might have observed, we questioned him.

"It was that Hard Winter," he went on, readily; "I'd hev to figger out what year, but most anybody on the East Side can tell you. Coal was clear up an' soarin', an' vittles was, too—everybody howlin' hard times, an' the winter just commenced. Make things worse, some phi-lanthropist had put up two model tenements in the block we was in, an' property alongside had shot up in value accordin' an' lugged rents with it. Everybody in my buildin' most was rowin' about it.

"But John Loneway, he wasn't rowin'. I met him on the stairs one mornin' early an' I says, 'Beg pardon, sir,' I says, 'but you ain't meanin' to make no change?' I ask him. He looks at me kind o' dazed—he was a wonderful clean-muscled little chap, with a crisscross o' veins on each temple an' big brown eyes back in his head. 'No,' he says. 'Change? I can't move. My wife's sick,' he says. That was news to me. I'd met her a couple o' times in the hall—pale little mite, hardly big as a baby, but pleasant spoken, an' with a way o' dressin' herself in shabby clo'es that made the other women in the house look like bundles tied up careless. But she walked awful slow, and she didn't go out much—they had only been in the house a couple o' weeks or so. 'Sick, is she?' I says. 'Too bad,' I says. 'Anything I can do?' I ask him. He stopped on the nex' step an' looked back at me. 'Got a wife?' he says. 'No,' says I, 'I ain't, sir. But they ain't never challenged my vote on 'count o' that, sir—no offence,' I says to him, respectful. 'All right,' he says, noddin' at me. 'I just thought mebbe she'd look in now and then. I'm gone all day,' he added, an' went off like he'd forgot me.

"I thought about the little thing all that mornin'—lyin' all alone up there in that room that wa'n't no bigger'n a coal-bin. It's bad enough to be sick anywheres, but it's like havin' both legs in a trap to be sick in New York. Towards noon I went into one o' the flats—first floor front it was—with the coal, an' I give the woman to understand they was somebody sick in the house. She was a great big creatur' that I'd never see excep' in red calico, an' I always thought she looked some like a tomato-ketchup bottle, with her apron for the label. She says, when I told her, 'You see if she wants anything,' she says. 'I can't climb all them stairs,' she answers me.

"Well, that afternoon I went down an' hunted up a rusty sleigh-bell I'd seen in the basement, an' I rubbed it up an' tied a string to it, an' long in the evenin' I went up-stairs an' rapped at Mr. Loneway's door.

"'I called,' I says, 'to ask after your wife, if I might.'

"'If you might,' he says, after me.

'I thank the Lord you're somebody that will. Come in,' he told me.

"They had two rooms. In one he was cookin' somethin' on a smelly oil-stove. In the other was his wife; but that room was all neat an' nice—curtains looped back, carpet an' all that, an' she was settin' up in bed. She had a black waist on, an' her hair pushed straight back, an' she was burnin' up with the fever.

"'Set down an' talk to her,' he says to me, 'while I get the dinner—will you? I've got to go out for the milk.'

"I did set down, feelin' some like a sawhorse in church. If she hadn't been so durn little, seems though I could 'a' talked with her, but I ketched sight of her hand on the quilt, an'—law! it wa'n't no bigger'n a butternut. She done the best thing she could do an' set me to work.

"'Mr. Bemus,' she says, first off—everybody else called me Peleg,—'Mr. Bemus,' she says, 'I wonder if you'd mind takin' an old newspaper—there's one somewheres around—an' stuffin' in the cracks of this window an' stop its rattlin'?'

"I laid my sleigh-bell down an' done as she says; an' while I fussed with the window, that seems though all Printin' House Square couldn't stuff up, she talked on, chipper as a squirrel, all about the buildin', an' who lived where, an' how many kids they was, an' wouldn't it be nice if they had an elevator like the model tenement we was payin' rent for, an' so on. I'd never 'a' dreamt she was sick if I hadn't looked 'round a time or two at her poor, burnin'-up face. Then bime-by he brought the supper in, an' when he went to lift her up she just naturally laid back an' fainted. But she was all right again in a minute, brave as two, an' she was like a child when she see what he'd brought her—a big platter for a tray, with milk toast an' an apple an' five cents' worth o' dates. She done her best to eat, too, and praised him up—an' the poor soul hung over her, watchin' every mouthful, feedin' her, coaxin' her, lookin' like nothin' more'n a boy himself. When I couldn't stand it no longer I took an' jingled the sleigh-bell.

"'I'm a-goin',' I says, 'to hang this outside the door here, an' run this nice long string through the transom. An'

to-morrow,' I says, 'when you want anything, just you pull the string a time or two, an' I'll be somewheres around.'

"She clapped her hands, her eyes shinin'.

"'Oh, goodey!' she says. 'Now I won't be alone. Ain't it nice,' she says, 'that there ain't no glass in the transom? If we lived in the model tenement, we couldn't do that,' she says, laughin' some.

"An' that young fellow, he followed me to the door an' just naturally shook hands with me, same 's though I'd been his kind. Then he followed me on out into the hall.

"'We had a little boy,' he says to me, low, 'an' it died four months ago yesterday, when it was six days old. She ain't ever been well since,' he says, kind of as if he wanted to tell somebody. But I didn't know what to say, an' so I found fault with the kerosene lamp in the hall, an' went on down.

"Nex' day I knew the doctor come twice. An' 'way 'long in the afternoon I was a-tinkerin' with the stair rail when I heard the sleigh-bell ring. I run up, an' she was settin' up just the same, in the black waist — but I thought her eyes was shiny with somethin' that wasn't fever—a sort o' scared excitement.

"'Mr. Bemus,' she says, 'I want you to do somethin' for me,' she says, 'an' not tell anybody. Will you?'

"'Why, yes,' I says, 'I will, Mis' Loneway,' I says. 'What is it?' I ask her.

"'There's a baby somewheres downstairs,' she says. 'I hear it cryin' sometimes. An' I want you to get it an' bring it up here.'

"That was a queer thing to ask, because kids isn't soothin' to the sick. But I went off down-stairs to the first floor front. The kid she meant belonged to the Tomato Ketchup woman. I knew they had one because it howled different times an', I judge, pounded its head on the floor some when it was maddest. It was the only real little one in the buildin'—the others was all the tonguey age. I told what I wanted.

"'For the land!' says Tomato Ketchup, 'I never see such nerve. Take my baby into a sick-room? Not if I know it. I s'pose you just come out o' there? Well, don't you stay here, bringin' diseases. A hospital's the true place fer the sick,' she says.

"I went back to Mis' Loneway, an' I guess I lied some. I said the kid was sick—had the croup, I thought, an' she'd hev to wait. Her face fell, but she said 'all right an' please not to say nothin',' an' then I went out an' done my best to borrow a kid for her. I ask all over the neighborhood, an' not a woman but looked on me as a cradle-snatcher—thought I wanted to abduct her child away from her. Bime-by I even told one woman what I want-ed it for.

"'My!' she says, 'if she ain't got one, she's got one less mouth to feed. Tell her to thank her stars.'

"After that I used to look into Mis' Loneway's frequent. The women on the same floor was quite decent to her, but they worked all day, an' mostly didn't get home till after her husband did. I found out somethin' about him, too. He was clerk in a big commission-house 'way down-town, an' his salary, as near as I could make out, was about what mine was, an' they wa'n't no estimatin' that by the cord at all. But I never heard a word out'n him about their not havin' much. He kep' on makin' milk toast an' bringin' in one piece o' fruit at a time an' once in a while a little meat. An' all the time anybody could see she wasn't gettin' no better. I knew she wasn't gettin' enough to eat, an' I knew he knew it, too. An' one night the doctor he outs with the truth.

"Mr. Loneway an' I was sittin' in the kitchen while the doctor was in the other room with her. I went there evenin's all the time by then—the young fellow seemed to like to hev me. We was keepin' warm over the oil stove because the real stove was in her room, an' the doctor come in an' stood over him.

"'My lad,' he says, gentle, 'there ain't half as much use o' my comin' here as there is o' her gettin' strengthenin' food. She's got to hev beef broth—cer'als—fresh this an' fresh that'—he went on to tell him, 'an' plenty of it,' he says. 'An' if we can make her strength hold out, I think,' he wound up, 'that we can save her—but she's gettin' weaker every day for lack o' food. Can you do anything more?' he ask him.

"I expected to see young Mr. Loneway go all to pieces at this, because I knew as it was he didn't ride in the street-car, he was pinchin' so to pay the doctor. But he sorter set up sudden an' squared his shoulders, an' he looked up an' says:

"'Yes!' he says. 'I've been thinkin' that to-night,' he says. 'An' I've hed a way to some good luck, you might call it —an' now I guess she can hev everything she wants,' he told him; an' he laughed some when he said it.

"That sort o' amazed me. I hadn't heard him sayin' anything about any ex-cruciatin' luck, an' his face hadn't been the face of a man on the brink of a bonanza. I wondered why he hadn't told her about this luck o' his, but I kep' quiet an' watched to see if he was bluffin'.

"I was cleanin' the walk off when he come home nex' night. Sure enough, there was his arms laid full o' bundles. An' his face—it done me good to see it.

"'Come on up an' help get dinner,' he yelled out like a kid, an' I thought I actually seen him smilin'.

"Soon's I could I went up-stairs, an' they wa'n't nothin' that man hadn't brought. They was everything the doctor had said, an' green things, an' a whol' basket o' fruit an' two bottles o' port, an' more things besides. They was lots o' fixin's, too, that there wa'n't a mite o' nourishment in—for he wa'n't no more practical nor medicinal 'n a wood-tick. But I knew how he felt.

"'Don't tell her,' he says. 'Don't tell her,' he says to me, hoppin' 'round the kitchen like a buzz-saw. 'I want to sur-prise her.'

"You can bet he did, too—if you'll overlook the liberty. When he was all ready he made me go in ahead.

"'To-ot!' says I, genial-like—they treated me jus' like one of 'em. 'To-ot! Lookey-at!'

"He set the big white platter down on the bed, an' when she see all the stuff—white grapes, mind you, an' fresh to-matoes, an' a glass for the wine—she just grabs his hand an' holds it up to her throat, an' says:

"'Jack! Oh, Jack!' she says—she called him that when she was pleased 'how did you? How did you?'

"'Never you mind,' he says, kissin' her an' lookin' as though he was goin' to bust out himself, 'never you ask. It's time I had some luck, ain't it? Like other men?'

"She was touchin' things here an' there, liftin' up the grapes, lookin' at 'em—poor little soul had lived on milk toast an' dates an' a apple now an' then for two weeks to my knowledge. But when he said that, she stopped an' looked at him, scared.

"'John!' she says, 'you ain't—'

"He laughed at that.

"'Gamblin'?' he says. 'No—never you fear.' I had thought o' that myself, only I didn't quite see when he'd had the chance since night before when the doctor told him. 'It's all owin' to the office,' he says to her; 'an' now you eat—lemme see you eat, Linda,' he says, an' that seemed to be food enough for him. He didn't half touch a thing. 'Eat all you want,' he says, 'an', Peleg, poke up the fire. There's half a ton o' coal comin' to-morrow. An' we're goin' to have this *every day*,' he told her.

"Land o' love! how happy she was! She made me eat some grapes, an' she sent a bunch to the woman on the same floor, because she had brought her an orange; an' then she begs Mr. Loneway to get an extry candle out of the top dresser draw'. An' when that was lit up she whispers to him, and he goes out an' fetches from somewheres a guitar with about half the strings left on; an' she set up an' picked away on 'em, an' we all three sung, though I can't carry a tune on more'n what I can carry a white-oak log.

"'Oh,' she says, 'I'm a-goin' to get well now. Oh,' she says, 'ain't it heaven to be rich?'

"No—you can say she'd ought to 'a' made him tell her where he got the money. But she trusted him, an' she'd been a-livin' on milk toast an' dates for so long that I can pretty well see how she took it all as what's-his-name took the wild honey, without askin' the Lord whose make it was. Besides, she was sick. An' milk toast an' dates 'd reconcile me to 'most any change for the better.

"It got so then that I went up-stairs every noon an' fixed up her lunch for her, an' one day she done what I'd been dreadin'. 'Mr. Bemus,' she says, 'that baby must be over the croup now. Won't you—won't you take it down this orange

an' see if you can't bring it up here a while?'

"I went down, but, law!—where was the use? The Ketchup woman grabs up her kid an' fair threw the orange at me. 'You don't know what disease you're bringin' in here,' she says—she had a voice like them gasoline wood-cutters. I see she'd took to heart some o' the model-tenement social-evenin' lectures on bugs an' worms in diseases. I carried the orange out an' give it to a kid in the ar'y, so's Mis' Loneway'd be makin' somebody some pleasure, anyhow. An' then I went back up-stairs an' told her the kid was worse. Seems the croup had turned into cholery infantum.

"'Why,' she says, 'I mus' send it down somethin' nice an' hot to-night,' an' so she did, and I slips it back in the Loneway kitchen unbeknownst. She wa'n't so very medicinal, either, bless her heart!

"'Tell me about that baby,' she says to me one noon. 'What's its name? Does it like to hev its mother love it?' she ask me.

"I knew the truth to be that it didn't let anybody do anything day or night within sight or sound of it, an' it looked to me like an imp o' the dark. But I fixed up a tol'able description, an' left out the freckles an' the temper, an' told her it was fat an' well an' a boy. That seemed to satisfy her. A fat, healthy boy is a woman's idea o' perfection in a kid. Its name, though, sort o' stumped me. The Tomato Ketchup called it mostly 'you-come-back-here-you-little-ape.' I heard that every day. So I said, just to piece out my information, that I thought its name might be April. That seemed to take her fancy, an' after that she was always askin' me how little April was—but not when Mr. Loneway was in hearin'. I see well enough she didn't want he should know that she was grievin' none.

"All the time kep' comin', every night, another armful o' good things. Land! that man he bought everything. Seems though he couldn't buy enough. Every night the big platter was heaped up an' runnin' over with everything under the sun, an' she was like another girl. I s'pose the things give her strength, but I reck'n the cheer helped most. She had the surprise to look forward to all day, an' there was plenty o' light, evenin's; an' the stove, that was kep' red hot. The doctor kep' sayin' she was better, too, an' everything seemed lookin' right up.

"Seems queer I didn't suspect from the first something was wrong. Seems though I ought to 'a' known money didn't grow out o' green wood the way he was pretendin'. It wasn't two weeks before he takes me down to the basement one night when he comes home, an' he owns up.

"'Peleg,' he says, 'I've got to tell somebody, an' God knows maybe it 'll be you that 'll hev to tell her. I've stole fifty-four dollars out o' the tray in the retail department,' says he, 'an' to-day they found me out. They wasn't no fuss made. Lovett, the assistant cashier, is the only one that knows. He took me aside quiet,' Mr. Loneway says, 'an' I made a clean breast. I said what I took it for. He's a married man himself, an' he told me if I'd make it up in three days he'd fix it so's nobody should know. The cashier's off for a week. In three days he's comin' back. But they might as well ask me to make up fifty-four hundred. I've got enough to keep on these three days so's she won't know,' he says, 'an' after that—'

"He hunched out his arms, an' I'll never forget his face.

"I says, 'Mr. Loneway, sir,' I says, 'chuck it. Tell her the whole thing an' give 'em back what you got left, an' do your best.'

"He turned on me like a crazy man.

"'Don't talk to me like that,' he says, fierce. 'You don't know what you're sayin',' he says. 'No man does till he has this happen to him. The judge on the bench that 'll send me to jail for it, he won't know what he's judgin'. My God—my God!' he says, leanin' up against the door o' the furnace-room, 'to see her sick like this—an' needin' things —when she give herself to me to take care of!'

"Course there wa'n't no talkin' to him. An' the nex' night an' the nex' he come home bringin' her truck just the same. Once he even hed her a bunch o' pinks. Seems though he was doin' the worst he could.

"The pinks come at the end of the second day of the three days the assistant cashier had give him to pay the money

back in. An' two things happened that night. I was in the kitchen helpin' him wash up the dishes while the doctor was in the room with Mis' Loneway. An' when the doctor come out o' there into the kitchen he shuts the door. I see right off somethin' was the matter. He took Mr. Loneway off to the back window, an' I rattled 'round with the dishes an' took on not to notice. Up until when the doctor goes out—an' then I felt Mr. Loneway's grip on my arm. I looked at him, an' I knew. She wasn't goin' to get well. He just slimpsed down on the chair an' put his face down in his arm, the way a schoolboy does—an' I swan he wa'n't much more'n a schoolboy, either. I s'pose if ever hell is in a man's heart— an' we mostly all see it there sometime even if we don't feel it—why, there was hell in his, then.

"All of a sudden there was a rap on the hall door. He never moved, an' so I went. I whistled, I rec'lect, so's she shouldn't suspect nothin' from our not goin' in where she was right off. An' a messenger-boy was out there in the passage with a letter for Mr. Loneway.

"I took it in to him. He turned himself around an' opened it, though I don't believe he knew half what he was doin'. An' what do you guess come tumblin' out o' that envelope? Fifty-four dollars in bills. Not a word with 'em.

"Then he broke down. 'It's Lovett,' he says, 'it's Lovett's done this—the assistant cashier. Maybe he's told some o' the other fellows at the desks next, an' they helped. They knew about her bein' sick. An' they can't none of 'em afford it,' he says, an' that seemed to cut him up worst of all. 'I'll give it back to him,' he says, resolute. 'I can't take it from 'em, Peleg.'

"I says, 'Hush up, Mr. Loneway, sir,' I says. 'You got to think o' her. Take it,' I told him, 'an' thank God it ain't as bad as it was. Who knows,' I asks him, 'but what the doctor might turn out wrong?'

"Pretty soon I got him to pull himself together some, an' I shoved him into the other room, an' I went with him, an' talked on like an idiot so nobody'd suspect—I didn't hev no idea what.

"She was settin' up in the same black waist. All of a sudden:

"'John!' says she.

" He went close by the bed.

" ' Is everything goin' on good?' she ask him.

" ' Everything,' he told her, right off.

" ' Splendid, John?' she ask him, pullin' his hand up by her cheek.

" ' Splendid,' he says, after her.

" ' We got a little money ahead?' she goes on.

" Bless me if he didn't do just what I had time to be afraid of. He hauls out them fifty-four dollars an' showed her.

" She claps her hands like a child.

" ' Oh, goodey!' she says; ' I'm so glad. I'm so glad. Now I can tell you,' she says to him.

" He took her in his arms an' kneeled down by the bed, an' I tried to slip out, but she called me back. So I stayed, like a axe in the parlor.

" ' John,' she says to him, ' do you know what Aunt Hettie told me before I was married? "You must always look the prettiest you know how," Aunt Hettie says,' she tells him, ' "for your husband. Because you must always be prettier for him than anybody else is." An', oh, dearest,' she says, ' you know I'd 'a' looked my best for you if I could— but I never had—an' it wasn't your fault!' she cries out, ' but things didn't go right. It wasn't anybody's fault. Only — I wanted to look nice for you. An' since I've been sick,' she says, ' it's made me wretched, wretched to think I didn't hev nothin' to put on but this black waist— this homely old black waist. You never liked me to wear black,' I rec'lect she says to him, ' an' it killed me to think— if anything should happen—you'd be rememberin' me like this. You think you'd remember me the way I was when I was well—but you wouldn't,' she says, earnest; ' people never, never do. You'd remember me here like I look now. Oh—an' so I thought—if there was ever so little money we could spare—won't you get me somethin'—somethin' so's you could remember me better? Somethin' to wear these few days,' she says.

" He breaks down then an' cries, with his face in her pillow.

" ' Don't—why, don't!' she says to him; ' if there wasn't any money, you might cry—only then I wouldn't never hev told you. But now—to-morrow—you can go an' buy me a little dressing-sack—the

kind they have in the windows on Broadway. Oh, Jack!' she says, ' is it wicked an' foolish for me to want you to remember me as nice as you can? It ain't—it ain't!' she says.

" Then I give out. I felt like a handful o' wet sawdust that's been squeezed. I slid out an' down-stairs, an' I guess I chopped wood near all night. The Tomato Ketchup's husband he pounded the floor for me to shut up, an' I told him— though I never was what you might call a impudent janitor—that if he thought he could chop it up any more soft, he'd better engage in it. But then the kid woke up, too, an' yelled some, an' I's afraid she'd hear it an' remember, an' so I quit.

" Nex' mornin' I laid for Mr. Loneway in the hall.

" ' Sir,' I says to him when he come down to go out, ' you won't do nothin' foolish?' I ask him.

" ' Mind your business,' he says, his face like a patch o' poplar ashes.

" I was in an' out o' their flat all day, an' I could see't Mis' Loneway she's happy as a lark. But I knew pretty well what was comin'. Mind you, this was the third day.

" That night I hed things goin' in the kitchen an' the kettle on, an' I's hesitatin' whether to put two eggs in the omelet or three, when he comes home. He laid a eternal lot o' stuff on the kitchen table, without one word, an' went in where she was. I heard paper rustlin', an' then I heard her voice—an' it wasn't no cryin', lemme say. An' so I says to myself, ' Well,' I says, ' she might as well hev a four-egg omelet, because it 'll be the last.' I knew if they's to arrest him she wouldn't never live the day out. So I goes on with the omelet, an' when he come out where I was I just told him if he'd cut open the grapefruit I hed ever'thing else ready. An' then he quit lookin' defiant, an' he calmed down some; an' pretty soon we took in the dinner.

" She was sittin' up in front o' her two pillows, pretty as a picture. An' she was in one o' the things I ain't ever see outside o' a store window. Lord! it was all the color o' roses, with craped-up stuff like the bark on a tree, an' rows an' rows o' lace, an' long, flappy ribbon. She was allus pretty, but she looked like an angel in that. An' I says to myself then, I says: 'If a woman *knows* she looks like that in them things, an' if she loves somebody an', livin' or dead, wants to look like that for him, I want to know who's to blame her? I ain't—Peleg Bemus, he ain't.' Mis' Loneway was as pretty as I ever see, not barrin' the stage. An' she was laughin', an' her cheeks was pinklike, an' she says,

"'Oh, Mr. Bemus,' she says, 'I feel like a queen,' she says, 'an' you must stay for dinner.'

"I never seen Mr. Loneway gayer. He was full o' fun an' funny sayin's, an' his face had even lost its chalky look an' he'd got some color, an' he laughed with her an' he made love to her—durned if it wasn't enough to keep a woman out o' the grave to be worshipped the way that man worshipped her. An' when she ask for the guitar I carried out the platter, an' I stayed an' straightened things some in the kitchen. An' all the while I could hear 'em singin' soft an' laughin' together . . . an' all the while I knew what was double sure to come.

"Well, in about an hour it did come. I was waitin' for it. Fact, I had filled up the coffee-pot expectin' it. An' when I heard the men comin' up the stairs I takes the coffee an' what rolls there was left an' I meets 'em in the hall, on the landing. They was two of 'em—constables, or somethin'—with a warrant for his arrest.

"'Gentlemen,' says I, openin' the coffee-pot careless so's the smell could get out an' circ'late—'gentlemen, he's up there in that room. There's only these one stairs, an' the only manhole's right here over your heads, so's you can watch that. You rec'lect that there ain't a roof on that side o' the house. Now, I'm a lonely beggar, an' I wisht you'd let me invite you to a cup o' hot coffee an' a hot buttered roll or two, right over there in that hall window. You can keep your eye peeled towards that door all the while,' I reminds 'em.

"Well, it was a bitter night, an' them two was flesh an' blood. They 'lowed that if he hadn't been there they'd 'a' had to wait for him anyway, so they finally set down. An' I doled 'em out the coffee. I 'lowed I could keep 'em an hour if I knew myself. Nobody could 'a' done any

different, with her an' him settin' up there singin' an' no manner o' doubt but what it was for the last time.

"I'd be'n 'round consid'able in my time an' I knew quite a batch o' stories. Well, I let 'em have 'em all, an' poured the coffee down 'em. They was willin' enough —it wa'n't cold in the halls to what it was outside, an' the coffee was boilin' hot. An' if anybody wants to blame me, they'd hev to see her first, all fluffed up, same as a kitten, in that pink jacket-thing, afore I'd give 'em a word o' hearin'.

"In the midst of it all I heard the Tomato Ketchup's kid yell. I remembered that this 'd be my last chanst fer *her* to see the kid when she could get any happiness out of it. I didn't think twice—I just filled up the cups o' them two, an' then I sails down-stairs, two at a time, an' opened the door o' first floor front without rappin'. The kid was there in its little nightgown, howlin' fer fair because it had be'n left alone with its boy brother. The Tomato Ketchup an' her husband was to a wake. I picked up the kid, rolled it in a blanket, grabbed brother by the arm, an' started up the stairs.

"'Is the house on f-f-fire?' says the boy brother.

"'Yes,' says I, 'it is. An' we're goin' up-stairs to hunt up a fire-escape,' I told him.

"At the top o' the stairs I sets him down on the floor an' promises him an orange, an' then I opens the door, with the kid on my arm. It had stopped yellin' by then, an' it was settin' up straight, with its eyes all round an' its cheeks all pinked up with havin' just woke up, an' it looked awful cute, in spite of its mother. Mis' Loneway was leanin' back, laughin', an' tellin' him what they was goin' to do the minute she got well; but when she see the baby she drops her husband's hand and sorter screams out, weak, an' holds out her arms. Mr. Loneway, he hardly heard me go in, I reckon—leastwise, he looks at me clean through me without seein' I was there. An' she hugs the kiddie up in her arms an' looks at me over the top of its head as much as to say she understood an' thanked me.

"'Its ma is went off,' I told 'em, apologetic, 'an' I thought maybe you'd look after it a while,' I told 'em.

Drawn by Lucius Wolcott Hitchcock

"SOMEHOW I KNEW THERE WASN'T NOTHIN' MORE TO WAIT FOR"

"Then I went out an' put oranges all around the boy brother on the hall floor, an' I hustled back down-stairs.

"'Gentlemen,' says I, brisk, 'I've got two dollars too much,' says I—an' I reck'n the cracks in them walls must 'a' winked at the notion. 'What do you say to a game o' dice on the bread plate?' I ask 'em.

"Well, one way an' another I kep' them two there for two hours. An' then, when the game was out, I knew I couldn't do nothin' else. So I stood up an' told 'em I'd go up an' let Mr. Loneway know they was there—along o' his wife bein' sick an' hadn't ought to be scared.

"I started up the stairs, feelin' like lead. Little more'n half way up I heard a little noise. I looked up, an' I see the boy brother a-comin', leakin' orange peel, with the kid slung over his shoulder, sleepin'. I looked on past him, an' the door o' Mr. Loneway's sittin'-room was open, an' I see Mr. Loneway standin' in the middle o' the floor. I must 'a' stopped still, because somethin' stumbled up against me from the back, an' the two constables was there, comin' close behind me. I could hear one of 'em breathin'.

"Then I went on up, an' somehow I knew there wasn't nothin' more to wait for. When we got to the top I see inside the room, an' she was layin' back on her pillow, all still an' quiet. An' the little new pink jacket never moved nor stirred, for there wa'n't no breath.

"Mr. Loneway, he come acrost the floor towards us.

"'Come in,' he says. 'Come right in,' he told us—an' I seen him smilin' some."

PROSPER'S OLD MOTHER
by Bret Harte

"IT'S all very well," said Joe Wynbrook, "for us to be sittin' here, slingin' lies easy and comfortable, with the wind whistlin' in the pines outside, and the rain just liftin' the ditches to fill our sluice-boxes with gold ez we're smokin' and waitin', but I tell you what, boys—it ain't home! No, sir, it ain't *home!*"

The speaker paused, glanced around the bright, comfortable bar-room, the shining array of glasses beyond, and the circle of complacent faces fronting the stove, on which his own boots were cheerfully steaming, lifted a glass of whiskey from the floor under his chair, and in spite of his deprecating remark, took a long draught of the spirits with every symptom of satisfaction.

"If ye mean," returned Cyrus Brewster, "that it ain't the old farm-house of our boyhood, 'way back in the woods, I'll agree with you; but ye'll just remember that there wasn't any gold-placers lying round on the medder on *that* farm. Not much! Ef thar had been, we wouldn't have left it."

"I don't mean that," said Joe Wynbrook, settling himself comfortably back in his chair; "it's the family hearth I'm talkin' of. The soothin' influence, ye know—the tidiness of the women folks."

"Ez to the soothin' influence," remarked the barkeeper, leaning his elbows meditatively on his counter, "afore I struck these diggin's I had a grocery and bar, 'way back in Mizzoori, where there was five old-fashioned farms jined. Blame my skin ef the men folks weren't a darned sight oftener over in my grocery, sittin' on barrils and histin' in their reg'lar corn juice, than ever any of you be here—with all these modern improvements."

"Ye don't catch on, any of you," returned Wynbrook, impatiently. "Ef it was a mere matter o' buildin' houses and becomin' family men, I reckon that this yer camp is about prosperous enough to do it, and able to get gals enough to marry us, but that would be only borryin' trouble, and lettin' loose a lot of jabberin' women to gossip again' each other and spile all our friendships. No, gentlemen! What we want here—each of us—is a good old mother! Nothin' newfangled or fancy, but the reg'lar oldfashioned mother we was used to when we was boys!"

The speaker struck a well-worn chord —rather the worse for wear, and one that had jangled falsely ere now, but which still produced its effect. The men were silent. Thus encouraged, Wynbrook proceeded:

"Think o' comin' home from the gulch a night like this and findin' yer old mother a-waitin' ye! No fumblin' around for the matches ye'd left in the gulch; no high old cussin' because the wood was wet or you forgot to bring it in; no bustlin' around for your dry things and findin' you forgot to dry 'em that mornin'— but everything waitin' for ye and ready. And then, mebbe, she brings ye in some doughnuts she's just cooked for ye— cooked ez only *she* kin cook 'em! Take Prossy Riggs—alongside of me here—for instance! *He's* made the biggest strike yet, and is puttin' up a high-toned house on the hill. Well! he'll hev it finished off and furnished slap-up style, you bet! with a Chinese cook, and a Biddy, and a Mexican *vaquero* to look after his horse— but he won't have no mother to housekeep! That is," he corrected himself, perfunctorily, turning to his companion, "you've never spoke o' your mother, so I reckon you're about fixed up like us."

The young man thus addressed flushed slightly, and then nodded his head with a sheepish smile. He had, however, listened to the conversation with an interest almost childish, and a reverent admiration of his comrades—qualities which, combined with an intellect not particularly brilliant, made him alternately the butt and the favorite of the camp. Indeed, he was supposed to possess that proportion of stupidity and inexperience which, in mining superstition, gives "luck" to its possessor. And this had been singularly proven in the fact that he had made the biggest "strike" of the season.

Joe Wynbrook's sentimentalism, albeit only argumentative and half-serious, had unwittingly touched a chord of "Prossy's" simple history, and the flush which had risen to his cheek was not entirely bashfulness. The home and relationship of which they spoke so glibly *he* had never known; he was a foundling! As he lay awake that night he remembered the charitable institution which had protected his infancy, the master to whom he had later been apprenticed;—that was all he knew of his childhood. In his simple way he had been greatly impressed by the strange value placed by his companions upon the family influence, and he had received their extravagance with perfect credulity. In his absolute ignorance and his lack of humor he had detected no false quality in their sentiment. And a vague sense of his responsibility, as one who had been the luckiest, and who was building the first "house" in the camp, troubled him. He lay staringly wide-awake, hearing the mountain wind, and feeling warm puffs of it on his face through the crevices of the log cabin, as he thought of the new house on the hill that was to be lathed and plastered and clapboarded, and yet void and vacant of that mysterious "mother"! And then, out of the solitude and darkness, a tremendous idea struck him that made him sit up in his bunk!

A day or two later "Prossy" Riggs stood on a sand-blown, wind-swept suburb of San Francisco, before a large building whose forbidding exterior proclaimed that it was an institution of formal charity. It was, in fact, a refuge for the various waifs and strays of ill-advised or hopeless immigration. As Prosper paused before the door, certain old recollections of a similar refuge were creeping over him, and, oddly enough, he felt as embarrassed as if he had been seeking relief for himself. The perspiration stood out on his forehead as he entered the room of the manager.

It chanced, however, that this official, besides being a man of shrewd experience of human weakness, was also kindly hearted, and having, after his first official scrutiny of his visitor and his resplendent watch-chain, assured himself that he was not seeking personal relief, courteously assisted him in his stammering request.

"If I understand you, you want some one to act as your housekeeper?"

"That's it! Somebody to kinder look arter things—and me—ginrally," returned Prosper, greatly relieved.

"Of what age?" continued the manager, with a cautious glance at the robust youth and good-looking simple face of Prosper.

"I ain't nowise partickler—ez long ez she's old—ye know. Ye follow me? Old —ez ef—betwixt you an' me, she might be my own mother."

The manager smiled inwardly. A certain degree of discretion was noticeable in this rustic youth! "You are quite right," he answered, gravely, "as yours is a mining camp where there are no other women. Still, you don't want any one *too* old or decrepit. There is an elderly maiden lady—" But a change was transparently visible on Prosper's simple face, and the manager paused.

"She oughter be kinder married, you know—ter be like a mother," stammered Prosper.

"Oh, aye. I see," returned the manager, again illuminated by Prosper's unexpected wisdom.

He mused for a moment. "There is," he began, tentatively, "a lady in reduced circumstances — not an inmate of this house, but who has received some relief from us. She was the wife of a whaling captain who died some years ago, and broke up her home. She was not brought up to work, and this, with her delicate health, has prevented her from seeking active employment. As you don't seem to require that of her, but rather want an overseer, and as your purpose, I gather, is somewhat philanthropical, you might induce her to accept a 'home' with you. Having seen better days, she is rather particular," he added, with a shrewd smile.

Simple Prosper's face was radiant. "She'll have a Chinaman and a Biddy to help her," he said, quickly. Then recollecting the tastes of his comrades, he added, half apologetically, half cautiously, " Ef she could, now and then, throw herself into a lemming pie or a pot of doughnuts, jest in a motherly kind o' way, it would please the boys."

" Perhaps you can arrange that too," returned the manager, " but I shall have to broach the whole subject to her, and you had better call again to-morrow, when I will give you her answer."

" Ye kin say," said Prosper, lightly, fingering his massive gold chain and somewhat vaguely recalling the language of advertisement, " that she kin have the comforts of a home and no questions asked, and fifty dollars a month."

Rejoiced at the easy progress of his plan, and half inclined to believe himself a miracle of cautious diplomacy, Prosper, two days later, accompanied the manager to the cottage on Telegraph Hill where the relict of the late Captain Pottinger lamented the loss of her spouse, in full view of the sea he had so often tempted. On their way thither the manager imparted to Prosper how, according to hearsay, that lamented seaman had carried into the domestic circle those severe habits of discipline which had earned for him the prefix of " Bully " and " Belaying-pin " Pottinger during his strenuous life. " They say that though she is very quiet and resigned, she once or twice stood up to the captain; but that's not a bad quality to have, in a rough community, as I presume yours is, and would insure her respect." Ushered at last into a small tanklike sitting - room, whose chief decorations consisted of large *abelone* shells, dried marine algæ, coral, and a sword-fish's broken weapon, Prosper's disturbed fancy discovered the widow, sitting, apparently, as if among her husband's remains at the bottom of the sea. She had a dejected yet somewhat ruddy face; her hair was streaked with white, but primly disposed over her ears like lappets, and her garb was cleanly but sombre. There was no doubt but that she was a lugubrious figure, even to Prosper's optimistic and inexperienced mind. He could not imagine her as beaming on his hearth! It was with some alarm that, after the introduction had been completed, he beheld the manager take his

leave. As the door closed, the bashful Prosper felt the murky eyes of the widow fixed upon him. A gentle cough, accompanied with the resigned laying of a black-mittened hand upon her chest, suggested a genteel prelude to conversation, with possible pulmonary complications.

" I am induced to accept your proposal temporarily," she said, in a voice of querulous precision, " on account of pressing pecuniary circumstances which would not have happened had my claim against the ship-owners for my dear husband's loss been properly raised. I hope you fully understand that I am unfitted both by ill health and early education from doing any menial or manual work in your household. I shall simply oversee and direct. I shall expect that the stipend you offer shall be paid monthly in advance. And as my medical man prescribes a certain amount of stimulation for my system, I shall expect to be furnished with such viands—or even "— she coughed slightly—" such beverages as may be necessary. I am far from strong —yet my wants are few."

" Ez far ez I am ketchin' on and followin' ye, ma'am," returned Prosper, timidly, " ye'll hev everything ye want— jest like it was yer own home. In fact," he went on, suddenly growing desperate as the difficulties of adjusting this unexpectedly fastidious and superior woman to his plan seemed to increase, " ye'll jest consider me ez yer—" But here her murky eyes were fixed on his and he faltered. Yet he had gone too far to retreat. " Ye see," he stammered, with a hysterical grimness that was intended to be playful —" ye see, this is jest a little secret betwixt and between you and me; there'll be only you and me in the house, and it would kinder seem to the boys more homelike—ef—ef—you and me had—you bein' a widder, you know—a kind of—of "— here his smile became ghastly—" close relationship."

The widow of Captain Pottinger here sat up so suddenly that she seemed to slip through her sombre and precise enwrappings with an exposure of the real Mrs. Pottinger that was almost improper. Her high color deepened; the pupils of her black eyes contracted in the light the innocent Prosper had poured into them. Leaning forward, with her fingers clasped on her bosom, she said: "Did you tell this to the manager?"

"Of course not," said Prosper; "ye see, it's only a matter 'twixt you and me."

Mrs. Pottinger looked at Prosper, drew a deep breath, and then gazed at the *abelone* shells for moral support. A smile, half querulous, half superior, crossed her face as she said: "This is very abrupt and unusual. There is, of course, a disparity in our ages! You have never seen me before—at least to my knowledge —although you may have heard of me. The Spraggs of Marblehead are well known—perhaps better than the Pottingers. And yet, Mr. Griggs—"

"Riggs," suggested Prosper, hurriedly.

"Riggs. Excuse me! I was thinking of young Lieutenant Griggs of the Navy, whom I knew in days now past. Mr. Riggs, I should say. Then you want me to—"

"To be my old mother, ma'am," said Prosper, tremblingly. "That is, to pretend and look ez ef you was! You see, I haven't any, but I thought it would be nice for the boys, and make it more like home in my new house, ef I allowed that *my* old mother would be comin' to live with me. They don't know I never had a mother to speak of. They'll never find it out! Say ye will, Mrs. Pottinger! Do!"

And here the unexpected occurred. Against all conventional rules and all accepted traditions of fiction, I am obliged to state that Mrs. Pottinger did *not* rise up and order the trembling Prosper to leave the house! She only gripped the arm of her chair a little tighter, leaned forward, and disdaining her usual precision and refinement of speech, said, quietly: "It's a bargain! If *that's* what you're wanting, my son, you can count upon me as becoming your old mother, Cecilia Jane Pottinger Riggs, every time!"

A few days later the sentimentalist Joe Wynbrook walked into the saloon of Wild Oat, where his comrades were drinking, and laid a letter down on the bar with every expression of astonishment and disgust. "Look," he said, "if that don't beat all! Ye wouldn't believe it, but here's Prossy Riggs writin' that he came across his mother — his *mother,* gentlemen—in 'Frisco; she hevin', unbe-

knownst to him, joined a party visiting the coast! And what does this blamed fool do? Why, he's goin' to bring her— that old woman—*here!* Here—gentlemen —to take charge of that new house—and spoil our fun. And the God-forsaken idiot thinks that we'll *like* it!"

. . . . . .

It was one of those rare mornings in the rainy season when there was a suspicion of spring in the air, and after a night of rainfall the sun broke through fleecy clouds with little islets of blue sky—when Prosper Riggs and his mother drove into Wild Cat Camp. An expression of cheerfulness was on the faces of his old comrades. For it had been recognized that, after all, "Prossy" had a perfect right to bring his old mother there—his well-known youth and inexperience preventing this baleful performance from being established as a precedent. For these reasons hats were cheerfully doffed, and some jackets put on, as the buggy swept up the hill to the pretty new cottage with its green blinds and white veranda, on the crest.

Yet I am afraid that Prosper was not perfectly happy, even in the triumphant consummation of his plans. Mrs. Pottinger's sudden and businesslike acquiescence in it, and her singular lapse from her genteel precision, were gratifying, but startling to his ingenuousness. And although from the moment she accepted the situation she was fertile in resources and full of precaution against any possibility of detection, he saw, with some uneasiness, that its control had passed out of his hands.

"You say your comrades know nothing of your family history?" she had said to him on the journey thither. "What are you going to tell them?"

"Nothin', 'cept your bein' my old mother," said Prosper, hopelessly.

"That's not enough, my son." (Another embarrassment to Prosper was her easy grasp of the maternal epithets.) "Now listen! You were born just six months after your father, Captain Riggs (formerly Pottinger) sailed on his first voyage. You remember very little of him, of course, as he was away so much."

"Hadn't I better know suthin' about his looks?" said Prosper, submissively.

"A tall dark man, that's enough," responded Mrs. Pottinger, sharply.

"Hadn't he better favor me?" said Prosper, with his small cunning recognizing the fact that he himself was a decided blond.

"Ain't at all necessary," said the widow, firmly. "You were always wild and ungovernable," she continued, "and ran away from school to join some Western emigration. That accounts for the difference of our styles."

"But," continued Prosper, "I oughter remember suthin' about our old times—runnin' arrants for you, and bringin' in the wood o' frosty mornin's, and you givin' me hot doughnuts," suggested Prosper, dubiously.

"Nothing of the sort," said Mrs. Pottinger, promptly. "We lived in the city, with plenty of servants. Just remember, Prosper dear, your mother wasn't *that* low down country style."

Glad to be relieved from further invention, Prosper was, nevertheless, somewhat concerned at this shattering of the ideal mother in the very camp that had sung her praises. But he could only trust to her recognizing the situation with her usual sagacity—of which he stood in respectful awe.

Joe Wynbrook and Cyrus Brewster had, as older members of the camp, purposely lingered near the new house to offer any assistance to "Prossy and his mother," and had received a brief and passing introduction to the latter. So deep and unexpected was the impression she made upon them that these two oracles of the camp retired down the hill in awkward silence for some time, neither daring to risk his reputation by comment or over-surprise. But when they approached the curious crowd below awaiting them, Cyrus Brewster ventured to say:

"Struck me ez ef that old gal was rather high-toned for Prossy's mother."

Joe Wynbrook instantly seized the fatal admission to show the advantage of superior insight:

"Struck *you!* Why, it was no more than *I* expected all along! What did we know of Prossy? Nothin'! What did he ever tell us? Nothin'! And why? 'Cos it was his secret. Lord! a blind mule could see that. All this foolishness and simplicity o' his come o' his bein' cuddled and pampered as a baby. Then, like ez not, he was either kidnapped or led away by some feller—and nearly broke his mother's heart. I'll bet my bottom dollar he has been advertised for afore this—only we didn't see the paper. Like ez not they had agents out seekin' him, and he jest ran into their hands in 'Frisco! I had a kind o' presentiment o' this when he left, though I never let on anything."

"I reckon, too, that she's kinder afraid he'll bolt agin. Did ye notice how she kept watchin' him all the time, and how she did the bossin' o' everything? And there's *one* thing sure! He's changed—yes! He don't look as keerless and free and foolish ez he uster."

Here there was an unmistakable chorus of assent from the crowd that had joined them. Every one—even those who had not been introduced to the mother—had noticed his strange restraint and reticence. In the impulsive logic of the camp, conduct such as this, in the face of that superior woman—his mother—could only imply that her presence was distasteful to him; that he was either ashamed of their noticing his inferiority to her, or ashamed of *them!* Wild and hasty as was their deduction, it was, nevertheless, voiced by Joe Wynbrook in a tone of impartial and even reluctant conviction "Well, gentlemen, some of ye may remember that when I heard that Prossy was bringin' his mother here I kicked—kicked because it only stood to reason that, being *his* mother, she'd be that foolish she'd upset the camp. There wasn't room enough for two such chuckle-heads—and one of 'em being a woman, she couldn't be shut up or sat upon ez we did to *him*. But now, gentlemen, ez we see she ain't that kind, but high-toned and level-headed, and that she's got the grip on Prossy—whether he likes it or not—we ain't goin' to let him go back on her! No, sir! we ain't goin' to let him break her heart the second time! He may think we ain't good enough for her, but ez long ez she's civil to us, we'll stand by her."

In this conscientious way were the shackles of that unhallowed relationship slowly riveted on the unfortunate Prossy.

In his intercourse with his comrades during the next two or three days their attitude was shown in frequent and ostentatious praise of his mother, and suggestive advice, such as: "I wouldn't stop at the saloon, Prossy; your old mother is wantin' ye;" or, "Chuck that 'ere tarpolin over your shoulders, Pross, and don't take your wet duds into the house that yer old mother's bin makin' tidy." Oddly enough, much of this advice was quite sincere, and represented—for at least twenty minutes—the honest sentiments of the speaker. Prosper was touched at what seemed a revival of the sentiment under which he had acted, forgot his uneasiness, and became quite himself again—a fact also noticed by his critics. "Ye've only to keep him up to his work and he'll be the widder's joy agin," said Cyrus Brewster. Certainly he was so far encouraged that he had a long conversation with Mrs. Pottinger that night, with the result that the next morning Joe Wynbrook, Cyrus Brewster, Hank Mann, and Kentucky Ike were invited to spend the evening at the new house. As the men, clean-shirted and decently jacketed, filed into the neat sitting-room with its bright carpet, its cheerful fire, its side table with a snowy cloth on which shining tea and coffee pots were standing, their hearts thrilled with satisfaction. In a large stuffed rocking-chair, Prossy's old mother, wrapped up in a shawl and some mysterious ill health which seemed to forbid any exertion, received them with genteel languor and an extended black mitten.

"I cannot," said Mrs. Pottinger, with sad pensiveness, "offer you the hospitality of my own home, gentlemen—you remember, Prosper dear, the large *salon* and our staff of servants at Lexington Avenue!—but since my son has persuaded me to take charge of his humble cot, I hope you will make all allowances for its deficiencies — even," she added, casting a look of mild reproach on the astonished Prosper "even if *he* cannot."

"I'm sure he oughter to be thankful to ye, ma'am," said Joe Wynbrook, quickly, "for makin' a break to come here to live, jest ez we're thankful—speakin' for the rest of this camp—for yer lightin' us up ez you're doin'! I reckon I'm speakin' for the crowd," he added, looking round him.

Murmurs of "That's so" and "You bet" passed through the company, and one or two cast a half-indignant glance at Prosper.

"It's only natural," continued Mrs. Pottinger, resignedly, "that having lived so long alone, my dear Prosper may at first be a little impatient of his old mother's control, and perhaps regret his invitation."

"Oh no, ma'am," said the embarrassed Prosper.

But here the mercurial Wynbrook interposed on behalf of amity and the camp's *esprit de corps*. "Why, Lord! ma'am, he's jest bin longin' for ye! Times and times agin he's talked about ye; sayin' how ef he could only get ye out of yer Fifth Avenue saloon to share his humble lot with him here, he'd die happy! *You've* heard him talk, Brewster?"

"Frequent," replied the accommodating Brewster.

"Part of the simple refreshment I have to offer you," continued Mrs. Pottinger, ignoring further comment, "is a viand the exact quality of which I am not familiar with, but which my son informs me is a great favorite with you. It has been prepared by Li Sing under my direction. Prosper dear, see that the — er — doughnuts — are brought in with the coffee."

Satisfaction beamed on the faces of the company, with perhaps the sole exception of Prosper. As a dish containing a number of brown glistening spheres of baked dough was brought in, the men's eyes shone in sympathetic appreciation. Yet that epicurean light was for a moment dulled as each man grasped a sphere, and then sat motionless with it in his hand, as if it was a ball and they were waiting the signal for playing.

"I am told," said Mrs. Pottinger, with a glance of Christian tolerance at Prosper, "that lightness is considered desirable by some—perhaps you gentlemen may find them heavy."

"Thar is two kinds," said the diplomatic Joe, cheerfully, as he began to nibble his, sideways, like a squirrel, "light and heavy; some likes 'em one way, and some another."

They were hard and heavy, but the men, assisted by the steaming coffee, finished them with heroic politeness. "And now, gentlemen," said Mrs. Pottinger, leaning back in her chair and calmly surveying the party, "you have my permission to light your pipes while you partake of some whiskey and water."

The guests looked up—gratified but astonished. "Are ye sure, ma'am, you don't mind it?" said Joe, politely.

"Not at all," responded Mrs. Pottinger, briefly. "In fact, as my physician advises the inhalation of tobacco smoke for my asthmatic difficulties, I will join you." After a moment's fumbling in a beaded bag that hung from her waist, she produced a small black clay pipe, filled it from the same receptacle, and lit it.

A thrill of surprise went round the company, and it was noticed that Prosper seemed equally confounded. Nevertheless, this awkwardness was quickly overcome by the privilege and example given them, and with a glass of whiskey and water before them, the men were speedily at their ease. Nor did Mrs. Pottinger disdain to mingle in their desultory talk. Sitting there with her black pipe in her mouth, but still precise and superior, she told a thrilling whaling adventure of Prosper's father (drawn evidently from the experience of the lamented Pottinger), which not only deeply interested her hearers, but momentarily exalted Prosper in their minds as the son of that hero. "Now you speak o' that, ma'am," said the ingenuous Wynbrook, "there's a good deal o' Prossy in that yarn o' his father's; same kind o' keerless grit! You remember, boys, that day the dam broke and he stood thar, the water up to his neck, heavin' logs in the break till he stopped it." Briefly, the evening, in spite of its initial culinary failure and its surprises, was a decided social success, and even the bewildered and doubting Prosper went to bed relieved. It was followed by many and more informal gatherings at the house, and Mrs. Pottinger so far unbent—if that term could be used of one who never altered her primness of manner—as to join in a game of poker— and even permitted herself to win.

But by the end of six weeks another change in their feelings towards Prosper seemed to insidiously creep over the camp. He had been received into his former fellowship, and even the presence of his mother had become familiar, but he began to be an object of secret commiseration. They still frequented the house, but among themselves afterwards they talked in whispers. There was no doubt to them that Prosper's old mother drank not only what her son had provided, but what she surreptitiously obtained from the saloon. There was the testimony of the barkeeper, himself concerned equally with the camp in the integrity of the Riggs household. And there was an even darker suspicion. But this must be given in Joe Wynbrook's own words:

"I didn't mind the old woman winnin' and winnin' reg'lar—for poker's an unsartin game;—it ain't the money that we're losin'—for it's all in the camp. But when she's developing a habit o' holdin' *four* aces when somebody else hez *two,* who don't like to let on because it's Prosper's old mother—it's gettin' rough! And dangerous too, gentlemen, if there happened to be an outsider in, or one of the boys should kick. Why, I saw Bilson grind his teeth—he holdin' a sequence flush—ace high—when the dear old critter laid down her reg'lar four aces and raked in the pile. We had to nearly kick his legs off under the table afore he'd understand—not havin' an old mother himself."

"Some un will hev to tackle her without Prossy knowin' it. For it would jest break his heart, arter all he's gone through to get her here!" said Brewster, significantly.

"Unless he *did* know it and it was that what made him so sorrowful when they first came. B'gosh! I never thought o' that," said Wynbrook, with one of his characteristic sudden illuminations.

"Well, gentlemen, whether he did or not," said the barkeeper, stoutly, "he must never know that *we* know it. No, not if the old gal cleans out my bar and takes the last scad in the camp."

And to this noble sentiment they responded as one man.

How far they would have been able to carry out that heroic resolve was never known. For an event occurred which eclipsed its importance. One morning at breakfast Mrs. Pottinger fixed a clouded eye upon Prosper.

"Prosper," she said, with fell deliberation, "you ought to know you have a sister."

"Yes, ma'am," returned Prosper, with that meekness with which he usually received these family disclosures.

"A sister," continued the lady, "whom you haven't seen since you were a child. A sister who for family reasons has been living with other relatives. A girl of nineteen."

"Yes, ma'am," said Prosper, humbly. "But ef you wouldn't mind writin' all that down on a bit o' paper—ye know my short memory!—I would get it by heart to-day in the gulch. I'd have it all pat enough by night, ef," he added, with a short sigh, "ye was kalkilatin' to make any allusions to it when the boys are here."

"Your sister Augusta," continued Mrs. Pottinger, calmly ignoring these details, "will be here to-morrow to make me a visit."

But here the worm Prosper not only turned, but stood up, nearly upsetting the table. "It can't be did, ma'am! it *mustn't* be did!" he said, wildly. "It's enough for me to hev played this camp with *you*—but now to run in—"

"Can't be did!" repeated Mrs. Pottinger, rising in her turn and fixing upon the unfortunate Prosper a pair of murky, piratical eyes that had once quelled the sea-roving Pottinger. "Do you, my adopted son, dare to tell me that I can't have my own flesh and blood beneath my roof?"

"Yes! I'd rather tell the whole story —I'd rather tell the boys I fooled them— than go on again!" burst out the excited Prosper.

But Mrs. Pottinger only set her lips implacably together. "Very well, tell them, then," she said, rigidly; "tell them how you lured me from my humble dependence in San Francisco with the prospect of a home with you; tell them how you compelled me to deceive their trusting hearts with your wicked falsehoods; tell them how you—a foundling—borrowed me for your mother, my poor dead husband for your father, and made me invent falsehood upon falsehood to tell them while you sat still and listened!"

Prosper gasped.

"Tell them," she went on, deliberately, "that when I wanted to bring my helpless child to her only home—*then,* only then—you determined to break your word to me, either because you meanly begrudged her that share of your house, or to keep your misdeeds from her knowledge! Tell them that, Prossy dear, and see what they'll say!"

Prosper sank back in his chair aghast. In his sudden instinct of revolt he had forgotten the camp! He knew, alas, too well what they would say! He knew that, added to their indignation at having been duped, their chivalry and absurd sentiment would rise in arms against the abandonment of two helpless women!

"P'r'aps ye're right, ma'am," he stammered. "I was only thinkin'," he added, feebly, "how *she'd* take it."

"She'll take it as I wish her to take it," said Mrs. Pottinger, firmly.

"Supposin', ez the camp don't know her, and I 'ain't bin talkin' o' havin' any *sister,* you ran her in here as my *cousin?* See? You bein' her aunt?"

Mrs. Pottinger regarded him with compressed lips for some time. Then she said, slowly and half meditatively: "Yes; it might be done! She will probably be willing to sacrifice her nearer relationship to save herself from passing as your sister. It would be less galling to her pride, and she wouldn't have to treat you so familiarly."

"Yes, ma'am," said Prosper, too relieved to notice the uncomplimentary nature of the suggestion. "And ye see I could call her 'Miss Pottinger,' which would come easier to me."

In its high resolve to bear with the weaknesses of Prosper's mother, the camp received the news of the advent of Prosper's cousin solely with reference to its possible effect upon the aunt's habits, and very little other curiosity. Prosper's own reticence, they felt, was probably due to the tender age at which he had separated from his relations. But when it was known that Prosper's mother had driven to the house with a very pretty girl of eighteen, there was a flutter of excitement in that impressionable community. Prosper, with his usual shyness, had evaded an early meeting with her, and was even loitering irresolutely on his way home from work, when, as he approached the house, to his discomfiture the door suddenly opened, the young lady appeared and advanced directly towards him.

She was slim, graceful, and prettily dressed, and at any other moment Prosper might have been impressed by her good looks. But her brows were knit, her dark eyes—in which there was an unmistakable reminiscence of Mrs. Pottinger—were glittering, and although she was apparently anticipating their meeting, it was evidently with no cousinly interest. When within a few feet of him she stopped. Prosper with a feeble smile offered his hand. She sprang back. "Don't touch me! Don't come a step nearer or I'll scream!"

Prosper, still with smiling inanity, stammered that he was only "goin' to shake hands," and moved sideways towards the house.

"Stop!" she said, with a stamp of her slim foot. "Stay where you are! We must have our talk out *here*. I'm not going to waste words with you in there, before *her*."

Prosper stopped.

"What did you do this for?" she said, angrily. "How dared you? How could you? Are you a man, or the fool she takes you for?"

"Wot did I do *wot* for?" said Prosper, sullenly.

"This! Making my mother pretend you were her son! Bringing her here among these men to live a lie!"

"She was willin'," said Prosper, gloomily. "I told her what she had to do, and she seemed to like it."

"But couldn't you see she was old and weak, and wasn't responsible for her actions? Or were you only thinking of yourself?"

This last taunt stung him. He looked up. He was not facing a helpless dependent old woman as he had been the day before, but a handsome clever girl in every way his superior—and in the right! In his vague sense of honor it seemed more creditable for him to fight it out with *her*. He burst out: "I never thought of myself! I never had an old mother; I never knew what it was to want one—but the men did! And as I couldn't get one for them, I got

one for myself—to share and share alike —I thought they'd be happier ef there was one in the camp!"

There was the unmistakable accent of truth in his voice. There came a faint twitching of the young girl's lips and the dawning of a smile. But it only acted as a goad to the unfortunate Prosper. "Ye kin laugh, Miss Pottinger, but it's God's truth! But one thing I didn't do. No! When your mother wanted to bring you in here as my sister, I kicked! I did! And you kin thank me, for all your laughin', that you're standing in this camp in your own name —and ain't nothin' but my cousin."

"I suppose you thought your precious friends didn't want a *sister* too?" said the girl, ironically.

"It don't make no matter wot they want now," he said, gloomily. "For," he added, with sudden desperation, "it's come to an end! Yes! You and your mother will stay here a spell so that the boys don't suspicion nothin' of either of ye. Then I'll give it out that you're takin' your aunt away on a visit. Then I'll make over to her a thousand dollars for all the trouble I've given her, and you'll take her away. I've bin a fool, Miss Pottinger, mebbe I am one now, but what I'm doin' is on the square, and it's got to be done!"

He looked so simple and so good—so like an honest school-boy confessing a fault and abiding by his punishment, for all his six feet of altitude and silky mustache—that Miss Pottinger lowered her eyes. But she recovered herself and said, sharply:

"It's all very well to talk of her going away! But she *won't*. You have made her like you—yes! like you better than me—than any of us! She says you're the only one who ever treated her like a mother—as a mother should be treated. She says she never knew what peace and comfort were until she came to you. There! Don't stare like that! Don't you understand? Don't you see? Must I tell you again that she is strange— that—that she was *always* queer and strange—and queerer on account of her unfortunate habits—surely you knew *them*, Mr. Riggs! She quarrelled with us all. I went to live with my aunt, and she took herself off to San Francisco with a silly claim against my father's ship-owners. Heaven only knows how she managed to live there; but she always impressed people with her manners, and some one always helped her! At last I begged my aunt to let me seek her, and I tracked her here. There! If you've confessed everything to me, you have made me confess everything to you, and about my own mother, too! Now, what is to be done?"

"Whatever is agreeable to you is the same to me, Miss Pottinger," he said, formally.

"But you mustn't call me 'Miss Pottinger' so loud. Somebody might hear you," she returned, mischievously.

"All right—'cousin,' then," he said, with a prodigious blush. "Supposin' we go in."

In spite of the camp's curiosity, for the next few days they delicately withheld their usual evening visits to Prossy's mother. "They'll be wantin' to talk o' old times, and we don't wanter be too previous," suggested Wynbrook. But their verdict, when they at last met the new cousin, was unanimous, and their praises extravagant. To their inexperienced eyes she seemed to possess all her aunt's gentility and precision of language, with a vivacity and playfulness all her own. In a few days the whole camp was in love with her. Yet she dispensed her favors with such tactful impartiality and with such innocent enjoyment—free from any suspicion of coquetry—that there were no heart-burnings, and the unlucky man who nourished a fancied slight would have been laughed at by his fellows. She had a town-bred girl's curiosity and interest in camp life, which she declared was like a "perpetual picnic," and her slim, graceful figure halting beside a ditch where the men were working seemed to them as grateful as the new spring sunshine. The whole camp became tidier; a coat was considered *de rigueur* at "Prossy's mother" evenings; there was less horseplay in the trails, and less shouting. "It's all very well to talk about 'old mothers,'" said the cynical barkeeper, "but that gal, single-handed, has done more in a week to make the camp decent than old Ma'am Riggs has in a month o' Sundays."

Since Prosper's brief conversation with Miss Pottinger before the house, the question "What is to be done?" had singularly lapsed, nor had it been referred to again by either. The young lady had apparently thrown herself into the diversions of the camp with the thoughtless gayety of a brief-holiday maker, and it was not for him to remind her—even had he wished to—that her important question had never been answered. He had enjoyed her happiness with the relief of a secret shared by her. Three weeks had passed; the last of the winter's rains had gone. Spring was stirring in underbrush and wildwood, in the pulse of the waters, in the sap of the great pines, in the uplifting of flowers. Small wonder if Prosper's boyish heart had stirred a little too.

In fact, he had been possessed by another luminous idea—a wild idea that to him seemed almost as absurd as the one which had brought him all this trouble. It had come to him like that one—out of a starlit night—and he had risen one morning with a feverish intent to put it into action! It brought him later to take an unprecedented walk alone with Miss Pottinger, to linger under green leaves in unfrequented woods, and at last seemed about to desert him as he stood in a little hollow with her hand in his—their only listener an inquisitive squirrel. Yet this was all the disappointed animal heard him stammer:

"So you see, dear, it would *then* be no lie—for—don't you see?—she'd be really *my* mother as well as *yours*."

The marriage of Prosper Riggs and Miss Pottinger was quietly celebrated at Sacramento, but Prossy's "old mother" did not return with the happy pair.

Of Mrs. Pottinger's later career some idea may be gathered from a letter which Prosper received a year after his marriage. "Circumstances," wrote Mrs. Pottinger, "which had induced me to accept the offer of a widower to take care of his motherless household, have since developed into a more enduring matrimonial position, so that I can always offer my dear Prosper a home with his mother, should he choose to visit this locality, and a second father in Hiram W. Watergates, Esq., her husband."

LOVE-LETTERS OF FALSTAFF
by James Branch Cabell

I

IT was, indeed, Sir John Falstaff; very old now, and very shaky after a night of hard drinking. He came into the room singing, as was often his custom when alone, and found Bardolph bending over the chest, while Mistress Quickly demurely stirred the fire, which winked at the old knight very knowingly.

"*Then came the bold Sir Caradoc,*" carolled Sir John. "Ah, mistress, what news?—*And eke Sir Pellinore.*—Did I rage last night, Bardolph? Was I a very Bedlamite?"

"As mine own bruises can testify," asserted Bardolph. "Had each one of them a tongue, they might raise a clamor whereby Babel were as an heir weeping for his rich uncle's death; their testimony would qualify you for any madhouse in England. And if their evidence go against the doctor's stomach, the watchman at the corner hath three teeth —or, rather, had until you knocked them out last night—that will, right willingly, aid him to digest it."

"Three, say you?" asked the knight, sinking into his great chair set ready for him beside the fire. "I would have my valor in all men's mouths, but not in this fashion; 'tis too biting a jest. I am glad it was no worse; I have a tender conscience, and that mad fellow of the north, Hotspur, sits heavily upon it; thus, Percy being slain, is *per se* avenged; a plague on him! We fought a long hour by Shrewsbury clock, but I gave no quarter, I promise you; though, i' faith, the jest is ill-timed. Three, say you? I would to God my name were not so terrible to the enemy as it is; I would I had 'bated my natural inclination somewhat, and slain less tall fellows by some threescore. I doubt Agamemnon slept not well o' nights. Three, say you? Give the fellow a crown apiece for his mouldy teeth, an thou hast them; an thou hast not, bid him eschew drunkenness,

whereby his misfortune hath befallen him."

"Indeed, sir," began Bardolph, "I doubt—"

"Doubt not, sirrah!" cried Sir John, testily. "Was not the apostle reproved for that same sin? Thou art a very Didymus, Bardolph;—a very incredulous paynim, a most unspeculative rogue! Have I carracks trading i' the Indies? Have I robbed the exchequer of late? Have I the Golden Fleece for a cloak? Sooth, 'tis very paltry gimlet; and that augurs not well for his suit. Does he take me for a raven to feed him in the wilderness? Tell him there are no such ravens hereabouts; else had I long since limed the house-tops and set springes in the gutters. Inform him, knave, that my purse is no better lined than his own broken costard; 'tis void as a beggar's protestations, or a butcher's stall in Lent; light as a famished gnat, or the sighing of a new-made widower; more empty than a last year's bird-nest, than a madman's eye, or, in fine, than the friendship of a king."

"But you have wealthy friends, Sir John," suggested the hostess of the Boar's Head Tavern, who had been waiting with considerable impatience for an opportunity to join in the conversation.

"Friends, dame?" asked the knight, and cowered closer to the fire, as though he were a little cold. "I have no friends since Hal is King. I had, I grant you, a few score of acquaintances whom I taught to play at dice; paltry young blades of the City, very unfledged juvenals! Setting my knighthood and my valor aside, if I did swear friendship with these, I did swear to a lie. 'Tis a censorious world: these sprouting aldermen, these bacon-fed rogues, have eschewed my friendship; my reputation hath grown somewhat more murky than Erebus; no matter! I walk alone, as one that hath the pestilence. No matter! but I grow old; I am not in the vaward of my youth, mistress."

He nodded his head very gravely; then reached for a cup of sack that Bardolph held at his elbow.

"Indeed, I know not what your worship will do," said Mistress Quickly, rather sadly.

"Faith!" answered Sir John, finishing the sack and grinning in a somewhat ghastly fashion, "unless the Providence that watches over the fall of a sparrow hath an eye to the career of Sir John Falstaff, Knight, and so comes to my aid shortly, I must needs convert my last doublet into a mask, and turn highwayman in my shirt. I will take purses yet, i' faith, as I did at Gadshill, where that scurvy Poins, and him that is now King, and some twoscore other knaves, did rob me; yet I peppered some of them, I warrant you!"

"You must be rid of me, then, master," interpolated Bardolph. "I have no need of a hempen collar wherein to dance on nothing."

"Ah, well!" said the knight, stretching himself in his chair as the warmth of the liquor coursed through his old blood, "I, too, would be loath to break the gallows' back! For fear of halters, we must alter our way of living; we must live close, Bardolph, till the wars make us either Croesuses or food for crows. Ah, go thy ways, old Jack; there live not three good men unhanged in England, and one of them is fat and grows old. We must live close, Bardolph; we must forswear drinking and wenching! There's lime in this sack, you rogue; give me another cup."

"I pray you, hostess," he continued, "remember that Doll Tearsheet sups with me to-night; have a capon of the best, and be not sparing of the wine. I'll repay you, i' faith, when we young fellows return from France, all laden with rings and brooches and such trumperies like your Lincolnshire peddlers at Christmas-tide. We will sack a town for you, and bring you back the Lord Mayor's beard to stuff you a cushion; the Dauphin shall be a tapster yet; we will walk on lilies, I warrant you."

"Indeed, sir," said Mistress Quickly, evidently in perfect earnest, "your worship is as welcome to my pantry as the mice—a pox on 'em!—think themselves; you are heartily welcome. Ah, well, old Puss is dead; I had her of Goodman Quickly these ten years since;—but I had thought you looked for the lady who was here but now;—she was a roaring lion among the mice."

"What lady?" cried Sir John, with great animation. "Was it Flint the mercer's wife, think you? Ah, she hath a liberal disposition, and will, without the aid of Prince Houssain's carpet or the horse of Cambuscan, transfer the golden shining pieces from her husband's coffers to mine."

"No mercer's wife, I think," answered Mistress Quickly, after consideration. "She came in her coach and smacked of gentility;—Master Dombledon's father was a mercer; but he had red hair;—she is old;—I could never abide red hair."

"No matter!" cried the knight. "I can love her, be she a very Witch of Endor. What a thing it is to be a proper man, Bardolph! She hath marked me;—in public, perhaps; on the street, it may be;—and then, I warrant you, made such eyes! and sighed such sighs! and lain awake o' nights, thinking of a pleasing portly man, whom, were my besetting sin not modesty, I might name;—and I, all this while, not knowing. Fetch me my Book of Riddles and my Sonnets, that I may speak smoothly. Why was my beard not combed this morning? Have I no better cloak than this?"

"By'r lady!" said Mistress Quickly, who had been looking out of the window, "your worship must begin with unwashed hands, for the coach is at the door."

"Avaunt, minions!" cried the knight. "Avaunt! Conduct the lady hither at once, hostess; Bardolph, another cup of sack. We will ruffle it, lad, and go to France all gold, like Midas! Are mine eyes too red? I must look sad, you know, and sigh very pitifully. Ah, we will ruffle it! Another cup of sack, Bardolph;—I am a rogue if I have drunk to-day. And avaunt! vanish! for the lady comes."

He threw himself into a graceful attitude, suggestive of one suddenly stricken with the palsy, and strutted like a turkey-cock towards the door to greet his unknown visitor.

II

She was by no means what he had expected in her personal appearance; for she was considerably over sixty. But time had treated her kindly: her form was still unbent, and her countenance, though very pale, bore the traces of great beauty; and, whatever the nature of her errand, the woman who stood in the doorway was unquestionably a person of breeding.

Sir John advanced towards her with such grace as he might muster; to speak plainly, his gout, coupled with his great bulk, did not permit an overpowering amount.

"*See, from the glowing East Aurora comes,*" he chirped. "Madam, permit me to welcome you to my poor apartments; they are not worthy of your—"

"I would see Sir John Falstaff, sir," said the lady, courteously, but with great reserve of manner, looking him full in the face as she said this.

"Indeed, madam," suggested Sir John, "an those bright eyes—whose glances have already cut my poor heart into as many pieces as the man i' the front of the almanac—will but do their proper duty, you will have little trouble in finding the man you seek."

"Are you Sir John?" asked the lady, as though suspecting a jest, or perhaps, in sheer astonishment. "The son of old Sir John Falstaff, of Norfolk?"

"His wife hath frequently assured me so," said Sir John, very gravely; "and to confirm her evidence I have a certain villanous thirst about me that did plague the old Sir John sorely in his lifetime, and came to me with his other chattels. The property I have expended long since; but no Jew will advance me a maravedi on the Falstaff thirst."

"I should not have known you," said the lady, wonderingly; "but," she added, "I have not seen you these forty years."

"Faith, madam," grinned the knight, "the great pilferer Time hath since then taken away a little from my hair, and added somewhat (saving your presence) to my paunch; and my face hath not been improved by being the grindstone for some hundred swords. But I do not know you."

"I am Sylvia Vernon," said the lady.

"I remember," said the knight, and his voice was strangely altered. Bardolph would not have known it; nor, perhaps, would he have recognized his master's manner as he handed the lady to a seat.

"Ah," continued the lady, sadly, after a pause during which the crackling of the fire was very audible, "time hath dealt harshly with us both, John;—the name hath a sweet savor. I am an old, old woman now."

"I should not have known you," said Sir John; then asked, almost resentfully, "What do you here?"

"My son goes to the wars," she answered, "and I am come to bid him farewell; yet I may not tarry in London, for my lord is very feeble now and hath need of me. And I, an old woman, am yet vain enough to steal these few moments from him who needs me to see for the last time, mayhap, him who was once my very dear friend."

"I was never your friend, Sylvia," said Sir John, softly.

"Ah, the old word!" said the lady, and smiled a little wistfully. "My dear and very honored lover, then; and I am come to see him here."

"Ay!" interrupted Sir John, rather hastily; then proceeded, glowing with benevolence: "A quiet, orderly place, where I bestow my patronage; the woman of the house had once a husband in my company. God rest his soul! he bore a good pike. He retired in his old age and 'stablished this tavern, where he passed his declining years, till death called him gently away from this naughty world. God rest his soul, say I!"

This was a somewhat poetical version of the taking-off of Goodman Quickly, who had been knocked over the head with a joint-stool while rifling the pockets of a drunken guest; but perhaps Sir John wished to speak well of the dead.

"And you for old memories' sake yet aid his widow?" murmured the lady; and continued, "'Tis like you, John."

There was another silence, and the fire crackled more loudly than ever.

"You are not sorry that I came?" asked the lady at last.

"Sorry?" echoed Sir John; and, ungallant as it was, hesitated a moment before replying: "No, i' faith! But there are some ghosts that will not easily bear raising, and you have raised one."

"We have raised no very fearful ghost, I think," said the lady; "at most, no worse than a pallid, gentle spirit that speaks—to me, at least—of a boy and a girl that loved one another and were very happy a great while ago."

"Are you come hither to seek that boy?" asked the knight, and chuckled, though not very merrily. "The boy that went mad and rhymed of you in those far-off years? He is quite dead, my lady; he was drowned, mayhap, in a cup of wine. Or he was slain, perchance, by a few light women. I know not how he died. But he is quite dead, my lady; and I was not haunted by his ghost until to-day."

He stared down at the floor as he ended; then choked, and broke into a fit of coughing that he would have given ten pounds, had he had them, to prevent.

"He was a dear boy," said the lady; "a boy who loved a woman very truly; a boy that, finding her heart given to another, yielded his right in her, and went forth into the world without protest."

"Faith!" admitted Sir John, "the rogue had his good points."

"Ah, John, you have not forgotten, I know," the lady said, looking up into his face; "and you will believe me that I am very, very heartily sorry for the pain I brought into your life?"

"My wounds heal easily," said Sir John.

"For though I might not accept your love," went on the lady, "I know its value; 'tis an honor that any woman might be proud of."

"Dear lady," suggested the knight, with a slight grimace, "the world is not altogether of your opinion."

"I know not of the world," she said; "for we live very quietly. But we have heard of you ever and anon; I have your life quite letter-perfect for these forty years or more."

"You have heard of me?" asked Sir John; and he looked rather uncomfortable.

"As a gallant and brave soldier," she answered; "of how you fought at sea with Mowbray that was afterward Duke of Norfolk; of your knighthood by King Richard; and how you slew the Percy at Shrewsbury; and captured Coleville o' late in Yorkshire; and how the Prince, that now is King, did love you above all men; and, in fine, I know not what."

Sir John heaved a sigh of relief; then said, with commendable modesty: "I have fought somewhat. But we are not Bevis of Southampton; we have slain no giants. Heard you naught else?"

"Little else of note," replied the lady; and went on, very quietly: "But we are very proud of you at home. And such tales as I have heard I have woven together in one story; and I have told it many times to my children as we sat on the old Chapel steps at evening, and the shadows lengthened across the lawn; and bid them emulate this, the most perfect knight and gallant gentleman that I have known. And they love you, I think, though but by repute."

Once more silence fell between them; and the fire grinned wickedly at its reflection in the old chest, as though it knew a most entertaining secret.

"Do you yet live at Winstead?" asked Sir John, half idly.

"Yes," she answered; "in the old house. It is little changed, but there are many changes about."

"Is Moll yet with you that did once carry our letters?" queried the knight.

"Married to Hodge, the tanner," the lady said; "and dead long since."

"And all our merry company?" Sir John went on. "Marian? And Hal? And Phyllis? And Kate? 'Tis like a breath of country air to speak the old names once more."

"All dead," she answered, in a hushed voice, "save Kate, and she is very old; for Robert was slain in the French wars, and she hath never married."

"All dead," Sir John informed the fire, very confidentially; then laughed, though his bloodshot eyes were not merry. "This same Death hath a wide maw. But you, at least, have had a happy life."

"I have been happy," she said, "but I am a little weary now. My dear lord is very feeble, and hath grown querulous of late, and I too am old."

"Faith!" agreed Sir John, "we are both very old; and I had not known it, my lady, until to-day."

Again there was silence, and again the fire leapt with delight at the jest.

The lady rose suddenly and cried, "I would I had not come!"

" 'Tis but a feeble sorrow you have brought," Sir John reassured her; and continued, slowly, " Our blood runs thinner than of yore; and we may no longer, I think, either sorrow or rejoice very deeply."

" It is true," she said; " but I must go; and, indeed, I would to God I had not come !"

Sir John was silent; he bowed his head, in acquiescence perhaps, in meditation it may have been; but he said nothing.

" Yet," she said, " there is something here that I must keep no longer; 'tis all the letters you ever writ me."

So saying, she handed Sir John a little packet of very old and very faded papers. He turned them over awkwardly in his hand for a moment; then stared at them; then at the lady.

" You have kept them—always?" he cried.

" Yes," she said, very wistfully; " but I must not any longer. 'Tis a villanous example to my grandchildren," she added, and smiled. " Farewell."

Sir John drew close to her and caught her by both wrists. He held himself very erect as he looked into her eyes for a moment—a habit to which he was not prone—and said, wonderingly, " How I loved you !"

" I know," she answered, gently; then looked into his bloated face, proudly and very tenderly. " And I thank you for your gift, my lover—O brave true 'lover, whose love I was ne'er ashamed to own! Farewell, my dear; yet a little while, and I go to seek the boy and girl we wot of."

" I shall not be long, madam," said Sir John. " Speak a kind word for me in heaven; for," he added, slowly, " I shall have sore need of it."

She had reached the door by now. " You are not sorry that I came?" asked she.

Sir John answered, very sadly: " There are many wrinkles now in your dear face, my lady; the great eyes are a little dimmed, and the sweet laughter is a little cracked; but I am not sorry to have seen you thus. For I have loved no woman truly save you alone; and I am not sorry. Farewell." And he bowed his old gray head for a moment over her lifted shrivelled fingers.

III

" Lord, Lord, how subject we old men are to the vice of lying !" chuckled Sir John, and threw himself back in his chair and mumbled over the jest.

" Yet 'twas not all a lie," he confided, in some perplexity, to the fire; " but what a coil over a youthful green-sickness 'twixt a lad and a wench some forty years syne!

" I might have had money of her for the asking," he went on; " yet I am glad I did not; which is a parlous sign and smacks of dotage."

He nodded very gravely over this new and alarming phase of his character.

" Were't not a quaint conceit, a merry tickle-brain of Fate," he asked, after a pause, of the leaping flames, " that this mountain of malmsey were once a delicate stripling with apple cheeks and a clean breath, smelling o' civet, and mad for love, I warrant you, as any Amadis of them all? For, if a man were to speak truly, I did love her.

" I had the special marks of the pestilence," he assured a particularly incredulous and obstinate-looking coal—a grim black fellow that, lurking in a corner, scowled forbiddingly and seemed to defy both the flames and Sir John: " not all the flagons and apples in the universe might have comforted me; I was wont to sigh like a leaky bellows; to weep like a wench that hath lost her grandam; to lard my speech with the fag-ends of ballads like a man milliner; and did, indeed, indite sonnets, canzonets, and what not of mine own.

" And Moll did carry them," he continued; " Moll that hath married Hodge, the tanner, and is dead long since." But the coal remained incredulous, and the flames crackled merrily.

" Lord, Lord, what did I not write?" said Sir John, drawing out a paper from the packet, and deciphering the faded writing by the fire-light.

" Have pity, Sylvia ! For without thy door
    Now stands with dolorous cry and clamoring
  Faint-hearted Love, that there hath stood of yore.
    Though winter draweth on, and no birds sing
    Within the woods, yet as in wanton spring

He follows thee; and never will have done,
  Though nakedly he die, from following
Whither thou leadest. Canst thou look
    upon
His woes, and laugh to see a goddess' son
Of wide dominion and great empery,
More strong than Jove, more wise than
    Solomon,
  Too weak to combat thy severity?
Have pity, Sylvia! And let Love be one
  Among those wights that bear thee com-
  pany.

"Is't not the very puling speech of your true lover?" he chuckled; and the flames spluttered assent. *"Among those wights that bear thee company,"* he repeated, and looked about him. "Faith, Adam Cupid hath forsworn my fellowship long since; he hath no score chalked up against him at the Boar's Head Tavern; or, if he hath, I doubt not a beggar might discharge it.

"And she hath commended me to her children as a very gallant gentleman and a true· knight," he went on, reflectively, then cast his eyes to the ceiling, and grinned at unseen deities. "Jove that sees all hath a goodly commodity of mirth; I doubt not his sides ache at times, as they had conceived another wine-god.

"Yet, by my honor," he insisted to the fire, then added, apologetically, "if I had any, which, to speak plain, I have not, I am glad; 'tis a good jest; and I did love her once."

He picked out another paper and read:

"'My dear lady,—That I am not with thee to-night is, indeed, no fault of mine; for Sir Thomas Mowbray hath need of me, he saith. Yet the service that I have rendered him thus far is but to cool my heels in his antechamber and dream of two great eyes and the gold hair that curls so wondrously about thy temples. For it heartens me—' And so on, and so on, the pen trailing most juvenal sugar, like a fly newly crept out of the honeypot. And ending with a posy, filched, I warrant you, from some ring.

"I remember when I did write her this," he explained to the fire, lest it might be disposed to question the authorship; "and 'twas sent with a sonnet, all of hell, and heaven, and your pagan gods, and other tricks o' speech. It should be somewhere."

He fumbled with uncertain fingers among the papers. "Ah, here 'tis," he said at last, and read:

"Cupid invaded Hell, and boldly drove
  Before him all the hosts of Erebus.
    Now he hath conquered; and grim Cer-
      berus
  Chaunts madrigals, the Furies rhyme of
    love,
  Old Charon sighs, and sonnets sound above
    The gloomy Styx. Yea, even as Tanta-
      lus,
  Is Proserpine discrowned in Tartarus,
And Cupid reigneth in the place thereof.

"Thus Love is monarch throughout Hell to-
      day;
  In Heaven we know his power was al-
    ways great;
  And Earth was ever his (as all men say)
    Since Sylvia's beauty overthrew us
      straight:
Thus Earth and Heaven and Hell his rule
    obey,
And Sylvia's heart alone is obdurate.

"Well, well," sighed Sir John, "'twas a goodly rogue that writ it, though the verse runs but lamely! A goodly rogue!

"He might," he suggested, tentatively, "have lived cleanly, and forsworn sack; he might have been a gallant gentleman, and begotten grandchildren, and had a quiet nook at the ingle-side to rest his old bones; but he is dead long since. He might have writ himself *armigero* in many a bill, or obligation, or quittance, or what not; he might have left something behind him save unpaid tavern bills; he might have heard cases, harried poachers, and quoted old saws; and slept through sermons yet unwrit, beneath his presentment, done in stone, and a comforting bit of Latin; but," he reassured the fire, "he is dead long since."

Sir John sat meditating for a while; it had grown quite dark in the room as he muttered to himself. Suddenly he rose with a start.

"By'r lady!" he cried, "I prate like a death's-head! I'll read no more of the rubbish."

He cast the packet into the heart of the fire; the yellow papers curled at the edges, rustled a little, and blazed up; he watched them burn slowly to the last spark.

"A cup of sack to purge the brain!" cried Sir John, and filled one to the brim. "And I'll go sup with Doll Tearsheet."

THE MONSTER
by Stephen Crane

I.

LITTLE JIM was, for the time, engine Number 36, and he was making the run between Syracuse and Rochester. He was fourteen minutes behind time, and the throttle was wide open. In consequence, when he swung around the curve at the flower-bed, a wheel of his cart destroyed a peony. Number 36 slowed down at once and looked guiltily at his father, who was mowing the lawn. The doctor had his back to this accident, and he continued to pace slowly to and fro, pushing the mower.

Jim dropped the tongue of the cart. He looked at his father and at the broken flower. Finally he went to the peony and tried to stand it on its pins, resuscitated, but the spine of it was hurt, and it would only hang limply from his hand. Jim could do no reparation. He looked again toward his father.

He went on to the lawn, very slowly, and kicking wretchedly at the turf. Presently his father came along with the whirring machine, while the sweet new grass blades spun from the knives. In a low voice, Jim said, "Pa!"

The doctor was shaving this lawn as if it were a priest's chin. All during the season he had worked at it in the coolness and peace of the evenings after supper. Even in the shadow of the cherry-trees the grass was strong and healthy. Jim raised his voice a trifle. "Pa!"

The doctor paused, and with the howl of the machine no longer occupying the sense, one could hear the robins in the cherry-trees arranging their affairs. Jim's hands were behind his back, and sometimes his fingers clasped and unclasped. Again he said, "Pa!" The child's fresh and rosy lip was lowered.

The doctor stared down at his son, thrusting his head forward and frowning attentively. "What is it, Jimmie?"

"Pa!" repeated the child at length. Then he raised his finger and pointed at the flower-bed. "There!"

"What?" said the doctor, frowning more. "What is it, Jim?"

After a period of silence, during which the child may have undergone a severe mental tumult, he raised his finger and repeated his former word—"There!" The father had respected this silence with perfect courtesy. Afterward his glance carefully followed the direction indicated by the child's finger, but he could see nothing which explained to him. "I don't understand what you mean, Jimmie," he said.

It seemed that the importance of the whole thing had taken away the boy's vocabulary. He could only reiterate, "There!"

The doctor mused upon the situation, but he could make nothing of it. At last he said, "Come, show me."

Together they crossed the lawn toward the flower-bed. At some yards from the broken peony Jimmie began to lag. "There!" The word came almost breathlessly.

"Where?" said the doctor.

Jimmie kicked at the grass. "There!" he replied.

The doctor was obliged to go forward alone. After some trouble he found the subject of the incident, the broken flower. Turning then, he saw the child lurking at the rear and scanning his countenance.

The father reflected. After a time he said, "Jimmie, come here." With an infinite modesty of demeanor the child came forward. "Jimmie, how did this happen?"

The child answered, "Now—I was playin' train—and—now—I runned over it."

"You were doing what?"

"I was playin' train."

The father reflected again. "Well, Jimmie," he said, slowly, "I guess you had better not play train any more to-day. Do you think you had better?"

"No, sir," said Jimmie.

During the delivery of the judgment the child had not faced his father, and afterward he went away, with his head lowered, shuffling his feet.

II.

It was apparent from Jimmie's manner that he felt some kind of desire to efface himself. He went down to the stable.

Henry Johnson, the negro who cared for the doctor's horses, was sponging the buggy. He grinned fraternally when he saw Jimmie coming. These two were pals. In regard to almost everything in life they seemed to have minds precisely alike. Of course there were points of emphatic divergence. For instance, it was plain from Henry's talk that he was a very handsome negro, and he was known to be a light, a weight, and an eminence in the suburb of the town, where lived the larger number of the negroes, and obviously this glory was over Jimmie's horizon; but he vaguely appreciated it and paid deference to Henry for it mainly because Henry appreciated it and deferred to himself. However, on all points of conduct as related to the doctor, who was the moon, they were in complete but unexpressed understanding. Whenever Jimmie became the victim of an eclipse he went to the stable to solace himself with Henry's crimes. Henry, with the elasticity of his race, could usually provide a sin to place himself on a footing with the disgraced one. Perhaps he would remember that he had forgotten to put the hitching-strap in the back of the buggy on some recent occasion, and had been reprimanded by the doctor. Then these two would commune subtly and without words concerning their moon, holding themselves sympathetically as people who had committed similar treasons. On the other hand, Henry would sometimes choose to absolutely repudiate this idea, and when Jimmie appeared in his shame would bully him most virtuously, preaching with assurance the precepts of the doctor's creed, and pointing out to Jimmie all his abominations. Jimmie did not discover that this was odious in his comrade. He accepted it and lived in its shadow with humility, merely trying to conciliate the saintly Henry with acts of deference. Won by this attitude, Henry would sometimes allow the child to enjoy the felicity of squeezing the sponge over a buggy-wheel, even when Jimmie was still gory from unspeakable deeds.

Whenever Henry dwelt for a time in sackcloth, Jimmie did not patronize him at all. This was a justice of his age, his condition. He did not know. Besides, Henry could drive a horse, and Jimmie had a full sense of this sublimity. Henry personally conducted the moon during the splendid journeys through the country roads, where farms spread on all sides, with sheep, cows, and other marvels abounding.

"Hello, Jim!" said Henry, poising his sponge. Water was dripping from the buggy. Sometimes the horses in the stalls stamped thunderingly on the pine floor. There was an atmosphere of hay and of harness.

For a minute Jimmie refused to take an interest in anything. He was very downcast. He could not even feel the wonders of wagon-washing. Henry, while at his work, narrowly observed him.

"Your pop done wallop yer, didn't he?" he said at last.

"No," said Jimmie, defensively; "he didn't."

After this casual remark Henry continued his labor, with a scowl of occupation. Presently he said: "I done tol' yer many's th' time not to go a-foolin' an' a-projjeckin' with them flowers. Yer pop don' like it nohow." As a matter of fact, Henry had never mentioned flowers to the boy.

Jimmie preserved a gloomy silence, so Henry began to use seductive wiles in this affair of washing a wagon. It was not until he began to spin a wheel on the tree, and the sprinkling water flew everywhere, that the boy was visibly moved. He had been seated on the sill of the carriage-house door, but at the beginning of this ceremony he arose and circled toward the buggy, with an interest that slowly consumed the remembrance of a late disgrace.

Johnson could then display all the dignity of a man whose duty it was to protect Jimmie from a splashing. "Look out, boy! look out! You done gwi' spile yer pants. I raikon your mommer don't 'low this foolishness, she know it. I ain't gwi' have you round yere spilin' yer pants, an' have Mis' Trescott light on me pressen'ly. 'Deed I ain't."

He spoke with an air of great irritation, but he was not annoyed at all. This tone was merely a part of his importance. In reality he was always delighted to have the child there to witness the business of the stable. For one thing, Jimmie was invariably overcome with reverence when he was told how beautifully a harness was polished or a horse groomed. Henry explained each detail of this kind with unction, procuring great joy from the child's admiration.

III.

After Johnson had taken his supper in the kitchen, he went to his loft in the carriage-house and dressed himself with much care. No belle of a court circle could bestow more mind on a toilet than did Johnson. On second thought, he was more like a priest arraying himself for some parade of the church. As he emerged from his room and sauntered down the carriage drive, no one would have suspected him of ever having washed a buggy.

It was not altogether a matter of the lavender trousers, nor yet the straw hat with its bright silk band. The change was somewhere far in the interior of Henry. But there was no cake-walk hyperbole in it. He was simply a quiet, well-bred gentleman of position, wealth, and other necessary achievements out for an evening stroll, and he had never washed a wagon in his life.

In the morning, when in his working-clothes, he had met a friend — "Hello, Pete!" "Hello, Henry!" Now, in his effulgence, he encountered this same friend. His bow was not at all haughty. If it expressed anything, it expressed consummate generosity— "Good-evenin', Misteh Washington." Pete, who was very dirty, being at work in a potato-patch, responded in a mixture of abasement and appreciation — "Good-evenin', Misteh Johnsing."

The shimmering blue of the electric arc-lamps was strong in the main street of the town. At numerous points it was conquered by the orange glare of the outnumbering gas-lights in the windows of shops. Through this radiant lane moved a crowd, which culminated in a throng before the post-office, awaiting the distribution of the evening mails. Occasionally there came into it a shrill electric street-car, the motor singing like a cageful of grasshoppers, and possessing a great gong that clanged forth both warnings and simple noise. At the little theatre, which was a varnish and red-plush miniature of one of the famous New York theatres, a company of strollers was to play *East Lynne*. The young men of the town were mainly gathered at

"NO ONE WOULD HAVE SUSPECTED HIM OF EVER
HAVING WASHED A BUGGY."

the corners, in distinctive groups, which expressed various shades and lines of chumship, and had little to do with any social gradations. There they discussed everything with critical insight, passing the whole town in review as it swarmed in the street. When the gongs of the electric cars ceased for a moment to harry the ears, there could be heard the sound of the feet of the leisurely crowd on the blue-stone pavement, and it was like the peaceful evening lashing at the shore of a lake. At the foot of the hill, where two lines of maples sentinelled the way, an electric lamp glowed high among the embowering branches, and made most wonderful shadow-etchings on the road below it.

When Johnson appeared amid the throng a member of one of the profane groups at a corner instantly telegraphed news of this extraordinary arrival to his companions. They hailed him. "Hello, Henry! Going to walk for a cake to-night?"

"Ain't he smooth?"

"Why, you've got that cake right in your pocket, Henry!"

"Throw out your chest a little more."

Henry was not ruffled in any way by these quiet admonitions and compliments. In reply he laughed a supremely good-natured, chuckling laugh, which nevertheless expressed an underground complacency of superior metal.

Young Griscom, the lawyer, was just emerging from Reifsnyder's barber shop, rubbing his chin contentedly. On the steps he dropped his hand and looked with wide eyes into the crowd. Suddenly he bolted back into the shop. "Wow!" he cried to the parliament; "you ought to see the coon that's coming!"

Reifsnyder and his assistant instantly poised their razors high and turned toward the window. Two belathered heads reared from the chairs. The electric shine in the street caused an effect like water to them who looked through the glass from the yellow glamour of Reifsnyder's shop. In fact, the people without resembled the inhabitants of a great aquarium that here had a square pane in it. Presently into this frame swam the graceful form of Henry Johnson.

"Chee!" said Reifsnyder. He and his assistant with one accord threw their obligations to the winds, and leaving their lathered victims helpless, advanced to the window. "Ain't he a taisy?" said Reifsnyder, marvelling.

But the man in the first chair, with a grievance in his mind, had found a weapon. "Why, that's only Henry Johnson, you blamed idiots! Come on now, Reif, and shave me. What do you think I am—a mummy?"

Reifsnyder turned, in a great excitement. "I bait you any money that vas not Henry Johnson! Henry Johnson! Rats!" The scorn put into this last word made it an explosion. "That man vas a Pullman-car porter or someding. How could that be Henry Johnson?" he demanded, turbulently. "You vas crazy."

The man in the first chair faced the barber in a storm of indignation. "Didn't

I give him those lavender trousers?" he roared.

And young Griscom, who had remained attentively at the window, said: "Yes, I guess that was Henry. It looked like him."

"Oh, vell," said Reifsnyder, returning to his business, "if you think so! Oh, vell!" He implied that he was submitting for the sake of amiability.

Finally the man in the second chair, mumbling from a mouth made timid by adjacent lather, said: "That was Henry Johnson all right. Why, he always dresses like that when he wants to make a front! He's the biggest dude in town —anybody knows that."

"Chinger!" said Reifsnyder.

Henry was not at all oblivious of the wake of wondering ejaculation that streamed out behind him. On other occasions he had reaped this same joy, and he always had an eye for the demonstration. With a face beaming with happiness he turned away from the scene of his victories into a narrow side street, where the electric light still hung high, but only to exhibit a row of tumble-down houses leaning together like paralytics.

The saffron Miss Bella Farragut, in a calico frock, had been crouched on the front stoop, gossiping at long range, but she espied her approaching caller at a distance. She dashed around the corner of the house, galloping like a horse. Henry saw it all, but he preserved the polite demeanor of a guest when a waiter spills claret down his cuff. In this awkward situation he was simply perfect.

The duty of receiving Mr. Johnson fell upon Mrs. Farragut, because Bella, in another room, was scrambling wildly into her best gown. The fat old woman met him with a great ivory smile, sweeping back with the door, and bowing low. "Walk in, Misteh Johnson, walk in. How is you dis ebenin', Misteh Johnson—how is you?"

Henry's face showed like a reflector as he bowed and bowed, bending almost from his head to his ankles. "Good-evenin', Mis' Fa'gut; good-evenin'. How is you dis evenin'? Is all you' folks well, Mis' Fa'gut?"

After a great deal of kowtow, they were planted in two chairs opposite each other in the living-room. Here they exchanged the most tremendous civilities, until Miss Bella swept into the room,

"HENRY JOHNSON! RATS!"

when there was more kowtow on all sides, and a smiling show of teeth that was like an illumination.

The cooking-stove was of course in this drawing-room, and on the fire was some kind of a long-winded stew. Mrs. Farragut was obliged to arise and attend to it from time to time. Also young Sim came in and went to bed on his pallet in the corner. But to all these domesticities the three maintained an absolute dumbness. They bowed and smiled and ignored and imitated until a late hour, and if they had been the occupants of the most gorgeous salon in the world they could not have been more like three monkeys.

After Henry had gone, Bella, who encouraged herself in the appropriation of phrases, said, "Oh, ma, isn't he divine?"

IV.

A Saturday evening was a sign always for a larger crowd to parade the thoroughfare. In summer the band played until ten o'clock in the little park. Most of the young men of the town affected to be superior to this band, even to despise it; but in the still and fragrant evenings they invariably turned out in force, because the girls were sure to attend this concert, strolling slowly over the grass, linked closely in pairs, or preferably in

threes, in the curious public dependence upon one another which was their inheritance. There was no particular social aspect to this gathering, save that group regarded group with interest, but mainly in silence. Perhaps one girl would nudge another girl and suddenly say, "Look! there goes Gertie Hodgson and her sister!" And they would appear to regard this as an event of importance.

On a particular evening a rather large company of young men were gathered on the sidewalk that edged the park. They remained thus beyond the borders of the festivities because of their dignity, which would not exactly allow them to appear in anything which was so much fun for the younger lads. These latter were careering madly through the crowd, precipitating minor accidents from time to time, but usually fleeing like mist swept by the wind before retribution could lay its hands upon them.

The band played a waltz which involved a gift of prominence to the bass horn, and one of the young men on the sidewalk said that the music reminded him of the new engines on the hill pumping water into the reservoir. A similarity of this kind was not inconceivable, but the young man did not say it because he disliked the band's playing. He said it because it was fashionable to say that manner of thing concerning the band. However, over in the stand, Billie Harris, who played the snare-drum, was always surrounded by a throng of boys, who adored his every whack.

After the mails from New York and Rochester had been finally distributed, the crowd from the post-office added to the mass already in the park. The wind waved the leaves of the maples, and, high in the air, the blue-burning globes of the arc lamps caused the wonderful traceries of leaf shadows on the ground. When the light fell upon the upturned face of a girl, it caused it to glow with a wonderful pallor. A policeman came suddenly from the darkness and chased a gang of obstreperous little boys. They hooted him from a distance. The leader of the band had some of the mannerisms of the great musicians, and during a pe-

riod of silence the crowd smiled when they saw him raise his hand to his brow, stroke it sentimentally, and glance upward with a look of poetic anguish. In the shivering light, which gave to the park an effect like a great vaulted hall, the throng swarmed, with a gentle murmur of dresses switching the turf, and with a steady hum of voices.

Suddenly, without preliminary bars, there arose from afar the great hoarse roar of a factory whistle. It raised and swelled to a sinister note, and then it sang on the night wind one long call that held the crowd in the park immovable, speechless. The band-master had been about to vehemently let fall his hand to start the band on a thundering career through a popular march, but, smitten by this giant voice from the night, his hand dropped slowly to his knee, and, his mouth agape, he looked at his men in silence. The cry died away to a wail, and then to stillness. It released the muscles of the company of young men on the sidewalk, who had been like statues, posed eagerly, lithely,

"THEY BOWED AND SMILED UNTIL A LATE HOUR."

"THE BAND PLAYED A WALTZ."

their ears turned. And then they wheeled upon each other simultaneously, and, in a single explosion, they shouted, "One!"

Again the sound swelled in the night and roared its long ominous cry, and as it died away the crowd of young men wheeled upon each other and, in chorus, yelled, "Two!"

There was a moment of breathless waiting. Then they bawled, "Second district!" In a flash the company of indolent and cynical young men had vanished like a snowball disrupted by dynamite.

V.

Jake Rogers was the first man to reach the home of Tuscarora Hose Company Number Six. He had wrenched his key from his pocket as he tore down the street, and he jumped at the spring-lock like a demon. As the doors flew back before his hands he leaped and kicked the wedges from a pair of wheels, loosened a tongue from its clasp, and in the glare of the electric light which the town placed before each of its hose-houses the next comers beheld the spectacle of Jake Rogers bent like hickory in the manfulness of his pulling, and the heavy cart was moving slowly towards the doors. Four men joined him at the time, and as they swung with the cart out into the street, dark figures sped towards them from the ponderous shadows back of the electric lamps. Some set up the inevitable question, "What district?"

"Second," was replied to them in a compact howl. Tuscarora Hose Company Number Six swept on a perilous wheel into Niagara Avenue, and as the men, attached to the cart by the rope which had been paid out from the windlass under the tongue, pulled madly in their fervor and abandon, the gong under the axle clanged incitingly. And sometimes the same cry was heard, "What district?"

"Second."

On a grade Johnnie Thorpe fell, and exercising a singular muscular ability, rolled out in time from the track of the on-coming wheel, and arose, dishevelled and aggrieved, casting a look of mournful disenchantment upon the black crowd that poured after the machine. The cart seemed to be the apex of a dark wave that was whirling as if it had been a broken dam. Back of the lad were stretches of lawn, and in that direction front doors were banged by men who hoarsely shouted out into the clamorous avenue, "What district?"

At one of these houses a woman came to the door bearing a lamp, shielding her face from its rays with her hands. Across the cropped grass the avenue represented to her a kind of black torrent, upon which, nevertheless, fled numerous miraculous figures upon bicycles. She did not know that the towering light at the corner was continuing its nightly whine.

Suddenly a little boy somersaulted around the corner of the house as if he had been projected down a flight of stairs by a catapultian boot. He halted himself in front of the house by dint of a rather extraordinary evolution with his legs. "Oh, ma," he gasped, "can I go? Can I, ma?"

She straightened with the coldness of the exterior mother-judgment, although the hand that held the lamp trembled slightly. "No, Willie, you had better come to bed."

Instantly he began to buck and fume like a mustang. "Oh, ma," he cried, contorting himself—"oh, ma, can't I go? Please, ma, can't I go? Can't I go, ma?"

"It's half past nine now, Willie."

He ended by wailing out a compromise: "Well, just down to the corner, ma? Just down to the corner?"

From the avenue came the sound of rushing men who wildly shouted. Somebody had grappled the bell-rope in the Methodist church, and now over the town rang this solemn and terrible voice, speaking from the clouds. Moved from its peaceful business, this bell gained a new spirit in the portentous night, and it swung the heart to and fro, up and down, with each peal of it.

"Just down to the corner, ma?"

"Willie, it's half past nine now."

VI.

The outlines of the house of Dr. Trescott had faded quietly into the evening, hiding a shape such as we call Queen Anne against the pall of the blackened sky. The neighborhood was at this time so quiet, and seemed so devoid of obstructions, that Hannigan's dog thought it a good opportunity to prowl in forbidden precincts, and so came and pawed Trescott's lawn, growling, and considering himself a formidable beast. Later, Peter

Washington strolled past the house and whistled, but there was no dim light shining from Henry's loft, and presently Peter went his way. The rays from the street, creeping in silvery waves over the grass, caused the row of shrubs along the drive to throw a clear, bold shade.

A wisp of smoke came from one of the windows at the end of the house and drifted quietly into the branches of a cherry-tree. Its companions followed it in slowly increasing numbers, and finally there was a current controlled by invisible banks which poured into the fruit-laden boughs of the cherry-tree. It was no more to be noted than if a troop of dim and silent gray monkeys had been climbing a grape-vine into the clouds.

After a moment the window brightened as if the four panes of it had been stained with blood, and a quick ear might have been led to imagine the fire-imps calling and calling, clan joining clan, gathering to the colors. From the street, however, the house maintained its dark quiet, insisting to a passer-by that it was the safe dwelling of people who chose to retire early to tranquil dreams. No one could have heard this low droning of the gathering clans.

Suddenly the panes of the red window tinkled and crashed to the ground, and at other windows there suddenly reared other flames, like bloody spectres at the apertures of a haunted house. This outbreak had been well planned, as if by professional revolutionists.

A man's voice suddenly shouted: "Fire! Fire! Fire!" Hannigan had flung his pipe frenziedly from him because his lungs demanded room. He tumbled down from his perch, swung over the fence, and ran shouting towards the front door of the Trescotts'. Then he hammered on the door, using his fists as if they were mallets. Mrs. Trescott instantly came to one of the windows on the second floor. Afterwards she knew she had been about to say, "The doctor is not at home, but if you will leave your name, I will let him know as soon as he comes."

Hannigan's bawling was for a minute incoherent, but she understood that it was not about croup.

"What?" she said, raising the window swiftly.

"Your house is on fire! You're all ablaze! Move quick if—" His cries were

resounding in the street as if it were
a cave of echoes. Many feet pattered
swiftly on the stones. There was one
man who ran with an almost fabulous
speed. He wore lavender trousers. A straw hat with a bright
silk band was held half crumpled in his hand.

As Henry reached the front
door, Hannigan had just broken
the lock with a kick.
A thick cloud of
smoke poured over
them, and Henry,
ducking his head,
rushed into it. From
Hannigan's clamor
he knew only one
thing, but it turn-
ed him blue with
horror. In the
hall a lick of
flame had found
the cord that sup-
ported "Signing
the Declaration."
The engraving
slumped sudden-
ly down at one
end, and then
dropped to the
floor, where it
burst with the
sound of a bomb.
The fire was al-
ready roaring like a winter wind among
the pines.

" WHAT DISTRICT ?"

At the head of the stairs Mrs. Trescott
was waving her arms as if they were two
reeds. "Jimmie! Save Jimmie!" she
screamed in Henry's face. He plunged
past her and disappeared, taking the long-
familiar routes among these upper chambers, where he had once held office as a
sort of second assistant house-maid.

Hannigan had followed him up the
stairs, and grappled the arm of the maniacal woman there. His face was black
with rage. "You must come down," he
bellowed.

She would only scream at him in reply:
"Jimmie! Jimmie! Save Jimmie!" But
he dragged her forth while she babbled at
him.

As they swung out into the open air a
man ran across the lawn, and seizing a
shutter, pulled it from its hinges and flung
it far out upon the grass. Then he frantically attacked the other shutters one by

one. It was a kind of temporary insanity.

"Here, you," howled Hannigan, "hold
Mrs. Trescott— And stop—"

The news had been telegraphed by a
twist of the wrist of a neighbor who had
gone to the fire-box at the corner, and
the time when Hannigan and his charge
struggled out of the house was the time
when the whistle roared its hoarse night
call, smiting the crowd in the park, causing the leader of the band, who was about
to order the first triumphal clang of a
military march, to let his hand drop slowly to his knees.

VII.

Henry pawed awkwardly through the
smoke in the upper halls. He had attempted to guide himself by the walls,
but they were too hot. The paper was
crimpling, and he expected at any moment to have a flame burst from under
his hands.

"Jimmie!"

He did not call very loud, as if in fear that the humming flames below would overhear him.

"Jimmie! Oh, Jimmie!"

Stumbling and panting, he speedily reached the entrance to Jimmie's room and flung open the door. The little chamber had no smoke in it at all. It was faintly illumined by a beautiful rosy light reflected circuitously from the flames that were consuming the house. The boy had apparently just been aroused by the noise. He sat in his bed, his lips apart, his eyes wide, while upon his little white-robed figure played caressingly the light from the fire. As the door flew open he had before him this apparition of his pal, a terror-stricken negro, all tousled and with wool scorching, who leaped upon him and bore him up in a blanket as if the whole affair were a case of kidnapping by a dreadful robber chief. Without waiting to go through the usual short but complete process of wrinkling up his face, Jimmie let out a gorgeous bawl, which resembled the expression of a calf's deepest terror. As Johnson, bearing him, reeled into the smoke of the hall, he flung his arms about his neck and buried his face in the blanket. He called twice in muffled tones: "Mam-ma! Mam-ma!"

When Johnson came to the top of the stairs with his burden, he took a quick step backwards. Through the smoke that rolled to him he could see that the lower hall was all ablaze. He cried out then in a howl that resembled Jimmie's former achievement. His legs gained a frightful faculty of bending sideways. Swinging about precariously on these reedy legs, he made his way back slowly, back along the upper hall. From the way of him then, he had given up almost all idea of escaping from the burning house, and with it the desire. He was submitting, submitting because of his fathers, bending his mind in a most perfect slavery to this conflagration.

He now clutched Jimmie as unconsciously as when, running toward the house, he had clutched the hat with the bright silk band.

Suddenly he remembered a little private staircase which led from a bedroom to an apartment which the doctor had fitted up as a laboratory and work-house, where he used some of his leisure, and also hours when he might have been

sleeping, in devoting himself to experiments which came in the way of his study and interest.

When Johnson recalled this stairway the submission to the blaze departed instantly. He had been perfectly familiar with it, but his confusion had destroyed the memory of it.

In his sudden momentary apathy there had been little that resembled fear, but now, as a way of safety came to him, the old frantic terror caught him. He was no longer creature to the flames, and he was afraid of the battle with them. It was a singular and swift set of alternations in which he feared twice without submission, and submitted once without fear.

"Jimmie!" he wailed, as he staggered on his way. He wished this little inanimate body at his breast to participate in his tremblings. But the child had lain limp and still during these headlong charges and countercharges, and no sign came from him.

Johnson passed through two rooms and came to the head of the stairs. As he opened the door great billows of smoke poured out, but gripping Jimmie closer, he plunged down through them. All manner of odors assailed him during this flight. They seemed to be alive with envy, hatred, and malice. At the entrance to the laboratory he confronted a strange spectacle. The room was like a garden in the region where might be burning flowers. Flames of violet, crimson, green, blue, orange, and purple were blooming everywhere. There was one blaze that was precisely the hue of a delicate coral. In another place was a mass that lay merely in phosphorescent inaction like a pile of emeralds. But all these marvels were to be seen dimly through clouds of heaving, turning, deadly smoke.

Johnson halted for a moment on the threshold. He cried out again in the negro wail that had in it the sadness of the swamps. Then he rushed across the room. An orange-colored flame leaped like a panther at the lavender trousers. This animal bit deeply into Johnson. There was an explosion at one side, and suddenly before him there reared a delicate, trembling sapphire shape like a fairy lady. With a quiet smile she blocked his path and doomed him and Jimmie. Johnson shrieked, and then ducked in the manner of his race in fights. He aimed to pass under the left guard of the sapphire lady. But she was swifter than eagles, and her talons caught in him as he plunged past her. Bowing his head as if his neck had been struck, Johnson lurched forward, twisting this way and that way. He fell on his back. The still form in the blanket flung from his arms, rolled to the edge of the floor and beneath the window.

Johnson had fallen with his head at the base of an old-fashioned desk. There was a row of jars upon the top of this desk. For the most part, they were silent amid this rioting, but there was one which seemed to hold a scintillant and writhing serpent.

Suddenly the glass splintered, and a ruby-red snakelike thing poured its thick length out upon the top of the old desk. It coiled and hesitated, and then began to swim a languorous way down the mahogany slant. At the angle it waved its sizzling molten head to and fro over the closed eyes of the man beneath it. Then, in a moment, with mystic impulse, it moved again, and the red snake flowed directly down into Johnson's upturned face.

Afterwards the trail of this creature seemed to reek, and amid flames and low explosions drops like red-hot jewels pattered softly down it at leisurely intervals.

VIII.

Suddenly all roads led to Dr. Trescott's. The whole town flowed toward one point. Chippeway Hose Company Number One toiled desperately up Bridge Street Hill even as the Tuscaroras came in an impetuous sweep down Niagara Avenue. Meanwhile the machine of the hook-and-ladder experts from across the creek was spinning on its way. The chief of the fire department had been playing poker in the rear room of Whiteley's cigar-store, but at the first breath of the alarm he sprang through the door like a man escaping with the kitty.

In Whilomville, on these occasions, there was always a number of people who instantly turned their attention to the bells in the churches and school-houses.

IN THE LABORATORY.

The bells not only emphasized the alarm, but it was the habit to send these sounds rolling across the sky in a stirring brazen uproar until the flames were practically vanquished. There was also a kind of rivalry as to which bell should be made to produce the greatest din. Even the Valley Church, four miles away among the farms, had heard the voices of its brethren, and immediately added a quaint little yelp.

Doctor Trescott had been driving homeward, slowly smoking a cigar, and feeling glad that this last case was now in complete obedience to him, like a wild animal that he had subdued, when he heard the long whistle, and chirped to his horse under the unlicensed but perfectly distinct impression that a fire had broken out in Oakhurst, a new and rather high-flying suburb of the town which was at least two miles from his own home. But in the second blast and in the ensuing silence he read the designation of his own district. He was then only a few blocks from his house. He took out the whip and laid it lightly on the mare. Surprised and frightened at this extraordinary action, she leaped forward, and as the reins straightened like steel bands, the doctor leaned backward a trifle. When the mare whirled him up to the closed gate he was wondering whose house could be afire. The man who had rung the signal-box yelled something at him, but he already knew. He left the mare to her will.

In front of his door was a maniacal woman in a wrapper. "Ned!" she screamed at sight of him. "Jimmie! Save Jimmie!"

Trescott had grown hard and chill. "Where?" he said. "Where?"

Mrs. Trescott's voice began to bubble. "Up—up—up—" She pointed at the second-story windows.

Hannigan was already shouting: "Don't go in that way! You can't go in that way!"

Trescott ran around the corner of the house and disappeared from them. He knew from the view he had taken of the main hall that it would be impossible to ascend from there. His hopes were fastened now to the stairway which led from the laboratory. The door which opened from this room out upon the lawn was fastened with a bolt and lock, but he kicked close to the lock and then close to the bolt. The door with a loud crash flew back. The doctor recoiled from the roll of smoke, and then bending low, he stepped into the garden of burning flowers. On the floor his stinging eyes could make out a form in a smouldering blanket near the window. Then, as he carried his son toward the door, he saw that the whole lawn seemed now alive with men and boys, the leaders in the great charge that the whole town was making. They seized him and his burden, and overpowered him in wet blankets and water.

But Hannigan was howling: "Johnson is in there yet! Henry Johnson is in there yet! He went in after the kid! Johnson is in there yet!"

These cries penetrated to the sleepy senses of Trescott, and he struggled with his captors, swearing, unknown to him and to them, all the deep blasphemies of his medical-student days. He arose to his feet and went again toward the door of the laboratory. They endeavored to restrain him, although they were much affrighted at him.

But a young man who was a brakeman on the railway, and lived in one of the rear streets near the Trescotts, had gone into the laboratory and brought forth a thing which he laid on the grass.

IX.

There were hoarse commands from in front of the house. "Turn on your wa-

"THEY DID NOT CARE MUCH FOR JOHN SHIPLEY."

ter, Five!" "Let 'er·go, One!" The gathering crowd swayed this way and that way. The flames, towering high, cast a wild red light on their faces. There came the clangor of a gong from along some adjacent street. The crowd exclaimed at it. "Here comes Number Three!" "That's Three a-comin'!" A panting and irregular mob dashed into view, dragging a hose-cart. A cry of exultation arose from the little boys. "Here's Three!" The lads welcomed Never-Die Hose Company Number Three as if it was composed of a chariot dragged by a band of gods. The perspiring citizens flung themselves into the fray. The boys danced in impish joy at the displays of prowess. They acclaimed the approach of Number Two. They welcomed Number Four with cheers. They were so deeply moved by this whole affair that they bitterly guyed the late appearance of the hook and ladder company, whose heavy apparatus had almost stalled them on the Bridge Street hill. The lads hated and feared a fire, of course. They did not particularly want to have anybody's house burn, but still it was fine to see the gathering of the companies, and amid a great noise to watch their heroes perform all manner of prodigies.

They were divided into parties over the worth of different companies, and supported their creeds with no small violence. For instance, in that part of the little city where Number Four had its home it would be most daring for a boy to contend the superiority of any other company. Likewise, in another quarter, when a strange boy was asked which fire company was the best in Whilomville, he was expected to answer "Number One." Feuds, which the boys forgot and remembered according to chance or the importance of some recent event, existed all through the town.

They did not care much for John Shipley, the chief of the department. It was true that he went to a fire with the speed of a falling angel, but when there he invariably lapsed into a certain still mood, which was almost a preoccupation, moving leisurely around the burning structure and surveying it, puffing meanwhile at a cigar. This quiet man, who even when life was in danger seldom raised his voice, was not much to their fancy. Now old Sykes Huntington, when he was chief, used to bellow continually like a bull and gesticulate in a sort of delirium. He was

much finer as a spectacle than this Shipley, who viewed a fire with the same steadiness that he viewed a raise in a large jack-pot. The greater number of the boys could never understand why the members of these companies persisted in re-electing Shipley, although they often pretended to understand it, because "My father says" was a very formidable phrase in argument, and the fathers seemed almost unanimous in advocating Shipley.

At this time there was considerable discussion as to which company had gotten the first stream of water on the fire. Most of the boys claimed that Number Five owned that distinction, but there was a determined minority who contended for Number One. Boys who were the blood adherents of other companies were obliged to choose between the two on this occasion, and the talk waxed warm.

But a great rumor went among the crowds. It was told with hushed voices. Afterward a reverent silence fell even upon the boys. Jimmie Trescott and Henry Johnson had been burned to death, and Dr. Trescott himself had been most savagely hurt. The crowd did not even feel the police pushing at them. They raised their eyes, shining now with awe, toward the high flames.

The man who had information was at his best. In low tones he described the whole affair. "That was the kid's room —in the corner there. He had measles or somethin', and this coon—Johnson— was a-settin' up with 'im, and Johnson got sleepy or somethin' and upset the lamp, and the doctor he was down in his office, and he came running up, and they all got burned together till they dragged 'em out."

Another man, always preserved for the deliverance of the final judgment, was saying: "Oh, they'll die sure. Burned to flinders. No chance. Hull lot of 'em. Anybody can see." The crowd concentrated its gaze still more closely upon these flags of fire which waved joyfully against the black sky. The bells of the town were clashing unceasingly.

A little procession moved across the lawn and toward the street. There were three cots, borne by twelve of the firemen. The police moved sternly, but it needed no effort of theirs to open a lane for this slow cortége. The men who bore the cots were well known to the crowd, but in this solemn parade during the

ringing of the bells and the shouting, and
with the red glare upon the sky, they
seemed utterly foreign, and Whilomville
paid them a deep respect. Each man in
this stretcher party had gained a reflected majesty. They were footmen to death,
and the crowd made subtle obeisance to
this august dignity derived from three
prospective graves. One woman turned
away with a shriek at sight of the covered body on the first stretcher, and people
faced her suddenly in silent and mournful indignation. Otherwise there was
barely a sound as these twelve important
men with measured tread carried their
burdens through the throng.

The little boys no longer discussed the
merits of the different fire companies.
For the greater part they had been routed. Only the more courageous viewed
closely the three figures veiled in yellow
blankets.

X.

Old Judge Denning Hagenthorpe, who
lived nearly opposite the Trescotts, had
thrown his door wide open to receive the
afflicted family. When it was publicly
learned that the doctor and his son and
the negro were still alive, it required a
specially detailed policeman to prevent
people from scaling the front porch and
interviewing these sorely wounded. One
old lady appeared with a miraculous poul-
tice, and she quoted most damning scrip-
ture to the officer when he said that she
could not pass him. Throughout the
night some lads old enough to be given
privileges or to compel them from their
mothers remained vigilantly upon the
kerb in anticipation of a death or some
such event. The reporter of the *Morning
Tribune* rode thither on his bicycle every
hour until three o'clock.

Six of the ten doctors in Whilomville
attended at Judge Hagenthorpe's house.

Almost at once they were able to know
that Trescott's burns were not vitally important. The child would possibly be
scarred badly, but his life was undoubtedly safe. As for the negro Henry Johnson, he could not live. His body was
frightfully seared, but more than that, he
now had no face. His face had simply
been burned away.

Trescott was always asking news of the
two other patients. In the morning he
seemed fresh and strong, so they told him
that Johnson was doomed. They then

saw him stir on the bed, and sprang quickly to see if the bandages needed readjust-
ing. In the sudden glance he threw from
one to another he impressed them as being both leonine and impracticable.

The morning paper announced the
death of Henry Johnson. It contained a
long interview with Edward J. Hannigan,
in which the latter described in full the
performance of Johnson at the fire. There
was also an editorial built from all the
best words in the vocabulary of the staff.
The town halted in its accustomed road
of thought, and turned a reverent attention to the memory of this hostler. In
the breasts of many people was the regret
that they had not known enough to give
him a hand and a lift when he was alive,
and they judged themselves stupid and
ungenerous for this failure.

The name of Henry Johnson became
suddenly the title of a saint to the little
boys. The one who thought of it first
could, by quoting it in an argument, at
once overthrow his antagonist, whether
it applied to the subject or whether it did
not.

> Nigger, nigger, never die,
> Black face and shiny eye.

Boys who had called this odious couplet
in the rear of Johnson's march buried the
fact at the bottom of their hearts.

Later in the day Miss Bella Farragut,
of No. 7 Watermelon Alley, announced
that she had been engaged to marry Mr.
Henry Johnson.

XI.

The old judge had a cane with an ivory head. He could never think at his
best until he was leaning slightly on this
stick and smoothing the white top with
slow movements of his hands. It was
also to him a kind of narcotic. If by
any chance he mislaid it, he grew at once
very irritable, and was likely to speak
sharply to his sister, whose mental inca-
pacity he had patiently endured for thirty years in the old mansion on Ontario
Street. She was not at all aware of her
brother's opinion of her endowments, and
so it might be said that the judge had
successfully dissembled for more than a
quarter of a century, only risking the
truth at the times when his cane was
lost.

On a particular day the judge sat in
his arm-chair on the porch. The sunshine sprinkled through the lilac-bushes

and poured great coins on the boards. The sparrows disputed in the trees that lined the pavements. The judge mused deeply, while his hands gently caressed the ivory head of his cane.

Finally he arose and entered the house, his brow still furrowed in a thoughtful frown. His stick thumped solemnly in regular beats. On the second floor he entered a room where Dr. Trescott was working about the bedside of Henry Johnson. The bandages on the negro's head allowed only one thing to appear, an eye, which unwinkingly stared at the judge. The latter spoke to Trescott on the condition of the patient. Afterward he evidently had something further to say, but he seemed to be kept from it by the scrutiny of the unwinking eye, at which he furtively glanced from time to time.

When Jimmie Trescott was sufficiently recovered, his mother had taken him to pay a visit to his grandparents in Connecticut. The doctor had remained to take care of his patients, but as a matter of truth he spent most of his time at Judge Hagenthorpe's house, where lay Henry Johnson. Here he slept and ate almost every meal in the long nights and days of his vigil.

At dinner, and away from the magic of the unwinking eye, the judge said, suddenly, "Trescott, do you think it is—" As Trescott paused expectantly, the judge fingered his knife. He said, thoughtfully, "No one wants to advance such ideas, but somehow I think that that poor fellow ought to die."

There was in Trescott's face at once a look of recognition, as if in this tangent of the judge he saw an old problem. He merely sighed and answered, "Who knows?" The words were spoken in a deep tone that gave them an elusive kind of significance.

The judge retreated to the cold manner of the bench. "Perhaps we may not talk with propriety of this kind of action, but I am induced to say that you are performing a questionable charity in preserving this negro's life. As near as I can understand, he will hereafter be a monster, a perfect monster, and probably with an affected brain. No man can observe you as I have observed you and not know that it was a matter of conscience with you, but I am afraid, my friend, that it is one of the blunders of

virtue." The judge had delivered his views with his habitual oratory. The last three words he spoke with a particular emphasis, as if the phrase was his discovery.

The doctor made a weary gesture. "He saved my boy's life."

"Yes," said the judge, swiftly—"yes, I know!"

"And what am I to do?" said Trescott, his eyes suddenly lighting like an outburst from smouldering peat. "What am I to do? He gave himself for—for Jimmie. What am I to do for him?"

The judge abased himself completely before these words. He lowered his eyes for a moment. He picked at his cucumbers.

Presently he braced himself straightly in his chair. "He will be your creation, you understand. He is purely your creation. Nature has very evidently given him up. He is dead. You are restoring him to life. You are making him, and he will be a monster, and with no mind."

"He will be what you like, judge," cried Trescott, in sudden, polite fury. "He will be anything, but, by God! he saved my boy."

The judge interrupted in a voice trembling with emotion: "Trescott! Trescott! Don't I know?"

Trescott had subsided to a sullen mood. "Yes, you know," he answered, acidly; "but you don't know all about your own boy being saved from death." This was a perfectly childish allusion to the judge's bachelorhood. Trescott knew that the remark was infantile, but he seemed to take desperate delight in it.

But it passed the judge completely. It was not his spot.

"I am puzzled," said he, in profound thought. "I don't know what to say."

Trescott had become repentant. "Don't think I don't appreciate what you say, judge. But—"

"Of course!" responded the judge, quickly. "Of course."

"It—" began Trescott.

"Of course," said the judge.

In silence they resumed their dinner.

"Well," said the judge, ultimately, "it is hard for a man to know what to do."

"It is," said the doctor, fervidly.

There was another silence. It was broken by the judge:

"Look here, Trescott; I don't want you to think—"

"No, certainly not," answered the doctor, earnestly.

"Well, I don't want you to think I would say anything to— It was only that I thought that I might be able to suggest to you that—perhaps—the affair was a little dubious."

With an appearance of suddenly disclosing his real mental perturbation, the doctor said: "Well, what would you do? Would you kill him?" he asked, abruptly and sternly.

"Trescott, you fool," said the old man, gently.

"Oh, well, I know, judge, but then—" He turned red, and spoke with new violence: "Say, he saved my boy—do you see? He saved my boy."

"You bet he did," cried the judge, with enthusiasm. "You bet he did." And they remained for a time gazing at each other, their faces illuminated with memories of a certain deed.

After another silence, the judge said, "It is hard for a man to know what to do."

XII.

Late one evening Trescott, returning from a professional call, paused his buggy at the Hagenthorpe gate. He tied the mare to the old tin-covered post, and entered the house. Ultimately he appeared with a companion—a man who walked slowly and carefully, as if he were learning. He was wrapped to the heels in an old-fashioned ulster. They entered the buggy and drove away.

After a silence only broken by the swift and musical humming of the wheels on the smooth road, Trescott spoke. "Henry," he said, "I've got you a home here with old Alek Williams. You will have everything you want to eat and a good place to sleep, and I hope you will get along there all right. I will pay all your expenses, and come to see you as often as I can. If you don't get along, I want you to let me know as soon as possible, and then we will do what we can to make it better."

The dark figure at the doctor's side answered with a cheerful laugh. "These buggy wheels don' look like I washed 'em yesterday, docteh," he said.

Trescott hesitated for a moment, and then went on insistently, "I am taking you to Alek Williams, Henry, and I—"

The figure chuckled again. "No, 'deed! No, seh! Alek Williams don' know a hoss! 'Deed he don't. He don' know a hoss from a pig." The laugh that followed was like the rattle of pebbles.

Trescott turned and looked sternly and coldly at the dim form in the gloom from the buggy-top. "Henry," he said, "I didn't say anything about horses. I was saying—"

"Hoss? Hoss?" said the quavering voice from these near shadows. "Hoss? 'Deed I don' know all erbout a hoss! 'Deed I don't." There was a satirical chuckle.

At the end of three miles the mare slackened and the doctor leaned forward, peering, while holding tight reins. The wheels of the buggy bumped often over out-cropping bowlders. A window shone forth, a simple square of topaz on a great black hill-side. Four dogs charged the buggy with ferocity, and when it did not promptly retreat, they circled courageously around the flanks, baying. A door opened near the window in the hill-side, and a man came and stood on a beach of yellow light.

"Yah! yah! You Roveh! You Susie! Come yah! Come yah this minit!"

Trescott called across the dark sea of grass, "Hello, Alek!"

"Hello!"

"Come down here and show me where to drive."

The man plunged from the beach into the surf, and Trescott could then only trace his course by the fervid and polite ejaculations of a host who was somewhere approaching. Presently Williams took the mare by the head, and uttering cries of welcome and scolding the swarming dogs, led the equipage toward the lights. When they halted at the door and Trescott was climbing out, Williams cried, "Will she stand, docteh?"

"She'll stand all right, but you better hold her for a minute. Now, Henry." The doctor turned and held both arms to the dark figure. It crawled to him painfully like a man going down a ladder. Williams took the mare away to be tied to a little tree, and when he returned he found them awaiting him in the gloom beyond the rays from the door.

He burst out then like a siphon pressed by a nervous thumb. "Hennery! Hennery, ma ol' frien'. Well, if I ain' glade. If I ain' glade!"

Trescott had taken the silent shape by the arm and led it forward into the full revelation of the light. "Well, now, Alek, you can take Henry and put him to bed, and in the morning I will—"

Near the end of this sentence old Williams had come front to front with Johnson. He gasped for a second, and then yelled the yell of a man stabbed in the heart.

For a fraction of a moment Trescott seemed to be looking for epithets. Then he roared: "You old black chump! You old black— Shut up! Shut up! Do you hear?"

Williams obeyed instantly in the matter of his screams, but he continued in a lowered voice: "Ma Lode amassy! Who'd ever think? Ma Lode amassy!"

Trescott spoke again in the manner of a commander of a battalion. "Alek!"

The old negro again surrendered, but to himself he repeated in a whisper, "Ma Lode!" He was aghast and trembling.

As these three points of widening shadows approached the golden doorway a hale old negress appeared there, bowing. "Good-evenin', docteh! Good-evenin'! Come in! come in!" She had evidently just retired from a tempestuous struggle to place the room in order, but she was now bowing rapidly. She made the effort of a person swimming.

"Don't trouble yourself, Mary," said Trescott, entering. "I've brought Henry for you to take care of, and all you've got to do is to carry out what I tell you." Learning that he was not followed, he faced the door, and said, "Come in, Henry."

Johnson entered. "Whee!" shrieked Mrs. Williams. She almost achieved a back somersault. Six young members of the tribe of Williams made simultaneous plunge for a position behind the stove, and formed a wailing heap.

XIII.

"You know very well that you and your family lived usually on less than three dollars a week, and now that Doctor Trescott pays you five dollars a week for Johnson's board, you live like millionaires. You haven't done a stroke of work since Johnson began to board with you— everybody knows that—and so what are you kicking about?"

The judge sat in his chair on the porch, fondling his cane, and gazing down at old Williams, who stood under the lilac-bushes. "Yes, I know, jedge," said the negro, wagging his head in a puzzled manner. "'Tain't like as if I didn't 'preciate what the docteh done, but—but—well, yeh see, jedge," he added, gaining a new impetus, "it's—it's hard wuk. This ol' man nev' did wuk so hard. Lode, no."

"Don't talk such nonsense, Alek," spoke the judge, sharply. "You have never really worked in your life—anyhow enough to support a family of sparrows, and now when you are in a more prosperous condition than ever before, you come around talking like an old fool."

The negro began to scratch his head. "Yeh see, jedge," he said at last, "my ol' 'ooman she cain't 'ceive no lady callahs, nohow."

"Hang lady callers!" said the judge, irascibly. "If you have flour in the barrel and meat in the pot, your wife can get along without receiving lady callers, can't she?"

"But they won't come anyhow, jedge," replied Williams, with an air of still deeper stupefaction. "Noner ma wife's frien's ner noner ma frien's 'll come near ma res'dence."

"Well, let them stay home if they are such silly people."

The old negro seemed to be seeking a way to elude this argument, but evidently finding none, he was about to shuffle meekly off. He halted, however. "Jedge," said he, "ma ol' 'ooman's near driv' abstracted."

"Your old woman is an idiot," responded the judge.

Williams came very close and peered solemnly through a branch of lilac. "Jedge," he whispered, "the chillens."

"What about them?"

Dropping his voice to funereal depths, Williams said, "They—they cain't eat."

"Can't eat!" scoffed the judge, loudly. "Can't eat! You must think I am as big an old fool as you are. Can't eat—the little rascals! What's to prevent them from eating?"

In answer, Williams said, with mournful emphasis, "Hennery." Moved with a kind of satisfaction at his tragic use of the name, he remained staring at the judge for a sign of its effect.

The judge made a gesture of irritation. "Come, now, you old scoundrel, don't beat around the bush any more. What are you up to? What do you want? Speak out like a man, and don't give me any more of this tiresome rigamarole."

"I ain't er-beatin' round 'bout nuffin, jedge," replied Williams, indignantly. "No, seh; I say whatter got to say right out. 'Deed I do."

"Well, say it, then."

"Jedge," began the negro, taking off his hat and switching his knee with it, "Lode knows I'd do jes 'bout as much fer five dollehs er week as any cul'd man, but—but this yere business is awful, jedge. I raikon 'ain't been no sleep in—in my house sence docteh done fetch 'im."

"Well, what do you propose to do about it?"

Williams lifted his eyes from the ground and gazed off through the trees. "Raikon I got good appetite, an' sleep jes like er dog, but he—he's done broke me all up. 'Tain't no good, nohow. I wake up in the night; I hear 'im, mebbe, er-whimperin' an' er-whimperin', an' I sneak an' I sneak until I try th' do' to see if he locked in. An' he keep me er-puzzlin' an' er-quakin' all night long. Don't know how 'll do in th' winter. Can't let 'im out where th' chillen is. He'll done freeze where he is now." Williams spoke these sentences as if he were talking to himself. After a silence of deep reflection he continued: "Folks go round sayin' he ain't Hennery Johnson at all. They say he's er devil!"

"What?" cried the judge.

"Yesseh," repeated Williams in tones of injury, as if his veracity had been challenged. "Yesseh. I'm er-tellin' it to yeh straight, jedge. Plenty cul'd people folks up my way say it is a devil."

"Well, you don't think so yourself, do you?"

"No. 'Tain't no devil. It's Hennery Johnson."

"Well, then, what is the matter with you? You don't care what a lot of foolish people say. Go on 'tending to your business, and pay no attention to such idle nonsense."

"'Tis nonsense, jedge; but he *looks* like er devil."

"What do you care what he looks like?" demanded the judge.

"Ma rent is two dollehs and er half er month," said Williams, slowly.

"It might just as well be ten thousand dollars a month," responded the judge. "You never pay it, anyhow."

"Then, anoth' thing," continued Williams, in his reflective tone. "If he was all right in his haid I could stan' it; but,

jedge, he's crazier 'n er loon. Then when he looks like er devil, an' done skears all ma frien's away, an' ma chillens cain't eat, an' ma ole 'ooman jes raisin' Cain all the time, an' ma rent two dollehs an' er half er month, an' him not right in his haid, it seems like five dollehs er week—"

The judge's stick came down sharply and suddenly upon the floor of the porch. "There," he said, "I thought that was what you were driving at."

Williams began swinging his head from side to side in the strange racial mannerism. "Now hol' on a minnet, jedge," he said, defensively. "'Tain't like as if I didn't 'preciate what the docteh done. 'Tain't that. Docteh Trescott is er kind man, an' 'tain't like as if I didn't 'preciate what he done; but—"

"But what? You are getting painful, Alek. Now tell me this: did you ever have five dollars a week regularly before in your life?"

Williams at once drew himself up with great dignity, but in the pause after that question he drooped gradually to another attitude. In the end he answered, heroically: "No, jedge, I 'ain't. An' 'tain't like as if I was er-sayin' five dollehs wasn't er lot er money for a man like me. But, jedge, what er man oughter git fer this kinder wuk is er salary. Yesseh, jedge," he repeated, with a great impressive gesture; "fer this kinder wuk er man oughter git er Salary." He laid a terrible emphasis upon the final word.

The judge laughed. "I know Dr. Trescott's mind concerning this affair, Alek; and if you are dissatisfied with your boarder, he is quite ready to move him to some other place; so, if you care to leave word with me that you are tired of the arrangement and wish it changed, he will come and take Johnson away."

Williams scratched his head again in deep perplexity. "Five dollehs is er big price fer bo'd, but 'tain't no big price fer the bo'd of er crazy man," he said, finally.

"What do you think you ought to get?" asked the judge.

"Well," answered Alek, in the manner of one deep in a balancing of the scales, "he looks like er devil, an' done skears e'rybody, an' ma chillens cain't eat, an' I cain't sleep, an' he ain't right in his haid, an'—"

"You told me all those things."

After scratching his wool, and beating his knee with his hat, and gazing off through the trees and down at the ground, Williams said, as he kicked nervously at the gravel, "Well, jedge, I think it is wuth—" He stuttered.

"Worth what?"

"Six dollehs," answered Williams, in a desperate outburst.

The judge lay back in his great armchair and went through all the motions of a man laughing heartily, but he made no sound save a slight cough. Williams had been watching him with apprehension.

"Well," said the judge, "do you call six dollars a salary?"

"No, seh," promptly responded Williams. "'Tain't a salary. No, 'deed! 'Tain't a salary." He looked with some anger upon the man who questioned his intelligence in this way.

"Well, supposing your children can't eat?"

"I—"

"And supposing he looks like a devil? And supposing all those things continue? Would you be satisfied with six dollars a week?"

Recollections seemed to throng in Williams's mind at these interrogations, and he answered dubiously. "Of co'se a man who ain't right in his haid, an' looks like er devil— But six dollehs—" After these two attempts at a sentence Williams suddenly appeared as an orator, with a great shiny palm waving in the air. "I tell yeh, jedge, six dollehs is six dollehs, but if I git six dollehs for bo'ding Hennery Johnson, I uhns it! I uhns it!"

"I don't doubt that you earn six dollars for every week's work you do," said the judge.

"Well, if I bo'd Hennery Johnson fer six dollehs er week, I uhns it! I uhns it!" cried Williams, wildly.

XIV.

Reifsnyder's assistant had gone to his supper, and the owner of the shop was trying to placate four men who wished to be shaved at once. Reifsnyder was very garrulous—a fact which made him rather remarkable among barbers, who, as a class, are austerely speechless, having been taught silence by the hammering reiteration of a tradition. It is the customers who talk in the ordinary event.

As Reifsnyder waved his razor down the cheek of a man in the chair, he turned often to cool the impatience of the others with pleasant talk, which they did not particularly heed.

"Oh, he should have let him die," said Bainbridge, a railway engineer, finally replying to one of the barber's orations. "Shut up, Reif, and go on with your business!"

Instead, Reifsnyder paused shaving entirely, and turned to front the speaker. "Let him die?" he demanded. "How vas that? How can you let a man die?"

"By letting him die, you chump," said the engineer. The others laughed a little, and Reifsnyder turned at once to his work, sullenly, as a man overwhelmed by the derision of numbers.

"How vas that?" he grumbled later. "How can you let a man die when he vas done so much for you?"

"'When he vas done so much for you?'" repeated Bainbridge. "You better shave some people. How vas that? Maybe this ain't a barber shop?"

A man hitherto silent now said, "If I had been the doctor, I would have done the same thing."

"Of course," said Reifsnyder. "Any man vould do it. Any man that vas not like you, you—old—flint-hearted—fish." He had sought the final words with painful care, and he delivered the collection triumphantly at Bainbridge. The engineer laughed.

The man in the chair now lifted himself higher, while Reifsnyder began an elaborate ceremony of anointing and combing his hair. Now free to join comfortably in the talk, the man said: "They say he is the most terrible thing in the world. Young Johnnie Bernard—that drives the grocery wagon—saw him up at Alek Williams's shanty, and he says he couldn't eat anything for two days."

"Chee!" said Reifsnyder.

"Well, what makes him so terrible?" asked another.

"Because he hasn't got any face," replied the barber and the engineer in duet.

"Hasn't got any face?" repeated the man. "How can he do without any face!"

"He has no face in the front of his head,
In the place where his face ought to grow."

Bainbridge sang these lines pathetically as he arose and hung his hat on a hook. The man in the chair was about to abdicate in his favor. "Get a gait on you now," he said to Reifsnyder. "I go out at 7.31."

As the barber foamed the lather on the cheeks of the engineer he seemed to be thinking heavily. Then suddenly he burst out. "How would you like to be with no face?" he cried to the assemblage.

"Oh, if I had to have a face like yours—" answered one customer.

Bainbridge's voice came from a sea of lather. "You're kicking because if losing faces became popular, you'd have to go out of business."

"I don't think it will become so much popular," said Reifsnyder.

"Not if it's got to be taken off in the way his was taken off," said another man. "I'd rather keep mine, if you don't mind."

"I guess so!" cried the barber. "Just think!"

The shaving of Bainbridge had arrived at a time of comparative liberty for him. "I wonder what the doctor says to himself?" he observed. "He may be sorry he made him live."

"It was the only thing he could do," replied a man. The others seemed to agree with him.

"Supposing you were in his place," said one, "and Johnson had saved your kid. What would you do?"

"Certainly!"

"Of course! You would do anything on earth for him. You'd take all the trouble in the world for him. And spend your last dollar on him. Well, then?"

"I wonder how it feels to be without any face?" said Reifsnyder, musingly.

The man who had previously spoken, feeling that he had expressed himself well, repeated the whole thing. "You would do anything on earth for him. You'd take all the trouble in the world for him. And spend your last dollar on him. Well, then?"

"No, but look," said Reifsnyder; "supposing you don't got a face!"

XV.

As soon as Williams was hidden from the view of the old judge he began to gesture and talk to himself. An elation had evidently penetrated to his vitals, and caused him to dilate as if he had been filled with gas. He snapped his fingers in the air, and whistled fragments of triumphal music. At times, in his progress toward his shanty, he indulged in a shuffling movement that was really a dance. It was to be learned from the intermediate monologue that he had emerged from his trials laurelled and proud. He was the unconquerable Alexander Williams. Nothing could exceed the bold self-reliance of his manner. His kingly stride, his heroic song, the derisive flourish of his hands—all betokened a man who had successfully defied the world.

On his way he saw Zeke Paterson coming to town. They hailed each other at a distance of fifty yards.

"How do, Broth' Paterson?"

"How do, Broth' Williams?"

They were both deacons.

"Is you' folks well, Broth' Paterson?"

"Middlin', middlin'. How's you' folks, Broth' Williams?"

Neither of them had slowed his pace in the smallest degree. They had simply begun this talk when a considerable space separated them, continued it as they passed, and added polite questions as they drifted steadily apart. Williams's mind seemed to be a balloon. He had been so inflated that he had not noticed that Paterson had definitely shied into the dry ditch as they came to the point of ordinary contact.

Afterward, as he went a lonely way, he burst out again in song and pantomimic celebration of his estate. His feet moved in prancing steps.

When he came in sight of his cabin, the fields were bathed in a blue dusk, and the light in the window was pale. Cavorting and gesticulating, he gazed joyfully for some moments upon this light. Then suddenly another idea seemed to attack his mind, and he stopped, with an air of being suddenly dampened. In the end he approached his home as if it were the fortress of an enemy.

Some dogs disputed his advance for a loud moment, and then discovering their lord, slunk away embarrassed. His reproaches were addressed to them in muffled tones.

Arriving at the door, he pushed it open with the timidity of a new thief. He thrust his head cautiously sideways, and his eyes met the eyes of his wife, who sat by the table, the lamp light defining a half of her face. "'Sh!" he said, uselessly. His glance travelled swiftly to the

"IF I GIT SIX DOLLEHS FOR BO'DING HENNERY JOHNSON, I UHNS IT!"

inner door which shielded the one bed-chamber. The pickaninnies, strewn upon the floor of the living-room, were softly snoring. After a hearty meal they had promptly dispersed themselves about the place and gone to sleep. "'Sh!" said Williams again to his motionless and silent wife. He had allowed only his head to appear. His wife, with one hand upon the edge of the table and the other at her knee, was regarding him with wide eyes and parted lips as if he were a spectre. She looked to be one who was living in terror, and even the familiar face at the door had thrilled her because it had come suddenly.

Williams broke the tense silence. "Is he all right?" he whispered, waving his eyes toward the inner door. Following his glance timorously, his wife nodded, and in a low tone answered,

"I raikon he's done gone t' sleep."

Williams then slunk noiselessly across his threshold.

He lifted a chair, and with infinite care placed it so that it faced the dreaded inner door. His wife moved slightly, so as to also squarely face it. A silence came

upon them in which they seemed to be waiting for a calamity, pealing and deadly.

Williams finally coughed behind his hand. His wife started, and looked upon him in alarm. "'Pears like he done gwine keep quiet ter-night," he breathed. They continually pointed their speech and their looks at the inner door, paying it the homage due to a corpse or a phantom. Another long stillness followed this sentence. Their eyes shone white and wide. A wagon rattled down the distant road. From their chairs they looked at the window, and the effect of the light in the cabin was a presentation of an intensely black and solemn night. The old woman adopted the attitude used always in church at funerals. At times she seemed to be upon the point of breaking out in prayer.

"He mighty quiet ter-night," whispered Williams. "Was he good ter-day?" For answer his wife raised her eyes to the ceiling in the supplication of Job. Williams moved restlessly. Finally he tiptoed to the door. He knelt slowly and without a sound, and placed his ear near the key-hole. Hearing a noise behind him, he turned quickly. His wife was staring at him aghast. She stood in front of the stove, and her arms were spread out in the natural movement to protect all her sleeping ducklings.

But Williams arose without having touched the door. "I raikon he ersleep," he said, fingering his wool. He debated with himself for some time. During this interval his wife remained, a great fat statue of a mother shielding her children.

It was plain that his mind was swept suddenly by a wave of temerity. With a sounding step he moved toward the door. His fingers were almost upon the knob when he swiftly ducked and dodged away, clapping his hands to the back of his head. It was as if the portal had threatened him. There was a little tumult near the stove, where Mrs. Williams's desperate retreat had involved her feet with the prostrate children.

After the panic Williams bore traces of a feeling of shame. He returned to the charge. He firmly grasped the knob with his left hand, and with his other hand turned the key in the lock. He pushed the door, and as it swung portentously open he sprang nimbly to one side like the fearful slave liberating the lion. Near the stove a group had formed, the terror-stricken mother with her arms stretched, and the aroused children clinging frenziedly to her skirts.

The light streamed after the swinging door, and disclosed a room six feet one way and six feet the other way. It was small enough to enable the radiance to lay it plain. Williams peered warily around the corner made by the door-post. Suddenly he advanced, retired, and advanced again with a howl. His palsied family had expected him to spring backward, and at his howl they heaped themselves wondrously. But Williams simply stood in the little room emitting his howls before an open window. "He's gone! He's gone! He's gone!" His eye and his hand had speedily proved the fact. He had even thrown open a little cupboard.

Presently he came flying out. He grabbed his hat, and hurled the outer door back upon its hinges. Then he tumbled headlong into the night. He was yelling: "Docteh Trescott! Docteh Trescott!" He ran wildly through the fields, and galloped in the direction of town. He continued to call to Trescott, as if the latter was within easy hearing. It was as if Trescott was poised in the contemplative sky over the running negro, and could heed this reaching voice—"Docteh Trescott!"

In the cabin, Mrs. Williams, supported by relays from the battalion of children, stood quaking watch until the truth of daylight came as a re-enforcement and made them arrogant, strutting, swashbuckler children, and a mother who proclaimed her illimitable courage.

XVI.

Theresa Page was giving a party. It was the outcome of a long series of arguments addressed to her mother, which had been overheard in part by her father. He had at last said five words, "Oh, let her have it." The mother had then gladly capitulated.

Theresa had written nineteen invitations, and distributed them at recess to her schoolmates. Later her mother had composed five large cakes, and still later a vast amount of lemonade.

So the nine little girls and the ten little boys sat quite primly in the dining-room, while Theresa and her mother plied them with cake and lemonade, and also with ice-cream. This primness sat now quite strangely upon them. It was owing to the presence of Mrs. Page. Previously in the parlor alone with their games they had overturned a chair; the boys had let more or less of their hoodlum spirit shine forth. But when circumstances could be possibly magnified to warrant it, the girls made the boys victims of an insufferable pride, snubbing them mercilessly. So in the dining-room they resembled a class at Sunday-school, if it were not for the subterranean smiles, gestures, rebuffs, and poutings which stamped the affair as a children's party.

Two little girls of this subdued gathering were planted in a settle with their backs to the broad window. They were beaming lovingly upon each other with an effect of scorning the boys.

Hearing a noise behind her at the window, one little girl turned to face it. Instantly she screamed and sprang away, covering her face with her hands. "What was it? What was it?" cried every one in a roar. Some slight movement of the eyes of the weeping and shuddering child informed the company that she had been frightened by an appearance at the window. At once they all faced the imperturbable window, and for a moment there

"THE DOOR SWUNG PORTENTOUSLY OPEN."

was a silence. An astute lad made an immediate census of the other lads. The prank of slipping out and looming spectrally at a window was too venerable. But the little boys were all present and astonished.

As they recovered their minds they uttered warlike cries, and through a side-door sallied rapidly out against the terror. They vied with each other in daring.

None wished particularly to encounter a dragon in the darkness of the garden, but there could be no faltering when the fair ones in the dining-room were present. Calling to each other in stern voices, they went dragooning over the lawn, attacking the shadows with ferocity, but still with the caution of reasonable beings. They found, however, nothing new to the peace of the night. Of course there was a lad who told a great lie. He described a grim figure, bending low and slinking off along the fence. He gave a number of details, rendering his lie more splendid by a repetition of certain forms which he recalled from romances. For instance, he insisted that he had heard the creature emit a hollow laugh.

Inside the house the little girl who had raised the alarm was still shuddering and weeping. With the utmost difficulty was she brought to a state approximating calmness by Mrs. Page. Then she wanted to go home at once.

Page entered the house at this time. He had exiled himself until he concluded that this children's party was finished and gone. He was obliged to escort the little girl home because she screamed again when they opened the door and she saw the night.

She was not coherent even to her mother. Was it a man? She didn't know. It was simply a thing, a dreadful thing.

XVII.

In Watermelon Alley the Farraguts were spending their evening as usual on the little rickety porch. Sometimes they howled gossip to other people on other rickety porches. The thin wail of a baby arose from a near house. A man had a terrific altercation with his wife, to which the alley paid no attention at all.

There appeared suddenly before the Farraguts a monster making a low and sweeping bow. There was an instant's pause, and then occurred something that resembled the effect of an upheaval of the earth's surface. The old woman hurled herself backward with a dreadful cry. Young Sim had been perched gracefully on a railing. At sight of the monster he simply fell over it to the ground. He made no sound, his eyes stuck out, his nerveless hands tried to grapple the rail to prevent a tumble, and then he vanished. Bella, blubbering, and with her hair suddenly and mysteriously dishevelled, was crawling on her hands and knees fearsomely up the steps.

Standing before this wreck of a family gathering, the monster continued to bow. It even raised a deprecatory claw. "Don' make no botheration 'bout me, Miss Fa'gut," it said, politely. "No, 'deed. I jes drap in ter ax if yer well this evenin', Miss Fa'gut. Don' make no botheration. No, 'deed. I gwine ax you to go to er daince with me, Miss Fa'gut. I ax you if I can have the magnifercent gratitude of you' company on that 'casion, Miss Fa'gut."

The girl cast a miserable glance behind her. She was still crawling away. On the ground beside the porch young Sim raised a strange bleat, which expressed both his fright and his lack of

MRS. FARRAGUT.

wind. Presently the monster, with a fashionable amble, ascended the steps after the girl.

She grovelled in a corner of the room as the creature took a chair. It seated itself very elegantly on the edge. It held an old cap in both hands. "Don' make no botheration, Miss Fa'gut. Don' make no botherations. No, 'deed. I jes drap in ter ax you if you won' do me the proud of acceptin' ma humble invitation to er daince, Miss Fa'gut."

She shielded her eyes with her arms and tried to crawl past it, but the genial monster blocked the way. "I jes drap in ter ax you 'bout er daince, Miss Fa'gut. I ax you if I kin have the magnifercent gratitude of you' company on that 'casion, Miss Fa'gut."

In a last outbreak of despair, the girl, shuddering and wailing, threw herself face downward on the floor, while the monster sat on the edge of the chair gabbling courteous invitations, and holding the old hat daintily to its stomach.

At the back of the house, Mrs. Farragut, who was of enormous weight, and who for eight years had done little more than sit in an arm-chair and describe her various ailments, had with speed and agility scaled a high board fence.

XVIII.

The black mass in the middle of Trescott's property was hardly allowed to cool before the builders were at work on another house. It had sprung upward at a fabulous rate. It was like a magical composition born of the ashes. The doctor's office was the first part to be completed, and he had already moved in his new books and instruments and medicines.

Trescott sat before his desk when the chief of police arrived. "Well, we found him," said the latter.

"Did you?" cried the doctor. "Where?"

"Shambling around the streets at daylight this morning. I'll be blamed if I can figure on where he passed the night."

"Where is he now?"

"Oh, we jugged him. I didn't know what else to do with him. That's what I want you to tell me. Of course we can't keep him. No charge could be made, you know."

"I'll come down and get him."

The official grinned retrospectively. "Must say he had a fine career while he was out. First thing he did was to break up a children's party at Page's. Then he went to Watermelon Alley. Whoo! He stampeded the whole outfit. Men, women, and children running pell-mell, and yelling. They say one old woman broke her leg, or something, shinning over a fence. Then he went right out on the main street, and an Irish girl threw a fit, and there was a sort of a riot. He began to run, and a big crowd chased him, firing rocks. But he gave them the slip somehow down there by the foundry and in the railroad yard. We looked for him all night, but couldn't find him."

"Was he hurt any? Did anybody hit him with a stone?"

"Guess there isn't much of him to hurt any more, is there? Guess he's been hurt up to the limit. No. They never touched him. Of course nobody really wanted to hit him, but you know how a crowd gets. It's like—it's like—"

"Yes, I know."

For a moment the chief of the police looked reflectively at the floor. Then he spoke hesitatingly. "You know Jake Winter's little girl was the one that he scared at the party. She is pretty sick, they say."

"Is she? Why, they didn't call me. I always attend the Winter family."

"No? Didn't they?" asked the chief, slowly. "Well—you know—Winter is —well, Winter has gone clean crazy over this business. He wanted—he wanted to have you arrested."

"Have me arrested? The idiot! What in the name of wonder could he have me arrested for?"

"Of course. He is a fool. I told him to keep his trap shut. But then you know how he'll go all over town yapping about the thing. I thought I'd better tip you."

"Oh, he is of no consequence; but then, of course, I'm obliged to you, Sam."

"That's all right. Well, you'll be down to-night and take him out, eh? You'll get a good welcome from the jailer. He don't like his job for a cent. He says you can have your man whenever you want him. He's got no use for him."

"But what is this business of Winter's about having me arrested?"

"Oh, it's a lot of chin about your having no right to allow this—this—this man to be at large. But I told him to tend to his own business. Only I thought I'd better let you know. And I might as well say right now, doctor, that there is a good deal of talk about this thing. If I were you, I'd come to the jail pretty late at night, because there is likely to be a crowd around the door, and I'd bring a—er—mask, or some kind of a veil, anyhow."

XIX.

Martha Goodwin was single, and well along into the thin years. She lived with her married sister in Whilomville. She performed nearly all the house-work in exchange for the privilege of existence. Every one tacitly recognized her labor as a form of penance for the early end of her betrothed, who had died of small-pox, which he had not caught from her.

But despite the strenuous and unceasing workaday of her life, she was a woman of great mind. She had adamantine opinions upon the situation in Armenia, the condition of women in China, the flirtation between Mrs. Minster of Niagara Avenue and young Griscom, the conflict in the Bible class of the Baptist Sunday-school, the duty of the United States toward the Cuban insurgents, and many other colossal matters. Her fullest experience of violence was gained on an occasion when she had seen a hound clubbed, but in the plan which she had made for the reform of the world she advocated drastic measures. For instance, she contended that all the Turks should be pushed into the sea and drowned, and that Mrs. Minster and young Griscom should be hanged side by side on twin gallows. In fact, this woman of peace, who had seen only peace, argued constantly for a creed of illimitable ferocity. She was invulnerable on these questions, because eventually she overrode all opponents with a sniff. This sniff was an active force. It was to her antagonists like a bang over the head, and none was known to recover from this expression of exalted contempt. It left them windless and conquered. They never again came forward as candidates for suppression. And Martha walked her kitchen with a stern brow, an invincible being like Napoleon.

Nevertheless her acquaintances, from the pain of their defeats, had been long in secret revolt. It was in no wise a conspiracy, because they did not care to state their open rebellion, but nevertheless it was understood that any woman who could not coincide with one of Martha's contentions was entitled to the support of others in the small circle. It amounted to an arrangement by which all were required to disbelieve any theory for which Martha fought. This, however, did not prevent them from speaking of her mind with profound respect.

Two people bore the brunt of her ability. Her sister Kate was visibly afraid of her, while Carrie Dungen sailed across from her kitchen to sit respectfully at Martha's feet and learn the business of the world. To be sure, afterwards, under another sun, she always laughed at Martha and pretended to deride her ideas, but in the presence of the sovereign she always remained silent or admiring. Kate, the sister, was of no consequence at all. Her principal delusion was that she did all the work in the upstairs rooms of the house, while Martha did it downstairs. The truth was seen only by the husband, who treated Martha with a kindness that was half banter, half deference. Martha herself had no suspicion that she was the only pillar of the domestic edifice. The situation was without definitions. Martha made definitions, but she devoted them entirely to the Armenians and Griscom and the Chinese and other subjects. Her dreams, which in early days had been of love of meadows and the shade of trees, of the face of a man, were now involved otherwise, and they were companioned in the kitchen curiously, Cuba, the hot-water kettle, Armenia, the washing of the dishes, and the whole thing being jumbled. In regard to social misdemeanors, she who was simply the mausoleum of a dead passion was probably the most sav-

age critic in town. This unknown woman, hidden in a kitchen as in a well, was sure to have a considerable effect of the one kind or the other in the life of the town. Every time it moved a yard, she had personally contributed an inch. She could hammer so stoutly upon the door of a proposition that it would break from its hinges and fall upon her, but at any rate it moved. She was an engine, and the fact that she did not know that she was an engine contributed largely to the effect. One reason that she was formidable was that she did not even imagine that she was formidable. She remained a weak, innocent, and pig-headed creature, who alone would defy the universe if she thought the universe merited this proceeding.

One day Carrie Dungen came across from her kitchen with speed. She had a great deal of grist. "Oh," she cried, "Henry Johnson got away from where they was keeping him, and came to town last night, and scared everybody almost to death."

Martha was shining a dish-pan, polishing madly. No reasonable person could see cause for this operation, because the pan already glistened like silver. "Well!" she ejaculated. She imparted to the word a deep meaning. "This, my prophecy, has come to pass." It was a habit.

The overplus of information was choking Carrie. Before she could go on she was obliged to struggle for a moment. "And, oh, little Sadie Winter is awful sick, and they say Jake Winter was around this morning trying to get Doctor Trescott arrested. And poor old Mrs. Farragut sprained her ankle in trying to climb a fence. And there's a crowd around the jail all the time. They put Henry in jail because they didn't know what else to do with him, I guess. They say he is perfectly terrible."

Martha finally released the dish-pan and confronted the headlong speaker. "Well!" she said again, poising a great brown rag. Kate had heard the excited new-comer, and drifted down from the novel in her room. She was a shivery little woman. Her shoulder-blades seemed to be two panes of ice, for she was constantly shrugging and shrugging. "Serves him right if he was to lose all his patients," she said suddenly, in bloodthirsty tones. She snipped her words out as if her lips were scissors.

"Well, he's likely to," shouted Carrie Dungen. "Don't a lot of people say that they won't have him any more? If you're sick and nervous, Doctor Trescott would scare the life out of you, wouldn't he? He would me. I'd keep thinking."

Martha, stalking to and fro, sometimes surveyed the two other women with a contemplative frown.

XX.

After the return from Connecticut, little Jimmie was at first much afraid of the monster who lived in the room over the carriage-house. He could not identify it in any way. Gradually, however, his fear dwindled under the influence of a weird fascination. He sidled into closer and closer relations with it.

One time the monster was seated on a box behind the stable basking in the rays of the afternoon sun. A heavy crêpe veil was swathed about its head.

Little Jimmie and many companions came around the corner of the stable. They were all in what was popularly known as the baby class, and consequently escaped from school a half-hour before the other children. They halted abruptly at sight of the figure on the box. Jimmie waved his hand with the air of a proprietor.

"There he is," he said.

"O-o-o!" murmured all the little boys —"o-o-o!" They shrank back, and grouped according to courage or experience, as at the sound the monster slowly turned its head. Jimmie had remained in the van alone. "Don't be afraid! I won't let him hurt you," he said, delighted.

"Huh!" they replied, contemptuously. "We ain't afraid."

Jimmie seemed to reap all the joys of the owner and exhibitor of one of the world's marvels, while his audience remained at a distance—awed and entranced, fearful and envious.

One of them addressed Jimmie gloomily. "Bet you dassent walk right up to him." He was an older boy than Jimmie, and habitually oppressed him to a small degree. This new social elevation of the smaller lad probably seemed revolutionary to him.

"Huh!" said Jimmie, with deep scorn. "Dassent I? Dassent I, hey? Dassent I?"

The group was immensely excited. It turned its eyes upon the boy that Jimmie addressed. "No, you dassent," he said, stolidly, facing a moral defeat. He could see that Jimmie was resolved. "No, you dassent," he repeated, doggedly.

"Ho!" cried Jimmie. "You just watch!—you just watch!"

Amid a silence he turned and marched toward the monster. But possibly the palpable wariness of his companions had an effect upon him that weighed more than his previous experience, for suddenly, when near to the monster, he halted dubiously. But his playmates immediately uttered a derisive shout, and it seemed to force him forward. He went to the monster and laid his hand delicately on its shoulder. "Hello, Henry," he said, in a voice that trembled a trifle. The monster was crooning a weird line of negro melody that was scarcely more than a thread of sound, and it paid no heed to the boy.

Jimmie strutted back to his companions. They acclaimed him and hooted his opponent. Amidst this clamor the larger boy with difficulty preserved a dignified attitude.

"I dassent, dassent I?" said Jimmie to him. "Now, you're so smart, let's see you do it!"

This challenge brought forth renewed taunts from the others. The larger boy puffed out his cheeks. "Well, I ain't afraid," he explained, sullenly. He had made a mistake in diplomacy, and now his small enemies were tumbling his prestige all about his ears. They crowed like roosters and bleated like lambs, and made many other noises which were supposed to bury him in ridicule and dishonor. "Well, I ain't afraid," he continued to explain through the din.

Jimmie, the hero of the mob, was pitiless. "You ain't afraid, hey?" he sneered. "If you ain't afraid, go do it, then."

"Well, I would if I wanted to," the other retorted. His eyes wore an expression of profound misery, but he preserved steadily other portions of a pot-valiant air. He suddenly faced one of his persecutors. "If you're so smart, why don't you go do it?" This persecutor sank promptly through the group to the rear. The incident gave the badgered one a breathing-spell, and for a moment even turned the derision in another direction. He took advantage of his interval. "I'll do it if anybody else will," he announced, swaggering to and fro.

Candidates for the adventure did not come forward. To defend themselves from this counter-charge, the other boys again set up their crowing and bleating. For a while they would hear nothing from him. Each time he opened his lips their chorus of noises made oratory impossible. But at last he was able to repeat that he would volunteer to dare as much in the affair as any other boy.

"Well, you go first," they shouted.

But Jimmie intervened to once more lead the populace against the large boy. "You're mighty brave, ain't you?" he said to him. "You dared me to do it, and I did—didn't I? Now who's afraid?" The others cheered this view loudly, and they instantly resumed the baiting of the large boy.

He shamefacedly scratched his left shin with his right foot. "Well, I ain't afraid." He cast an eye at the monster. "Well, I ain't afraid." With a glare of hatred at his squalling tormentors, he finally announced a grim intention. "Well, I'll do it, then, since you're so fresh. Now!"

The mob subsided as with a formidable countenance he turned toward the impassive figure on the box. The advance was also a regular progression from high daring to craven hesitation. At last, when some yards from the monster, the lad came to a full halt, as if he had encountered a stone wall. The observant little boys in the distance promptly hooted. Stung again by these cries, the lad sneaked two yards forward. He was crouched like a young cat ready for a backward spring. The crowd at the rear, beginning to respect this display, uttered some encouraging cries. Suddenly the lad gathered himself together, made a white and desperate rush forward, touched the monster's shoulder with a far-outstretched finger, and sped away, while his laughter rang out wild, shrill, and exultant.

The crowd of boys reverenced him at once, and began to throng into his camp, and look at him, and be his admirers. Jimmie was discomfited for a moment, but he and the larger boy, without agreement or word of any kind, seemed to recognize a truce, and they swiftly combined and began to parade before the others.

"Why, it's just as easy as nothing," puffed the larger boy. "Ain't it, Jim?"

"Course," blew Jimmie. "Why, it's as e-e-easy."

They were people of another class. If they had been decorated for courage on twelve battle-fields, they could not have made the other boys more ashamed of the situation.

Meanwhile they condescended to explain the emotions of the excursion, expressing unqualified contempt for any one who could hang back. "Why, it ain't nothin'. He won't do nothin' to you," they told the others, in tones of exasperation.

One of the very smallest boys in the party showed signs of a wistful desire to distinguish himself, and they turned their attention to him, pushing at his shoulders while he swung away from them, and hesitated dreamily. He was eventually induced to make furtive expedition, but it was only for a few yards. Then he paused, motionless, gazing with open mouth. The vociferous entreaties of Jimmie and the large boy had no power over him.

Mrs. Hannigan had come out on her back porch with a pail of water. From this coign she had a view of the secluded portion of the Trescott grounds that was behind the stable. She perceived the group of boys, and the monster on the box. She shaded her eyes with her hand to benefit her vision. She screeched then as if she was being murdered. "Eddie! Eddie! You come home this minute!"

Her son querulously demanded, "Aw, what for?"

"You come home this minute. Do you hear?"

The other boys seemed to think this visitation upon one of their number required them to preserve for a time the hang-dog air of a collection of culprits, and they remained in guilty silence until the little Hannigan, wrathfully protesting, was pushed through the door of his home. Mrs. Hannigan cast a piercing glance over the group, stared with a bitter face at the Trescott house, as if this new and handsome edifice was insulting her, and then followed her son.

There was wavering in the party. An inroad by one mother always caused them to carefully sweep the horizon to see if there were more coming. "This is my yard," said Jimmie, proudly. "We don't have to go home."

The monster on the box had turned its black crêpe countenance toward the sky, and was waving its arms in time to a

religious chant. "Look at him now,"
cried a little boy. They turned, and
were transfixed by the solemnity and mystery of the
indefinable gestures. The
wail of the melody was
mournful and slow.
They drew back. It
seemed to spellbind
them with the power
of a funeral. They
were so absorbed that
they did not hear the
doctor's buggy drive
up to the stable. Tres-
cott got out, tied his
horse, and approached
the group. Jimmie saw
him first, and at
his look of dis-
may the others
wheeled.

"What's all this,
Jimmie?" asked
Trescott, in sur-
prise.

The lad ad-
vanced to the
front of his com-
panions, halted,
and said nothing.
Trescott's face
gloomed slightly
as he scanned the
scene.

"What were you
doing, Jimmie?"

"We was play-
in'," answered
Jimmie, huskily.

"Playing at
what?"

"Just playin'."

Trescott looked

"IF YOU AIN'T AFRAID, GO DO IT THEN."

gravely at the other boys, and asked
them to please go home. They proceeded
to the street much in the manner of frus-
trated and revealed assassins. The crime
of trespass on another boy's place was
still a crime when they had only accepted
the other boy's cordial invitation, and
they were used to being sent out of all
manner of gardens upon the sudden appearance of a father or a mother. Jimmie
had wretchedly watched the departure of
his companions. It involved the loss of
his position as a lad who controlled the
privileges of his father's grounds, but then
he knew that in the beginning he had

no right to ask so many boys to be his
guests.

Once on the sidewalk, however, they
speedily forgot their shame as tres-
passers, and the large boy launched forth
in a description of his success in the late
trial of courage. As they went rapidly
up the street, the little boy who had
made the furtive expedition cried out confidently from the rear. "Yes, and I went
almost up to him, didn't I, Willie?"

The large boy crushed him in a few
words. "Huh!" he scoffed. "You only
went a little way. I went clear up to
him."

The pace of the other boys was so manly that the tiny thing had to trot, and he remained at the rear, getting entangled in their legs in his attempts to reach the front rank and become of some importance, dodging this way and that way, and always piping out his little claim to glory.

XXI.

"By-the-way, Grace," said Trescott, looking into the dining-room from his office door, "I wish you would send Jimmie to me before school-time."

When Jimmie came, he advanced so quietly that Trescott did not at first note him. "Oh," he said, wheeling from a cabinet, "here you are, young man."

"Yes, sir."

Trescott dropped into his chair and tapped the desk with a thoughtful finger. "Jimmie, what were you doing in the back garden yesterday—you and the other boys—to Henry?"

"We weren't doing anything, pa."

Trescott looked sternly into the raised eyes of his son. "Are you sure you were not annoying him in any way? Now what were you doing, exactly?"

"Why, we — why, we — now — Willie Dalzel said I dassent go right up to him, and I did; and then he did; and then— the other boys were 'fraid; and then—you comed."

Trescott groaned deeply. His countenance was so clouded in sorrow that the lad, bewildered by the mystery of it, burst suddenly forth in dismal lamentations. "There, there. Don't cry, Jim," said Trescott, going round the desk. "Only—" He sat in a great leather reading-chair, and took the boy on his knee. "Only I want to explain to you—"

After Jimmie had gone to school, and as Trescott was about to start on his round of morning calls, a message arrived from Doctor Moser. It set forth that the latter's sister was dying in the old homestead, twenty miles away up the valley, and asked Trescott to care for his patients for the day at least. There was also in the envelope a little history of each case and of what had already been done. Trescott replied to the messenger that he would gladly assent to the arrangement.

He noted that the first name on Moser's list was Winter, but this did not seem to strike him as an important fact. When its turn came, he rang the Winter bell.

"Good-morning, Mrs. Winter," he said, cheerfully, as the door was opened. "Doctor Moser has been obliged to leave town to-day, and he has asked me to come in his stead. How is the little girl this morning?"

Mrs. Winter had regarded him in stony surprise. At last she said: "Come in! I'll see my husband." She bolted into the house. Trescott entered the hall, and turned to the left into the sitting-room.

Presently Winter shuffled through the door. His eyes flashed toward Trescott. He did not betray any desire to advance far into the room. "What do you want?" he said.

"What do I want? What do I want?" repeated Trescott, lifting his head suddenly. He had heard an utterly new challenge in the night of the jungle.

"Yes, that's what I want to know," snapped Winter. "What do you want?"

Trescott was silent for a moment. He consulted Moser's memoranda. "I see that your little girl's case is a trifle serious," he remarked. "I would advise you to call a physician soon. I will leave you a copy of Doctor Moser's record to give to any one you may call." He paused to transcribe the record on a page of his note-book. Tearing out the leaf, he extended it to Winter as he moved toward the door. The latter shrunk against the wall. His head was hanging as he reached for the paper. This caused him to grasp air, and so Trescott simply let the paper flutter to the feet of the other man.

"Good-morning," said Trescott from the hall. This placid retreat seemed to suddenly arouse Winter to ferocity. It was as if he had then recalled all the truths which he had formulated to hurl at Trescott. So he followed him into the hall, and down the hall to the door, and through the door to the porch, barking in fiery rage from a respectful distance. As Trescott imperturbably turned the mare's head down the road, Winter stood on the porch, still yelping. He was like a little dog.

XXII.

"Have you heard the news?" cried Carrie Dungen, as she sped toward Martha's kitchen. "Have you heard the news?" Her eyes were shining with delight.

"No," answered Martha's sister Kate, bending forward eagerly. "What was it? What was it?"

Carrie appeared triumphantly in the open door. "Oh, there's been an awful scene between Doctor Trescott and Jake Winter. I never thought that Jake Winter had any pluck at all, but this morning he told the doctor just what he thought of him."

"Well, what did he think of him?" asked Martha.

"Oh, he called him everything. Mrs. Howarth heard it through her front blinds. It was terrible, she says. It's all over town now. Everybody knows it."

"Didn't the doctor answer back?"

"No! Mrs. Howarth—she says he never said a word. He just walked down to his buggy and got in, and drove off as co-o-o-l. But Jake gave him jinks, by all accounts."

"But what did he say?" cried Kate, shrill and excited. She was evidently at some kind of a feast.

"Oh, he told him that Sadie had never been well since that night Henry Johnson frightened her at Theresa Page's party, and he held him responsible, and how dared he cross his threshold—and—and—and—"

"And what?" said Martha.

"Did he swear at him?" said Kate, in fearsome glee.

"No—not much. He did swear at him a little, but not more than a man does anyhow when he is real mad, Mrs. Howarth says."

"O-oh!" breathed Kate. "And did he call him any names?"

Martha, at her work, had been for a time in deep thought. She now interrupted the others. "It don't seem as if Sadie Winter had been sick since that time Henry Johnson got loose. She's been to school almost the whole time since then, hasn't she?"

They combined upon her in immediate indignation. "School? School? I should say not. Don't think for a moment. School!"

Martha wheeled from the sink. She held an iron spoon, and it seemed as if she was going to attack them. "Sadie Winter has passed here many a morning since then carrying her school-bag. Where was she going? To a wedding?"

The others, long accustomed to a mental tyranny, speedily surrendered.

"Did she?" stammered Kate. "I never saw her."

Carrie Dungen made a weak gesture.

"If I had been Doctor Trescott," exclaimed Martha, loudly, "I'd have knocked that miserable Jake Winter's head off."

Kate and Carrie, exchanging glances, made an alliance in the air. "I don't see why you say that, Martha," replied Carrie, with considerable boldness, gaining support and sympathy from Kate's smile. "I don't see how anybody can be blamed for getting angry when their little girl gets almost scared to death and gets sick from it, and all that. Besides, everybody says—"

"Oh, I don't care what everybody says," said Martha.

"Well, you can't go against the whole town," answered Carrie, in sudden sharp defiance.

"No, Martha, you can't go against the whole town," piped Kate, following her leader rapidly.

"'The whole town,'" cried Martha. "I'd like to know what you call 'the whole town.' Do you call these silly people who are scared of Henry Johnson 'the whole town'?"

"Why, Martha," said Carrie, in a reasoning tone, "you talk as if you wouldn't be scared of him!"

"No more would I," retorted Martha.

"O-oh, Martha, how you talk!" said Kate. "Why, the idea! Everybody's afraid of him."

Carrie was grinning. "You've never seen him, have you?" she asked, seductively.

"No," admitted Martha.

"Well, then, how do you know that you wouldn't be scared?"

Martha confronted her. "Have you ever seen him? No? Well, then, how do you know you *would* be scared?"

The allied forces broke out in chorus: "But, Martha, everybody says so. Everybody says so."

"Everybody says what?"

"Everybody that's seen him say they were frightened almost to death. 'Tisn't only women, but it's men too. It's awful."

Martha wagged her head solemnly. "I'd try not to be afraid of him."

"But supposing you could not help it?" said Kate.

"Yes, and look here," cried Carrie. "I'll tell you another thing. The Hannigans are going to move out of the house next door."

"On account of him?" demanded Martha.

Carrie nodded. "Mrs. Hannigan says so herself."

"Well, of all things!" ejaculated Martha. "Going to move, eh? You don't say so! Where they going to move to?"

"Down on Orchard Avenue."

"Well, of all things! Nice house?"

"I don't know about that. I haven't heard. But there's lots of nice houses on Orchard."

"Yes, but they're all taken," said Kate. "There isn't a vacant house on Orchard Avenue."

"Oh yes, there is," said Martha. "The old Hampstead house is vacant."

"Oh, of course," said Kate. "But then I don't believe Mrs. Hannigan would like it there. I wonder where they can be going to move to?"

"I'm sure I don't know," sighed Martha. "It must be to some place we don't know about."

"Well," said Carrie Dungen, after a general reflective silence, "it's easy enough to find out, anyhow."

"Who knows around here?" asked Kate.

"Why, Mrs. Smith, and there she is in her garden," said Carrie, jumping to her feet. As she dashed out of the door, Kate and Martha crowded at the window. Carrie's voice rang out from near the steps. "Mrs. Smith! Mrs. Smith! Do you know where the Hannigans are going to move to?"

XXIII.

The autumn smote the leaves, and the trees of Whilomville were panoplied in crimson and yellow. The winds grew stronger, and in the melancholy purple of the nights the home shine of a window became a finer thing. The little boys, watching the sear and sorrowful leaves drifting down from the maples, dreamed of the near time when they could heap bushels in the streets and burn them during the abrupt evenings.

Three men walked down the Niagara Avenue. As they approached Judge Hagenthorpe's house he came down his walk to meet them in the manner of one who has been waiting.

"Are you ready, judge?" one said.

"All ready," he answered.

The four then walked to Trescott's house. He received them in his office, where he had been reading. He seemed surprised at this visit of four very active

and influential citizens, but he had nothing to say of it.

After they were all seated, Trescott looked expectantly from one face to another. There was a little silence. It was broken by John Twelve, the wholesale grocer, who was worth $400,000, and reported to be worth over a million.

"Well, doctor," he said, with a short laugh, "I suppose we might as well admit at once that we've come to interfere in something which is none of our business."

"Why, what is it?" asked Trescott, again looking from one face to another. He seemed to appeal particularly to Judge Hagenthorpe, but the old man had his chin lowered musingly to his cane, and would not look at him.

"It's about what nobody talks of—much," said Twelve. "It's about Henry Johnson."

Trescott squared himself in his chair. "Yes?" he said.

Having delivered himself of the title, Twelve seemed to become more easy. "Yes," he answered, blandly, "we wanted to talk to you about it."

"Yes?" said Trescott.

Twelve abruptly advanced on the main attack. "Now see here, Trescott, we like you, and we have come to talk right out about this business. It may be none of our affairs and all that, and as for me, I don't mind if you tell me so; but I am not going to keep quiet and see you ruin yourself. And that's how we all feel."

"I am not ruining myself," answered Trescott.

"No, maybe you are not exactly ruining yourself," said Twelve, slowly, "but you are doing yourself a great deal of harm. You have changed from being the leading doctor in town to about the last one. It is mainly because there are always a large number of people who are very thoughtless fools, of course, but then that doesn't change the condition."

A man who had not heretofore spoken said, solemnly, "It's the women."

"Well, what I want to say is this," resumed Twelve: "Even if there are a lot of fools in the world, we can't see any reason why you should ruin yourself by opposing them. You can't teach them anything, you know."

"I am not trying to teach them anything." Trescott smiled wearily. "I— It is a matter of—well—"

"'IT'S ABOUT WHAT NOBODY TALKS OF—MUCH,' SAID TWELVE."

"And there are a good many of us that admire you for it immensely," interrupted Twelve; "but that isn't going to change the minds of all those ninnies."

"It's the women," stated the advocate of this view again.

"Well, what I want to say is this," said Twelve. "We want you to get out of this trouble and strike your old gait again. You are simply killing your practice through your infernal pig-head-edness. Now this thing is out of the ordinary, but there must be ways to—to beat the game somehow, you see. So we've talked it over—about a dozen of us—and, as I say, if you want to tell us to mind our own business, why, go ahead; but we've talked it over, and we've come to the conclusion that the only way to do is to get Johnson a place somewhere off up the valley, and—"

Trescott wearily gestured. "You don't

know, my friend. Everybody is so afraid of him, they can't even give him good care. Nobody can attend to him as I do myself."

"But I have a little no-good farm up beyond Clarence Mountain that I was going to give to Henry," cried Twelve, aggrieved. "And if you—and if you— if you — through your house burning down, or anything — why, all the boys were prepared to take him right off your hands, and—and—"

Trescott arose and went to the window. He turned his back upon them. They sat waiting in silence. When he returned he kept his face in the shadow. "No, John Twelve," he said, "it can't be done."

There was another stillness. Suddenly a man stirred on his chair.

"Well, then, a public institution—" he began.

"No," said Trescott; "public institutions are all very good, but he is not going to one."

In the background of the group old Judge Hagenthorpe was thoughtfully smoothing the polished ivory head of his cane.

XXIV.

Trescott loudly stamped the snow from his feet and shook the flakes from his shoulders. When he entered the house he went at once to the dining-room, and then to the sitting-room. Jimmie was there, reading painfully in a large book concerning giraffes and tigers and crocodiles.

"Where is your mother, Jimmie?" asked Trescott.

"I don't know, pa," answered the boy. "I think she is upstairs."

Trescott went to the foot of the stairs and called, but there came no answer. Seeing that the door of the little drawing-room was open, he entered. The room was bathed in the half-light that came from the four dull panes of mica in the front of the great stove. As his eyes grew used to the shadows he saw his wife curled in an arm-chair. He went to her. "Why, Grace," he said, "didn't you hear me calling you?"

She made no answer, and as he bent over the chair he heard her trying to smother a sob in the cushion.

"Grace!" he cried. "You're crying!"

She raised her face. "I've got a headache, a dreadful headache, Ned."

"A headache?" he repeated, in surprise and incredulity.

He pulled a chair close to hers. Later, as he cast his eye over the zone of light shed by the dull red panes, he saw that a low table had been drawn close to the stove, and that it was burdened with many small cups and plates of uncut teacake. He remembered that the day was Wednesday, and that his wife received on Wednesdays.

"Who was here to-day, Gracie?" he asked.

From his shoulder there came a mumble, "Mrs. Twelve."

"Was she — um," he said. "Why—didn't Anna Hagenthorpe come over?"

The mumble from his shoulder continued, "She wasn't well enough."

Glancing down at the cups, Trescott mechanically counted them. There were fifteen of them. "There, there," he said. "Don't cry, Grace. Don't cry."

The wind was whining round the house, and the snow beat aslant upon the windows. Sometimes the coal in the stove settled with a crumbling sound, and the four panes of mica flashed a sudden new crimson. As he sat holding her head on his shoulder, Trescott found himself occasionally trying to count the cups. There were fifteen of them.

CRAPY CORNELIA
by Henry James

THREE times within a quarter of an hour—shifting the while his posture on his chair of contemplation—had he looked at his watch as for its final sharp hint that he should decide, that he should get up. His seat was one of a group fairly sequestered, unoccupied save for his own presence, and from where he lingered he looked off at a stretch of lawn freshened by recent April showers and on which sundry small children were at play. The trees, the shrubs, the plants, every stem and twig just ruffled as by the first touch of the light finger of the relenting year, struck him as standing still in the blest hope of more of the same caress; the quarter about him held its breath after the fashion of the child who waits with the rigor of an open mouth and shut eyes for the promised sensible effect of his having been good. So, in the windless, sun-warmed air of the beautiful afternoon, the Park of the winter's end had struck White-Mason as waiting; even New York, under such an impression, was "good," good enough—for *him;* its very sounds were faint, were almost sweet, as they reached him from so seemingly far beyond the wooded horizon that formed the remoter limit of his large shallow glade. The tones of the frolic infants ceased to be nondescript and harsh — were in fact almost as fresh and decent as the frilled and puckered and ribboned garb of the little girls, which had always a way, in those parts, of so portentously flaunting the daughters of the strange native—that is of the overwhelmingly alien—populace at him.

Not that these things in particular were his matter of meditation now; he had wanted, at the end of his walk, to sit apart a little and think—and· had been doing that for twenty minutes, even though as yet to no break in the charm of procrastination. But he had looked without seeing and listened without hearing: all that had been positive for him was that he hadn't failed vaguely to feel. He had felt in the first place, and he continued to feel—yes, at forty-eight quite as much as at any point of the supposed reign of younger intensities—the great spirit of the air, the fine sense of the season, the supreme appeal of Nature, he might have said, to his time of life; quite as if she, easy, indulgent, indifferent, cynical Power, were offering him the last chance it would rest with his wit or his blood to embrace. Then with that he had been entertaining, to the point and with the prolonged consequence of accepted immobilization, the certitude that if he did call on Mrs. Worthingham and find her at home he couldn't in justice to himself not put to her the question that had lapsed the other time, the last time, through the irritating and persistent, even if accidental, presence of others. What friends she had—the people who so stupidly, so wantonly stuck! If they *should,* he and she, come to an understanding, that would presumably have to include certain members of her singularly ill-composed circle, in whom it was incredible to him that he should ever take an interest. This defeat, to do himself justice—he was bent rather predominantly on *that,* you see; ideal justice to *her,* with her possible conception of what it should consist of, being another and quite a different matter—he had had the fact of the Sunday afternoon to thank for; she didn't "keep" that day for him, since they hadn't, up to now, quite begun to cultivate the appointment or assignation founded on explicit sacrifices. He might at any rate look to find this pleasant practical Wednesday — should he indeed, at his actual rate, stay it before it ebbed—more liberally and intendingly given him.

The sound he at last most wittingly distinguished in his nook was the single deep note of half past five borne to him from some high-perched public clock. He finally got up with the sense that the time from then on *ought* at least to be felt as sacred to him. At this juncture it was—while he stood there shaking his garments, settling his hat, his necktie, his shirt-cuffs, fixing the high polish of his fine shoes as if for some reflection in it of his straight and spare and grizzled, his refined and trimmed and dressed, his altogether distinguished person, that of a gentleman abundantly settled, but of a bachelor markedly nervous—at this crisis it was, doubtless, that he at once most measured and least resented his predicament. If he should go he'd almost to a certainty find her, and if he should find her he'd almost to a certainty come to the point. He wouldn't put it off again—there was that high consideration for him of justice at least to himself. He had never yet denied himself anything so apparently fraught with possibilities as the idea of proposing to Mrs. Worthingham—never yet, in other words, denied himself anything he had so distinctly wanted to do; and the results of that wisdom had remained for him precisely the precious parts of experience. Counting only the offers of his honorable hand, these had been on three remembered occasions at least the consequence of an impulse as sharp and a self-respect as reasoned; a self-respect that hadn't in the least suffered, moreover, from the failure of each appeal. He had been met in the three cases—the only ones he at all compared with his present case—by the frank confession that he didn't somehow, charming as he was, cause himself to be superstitiously believed in; and the lapse of life, afterwards, had cleared up many doubts.

It *wouldn't* have done, he eventually, he lucidly saw, each time he had been refused; and the candor of his nature was such that he could live to think of these very passages as a proof of how right he had been—right, that is, to have put himself forward always, by the happiest instinct, only in impossible conditions. He had the happy consciousness of having exposed the important question to the crucial test, and of having escaped, by that persistent logic, a grave mistake. What better proof of his escape than the fact that he was now free to renew the all-

interesting inquiry, and should be, exactly, about to do so in different and better conditions? The conditions were better by as much more—as much more of his career and character, of his situation, his reputation he could even have called it, of his knowledge of life, of his somewhat extended means, of his possibly augmented charm, of his certainly improved mind and temper—as was involved in the actual impending settlement. Once he had got into motion, once he had crossed the Park and passed out of it, entering, with very little space to traverse, one of the short new streets that abutted on its east side, his step became that of a man young enough to find confidence, quite to find felicity, in the sense, in almost any sense, of action. He could still enjoy almost anything, absolutely an unpleasant thing, in default of a better, that might still remind him he wasn't so old. The standing newness of everything about him would, it was true, have weakened this cheer by too much presuming on it; Mrs. Worthingham's house, before which he stopped, had that gloss of new money, that glare of a piece fresh from the mint and ringing for the first time on any counter, which seems to claim for it, in any transaction, something more than the "face" value.

This could but be yet more the case for the impression of the observer introduced and committed; on our friend's part I mean, after his admission and while still in the hall, the sense of the general shining immediacy, of the still unhushed clamor of the shock, was perhaps stronger than he had ever known it. That broke out from every corner as the high pitch of interest, and with a candor that—no, certainly—he had never seen equalled; every particular expensive object shrieking at him in its artless pride that it had just "come home." He met the whole vision with something of the grimace produced on persons without goggles by the passage from a shelter to a blinding light; and if he had—by a perfectly possible chance—been "snap-shotted" on the spot, would have struck you as showing for his first tribute to the temple of Mrs. Worthingham's charming presence a scowl almost of anguish. He wasn't constitutionally, it may at once be explained for him, a goggled person; and he was condemned, in New York, to this frequent violence of transition—having to reckon with it whenever he went out, as who should say, from himself. The high pitch of interest, to his taste, was the pitch of history, the pitch of acquired and earned suggestion, the pitch of association, in a word; so that he lived by preference, incontestably, if not in a rich gloom, which would have been beyond his means and spirits, at least amid objects and images that confessed to the tone of time.

He had ever felt that an indispensable presence—with a need of it moreover that interfered at no point with his gentle habit, not to say his subtle art, of drawing out what was left him of his youth, of thinly and thriftily spreading the rest of that choicest jam-pot of the cupboard of consciousness over the remainder of a slice of life still possibly thick enough to bear it; or in other words of moving the melancholy limits, the significant signs, constantly a little further on, very much as property-marks or staked boundaries are sometimes stealthily shifted at night. He positively cherished in fact, as against the too inveterate gesture of distressfully guarding his eyeballs — so many New York aspects seemed to keep him at it—an ideal of adjusted appreciation, of courageous curiosity, of fairly letting the world about him, a world of constant breathless renewals and merciless substitutions, make its flaring assault on its own inordinate terms. Newness *was* value in the piece— for the acquisitor, or at least sometimes might be, even though the act of "blowing" hard, the act marking a heated freshness of arrival, or other form of irruption, could never minister to the peace of those already and long on the field; and this if only because maturer tone was after all most appreciable and most consoling when one staggered back to it, wounded, bleeding, blinded, from the riot of the raw—or, to put the whole experience more prettily, no doubt, from excesses of light.

If he went in, however, with something of his more or less inevitable scowl, there were really, at the moment, two rather valid reasons for screened observation;

the first of these being that the whole place seemed to reflect as never before the lustre of Mrs. Worthingham's own polished and prosperous little person— to smile, it struck him, with her smile, to twinkle not only with the gleam of her lovely teeth, but with that of all her rings and brooches and bangles and other gewgaws, to curl and spasmodically cluster as in emulation of her charming complicated yellow tresses, to surround the most animated of pink-and-white, of ruffled and ribboned, of frilled and festooned Dresden china shepherdesses with exactly the right system of rococo curves and convolutions and other flourishes, a perfect bower of painted and gilded and moulded conceits. The second ground of this immediate impression of scenic extravagance, almost as if the curtain rose for him to the first act of some small, expensively mounted comic opera, was that she hadn't, after all, awaited him in fond singleness, but had again just a trifle inconsiderately exposed him to the drawback of having to reckon, for whatever design he might amiably entertain, with the presence of a third and quite superfluous person, a small black insignificant but none the less oppressive stranger. It was odd how, on the instant, the little lady engaged with her did affect him as comparatively black— very much as if that had absolutely, in such a medium, to be the graceless appearance of any item not positively of some fresh shade of a light color or of some pretty pretension to a charming twist. Any witness of their meeting, his hostess should surely have felt, would have been a false note in the whole rosy glow; but what note so false as that of the dingy little presence that she might actually, by a refinement of her perhaps always too visible study of effect, have provided as a positive contrast or foil? whose name and intervention, moreover, she appeared to be no more moved to mention and account for than she might have been to "present"—whether as stretched at her feet or erect upon disciplined haunches—some shaggy old domesticated terrier or poodle.

Extraordinarily, after he had been in the room five minutes—a space of time during which his fellow visitor had neither budged nor uttered a sound—he had made Mrs. Worthingham out as all at once perfectly pleased to see him, completely aware of what he had most in mind, and singularly serene in face of his sense of their impediment. It was as if for all the world she didn't take it for one, the immobility, to say nothing of the seeming equanimity, of their tactless companion; at whom meanwhile indeed our friend himself, after his first ruffled perception, no more adventured a look than if advised by his constitutional kindness that to notice her in any degree would perforce be ungraciously to glower. He talked after a fashion with the woman as to whose power to please and amuse and serve him, as to whose really quite organized and indicated fitness for lighting up his autumn afternoon of life his conviction had lately strained itself so clear; but he was all the while carrying on an intenser exchange with his own spirit and trying to read into the charming creature's behavior, as he could only call it, some confirmation of his theory that she also had her inward flutter and anxiously counted on him. He found support, happily for the conviction just named, in the idea, at no moment as yet really repugnant to him, the idea bound up in fact with the finer essence of her appeal, that she had her own vision too of her quality and her price, and that the last appearance she would have liked to bristle with was that of being forewarned and eager.

He had, if he came to think of it, scarce definitely warned her, and he probably wouldn't have taken to her so consciously in the first instance without an appreciative sense that, as she was a little person of twenty superficial graces, so she was also a little person with her secret of pride. She might just have planted her mangy lion—not to say her muzzled house-dog—there in his path as a symbol that she wasn't cheap and easy; which would be a thing he couldn't possibly wish his future wife to have shown herself in advance, even if to him alone. That she could make him put himself such questions was precisely part of the attaching play of her iridescent surface, the shimmering interfusion of her various aspects; that of her youth with her independence—her pecuniary perhaps in particular, that of her vivacity with her

beauty, that of her facility above all with her odd novelty; the high modernity, as people appeared to have come to call it, that made her so much more " knowing " in some directions than even he man of the world as he certainly was, could pretend to be, though all on a basis of the most unconscious and instinctive and luxurious assumption. She was " up " to everything, aware of everything—if one counted from a short enough time back (from week before last, say, and as if quantities of history had burst upon the world within the fortnight); she was likewise surprised at nothing, and in that direction one might reckon as·far ahead as the rest of her lifetime, or at any rate as the rest of his, which was all that would concern him: it was as if the suitability of the future to her personal and rather pampered tastes was what she most took for granted, so that he could see her, for all her Dresden-china shoes and her flutter of wondrous befrilled contemporary skirts, skip by the side of the coming age as over the floor of a ball-room, keeping step with its monstrous stride and prepared for every figure of the dance.

Her outlook took form to him suddenly as a great square sunny window that hung in assured fashion over the immensity of life. There rose toward it as from a vast swarming *plaza* a high tide of motion and sound; yet it was at the same time as if even while he looked her light gemmed hand, flashing on him in addition to those other things the perfect polish of the prettiest pink fingernails in the world, had touched a spring, the most ingenious of recent devices for instant ease, which dropped half across the scene a soft - colored mechanical blind, a fluttered, fringed awning of charmingly toned silk, such as would make a bath of cool shade for the favored friend leaning with her there—that is for the happy couple itself—on the balcony. The great view would be the prospect and privilege of the very state he coveted—since didn't he covet it?—the state of being so securely at her side; while the wash of privacy, as one might count it, the broad fine brush dipped into clear umber and passed, full and wet, straight across the strong scheme of color, would represent the security itself.

all the uplifted inner elegance, the condition, so ideal, of being shut out from nothing and yet of having, so gayly and breezily aloft, none of the burden or worry of anything. Thus, as I say, for our friend, the place itself, while his vivid impression lasted, portentously opened and spread, and what was before him took, to his vision, though indeed at so other a crisis, the form of the "glimmering square" of the poet; yet, for a still more remarkable fact, with an incongruous object usurping at a given instant the privilege of the frame and seeming, even as he looked, to block the view.

The incongruous object was a woman's head, crowned with a little sparsely feathered black hat, an ornament quite unlike those the women mostly noticed by White-Mason were now "wearing," and that grew and grew, that came nearer and nearer, while it met his eyes, after the manner of images in the cinematograph. It had presently loomed so large that he saw nothing else—not only among the things at a considerable distance, the things Mrs. Worthingham would eventually, yet unmistakably, introduce him to, but among those of this lady's various attributes and appurtenances as to which he had been in the very act of cultivating his consciousness. It was in the course of another minute the most extraordinary thing in the world: everything had altered, dropped, darkened, disappeared; his imagination had spread its wings only to feel them flop all grotesquely at its sides as he recognized in his hostess's quiet companion, the oppressive alien who hadn't indeed interfered with his fanciful flight, though she had prevented his immediate declaration and brought about the thud, not to say the felt violent shock, of his fall to earth, the perfectly plain identity of Cornelia Rasch. It was she who had remained there at attention; it was she their companion hadn't introduced; it was she he had forborne to face with his fear of incivility. He stared at her—everything else went.

"Why it has been *you* all this time?" Miss Rasch fairly turned pale. "I was waiting to see if you'd know me."

"Ah, my dear Cornelia "—he came straight out with it—" rather!"

"Well it isn't," she returned with a quick change to red now, "from having taken much time to look at me!"

She smiled, she even laughed, but he could see how she had felt his unconsciousness, poor thing; the acquaintance, quite the friend of his youth, as she had been, the associate of his childhood, of his early manhood, of his middle age in fact, up to a few years back, not more than ten at the most; the associate too of so many of his associates and of almost all of his relations, those of the other time, those who had mainly gone forever; the person in short whose noted disappearance, though it might have seemed final, had been only of recent seasons. She was present again now, all unexpectedly—he had heard of her having at last, left alone after successive deaths and with scant resources, sought economic salvation in Europe, the promised land of American thrift—she was present as this almost ancient and this oddly unassertive little rotund figure whom one seemed no more obliged to address than if she had been a black satin ottoman "treated" with buttons and gimp; a class of object as to which the policy of blindness was imperative. He felt the need of some explanatory plea, and before he could think had uttered one at Mrs. Worthingham's expense. "Why, you see we weren't introduced—!"

"No—but I didn't suppose I should have to be named to you."

"Well, my dear woman, you haven't—do me that justice!" He could at least make this point. "I felt all the while—!" However it would have taken him long to say what he had been feeling; and he was aware now of the pretty projected light of Mrs. Worthingham's wonder. She looked as if, out for a walk with her, he had put her to the inconvenience of his stopping to speak to a strange woman in the street.

"I never supposed you knew her!"—it was to him his hostess excused herself.

This made Miss Rasch spring up, distinctly flushed, distinctly strange to behold, but not vulgarly nettled—Cornelia was incapable of that; only rather funnily bridling and laughing, only showing that this was all she had waited for, only saying just the right thing, the thing she could make so clearly a jest. "Of course if you *had* you'd have presented him."

Mrs. Worthingham looked while answering at White-Mason. "I didn't want you to go—which you see you do as soon as he speaks to you. But I never dreamed—!"

"That there was anything between us? Ah, there are no end of things!" He, on his side, though addressing the younger and prettier woman, looked at his fellow guest; to whom he even continued: "When did you get back? May I come and see you the very first thing?"

Cornelia gasped and wriggled—she practically giggled; she had lost every atom of her little old, her little young, though always unaccountable prettiness, which used to peep so, on the bare chance of a shot, from behind indefensible features, that it almost made watching her a form of sport. He had heard vaguely of her, it came back to him (for there had been no letters; their later acquaintance, thank goodness, hadn't involved that) as experimenting, for economy, and then as settling, to the same rather dismal end, somewhere in England, at one of those intensely English places. St. Leonards, Cheltenham, Bognor, Dawlish —which, awfully, *was it?*—and she now affected him for all the world as some small squirming, exclaiming, genteelly conversing old maid of a type vaguely associated with the three-volume novels he used to feed on (besides his so often encountering it in "real life.") during a far-away stay of his own at Brighton. Odder than any element of his ex-gossip's identity itself, however, was the fact that she somehow, with it all, rejoiced his sight. Indeed the supreme oddity was that the manner of her reply to his request for leave to call should have absolutely charmed his attention. She didn't look at him; she only, from under her frumpy, crapy, curiously exotic hat, and with her good little near-sighted insinuating glare, expressed to Mrs. Worthingham, while she answered him, wonderful arch things, the overdone things of a shy woman. "Yes, you may call—but only when this dear lovely lady has done with you!" The moment after which she was gone.

Forty minutes later he was taking his way back from the queer miscarriage of his adventure; taking it, with no conscious positive felicity, through the very spaces that had witnessed shortly before the considerable serenity of his assurance. He had said to himself then, or had as good as said it, that, since he might do perfectly as he liked, it couldn't fail for him that he must soon retrace those steps, humming, to all intents, the first bars of a wedding-march; so beautifully had it cleared up for him that he was "going to like" letting Mrs. Worthingham accept him. He was to have hummed no wedding-march, as it seemed to be turning out—he had none, up to now, to hum; and yet, extraordinarily, it wasn't in the least because she had refused him. Why then hadn't he liked as much as he had intended to like it putting the pleasant act, the act of not refusing him, in her power? Could it all have come from the awkward minute of his failure to decide sharply, on Cornelia's departure, whether or no he would attend her to the door? He hadn't decided at all—what the deuce had been in him?—but had danced to and fro in the room, thinking better of each impulse and then thinking worse. He had hesitated like an ass, erect on absurd hind-legs, between two bundles of hay; the upshot of which must have been his giving the falsest impression. In what way that was to be for an instant considered had their common past committed him to crapy Cornelia? He repudiated with a whack on the gravel any ghost of an obligation.

What he could get rid of with scanter success, unfortunately, was the peculiar sharpness of his sense that, though mystified by his visible flurry—and yet not mystified enough for a sympathetic question either—his hostess had been, on the whole, even more frankly diverted: which was precisely an example of that newest, freshest, finest freedom in her, the air and the candor of assuming, not "heartlessly," not viciously, not even very consciously, but with a bright pampered confidence which would probably end by affecting one's nerves as the most impertinent stroke in the world, that every bleat thing coming up for her in any connection was somehow matter for her general recreation. There she was again with the innocent egotism, the gilded and overflowing anarchism, really, of her doubtless quite unwitting but none the less rabid modern note. Her grace of ease was perfect, but it was all grace of ease, not a single shred of it grace of uncertainty or of difficulty—which meant, when you came to see, that, for its happy working, not a grain of provision was left by it to mere manners. This was clearly going to be the music of the future—that if people were but rich enough and furnished enough and fed enough, exercised and sanitated and manicured, and generally advised and advertised and made "knowing" enough, *avertis* enough, as the term appeared to be nowadays in Paris, all they had to do for civility was to take the amused ironic view of those who might be less initiated. In *his* time, when he was young or even when he was only but a little less middle-aged, the best manners had been the best kindness, and the best kindness had mostly been some art of not insisting on one's luxurious differences, of concealing rather, for common humanity, if not for common decency, a part at least of the intensity or the ferocity with which one might be "in the know."

Oh, the "know"—Mrs. Worthingham was in it, all instinctively, inevitably, and as a matter of course, up to her eyes; which didn't, however, the least little bit prevent her being as ignorant as a fish of everything that really and intimately and fundamentally concerned *him,* poor dear old White-Mason. She didn't, in the first place, so much as know who he was—by which he meant know who and what it was to *be* a White-Mason, even a poor and a dear and old one, "anyway." That indeed—he did her perfect justice—was of the very essence of the newness and freshness and beautiful, brave, social irresponsibility by which she had originally dazzled him: just exactly that circumstance of her having no instinct for any old quality or quantity or identity, a single historic or social value, as he might say, of the New York of his already almost legendary past; and that additional one of his, on his side, having, so far as this went, cultivated blankness, cultivated positive prudence, as to her own personal background—the vagueness, at the best, with which all honest gentlefolk, the New-Yorkers of his approved stock and conservative genera-

tion, were content, as for the most part they were indubitably wise, to surround the origins and antecedents and queer unimaginable early influences of persons swimming into their ken from those parts of the country that quite necessarily and naturally figured to their view as "God-forsaken" and generally impossible.

The few scattered surviving representatives of a society once "good"—*rari nantes in gurgite vasto*— were liable, at the pass things had come to, to meet, and even amid old shades once sacred, or what was left of such, every form of social impossibility, and, more irresistibly still, to find these apparitions often carry themselves (often at least in the case of the women) with a wondrous wild gallantry, equally imperturbable and inimitable, the sort of thing that reached its maximum in Mrs. Worthingham. Beyond that who ever wanted to look up their annals, to reconstruct their steps and stages, to dot their i's in fine, or to "go behind" anything that was theirs? One wouldn't do that for the world—a rudimentary discretion forbade it; and yet this check from elementary undiscussable taste quite consorted with a due respect for them, or at any rate with a due respect for one's self in connection with them; as was just exemplified in what would be his own, what would be poor dear old White-Mason's, insurmountable aversion to having, on any pretext, the doubtless very queer spectre of the late Mr. Worthingham presented to him. No question had he asked, or would he ever ask, should his life—that is should the success of his courtship— even intimately depend on it, either about that obscure agent of his mistress's actual affluence or about the happy head-spring itself, and the apparently copious tributaries, of the golden stream.

From all which marked anomalies, at any rate, what was the moral to draw? He dropped into a Park chair again with that question, he lost himself in the wonder of why he had come away with his homage so very much unpaid. Yet it didn't seem at all, actually, as if he could say or conclude, as if he could do anything but keep on worrying—just in conformity with his being a person who, whether or no familiar with the need to make his conduct square with his conscience and his taste was never wholly exempt from that of making his taste and his conscience square with his conduct. To this latter occupation he further abandoned himself, and it didn't release him from his second brooding session till the sweet spring sunset had begun to gather and he had more or less cleared up, in the deepening dusk, the effective relation between the various parts of his ridiculously agitating experience. There were vital facts he seemed thus to catch, to seize, with a nervous hand, and the twilight helping, by their vaguely-whisked tails; unquiet truths that swarmed out after the fashion of creatures bold only at eventide, creatures that hovered and circled, that verily brushed his nose, in spite of their shyness. Yes, he had practically just sat on with his "mistress" —heaven save the mark!—as if *not* to come to the point; as if it had absolutely come up that there would be something rather vulgar and awful in doing so. The whole stretch of his stay after Cornelia's withdrawal had been consumed by his almost ostentatiously treating himself to the opportunity of which he was to make nothing. It was as if he had sat and watched himself—that came back to him: Shall I now or sha'n't I? Will I now or won't I? Say within the next three minutes, say by a quarter past six, or by twenty minutes past, at the furthest—always if nothing more comes up to prevent.

What had already come up to prevent was, in the strangest and drollest, or at least in the most preposterous, way in the world, that not Cornelia's presence, but her very absence, with its distraction of his thoughts, the thoughts that lumbered after her, had made the difference; and without his being the least able to tell why and how. He put it to himself after a fashion by the image that, this distraction once created, his working round to his hostess again, his reverting to the matter of his errand, began suddenly to represent a return from so far. That was simply all—or rather a little less than all; for something else had contributed. "I never dreamed you knew her," and "I never dreamed *you* did," was inevitably what had been exchanged between them — supplemented by Mrs. Worthingham's mere scrap of an expla-

nation: "Oh yes—to the small extent you see. Two years ago in Switzerland when I was at a high place for an 'after-cure,' during twenty days of incessant rain, she was the only person in an hotel full of roaring, gorging, smoking Germans with whom I could have a word of talk. She and I were the only speakers of English, and were thrown together like castaways on a desert island and in a raging storm. She was ill besides, and she had no maid, and mine looked after her, and she was very grateful—writing to me later on and saying she should certainly come to see me if she ever returned to New York. She *has* returned, you see—and there she was, poor little creature!" Such was Mrs. Worthingham's tribute—to which even his asking her if Miss Rasch had ever happened to speak of him caused her practically to add nothing. Visibly she had never thought again of any one Miss Rasch had spoken of or anything Miss Rasch had said; right as she was, naturally, about her being a little clever queer creature. This was perfectly true, and yet it was probably—by being *all* she could dream of about her—what had paralyzed his proper gallantry. Its effect had been not in what it simply stated, but in what, under his secretly disintegrating criticism, it almost luridly symbolized.

He had quitted his seat in the Louis Quinze drawing-room without having, as he would have described it, done anything but give the lady of the scene a superior chance not to betray a defeated hope—not, that is, to fail of the famous "pride" mostly supposed to prop even the most infatuated women at such junctures; by which chance, to do her justice, she had thoroughly seemed to profit. But he finally rose from his later station with a feeling of better success. He had by a happy turn of his hand got hold of the most precious, the least obscure of the flitting, circling things that brushed his ears. What he wanted—as justifying for him a little further consideration—was there before him from the moment he could put it that Mrs. Worthingham had no data. He almost hugged that word—it suddenly came to mean so much to him. No data, he felt, for a conception of the sort of thing the New York of "his time" had been in his personal life—the New York so unexpectedly, so vividly and, as he might say, so perversely called back to all his senses by its identity with that of poor Cornelia's time: since even she had had a time, small show as it was likely to make now, and his time and hers had been the same. Cornelia figured to him while he walked away as, by contrast and opposition, a massive little bundle of data; his impatience to go to see her sharpened as he thought of this: so certainly should he find out that wherever he might touch her, with a gentle though firm pressure, he would, as the fond visitor of old houses taps and fingers a disfeatured, overpapered wall with the conviction of a wainscot-edge beneath, recognize some small extrusion of history.

There would have been a wonder for us meanwhile in his continued use, as it were, of his happy formula—brought out to Cornelia Rasch within ten minutes, or perhaps only within twenty, of his having settled into the quite comfortable chair that, two days later, she indicated to him by her fireside. He had arrived at her address through the fortunate chance of his having noticed her card, as he went out, deposited, in the good old New York fashion, on one of the rococo tables of Mrs. Worthingham's hall. His eye had been caught by the pencilled indication that was to affect him, the next instant, as fairly placed there for his sake. This had really been his luck, for he shouldn't have liked to write to Mrs. Worthingham for guidance —*that* he felt, though too impatient just now to analyze the reluctance. There was nobody else he could have approached for a clue, and with this reflection he was already aware of how it testified to their rare little position, his and Cornelia's —position as conscious, ironic, pathetic survivors together of a dead and buried society—that there would have been, in all the town, under such stress, not a member of their old circle left to turn to. Mrs. Worthingham had practically, even if accidentally, helped him to knowledge; the last nail in the coffin of the poor dear extinct past had been planted for him by his having thus to reach his antique contemporary through perforation of the newest newness. The note of this

particular recognition was in fact the more prescribed to him that the ground of Cornelia's return to a scene swept so bare of the associational charm was certainly inconspicuous. What had she then come back for?—he had asked himself that; with the effect of deciding that it probably would have been, a little, to "look after" her remnant of property. Perhaps she had come to save what little might still remain of that shrivelled interest; perhaps she had been, by those who took care of it for her, further swindled and despoiled, so that she wished to get at the facts. Perhaps on the other hand—it was a more cheerful chance—her investments, decently administered, were making larger returns, so that the rigorous thrift of Bognor could be finally relaxed.

He had little to learn about the attraction of Europe, and rather expected that in the event of his union with Mrs. Worthingham he should find himself pleading for it with the competence of one more in the "know" about Paris and Rome, about Venice and Florence, than even she could be. He could have lived on in *his* New York, that is in the sentimental, the spiritual, the more or less romantic visitation of it; but had it been positive for him that he could live on in hers?—unless indeed the possibility of this had been just (like the famous *vertige de l'abîme,* like the solicitation of danger, or otherwise of the dreadful) the very hinge of his whole dream. However that might be, his curiosity was occupied rather with the conceivable hinge of poor Cornelia's: it was perhaps thinkable that even Mrs. Worthingham's New York, once it should have become possible again at all, might have put forth to this lone exile a plea that wouldn't be in the chords of Bognor. For himself, after all, too, the attraction had been much more of the Europe over which one might move at one's ease, and which therefore could but cost, and cost much, right and left, than of the Europe adapted to scrimping. He saw himself on the whole scrimping with more zest even in Mrs. Worthingham's New York than under the inspiration of Bognor. Apart from which it was yet again odd, not to say perceptibly pleasing to him, to note where the emphasis of his interest fell in this fumble of fancy over such felt oppositions as the new, the latest, the luridest power of money and the ancient reserves and moderations and mediocrities. These last struck him as showing by contrast the old brown surface and tone as of velvet rubbed and worn, shabby, and even a bit dingy, but all soft and subtle and still velvety—which meant still dignified; whereas the angular facts of current finance were as harsh and metallic and bewildering as some stacked " exhibit " of ugly patented inventions, things his mediæval mind forbade his taking in. He had for instance the sense of knowing the pleasant little old Rasch fortune—pleasant as far as it went; blurred memories and impressions of what it had been and what it hadn't, of how it had grown and how languished and how melted; they came back to him and put on such vividness that he could almost have figured himself testify for them before a bland and encouraging Board. The idea of taking the field in any manner on the subject of Mrs. Worthingham's resources would have affected him on the other hand as an odious ordeal, some glare of embarrassment and exposure in a circle of hard unhelpful attention, of converging, derisive, unsuggestive eyes.

In Cornelia's small and quite cynically modern flat—the house had a grotesque name, " The Gainsborough," but at least wasn't an awful boarding-house, as he had feared, and she could receive him quite honorably, which was so much to the good—he would have been ready to use at once to her the greatest freedom of friendly allusion: " Have you still your old ' family interest ' in those two houses in Seventh Avenue?—one of which was next to a corner grocery, don't you know? and was occupied as to its lower part by a candy-shop where the proportion of the stock of suspectedly stale popcorn to that of rarer and stickier joys betrayed perhaps a modest capital on the part of your father's, your grandfather's or whoever's tenant, but out of which I nevertheless remember once to have come as out of a bath of sweets, with my very garments, and even the separate hairs of my head, glued together. The other of the pair, a tobacconist's, further down, had before it a

wonderful huge Indian who thrust out wooden cigars at an indifferent world (you could buy candy cigars too, at the popcorn shop, and I greatly preferred them to the wooden); I remember well, how I used to gape in fascination at the Indian and wonder if the last of the Mohicans was like him—besides admiring so the resources of a family whose ' property ' was in such forms. I haven't been round there lately—we must go round together; but don't tell me the forms have utterly perished!" It was after *that* fashion he might easily have been moved, and with almost no transition, to break out to Cornelia quite as if taking up some old talk, some old community of gossip, just where they had left it; and even with the consciousness perhaps of overdoing a little, of putting at its maximum, for the present harmony, recovery, recapture (what should he call it?) the pitch and quantity of what the past had held for them.

He didn't in fact, no doubt, dart straight off to Seventh Avenue, there being too many other old things and much nearer and long subsequent; the point was only that for everything they spoke of after he had fairly begun to lean back and stretch his legs, and after she had let him, above all, light the first of a succession of cigarettes—for everything they spoke of he positively cultivated extravagance and excess, piling up the crackling twigs as on the very altar of memory; and that by the end of half an hour she had lent herself, all gallantly, to their game. It was the game of feeding the beautiful iridescent flame, ruddy and green and gold, blue and pink and amber and silver, with anything they could pick up, anything that would burn and flicker. Thick-strown with such gleanings the occasion seemed indeed, in spite of the truth that they perhaps wouldn't have proved, under cross-examination, to have rubbed shoulders in the other life so very hard. Casual contacts, qualified communities enough, there had doubtless been, but not particular " passages," nothing that counted, as he might think of it, for their " very own " together, for nobody's else at all. These shades of historic exactitude didn't signify; the more and the less that there had been made perfect terms—and just by his being there and by her rejoicing in it—with their present need to have *had* all their past could be made to appear to have given them. It was to this tune they proceeded, the least little bit as if they knowingly pretended—he giving her the example and setting her the pace of it, and she, poor dear, after a first inevitable shyness, an uncertainty of wonder, a breathlessness of courage, falling into step and going whatever length he would.

She showed herself ready for it, grasping gladly at the perception of what he must mean; and if she didn't immediately and completely fall in—not in the first half-hour, not even in the three or four others that his visit, even whenever he consulted his watch, still made nothing of—she yet understood enough as soon as she understood that, if their finer economy hadn't so beautifully served, he might have been conveying this, that and the other incoherent and easy thing by the comparatively clumsy method of sound and statement. "No, I never made love to you; it would in fact have been absurd, and I don't care—though I almost know, in the sense of almost remembering!—who did and who didn't; but you were always about, and so was I, and, little as you may yourself care who *I* did it to, I dare say you remember (in the sense of having known of it!) any old appearances that told. But we can't afford at this time of day not to help each other to have had—well, everything there was, since there's no more of it now, nor any way of coming by it *except so;* and therefore let us *make* together, let us make over and re-create, our lost world: for which we have after all and at the worst such a lot of material. You were in particular my poor dear sisters' friend—they thought you the funniest little brown thing possible; so isn't that again to the good? You were mine only to the extent that you were so much in and out of the house —as how much, if we come to that, wasn't one in and out, south of Thirtieth Street and north of Washington Square, in those days, those spacious, sociable, Arcadian days, that we flattered ourselves we filled with the modern fever, but that were so different from any of *these* arrangements of pretended

hourly Time that dash themselves forever to pieces as from the fiftieth floors of sky-scrapers."

This was the kind of thing that was in the air, whether he said it or not, and that could hang there even with such quite other things as more crudely came out; came in spite of its being perhaps calculated to strike us that these last would have been rather and most the unspoken and the indirect. They were Cornelia's contribution, and as soon as she had begun to talk of Mrs. Worthingham—*he* didn't begin it!—they had taken their place bravely in the centre of the circle. There they made, the while, their considerable little figure, but all within the ring formed by fifty other allusions, fitful but really intenser irruptions that hovered and wavered and came and went, joining hands at moments and whirling round as in chorus, only then again to dash at the slightly huddled centre with a free twitch or peck or push or other taken liberty, after the fashion of irregular frolic motions in a country dance or a Christmas game.

"You're so in love with her and want to marry her!"—she said it all sympathetically and yearningly, poor crapy Cornelia; as if it were to be quite taken for granted that she knew all about it. And then when he had asked how she knew—why she took so informed a tone about it; all on the wonder of her seeming so much more "in" it just at that hour than he himself quite felt he could figure for: "Ah, how but from the dear lovely thing herself? Don't you suppose *she* knows it?"

"Oh, she absolutely 'knows' it, does she?"—he fairly heard himself ask that; and with the oddest sense at once of sharply wanting the certitude and yet of seeing the question, of hearing himself say the words, through several thicknesses of some wrong medium. He came back to it from a distance; as he would have had to come back (this was again vivid to him) should he have got round again to his ripe intention three days before—after his now present but then absent friend, that is, had left him planted before his now absent but then present one for the purpose. "Do you mean she —at all confidently!—expects?" he went on, not much minding if it couldn't but sound foolish; the time being given it for him meanwhile by the sigh, the wondering gasp, all charged with the unutterable, that the tone of his appeal set in motion. He saw his companion look at him, but it might have been with the eyes of thirty years ago; when—very likely!—he had put her some such question about some girl long since dead. Dimly at first, then more distinctly, didn't it surge back on him for the very strangeness that there had been some such passage as this between them—yes, about Mary Cardew!—in the autumn of '68?

"Why, don't you realize your situation?" Miss Rasch struck him as quite beautifully wailing—above all to such an effect of deep interest, that is, on her own part and in him.

"My situation?"—he echoed, he considered; but reminded afresh, by the note of the detached, the far-projected in it, of what he had last remembered of his sentient state on his once taking ether at the dentist's.

"Yours and hers—the situation of her adoring you. I suppose you at least know it," Cornelia smiled.

Yes, it was like the other time and yet it wasn't. *She* was like—poor Cornelia was—everything that used to be; that somehow was most definite to him. Still he could quite reply "Do you call it— her adoring me—*my* situation?"

"Well, it's a part of yours, surely—if you're in love with her."

"Am I, ridiculous old person! in love with her?" White-Mason asked.

"I may be a ridiculous old person," Cornelia returned—"and, for that matter of course I *am!* But she's young and lovely and rich and clever: so what could be more natural?"

"Oh, I was applying that opprobrious epithet—!" He didn't finish, though he meant he had applied it to himself. He had got up from his seat; he turned about and, taking in, as his eyes also roamed, several objects in the room, serene and sturdy, not a bit cheap-looking, little old New York objects of '68, he made, with an inner art, as if to recognize them—made so, that is, for himself; had quite the sense for the moment of asking them, of imploring them, to recognize *him*, to be for him things of his

own past. Which they truly were, he could have the next instant cried out: for it meant that if three or four of them, small sallow carte-de-visite photographs, faithfully framed but spectrally faded, hadn't in every particular, frames and balloon skirts and false "property" balustrades of unimaginable terraces and all, the tone of time, the secret for warding and easing off the perpetual imminent ache of one's protective scowl, one would verily but have to let the scowl stiffen, or to take up seriously the question of blue goggles, during what might remain of life.

What he actually took up from a little old Twelfth-Street table that piously preserved the plain mahogany circle, with never a curl nor a crook nor a hint of a brazen flourish, what he paused there a moment for commerce with, his back presented to crapy Cornelia, who sat taking that view of him, during this opportunity, very protrusively and frankly and fondly, was one of the wasted mementos just mentioned, over which he both uttered and suppressed a small comprehensive cry. He stood there another minute to look at it, and when he turned about still kept it in his hand, only holding it now a little behind him. "You *must* have come back to stay—with all your beautiful things. What else does it mean?"

"'Beautiful'?" his old friend commented with her brow all wrinkled and her lips thrust out in expressive dispraise. They might at that rate have been scarce more beautiful than she herself. "Oh, don't talk so—after Mrs. Worthingham's! *They're* wonderful, if you will: such things, such things! But one's own poor relics and odds and ends are one's own at least; and one *has*—yes —come back to them. They're all I have in the world to come back to. They were stored, and what I was paying—!" Miss Rasch wofully added.

He had possession of the small old picture; he hovered there; he put his eyes again to it intently; then again held it a little behind him as if it might have been snatched away or the very feel of it, pressed against him, was good to his palm. "Mrs. Worthingham's things? You think them beautiful?"

Cornelia did now, if ever, show an odd face. "Why certainly prodigious, or whatever. Isn't that conceded?"

"No doubt every horror, at the pass we've come to, is conceded. That's just what I complain of."

"Do you *complain?*"—she drew it out as for surprise: she couldn't have imagined such a thing.

"To me her things are awful. They're the newest of the new."

"Ah, but the old forms!"

"Those are the most blatant. I mean the swaggering reproductions."

"Oh but," she pleaded, "we can't all be *really* old."

"No, we can't, Cornelia. But *you* can—!" said White-Mason with the frankest appreciation.

She looked up at him from where she sat as he could imagine her looking up at the curate at Bognor. "Thank you, sir! If that's all you want—!"

"It *is*," he said, "all I want—or almost."

"Then no wonder such a creature as that," she lightly moralized, "won't suit you!"

He bent upon her, for all the weight of his question, his smoothest stare. "You hold she certainly won't suit me?"

"Why, what can I tell about it? Haven't you by this time found out?"

"No, but I think I'm finding." With which he began again to explore.

Miss Rasch immensely wondered. "You mean you don't expect to come to an understanding with her?" And then as even to this straight challenge he made at first no answer: "Do you mean you give it up?"

He waited some instants more, but not meeting her eyes—only looking again about the room. "What do you think of my chance?"

"Oh," his companion cried, "what has what I think to do with it? How can I think anything but that she must like you?"

"Yes—of course. But how much?"

"Then don't you really know?" Cornelia asked.

He kept up his walk, oddly preoccupied and still not looking at her. "Do you, my dear?"

She waited a little. "If you haven't really put it to her I don't suppose she knows."

This at last pulled him up again. "My dear Cornelia, she doesn't know—!"

He had paused as for the desperate tone, or at least the large emphasis of it, so that she took him up. "The more reason then to help her to find it out."

"I mean," he explained, "that she doesn't know anything."

"Anything?"

"Anything else, I mean—even if she does know *that*."

Cornelia considered of it. "But what else need she—in particular—know? Isn't that the principal thing?"

"Well"—and he resumed his circuit —"she doesn't know anything that *we* know. But nothing," he re-emphasized— "nothing whatever!"

"Well, can't she do without that?"

"Evidently she can—and evidently she does, beautifully. But the question is whether *I* can!"

He had paused once more with his point—but she glared, poor Cornelia, with her wonder. "Surely if you know for yourself—!"

"Ah, it doesn't seem enough for me to know for myself! One wants a woman," he argued—but still, in his prolonged tour, quite without his scowl—"to know *for* one, to know *with* one. That's what you do now," he candidly put to her.

It made her again gape. "Do you mean you want to marry *me?*"

He was so full of what he did mean, however, that he failed even to notice it. "She doesn't in the least know, for instance, how old I am."

"That's because you're so young!"

"Ah, there you are!"—and he turned off afresh and as if almost in disgust. It left her visibly perplexed—though even the perplexed Cornelia was still the exceedingly pointed; but he had come to her aid after another turn. "Remember, please, that I'm pretty well as old as you."

She had all her point at least, while she bridled and blinked, for this. "You're exactly a year and ten months older."

It checked him there for delight. "You remember my birthday?"

She twinkled indeed like some far-off light of home. "I remember every one's. It's a little way I've always had—and that I've never lost."

He looked at her accomplishment,

across the room, as at some striking, some charming phenomenon. "Well, *that's* the sort of thing I want!" All the ripe candor of his eyes confirmed it.

What could she do therefore, she seemed to ask him, but repeat her question of a moment before?—which indeed, presently she made up her mind to. "Do you want to marry *me?*"

It had this time better success—if the term may be felt in any degree to apply. All his candor, or more of it at least, was in his slow, mild, kind, considering head-shake. "No, Cornelia—not to *marry* you."

His discrimination was a wonder; but since she was clearly treating him now as if everything about him was, so she could as exquisitely meet it. "Not at least," she convulsively smiled, "until you've honorably tried Mrs. Worthingham. Don't you really *mean* to?" she gallantly insisted.

He waited again a little; then he brought out: "I'll tell you presently." He came back, and as by still another mere glance over the room, to what seemed to him so much nearer. "That table *was* old Twelfth-Street?"

"Everything here was."

"Oh, the pure blessings! With you, ah, with you, I haven't to wear a green shade." And he had retained meanwhile his small photograph which he again showed himself. "Didn't we talk of Mary Cardew?"

"Why, do you remember it?"—she marvelled to extravagance.

"You make me. You connect me with it. You connect it with *me*." He liked to display to her this excellent use she thus had, the service she rendered. "There are so many connections—there will *be* so many. I feel how, with you, they must all come up again for me: in fact you're bringing them out already, just while I look at you, as fast as ever you can. The fact that you knew every one—!" he went on; yet as if there were more in that too than he could quite trust himself about.

"Yes, I knew every one," said Cornelia Rasch; but this time with perfect simplicity. "I knew, I imagine, more than you do—or more than you did."

It kept him there, it made him wonder with his eyes on her. "Things about *them*—our people?"

"Our people. Ours only now."

Ah, such an interest as he felt in this—taking from her while, so far from scowling, he almost gaped, all it might mean! "Ours indeed—and it's awfully good they are; or that we're still here for them! Nobody else is—nobody but you: not a cat!"

"Well, I *am* a cat!" Cornelia grinned.

"Do you mean you can tell me things—?" It was too beautiful to believe.

"About what really *was?*" she artfully considered, holding him immensely now. "Well, unless they've come to you with time; unless you've learned—or found out."

"Oh," he reassuringly cried—reassuringly, it most seemed, for himself—"nothing has come to me with time, everything has gone from me. How I find out now? What creature has an idea—?"

She threw up her hands with the shrug of old days—the sharp little shrug his sisters used to imitate and that she hadn't had to go to Europe for. The only thing was that he blessed her for bringing it back. "Ah, the ideas of people now—!"

"Yes, their ideas are certainly not about *us*." But he ruefully faced it. "We've none the less, however, to live with them."

"With their ideas—?" Cornelia questioned.

"With *them*—these modern wonders; such as they are!" Then he went on: "It must have been to help me you've got back."

She said nothing for an instant about that, only nodding instead at his photograph. "What has become of yours? I mean of *her*."

This time it made him turn pale. "You remember I *have* one?"

She kept her eyes on him. "In a 'pork-pie' hat, with her hair in a long net. That was so 'smart' then; especially with one's skirt looped up, over one's hooped magenta petticoat, in little festoons, and a row of very big onyx beads over one's braided velveteen sack—braided quite plain and very broad, don't you know?"

He smiled for her extraordinary possession of these things—she was as prompt as if she had had them before her.

"Oh, rather—'don't I know?' You wore brown velveteen, and, on those remarkably small hands, funny gauntlets—like mine."

"Oh, do *you* remember? But like yours?" she wondered.

"I mean like hers in my photograph." But he came back to the present picture. "This is better, however, for really showing her lovely head."

"Mary's head was a perfection!" Cornelia testified.

"Yes—it was better than her heart."

"Ah, don't say that!" she pleaded. "You weren't fair."

"Don't you think I was fair?" It interested him immensely—and the more that he indeed mightn't have been; which he seemed somehow almost to hope. "She didn't think so—to the very end."

"She didn't?"—ah the right things Cornelia said to him! But before she could answer he was studying again closely the small faded face. "No, she doesn't, she doesn't. Oh, her charming sad eyes and the way they *say* that, across the years, straight into mine! But I don't know, I don't know!" White-Mason quite comfortably sighed.

His companion appeared to appreciate this effect. "That's just the way you used to flirt with her, poor thing. Wouldn't you like to have it?" she asked.

"This—for my very own?" He looked up delighted. "I really may?"

"Well, if you'll give me yours. We'll exchange."

"That's a charming idea. We'll exchange. But you must come and get it at my rooms—where you'll see my things."

For a little she made no answer—as if for some feeling. Then she said: "You asked me just now why I've come back."

He stared as for the connection; after which with a smile: "Not to do *that*—?"

She waited briefly again, but with a queer little look. "I can do those things now; and—yes!—that's in a manner why. I came," she then said, "because I knew of a sudden one day—knew as never before—that I was old."

"I see. I see." He quite understood —she had notes that so struck him. "And how did you like it?"

She hesitated—she decided. "Well, if I liked it, it was on the principle perhaps on which some people like high game!"

"High game—that's good!" he laughed. "Ah, my dear, we're 'high'!"

She shook her head. "No, not you— yet. I at any rate didn't want any more adventures," Cornelia said.

He showed their small relic again with assurance. "You wanted *us*. Then here we are. Oh how we can talk!—with all those things you know! You *are* an invention. And you'll see there are things *I* know. I shall turn up here—well, daily."

She took it in, but after a moment only answered. "There was something you said just now you'd tell me. Don't you mean to try—?"

"Mrs. Worthingham?" He drew from within his coat his pocketbook and carefully found a place in it for Mary Cardew's carte-de-visite, over which, folding it together with deliberation, he put it back. Finally he spoke. "No—I've decided. I can't—I don't want to."

Cornelia marvelled—or looked as if she did. "Not for all she has?"

"Yes—I know all she . has. But I also know all she hasn't. And, as I told you, she herself doesn't—hasn't a glimmer of a suspicion of it; and never will have."

Cornelia magnanimously thought. "No —but she knows other things."

He shook his head as at the portentous heap of them. "Too many—too many. And other indeed — so other! Do you know," he went on, "that it's as if *you*—by turning up for me—had brought that home to me?"

"'For you'?" she candidly considered. "But what—since you can't marry me!— can you do with me?"

Well, he seemed to have it all. "Everything. I can live with you—just this way." To illustrate which he dropped into the other chair by her fire; where, leaning back, he gazed at the flame. "I can't give you up. It's very curious. It has come over me as it did over you when you renounced Bognor. That's it—I know it at last, and I see one can like it. I'm 'high.' You needn't deny it. That's my taste. I'm old." And in spite of the considerable glow there of her little household altar he said it without the scowl.

THE RECKONING
by Edith Wharton

"THE marriage law of the new dispensation will be: *Thou shalt not be unfaithful—to thyself.*"

A discreet murmur of approval filled the studio, and through the haze of cigarette smoke Mrs. Clement Westall, as her husband descended from his improvised platform, saw him merged in a congratulatory group of ladies. Westall's informal talks on "The New Ethics" had drawn about him an eager following of the mentally unemployed—those who, as he had once phrased it, liked to have their brain-food cut up for them. The talks had begun by accident. Westall's ideas were known to be "advanced," but hitherto their advance had not been in the direction of publicity. He had been, in his wife's opinion, almost pusillanimously careful not to let his personal views endanger his professional standing. Of late, however, he had shown a puzzling tendency to dogmatize, to throw down the gauntlet, to flaunt his private code in the face of society; and the relation of the sexes being a topic always sure of an audience, a few admiring friends had persuaded him to give his after-dinner opinions a larger circulation by summing them up in a series of talks at the Van Sideren studio.

The Herbert Van Siderens were a couple who subsisted, socially, on the fact that they had a studio. Van Sideren's pictures were chiefly valuable as accessories to the *mise en scène* which differentiated his wife's "afternoons" from the blighting functions held in long New York drawing-rooms, and permitted her to offer their friends whiskey-and-soda instead of tea. Mrs. Van Sideren, for her part, was skilled in making the most of the kind of atmosphere which a lay-figure and an easel create; and if at times she found the illusion hard to maintain, and lost courage to the extent of almost wishing that Herbert could paint, she promptly overcame such moments of weakness by calling in some fresh talent, some extraneous re-enforcement of the "artistic" impression. It was in quest of such aid that she had seized on Westall, coaxing him, somewhat to his wife's surprise, into a flattered participation in her fraud. It was vaguely felt, in the Van Sideren circle, that all the audacities were artistic, and that a teacher who pronounced marriage immoral was somehow as distinguished as a painter who depicted purple grass and a green sky. The Van Sideren set were tired of the conventional color-scheme in art and conduct.

Julia Westall had long had her own views on the immorality of marriage; she might indeed have claimed her husband as a disciple. In the early days of their union she had secretly resented his disinclination to proclaim himself a follower of the new creed; had been inclined to tax him with moral cowardice, with a failure to live up to the convictions for which their marriage was supposed to stand. That was in the first burst of propagandism, when, womanlike, she wanted to turn her disobedience into a law. Now she felt differently. She could hardly account for the change, yet being a woman who never allowed her impulses to remain unaccounted for, she tried to do so by saying that she did not care to have the articles of her faith misinterpreted by the vulgar. In this connection, she was beginning to think that almost every one was vulgar; certainly there were few to whom she would have cared to intrust the defence of so esoteric a doctrine. And it was precisely at this point that Westall, discarding his unspoken principles, had chosen to descend from the heights of privacy, and stand hawking his convictions at the street-corner!

It was Una Van Sideren who, on this occasion, unconsciously focussed upon herself Mrs. Westall's wandering resentment. In the first place, the girl had no

UNA VAN SIDEREN

business to be there. It was "horrid"— Mrs. Westall found herself slipping back into the old feminine vocabulary—simply "horrid" to think of a young girl's being allowed to listen to such talk. The fact that Una smoked cigarettes and sipped an occasional cocktail did not in the least tarnish a certain radiant innocency which made her appear the victim, rather than the accomplice, of her parents' vulgarities. Julia Westall felt in a hot helpless way that something ought to be done —that some one ought to speak to the girl's mother. And just then Una glided up.

"Oh, Mrs. Westall, how beautiful it was!" Una fixed her with large limpid eyes. "You believe it all, I suppose?" she asked with seraphic gravity.

"All—what, my dear child?"

The girl shone on her. "About the higher life—the freer expansion of the individual—the law of fidelity to one's self," she glibly recited.

Mrs. Westall, to her own wonder, blushed a deep and burning blush.

"My dear Una," she said, "you don't in the least understand what it's all about!"

Miss Van Sideren stared, with a slowly answering blush. "Don't you, then?" she murmured.

Mrs. Westall laughed. "Not always— or altogether! But I should like some tea, please."

Una led her to the corner where innocent beverages were dispensed. As Julia received her cup she scrutinized the girl more carefully. It was not such a girlish face, after all—definite lines were forming under the rosy haze of youth. She reflected that Una must be six-and-twenty, and wondered why she had not married. A nice stock of ideas she would have as her dower! If they were to be a part of the modern girl's trousseau—

Mrs. Westall caught herself up with a start. It was as though some one else had been speaking—a stranger who had borrowed her own voice: she felt herself the dupe of some fantastic mental ventriloquism. Concluding suddenly that the room was stifling and Una's tea too sweet, she set down her cup, and looked about for Westall: to meet his eyes had long been her refuge from every uncertainty. She met them now, but only, as she felt,

in transit; they included her parenthetically in a larger flight. She followed the flight, and it carried her to a corner to which Una had withdrawn—one of the palmy nooks to which Mrs. Van Sideren attributed the success of her Saturdays. Westall, a moment later, had overtaken his look, and found a place at the girl's side. She bent forward, speaking eagerly; he leaned back, listening, with the depreciatory smile which acted as a filter to flattery, enabling him to swallow the strongest doses without apparent grossness of appetite. Julia winced at her own definition of the smile.

On the way home, in the deserted winter dusk, Westall surprised his wife by a sudden boyish pressure of her arm. "Did I open their eyes a bit? Did I tell them what you wanted me to?" he asked gaily.

Almost unconsciously, she let her arm slip from his. "What I wanted—?"

"Why, haven't you—all this time?" She caught the honest wonder of his tone. "I somehow fancied you'd rather blamed me for not talking more openly—before—. You've almost made me feel, at times, that I was sacrificing principles to expediency."

She paused a moment over her reply; then she asked quietly: "What made you decide not to—any longer?"

She felt again the vibration of a faint surprise. "Why — the wish to please you!" he answered, almost too simply.

"I wish you would not go on, then," she said abruptly.

He stopped in his quick walk, and she felt his stare through the darkness.

"Not go on—?"

"Call a hansom, please. I'm tired," broke from her with a sudden rush of physical weariness.

Instantly his solicitude enveloped her. The room had been infernally hot—and then that confounded cigarette smoke— he had noticed once or twice that she looked pale—she mustn't come to another Saturday. She felt herself yielding, as she always did, to the warm influence of his concern for her, the feminine in her leaning on the man in him with a conscious intensity of abandonment. He put her in the hansom, and her hand stole into his in the darkness. A tear or two rose, and she let them fall. It was so delicious to cry over imaginary troubles!

That evening, after dinner, he surprised her by reverting to the subject of his talk. He combined a man's dislike of uncomfortable questions with an almost feminine skill in eluding them; and she knew that if he returned to the subject he must have some special reason for doing so.

"You seem not to have cared for what I said this afternoon. Did I put the case badly?"

"No—you put it very well."

"Then what did you mean by saying that you would rather not have me go on with it?"

She glanced at him nervously, her ignorance of his intention deepening her sense of helplessness.

"I don't think I care to hear such things discussed in public."

"I don't understand you," he exclaimed. Again the feeling that his surprise was genuine gave an air of obliquity to her own attitude. She was not sure that she understood herself.

"Won't you explain?" he said with a tinge of impatience.

Her eyes wandered about the familiar drawing-room which had been the scene of so many of their evening confidences. The shaded lamps, the quiet-colored walls hung with mezzotints, the pale spring flowers scattered here and there in Venice glasses and bowls of old Sèvres, recalled, she hardly knew why, the apartment in which the evenings of her first marriage had been passed—a wilderness of rosewood and upholstery, with a picture of a Roman peasant above the mantel-piece, and a Greek slave in "statuary marble" between the folding-doors of the back drawing-room. It was a room with which she had never been able to establish any closer relation than that between a traveller and a railway station; and now, as she looked about at the surroundings which stood for her deepest affinities—the room for which she had left that other room—she was startled by the same sense of strangeness and unfamiliarity. The prints, the flowers, the subdued tones of the old porcelains, seemed to typify a superficial refinement that had no relation to the deeper significances of life.

Suddenly she heard her husband repeating his question.

"I don't know that I can explain," she faltered.

He drew his arm-chair forward so that he faced her across the hearth. The light of a reading-lamp fell on his finely drawn face, which had a kind of surface-sensitiveness akin to the surface-refinement of its setting.

"Is it that you no longer believe in our ideas?" he asked.

"In our ideas—?"

"The ideas I am trying to teach. The ideas you and I are supposed to stand for." He paused a moment. "The ideas on which our marriage was founded."

The blood rushed to her face. He had his reasons, then—she was sure now that he had his reasons! In the ten years of their marriage, how often had either of them stopped to consider the ideas on which it was founded? How often does a man dig about the basement of his house to examine its foundation? The foundation is there, of course—the house rests on it—but one lives abovestairs and not in the cellar. It was she, indeed, who in the beginning had insisted on reviewing the situation now and then, on recapitulating the reasons which justified her course, on proclaiming, from time to time, her adherence to the religion of personal independence; but she had long ceased to feel the need of any such ideal standards, and had accepted her marriage as frankly and naturally as though it had been based on the primitive needs of the heart, and needed no special sanction to explain or justify it.

"Of course I still believe in our ideas!" she exclaimed.

"Then I repeat that I don't understand. It was a part of your theory that the greatest possible publicity should be given to our view of marriage. Have you changed your mind in that respect?"

She hesitated. "It depends on circumstances—on the public one is addressing. The set of people that the Van Siderens get about them don't care for the truth or falseness of a doctrine. They are attracted simply by its novelty."

"And yet it was in just such a set of people that you and I met, and learned the truth from each other."

"That was different."

"In what way?"

"I was not a young girl, to begin with. It is perfectly unfitting that young girls should be present at—at such times—should hear such things discussed—"

"I thought you considered it one of the deepest social wrongs that such things never *are* discussed before young girls; but that is beside the point, for I don't remember seeing any young girl in my audience to-day—"

"Except Una Van Sideren!"

He-turned slightly and pushed back the lamp at his elbow.

"Oh, Miss Van Sideren—naturally—"

"Why naturally?"

"The daughter of the house—would you have had her sent out with her governess?"

"If I had a daughter I should not allow such things to go on in my house!"

Westall, stroking his mustache, leaned back with a faint smile. "I fancy Miss Van Sideren is quite capable of taking care of herself."

"No girl knows how to take care of herself—till it's too late."

"And yet you would deliberately deny her the surest means of self-defence?"

"What do you call the surest means of self-defence?"

"Some preliminary knowledge of human nature in its relation to the marriage tie."

She made an impatient gesture. "How should you like to marry that kind of a girl?"

"Immensely—if she were my kind of girl in other respects."

She took up the argument at another point.

"You are quite mistaken if you think such talk does not affect young girls. Una was in a state of the most absurd exaltation—" She broke off, wondering why she had spoken.

Westall reopened a magazine which he had laid aside at the beginning of their discussion. "What you tell me is immensely flattering to my oratorical talent—but I fear you overrate its effect. I can assure you that Miss Van Sideren doesn't have to have her thinking done for her. She's quite capable of doing it herself."

"You seem very familiar with her mental processes!" flashed unguardedly from his wife.

He looked up quietly from the pages he was cutting.

"I should like to be," he answered. "She interests me."

II

If there be a distinction in being misunderstood, it was one denied to Julia Westall when she left her first husband. Every one was ready to excuse and even to defend her. The world she adorned agreed that John Arment was "impossible," and hostesses gave a sigh of relief at the thought that it would no longer be necessary to ask him to dine.

There had been no scandal connected with the divorce: neither side had accused the other of the offence euphemistically described as "statutory." The Arments had indeed been obliged to transfer their allegiance to a State which recognized desertion as a cause for divorce, and construed the term so liberally that the seeds of desertion were shown to exist in every union. Even Mrs. Arment's second marriage did not make traditional morality stir in its sleep. It was known that she had not met her second husband till after she had parted from the first, and she had, moreover, replaced a rich man by a poor one. Though Clement Westall was acknowledged to be a rising lawyer, it was generally felt that his fortunes would not rise as rapidly as his reputation. The Westalls would probably always have to live quietly and go out to dinner in cabs. Could there be better evidence of Mrs. Arment's complete disinterestedness?

If the reasoning by which her friends justified her course was somewhat cruder and less complex than her own elucidation of the matter, both explanations led to the same conclusion: John Arment was impossible. The only difference was that, to his wife, his impossibility was something deeper than a social disqualification. She had once said, in ironical defence of her marriage, that it had at least preserved her from the necessity of sitting next to him at dinner; but she had not then realized at what cost the immunity was purchased. John Arment was impossible; but the sting of his impossibility lay in the fact that he made it

impossible for those about him to be other
than himself. By an unconscious process of elimination he had excluded from
the world everything of which he did not
feel a personal need: had become, as it
were, a climate in which only his own requirements survived. This might seem
to imply a deliberate selfishness; but
there was nothing deliberate about Arment. He was as instinctive as an animal or a child. It was this childish element in his nature which sometimes for
a moment unsettled his wife's estimate
of him. Was it possible that he was simply undeveloped, that he had delayed,
somewhat longer than is usual, the la-
borious process of growing up? He had
the kind of sporadic shrewdness which
causes it to be said of a dull man that he
is "no fool"; and it was this quality
that his wife found most trying. Even to
the naturalist it is annoying to have his
deductions disturbed by some unforeseen
aberrancy of form or function; and how
much more so to the wife whose estimate
of herself is inevitably bound up with her
judgment of her husband!

Arment's shrewdness did not, indeed,
imply any latent intellectual power; it
suggested, rather, potentialities of feeling,
of suffering, perhaps, in a blind rudimentary way, on which Julia's sensibilities
naturally declined to linger. She so fully
understood her own reasons for leaving
him that she disliked to think they were
not as comprehensible to her husband.
She was haunted, in her analytic moments, by the look of perplexity, too inarticulate for words, with which he had
acquiesced in her explanations.

These moments were rare with her,
however. Her marriage had been too
concrete a misery to be surveyed philo-
sophically. If she had been unhappy for
complex reasons, the unhappiness was as
real as though it had been uncompli-
cated. Soul is more bruisable than flesh,
and Julia was wounded in every fibre of
her spirit. Her husband's personality
seemed to be closing gradually in on her,
obscuring the sky and cutting off the air,
till she felt herself shut up among the
decaying bodies of · her starved hopes.
A sense of having been decoyed by some
world-old conspiracy into this bondage of
body and soul filled her with despair. If
marriage was the slow life-long acquittal

of a debt contracted in ignorance, then
marriage was a crime against human nature. She, for one, would have no share
in maintaining the pretence of which she
had been a victim: the pretence that a
man and a woman, forced into the nar-
rowest of personal relations, must remain there till the end, though they
may have outgrown the span of each
other's natures as the mature tree out-
grows the iron brace about the sapling.

It was in the first heat of her moral indignation that she had met Clement
Westall. She had seen at once that he
was "interested," and had fought off the
discovery, dreading any influence that
should draw her back into the bondage
of conventional relations. To ward off
the peril she had, with an almost crude
precipitancy, revealed her opinions to
him. To her surprise, she found that he
shared them. She was attracted by the
frankness of a suitor who, while pressing
his suit, admitted that he did not believe
in marriage. Her worst audacities did
not seem to surprise him: he had thought
out all that she had felt, and they had
reached the same conclusion. People
grew at varying rates, and the yoke that
was an easy fit for the one might soon
become galling to the other. That was
what divorce was for: the readjustment
of personal relations. As soon as their
necessarily transitive nature was recognized they would gain in dignity as well
as in harmony. There would be no farther
need of the ignoble concessions and con-
nivances, the perpetual sacrifice of personal delicacy and moral pride, by means
of which imperfect marriages were now
held together. Each partner to the contract would be on his mettle, forced to
live up to the highest standard of self-
development, on pain of losing the other's
respect and affection. The low nature
could no longer drag the higher down,
but must struggle to rise, or remain
alone on its inferior level. The only
necessary condition to a harmonious marriage was a frank recognition of this
truth, and a solemn agreement between
the contracting parties to keep faith with
themselves, and not to live together for
a moment after complete accord had
ceased to exist between them. The new
adultery was unfaithfulness to self.

It was, as Westall had just reminded

her, on this understanding that they had married. The ceremony was an unimportant concession to social prejudice: now that the door of divorce stood open, no marriage need be an imprisonment, and the contract therefore no longer involved any diminution of self-respect. The nature of their attachment placed them so far beyond the reach of such contingencies that it was easy to discuss them with an open mind; and Julia's sense of security made her dwell with a tender insistence on Westall's promise to claim his release when he should cease to love her. The exchange of these vows seemed to make them, in a sense, champions of the new law, pioneers in the forbidden realm of individual freedom: they felt that they had somehow achieved beatitude without martyrdom.

This, as Julia now reviewed the past, she perceived to have been her theoretical attitude toward marriage. It was unconsciously, insidiously, that her ten years of happiness with Westall had developed another conception of the tie; a reversion, rather, to the old instinct of passionate dependency and possessorship that now made her blood revolt at the mere hint of change. Change? Renewal? Was that what they had called it, in their foolish jargon? Destruction, extermination rather—this rending of a myriad fibres interwoven with another's being! Another? But he was not other! He and she were one, one in the mystic sense which alone gave marriage its significance. The new law was not for them, but for the disunited creatures forced into a mockery of union. The gospel she had felt called on to proclaim had no bearing on her own case.... She sent for the doctor and told him she was sure she needed a nerve tonic.

She took the nerve tonic diligently, but it failed to act as a sedative to her fears. She did not know what she feared; but that made her anxiety the more pervasive. Her husband had not reverted to the subject of his Saturday talks. He was unusually kind and considerate, with a softening of his quick manner, a touch of shyness in his consideration, that sickened her with new fears. She told herself that it was because she looked badly—because he knew about the doctor and the nerve tonic—that he showed this

deference to her wishes, this eagerness to screen her from moral draughts; but the explanation simply cleared the way for fresh inferences.

The week passed slowly, vacantly, like a prolonged Sunday. On Saturday the morning post brought a note from Mrs. Van Sideren. Would dear Julia ask Mr. Westall to come half an hour earlier than usual, as there was to be some music after his "talk"? Westall was just leaving for his office when his wife read the note. She opened the drawing-room door and called him back to deliver the message.

He glanced at the note and tossed it aside. "What a bore! I shall have to cut my game of racquets. Well, I suppose it can't be helped. Will you write and say it's all right?"

Julia hesitated a moment, her hand stiffening on the chair-back against which she leaned.

"You mean to go on with these talks?" she asked.

"I—why not?" he returned; and this time it struck her that his surprise was not quite unfeigned. The discovery helped her to find words.

"You said you had started them with the idea of pleasing me—"

"Well?"

"I told you last week that they didn't please me."

"Last week? Oh—" He seemed to make an effort of memory. "I thought you were nervous then; you sent for the doctor the next day."

"It was not the doctor I needed; it was your assurance—"

"My assurance?"

Suddenly she felt the floor fail under her. She sank into the chair with a choking throat, her words, her reasons slipping away from her like straws down a whirling flood.

"Clement," she cried, "isn't it enough for you to know that I hate it?"

He turned to close the door behind them; then he walked toward her and sat down. "What is it that you hate?" he asked gently.

She had made a desperate effort to rally her routed argument.

"I can't bear to have you speak as if —as if—our marriage—were like the other kind—the wrong kind. When I heard you there, the other afternoon, before all those inquisitive gossiping people, proclaiming that husbands and wives had a right to leave each other whenever they were tired—or had seen some one else—"

Westall sat motionless, his eyes fixed on a pattern of the carpet.

"You *have* ceased to take this view, then?" he said as she broke off. "You no longer believe that husbands and wives *are* justified in separating—under such conditions?"

"Under such conditions?" she stammered. "Yes—I still believe that—but how can we judge for others? What can we know of the circumstances—?"

He interrupted her. "I thought it was a fundamental article of our creed that the special circumstances produced by marriage were not to interfere with the full assertion of individual liberty." He paused a moment. "I thought that was your reason for leaving Arment."

She flushed to the forehead. It was not like him to give a personal turn to the argument.

"It was my reason," she said simply.

"Well, then—why do you refuse to recognize its validity now?"

"I don't—I don't—I only say that one can't judge for others."

He made an impatient movement. "This is mere hair-splitting. What you mean is that, the doctrine having served your purpose when you needed it, you now repudiate it."

"Well," she exclaimed, flushing again, "what if I do? What does it matter to us?"

Westall rose from his chair. He was excessively pale, and stood before his wife with something of the formality of a stranger.

"It matters to me," he said in a low voice, "because I do *not* repudiate it."

"Well—?"

"And because I had intended to invoke it as"—

He paused and drew his breath deeply. She sat silent, almost deafened by her heart-beats.

—"as a complete justification of the course I am about to take."

Julia remained motionless. "What course is that?" she asked.

He cleared his throat. "I mean to claim the fulfilment of your promise."

For an instant the room wavered and

darkened; then she recovered a torturing acuteness of vision. Every detail of her surroundings pressed upon her: the tick of the clock, the slant of sunlight on the wall, the hardness of the chair-arms that she grasped, were a separate wound to each sense.

"My promise—" she faltered.

"Your part of our mutual agreement to set each other free if one or the other should wish to be released."

She was silent again. He waited a moment, shifting his position nervously; then he said, with a touch of irritability: "You acknowledge the agreement?"

The question went through her like a shock. She lifted her head to it proudly. "I acknowledge the agreement," she said.

"And—you don't mean to repudiate it?"

A log on the hearth fell forward, and mechanically he advanced and pushed it back.

"No," she answered slowly, "I don't mean to repudiate it."

There was a pause. He remained near the hearth, his elbow resting on the mantel-shelf. Close to his hand stood a little cup of jade that he had given her on one of their wedding anniversaries. She wondered vaguely if he noticed it.

"You intend to leave me, then?" she said at length.

His gesture seemed to deprecate the crudeness of the allusion.

"To marry some one else?"

Again his eye and hand protested. She rose and stood before him.

"Why should you be afraid to tell me? Is it Una Van Sideren?"

He was silent.

"I wish you good luck," she said.

III

She looked up, finding herself alone. She did not remember when or how he had left the room, or how long afterward she had sat there. The fire still smouldered on the hearth, but the slant of sunlight had left the wall.

Her first conscious thought was that she had not broken her word, that she had fulfilled the very letter of their bargain. There had been no crying out, no vain appeal to the past, no attempt at temporizing or evasion. She had march-ed straight up to the guns.

Now that it was over, she sickened to find herself alive. She looked about her, trying to recover her hold on reality. Her identity seemed to be slipping from her, as it disappears in a physical swoon. "This is my room—this is my house," she heard herself saying. Her room? Her house? She could almost hear the walls laugh back at her.

She stood up, a dull ache in every bone. The silence of the room frightened her. She remembered, now, having heard the front door close a long time ago: the sound suddenly re-echoed through her brain. Her husband must have left the house, then—her *husband?* She no longer knew in what terms to think: the simplest phrases had a poisoned edge. She sank back into her chair, overcome by a strange weakness. The clock struck ten —it was only ten o'clock! Suddenly she remembered that she had not ordered dinner... or were they dining out that evening? *Dinner—dining out*—the old meaningless phraseology pursued her! She must try to think of herself as she would think of some one else, a some one dissociated from all the familiar routine of the past, whose wants and habits must gradually be learned, as one might spy out the ways of a strange animal. . .

The clock struck another hour—eleven. She stood up again and walked to the door: she thought she would go up stairs to her room. *Her* room? Again the word derided her. She opened the door, crossed the narrow hall, and walked up the stairs. As she passed, she noticed Westall's sticks and umbrellas: a pair of his gloves lay on the hall table. The same stair-carpet mounted between the same walls; the same old French print, in its narrow black frame, faced her on the landing. This visual continuity was intolerable. Within, a gaping chasm; without, the same untroubled and familiar surface. She must get away from it before she could attempt to think. But, once in her room, she sat down on the lounge, a stupor creeping over her. . .

Gradually her vision cleared. A great deal had happened in the interval—a wild marching and countermarching of emotions, arguments, ideas—a fury of insurgent impulses that fell back spent upon themselves. She had tried, at first, to rally, to organize these chaotic forces. There must be help somewhere, if only she could master the inner tumult. Life could not be broken off short like this, for a whim, a fancy; the law itself would side with her, would defend her. The law? What claim had she upon it? She was the prisoner of her own choice: she had been her own legislator, and she was the predestined victim of the code she had devised. But this was grotesque, intolerable—a mad mistake, for which she could not be held accountable! The law she had despised was still there, might still be invoked . . . invoked, but to what end? Could she ask it to chain Westall to her side? *She* had been allowed to go free when she claimed her freedom—should she show less magnanimity than she had exacted? Magnanimity? The word lashed her with its irony—one does not strike an attitude when one is fighting for life! She would threaten, grovel, cajole... she would yield anything to keep her hold on happiness. Ah, but the difficulty lay deeper! The law could not help her—her own apostasy could not help her. She was the victim of the theories she renounced. It was as though some giant machine of her own making had caught her up in its wheels and was grinding her to atoms. . .

It was afternoon when she found herself out-of-doors. She walked with an aimless haste, fearing to meet familiar faces. The day was radiant, metallic: one of those searching American days so calculated to reveal the shortcomings of our street-cleaning and the excesses of our architecture. The streets looked bare and hideous; everything stared and glittered. She called a passing hansom, and gave Mrs. Van Sideren's address. She did not know what had led up to the act; but she found herself suddenly resolved to speak, to cry out a warning. It was too late to save herself—but the girl might still be told. The hansom rattled up Fifth Avenue; she sat with her eyes fixed, avoiding recognition. At the Van Sideren's door she sprang out and rang the bell. Action had cleared her brain, and she felt calm and self-possessed. She knew now exactly what she meant to say.

The ladies were both out ... the parlor-maid stood waiting for a card. Julia, with a vague murmur, turned away from the door and lingered a moment on the

"YOU INTEND TO LEAVE ME, THEN?" SHE SAID AT LENGTH

sidewalk. Then she remembered that she had not paid the cab-driver. She drew a dollar from her purse and handed it to him. He touched his hat and drove off, leaving her alone in the long empty street. She wandered away westward, toward strange thoroughfares, where she was not likely to meet acquaintances. The feeling of aimlessness had returned. Once she found herself in the afternoon torrent of Broadway, swept past tawdry shops and flaming theatrical posters, with a succession of meaningless faces gliding by in the opposite direction. . .

A feeling of faintness reminded her that she had not eaten since morning. She turned into a side street of shabby houses, with rows of ash-barrels behind bent area railings. In a basement window she saw the sign *Ladies' Restaurant:* a pie and a dish of doughnuts lay against the dusty pane like petrified food in an ethnological museum. She entered, and a young woman with a weak mouth and a brazen eye cleared a table for her near the window. The table was covered with a red and white cotton cloth and adorned with a bunch of celery in a thick tumbler and a salt-cellar full of grayish lumpy salt. Julia ordered tea, and sat a long time waiting for it. She was glad to be away from the noise and confusion of the streets. The low-ceilinged room was empty, and two or three waitresses with thin pert faces lounged in the background staring at her and whispering together. At last the tea was brought in a discolored metal teapot. Julia poured a cup and drank it hastily. It was black and bitter, but it flowed through her veins like an elixir. She was almost dizzy with exhilaration. Oh, how tired, how unutterably tired she had been!

She drank a second cup, blacker and bitterer, and now her mind was once more working clearly. She felt as vigorous, as decisive, as when she had stood on the Van Siderens' door-step—but the wish to return there had subsided. She saw now the futility of such an attempt—the humiliation to which it might have exposed her. . . The pity of it was that she did not know what to do next. The short winter day was fading, and she realized that she could not remain much longer in the restaurant without attracting notice. She paid for her tea and went out into the street. The lamps were alight, and here and there a basement shop cast an oblong of gas-light across the fissured pavement. In the dusk there was something sinister about the aspect of the street, and she hastened back toward Fifth Avenue. She was not used to being out alone at that hour.

At the corner of Fifth Avenue she paused and stood watching the stream of carriages. At last a policeman caught sight of her and signed to her that he would take her across. She had not meant to cross the street, but she obeyed automatically, and presently found herself on the farther corner. There she paused again for a moment; but she fancied the policeman was watching her, and this sent her hastening down the nearest side street. . . After that she walked a long time, vaguely. . . Night had fallen, and now and then, through the windows of a passing carriage, she caught the expanse of an evening waistcoat or the shimmer of an opera cloak. . .

Suddenly she found herself in a familiar street. She stood still a moment, breathing quickly. She had turned the corner without noticing whither it led; but now, a few yards ahead of her, she saw the house in which she had once lived —her first husband's house. The blinds were drawn, and only a faint translucence marked the windows and the transom above the door. As she stood there she heard a step behind her, and a man walked by in the direction of the house. He walked slowly, with a heavy middle-aged gait, his head sunk a little between the shoulders, the red crease of his neck visible above the fur collar of his overcoat. He crossed the street, went up the steps of the house, drew forth a latch-key, and let himself in. . .

There was no one else in sight. Julia leaned for a long time against the area-rail at the corner, her eyes fixed on the front of the house. The feeling of physical weariness had returned, but the strong tea still throbbed in her veins and lit her brain with an unnatural clearness. Presently she heard another step draw near, and moving quickly away, she too crossed the street and mounted the steps of the house. The impulse which had carried her there prolonged itself in a quick pressure of the electric bell—

then she felt suddenly weak and tremulous, and grasped the balustrade for support. The door opened and a young footman with a fresh inexperienced face stood on the threshold. Julia knew in an instant that he would admit her.

"I saw Mr. Arment going in just now," she said. "Will you ask him to see me for a moment?"

The footman hesitated. "I think Mr. Arment has gone up to dress for dinner, madam."

Julia advanced into the hall. "I am sure he will see me—I will not detain him long," she said. She spoke quietly, authoritatively, in the tone which a good servant does not mistake. The footman had his hand on the drawing-room door.

"I will tell him, madam. What name, please?"

Julia trembled: she had not thought of that. "Merely say a lady," she returned carelessly.

The footman wavered and she fancied herself lost; but at that instant the door opened from within and John Arment stepped into the hall. He drew back sharply as he saw her, his florid face turning sallow with the shock; then the blood poured back to it, swelling the veins on his temples and reddening the lobes of his thick ears.

It was long since Julia had seen him, and she was startled at the change in his appearance. He had thickened, coarsened, settled down into the enclosing flesh. But she noted this insensibly: her one conscious thought was that, now she was face to face with him, she must not let him escape till he had heard her. Every pulse in her body throbbed with the urgency of her message.

She went up to him as he drew back. "I must speak to you," she said.

Arment hesitated, red and stammering. Julia glanced at the footman, and her look acted as a warning. The instinctive shrinking from a "scene" predominated over every other impulse, and Arment said slowly: "Will you come this way?"

He followed her into the drawing-room and closed the door. Julia, as she advanced, was vaguely aware that the room at least was unchanged: time had not mitigated its horrors. The contadina still lurched from the chimney-breast, and the Greek slave obstructed the threshold of the inner room. The place was alive with memories: they started out from every fold of the yellow satin curtains and glided between the angles of the rosewood furniture. But while some subordinate agency was carrying these impressions to her brain, her whole conscious effort was centred in the act of dominating Arment's will. The fear that he would refuse to hear her mounted like fever to her brain. She felt her purpose melt before it, words and arguments running into each other in the heat of her longing. For a moment her voice failed her, and she imagined herself thrust out before she could speak; but as she was struggling for a word, Arment pushed a chair forward, and said quietly: "You are not well."

The sound of his voice steadied her. It was neither kind nor unkind—a voice that suspended judgment, rather, awaiting unforeseen developments. She supported herself against the back of the chair and drew a deep breath. "Shall I send for something?" he continued, with a cold embarrassed politeness.

Julia raised an entreating hand. "No —no—thank you. I am quite well."

He paused midway toward the bell, and turned on her. "Then may I ask—?"

"Yes," she interrupted him. "I came here because I wanted to see you. There is something I must tell you."

Arment continued to scrutinize her. "I am surprised at that," he said. "I should have supposed that any communication you may wish to make could have been made through our lawyers."

"Our lawyers!" She burst into a little laugh. "I don't think they could help me—this time."

Arment's face took on a barricaded look. "If there is any question of help— of course—"

It struck her, whimsically, that she had seen that look when some shabby devil called with a subscription-book. Perhaps he thought she wanted him to put his name down for so much in sympathy—or even in money. . . The thought made her laugh again. She saw his look change slowly to perplexity. All his facial changes were slow, and she remembered, suddenly, how it had once diverted her to shift that lumbering scenery with a word. For the first time it struck her

HE DREW BACK SHARPLY AS HE SAW HER

that she had been cruel. "There *is* a question of help," she said in a softer key; "you can help me; but only by listening. . . I want to tell you something. . ."

Arment's resistance was not yielding. "Would it not be easier to—write?" he suggested.

She shook her head. "There is no time to write. . . and it won't take long." She raised her head and their eyes met. "My husband has left me," she said.

"Westall—?" he stammered, reddening again.

"Yes. This morning. Just as I left you. Because he was tired of me."

The words, uttered scarcely above a whisper, seemed to dilate to the limit of the room. Arment looked toward the door; then his embarrassed glance returned to Julia.

"I am very sorry," he said awkwardly.

"Thank you," she murmured.

"But I don't see—"

"No—but you will—in a moment. Won't you listen to me? Please!" Instinctively she had shifted her position, putting herself between him and the door. "It happened this morning," she went on in short breathless phrases. "I never suspected anything—I thought we were—perfectly happy. . . Suddenly he told me he was tired of me. . . there is a girl he likes better. . . He has gone to her. . ." As she spoke, the lurking anguish rose upon her, possessing her once more to the exclusion of every other emotion. Her eyes ached, her throat swelled with it, and two painful tears burnt a way down her face.

Arment's constraint was increasing visibly. "This—this is very unfortunate," he began. "But I should say the law—"

"The law?" she echoed ironically. "When he asks for his freedom?"

"You are not obliged to give it."

"You were not obliged to give me mine —but you did."

He made a protesting gesture.

"You saw that the law couldn't help you—didn't you?" she went on. "That is what I see now. The law represents material rights—it can't go beyond. If we don't recognize an inner law . . . the obligation that love creates . . . being loved as well as loving . . . there is nothing

to prevent our spreading ruin unhindered . . . is there?" She raised her head plaintively, with the look of a bewildered child. "That is what I see now . . . what I wanted to tell you. He leaves me because he's tired . . . but *I* was not tired; and I don't understand why he is. That's the dreadful part of it—the not understanding: I hadn't realized what it meant. But I've been thinking of it all day, and things have come back to me— things I hadn't noticed . . . when you and I . . ." She moved closer to him, and fixed her eyes on his with the gaze that tries to reach beyond words. "I see now that *you* didn't understand—did you?"

Their eyes met in a sudden shock of comprehension: a veil seemed to be lifted between them. Arment's lip trembled.

"No," he said, "I didn't understand."

She gave a little cry, almost of triumph. "I knew it! I knew it! You wondered —you tried to tell me—but no words came. . . You saw your life falling in ruins . . . the world slipping from you . . . and you couldn't speak or move!"

She sank down on the chair against which she had been leaning. "Now I know—now I know," she repeated.

"I am very sorry for you," she heard Arment stammer.

She looked up quickly. "That's not what I came for. I don't want you to be sorry. I came to ask you to forgive me. . . for not understanding that *you* didn't understand. . . That's all I wanted to say." She rose with a vague sense that the end had come, and put out a groping hand toward the door.

Arment stood motionless. She turned to him with a faint smile.

"You forgive me?"

"There is nothing to forgive—"

"Then will you shake hands for good-by?" She felt his hand in hers: it was nerveless, reluctant.

"Good-by," she repeated. "I understand now."

She opened the door and passed out into the hall. As she did so, Arment took an impulsive step forward; but just then the footman, who was evidently alive to his obligations, advanced from the background to let her out. She heard Arment fall back. The footman threw open the door, and she found herself outside in the darkness.

LA TINAJA BONITA
by Owen Wister

"And it came to pass after a while that the brook dried up, because there had been no rain in the land."—1 Kings, xvii. 7.

A PRETTY girl was kneeling on the roof of a flat mud cabin, a harvest of red peppers round her knees. On the ground below her stood a swarthy young man, the bloom on his Mexican cheeks rich and dusky, like her own. His face was irresponsible and winning, and his watching eyes shone upon her with admiration and desire. She on the roof was entertained by her visitor's attention, but unfavorable to it. Through the livelong sunny day she had parried his love-talk with light and complete skill, enjoying herself, and liking him very well, as she had done since they were two children playing together in the Arizona desert. She was quite mistress of the situation, because she was a woman, and he as yet merely a boy; he was only twenty-two; she was almost sixteen. The Mexican man at twenty-two may be as experienced as his Northern brother of thirty, but at sixteen the Mexican woman is also mature, and can competently deal with the man. ~ So this girl had relished the thoughtless morning and noon as they passed; but twice lately she had glanced across the low tree-tops of her garden down the trail, where the cañon descended to the silent plain below.

"I think I must go back now," said the young man, not thinking so. He had a guitar from the cabin.

"Oh!" said she, to whom he was transparent. "Well, if you think it so late." She busied herself with the harvest. Her red handkerchief and strands of her black hair had fallen loosely together from her head to her shoulders. The red peppers were heaped thick, hiding the whole roof, and she stooped among them, levelling them to a ripening layer with buckskin gloves (for peppers sting sharper than mustard), sorting and turning them in the bright sun. The youth looked at her most wistfully.

"It is not precisely late—yet," said he.

"To be sure not," she assented, consulting the sky. "We have still three hours of day."

He brightened as he lounged against a water-barrel. "But after night it is so very dark on the trail to camp," he insincerely objected.

"I never could have believed you were afraid of the dark."

"It is for the horse's legs, Lolita. Of course I fear nothing."

"Bueno! I was sure of it. Do you know, Luis, you have become a man quite suddenly? That mustache will be beautiful in a few years. And you have a good figure."

"I am much heavier than last year," said he. "My arm—"

"I can see, I can see. I am not sure I shall let you kiss me any more. You didn't offer to when you came this morning—and that shows you men perceive things more quickly than we can. But don't go yet. You can lead your horse. His legs will come to no harm, eased of your weight. I should have been lonely to-day, and you have made it pass so quickly. You have talked so much that my peppers are not half spread."

"We could finish them in five minutes together," said the youth, taking a step.

"Two up here among all these peppers? Oh no, Luis. We should tread on them, and our ankles would burn all night. If you want to help me, go bring some fresh water. The barrel is almost empty."

But Luis stood ardently gazing up at the roof.

"Very well, then," said Lolita. "If you like this better, finish the peppers, and I'll go for the water."

"Why do you look down the trail so often?" said the baffled love-maker, petulantly.

"Because Uncle Ramon said the American would be coming to-day," the girl replied, softly.

"Was it Uncle Ramon said that? He told you that?"

"Why not?" She shaded her eyes, and looked where the cañon's widening slit gave view of a slant of sand merging fan-spread into a changeless waste of plain. Many watercourses, crooked and straight, came out of the gaps, creasing the sudden Sierra, descending to the flat through bushes and leaning margin trees, but in these empty shapes not a rill tinkled to refresh the silence, nor did a drop slide over the glaring rocks, or even dampen the heated cheating sand. Lolita strained her gaze at the dry distance, and stooped again to her harvest.

"What does he come here for?" demanded Luis.

"The American? We buy white flour of him sometimes."

"Sometimes! That must be worth his while! He will get rich!" Luis lounged back against his water-barrel, and was silent. As he watched Lolita, serenely working, his silver crescent ear-rings swung a little with the slight tilting of his head, and his fingers, forgotten and unguided by his thoughts, ruffled the strings of the guitar, drawing from it gay purposeless tendrils of sound. Occasionally, when Lolita knew the song, she would hum it on the roof, inattentively, busy rolling her peppers:

> "Soy purita mejicana;
> Nada tengo español."

("I am pure Mexican. I have nothing Spanish about me.") And this melodious inattention of Lolita's, Luis felt to be the extreme of slight.

"Have you seen him lately?" he asked, sourly.

"Not very. Not since the last time he came to the mines from Maricopa."

"I heard a man at Gun Sight say he was dead," snapped Luis.

But she made no sign. "That would be a pity," she said, humming gayly.

"Very sad. Uncle Ramon would have to go himself to Maricopa for that white flour."

Pleased with this remark, the youth took to song himself; and there they were like two mischievous birds. Only the bird on the ground was cross with a sense of failure. "El telele se murió," he sang.

"The hunchback is dead.
Ay! Ay! Ay!
And no one could be found to bury him except—"

"Luis, aren't you going to get my water for me?"

"Poco tiempo: I'll bring it directly."

"You have to go to the Tinaja Bonita for it."

The Pretty Spring—or water-hole, or tank—was half a mile from the cabin.

"Well, it's not nice out there in the sun. I like it better in here, where it is pleasant.

"And no one could be found to bury him except
Five dragoons and a corporal
And the sacristan's cat."

Singing resentfully, young Luis staid in here, where it was pleasant. Bright green branches of fruit trees and small cottonwoods and a fenced irrigated square of green growing garden hid the tiny adobe home like a nut, smooth and hard and dry in their clustered midst. The lightest air that could blow among these limber ready leaves set going at once their varnished twinkling round the house. Their white and dark sides gleamed and went out with chasing lights that quickened the torpid place into a holiday of motion. Closed in by this cool green, you did not have to see or think of Arizona, just outside; you could forget, and play at love-making, and be spiteful about hunchbacks.

"Where is Uncle Ramon to-day?" inquired Luis, dropping his music.

She sighed. "He has gone to drive our cattle to a new spring. There is no pasture at the Tinaja Bonita. Our streams and ditches went dry last week. They have never done so in all the years before. I don't know what is going to happen to us." The anxiety in the girl's face seemed to come outward more plainly for a moment, and then recede to its permanent abiding-place.

"There cannot be much water to keep flour-sellers alive on the trail to Maricopa," chirped the bird on the ground.

She made no answer to this. "What are you doing nowadays?" she asked.

"I have been working very hard on the wood contract for the American soldiers," he replied, promptly.

"By Tucson?"

"No. Huachuca."

"Away over there again? I thought you had cut all they wanted last May."

"It is of that enterprise of which I speak, Lolita."

"But it's October now!" Lolita lifted her face, ruddy with stooping, and broke into laughter.

"I do not see why you mock me. No one has asked me to work since."

"Have you asked any one for work?"

"It is not my way to beg."

"Luis, I don't believe you're quite a man yet, in spite of your mustache. You complain there's no money for Mexicans in Arizona because the Americans get it all. Why don't you go back to Sonora, then, and be rich in five minutes? It would sound finely: 'Luis Romero, Merchant, Hermosillo.' Or perhaps gold would fall more quickly into your lap at Guaymas. You would live in a big house, perhaps with two stories, and I would come and visit you at Easter—if your wife would allow it." Here Lolita threw a pepper at him.

The guitar grated a few pretty notes; otherwise there was silence.

"And it was Uncle Ramon persuaded them to hire you in May. He told the American contractor you owned a strong burro good for heavy loads. He didn't say much about you," added the little lady.

"Much good it did me! The American contractor-pig retained my wages to pay for the food he supplied us. They charge you extra for starvation, those gringos. They are all pigs. Ah, Lolita, a man needs a wife, so he may strive to win a home for her."

"I have heard men say that they needed a home before they could strive to win a wife for it. But you go about it the other way."

"I am not an American pig, I thank the Virgin! I have none of their gringo customs."

"You speak truly indeed," murmured Lolita.

"It is you who know about them," the boy said, angry like a child. He had seen her eye drawn to the trail again as by a magnet. "They say you prefer gringos to your own people."

"Who dares say that?"

The elated Luis played loudly on the guitar. He had touched her that time.

But Lolita's eye softened at the instant of speaking, and she broke into her sweet laugh. "There!" she said, recapturing the situation; "is it not like old times for you and me to be fighting?"

"Me? I am not fighting."

"You relieve me."

"I do not consider a gringo worth my notice."

"Sensible boy! You speak as wisely as one who has been to school in a large city. Luis, do you remember the day Uncle Ramon locked me up for riding on the kicking burro, and you came and unlocked me when uncle was gone? You took me walking, and lost us both in the mountains. We were really only a little, little way from home, but I thought we had got into another country where they eat children. I was six, and I beat you for losing me, and cried, and you were

big, and you kissed me till I stopped crying. Do you remember?"

"No."

"Don't you remember?"

"I don't remember child's tricks."

"Luis, I have come to a conclusion. You are still young enough for me to kiss quite safely. Every time you fight with me—I shall kiss you. Won't you get me some fresh water now?"

He lounged, sulky, against his barrel.

"Come, querido! Must I go all that way myself? Well, then, if you intend to stand and glare at me till the moon rises— Ah! he moves!"

Luis laid the guitar gradually down, and gradually lifting a pail in which the dipper rattled with emptiness, he proceeded to crawl on his journey.

"You know that is not the one we use, muchacho, little boy," remarked Lolita.

"Keep your kisses for your gringo," the water-carrier growled, with his back to her.

"I shall always save some for my little cousin."

The pail clattered on the stones, and the child stopped crawling. She on the roof stared at this performance for an open-mouthed moment, gloves idle among the spicy peppers. Then, laughing, she sprang to her feet, descended, and catching up the water-jar, the olla de agua, overtook him, and shook it in his face with the sweetest derision. "Now we'll go together," said she, and started gayly through the green trees and the garden. He followed her, two paces behind, half ashamed, and gazing at her red handkerchief, and the black hair blowing a little; thus did they cross the tiny cool home acre through the twinkling pleasantness of the leaves, and pass at once outside the magic circle of irrigation into Arizona's domain, among a prone herd of carcasses upon the ground. Dead cattle, two seasons dead now, hunted to this sanctuary by the drought, killed in the sanctuary by cold water.

A wise quiet man, with a man's will, may sometimes after three days of thirst still hold grip enough upon his slipping mind to know, when he has found the water, that he must not drink it, must only dampen his lips and tongue in a drop-by-drop fashion until he has endured the passing of many slow insidious hours. Even a wise man had best have a friend by his side then, who shall fight and tear him from the perilous excesses that he craves, knock him senseless if he cannot pin him down; but cattle know nothing of drop by drop, and you cannot pin down a hundred head that have found water after three days. So these hundred had drunk themselves swollen, and died. Cracked hide and white bone they lay, brown, dry, gaping humps straddled stiff askew in the last convulsion; and over them presided Arizona—silent, vast, all sunshine everlasting.

Luis saw these corpses that had stumbled to their fate, and he remembered; with Lolita in those trees all day, he had forgotten for a while. He pointed to the wide-strewn sight, familiar, monotonous as misfortune. "There will be many more," he said. "Another rainy season is gone without doing anything for the country. It cannot rain now for another year, Lolita."

"God help us and our cattle, and travellers!" she whispered.

Luis musingly repeated a saying of the country about the Tinaja Bonita,

> "When you see the Black Cross dry,
>   Fill the wagon cisterns high"

—a doggerel in homely Spanish metre, unwritten mouth-to-mouth wisdom, stable as a proverb, enduring through generations of unrecorded wanderers, that repeated it for a few years, and passed beneath the desert.

"But the Black Cross has never been dry yet," Luis said.

"You have not seen it lately," said Lolita.

"Lolita! do you mean—" He looked in her troubled eyes, and they went on in silence together. They left behind them the bones and the bald level on which they lay, and came to where the cañon's broader descent quickened until they sank below that sight of the cattle, and for a while below the home and trees. They went down steeply by cactus and dry rock to a meeting of several cañons opening from side rifts in the Sierra, furrowing the main valley's mesa with deep watercourses that brought no water. Finding their way in this lumpy meeting-ground, they came upon the lurking-place of the Tinaja Bonita. They stood above it at the edge of a pitch of rock, watching the motionless crystal of the pool.

"How well it hides down there in its own cañon!" said Luis. "How pretty and clear! But there's plenty of water, Lolita."

"Can you see the Black Cross?"

"Not from here."

They began descending around the sides of the crumbled slate-rock face that tilted too steep for foothold.

"The other well is dry, of course," said Lolita. In the slaty, many-ledged formation a little lower down the cañon, towards the peep of outlying open country which the cloven hills let in, was a second round hole, twin of the first. Except after storms, water was never in this place, and it lay dry as a kiln nine-tenths of the year. But in size and depth and color, and the circular fashion of its shaft, that seemed man's rather than nature's design, it might have been the real Tinaja's reflection, conjured in some evil mirror that gave all of its likeness except alone the living water that made it precious.

"It must have been a real well once," said Luis.

"Once, yes."

"And what made it go dry?"

"Who knows?"

"How strange it should be the lower well that failed, Lolita!"

The boy and girl were climbing down slowly, drawing near each other as they reached the bottom of the hollow. The peep of open country was blocked, and the tall tops of the mountains were all of the outer world they could see, choked in down here below the mesa's level, amid a silence more ancient than the spheres.

"Do you believe it ever can go dry?" asked Luis. They were now on the edge of the Tinaja.

"Father Rafael says that it is miraculous," said the girl, believingly.

Opposite, and everywhere except where they were, the walls went sheer down, not slate-colored, but white, with a sudden upcropping formation of brick-shaped stones. These also were many-layered and crumbling, cracking off into the pool if the hand hung or the foot weighed on them. No safe way went to the water but at this lower side, where the riven, tumbled white blocks shelved easily to the bottom; and Luis and Lolita looked down these natural stairs at the portent in the well. In that white formation shot up from the earth's bowels, arbitrary and irrelevant amid the surrounding alien layers of slate, four black stones were lodged as if built into the wall by some hand—four small stones shaping a cross, black against the white, symmetrical and plain beyond need of imagination.

"It has come further—more uncovered since yesterday," Lolita whispered.

"Can the Tinaja sink altogether?" repeated Luis. The arms of the cross were a measurable space above the water-line, and he had always seen it entirely submerged.

"How could it sink?" said Lolita, simply. "It will stop when the black stones are wholly dry."

"You believe Father Rafael," Luis said, always in a low voice; "but it was only Indians, after all, who told the mission fathers at the first."

"That was very long ago," said she, "and there has always been water in the Tinaja Bonita."

Boy and girl had set the jar down, and forgotten it and why they had come. Luis looked uneasily at the circular pool, and up from this creviced middle of the cañon to the small high tops of the mountains rising in the free sky.

"This is an evil place," he said. "As for the water—no one, no three, can live long enough to be sure."

But it was part of Lolita's religion. "I am sure," said she.

The young Mexican's eyes rested on the face of the girl beside him, more beautiful just then with some wave of secret fear and faith.

"Come away with me, Lolita!" he pleaded, suddenly. "I can work. I can be a man. It is fearful for you to live here alone."

"Alone, Luis?" His voice had called her from her reverie back to her gay, alert self. "Do you consider Uncle Ramon nobody to live with?"

"Yes. Nobody—for you."

"Promise me never to tell that to uncle. He is so considerate that he might make me marry somebody for company. And then, you know, my husband would be certain to be stupid about your coming to see me, querido."

"Why do you always mock me, Lolita?"

"Mock you? What a fancy! Oh, see how the sun's going! If we do not get our water, your terrible Tinaja will go dry before supper. Come, Luis, I carried the olla. Must I do everything?"

He looked at her disconsolate. "Ah!" he vibrated, revelling in deep imaginary passion.

"Go! go!" she cried, pushing him. "Take your olla."

Upon any passing puff of sentiment the Southern breast can heave with every genuine symptom of storm except wreck. Of course she stirred his gregarious heart. Was she not lovely and he twenty-two? He went down the natural stairs and came slowly up with the water, stopping a step below her. "Lolita," he said, "don't you love me at all? not a very little?"

"You are my dearest, oldest friend, Luis," she said, looking at him with such full sweetness that his eyes fell. "But why do you pretend five beans make ten?"

"Of course they only make ten with gringos."

She held up a warning finger.

"Oh yes, oh yes! Strangers make fine lovers!" With this he swelled to a fond, dangerous appearance, and muttered, "It is not difficult to kill a man, Lolita."

"Fighting! after what I told you!" Lolita stooped and kissed her cousin Luis, and he instantly made the most of that chance.

"As often as you please," he said, as she released herself angrily, and then a stroke of sound struck their two hearts still. They jumped apart, trembling. Some of the rock slide had rattled down and plunged into the Tinaja with a gulping resonance. Loitering strings of sand strewed after it, and the boy's and girl's superstitious eyes looked up from the ringed waving water to the ledge. Lolita's single shriek of terror turned to joy as she uttered it.

"I thought—I thought you would not come!" she cried out.

The dismounted horseman above made no sign of understanding her words. He stepped carefully away from the ledge his foot had crumbled, and they saw him using his rifle like a staff, steadying its stock in successive niches, and so working back to his horse. There he slid the rifle into its leather sling along the left side of his saddle.

"So he is not dead," murmured Luis, "and we need not live alone."

"Come down!" the girl called, and waved her hand. But the new-comer stood by his horse like an apparition.

"Perhaps he is dead, after all," Luis said. "You might say some of the Mass, only he was a heretic. But his horse is Mexican and a believer."

Lolita had no eyes or ears for Luis any more. He prattled away on the stone stairs of the Tinaja, elated into flippancy after a piercing shock of fear. To him, unstrung by the silence and the Black Cross and the presence of the sinking pool, the stone had crashed like a clap of sorcery, and he had started and stared to see—not a spirit, but a man, dismounted from his horse, with a rifle. At that his heart clutched him like talons, and in the flashing spasm of his mind came a picture—smoke from the rifle, and himself bleeding in the dust. Costly love-making! But why else that rifle on the ledge? For a staff merely? Luis thanked the Virgin for the stone that fell and frightened him. He had chattered himself cool now, and ready. Lolita was smiling at the man on the hill, glowing without concealment of her heart's desire.

"Come down!" she repeated. "Come round the side." And lifting the olla, she tapped it, and signed the way to him.

"He has probably brought too much white flour for Uncle Ramon to care to climb more than he must," said Luis. But the man had stirred at last from his sentinel stillness, and began leading his horse down. Presently he was near enough for Luis to read his face. "Your gringo is a handsome fellow certainly," he commented. "But he does not like me to-day."

"Like you? He doesn't think about you," said Lolita.

"Ha! That's your opinion?"

"It is also his opinion—if you'll ask him."

"He is afraid of Cousin Luis," stated the youth.

"Cousin grasshopper! He could eat you—if he could see you."

"There are other things in this world besides brute muscle, Lolita. Your gringo thinks I am worth notice, if you do not."

"How little he knows you!"

"It is you he does not know very well," the boy said, with a pang.

The scornful girl stared.

"Oh, the innocent one!" sneered Luis. "Grasshopper, indeed! Well, one man can always recognize another, and the women don't know much."

But Lolita had run off to meet her chosen lover. She did not stop to read his face. He was here; and as she hurried towards him she had no thought except that he was come at last. She saw his eyes and lips, and to her they were only the eyes and lips that she had longed for. "You have come just in time," she called out to him. At the voice, he looked at her one instant, and looked away; but the nearer sight of her sent a tide of scarlet across his face. His actions he could control, his bearing, and the steadiness of his speech, but not the coursing of his blood. It must have been a minute he had stood on the ledge above, getting a grip of himself. "Luis was becoming really afraid that he might have to do some work," continued Lolita, coming up the stony hill. "You know Luis!"

"I know him."

"You can fill your two canteens and carry the olla for us," she pursued, arriving eagerly beside him, her face lifted to her strong tall lover.

"I can."

At this second chill of his voice, and his way of meeting her when she had come running, she looked at him bewildered, and the smile fluttered on her lips and left them. She walked beside him, talking no more; nor could she see his furtive other hand mutely open and shut, helping him keep his grip.

Luis also looked at the man who had taken Lolita's thoughts away from him and all other men. "No, indeed, he does not understand her very well," he repeated, bitter in knowing the man's suspicion and its needlessness. Something—disappointment, it may be—had wrought more reality in the young Mexican's easy-going love. "And she likes this gringo because—because he is light-colored!" he said, watching the American's bronzed Saxon face, almost as young as his own, but of sterner stuff. Its look left him no further doubt, and he held himself forewarned. The American came to the bottom, powerful, blue-eyed, his mustache golden, his cheek clean-cut, and beaten to shining health by the weather. He swung his blue-overalled leg over his saddle and rode to the Tinaja, with a short greeting to the watcher, while the pale Lolita unclasped the canteen straps and brought the water herself, brushing coldly by Luis to hook the canteens to the saddle again. This slighting touch changed the Mexican boy's temper to diversion and malice. Here were mountains from mole-hills! Here were five beans making ten with a vengeance!

"Give me that," said the American; and Luis handed up the water-jar to him with such feline politeness that the American's blue eye filled with fire and rested on him for a doubtful second. But Luis was quite ready, and more diverted than ever over the suppressed violence of his Saxon friend. The horseman wheeled at once, and took a smooth trail out to the top of the mesa, the girl and boy following.

As the three went silent up the cañon, Luis caught sight of Lolita's eyes shining with the hurt of her lover's rebuff, and his face sparkled with further mischief. "She has been despising me all day," he said to himself. "Very well, very well. —Señor Don Ruz," he speechified aloud, elaborately, "we are having a bad drought."

The American rode on, inspecting the country.

"I know at least four sorts of kisses," reflected the Mexican trifler. "But there! very likely to me also they would appear alike from the top of a rock." He looked the American over, the rifle under his leg, his pistol, and his knife. "How clumsy these gringos are when it's about a girl!" thought Luis. "Any fool could fool them. Now I should take much care to be friendly if ever I did want to kill a man in earnest. Comical gringo! —Yes, very dry weather, Don Ruz. And the rainy season gone!"

The American continued to inspect the country, his supple, flannel-shirted back hinting no interest in the talk.

"Water is getting scarce, Don Ruz," persisted the gadfly, lighting again. "Don Ramon's spring does not run now, and so we must come to the Tinaja Bonita, you see. Don Ramon removed the cattle yesterday. Everybody absent from home, except Lolita." Luis thought he could see his Don Ruz listening to that last piece of gossip, and his smile over himself and his skill grew more engaging. "Lolita has been telling me all to-day that even the Tinaja will go dry."

"It was you said that!" exclaimed the brooding, helpless Lolita.

"So I did. And it was you said no. Well, we found something to disagree about." The gadfly was mirthful now at the expression of the flannel shirt.

"No sabe cuantos son cinco," he whispered, stepping close to Lolita. "Your gringo could not say boo to a goose just now." Lolita drew away from her cousin, and her lover happened to turn his head slightly, so that he caught sight of her drawing away. "But what do you say yourself, Don Ruz?" inquired Luis, pleased at this slight coincidence—"will the Tinaja go dry, do you think?"

"I expect guessing won't interfere with the water's movements much," finally remarked Don Ruz—Russ Genesmere. His drawl and the body in his voice were not much like the Mexican's light fluency. They were music to Lolita, and her gaze went to him once more, but got no answer. The bitter Luis relished this too.

"You are right, Don Ruz. Guessing is idle. Yet how can we help wondering about this mysterious Tinaja? I am sure that you can never have seen so much of the cross out of water. Lolita says—"

"So that's that place," said Genesmere, roughly.

Luis looked inquiring.

"Down there," Genesmere explained, with a jerk of his head back along the road they had come.

Luis was surprised that Don Ruz, who knew this country so well, should never have seen the Tinaja Bonita until to-day.

"I'd have seen it if I'd had any use for it," said Genesmere.

"To be sure, it lay off the road of travel," Luis assented. And of course Don Ruz knew all that was needful—how to find it. He knew what people said—did he not? Father Rafael, Don Ramon, everybody? Lolita perhaps had told him? And that if the cross ever rose entirely above the water, that was a sign all other water-holes in the region were empty. Therefore it was a good warning for travellers, since by it they could judge how much water to carry on a journey. But certainly he and Lolita were surprised to see how low the Tinaja had fallen to-day. No doubt what the Indians said about the great underground snake that came and sucked all the wells dry in the lower country, and in consequence was nearly satisfied before he reached the Tinaja, was untrue.

To this tale of Jesuits and peons the American listened with unexpressed contempt, caring too little to mention that he had heard some of it before, or even to say that in the last few days he had crossed the desert from Tucson and found water on the trail as usual where he expected. He rode on, leading the way slowly up the cañon, suffering the glib Mexican to talk unanswered. His own suppressed feelings still smouldered in his eye, still now and then knotted the muscles in his cheeks; but of Luis's chatter he said his whole opinion in one word, a single English syllable, which he uttered quietly for his own benefit. Luis, however, understood that order of English, and, overhearing, was glad, and commended himself for playing so tellingly the lover who but ill conceals his successes. He would sustain this part to a last delicate finish.

They passed through the hundred corpses to the home and the green trees, where the sun was setting against the little shaking leaves.

"So you will camp here to-night, Don Ruz?" said Luis, perceiving the American's pack-mules. Genesmere had come over from the mines at Gun Sight, found the cabin empty, and followed Lolita's and her cousin's trail, until he had suddenly seen the two from that ledge above the Tinaja. "You are always welcome to what we have at our camp, you know, Don Ruz. All that is mine is yours also. To-night it is probably frijoles. But no doubt you have white flour here." He was giving his pony water from the barrel, and next he threw the saddle on and mounted. "I must be going back, or they will decide I am not coming till to-morrow, and quickly eat my supper." He spoke jauntily from his horse, arm akimbo, natty short jacket put on for to-day's courting, gray steeple-hat silver-embroidered, a spruce pretty boy, not likely to toil severely at wood contracts so long as he could hold soul and body together and otherwise be merry, and the hand of that careless arm soft on his pistol, lest Don Ruz should abruptly dislike him too much; for Luis contrived a tone for his small-talk that would have disconcerted the most sluggish, sweet to his own mischievous ears, healing to his galled self-esteem. "Good-night, Don Ruz. Good-night, Lolita. Perhaps I shall come to-morrow, mañana en la mañana."

"Good-night," said Lolita, harshly, which increased his joy; "I cannot stop you from passing my house."

Genesmere said nothing, but sat still on his white horse, hands folded upon

the horns of his saddle, and Luis, always engaging and at ease, ambled away with his song about the hunchback. He knew that the American was not the man to wait until his enemy's back was turned.

"El telele se murió
A enterrar ya le llevan—"

The tin-pan Mexican voice was empty of melody and full of rhythm.

"Ay! Ay! Ay!"

Lolita and Genesmere stood as they had stood, not very near each other, looking after him and his gayety that the sun shone bright upon. The minstrel truly sparkled. His clothes were more elegant than the American's shirt and overalls, and his face luxuriant with thoughtlessness. Like most of his basking Southern breed, he had no visible means of support, and nothing could worry him for longer than three minutes. Frijoles do not come high, out-of-doors is good enough to sleep in if you or your friend have no roof, and it is not a hard thing to sell some other man's horses over the border and get a fine coat and hat.

"Cinco dragones y un cabo,
Oh, no no no no no!
Y un gato de sacristan."

Coat and hat were getting up the cañon's side among the cactus, the little horse climbing the trail shrewdly with his light-weight rider; and dusty unmusical Genesmere and sullen Lolita watched them till they went behind a bend, and nothing remained but the tin-pan song singing in Genesmere's brain. The gadfly had stung more poisonously than he knew, and still Lolita and Genesmere stood watching nothing, while the sun— the sun of Arizona at the day's transfigured immortal passing—became a crimson coal in a lake of saffron, burning and beating like a heart, till the desert seemed no longer dead, but only asleep, and breathing out wide rays of rainbow color that rose and expanded over earth and sky.

Then Genesmere spoke his first volunteered word to Lolita. "I didn't shoot because I was afraid of hitting you," he said.

So now she too realized clearly. He had got off his horse above the Tinaja to kill Luis during that kiss. Complete innocence had made her stupid and slow.

"GOOD-NIGHT! PERHAPS I SHALL COME TO-MORROW."

"Are you going to eat?" she inquired.

"Oh yes. I guess I'll eat."

She set about the routine of fire-lighting and supper as if it had been Uncle Ramon, and this evening like all evenings. He, not so easily, and with small blunderings that he cursed, attended to his horse and mules, coming in at length to sit against the wall where she was cooking.

"It is getting dark," said Lolita. So he found the lamp and lighted it, and sat down again.

"I've never hurt a woman," he said presently, the vision of his rifle's white front sight held steady on the two below the ledge once more flooding his brain. He spoke slowly.

"Then you have a good chance now," said Lolita, quickly, busy over her cooking. In her Southern ears such words sounded a threat. It was not in her blood to comprehend this Northern way of speaking and walking and sitting, and being one thing outside and another inside.

"And I wouldn't hurt a woman"—he was hardly talking to her—"not if I could think in time."

"Men do it," she said, with the same defiance. "But it makes talk."

"Talk's nothing to me," said Genesmere, flaming to fierceness. "Do I care for opinions? Only my own." The fierceness passed from his face, and he was remote from her again. Again he fell to musing aloud, changing from Mexican to his mother-tongue. "I wouldn't want to have to remember a thing like that." He stretched himself, and leaned his elbows on his knees and his head in his hands, the yellow hair hiding his fingers. She had often seen him do this when he felt lazy; it was not a sign by which she could read a spiritual standstill, a quivering wreck of faith and passion. "I have to live a heap of my life alone," the lounger went on. "Journey alone. Camp alone. Me and my mules. And I don't propose to have thoughts a man should be ashamed of." Lolita was throwing a cloth over the table and straightening it. "I'm twenty-five, and I've laid by no such thoughts yet. Church folks might say different."

"It is ready," said Lolita, finishing her preparations.

He looked up, and seeing the cloth and the places set, pulled his chair to the table, and passively took the food she brought him. She moved about the room between shelves and fire, and when she had served him, seated herself at leisure to begin her own supper. Uncle Ramon was a peon of some substance, doing business in towns and living comparatively well. Besides the shredded spiced stew of meat, there were several dishes for supper. Genesmere ate the meal deliberately, attending to his plate and cup, and Lolita was as silent as himself, only occasionally looking at him; and in time his thoughts came to the surface again in words. He turned and addressed Lolita in Mexican: "So, you see, you saved his life down there."

She laid her fork down and gave a laugh, hard and harsh; and she said nothing, but waited for what next.

"You don't believe that. You don't know that. He knows that."

She laughed again, more briefly.

"You can tell him so. From me."

Replies seemed to struggle together on Lolita's lips and hinder each other's escaping.

"And you can tell him another thing. He wouldn't have stopped. He'd have shot. Say that. From me. He'd have shot, because he's a Spaniard, like you."

"You lie!" This side issue in some manner set free the girl's tongue. "I am not Spanish. I care nothing for Spaniards or what they may do. I am Mexican, and I waited to see you kill him. I wanted to watch his blood. But you! you listened to his false talk, and believed him, and let him go. I save his life? Go after him now! Do it with this knife, and tell him it is Lolita's. But do not sit there and talk any more. I have had enough of men's talk to-day. Enough, enough, enough!"

Genesmere remained in his chair, while she had risen to her feet. "I suppose," he said, very slowly, "that folks like you folks can't understand about love—not about the kind I mean."

Lolita's two hands clinched the edge of the table, and she called upon her gods.

"Believe it, then! Believe it! And kill me, if that will make you contented. But do not talk any more. Yes, he told me that he loved me. Yes, I kissed him; I have kissed him hundreds of times, always, since before I can remember. And I had been laughing at him to-day, having nothing in my heart but you. All day it had rejoiced me to hear his folly and think of you, and think how little he knew, and how you would come soon. But your folly is worse. Kill me in this house to-night, and I will tell you, dying, that I love you, and that it is you who are the fool."

She looked at her lover, and seeing his face and eyes she had sought to bring before her in the days that she had waited for him, she rushed to him.

"Lolita!" he whispered. "Lolita!"

But she could only sob as she felt his arms and his lips. And when presently he heard her voice again murmuring brokenly to him in the way that he knew and had said over in his mind and dwelt upon through the desert stages he had ridden, he trembled, and with savage triumph drew her close, and let his doubt and the thoughts that had chilled and changed him sink deep beneath the flood of this present rapture. "My life!" she said. "Toda mi vida. All my life!" Through the open door the air of the cañon blew cool into the little room that the fire and the lamp oppressed, and in time they grew aware of the endless rustling of the trees, and went out and stood in the darkness together, until it ceased to be darkness, and their eyes could discern the near and distant shapes of their world. The sky was black and splendid, with four or five planets too bright for lesser stars to show, and the promontories of the keen mountains shone almost as in moonlight. A certain hill down towards the Tinaja and its slate ledge caught Genesmere's eye, and Lolita felt him shudder, and she wound her arm more tightly about him.

"What is it?" she said.

"Nothing." He was staring at the hill. "Nothing," he replied to himself.

"Dreamer, come!" said Lolita, pulling him. "It is cold here in the night—and if you choose to forget, I choose you shall remember."

"What does this girl want now?"

"The cards! our cards!"

"Why, to be sure!" He ran after her,

and joy beat in her heart at the fleet kiss
he tried for and half missed. She escaped
into the room, laughing for delight at her
lover's being himself again—his own right
self that she talked with always in the
long days she waited alone.

"Take it!" she cried out, putting the
guitar at him so he should keep his distance. "There! now you have broken
it, songless Americano! You shall buy
me another." She flung the light instrument, that fell in a corner with a loud
complaint of all the strings together, col-
lapsing to a blurred hollow humming, and
silence.

"Now you have done it!" said Genesmere, mock serious.

"I don't care. I am glad. He played
on that to-day. He can have it, and you
shall give me a new one. 'Yo soy purita
mejicana; nada tengo español,'" sang the
excited, breathless Lolita to her American, and seated herself at the table, beginning a brisk shuffle of a dim, dog-eared
pack. "You sit there!" She nodded to
the opposite side of the table. "Very
well, move the lamp, then." Genesmere
had moved it because it hid her face from
him. "He thinks I cheat! Now, Señor
Don Ruz, it shall be for the guitar. Do
you hear?"

"Too many pesos, señorita."

"Oh, oh! the miser!"

"I'm not going broke on any señori-
tas—not even my own girl!"

"Have you no newer thing than poverty to tell me? Now if you look at me
like that I cannot shuffle properly."

"How am I to look, please?" He held
his glance on her.

"Not foolish like a boy. There, take
them, then!" She threw the cards at him,
blushing and perturbed by his eyes, while
he scrambled to punish her across the table.

"Generous one!" she said. "Ardent
pretender! He won't let me shuffle because he fears to lose."

"You shall have a silk handkerchief
with flowers on it," said he, shuffling.

"I have two already. I can see you
arranging those cards, miser!"

It was the custom of their meetings,
whether at the cabin or whether she stole
out to his camp, to play for the token he
should bring for her when he next came
from town. She named one thing, he
some other, and the cards judged between
them. And to see Genesmere in these

hours, his oldest friend could not have
known him any more than he knew himself. Never had a woman been for him
like Lolita, conjuring the Saxon to forget
himself and bask openly in that Southern joy and laughter of the moment.

"Say my name!" he ordered; and at
the child effort she made over "Russ" he
smiled with delight. "Again!" he exclaimed, bending to catch her R and the
whole odd little word she made. "More!"

"No," pouted the girl, and beat at him,
blushing again.

"Make your bet!" he said, laying out
the Mexican cards before him. "Quick!
Which shall it be?"

"The caballo. Oh, my dear, I wanted
to die this afternoon, and now I am so
happy!"

It brought the tears to her eyes, and
almost to his, till he suddenly declared
she had stolen a card, and with that they
came to soft blows and laughing again.
So did the two sit and wrangle, seizing
the pack out of turn, feigning rage at
being cheated, until he juggled to make
her win three times out of five; and when
chance had thus settled for the guitar,
they played for kisses, and so forgot the
cards at last. And at last Genesmere began to speak of the next time, and Lolita
to forbid such talk as that so soon. She
laid her hand over his lips, at which he
yielded for a little, and she improvised
questions of moment to ask him, without
time for stopping, until she saw that this
would avail no longer. Then she sighed,
and let him leave her to see to his animals, while she lighted the fire again to
make breakfast for him. At that parting
meal an anxiety slowly came in her face,
and it was she that broke their silence
after a while.

"Which road do you go this time,
querido?" she asked.

"Tucson, Maricopa, and then straight
here to you."

"From Maricopa? That is longer across
the desert."

"Shorter to my girl."

"I—I wish you would not come that
way."

"Why?"

"That—that desert!"

"There's desert both ways—all ways.
The other road puts an extra week between you and me."

"Yes, yes. I have counted."

"What is all this, Lolita?"

Once more she hesitated, smiling uneasily beneath his scrutiny. "Yo no sé. I don't know. You will laugh. You do not believe the things that I believe. The Tinaja Bonita—"

"That again!"

"Yes," she half whispered. "I am afraid."

He looked at her steadily.

"Return the same road by Tucson," she urged. "That way is only half so much desert, and you can carry water from Poso Blanco. Do not trust the Coyote Wells. They are little and shallow, and if the Black Cross— Oh, my darling, if you do not believe, do this for me because you love me, love me!"

He did not speak at once. The two had risen, and stood by the open door, where the dawn was entering and mixing with the lamp. "Because I love you," he repeated at length, slowly, out of his uncertain thoughts.

She implored him, and he studied her in silence.

Suddenly hardness stamped his face. "I'll come by Tucson, then—since I love you!" And he walked at once out of the door. She followed him to his horse, and there reached up and pulled him round to her, locking her fingers behind his neck. Again his passion swept him and burned the doubt from his eyes. "I believe you love me!" he broke out.

"Ah, why need you say that?"

"Adios, chiquita." He was smiling, and she looked at his white teeth and golden mustache. She felt his hands begin to unlock her own.

"Not yet—not yet!"

"Adios, chiquita."

"O mi querido!" she murmured; "with you I forget day and night!"

"Bastante!" He kissed her once for all.

"Good-by! good-by! Mis labios van estar frios hasta que tu los toques otra vez. My lips will be cold until you touch them again."

He caught her two hands, as if to cling to something. "Say that once more. Tell me that once more."

She told him with all her heart and soul, and he sprang into his saddle. She went beside him through the cold pale-lighted trees to the garden's edge, and there stood while he took his way across the barren ground among the carcasses. She watched the tip of his mustache that came beyond the line of his cheek, and when he was further, his whole strong figure, while the clack of the hoofs on the dead ground grew fainter. When the steeper fall of the cañon hid him from her she ran to the house, and from its roof among her peppers she saw him come into sight again below, the wide foreshortened slant of ground between them, the white horse and dark rider and the mules, until they became a mere line of something moving, and so vanished into the increasing day.

Genesmere rode, and took presently to smoking. Coming to a sandy place, he saw prints of feet and of a shod horse in the trail heading the other way. That was his own horse, and the feet were Lolita's and Luis's—the record and the memory of yesterday afternoon. He looked up from the trail to the hills, now lambent with violet and shifting orange, and their shapes as they moved out into his approaching view were the shapes of yesterday afternoon. He came soon to the forking of the trails, one for Tucson, and the other leading down into the lumpy country, and here again were the prints in the sand, the shod horse, the man and the woman, coming in from the lumpy country that lay to the left; and Genesmere found himself stock-still by the forking trails, looking at his watch. His many-journeyed mules knew which was the Tucson trail, and not understanding why he turned them from their routine, walked asunder, puzzled at being thus driven in the wrong direction. They went along a strange up-and-down path, loose with sliding stones, and came to an end at a ledge of slate, and stood about on the tricky footing looking at their master and leaning their heads together. The master sat quiet on his horse, staring down where a circular pool lay below; and the sun rose everywhere, except in his mind. So far had he come yesterday with that mind easy over his garnered prosperity, free and soaring on its daily flight among the towers of his hopes— those constructions that are common with men who grow fond: the air-castle rises and reaches, possessing the architect, who cherishes its slow creation with hourly changes and additions to the plan. A house was part of Genesmere's castle, a home with a wife inside, and no more camping alone. Thus far, to this exact ledge, the edifice had gone forward fortunately, and then a blast had crumbled house and days to come into indistinguishable dust. The heavy echo jarred in Genesmere, now that he had been lured to look again upon the site of the disaster, and a lightning violence crossed his face. He saw the two down there as they had stood, the man with his arms holding the woman, before the falling stone had startled them. Were the Mexican present now in the flesh, he would destroy him just for what he had tried to do. If she were true— She was true—that was no thanks to the Mexican. Genesmere was sorry second thoughts had spared that fellow yesterday, and he looked at his watch again. It was time to be starting on the Tucson trail, and the mules alertly turned their steps from the Tinaja Bonita. They could see no good in having come here. Evidently it was not to get water. Why, then? What use was there in looking down a place into a hole? The mules gave it up. Genesmere himself thought the Tinaja poorly named. It was not pretty. In his experience of trail and cañon he knew no other such hole. He was not aware of the twin, dried up, thirty yards below, and therefore only half knew the wonders of the spot.

He rode back to the forks across the rolling steepness, rebuilding the castle; then, discovering something too distant to be sure about, used his glass quickly. It was another rider, also moving slowly among the knolls and gullies of the mesa, and Genesmere could not make him out. He was going towards the cabin, but it was not the same horse that Luis had ridden yesterday. This proved nothing, and it would be easy to circle and see the man closer—only not worth the trouble. Let the Mexican go to the cabin. Let him go every day. He probably would, if she permitted. Most likely she would tell him to keep away from her. She ought to. She might hurt him if he annoyed her. She was a good shot with a pistol. But women work differently from men—and then she was Mexican. She might hide her feelings and make herself pleasant for three weeks. She would tell him when he returned, and they would laugh together over how she had fooled this Luis. After all, shooting would have been too much punishment. A man with a girl like Lolita must expect to find other men after her. It depends on your girl.

You find that out when you go after other men's girls. When a woman surely loves some other man she will not look at you. And Lolita's love was a sure thing. A woman can say love and a man will believe her—until he has experienced the genuine article once; after that he can always tell. And to have a house, with her inside waiting for you! Such a turn was strange luck for a man, not to be accounted for. If anybody had said last year—why, as late as the 20th of last March—that settling down was what you were coming to—and now— Genesmere wondered how he could ever have seen anything in riding a horse up and down the earth and caring nothing for what next. "No longer alone!" he said aloud, suddenly, and surprised the white horse.

The song about the hunchback and the sacristan's cat stirred its rhythm in his mind. He was not a singer, but he could think the tune, trace it, naked of melody, in the dry realm of the brain. And it was a diversion to piece out the gait of the phantom notes, low after high, quick after slow, until they went of themselves. Lolita would never kiss Luis again; would never want to — not even as a joke. Genesmere turned his head back to take another look at the rider, and there stood the whole mountains like a picture, and himself far out in the flat country, and the bare sun in the sky. He had come six miles on the road since he had last noticed. Six miles, and the air-castle was rebuilt and perfect, with no difference from the old one except its foundation, which was upon sand. To see the unexpected plain around him, and the islands of blue sharp peaks lying in it, drove the tune from his head, and he considered the well-known country, reflecting that man could not be meant to live here. The small mountain-islands lay at all distances, blue in a dozen ways, amid the dead calm of this sand archipelago. They rose singly from it, sheer and sudden, toothed and triangled like icebergs, hot as stoves. The channels to the north, Santa Rosa way, opened broad and yellow, and ended without shore upon the clean horizon, and to the south narrowed with lagoons into Sonora. Genesmere could just see one top of the Sierra de la Quitabac jutting up from below the earthline, splitting the main channel, the faintest blue of all. They could be having no trouble over their water down there, with

the Laguna Esperanca and the Poso de
Mazis. Genesmere killed some more of
the way rehearsing the trails and water-
holes of this country, known to him like
his pocket; and by-and-by food-cooking
and mule-feeding and the small machine
repetitions of a camp and a journey
brought the Quijotoa Mountains behind
him to replace Gun Sight and the Sierra
de la Naril; and later still the Cababi hid
the Quijotoa, and Genesmere counted days

now noticed steadily running in his head
again, beneath the random surface of his
thoughts. "Cinco dragones y un cabo y
un gato de sacristan." That made no
sense either; but Mexicans found something in it. Liked it. Now American
songs had some sense:

"They bathed his head in vinegar
  To fetch him up to time,
And now he drives a mule team on
  The Denver City line."

"BUSINESS AND PLEASURE WERE WAITING IN TUCSON."

and nights to the good, and was at the
Coyote Wells.

These were holes in rocks, but shallow,
as Lolita said. No shallower than ordinary, however; he would see on the way
back if they gave signs of failing. No
wonder if they did, with this spell of
drought—but why mix up a plain thing
with a lot of nonsense about a black cross
down a hole? Genesmere was critically
struck with the words of the tune he

A man could understand that. A proud
stage-driver makes a mistake about a female passenger. Thinks he has got an
heiress, and she turns out to peddle sarsa-
parilla. "So he's naturally used up,"
commented Genesmere. "You estimate
a girl as one thing, and she—" Here the
undercurrent welled up, breaking the surface. "Did she mean that? Was that
her genuine reason?" In memory he took
a look at his girl's face, and repeated her

words when she besought him to come the longer way and hesitated over why. Was that shame at owning she believed such stuff? True, after asking him once about his religion and hearing what he said, she had never spoken of these things again. That must be a woman's way when she loved you first—to hide her notions that differed from yours, and not ruffle happy days. "Return the same road by Tucson!" He unwrapped a clean, many-crumpled handkerchief, and held Lolita's photograph for a while. Then he burst into an unhappy oath, and folded the picture up again. What if her priest did tell her? He had heard the minister tell about eternal punishment when he was a boy, and just as soon as he started thinking it over he knew it was a lie. And this quack Tinaja was worse foolishness, and had nothing to do with religion. Lolita afraid of his coming to grief in a country he had travelled hundreds, thousands of miles in! Perhaps she had never started thinking for herself yet. But she had. She was smarter than any girl of her age he had ever seen. She did not want him back so soon. That was what it was. Yet she had looked true; her voice had sounded that way. Again he dwelt upon her words and caresses; and harboring these various thoughts, he killed still more of the long road, until, passing after a while Poso Blanco, and later Marsh's ranch-well at the forks where the Sonora road comes in, he reached Tucson a man divided against himself. Divided beyond his will into two selves—one of faith besieged, and one of besieging inimical reason—the inextricable error!

Business and pleasure were waiting in Tucson, and friends whose ways and company had not been of late for him; but he frequented them this time, tasting no pleasure, yet finding the ways and company better than his own. After the desert's changeless unfathomed silence, in which nothing new came day or night to break the fettering spell his mind was falling under, the clink and knocking of bottles was good to hear, and he listened for more, craving any sound that might wake him from his looming doubt. Abstaining himself, he moved his chair near others who sat lively in saloons. His boots, that for days had trod upon the unwatered earth beneath sun and stars, stepped now in spilled liquids on floors, and so beneath a roof among tobacco

smoke he hid himself from the exorcism of the desert. Later the purring tinkle of guitars reminded him of that promised present, and the next morning he was the owner of the best instrument that he could buy. Leaving it with a friend to keep until he should come through again from Maricopa, he departed that way with his mules, finding in the new place the same sort of friends and business, and by night looking upon the same untasted pleasures. He went about town with some cattlemen, carousing bankrupts, who remembered their ruin in the middle of whiskey, and broke off to curse it and the times and climate, and their starved herds that none would buy at any price. Genesmere touched nothing, yet still drew his chair among these drinkers.

"Aren't you feeling good to-night, Russ?" asked one at length.

And Genesmere's eyes roused from seeing visions, and his ears became aware of the loud company. In Tucson he had been able to sit in the smoke, and compass a cheerful deceit of appearance even to himself. Choosing and buying the guitar had lent reality to his imitated peace of mind; he had been careful over its strings, selecting such as Lolita preferred, wrapt in carrying out this spiritual forgery of another Genesmere. But here they had noticed him; appearances had slipped from him. He listened to a piece of late Arizona news some one was in the middle of telling—the trial of several Mormons for robbing a paymaster near Cedar Springs. This was the fourth time he had heard the story, because it was new; but the present narrator dwelt upon the dodgings of a witness, a negress, who had seen everything and told nothing, outwitting the government, furnishing no proofs. This brought Genesmere quite bald.

"No proofs!" he muttered. "No proofs!" He laughed and became alert. "She lied to them good, did she?"

They looked at him, because he had not spoken for so long; and he was told that she had certainly lied good.

"Fooled them clean through, did she? On oath! Tell about her."

The flattered narrator, who had been in court, gave all he knew, and Genesmere received each morsel of perjury gravely with a nod. He sat still when the story was done.

"Yes," he said, after a time. "Yes."

"YOU DON'T WANT TO TALK THIS WAY. YOU'RE ALONE."

And again, "Yes." Then he briefly bade the boys good-night, and went out from the lamps and whiskey into the dark.

He walked up and down alone, round the corral where his mules stood, round the stable where his bed-blankets were; and one or two carousers came by, who suggested further enjoyments to him. He went to the edge of the town and walked where passers would not meet him, turning now and then to look in the direction of Tucson, where the guitar was waiting. When he felt the change of dawn he went to the stable, and by the first early gray had his mules packed. He looked once again towards Tucson, and took the road he had promised not to take, leaving the guitar behind him altogether. Besieged faith scarcely stirred in protest, starved in the citadel; victorious, well-fed reason hit upon the mockery that he had "come by Tucson," according to his literal word. It is a comfort to be divided no longer against one's self. Genesmere was at ease in his thraldom to the demon with whom he had wrestled through the dark hours. As the day brightened he wondered how he had come to fool a night away over a promise such as that. He took out the face in the handkerchief, and gave it a curious defiant smile. She had said waiting would be long. She should have him quickly. And he was going to know about that visitor at the cabin, the steeple-hatted man he saw in his visions. So Maricopa drew behind him, small, clear-grouped in the unheated morning, and the sun found the united man and his mules moving into the desert.

By the well in the bottom of the Santa Cruz River he met with cattle and little late-born calves trying to trot. Their mothers, the foreman explained, had not milk enough for them, nor the cursed country food or water for the mothers. They could not chew cactus. These animals had been driven here to feed and fatten inexpensively, and get quick money for the owner. But, instead, half of them had died, and the men were driving the rest to new pastures, as many, that is, as could still walk. Genesmere knew, the foreman supposed, that this well was the last for more than a hundred miles? Funny to call a thing like that Santa Cruz a river! Well, it was an Arizona river; all right enough, no doubt, somewhere a thousand feet or so underground.

Pity you weren't a prairie-dog that eats sand when he gets a thirst on him. Got any tobacco? Good-by.

Think of any valleys that you know between high mountains. Such was southern Arizona once—before we came. Then fill up your valleys with sand until the mountains show no feet or shoulders, but become as men buried to the neck. That is what makes separate islands of their protruding peaks, and that is why water slinks from the surface whenever it can and flows useless underneath, entombed in the original valley. This is Arizona now—since the pterodactyls have gone. Nor does no rain to speak of for three years help things. In such a place the traveller turns mariner, only, instead of the stars, he studies the water-wells, shaping his course by these. Not sea-gulls, but ravens, fly over this waste, seeking their meal. Some were in front of Genesmere now, settled black in the recent trail of the cattle. He did not much care that the last well was gone by, for he was broken in by long travel to the water of the 'dobe-holes that people rely upon through this journey. These 'dobe-holes are occasional wallows in clayey spots, and men and cattle know each one. The cattle, of course, roll in them, and they become worn into circular hollows, their edges tramped into muck, and surrounded by a thicket belt of mesquite. The water is not good, but will save life. The first one lay two stages from the well, and Genesmere accordingly made an expected dry camp the first night, carrying water from the well in the Santa Cruz, and dribbling all of it but a cupful among his animals, and the second night reached his calculated 'dobe-hole. The animals rolled luxuriously in the brown dungy mixture, and Genesmere made his coffee strong. He had had no shade at the first camp, and here it was good under the tangle of the mesquite, and he slept sound. He was early awakened by the ravens, whose loose dislocated croaking came from where they sat at breakfast on the other side of the wallow. They had not suspected his presence among the mesquite, and when he stepped to the mud-hole and dipped its gummy fluid in his coffee-pot they rose hoarse and hovering, and flapped twenty yards away, and sat watching until he was gone into the desert, when they clouded back again round their carrion.

This day was over ground yellow and hard with dearth, until afternoon brought a footing of sifting sand heavy to travel in. He had plenty of time for thinking. His ease after the first snapping from his promise had changed to an eagerness to come unawares and catch the man in the steeple-hat. Till that there could be no proofs. Genesmere had along the road nearly emptied his second canteen of its brown-amber drink, wetting the beasts' tongues more than his own. The neighborhood of the next 'dobe-hole might be known by the three miles of cactus you went through before coming on it, a wide-set plantation of the yucca. The posted plants deployed over the plain in strange extended order like legions and legions of figures, each shock-head of spears bunched bristling at the top of its lank, scaly stalk, and out of that stuck the blossom-pole, a pigtail on end, with its knot of bell-flowers seeded to pods ten feet in the air. Genesmere's horse started and nearly threw him, but it was only a young calf lying for shade by a yucca. Genesmere could tell from its unlicked hide that the mother had gone to hunt water, and been away for some time. This unseasonable waif made a try at running away, but fell in a heap, and lay as man and mules passed on. Presently he passed a sentinel cow. She stood among the thorns guarding the calves of her sisters till they should return from getting their water. The desert cattle learn this shift, and the sentinel now, at the stranger's approach, lowered her head, and with a feeble but hostile sound made ready to protect her charge, keeping her face to the passing enemy. Further along gaunt cows stood or lay under the perpetual yuccas, an animal to every plant. They stared at Genesmere passing on; some rose to look after him; some lifted their heads from the ground, and seeing, laid them down again. He came upon a calf watching its mother, who had fallen in such a position that the calf could not suck. The cow's fore leg was caught over her own head, and so she held herself from rising. The sand was rolled and grooved into a wheel by her circlings; her body heaved and fell with breathing, and the sand was wet where her pivot nostrils had ground it. While Genesmere untangled her and gave her tongue the last of his canteen the calf walked round and round. He placed the cow upon her feet, and as soon

as he moved away to his horse the calf came to its mother, who began to lick it. He presently marked ahead the position of the coming 'dobe-hole by the ravens assembled in the air, continually rising and lighting. The white horse and mules quickened their step, and the trail became obliterated by hundreds of hoof-marks leading to the water. As a spider looks in the centre of an empty web, so did the round wallow sit in the middle of the plain, with threaded feet conducting from everywhere to it. Mules and white horse scraped through the scratching mesquite, and the ravens flapped up. To Genesmere their croaking seemed suddenly to fill all space with loud total clamor, for no water was left, only mud. He eased the animals of their loads and saddles, and they rolled in the stiff mud, squeezing from it a faint ooze, and getting a sort of refreshment. Genesmere chewed the mud, and felt sorry for the beasts. He turned both canteens upside down and licked the bungs. A cow had had his last drink. Well, that would keep her alive several hours more. Hardly worth while; but spilled milk decidedly. Milk! That was an idea. He caught animal after animal, and got a few sickly drops. There was no gain in camping at this spot, no water for coffee; so Genesmere moved several hundred yards away to be rid of the ravens and their all-day-long meal and the smell. He lay thinking what to do. Go back? At the rate he could push the animals now that last hole might be used up by the cattle before he got there—and then it was two stages more to the Santa Cruz well. And the man would be gaining just so many more days unhindered at the cabin. Out of the question. Forward, it was one shortish drive to the next hole. If that were dry, he could forsake the trail and make a try by a short-cut for that Tinaja place. And he must start soon, too, as soon as the animals could stand it, and travel by night and rest when the sun got bad. What business had October to be hot like this? So in the darkness he mounted again, and noon found him with eyes shut under a yucca. It was here that he held a talk with Lolita. They were married, and sitting in a room with curtains that let you see flowers growing outside by the window, as he had always intended. Lolita said to him that there was no fool like an old fool, and he was telling her that love could make a man more a fool than age, when she threw the door open, letting in bright light, and said, "No proofs." The bright light was the real sun coming round the yucca on his face, and he sat up and saw the desert. No cows were here, but he noticed the roughened hides and sunk eyes of his own beasts, and spoke to them.

"Cheer up, Jeff! Stonewall!" He stopped at the pain. It was in his lips and mouth. He put up his hand, and the feel of his tongue frightened him. He looked round to see what country he was in, and noted the signs that it was not so very far now. The blue crags of the islands were showing, and the blue sterile sky spread over them and the ceaseless sunlight like a plague. Man and horse and mules were the only life in the naked bottom of this caldron. The mirage had caught the nearest island, and blunted and dissolved its points and frayed its base away to a transparent fringe.

"Like a lump of sugar melts in hot tod," remarked Genesmere, aloud, and remembered his thickened mouth again. "I can stand it off for a while yet, though —if they can travel." His mules looked at him when he came—looked when he tightened their cinches. "I know, Jeff," he said, and inspected the sky. "No heaven's up there. Nothing's back of that thing, unless it's hell."

He got the animals going, and the next 'dobe-hole was like the last, and busy with the black flapping of the birds. "You didn't fool me," said Genesmere, addressing the mud. "I knew you'd be dry." His eye ran over the cattle, that lay in various conditions. "That foreman was not too soon getting his live-stock out of your country," he continued to the hole, his tongue clacking as it made his words. "This live-stock here's not enjoying itself like its owners in town. This live-stock was intended for Eastern folks' dinner.—But you've got ahead of 'em this trip," he said to the ravens. He laughed loudly, and hearing himself, stopped, and his face became stern. "You don't want to talk this way, Russ Genesmere. Shut your head. You're alone. —I wish I'd never known!" he suddenly cried out.

He went to his animals and sat down by them, clasping and unclasping his hands. The mules were lying down on the baked mud of the wallow with their loads

on, and he loosed them. He stroked his white horse for some little while, thinking; and it was in his heart that he had brought these beasts into this scrape. It was sunset and cool. Against the divine fires of the west the peaks towered clear in splendor impassive, and forever aloof, and the universe seemed to fill with infinite sadness. "If she'll tell me it's not so," he said, "I'll believe her. I will believe her now. I'll make myself. She'll help me to." He took what rest he dared, and started up from it much later than he had intended, having had the talk with Lolita again in the room with the curtains. It was nine when he set out for the short-cut under the moon, dazed by his increasing torture. The brilliant disk, blurring to the eye, showed the mountains unearthly plain, beautiful, and tall in the night. By-and-by a mule fell and could not rise, and Genesmere decided it was as well for all to rest again. The next he knew it was blazing sunshine, and the sky at the same time bedded invisible in black clouds. And when his hand reached for a cloud that came bellying down to him, it changed into a pretzel, and salt burned in his mouth at the sight of it. He turned away, and saw the hot unshaded mountains wrinkled in the sun, glazed and shrunk, gullied like the parchment of an old man's throat; and then he saw a man in a steeple-hat. He could no more lay the spectre that wasted his mind than the thirst-demon which raged in his body. He shut his eyes, and then his arm was beating at something to keep it away. Pillowed on his saddle, he beat until he forgot. A blow at the corner of his eye brought him up sitting, and a raven jumped from his chest.

"You're not experienced," said Genesmere. "I'm not dead yet. But I'm obliged to you for being so enterprising. You've cleared my head. Quit that talk, Russ Genesmere." He went to the mule that had given out during the night. "Poor Jeff! We must lighten your pack. Now if that hunchback had died here, the birds would have done his business for him without help from any of your cats. Am I saying that, now, or only thinking it? I know I'm alone. I've travelled that way in this world. Why?" He turned his face, expecting some one to answer, and the answer came in a fierce voice: "Because you're a man, and can stand this world off by yourself. You look to no one." He suddenly took out the handkerchief and tore the photograph to scraps. "That's lightened my pack all it needs. Now for these boys, or they'll never make camp." He took what the mules carried, his merchandise, and hid it carefully between stones—for they had come near the mountain country—and looking at the plain he was leaving, he saw a river. "Ha, ha!" he said, slyly; "you're not there, though. And I'll prove it to you." He chose another direction, and saw another flowing river. "I was expecting you," he stated, quietly. "Don't bother me. I'm thirsty."

But presently as he journeyed he saw lying to his right a wide fertile place with fruit trees and water everywhere. "Peaches too!" he sang out, and sprang off to run, but checked himself in five steps. "I don't seem able to stop your foolish talking," he said, "but you shall not chase around like that. You'll stay with me. I tell you that's a sham. Look at it." Obedient, he looked hard at it, and the cactus and rocks thrust through the watery image of the lake like two photographs on the same plate. He shouted with strangling triumph, and continued shouting until brier-roses along a brook and a farm-house unrolled to his left, and he ran half-way there, calling his mother's name. "Why, you fool, she's dead!" He looked slowly at his cut hands, for he had fallen among stones. "Dead, back in Kentucky, ever so long ago," he murmured, softly. "Didn't stay to see you get wicked." Then he grew stern again. "You've showed yourself up, and you can't tell land from water. You're going to let the boys take you straight. I don't trust you."

He started the mules, and caught hold of his horse's tail, and they set out in single file, held steady by their instinct, stumbling ahead for the water they knew among the mountains. Mules led, and the shouting man brought up the rear, clutching the white tail like a rudder, his feet sliding along through the stones. The country grew higher and rougher, and the peaks blazed in the hot sky; slate and sand and cactus below, gaping cracks and funnelled erosions above, rocks like monuments slanting up to the top pinnacles; supreme Arizona, stark and dead in space, like an extinct planet, flooded blind with eternal brightness. The perpetual dominating peaks caught Genesmere's attention. "Toll on!" he cried to them. "Toll on, you tall mountains. What do you care? Summer and winter, night and day, I've known you, and I've heard you all along. A man can't look but he sees you walling God's country from him, ringing away with your knell."

He must have been lying down during some time, for now he saw the full moon again, and his animals near him, and a fire blazing that himself had evidently built. The coffee-pot sat on it, red-hot and split open. He felt almost no suffering at all, but stronger than ever in his life, and he heard something somewhere screaming "water, water, water," fast and unceasing, like an alarm-clock. A rattling of stones made him turn, and there stood a few staring cattle. Instantly he sprang to his feet, and the screaming stopped. "Round 'em up, Russ Genesmere. It's getting late," he yelled, and ran among the cattle, whirling his rope. They dodged weakly this way and that, and next he was on the white horse urging him after the cows, who ran in a circle. One struck the end of a log that stuck out from the fire, splintering the flames and embers, and Genesmere followed on the tottering horse through the sparks, swinging his rope and yelling in the full moon. "Round 'em up! round 'em up! Don't you want to make camp? All the rest of the herd's bedded down along with the ravens."

The white horse fell and threw him by the edge of a round hole, but he did not know it till he opened his eyes and it was light again, and the mountains still tolling. Then like a crash of cymbals the Tinaja beat into his recognition. He knew the slate rock; he saw the broken natural stairs. He plunged down them, arms forward like a diver's, and ground his forehead against the bottom. It was dry. His bloodshot eyes rolled once up round the sheer walls. Yes, it was the Tinaja, and his hands began to tear at the gravel. He flung himself to fresh places, fiercely grubbing with his heels, biting into the sand with his teeth; while above him in the cañon his placid animals lay round the real Tinaja Bonita, having slaked their thirst last night, in time, some thirty yards from where he now lay bleeding and fighting the dust in the dry twin hole.

He heard voices, and put his hands up

to something round his head. He was now lying out in the light, with a cold bandage round his forehead, and a moist rag on his lips.

"Water!" He could just make the whisper.

But Lolita made a sign of silence.

"Water!" he gasped.

She shook her head, smiling, and moistened the rag. That must be all just now.

His eye sought and travelled, and stopped short, dilating; and Lolita screamed at his leap for the living well.

"Not yet! Not yet!" she said in terror, grappling with him. "Help! Luis!"

So this was their plot, the demon told him — to keep him from water! In a frenzy of strength he seized Lolita. "Proved! Proved!" he shouted, and struck his knife into her. She fell at once to the earth and lay calm, eyes wide open, breathing in the bright sun. He rushed to the water and plunged, swallowing and rolling.

Luis ran up from the cows he was gathering, and when he saw what was done, sank by Lolita to support her. She pointed to the pool.

"He is killing himself!" she managed to say, and her head went lower.

"And I'll help you die, caberon! I'll tear your tongue. I'll—"

But Lolita, hearing Luis's terrible words, had raised a forbidding hand. She signed to leave her and bring Genesmere to her.

The distracted Luis went down the stone stairs to kill the American in spite of her, but the man's appearance stopped him. You could not raise a hand against one come to this. The water-drinking was done, and Genesmere lay fainting, head and helpless arms on the lowest stone, body in the water. The Black Cross stood dry above. Luis heard Lolita's voice, and dragged Genesmere to the top as quickly as he could. She, seeing her lover, cried his name once and died; and Luis cast himself on the earth.

"Fool! fool!" he repeated, catching at the ground, where he lay for some while until a hand touched him. It was Genesmere.

"I'm seeing things pretty near straight now," the man said. "Come close. I can't talk well. Was—was that talk of yours, and singing—was that bluff?"

"God forgive me!" said poor Luis.

"You mean forgive me," said Genes-

mere. He lay looking at Lolita. "Close her eyes," he said. And Luis did so. Genesmere was plucking at his clothes, and the Mexican helped him draw out a handkerchief, which the lover unfolded like a treasure. "She used to look like this," he began. He felt and stopped. "Why, it's gone!" he said. He lay evidently seeking to remember where the picture had gone, and his eyes went to the hills whence no help came. Presently Luis heard him speaking, and leaning to hear, made out that he was murmuring his own name, Russ, in the way Lolita had been used to say it. The boy sat speechless, and no thought stirred in his despair as he watched. The American moved over, and put his arms round Lolita, Luis knowing that he must not offer to help him do this. He remained so long that the boy, who would never be a boy again, bent over to see. But it was only another fainting fit. Luis waited; now and then the animals moved among the rocks. The sun crossed the sky, bringing the many-colored evening, and Arizona was no longer terrible, but once more infinitely sad. Luis started, for the American was looking at him and beckoning.

"She's not here," Genesmere said, distinctly.

Luis could not follow.

"Not here, I tell you." The lover touched his sweetheart. "This is not her. My punishment is nothing," he went on, his face growing beautiful. "See there!"

Luis looked where he pointed.

"Don't you see her? Don't you see her fixing that camp for me? We're going to camp together now."

But these were visions alien to Luis, and he stared helpless, anxious to do anything that the man might desire. Genesmere's face darkened wistfully.

"Am I not making camp?" he said.

Luis nodded to please him, without at all comprehending.

"You don't see her." Reason was warring with the departing spirit until the end. "Well, maybe you're right. I never was sure. But I'm mortal tired of travelling alone. I hope—"

That was the end, and Russ Genesmere lay still beside his sweetheart. It was a black evening at the cabin, and a black day when Luis and old Ramon raised and fenced the wooden head-stone, with its two forlorn names.

THE CHINAGO
by Jack London

"The coral waxes, the palm grows, but man departs."—*Tahitian proverb.*

AH CHO did not understand French. He sat in the crowded court-room, very weary and bored, listening to the unceasing, explosive French that now one official and now another uttered. It was just so much gabble to Ah Cho, and he marvelled at the stupidity of the Frenchmen who took so long to find out the murderer of Chung Ga, and who did not find him at all. The five hundred coolies on the plantation knew that Ah San had done the killing, and here was Ah San not even arrested. It was true that all the coolies had agreed secretly not to testify against one another; but then, it was so simple, the Frenchmen should have been able to discover that Ah San was the man. They were very stupid, these Frenchmen.

Ah Cho had done nothing of which to be afraid. He had had no hand in the killing. It was true he had been present at it, and Schemmer, the overseer on the plantation, had rushed into the barracks immediately afterward and caught him there, along with four or five others; but what of that? Chung Ga had been stabbed only twice. It stood to reason that five or six men could not inflict two stab-wounds. At the most, if a man had struck but once, only two men could have done it.

So it was that Ah Cho reasoned, when he, along with his four companions, had lied and blocked and obfuscated in their statements to the court concerning what had taken place. They had heard the sounds of the killing, and, like Schemmer, they had run to the spot. They had got there before Schemmer—that was all. True, Schemmer had testified that, attracted by the sound of quarrelling as he chanced to pass by, he had stood for at least five minutes outside; that then, when he entered, he found the prisoners already inside; and that they had not

entered just before, because he had been standing by the one door to the barracks. But what of that? Ah Cho and his four fellow prisoners had testified that Schemmer was mistaken. In the end they would be let go. They were all confident of that. Five men could not have their heads cut off for two stab-wounds. Besides, no foreign devil had seen the killing. But these Frenchmen were so stupid. In China, as Ah Cho well knew, the magistrate would order all of them to the torture and learn the truth. The truth was very easy to learn under torture. But these Frenchmen did not torture—bigger fools they! Therefore they would never find out who killed Chung Ga.

But Ah Cho did not understand everything. The English Company that owned the plantation had imported into Tahiti, at great expense, the five hundred coolies. The stockholders were clamoring for dividends, and the Company had not yet paid any; wherefore the Company did not want its costly contract laborers to start the practice of killing one another. Also, there were the French, eager and willing to impose upon the Chinagos the virtues and excellences of French law. There was nothing like setting an example once in a while; and, besides, of what use was New Caledonia except to send men to live out their days in misery and pain in payment of the penalty for being frail and human?

Ah Cho did not understand all this. He sat in the court-room and waited for the baffled judgment that would set him and his comrades free to go back to the plantation and work out the terms of their contracts. This judgment would soon be rendered. Proceedings were drawing to a close. He could see that. There was no more testifying, no more gabble of tongues. The French devils were tired, too, and evidently waiting for the judgment. And as he waited he remembered back in his life to the time when he had signed the contract and set sail in the ship for Tahiti. Times had been hard in his seacoast village, and when he indentured himself to labor for five years in the South Seas at fifty cents Mexican a day, he had thought himself fortunate. There were men in his village who toiled a whole year for ten dollars Mexican, and there were women who made nets all the year round for five dollars, while in the houses of shopkeepers there were maid servants who received four dollars for a year of service. And here he was to receive fifty cents a day; for one day, only one day, he was to receive that princely sum! What if the work were hard? At the end of the five years he would return home—that was in the contract—and he would never have to work again. He would be a rich man for life, with a house of his own, a wife, and children growing up to venerate him. Yes, and back of the house he would have a small garden, a place of meditation and repose, with goldfish in a tiny lakelet, and wind-bells tinkling in the several trees, and there would be a high wall all around so that his meditation and repose should be undisturbed.

Well, he had worked out three of those five years. He was already a wealthy man (in his own country), through his earnings, and only two years more intervened between the cotton plantation on Tahiti and the meditation and repose that awaited him. But just now he was losing money because of the unfortunate accident of being present at the killing of Chung Ga. He had lain three weeks in prison, and for each day of those three weeks he had lost fifty cents. But now judgment would soon be given and he would go back to work.

Ah Cho was twenty-two years old. He was happy and good-natured, and it was easy for him to smile. While his body was slim in the Asiatic way, his face was rotund. It was round, like the moon, and it irradiated a gentle complacence and a sweet kindliness of spirit that was unusual among his countrymen. Nor did his looks belie him. He never caused trouble, never took part in wrangling. He did not gamble. His soul was not harsh enough for the soul that must belong to a gambler. He was content with little things and simple pleasures. The hush and quiet in the cool of the day after the blazing toil in the cotton field was to him an infinite satisfaction. He could sit for hours gazing at a solitary flower and philosophizing about the mysteries and riddles of being. A blue heron on a tiny crescent of sandy beach, a silvery splatter of flying-fish, or a sunset of pearl and rose across the lagoon, could entrance him to all forgetfulness of the procession of wearisome days and of the heavy lash of Schemmer.

Schemmer, Karl Schemmer, was a brute, a brutish brute. But he earned his salary. He got the last particle of strength out of the five hundred slaves; for slaves they were until their term of years was up. Schemmer worked hard to extract the strength from those five hundred sweating bodies and to transmute it into bales of fluffy cotton ready for export. His dominant, iron-clad, primeval brutishness was what enabled him to effect the transmutation. Also, he was assisted by a thick leather belt, three inches wide and a yard in length, with which he always rode and which, on occasion, could come down on the naked back of a stooping coolie with a report like a pistol-shot. These reports were frequent when Schemmer rode down the furrowed field.

Once, at the beginning of the first year of contract labor, he had killed a coolie with a single blow of his fist. He had not exactly crushed the man's head like an egg-shell, but the blow had been sufficient to addle what was inside, and, after being sick for a week, the man had died. But the Chinese had not complained to the French devils that ruled over Tahiti. It was their own lookout. Schemmer was their problem. They must avoid his wrath as they avoided the venom of the centipedes that lurked in the grass or crept into the sleeping-quarters on rainy nights. The Chinagos—such they were called by the indolent, brown-skinned island folk—saw to it that they did not displease Schemmer too greatly. This was equivalent to rendering up to him a full measure of efficient toil. That blow of Schemmer's fist had been worth thousands of dollars to the Company, and no trouble ever came of it to Schemmer.

The French, with no instinct for colonization, futile in their childish playgame of developing the resources of the island, were only too glad to see the English Company succeed. What matter of Schemmer and his redoubtable fist? The Chinago that died? Well, he was only a Chinago. Besides, he died of sunstroke, as the doctor's certificate attested. True, in all the history of Tahiti no one had ever died of sunstroke. But it was that, precisely that, which made the death of this Chinago unique. The doctor said as much in his report. He was very candid. Dividends must be paid, or else one more failure would be added to the long history of failure in Tahiti.

There was no understanding these white devils. Ah Cho pondered their inscrutableness as he sat in court-room waiting the judgment. There was no telling what went on at the back of their minds. He had seen a few of the white devils. They were all alike—the officers and sailors on the ship, the French officials, the several white men on the plantation, including Schemmer. Their minds all moved in mysterious ways there was no getting at. They grew angry without apparent cause, and their anger was always dangerous. They were like wild beasts at such times. They worried about little things, and on occasion could outtoil even a Chinago. They were not temperate as Chinagos were temperate; they were gluttons, eating prodigiously and drinking more prodigiously. A Chinago never knew when an act would please them or arouse a storm of wrath. A Chinago could never tell. What pleased one time, the very next time might provoke an outburst of anger. There was a curtain behind the eyes of the white devils that screened the backs of their minds from the Chinago's gaze. And then, on top of it all, was that terrible efficiency of the white devils, that ability to do things, to make things go, to work results, to bend to their wills all creeping, crawling things, and the powers of the very elements themselves. Yes, the white men were strange and wonderful, and they were devils. Look at Schemmer.

Ah Cho wondered why the judgment was so long in forming. Not a man on trial had laid hand on Chung Ga. Ah

San alone had killed him. Ah San had done it, bending Chung Ga's head back with one hand by a grip of his queue, and with the other hand, from behind, reaching over and driving the knife into his body. Twice had he driven it in. There in the court-room, with closed eyes, Ah Cho saw the killing acted over again—the squabble, the vile words bandied back and forth, the filth and insult flung upon the venerable ancestors, the curses laid upon unbegotten generations, the leap of Ah San, the grip on the queue of Chung Ga, the knife that sank twice into his flesh, the bursting open of the door, the irruption of Schemmer, the dash for the door, the escape of Ah San, the flying belt of Schemmer that drove the rest into the corner, and the firing of the revolver as a signal that brought help to Schemmer. Ah Cho shivered as he lived it over. One blow of the belt had bruised his cheek, taking off some of the skin. Schemmer had pointed to the bruises when, on the witness-stand, he had identified Ah Cho. It was only just now that the marks had become no longer visible. That had been a blow. Half an inch nearer the centre and it would have taken out his eye. Then Ah Cho forgot the whole happening in a vision he caught of the garden of meditation and repose that would be his when he returned to his own land.

He sat with impassive face, while the magistrate rendered the judgment. Likewise were the faces of his four companions impassive. And they remained impassive when the interpreter explained that the five of them had been found guilty of the murder of Chung Ga, and that Ah Chow should have his head cut off, Ah Cho serve twenty years in prison in New Caledonia, Wong Li twelve years, and Ah Tong ten years. There was no use in getting excited about it. Even Ah Chow remained expressionless as a mummy, though it was his head that was to be cut off. The magistrate added a few words, and the interpreter explained that Ah Chow's face having been most severely bruised by Schemmer's strap had made his identification so positive that, since one man must die, he might as well be that man. Also, the fact that Ah Cho's face also had been severely bruised, conclusively proving his presence at the murder and his undoubted participation, had merited him the twenty years of penal servitude. And down to the ten years of Ah Tong, the proportioned reason for each sentence was explained. Let the Chinagos take the lesson to heart, the Court said finally, for they must learn that the law would be fulfilled in Tahiti though the heavens fell.

The five Chinagos were taken back to jail. They were not shocked nor grieved. The sentences being unexpected was quite what they were accustomed to in their dealings with the white devils. From them a Chinago rarely expected more than the unexpected. The heavy punishment for a crime they had not committed was no stranger than the countless strange things the white devils did. In the several weeks that followed, Ah Cho several times contemplated Ah Chow with mild curiosity. His head was to be cut off by the guillotine that was being erected on the plantation. For him there would be no declining years, no gardens of tranquillity. Ah Cho philosophized and speculated about life and death. As for himself, he was not perturbed. Twenty years were merely twenty years. By that much was his garden removed from him—that was all. He was young, and the patience of Asia was in his bones. He could wait those twenty years, and by that time the heats of his blood would be assuaged and he would be better fitted for that garden of calm delight. He thought of a name for it; he would call it The Garden of the Morning Calm. He was made happy all day by the thought, and he was inspired to devise a moral maxim on the virtue of patience, which maxim proved a great comfort, especially to Wong Li and Ah Tong. Ah Chow, however, did not care for the maxim. His head was to be separated from his body in so short a time that he had no need for patience to wait for that event. He smoked well, ate well, slept well, and did not worry about the slow passage of time.

Cruchot was a gendarme. He had seen twenty years of service in the colonies, from Nigeria and Senegal to the South Seas, and those twenty years had not perceptibly brightened his dull mind. He was as slow-witted and stupid as in his peasant days in the south of France.

He knew discipline and fear of authority, and from God down to the sergeant of gendarmes the only difference to him was the measure of slavish obedience which he rendered. In point of fact, the sergeant bulked bigger in his mind than God, except on Sundays when God's mouthpieces had their say. God was usually very remote, while the sergeant was ordinarily very close at hand.

Cruchot it was who received the order from the Chief Justice to the jailer commanding that functionary to deliver over to Cruchot the person of Ah Chow. Now, it happened that the Chief Justice had given a dinner the night before to the captain and officers of the French man-of-war. His hand was shaking when he wrote out the order, and his eyes were aching so dreadfully that he did not read over the order. It was only a Chinago's life he was signing away anyway. So he did not notice that he had omitted the final letter in Ah Chow's name. The order read "Ah Cho," and, when Cruchot presented the order, the jailer turned over to him the person of Ah Cho. Cruchot took that person beside him on the seat of a wagon, behind two mules, and drove away.

Ah Cho was glad to be out in the sunshine. He sat beside the gendarme and beamed. He beamed more ardently than ever when he noted the mules headed south toward Atimaono. Undoubtedly Schemmer had sent for him to be brought back. Schemmer wanted him to work. Very well, he would work well. Schemmer would never have cause to complain. It was a hot day. There had been a stoppage of the trades. The mules sweated, Cruchot sweated, and Ah Cho sweated. But it was Ah Cho that bore the heat with the least concern. He had toiled three years under that sun on the plantation. He beamed and beamed with such genial good nature that even Cruchot's heavy mind was stirred to wonderment.

"You are very funny," he said at last.

Ah Cho nodded and beamed more ardently. Unlike the magistrate, Cruchot spoke to him in the Kanaka tongue, and this, like all Chinagos and all foreign devils, Ah Cho understood.

"You laugh too much," Cruchot chided. "One's heart should be full of tears on a day like this."

"I am glad to get out of the jail."

"Is that all?" The gendarme shrugged his shoulders.

"Is it not enough?" was the retort.

"Then you are not glad to have your head cut off?"

Ah Cho looked at him in abrupt perplexity and said:

"Why, I am going back to Atimaono to work on the plantation for Schemmer. Are you not taking me to Atimaono?"

Cruchot stroked his long mustaches reflectively. "Well, well," he said, finally, with a flick of the whip at the off mule, "so you don't know?"

"Know what?" Ah Cho was beginning to feel a vague alarm. "Won't Schemmer let me work for him any more?"

"Not after to-day." Cruchot laughed heartily. It was a good joke. "You see, you won't be able to work after to-day. A man with his head off can't work, eh?" He poked the Chinago in the ribs and chuckled.

Ah Cho maintained silence while the mules trotted a hot mile. Then he spoke: "Is Schemmer going to cut off my head?"

Cruchot grinned as he nodded.

"It is a mistake," said Ah Cho, gravely. "I am not the Chinago that is to have his head cut off. I am Ah Cho. The honorable judge has determined that I am to stop twenty years in New Caledonia."

The gendarme laughed. It was a good joke, this funny Chinago trying to cheat the guillotine. The mules trotted through a cocoanut grove and for half a mile beside the sparkling sea before Ah Cho spoke again.

"I tell you I am not Ah Chow. The honorable judge did not say that my head was to go off."

"Don't be afraid," said Cruchot, with the philanthropic intention of making it easier for his prisoner. "It is not difficult to die that way." He snapped his fingers. "It is quick—like that. It is not like hanging on the end of a rope and kicking and making faces for five minutes. It is like killing a chicken with a hatchet. You cut its head off, that is all. And it is the same with a man. Pouf!—it is over. It doesn't hurt. You don't even think it hurts.

You don't think. Your head is gone, so you cannot think. It is very good. That is the way I want to die—quick, ah, quick. You are lucky to die that way. You might get the leprosy and fall to pieces slowly, a finger at a time, and now and again a thumb, also the toes. I knew a man who was burned by hot water. It took him two days to die. You could hear him yelling a kilometre away. But you? Ah! so easy! Chck!—the knife cuts your neck like that. It is finished. The knife may even tickle. Who can say? Nobody who died that way ever came back to say."

He considered this last an excruciating joke, and permitted himself to be convulsed with laughter for half a minute. Part of his mirth was assumed, but he considered it his humane duty to cheer up the Chinago.

"But I tell you I am Ah Cho," the other persisted. "I don't want my head cut off."

Cruchot scowled. The Chinago was carrying the foolishness too far.

"I am not Ah Chow—" Ah Cho began.

"That will do," the gendarme interrupted. He puffed up his cheeks and strove to appear fierce.

"I tell you I am not—" Ah Cho began again.

"Shut up!" bawled Cruchot.

After that they rode along in silence. It was twenty miles from Papeete to Atimaono, and over half the distance was covered by the time the Chinago again ventured into speech.

"I saw you in the court-room, when the honorable judge sought after our guilt," he began. "Very good. And do you remember that Ah Chow, whose head is to be cut off—do you remember that he—Ah Chow—was a tall man? Look at me."

He stood up suddenly, and Cruchot saw that he was a short man. And just as suddenly Cruchot caught a glimpse of a memory picture of Ah Chow, and in that picture Ah Chow was tall. To the gendarme all Chinagos looked alike. One face was like another. But between tallness and shortness he could differentiate, and he knew that he had the wrong man beside him on the seat. He pulled up the mules abruptly, so that the pole shot ahead of them, elevating their collars.

"You see, it was a mistake," said Ah Cho, smiling pleasantly.

But Cruchot was thinking. Already he regretted that he had stopped the wagon. He was unaware of the error of the Chief Justice, and he had no way of working it out; but he did know that he had been given this Chinago to take to Atimaono and that it was his duty to take him to Atimaono. What if he was the wrong man and they cut his head off? It was only a Chinago when all was said, and what was a Chinago anyway? Besides, it might not be a mistake. He did not know what went on in the minds of his superiors. They knew their business best. Who was he to do their thinking for them? Once, in the long ago, he had attempted to think for them, and the sergeant had said: "Cruchot, you are a fool! The quicker you know that, the better you will get on. You are not to think; you are to obey and leave thinking to your betters." He smarted under the recollection. Also, if he turned back to Papeete he would delay the execution at Atimaono, and if he were wrong in turning back he would get a reprimand from the sergeant who was waiting for the prisoner. And, furthermore, he would get a reprimand at Papeete as well.

He touched the mules with the whip and drove on. He looked at his watch. He would be half an hour late as it was, and the sergeant was bound to be angry. He put the mules into a faster trot. The more Ah Cho persisted in explaining the mistake, the more stubborn Cruchot became. The knowledge that he had the wrong man did not make his temper better. The knowledge that it was through no mistake of his confirmed him in the belief that the wrong he was doing was the right. And, rather than incur the displeasure of the sergeant, he would willingly have assisted a dozen wrong Chinagos to their doom.

As for Ah Cho, after the gendarme had struck him over the head with the butt of the whip and commanded him in a loud voice to shut up, there remained nothing for him to do but to shut up. The long ride continued in silence. Ah Cho pondered the strange ways of the foreign devils. There was no explaining them. What they were doing with him was of a piece with everything they did. First they found guilty five innocent men, and next they cut off the head of the man that even they, in their benighted ignorance, had deemed meritorious of no more than twenty years' imprisonment. And there was nothing he could do. He could only sit idly and take what these lords of life measured out to him. Once, he got in a panic, and the sweat upon his body turned cold; but he fought his way out of it. He endeavored to resign himself to his fate by remembering and repeating certain passages from the "Yin Chih Wen" ("The Tract of the Quiet Way"); but, instead, he kept seeing his dream-garden of meditation and repose. This bothered him, until he abandoned himself to the dream and sat in his garden listening to the tinkling of the wind-bells in the several trees. And lo! sitting thus, in the dream, he was able to remember and repeat the passages from the "Tract of the Quiet Way."

So the time passed nicely until Atimaono was reached and the mules trotted up to the foot of the scaffold, in the shade of which stood the impatient sergeant. Ah Cho was hurried up the ladder of the scaffold. Beneath him on one side he saw assembled all the coolies of the plantation. Schemmer had decided that the event would be a good object lesson, and so had called in the coolies from the fields and compelled them to be present. As they caught sight of Ah Cho they gabbled among themselves in low voices. They saw the mistake; but they kept it to themselves. The inexplicable white devils had doubtlessly changed their minds. Instead of taking the life of one innocent man they were taking the life of another innocent man. Ah Chow or Ah Cho—what did it matter which? They could never understand the white dogs any more than could the white dogs understand them. Ah Cho was going to have his head cut off, but they, when their two remaining years of servitude were up, were going back to China.

Schemmer had made the guillotine himself. He was a handy man, and though he had never seen a guillotine, the French officials had explained the principle to him. It was on his suggestion that they had ordered the execution to take place at Atimaono instead of at Papeete. The scene of the crime, Schemmer had argued, was the best possible place for the punishment, and, in addition, it would have a salutary influence upon the half-thousand Chinagos on the plantation. Schemmer had also volunteered to act as executioner, and in that capacity he was now on the scaffold, experimenting with the instrument he had made. A banana tree, of the size and consistency of a man's neck, lay under the guillotine. Ah Cho watched with fascinated eyes. The German, turning a small crank, hoisted the blade to the top of the little derrick he had rigged. A jerk on a stout piece of cord loosed the blade and it dropped with a flash, neatly severing the banana trunk.

"How does it work?" The sergeant, coming out on top the scaffold, had asked the question.

"Beautifully," was Schemmer's exultant answer. "Let me show you."

Again he turned the crank that hoisted the blade, jerked the cord, and sent the blade crashing down on the soft tree. But this time it went no more than two-thirds of the way through.

The sergeant scowled. "That will not serve," he said.

Schemmer wiped the sweat from his forehead. "What it needs is more weight," he announced. Walking up to the edge of the scaffold, he called his orders to the blacksmith for a twenty-five-pound piece of iron. As he stooped over to attach the iron to the broad top of the blade, Ah Cho glanced at the sergeant and saw his opportunity.

"The honorable judge said that Ah Chow was to have his head cut off," he began.

The sergeant nodded impatiently. He was thinking of the fifteen-mile ride before him that afternoon, to the windward side of the island, and of Berthe, the pretty half-caste daughter of Lafière, the pearl-trader, who was waiting for him at the end of it.

"Well, I am not Ah Chow. I am Ah Cho. The honorable jailer has made a mistake. Ah Chow is a tall man, and you see I am short."

The sergeant looked at him hastily and saw the mistake. "Schemmer!" he called, imperatively. "Come here."

The German grunted, but remained bent over his task till the chunk of iron was lashed to his satisfaction. "Is your Chinago ready?" he demanded.

"Look at him," was the answer. "Is he the Chinago?"

Schemmer was surprised. He swore tersely for a few seconds, and looked regretfully across at the thing he had made with his own hands and which he was eager to see work. "Look here," he said, finally, "we can't postpone this affair. I've lost three hours' work already out of those five hundred Chinagos. I can't afford to lose it all over again for the right man. Let's put the performance through just the same. It is only a Chinago."

The sergeant remembered the long ride before him, and the pearl-trader's daughter, and debated with himself.

"They will blame it on Cruchot—if it is discovered," the German urged. "But there's little chance of its being discovered. Ah Chow won't give it away, at any rate."

"The blame won't lie with Cruchot anyway," the sergeant said. "It must have been the jailer's mistake."

"Then let's go on with it. They can't blame us. Who can tell one Chinago from another? We can say that we merely carried out instructions with the Chinago that was turned over to us. Besides, I really can't take all those coolies a second time away from their labor."

They spoke in French, and Ah Cho, who did not understand a word of it, nevertheless knew that they were determining his destiny. He knew, also, that the decision rested with the sergeant, and he hung upon that official's lips.

"All right," announced the sergeant. "Go ahead with it. He is only a Chinago."

"I'm going to try it once more, just to make sure." Schemmer moved the banana trunk forward under the knife, which he had hoisted to the top of the derrick.

Ah Cho tried to remember maxims from "The Tract of the Quiet Way." "Live in concord," came to him; but it was not applicable. He was not going to live. He was about to die. No, that would not do. "Forgive malice"—yes, but there was no malice to forgive.

Schemmer and the rest were doing this thing without malice. It was to them merely a piece of work that had to be done, just as clearing the jungle, ditching the water, and planting cotton were pieces of work that had to be done. Schemmer jerked the cord, and Ah Cho forgot "The Tract of the Quiet Way." The knife shot down with a thud, making a clean slice of the tree.

"Beautiful!" exclaimed the sergeant, pausing in the act of lighting a cigarette. "Beautiful, my friend."

Schemmer was pleased at the praise.

"Come on, Ah Chow," he said, in the Tahitian tongue.

"But I am not Ah Chow—" Ah Cho began.

"Shut up!" was the answer. "If you open your mouth again I'll break your head."

The overseer threatened him with a clenched fist, and he remained silent. What was the good of protesting? Those foreign devils always had their way. He allowed himself to be lashed to the vertical board that was the size of his body. Schemmer drew the buckles tight—so tight that the straps cut into his flesh and hurt. But he did not complain.

The hurt would not last long. He felt the board tilting over in the air toward the horizontal, and closed his eyes. And in that moment he caught a last glimpse of his garden of meditation and repose. It seemed to him that he sat in the garden. A cool wind was blowing, and the bells in the several trees were tinkling softly. Also, birds were making sleepy noises, and from beyond the high wall came the subdued sound of village life.

Then he was aware that the board had come to rest, and from muscular pressures and tensions he knew that he was lying on his back. He opened his eyes. Straight above him he saw the suspended knife blazing in the sunshine. He saw the weight which had been added and noted that one of Schemmer's knots had slipped. Then he heard the sergeant's voice in sharp command. Ah Cho closed his eyes hastily. He did not want to see that knife descend. But he felt it—for one great fleeting instant. And in that instant he remembered Cruchot and what Cruchot had said. But Cruchot was wrong. The knife did not tickle. That much he knew before he ceased to know.

A SILHOUETTE
by Rebecca Harding Davis

IT was the second day of Lucy Coyt's journey from home. For years she had looked forward to the time when she should set out to earn her living in that mysterious "South" which, before the war, was like a foreign land to most Northern women. At that time families of the class to which Lucy belonged trained their clever daughters as teachers to go to the cotton States, precisely as they now fit their sons to go to Colorado or Dakota. In any case they would do better than at home, and they might open up a gold mine in the shape of a rich widower or susceptible young planter. Two or three of Miss Coyt's class-mates had disappeared victoriously in this way. She fancied them as reigning over a legion of slaves, and adored by a swarthy, fiery Don Furioso; and natur-ally the possibility of such a fate for herself glimmered hazily in the distance. Though, of course, it was wrong to hold slaves; at least, she was feebly confident that was her belief ever since David Pettit had talked to her about it the other evening. The Reverend David had brought some queer new notions back with him from the theological school.

"He'll wait a long time for a call in our Synod if they suspect he's an aboli-tionist," thought Lucy as the train whizzed swiftly on. "I wish I'd given him a hint; though he wouldn't have taken it. Dave was a nice sort of a girl-boy when he used to help me skim the cream. But he has grown real coarse and conceited, with his white cravat and radical talk." She drew a book from her bag which he had slipped into her hand just as the stage was starting. "*Imitation of Christ?*" eyeing the cross on the back suspiciously. "It reads like sound doc-trine enough. But Dave will have to be on his guard. If he brings any papistical notions into our Synod, his chance for a call is over."

She leaned back, uneasily feeling that if she could have staid and watched him, poor Miss Daisy (as the Fairview boys used to call him) would have had a better chance, when the train suddenly stopped. Miss Coyt had been expecting adventures ever since they started. Now they had begun. The train (she was on a railway in Lower Virginia) was rush-ing across a trestle bridge, when, with a shrill screech of steam, it stopped. Half of the men in the car crowded to the door, where a brakeman stood barring the way.

"Run over a cow?"

"No. Hush-h! Don't skeer the ladies!"

Miss Coyt laughed to herself. Jake Carr, the brakeman on the Fairview road, would have thrust his head in and yelled, "Keep you seats, gents!" These Southerners were ridiculously gentle and soft whenever they came near a woman. This brakeman was mild-mannered enough to have kept sheep in Arcadia. It was plain that Fairview was many hundred miles back; this was a different world. Lucy's quick eyes had noted all the differences, although she was miser-ably abashed by the crowd—so abashed, indeed, that she had been parched with thirst since morning, and could not summon courage to go to the water-cooler for a drink.

Looking out of the window, she saw on the bank below the bridge a hunched heap of grey flannel and yellow calico. The men from the train ran toward it. "Something's wrong. I'd better take right hold at once," thought Miss Coyt. She took her purse out of her bag and put it in her pocket, lest there might be a thief in the car, and then hurried out after the men. She had a very low opinion of the intelligence of men in any emergency. At home, she always had pulled the whole household of father and brothers along. She was the little steam-tug; they the heavy scows, dragged un-willingly forward.

She reached the quivering heap on the bank. It was a woman. Miss Coyt straightened the clothes, kneeled down and lifted her head. The grey hair was clotted with blood. "Why, she's old! Her hair's white!" cried Lucy, excitedly, catching the head up to her breast. "Oh dear! oh dear!"

"It's old Mis' Crocker!" said a train man. "Yon's her cabin down on the branch. I see her on the bridge, 'n' she heerd the train comin', 'n' she jumped, 'n'—"

"Don't stand there chattering. Go for a doctor!" said Miss Coyt.

"I am a doctor," said one of the pas-sengers, quietly, stooping to examine the woman. "She is not dead. Not much hurt. An arm broken."

The men carried Mrs. Crocker to her cabin. She had caught Lucy's hand, and so led her along. The other women craned their necks out of the car watching her. They were just as sorry as Lucy, but they were in the habit of leaving great emergencies in the hands of men.

" What can that bold gyurl do ? " they said. " The gentlemen will attend to it."

The men, having seen Mrs. Crocker open her eyes, straggled back to the train.

" Time's up, doctor ! " shouted the conductor. " Express is due in two minutes."

The doctor was leisurely cutting away Mrs. Crocker's flannel sleeve. " I shall want bandages," he said, without looking up. Lucy looked about the bare little cabin, half drew out her handkerchief, and put it back. It was one of her half-dozen newest and best. Then she espied a pillow-cover, and tore it into strips. The doctor dressed the arm as composedly as if the day was before him. Miss Coyt kept her eye on the puffing engine. All the clothes she had in the world were in her trunk on that train. What intolerable dawdlers these Southerners were! There! They were going ! She could not leave the woman— But her clothes !

There was a chorus of shouts from the train, a puff of steam, and then the long line of cars shot through the hills, leaving but a wisp of smoke clinging to the closing forest. The doctor fastened his last bandage. Miss Coyt, with a choking noise in her throat, rushed to the door. The doctor looked at his companion for the first time. Then he quickly took off his hat, and came up to her with that subtle air of homage which sets the man in that region so thoroughly apart from the woman.

" I beg of you not to be alarmed," he said.

" But they are gone ! "

" You have your ticket ? There will be another train before night, and you will find your baggage awaiting you at Abingdon."

" Oh, thank you ! " gasped Lucy, suddenly ashamed of her tear-dabbled face. " It was very silly in me. But I never travelled alone before."

The doctor had always supposed Northern women to be as little afflicted with timidity as life-insurance agents. His calm eyes rested an instant on Miss Coyt as he folded his pocket-book. " It was my fault that you were detained, madam," he said. " If you will permit me, I will look after your baggage when we reach Abingdon."

Lucy thanked him again, and turned to help Mrs. Crocker, who was struggling to her feet. How lucky she was to meet this good-natured, fatherly doctor in this adventure ! It might have been some conceited young man. The doctor, too, was of a very different human species from the ox-like Fairview farmers whom she had left behind, or neat, thin-blooded Davy Pettit. Miss Coyt had known no other men than these. But in the intervals of pie-making and milking on the farm she has gone to the Fairview Female Seminary, and had read Carlyle, and the Autocrat in the *Atlantic*, and *Beauties of German Authors;* and so felt herself an expert in human nature, and quite fitted to criticise any new types which the South might offer to her.

Mrs. Crocker went out to the doctor, who was sitting on the log which served as a step. She looked at the bridge.

" Powerful big fall thet wur," she said, complacently. " Ther's not another woman in Wythe County as could hev done it athout breakin' her neck."

" Ah, you've twenty good years of life in you yet, mother," he said, good-humouredly, glancing at her muscular limbs and skin, tanned to a fine leather-colour by wind and sun.

" Oh, I'm tough enough. Brought up eleven children right hyar on the branch. All gone—dead or married. I helped build this hyar house with my own hands twelve year ago. What d'ye think o' thet corn ? Ploughed and hoed every hill of it."

" It's outrageous ! " said Lucy, authoritatively. " At your age a woman's children should support her. I would advise you to give up the house at once, divide the year among them, and rest."

" No, missy ; I never war one for jauntin' round. Once, when I wur a gyurl, I wur at Marion. But I wur born right hyar on the branch seventy year back, 'n' I reckon I'll make an eend on't hyar."

" Seventy years ! — here ! " thought

Lucy. Her eyes wandered over the gorge lined with corn, the pig-pen, the unchinked, dirty cabin. The doctor watched her expressive face with an amused smile. Mrs. Crocker went in to stir the fire.

"Better, you think, not to live at all?" he replied to her looks.

"I do not call it living," she said, promptly. "I've seen it often on farms. Dropping corn and eating it; feeding pigs and children until both were big enough to be sent away; and that for seventy years! It is no better life than that fat worm's there beside you."

The doctor laughed, and lazily put down his hand that the worm might crawl over it. "Poor old woman! Poor worm!" he said. "There is nothing as merciless as a woman—like you," hesitating, but not looking up. "She would leave nothing alive that was not young and beautiful and supreme as herself. You should consider. The world was not made for the royal family alone. You must leave room in it for old women, and worms, and country doctors."

Lucy laughed, but did not reply. She did not understand this old gentleman, who was bestowing upon her very much the same quizzical, good-humoured interest which he gave to the worm.

"I don't know how you can touch the loathsome thing, anyhow," she said, tartly. "It creeps up into your hand as if it knew you were taking its part."

"It does know. If I wanted it for bait, it would not come near me. I fancy all creatures know their friends. Watch a moment."

He walked a few steps into the edge of the woods, and threw himself down into the deep grass, his face upward. Whether he made signs or whistled Lucy could not tell, but presently a bird from a neighbouring bough came circling down and perched beside him; another and another followed, until, when he rose, it seemed to her that the whole flock hovered about him, chirping excitedly. He stopped by the bee-hives as he came back, and the bees, disturbed, swarmed about him, settling black on his head and shoulders. Lucy ran to him, as he stood unhurt, gently brushing them off, pleased and flushed with his little triumph.

"One would really think you knew what they said."

"I wish I did!" he said, looking thoughtfully at the birds flying upward. There was a certain sentimentalism, a straining after scenic pose and effect, which would have seemed ridiculous to her in Dave Pettit; but she found it peculiarly attractive now.

"You have no charm?"

"No. Only that I have been friends with them all since I was a child, and they know it. I remember when I was a baby sitting with the black pickaninnies on the ground playing with frogs. Even then" (with the same touch of grandiloquence in his tone) "I did not find anything that was alive loathsome or unfriendly. I beg your pardon," suddenly. "I did not mean to bore you with the history of my infancy."

"Bore me! Why, I never met with so singular a trait in anybody before."

Miss Coyt was now satisfied that this was not only a most extraordinary man in intellect, but in goodness. She could imagine what life and strength, living so close to nature as he did, he would carry to a sick or dying bed! It was like the healing power of the old saints. There was the advantage of travel! How long would she have lived in Fairview without meeting anybody with traits so abnormal and fine! She began to have a sense of ownership in this her discovery. Now that she examined the doctor, he was not even middle-aged: how could she have thought him old? What womanish tenderness was in the cut of his mouth! Indeed, this astute young woman found the close-shaven jaws indicated a benevolence amounting to weakness. The eyes were less satisfactory: they were grey and bright, but they said absolutely nothing to her, no more than if they belonged to a species of animal which was unknown to her. This only whetted her interest. Was he married? Was he a church member? What would he probably think of that favourite passage of hers in Jean Paul? This young woman, we should have stated earlier, was neither engaged nor in love. She intended to be in love some day, however; and there were certain tests which she applied as she went through life to each man whom she met, just as she might idly try to set different words to some melody known only to herself.

The man (who was not in want of a

mate) had quite forgotten the woman. He had gone into the kitchen, and finding some bacon and fresh mountain trout, had set about cooking dinner as if he were in camp. A mess was already simmering on the fire. He fastened a towel before him for an apron, lifted the lid from the frying-pan and dropped something into it from a case of vials which he took out of his pocket.

"Always carry my own sauces," he said, as Lucy came up. "Smell that!" sniffing up the savoury steam with an unctuous smile. "Ah-h!"

Lucy ate the dinner when it was ready in a kind of fervour. She had never met a gourmand before. There was a fine individual trait in this exceptional character.

This fair-haired stout doctor, with his birds and his cookery and his jokes and his pale impenetrable eyes, seemed to her for some reason a bigger and more human man than any she had ever guessed were in the world. If she were only a man and could make a comrade of him! She had never made a comrade of her father or brothers; they were always taken up with pigs, or politics, or county railroad business. And the ideal companion she had picked out for herself from religious novels was unsatisfactory—as a matter of fact. She looked speculatively at the broad-backed linen duster in the doorway. She was as unconscious of the speculation in her eyes as the polyp fastened to a rock is of the movement of its tentacles groping through the water for food.

The doctor had no curiosity about her. When Mrs. Crocker questioned her as to her name and age, he whistled to the farm dog, not listening to the answer.

"What you doin' har in Vuhginny, ennyhow?"

"I came from Pennsylvania to teach a school in a place called Otoga, in Carolina," said Lucy.

"Hev some friends in these parts, I reckon?"

"No, none at all. Unless I may call you one, Mrs. Crocker," with a nervous laugh.

"Reckon you'll not see much more o' me, ma'am. Otoga, hey? My son Orlando lives thar. 'Pears to me I'd keep clar o' thet town ef I wur a young woman 'thout protection. Orlan's tole me a heap about it."

"Why, what is the matter with Otoga?" exclaimed Lucy, rising uncertainly. "I must go there. My engagement—"

"Matter? Nothin', only it's ther the Van Cleves hev gone to live. You've heerd o' them, o' course?"

"No. Van Cleves?"

The doctor came up to the open door, watch in hand.

"The train will be due in twenty minutes."

"I am ready. Who are these people, Mrs. Crocker? I must live among them."

"They won't hurt you, I reckon. Ther's no higher toned people than the Van Cleves and the Suydams. Only it's sort of unpleasant whar they are, sometimes. You see," leisurely lighting her pipe with a brand, "them two famblies swore death agin each other nigh a hundred year ago, an' since then ther's not a man of them hes died in his bed. They live in Tennessee. Orlan he tole me the rights of it. Four brothers of the Van Cleves barricaded the Suydams up in their house for five weeks, an' when they were fairly starved an' crep out, they shot them dead. Thet wur the grandfathers o' this present stock. But they hev kep at it stiddy. Not a man o' them but died in his boots. Ther's but one Suydam left, 'n' thet's Cunnel Abram. His father wur shot by the Van Cleves. So when Abram wur a boy, he says, says he, 'Now I'm gwine to put a final eend to this whole thing.' So he went at it practisin' with his pistol, 'n' when he thought he wur ready he challenges Jedge Van Cleve, 'n' shoots him plumb through the head. Oh, Orlan says it wur a fah dooel, no murder. Ther wur two Van Cleves left, jess boys, nepheys of the jedge, 'n' they'd gone to Californy. But Cunnel Abram he followed them, 'n' shot one on the deck of a ship bound for Chiny. T'other he dodged him somehow 'n' come back, 'n' is living in Otoga. But he'll be found. Cunnel Abram 'll track him down," wagging her head with the zest of horror.

"But is there no law at all here?" cried Lucy. "I can't believe such a wretch would go unhung anywhere."

The doctor tapped on the window. "The train is in sight. You must bid our friend good-bye."

Lucy shook hands hurriedly with the old woman. She had some money in her hand to give her, but after a moment's hesitation, dropped it back into her pocket, and handed her a tract instead. "Religion will do her more real good," she thought afterward, quieting an uneasy inward twinge; "at least it ought to."

When they had boarded the train the doctor arranged her seat with gentle, leisurely movements, and brought her last week's Richmond paper. He did not, as she expected, take the vacant seat beside her, but disappeared, only returning when the train reached Abingdon.

"This carriage will take you to the hotel, madam. I have written a note to the landlord, who will show you every attention. No, no thanks," shutting her in, his fat, agreeable face showing an instant smiling over the door. He did not offer his hand, as all the men whom Lucy had known would have done. He lifted his hat, hesitating a moment before he added, half reluctantly: "It is probable that I may meet you again. My business calls me to Otoga."

Miss Coyt bowed civilly, but as the carriage rattled up the street she laughed aloud and blushed. She herself did not know why. It was certainly very lonely and dangerous for a woman adventuring among murderers and assassins. . . .

Three days after she left Abingdon, Lucy, rumbling along the mountain-side in an old waggon, came in sight of a dozen grey, weather-beaten houses huddled on the edge of a creek in the gorge below.

"Yon's Otoga," said the driver, pointing with his whip.

"Hi, Dumfort!" shouted a man's voice. "Hold on thar!" and a big young fellow in butternut flannel appeared in the under-brush, "You cahn't go to Otoga. Yellow Jack's thar afore you. Six men dead since yes'day mawnin'."

"The devil!" Dumfort pulled up his mules.

"So I say. Six. I and my wife hev been on the lookout for you since mawnin'."

"'Bleeged, captain. Six? That about halves them down thar. T! T! I dunno 's ever I was more interruptid than this afore!" snapping his whip meditatively.

Lucy, peeping through the oil-skin blind, could see the bold, merry face of the young countryman. He stood pulling his red beard and frowning with decent regret for his neighbours. Of course he was sorry, but he had so much life and fun in him that he could not help being happy and comforable if the whole State of Carolina were dead with yellow fever.

"I've got the mail, too. An' a passenger," said Dumfort, jerking his head back to the waggon. "What in the mischief am I to do?"

"The mail 'll keep. Drive right up to my house, an' my wife 'll give you an' the other man shake-downs till the mawnin'."

"'Tain't another man."

The young man stepped quickly forward, with an instantaneous change of manner. He jerked off his quilted wide-rimmed hat ("made out of his wife's old dress," thought Lucy). "I did not know thet ther' was a lady inside," he said. "I was too rough with my news. Come up to my house. My wife 'll tell you there's no danger."

"I shall be very glad to go," said Miss Coyt.

Dumfort drove up a rutted mountain road and stopped before a log cabin. Of all houses in the world, it was plainly the first venture in life of two poor young people. Lucy read the whole story at a glance. There was the little clearing on the mountainside; the patch of corn and potatoes (just enough for two); the first cow; the house itself, walls, ceiling, and floor made of planed planks of the delicately veined poplar; the tidy supper table, with its two plates; the photographs of the bride's father and mother hung over the mantel-shelf in frames which she had made of bits of mica from the mine yonder. Here was a chair made out of a barrel and trimmed with pink muslin, there a decorated ginger jar, a chromo of the Death of Andrew Jackson on the wall. Lucy was on the same rung of the ladder of culture as her hostess.

"She has a very refined taste," she thought. "That tidy stitch was just coming in at Fairview." Hurrying in from the field, her baby in her arms, came a plump, freckled, blue-eyed woman.

"Mistress Thomas," said Dumfort, ponderously, "let me make you acquainted with Miss Coyt. She war a-goin' to Otoga to teach school."

The two women exchanged smiles and keen glances. "Baby's asleep," whispered the mother. "I'll shake hands when I lay him down."

Lucy ran to turn down the crib quilt. "He's tremendously big," she whispered, helping to tuck him in.

"Now, Dorcas, let's have supper," called the farmer from the door, where he sat smoking with Dumfort. "Our friends must be hungry as bars."

Dorcas smiled, and with intolerably lazy slowness tucked up her sleeves from her white arms and began the inevitable chicken frying. Lucy suddenly remembered how unbusinesslike was the whole proceeding. She went up to her hostess, who was stooping over the big log fire.

"What do you charge for board?" she said. "I should like to stay here until the sickness is over in Otoga. That is, if your charges are reasonable," eyeing her keenly. Her rule always was to make her bargain before buying, then she never was cheated.

Mrs. Dorcas's fair face burned red. "We *don't* take folks in to *board*," she drawled in her sweet voice, looking at Lucy curiously. "But we'll be *mighty* glad if you'll stay 's long 's you can. It's powerful lonesome hyah on the mountains. We'll take it as *very* kyind in you to stay."

"It is you who are kind," said Lucy, feeling miserably small and vulgar. But how could she have known? They did not use strangers in this ridiculously generous way in Fairview.

Mistress Dorcas shot an amused speculative glance after her, and went on with her frying. Miss Coyt, presently finding the baby awake, took him up and went out to the steps where his father and Dumfort still smoked and gossiped in the slanting yellow beams of the lowering sun. The baby, who was freckled and soft-eyed as his mother, replied to Lucy's cooing and coddling by laughing and thrusting his tiny fat fist into her eyes. Lucy stooped and kissed him furtively. She felt lonely and far from home just then.

"What do you call baby?" she asked.

Mrs. Dorcas came to the door. "His real name is Humpty. But he was baptized Alexander — Alexander Van Cleve."

Lucy sprang to her feet. "Van Cleve!" staring at the farmer. "I thought your name was Thomas?"

"Thomas Van Cleve," smiling. "Why, what's wrong with that?"

Lucy felt as though a blow had been struck at her, which made her knees totter. "They told me in Virginia that the Suydams were on your track."

There was a sudden silence, but Miss Coyt, being greatly shaken, stumbled on. "I did not expect to come in your way —I'm not used to such things—and this poor baby," hugging it passionately. "It's a Van Cleve too?"

The young man took the boy. "Quiet yourself. Humpty will not be hurt by —any one," he said, and putting him up on his shoulder he walked down to the chicken-yard. His wife went in without a word, and shut the door. Lucy sat down. After a long time she said to Dumfort:

"I have made a mistake."

"Yes. But you couldn't be expected to know. I have never heard a Suydam's name mentioned to a Van Cleve afore. It was so surprisin', it didn't seem decent, somehow.

"I don't understand why," groaned Lucy.

"No? Ther's things what ain't never talked of. Now ther's the Peterses in the Smoky Mountains. There used to be a disease in the Peters fambly which attacked one leg. But it turned out to be true Asiatic leprosy. Well, it isn't reckoned civil hyarabouts to talk of legs afore a Peters. Now this fambly's got a —a discussion hangin' on with the Suydams for a hundred year, as onfortinit 's leprosy. An' well, probably you're the first person's ever mentioned it to them."

They relapsed into silence until they were called into supper. Lucy felt as if a thin glaze of ice had risen between her and the Van Cleves. They were afraid of her. As for her, her food choked her. But after supper Mrs. Dorcas brought out a flannel slip which she was making for baby, and Lucy insisted on trying it on. She was fond of babies. She had a sacque in her trunk which she had been braiding for her brother Joe's child.

"I'll bring it down to give you the idea," she said, and ran up for it.

Van Cleve looked at it over his wife's shoulder when it came. "Try that thing on Humpty, Miss Coyt," he said, and when it was on he held the boy up on his outstretched arm. "Pretty's a picture, hey, Dumfort?"

"I'll finish it for him," exclaimed Lucy, with a gush of generosity. "I can make Sam another."

Mrs. Dorcas broke into a delighted flood of thanks. She jumped up to fit and button it on the boy, while her husband, quite as vain and pleased as she, held him. It seemed incredible to Lucy that this ghastly horror, which never could be mentioned, stood like a shadow behind the three; that this commonplace, jolly little family went to bed, rose, sat down to eat, with Death as their perpetual companion, dumb, waiting to strike.

The next morning was that of an April day. The whole world was swathed in fog and grey dampness, and the next moment it flashed and sparkled in the sunlight, every leaf quivering back in brilliance. Young Van Cleve had set off by daylight, whistling behind his steers. Before noon he came up the mountain, his head sunk, silent, and morose. Even the ruddy colour was gone: his thick-featured, jolly face was nipped as with age.

Dorcas ran to meet him. "Are you sick, Tom?"

"No."

"Have you"—she glanced swiftly around—"have you heard—anything?"

"Nothing. I thought it best to throw off work to-day."

He drove the steers into the inclosure. As he unyoked them he sent keen, furtive glances into the darkening woods. Meanwhile the sky had lowered. Clouds walled in the mountain plateau; the day had grown heavy and foreboding.

Dumfort came to Lucy, who was sitting on the steps with the baby.

"Thomas has hed a warnin'," he said, in a low tone. "Cunnel Abram's on his track."

"He has seen him!" She started up, catching up Humpty in her arms. "He is coming here?"

"So I think. But Thomas hain't seen him. He's ben warned. I've heerd

that them Van Cleves allays kin tell when a Suydam is near them."

"Nonsense!" Lucy set the child down again.

"Jess as some men," pursued Dumfort, calmly, "kin tell when there's a rattlesnake in the grass nigh; an' others creep with cold ef a cat's in the room."

Miss Coyt, still contemptuous, watched Van Cleve sharply as he passed into the house. "Dorcas," he said, quietly, as he passed, "bring Humpty in. Keep indoors to-day." He went up to the loft, closing the trap-door behind him, and Lucy fancied that she heard the click of fire-arms.

Dumfort's pipe went out in his mouth with his smothered excitement. "He's loadin'! Suydam's comin'!" he whispered. "Thomas ain't the same man he was this mawnin'! He's layin' to, 'n' waitin'."

"To murder another man! And he calls himself a Christian! He had family prayers this morning!"

"What's that got to do with it?" demanded Dumfort, fiercely. "Thomas's got his dooty laid out. He's got the murderer of his brother to punish. The law's left it to them two famblies to settle with each other. God's left it to them. Them old Jews sent the nearest of kin to avenge blood. The Suydams hev blood to avenge." He got up abruptly and walked uneasily up and down the barn-yard. Dorcas had left her work, and with Humpty in her arms sat by the window, her keen eyes fixed on the thicket of pines that fenced in the house, black and motionless in the breathless air.

No rain had fallen as yet, but the forest, the peaks of the mountains beyond, the familiar objects in the barn-yard, had drawn closer with that silent hush and peculiar dark distinctness that precedes a storm. They, too, listened and waited. Lucy heard a step in the house. Van Cleve came heavily down from the loft and seated himself, his face turned toward the road by which a stranger must approach.

Lucy stood irresolute for a few minutes; she felt as if she could not draw her breath; the air was full of death. Pulling the hood of her waterproof over her head, she crossed the stile and walked down the road. "I will be first to meet the wolf," she said aloud, laughing nervously.

The road wound through the unbroken forest down to the creek. As she came nearer to the water she heard the plash of a horse's feet crossing the ford. She tried to cry out that he was coming, to warn them, but her mouth would not make a sound; her legs shook under her; she caught by a tree, possessed by childish, abject fear. When the horse and rider came into sight she laughed hysterically.

It was the good-humoured doctor. He turned quietly at her cry, and smiled placidly. Nothing would startle that phlegmatic mass of flesh. He alighted, tied his horse, and came to her with the leisurely, noiseless movements peculiar to him.

"You are frightened. What are you afraid of, Miss Coyt?"

"Oh, of a monster!"—laughing feebly —"a human beast of prey that is in these mountains. Every time a branch moved I expected to see his murderous face coming toward his victim."

She wanted to pour out the whole story, but he stood stolid and incurious, asking no questions. She hesitated and stopped.

"I saw nobody," he said, composedly.

Whether he was interested or not, she must tell him. He was so wise and kind; he was a man used to control others. If he would interfere he could doubtless put an end to it all.

"It is a vendetta," she began. "You heard of it at the time of the accident."

"You should not allow yourself to be excited by the gossip of the mountains," he interrupted, gently; but his eyes, smiling down at her, suddenly seemed to her as hard and impenetrable as granite. "I fear I must leave you. I must reach Otoga before noon."

"You must not go to Otoga," catching him by the arm. "The yellow fever is there. Half of the population are dead."

"Worse than that, I am afraid," he said, gravely. "We heard this morning that there was now neither doctor, nurse, nor anybody to bury the dead."

"And you are going to help them?" drawing back with a kind of awe.

"I am a doctor," he said, indifferently, "and I can nurse in a fashion, and if the worst comes to the worst, I can dig a grave."

"I'm sure it is—very heroic," gasped Lucy. The tears came to her eyes.

He frowned irritably. "Nothing of the kind. Somebody must go, of course. The physicians in Abingdon are married men. I am a stranger, and have nobody. There is nothing to keep me in this world but a little business which I have to do, and that lies in Otoga. I really must ride on. But I will take you safely home first. Where are you staying?"

"At the cabin yonder. Behind the pines. Thomas Van Cleve's."

The doctor had stepped before her to bend aside the bushes. He stopped short, and stood motionless a moment, his back to her. When he turned there was an alteration in his face which she could not define. The actor was gone; the real man looked out for an instant from behind the curtain.

"Young Van Cleve lives in that cabin?"

"Yes, with his wife and child."

"A child? Is it a boy?"

"Yes, the dearest little fellow. Why do you ask?"

A smile, or it might have been a nervous contortion, flickered over the fat, amiable face. His tones became exceedingly soft and lazy.

"It is with Van Cleve I had business to settle. I have been looking for him a long time."

"Then you will come to the house with me?"

She would have passed on, but stopped, troubled and frightened, she knew not why. The man had not heard her; he stood slowly stroking his heavy chin, deliberating. Certainly there was nothing dramatic in the stout figure in its long linen coat, low hat, and boots sunk in the mud—there was not a trace of emotion on the flabby, apathetic features, yet Lucy cowered as though she had been brought face to face with a naked soul in the crisis of its life.

"I have been looking for him a long time," he repeated, talking to himself. "But there is Otoga. They need me in Otoga."

There was not a sound. Not the fall of a leaf. Even the incessant sough of the wind through the gorges was still. The world seemed to keep silence. The time comes to every man when the devil of his life-long appetites and passions rises to face the God that is in him for a final struggle.

He looked up at the cabin; it was but a step. He had been following Van Cleve for years. He drew his breath quickly once, thrust the bushes aside, and began to climb the rock.

The sun suddenly flashed out; a bird fluttered up from the thicket, and perched on a bough close beside him, sending out a clear trill of song. He stopped short, a quick, pleased heat coming to his face.

"Pretty little thing, hey? It knows me, d'ye see? It's watching me."

He waited a moment until the song ceased, and then nervously adjusted his hat.

"I'll go to those poor devils in Otoga. I reckon that's the right thing to do." And turning, he hastily mounted his horse.

Lucy felt that he was going to his death, and he seemed like an old friend. She ran across the road and put her hands up on the horse's neck.

"Good-bye," she said.

"Good-bye, Miss Coyt."

"I will never see you again! God bless you!"

"*Me?*" He looked at her, bewildered. "God? Oh yes. Well, perhaps so." He rode down the road, and the stout figure and flapping linen coat disappeared in the fog.

Four days passed. Dumfort, who appeared to be a man of leisure, lounged about the cabin, helping with the work, and occasionally bringing news from Otoga, gathered from some straggler who was flying from the fever. He came in one morning and beckoned Van Cleve out.

"There's one of them poor wretches fallen by the wayside. He's got the plague. It's my belief there's not an hour's life in him."

"I'll come." Van Cleve hastily gathered some simple remedies; he had not heroism enough to leave his family and sacrifice his life for his neighbours, but he was a kindly fellow, and could not turn back from any dying creature creeping to his door. The two men went down the mountain together.

"I wanted," said Dumfort, "to pull him under a rock. But he said, 'No, let me die out-of-doors.'"

"That was a queer notion."

"Yes." Dumfort glanced askance at his companion. "He's ben down doctorin' in Otoga. Went there voluntarily. I hearn of him two days ago." After an embarrassed pause, he added, "He wants to see you, Thomas. You personally."

"Me? Who is he?" (halting).

Dumfort lowered his voice to a quick whisper. "It's the man that's ben follerin' you an' your'n, Thomas."

Van Cleve uttered an oath, but it choked on his lips. "An' he's dying? What does he want of me?"

"God knows, I don't." The men stood silent. "He's been doctorin' them pore souls in Otoga," ventured Dumfort, presently.

Still Van Cleve did not move. Then, with a jerk, he started down-hill. "I'll go to him. Bring them other medicines, Dumfort."

But when he reached the dying man he saw that it was too late for medicines. He kneeled beside him and lifted his head, motioning Dumfort to stand back out of hearing.

What passed between them no one but God ever knew.

As the sun was setting that day Van Cleve came to the cabin. He was pale and haggard, but he tried to speak cheerfully.

"It was a poor fellow, Dorcas, down in the woods as died of the fever. Dumfort an' I have buried him. But I'd like you an' Miss Coyt to come to the grave. It 'd seem kinder, somehow." He carried the baby in his arms, and when they reached the place—it was a patch of sunny sward, where the birds sang overhead—he said: "Humpty, I wish you'd kneel down on the grave an' say your little prayer. I think he'd know, an' 'd feel better of it; an'—there's another reason."

The next week Miss Coyt received a letter from home, which, with very red cheeks, she told Dorcas would compel her immediate return home. Mr. Pettit, of whom she had told her, had received a call, and had asked her to be his wife, and this would put an end to her experiment of teaching in the South. In a day or two Dumfort drove her back to Abingdon, and the little family in the cabin returned to their usual quiet routine of life.

MRS NOAH'S ARK
by Gelett Burgess

MRS. NOAH FIGTRY stood upon the huge front gallery, between the Doric columns of the "big house," her hands clasped beneath her blue gingham apron, dispiritedly regarding the main road, a hundred yards away. Her pursed New England lips expressed disapproval. It was March, and March is disconsolate enough anywhere, but the cold gray day made the down-at-the-heels plantation seem more ruinous than ever. Mrs. Noah was alone in temporary possession of the house, having come from New England to take charge during her son-in-law's absence. The prospect of two weeks' loneliness in this dreary environment was, to a person of her lively temperament, depressing.

"If the Lord would only send *something* interesting, I wouldn't mind, if it was only a plaid pig," she mused.

As if in answer to this prayer, at that moment a little procession appeared coming round a turn of the road. It was led by a pleasant-looking man in blue overalls, who guided with his hands the shafts of a highly decorated circus cage on gilded wheels, which was pushed by a solemn, wrinkled, muddy elephant, bending his forehead to the rear of the car. The beast was directed in his labors by a barelegged Oriental-looking person with a turban and white blouse, who walked alongside. Behind this group stalked a giraffe, who bore, seated perilously astride, a buxom, smiling woman of some forty years.

"For the land sakes!" Mrs. Noah ejaculated, "if that don't beat the Book of Revelation! I wonder if I'm dreamin' 'em, or are they really alive? If that ain't the tag-end of a circus, I never see a wild-beast show in *my* life. I do believe they're turnin' in here, and me in my apron and curl-papers!"

Directly in front of the door the elephant, at a word from his driver, stopped, and the procession came to a standstill.

The woman slid gracefully down from her perch, with a sigh of relief; the man in blue overalls dropped his shafts and came up to the front steps, taking off his hat.

"Good afternoon," he said, politely. "Pretty muddy roads you have along here."

"What in the world did you bring them critters in here for?" was Mrs. Noah's rejoinder. "If you expect to set up a show in my front yard, I may as well tell you that it ain't worth the trouble. They ain't nobody here but me and the malaria."

"Lady, I'd like to introduce the Princess Ziffio, the snake-charmer and contortionist, and Ramo Bung, the elephant-driver, late of Sorrowtop's Circus," the man explained. "My name is Steggins, and I'm a lion-tamer from the same show."

"I'm proud to know you. It ain't often I meet celebrities in these parts," was Mrs. Noah's welcome, as she placidly awaited further developments.

"You see, it's this way, lady," Mr. Steggins went on, affably: "The show's bust up on account of a small financial difficulty, bringing on a seizure by the sheriff. Now, as me and my partners ain't been paid our salaries for two months, we just laid our hands on what we could find last night and are holding them as security for the money that's due us. It ain't our fault that the manager was crooked, and we don't propose to pay his debts; so what we want you to do is to let us hide the animals in your place until we can find a scow to take 'em down the river and sell 'em."

"What in the world do you mean?" Mrs. Noah exclaimed. "I ain't got any tent, nor even a barn. I'm real sorry for you, but I don't see what I can do— There's the old mill down by the river."

"That won't do at all," said Steggins, uneasily; "the sheriff will look there first thing. It ain't so easy to hide an elephant and a giraffe. We got to put 'em in some place where people won't be likely to suspect. See here; if you'll let us hide our property in your house for a week, we'll agree to pay you two hundred and fifty dollars as soon as we've sold the beasts."

"Why, you can't ever get that critter through the front door, much less upstairs," said Mrs. Noah, pointing to the elephant.

Ramo Bung now broke in excitedly. "Oh yes, yes!" he exclaimed; "it is a just perfection of sizes. You regard with pleasure?" He snatched a hoe from the ground by the front steps and applied it to the elephant's side in measurement. The creature was not a large one, being only one and a half hoe-handles in height. Running up to the double front doors, the Hindu demonstrated the possibility of entrance. "You accept the certainty? Even he can with kneeling crawl, I guiding in wisdom!"

Mrs. Noah Figtry had already rapidly estimated what two hundred and fifty dollars could do to improve her son-in-law's place. In an instant her mind was made up, her cool practical head defeated by her childlike emotions and kind, indulgent heart.

"Well," she said, "when Ebeneezer left I didn't calculate to take in no boarders, but if you think you can get that elephant into the parlor, I don't know but what I'll let you try it, just to see how you come out. I can't think what you can do with a giraffe, unless you put his head up a chimney somewheres. But perhaps he can be made to go in the bath-room with a little squeezin'. What you got in that bag, anyway? Looks like it was boilin'. I won't tolerate no rabbits! Of all things, I do hate a rabbit."

The Princess Ziffio was already loosening the ropes which bound the sack, and at this moment the mass fell to the ground and began to squirm convulsively.

"Snakes, I do declare! I can't abide snakes. I couldn't sleep a wink at night! You just take that bag of varmints as far away from the house as you can get it."

"Oh, he won't hurt you," asserted the Princess; "he's only a boy-constrictor, and he's got thawed out in the sun, that's all. We'll just put him in a cool place, and he won't give you a bit of trouble."

"There ain't no cellar to this house, and the coolest place I know is the ice-chest. He might possibly scrouge in there, though I can't say as I'd be at all easy in my mind about it. They ain't any lock on the door." Mrs. Noah was still holding her skirts raised, and kept at a safe distance.

Hardly had she said this, when a terrific and prolonged roar of blood-curdling intensity shook the shutters of the cage. Mrs. Noah was inside the house in an instant, behind barred doors. She reappeared later at the parlor window, which she gently raised a quarter of an inch. "You never said nothin' about lions," she cried, hysterically. "I consider I'm doin' considerable to welcome an elephant into my front parlor, and a giraffe in the bath-room, but roarin' lions is altogether *too* much. You go along and don't bother me any more."

Mr. Steggins reassured her with a laughing voice. "Why, lady," he said, "Joshua wouldn't hurt a fly. He was born in captivity, and he's forty years old, without a tooth in his head. He's tame as a puppy. I can have him right in my room. He wouldn't roar if he wa'n't so hungry, but he hasn't been fed for two days, and then only bones and sawdust."

Mrs. Noah timidly emerged again. "You ain't got any seven-horned beasts or nothin', have you? That roar did give me a start, but I don't know but I might as well be hung for a sheep as a lamb if I've got to keep house for a whole menagerie. It does seem a shame to leave a dumb animal outside without a roof to help himself to, don't it? I'll go up and sit on the ridge-pole while you get that critter into the house; and mind you lock the door after him when you get him up-stairs. I ain't goin' to be devoured by a ragin', rampin' lion at *my* time of life." At that she scurried up-stairs, and, a little later, appeared on the flat roof, from which post of security she surveyed the installation over the eaves.

One shutter was removed from the side of the cage, and Joshua—a tawny, dignified Numidian lion—was discovered, his eyes blinking with the unaccustomed glare. Into his den Steggins entered nonchalantly by a door in the rear, and threw a noose round the beast's neck. The lion arose and shook himself like a dog, and then, urged by a slap on the rump, slowly descended from the cage and was dragged unresistingly into the house.

Mrs. Noah, who had been gazing in terror, now breathed freer. After the interval her caution demanded she descended from the roof, and hurrying breathlessly down-stairs, joined the perspiring group on the portico. Princess Ziffio informed her that the serpent had already been safely removed to its new abode.

All the lighter pieces of furniture having been moved into the back room, proceedings were now begun with the elephant, who was manœuvred clumsily up the creaking front steps under the guidance of Ramo Bung, who emitted a stream of directions in Hindustani. A violent percussion against the doorjambs, the crash of a newel-post, and the overturning of a hat-rack marked his progress into the front parlor, where he rested quietly, exploring the precincts within range of his trunk.

Only the giraffe now remained, patiently grazing on the Virginia creeper that grew over the columns.

His entrance was effected with a grotesque awkwardness that made Mrs. Noah laugh, in spite of her fear for the transom. His neck was bent stiffly down like a pump-handle by the weight of Steggins, who was forced to climb a chair to reach the animal's horns. But once inside the hallway, he was propelled rapidly, though reluctantly, into the bath-room. The upper sash of the window was dropped, and the animal took advantage of the aperture to gaze at the levee on the bank of the Mississippi, about a mile distant.

The four conspirators entered the house at last, fairly safe against discovery. The lion-tamer and the Hindu left to complete their preparations for the animals' comfort, while Mrs. Noah and Princess Ziffio set about getting dinner in the kitchen.

"Well," said the hostess, when the quartet was assembled about the dining-room table, "I've often seen 'Entertainment for Man and Beast' on tavern signboards, but the last thing I ever thought I'd be doin' was that! What do you feed the critters, anyway?"

"Those sucking-pigs will do just right for the lion. One a day is enough," Mr. Steggins said. "Hay or corn-husks for the elephant and giraffe."

"Do tell! Why, I thought you fed elephants on peanuts!" was Mrs. Noah's comment. She turned to the Princess: "What do you want to give your snake in the ice-box? Eggs, I s'pose."

"Oh, he won't need anything at all. He was fed only last New-year's day."

"My land! He'd make a prime husband for a lazy woman, wouldn't he?" said Mrs. Noah. Then she looked curiously at the woman.

"Whatever are you Princess of, anyway?" she inquired, regarding the snake-charmer's good-natured, stupid face, her heavy coils of straight black hair and the elaborate curl swinging over her nose. "I'd never suspect your father was a king, though they *do* say emperors and sultans and such are as thick as flies in August out in them heathen lands of Asia."

"Oh, Mr. Gentry, our advertising man, made up that name for me. I'm really Mrs. Bung. Ramo here is my husband, though we was married only last month."

Ramo Bung showed a score of glittering white teeth as he clasped his wife's fat, pudgy hand ecstatically. "Yes, yes, we are allies quite undoubtedly!" he proclaimed. "Even the honeymoon is not yet out, and our hearts are packed to tightening with quite absolute blisses!"

"By the way, don't you think you could get your elephant's feet out the side window, one at a time, and wash them off with a pail of water?" Mrs. Noah asked the Hindu, anxiously. "I'm afraid he's goin' to make dreadful unsightly work of that body-Brussels carpet in spite of the straw, stompin' around."

Ramo Bung bowed with immense deference. "It shall doubtless be experimented at, Mrs. Lady. I will be endeavoring to Jumbo the Junior with the next morning. He is being at this time unremittingly fastened against the leg of piano. Only to-night with careless training he shall acquire the machination of the folding-bed for helpfulness of myself. It can be opened and shut easily, assisted by proboscis, doubtlessly."

Steggins, who felt an unfeigned fondness for his own charge, now spoke up:

"LADY, I'D LIKE TO INTRODUCE THE PRINCESS ZIFFIO AND RAMO BUNG"

"Mrs. Figtry, you really ought to know Joshua better. You'd learn to like him like I do when you see how affectionate he is. Why, if you rub his neck, he'll purr like a kitten, and I'd sleep with him if only he didn't snore so. I left him all curled up on that four-post bed of yours, and I'll be darned if he didn't wave his paw at me like a baby when I left."

"I suppose lions ain't really no more than great big cats, after all," said Mrs. Noah, "but I never looked at 'em in that light before. I expect he might like some milk to-night. I could spare you a wash-bowl full just as well as not, if you promise he wouldn't spill it. I would like to have him get after the rats in the woodshed. They do beat all Greely out there."

The Hindu interposed excitedly. "Have a fear, have a fear!" he cried; "Jumbo the Junior is distracted of mice from out his brains, yes! Even in the number of one small mouse his insides turn, and he trumpets of extremest caution. Two mouses will he break his constriction — very so, indeed! How say further what mices of three will obtain by him? It is of fury certainly. I must

be vigilant with candles all inside the night-time."

Mrs. Noah gasped. "Dear me suz!" she exclaimed, "elephants are just as bad as womenfolks, ain't they? I do hope he won't jump on that parlor table if he's frightened. They ain't nothin' can happen to your snake, is they?" she inquired of the Princess. "I do believe I left a lot of broilers in the ice-chest. Well, never mind; I expect they are about half a mile down his throat by this time."

After dinner, their extraordinary live stock having been fed and watered and the dishes washed, Mrs. Noah was persuaded to visit her four-footed guests. She waited outside the upper bedroom door until Steggins had entered, lighted a lamp, and tied the lion to the bedpost. Then she went in on tiptoe, as if visiting a sick-room, speaking in a hushed whisper.

"Well, of all things! Ain't he too cute for anything?" she said. "I never thought a wild lion could feel so much to home in a back bedroom."

Joshua was crouching in a kitten-

RAMO BUNG MANOEUVRED HIM INTO THE FRONT PARLOR

ish pose upon the braided rag rug, lazily licking his paws. He raised his heavy head to blink with yellow eyes at his landlady.

"Well, as I'm a sinner, he's getting bald!" she exclaimed. "I'll bet a hairpin I could cure him and keep his mane from falling out!" In her interest she approached the brute fearlessly and laid a hand upon his neck. Joshua purred with a basso - profundo church - organ vibration. "Dandruff! I thought so. Looks like a snow-storm. Here, Mr. Steggins, you just reach me that bottle of Paderewski Hirsutine in the medicine-closet over your head, and I'll have a good growth of new hair started in less than a week. Say, does lion's hair ever turn gray? I've got some Brunette Rejuvenator that 'll fix his color just as natural as life. Or I don't know but what you'd call him a blond, after all. Seems to me he's kind o' betwixt an' between. He's sandy-complected, I should say." She regarded him judicially. "I believe I'll look up a ball of yarn for him

to play with," she said, as she left. "I had no idea lions behaved so clever. Why, they're as much like folks as second cousins."

Her next visit was to the front parlor, where Jumbo Junior stood rocking to and fro like a ship at anchor in a swell, his lithe trunk questing the air with sinuous curves. He held it out to her inquisitively. She attempted to shake hands with him, but he drew back. "You ought to teach that critter better manners," she remarked to the Hindu. "Though, to be sure, I never did quite know whether an elephant's trunk was most like a hand or a nose. Will you look at them toe-nails! I do hope there aren't any of them ingrowin'. What does he want, anyway?"

Jumbo Junior himself answered her question by deftly removing her stick-pin from the front of her dress and carefully inserting it in the ceiling. After this, he waved his trunk aloft, broke a piece of glass from the hanging-lamp shade, and threw it on the floor.

"My stars and garters, ain't he sassy! Now I've always heard that elephants had more intelligence than all the other animals put together. You'd think he'd know he'd got to walk round this room barefoot. How much do you suppose he could lift?"

"Entire immenseness, past eight horse," said the Hindu. "In Cawnpore, I did see a lonesome elephant push a house downside."

Mrs. Noah gazed musingly upon the elephant's bulk: "I've often wished that piano could be moved into the back room, but these niggers here ain't no more use than woodchucks. If you want to give him a stint, there's lots of chores round the house he'll be real handy at. . . . But I expect you hadn't ought to require a parlor-boarder to exert himself too much. If he's cold in the night, I've got a spare bedspread up in the garret. Now try to shake hands again, Jumbo. You must act genteel when you're in my parlor." And after shak-

ing the elephant's trunk cordially, she left the room.

Then she visited the giraffe in the bath-room. Accompanied by the Princess, she opened the door, to find the animal still standing at the window, gazing pensively out into the night. As they entered, the giraffe's head turned in their direction, and a pair of melting brown eyes gazed down at them. Her mouth opened and emitted a noise that was something between a wheeze and a whinny.

"Now I was *afraid* that giraffe was going to catch his death of cold!" cried Mrs. Noah, her quick benevolence instantly aroused.

The Princess Ziffio laughed. "Oh, Milly, she's all right. I reckon she just smells the hay, that's all."

"Hay-fever! Just what I thought! I can't see a dumb beast suffer under my roof. I've got some of Dr. Surenuff's Celebrated Specific handy, and I'm goin' to rub it on his throat. It may take

"I LEFT HIM ALL CURLED UP ON THAT FOUR-POST BED OF YOURS"

seven or eight bottles, but it's fortunate I've got plenty of it in the house. Just move in that step-ladder you'll see in the hall closet, please, and I'll go and get the remedy."

In a few minutes more she had mounted a somewhat unsteady perch and began to administer the lotion. "Strange how much this creature's eyes favor Lucy's," she said to herself, massaging energetically. "I always *did* admire brown eyes. Ebeneezer always used to say you can get a black eye too easy for 'em to be pretty. Lucy admires to get herself up in low-cut gowns; I s'pose she would even if she had a neck like this. Say, Princess, hand me up a couple of them crash bath-towels, will you? I think Milly ought to have a regular bandage. I'll take my needle and thread and sew 'em on good. Don't you think I might tie the top onto his horns so it won't slip down? Hold your head still, won't you, please! My land! the airs this critter puts on! Bridles like a girl of sixteen. There! I guess that 'll keep her from gettin' any worse. She does look ridiculous, don't she? If I once stop to laugh, I'll fall off this step-ladder."

The Princess gazed stolidly at the result. "You got an awful good heart, Mrs. Figtry," she said, "but I don't reckon dumb animals suffer much like us folks."

"What! With all that throat to be sore!" cried Mrs. Noah, descending the steps. "Don't you believe it! Animals have got organs and innerds just like ours. If you'd cleaned and drawn as many chickens as I have, you'd known that. Now what that animal wants is a good hot bath and then be well wrapped up. But I don't suppose we could get her in the tub; that zinc's too slippery; and then the water 'd never reach up beyond her knees, anyway. But I tell you what I'm goin' to do I'm goin' to fill a hot-water bottle and fasten it on this giraffe's chest. That 'll do more good than anything else. But where in the world her neck leaves off and her chest begins I'm jiggered if I can tell! I hope your snake won't get sick, Princess, for I consider I'd have to draw the line at reptiles. They don't hardly seem to deserve even pity from a Christian, but I hope I won't be tempted to allow him to suffer."

Mrs. Noah's ministrations were at last finished by means of a complicated net of tapes, and the two women bade the men good night and prepared for bed. Their repose was somewhat broken, however, by the snoring of the trio of quadrupeds. Joshua's almost continuous performance reverberated through the night. Occasionally the plaintive wheezing of the giraffe in the bath-room awoke Mrs. Noah, and she made several trips of visitation in her nightgown to renew the temperature of the hot-water bottle by means of an alcohol-lamp and a tea-kettle. The Princess, however, slept on serenely. A heavy jar at midnight and a rattle of window-panes at four o'clock in the morning marked the limits of Jumbo Junior's deep sleep. From the ice-chest no sound was heard.

So a few days passed, during which time Mr. Steggins scoured the neighborhood to find some raft or barge upon which to make his voyage to Memphis. During his absence his hostess's acquaintance with the three animals and the married couple progressed toward friendship.

A feature of Mrs. Noah's methodical habits was her diary—a small octavo bound in faded morocco—the week-days laboriously altered from 1887, the year of its publication, to the current calendar. A few excerpts from this volume would indicate the progress of events in her household:

"*Tuesday, March 27.*—Last night I heard Jumbo Junior whining in his sleep. Thought he might have a tusk-ache. Went down-stairs with a bottle of oil of clove and a wash-rag. Stepped on something at foot of stairs. Felt just like a big sausage, only more energetic. Screamed. The Princess (found out she really comes from Hoboken) come down in her shawl. It was the big snake. Sat on banisters while she gave it two soup-ladles full of soothing-syrup. Ramo came out in Ebeneezer's smoking-jacket and helped lift the snake into the ice-chest. Elephant didn't have toothache, after all.

"*Wednesday, March 28.*—Cloudy, S W. wind. Giraffe still enjoying poor health. Tried hot applications and tied two pairs of bed-socks on her feet. Wrapped Ebeneezer's flannelette bath-robe round her shoulders. Found later

MRS. NOAH MADE SEVERAL TRIPS OF VISITATION

she had succeeded in getting a packet of pennyroyal, four moth-balls, and a cigar out of the left-hand pocket and was chewing them. Her swallow is 'way up on top of her neck, not half-way down as I naturally expected. Have been trying to teach Jumbo Junior to shake hands. He can drink a tumbler of molasses very nicely. Joshua's hair seems to be im-proving. Tried a little Hirsutine on his tail, at the end. He got into my room and woke me up at 3 A.M. Must have left his door open. Only two pigs left."

So a week passed without Mrs. Noah's interesting family having been discovered by the sheriff, and each day she be-came more fond of her new friends. She watched, as with a doting mother's eye, the improvement which she believed was apparent in Joshua's coat and the gentle Milly's voice, while Jumbo Junior's adaptability to instruction pleased her beyond words. The silent, inscrutable Princess baffled her, but the Hindu's vocabulary and diction kept her in a continual glee.

"Oh, there is so muchness!" cried Ramo Bung, when he was shown the Mississippi. "Oh, be astonished beyond utterness!"

And so, when at last Steggins procured a raft and moored it to the pier by the molasses-sheds, the kind-hearted hostess wiped away the tears that came to her eyes. The boa-constrictor she was indeed glad to be rid of, for it was the one cloud on her week of happiness, but when Milly's plaintive eyes had looked their last at her, and Joshua had been dragged, whining, aboard, it was all she could do to speak. It only remained for Jumbo Junior, of his own accord, to offer her his trunk for her to break down with emotion.

"I don't know *when* I've had such a pleasant time," she said. "I do hope you'll get to Memphis all right; and be sure and send me word how you get along and how Joshua stood the trip. Now here's four bottles of Smiley's Embrocation for Milly's neck and feet. Be sure you rub it well in, night and morning. If I only had a bottle of aconite pills, I'd like her to have them."

Steggins took her hand with a fierce grip. "Good-by, Mis' Figtry," he said. "You treated us square, and we'll treat you square. Just as soon as I get to Memphis and sell the animals I'll send you the money. You've been a good friend to Joshua, and he'll never forget you, I know."

Ramo Bung prostrated himself before her in an elaborate salaam. "Good-by with condescension," he cried. "Bung family are in salutement to your home with excellence. There is a doubtless explosion of violent heart on my interior. Ever so much blessing come against you."

"Well," said Mrs. Noah, "now you've found the way I hope you'll come again sometime. The world ain't such a big place but that we may meet again."

Mrs. Noah sobbed as she watched the little expedition sweep away. Then, just as they were abreast of the house, a long, muffled roar came to her over the rushing waters, as Joshua lifted up his voice in mournful lament. In spite of herself she smiled through her tears.

Soon the barge was far away, rapidly diminishing in the distance. When at last it drifted out of her sight she turned to her cook-stove and brewed a pot of strong tea.

"Well," she said over the third cup, "what can't be cured must be endured. I must say this place looks like Sam Patch in a hail-storm—I guess it'll do me good to go to spring cleanin'!"

The month of April, a year later, found Mrs. Noah Figtry home again in Duxbury, immersed in the quiet of New England life. From the quaint collection of friends that she had made in Tennessee no word had come, except a draft for two hundred and fifty dollars and a short misspelled letter from Mr. Steggins, announcing their safe arrival in Memphis and subsequent sale of the animals, and employment by Wilder's Triplex Conglomeration.

It was with a feeling of keen disappointment, then, that, returning late one Saturday night from a week's visit in Boston, she learned that Wilder's circus had been in town. It was breaking camp that very night, and would on Sunday proceed to Plymouth. Mrs. Noah, eagerly interrogating her neighbors, found scant satisfaction in their reports. The show, it was true, boasted a small menagerie, including a lion, a giraffe, and two elephants, but it was not easy to identify the animals from the meagre descriptions she received.

"I should know Joshua anywhere by a scar on his left cheek," Mrs. Noah declared, "but as for Jumbo Junior and Milly, I ain't so sure I'd recognize them, unless I met a wheezing giraffe and an elephant that volunteered to shake hands with me. But it seems strange that nobody saw that mealy-mouthed Hindu and the snake-princess. As for Mr. Steggins, he ain't the kind of man that's likely to keep any job long, and maybe he's in Terra del Fuego by this time. Howsomever, I'm determined to go over

"Don't you know me, Joshua?"

to Plymouth on Monday to see the show. I'll spear around, and if I don't see any folks or critters I know, I'll inquire. They say these show-people all know each other."

On Sunday morning Mrs. Noah Figtry proceeded decorously to church. As she approached the meeting-house, she observed an unusual stir amongst the villagers on the street, and upon the steps of the edifice were groups of church members excitedly discussing some surprising piece of news. A band of small boys charged by her on the run, their faces lighted by adventurous anticipation. Deftly capturing one by the arm, Mrs. Noah demanded information. The answer was sufficiently alarming. Wilder's Triplex Conglomeration, *en route* for Plymouth, had discovered that the door of the lion's cage had been left open and its occupant was missing. Somewhere between Kingston and Duxbury a lion was at large, and a party of searchers from the circus was now on the animal's trail.

The second bell had already rung, but no one felt in a devotional mood, and the minister himself soon came out to learn the latest developments of the situation. A dozen plans for the capture of the beast were offered and debated. Mrs. Noah, an acknowledged authority on lions, was at her best, and became the centre of an admiring audience, to whom she described, as one with experience, the power of the human eye, the influence of kindness.

She was in the midst of her discourse, when of a sudden came a chorus of shrieks from down the road. A stampede of small boys swept back towards the growing concourse of people, and a prolonged roar in the distance proclaimed that the approach of the lion was imminent. In an instant the street was cleared. The crowd scuttled into the church, slammed the doors, and flew to the windows. On the steps only the bolder members of the congregation remained, anxiously peering down the road. Amongst these men and boys Mrs. Noah stood calm and dignified, the only woman who dared venture out.

Then around the curve by the post-office came a galloping tawny brute, scattering the dust in clouds as he ran. The watchers on the church steps, terrified by the sight, burst inside the church, leaving Mrs. Noah alone to confront the situation. She grasped the handle of her parasol tighter, and waited with supreme confidence till the last possible moment. The lion had now settled into a stealthy trot, and seemed about to pass the building without molesting its occupants, when Mrs. Noah, who had been gazing intently at him, took a step forward.

"It *is* Joshua, as I live!" she exclaimed; "there's that selfsame scar on his cheek, I declare!"

At the sound of her voice the lion stopped immediately and stood, lashing his tail. Then his heavy muzzle was raised, his fangless jaws opened, and he emitted a mournful roar. Mrs. Figtry stood her ground.

"Joshua, Joshua," she called to him, as one calls to a stray poodle; "don't you know me, Joshua?" and she started down the steps.

From the windows and through a hazardous slit of half-opened door the astonished members of the congregation stared upon a marvel. They saw her boldly approach the beast and lay her hand calmly upon his head. They saw his bloodthirsty rage wilt into docility as Joshua recognized his former benefactor. One by one the church-goers crept out upon the steps to witness this unwonted scene, the men first, the women following, timid but curious, ready at a moment's notice to bolt back into their refuge.

"You needn't be a bit scared," Mrs. Noah was saying. "I'll tend to this lion," grabbing him by the ear and swinging him round. "He's all heat up, anyhow. Deacon Skinner, can't you let me take your overcoat to wrap him up with? This southwest wind isn't like what he's used to in the tropics of Sahara, and I'm afraid he'll catch cold, perspiring so."

She took the overcoat that was hesitatingly offered her, spread it carefully on Joshua's back, pinning the sleeves around his neck. Then she sat herself upon his hind quarters as he lay in the middle of the road, and proceeded to give further orders.

"Now, Deacon Skinner, I want you should bring your buggy round here. I've got to take this lion home. It wouldn't do for him to stay here, and if he walks I'm afraid he'll be run into by some team. He ain't much used to travellin' afoot."

Deacon Skinner was meekly obedient, and going round to the sheds, untied his horse and led him back. But at the first sight of the lion the horse became paralyzed with terror. Nothing could induce him to move forward. The dilemma seemed unsolvable. Mrs. Figtry looked up and down the road in despair. Then the rhythmic thud of machinery was heard as an automobile touring-car came rapidly towards them.

Without a word, but with lips compressed, Mrs. Figtry stepped directly into its path. There, holding her parasol in front of her, she opened and shut it rapidly, making frantic signals to the chauffeur. He came to a stop a few feet away from her. There was no one else in the car.

"See here," she cried to him; "can't you take me and this lion back to the circus in your steam-engine? It's nothing more nor less than cruelty to animals to let him stay here, and horses are scared to death of him." She paused for his reply.

The chauffeur, with a grin, pulled off his mask of goggles. It was Steggins. "Why, how-de-do, Mis' Figtry?" he cried. "I'm proud to see you! Step right in. I never calculated to see you or Joshua again, least of all together. Come, Joshua," he commanded.

At the sound of his master's voice the old lion leaped into the automobile. Here he was pushed into a back seat. Mrs. Figtry, after seeing that the overcoat was well wrapped about the animal's shoulders, got in beside him. In another instant the car had bounded off down the road. The awestruck congregation watched its heroine well round the turn and then filed in to church.

MY COUSIN THE COLONEL
by *Thomas Bailey Aldrich*

I.

MRS. WATTLES frequently embarrasses me by remarking in the presence of other persons — our intimate friends, of course — "Wattles, you are not brilliant, but you are good."

From Mrs. Wattles's outlook, which is that of a very high ideal, there is nothing uncomplimentary in the remark, nothing so intended, but I must confess that I have sometimes felt as if I were paying a rather large price for character. Yet when I reflect on my cousin the colonel, and my own action in the matter, I am ready with gratitude to accept Mrs. Wattles's estimate of me, for if I am not good, I am not anything. Perhaps it is an instance of my lack of brilliancy that I am willing to relate certain facts which strongly tend to substantiate this. My purpose, however, is not to prove either my goodness or my dulness, but to leave some record, even if slight and imperfect, of my only relative. When a family is reduced like ours to a single relative, it is well to make the most of him. One should celebrate him annually, as it were.

One morning in the latter part of May, a few weeks after the close of the war of the rebellion, as I was hurrying down Sixth Avenue in pursuit of a heedless horse-car, I ran against a young person whose shabbiness of aspect was all that impressed itself upon me in the instant of collision. At a second glance I saw that this person was clad in the uniform of a Confederate soldier—an officer's uniform originally, for there were signs that certain insignia of rank had been removed from the cuffs and collar of the threadbare coat. He wore a wide-brimmed felt hat of a military fashion, decorated with a tarnished gilt cord, the two ends of which, terminating in acorns, hung down over his nose. His butternut trousers were tucked into the tops of a pair of high cavalry boots, of such primitive workmanship as to suggest the possibility that the wearer had made them himself. In fact, his whole appearance had an impromptu air about it. The young man eyed me gloomily for half a minute; then a light came into his countenance.

"Wattles—Tom Wattles!" he exclaimed. "Dear old boy!"

To be sure I was Thomas Wattles, and, under conceivable circumstances, dear old boy; but who on earth was he?

"You don't know me?" he said, laying a hand on each of my shoulders, and leaning back as he contemplated me with a large smile in anticipatory enjoyment of my surprise and pleasure when I should come to know him. "I am George W. Flagg, and long may I wave!"

My cousin Flagg! It was no wonder that I didn't recognize him.

When the Flagg family, consisting of father and son, removed to the South, George was ten years old and I was thirteen. It was twenty years since he and I had passed a few weeks together on Grandfather Wattles's farm in New Jersey. Our intimacy began and ended there, for it had not ripened into letters; perhaps because we were too young when we parted. Later I had had a hundred intermittent impulses to write to him, but did not. Meanwhile separation and silence had clothed him in my mind with something of the mistiness of a half-remembered dream. Yet the instant Washington Flagg mentioned his name, the boyish features began rapidly to define themselves behind the maturer mask, until he stood before me in the crude form in which my memory had slyly embalmed him.

Now my sense of kinship is particularly strong, for reasons which I shall presently touch upon, and I straightway grasped my cousin's hand with a warmth that would have seemed exaggerated to a bystander, if there had been a by-stander; but it was early in the day, and the avenue had not yet awakened to life. As this bitter world goes, a sleek, prosperous, well-dressed man does not usually throw much heartiness into his manner when he is accosted on the street by so unpromising and dismal an object as my cousin Washington Flagg was that morning. Not at all in the way of sounding the trumpet of my own geniality, but simply as the statement of a fact, I will say that I threw a great deal of heartiness into my greeting. This man to me meant Family.

I stood curiously alone in the world. My father died before I was born, and my mother shortly afterwards. I had neither brother nor sister. Indeed, I never had any near relatives except a grandfather until my sons came along. Mrs. Wattles, when I married her, was not merely an only child, but an orphan. Fate denied me even a mother-in-law. I had one uncle and one cousin. The former I do not remember ever to have seen, and my association with the latter, as has been stated, was of a most limited order. Perhaps I should have had less sentiment about family ties if I had had more of them. As it was, Washington Flagg occupied the position of sole kinsman, always excepting the little Wattleses, and I was as glad to see him that May morning in his poverty as if he had come to me loaded with the title-deeds of those vast estates which our ancestors (I wonder that I was allowed any ancestors: why wasn't I created at once out of some stray scrap of protoplasm?) were supposed to have held in the colonial period. As I gazed upon Washington Flagg I thrilled with the sense that I was gazing upon the materialization in a concrete form of all the ghostly brothers and sisters and nephews and nieces which I had never had.

"Dear old boy!" I exclaimed, in my turn, holding on to his hand as if I were going to lose him again for another twenty years. "Bless my stars! where did you come from?"

"From Dixie's Land," he said, with a laugh. "'Way down in Dixie."

In a few words, and with a picturesqueness of phrase in which I noted a rich Southern flavor, he explained the phenomenon of his presence in New York. After Lee's surrender at Appomattox Court House, my cousin had managed to reach Washington, where he was fortunate enough to get a free pass to Baltimore. He had nearly starved to death in making his way out of Virginia. To quote his words, "The wind that is supposed to be tempered expressly for shorn lambs was not blowing very heavily about that time." At Baltimore he fell in with a former Mobile acquaintance, from whom he borrowed a sum sufficient to pay the fare to New York—a humiliating necessity, as my cousin remarked, for a man who had been a colonel in Stonewall Jackson's brigade. Flagg had reached the city before daybreak, and had wandered

for hours along the water-front, waiting for some place to open, in order that he might look up my address in the Directory, if I were still in the land of the living. He had had what he described as an antediluvian sandwich the previous day at two o'clock, since which banquet no food had passed his lips.

"And I'll be hanged," he said, "if the first shop that took down its shutters wasn't a restaurant, with a cursed rib of roast beef, flanked with celery, and a ham in curl-papers staring at me through the window-pane. A little tin sign, with 'Meals at All Hours' painted on it, knocked the breath clean out of me. I gave one look, and ploughed up the street, for if I had staid fifteen seconds longer in front of that plate-glass, I reckon I would have burst it in. Well, I put distance between me and temptation, and by-and-by I came to a newspaper office, where I cornered a Directory. I was on the way to your house when we collided; and now, Tom Wattles, for Heaven's sake introduce me to something to eat. There is no false pride about me; I'd shake hands with a bone."

The moisture was ready to gather in my eyes, and for a second or two I was unable to manage my voice. Here was my only kinsman on the verge of collapse— one miserable sandwich, like a thin plank, between him and destruction. My own plenteous though hasty morning meal turned into reproachful lead within me.

"Dear old boy!" I cried again. "Come along! I can see that you are nearly famished."

"I've a right smart appetite, Thomas, there's no mistake about that. If appetite were assets, I could invite a whole regiment to rations."

I had thrust my hand under his arm, and was dragging him towards a small oyster shop, whose red balloon in a side street had caught my eye, when I suddenly remembered that it was imperative on me to be at the office at eight o'clock that morning, in order to prepare certain papers wanted by the president of the board, previous to a meeting of the directors. (I was at that time under-secretary of the Savonarola Fire-insurance Company.) The recollection of the business which had caused me to be on foot at this unusual hour brought me to a dead halt. I dropped my cousin's arm, and stood looking at him helplessly. It seemed so inhospita-

"'YOU DON'T KNOW ME?' HE SAID."

ble, not to say cold-blooded, to send him off to get his breakfast alone. Flagg misunderstood my embarrassment.

"Of course," he said, with a touch of dignity which pierced me through the bosom, "I do not wish to be taken to any place where I would disgrace you. I know how impossible I am. Yet this suit of clothes cost me twelve hundred dollars in Confederate scrip. These boots are not much to look at, but they were made by a scion of one of the first families of the South; I paid him two hundred dollars for them, and he was right glad to get it. To such miserable straits have Southern gentlemen been reduced by the vandals of the North. Perhaps you don't like the Confederate gray?"

"Bother your boots and your clothes!" I cried. "Nobody will notice them here." (Which was true enough, for in those days the land was strewed with shreds and patches of the war. The drivers and conductors of street cars wore overcoats made out of shoddy army blankets, and the dustmen went about in cast-off infantry caps.) "What troubles me is that I can't wait to start you on your breakfast."

"I reckon I don't need much starting."

I explained the situation to him, and suggested that instead of going to the restaurant, he should go directly to my house, and be served by Mrs. Wattles, to whom I would write a line on a leaf of my memorandum-book. I did not suggest this step in the first instance because the little oyster saloon, close at hand, had seemed to offer the shortest cut to my cousin's relief.

"So you're married?" said he.

"Yes—and you?"

"I haven't taken any matrimony in mine."

"I've been married six years, and have two boys."

"No! How far is your house?" he inquired. "Will I have to take a caar?"

"A 'caar'? Ah, yes—that is to say, no. A car isn't worth while. You see that bakery two blocks from here, at the right? That's on the corner of Clinton Place. You turn down there. You'll notice in looking over what I've written to Mrs. Wattles that she is to furnish you with some clothes, such as are worn by—by vandals of the North in comfortable circumstances."

"Tom Wattles, you are as good as a straight flush. If you ever come down South, when this cruel war is over, our people will treat you like one of the crowned heads—only a devilish sight better, for the crowned heads rather went back on us. If England had recognized the Southern Confederacy—"

"Never mind that; your tenderloin steak is cooling."

"Don't mention it! I go. But I say, Tom—Mrs. Wattles? Really, I am hardly presentable. Are there other ladies around?"

"There's no one but Mrs. Wattles."

"Do you think I can count on her being glad to see me at such short notice?"

"She will be a sister to you," I said, warmly.

"Well, I reckon that you two are a pair of trumps. *Au revoir.* Be good to yourself."

With this, my cousin strode off, tucking my note to Mrs. Wattles inside the leather belt buckled tightly around his waist. I lingered a moment on the curb-stone, and looked after him with a sensation of mingled pride, amusement, and curiosity. That was my Family, there it was, in that broad back and those not ungraceful legs, striding up Sixth Avenue, with its noble intellect intent on thoughts of breakfast. I was thankful that it had not been written in the book of fate that this limb of the closely pruned Wattles tree should be lopped off by the sword of war. But as Washington Flagg turned into Clinton Place, I had a misgiving. It was hardly to be expected that a person of his temperament, fresh from a four years' desperate struggle and a disastrous defeat, would refrain from expressing his views on the subject. That those views would be somewhat lurid, I was convinced by the phrases which he had dropped here and there in the course of our brief conversation. He was, to all intents and purposes, a Southerner. He had been a colonel in Stonewall Jackson's brigade. And Mrs. Wattles was such an uncompromising patriot! It was in the blood. Her great-grandfather, on the mother's side, had frozen to death at Valley Forge in the winter of 1778, and her grand-father, on the paternal side, had had his head taken off by a round shot from his Majesty's sloop of war *Porpoise* in 1812. I believe that Mrs. Wattles would have applied for a divorce from me if I had not served a year in the army at the beginning of the war.

I began bitterly to regret that I had been obliged to present my cousin to her so abruptly. I wished it had occurred to me to give him a word or two of caution, or that I had had sense enough to adhere to my first plan of letting him feed himself at the little oyster establishment round the corner. But wishes and regrets could not now mend the matter; so I hailed an approaching horse-car, and comforted myself on the rear platform with the reflection that perhaps the colonel would not wave the palmetto leaf too vigorously, if he waved it at all, in the face of Mrs. Wattles.

II.

The awkwardness of the situation disturbed me more or less during the forenoon; but fortunately it was a half-holiday, and I was able to leave the office shortly after one o'clock.

I do not know how I came to work myself into such a state of mind on the way up town, but as I stepped from the horse-car and turned into Clinton Place, I had a vague apprehension that I should find some unpleasant change in the facial aspect of the little red brick building I occupied — a scowl, for instance, on the brownstone eyebrow over the front door. I actually had a feeling of relief when I saw that the façade presented its usual unaggressive appearance.

As I entered the hall, Mrs. Wattles, who had heard my pass-key grating in the lock, was coming down stairs.

"Is my cousin here, Clara?" I asked, in the act of reaching up to hang my hat on the rack.

"No," said Mrs. Wattles. There was a tone in that monosyllable that struck me.

"But he has been here?"

"He has been here," replied Mrs. Wattles. "Possibly you noticed the bell-knob hanging out one or two inches. Is Mr. Flagg in the habit of stretching the bell-wire of the houses he visits, when the door is not opened in a moment? Has he escaped from somewhere?"

"'Escaped from somewhere!'" I echoed.

"I only asked; he behaved so strangely."

"Good heavens, Clara! what has the man done? I hope that nothing unpleasant has happened. Flagg is my only surviving relative — I may say *our* only surviving relative — and I should be pained to have any misunderstanding. I want you to like him."

"There was a slight misunderstanding at first," said Clara, and a smile flitted across her face, softening the features, which had worn an air of unusual seriousness and preoccupation. "But it is all right now, dear. He has eaten everything in the house, the bit of spring lamb I saved expressly for you; and has gone down town 'on a raid,' as he called it, in your second-best suit—the checked tweed. I did all I could for him."

"My dear, something has ruffled you. What is it?"

"Wattles," said my wife, slowly, and in a perplexed way, "I have had so few relatives that perhaps I don't know what to do with them, or what to say to them."

"You always say and do what is just right."

"I began unfortunately with Mr. Flagg, then. Mary was washing the dishes when he rang, and I went to the door. If he *is* our cousin, I must say that he cut a remarkable figure on the door-step."

"I can imagine it, my dear, coming upon you so unexpectedly. There *were* peculiarities in his costume."

"For an instant," Mrs. Wattles went on, "I took him for the ashman, though the ashman always goes to the area door, and never comes on Tuesdays; and then, before the creature had a chance to speak, I said, 'We don't want any,' supposing he had something to sell. Instead of going away quietly, as I expected him to do, the man made a motion to come in, and I slammed the door on him."

"Dear! dear!"

"What else could I do, all alone in the hall? How was I to know that he was one of the family?"

"What happened next?"

"Well, I saw that I had shut the lapel of his coat in the door, and that the man couldn't go away if he wanted to ever so much. Wasn't it dreadful? Of course I didn't dare to open the door, and there he was! He instantly began pounding on the panels and ringing the bell in a manner to curdle one's blood. He rang the bell at least a hundred times in succession. I stood there with my hand on the bolt, not daring to move or breathe. I called to Mary to put on her things, steal out the lower way, and bring the police. Suddenly everything was still outside, and presently I saw a piece of paper slyly slipping in over the threshold, oh, so slyly! I felt my hands and feet grow cold.

"OF COURSE I GOT BREAKFAST FOR HIM."

I felt that the man himself was about to follow that narrow strip of paper, that he was bound to get in that way, or through the key-hole, or somehow. Then I recognized your handwriting. My first thought was that you had been killed in some horrible accident—"

"And had dropped you a line?"

"I didn't reason about it, Wattles; I was paralyzed. I picked up the paper, and read it, and opened the door, and Mr. Flagg rushed in as if he had been shot out of something. 'Don't want any?' he shouted. 'But I do! I want some breakfast!' You should have heard him."

"He stated a fact, at any rate. Of course he might have stated it less vivaciously." I was beginning to be amused.

"After that he was quieter, and tried to make himself agreeable, and we laughed a little together over my mistake—that is, *he* laughed. Of course I got breakfast for him—and such a breakfast!"

"He had been without anything to eat since yesterday."

"I should have imagined," said Clara, "that he had eaten nothing since the war broke out."

"Did he say anything in particular about himself?" I asked, with a recurrent touch of anxiety.

"He wasn't particular what he said about himself. Without in the least seeing the horror of it, he positively boasted of having been in the rebel army."

"Yes—a colonel."

"That makes it all the worse," replied Clara.

"But they had to have colonels, you know."

"Is Mr. Flagg a Virginian, or a Mississippian, or a Georgian?"

"No, my dear; he was born in the State of Maine; but he has lived so long in the South that he's quite one of them for the present. We must make allowances for him, Clara. Did he say anything else?"

"Oh yes."

"What did he say?"

"He said he'd come back to supper."

It was clear that Mrs. Wattles was not favorably impressed by my cousin, and, indeed, the circumstances attending his advent were not happy. It was likewise clear that I had him on my hands, temporarily at least. I almost reproach myself even now for saying "on my hands," in connection with my own flesh and blood. The responsibility did not so define itself at the time. It took the shape of a novel and pleasing duty. Here was my only kinsman, in a strange city, without friends, money, or hopeful outlook. My course lay before me as straight as a turnpike. I had a great deal of family pride, even if I did not have any family to speak of, and I was resolved that what little I had should not perish for want of proper sustenance.

Shortly before six o'clock Washington Flagg again presented himself at our door-step, and obtained admission to the house with fewer difficulties than he had encountered earlier in the day.

I do not think I ever saw a man in destitute circumstances so entirely cheerful as my cousin was. Neither the immediate past, which must have been full of hardships, nor the immediate future, which was not lavish of its promises, seemed to give him any but a momentary and impersonal concern. At the supper table he talked much and well, exceedingly well, I thought, except when he touched on the war, which he was continually doing, and then I was on tenter-hooks. His point of view was so opposed to ours as to threaten in several instances to bring on an engagement all along the line. This calamity was averted by my passing something to him at the critical moment. Now I checked his advance by a slice of cold tongue, and now I turned his flank with another cup of tea; but I questioned my ability to preserve peace throughout the evening. Before the meal was at an end there had crept into Clara's manner a polite calmness which I never like to see. What was I going to do with these two after supper, when my cousin Flagg, with his mind undistracted by relays of cream toast, could give his entire attention to the Lost Cause?

As we were pushing the chairs back from the table, I was inspired with the idea of taking our guest off to a café concert over in the Bowery—a *volksgarten* very popular in those days. While my whispered suggestion was meeting Clara's cordial approval, our friend Bleeker dropped in. So the colonel and Bleeker and I passed the evening with "lager-beer and Meyerbeer," as my lively kinsman put it; after which he spent the night on the sofa in our sitting-room, for we had no spare chamber to place at his disposal.

"I shall be very snug here," he said, smiling down my apologies. "I'm a 'possum for adapting myself to any odd hollow."

The next morning my cousin was early astir, possibly not having found that narrow springless lounge all a 'possum could wish, and joined us in discussing a plan which I had proposed overnight to Mrs. Wattles, namely, that he should hire an apartment in a quiet street near by, and take his meals—that was to say, his dinner—with us, until he could make such arrangements as would allow him to live more conveniently. To return South, where all the lines of his previous business connections were presumably broken, was at present out of the question.

"The war has ruined our people," said the colonel. "I will have to put up for a while with a place in a bank or an insurance office, or something in that small way. The world owes me a living, north or south."

His remark nettled me a little, though he was, of course, unaware of my relations with the Savonarola Fire-insurance Company, and had meant no slight.

"I don't quite see that," I observed.

"Don't see what?"

"How the world contrived to get so deeply into your debt—how all the points of the compass managed it."

"Thomas, I didn't ask to be born, did I?"

"Probably not."

"But I was born, wasn't I?"

"To all appearances."

"Well, then!"

"But you cannot hold the world in

"FLAGG GLANCED OVER THE 'WANTS' COLUMN IN THE EVENING JOURNAL."

general responsible for your birth. The responsibility narrows itself down to your parents."

"Then I am euchred. By one of those laws of nature which make this globe a sweet spot to live on, they were taken from me just when I needed them most—my mother in my infancy, and my father in my childhood."

"But your father left you something?"

"The old gentleman left me nothing, and I've been steadily increasing the legacy ever since."

"What did you do before the war?" inquired Mrs. Wattles, sympathetically. His mention of his early losses had touched her.

"Oh, a number of things. I read law for a while. At one time I was interested in a large concern for the manufacture of patent metallic burial cases; but nobody seemed to die that year. Good health raged like an epidemic all over the South.

Latterly I dabbled a little in stocks—and stocks dabbled in me."

"You were not successful, then?" I said.

"I was at first, but when the war fever broke out and the Southern heart was fired, everything that didn't go down went up."

"And you couldn't meet your obligations?"

"That wasn't the trouble—I couldn't get away from them," replied the colonel, with a winsome smile. "I met them at every corner."

The man had a fashion of turning his very misfortunes into pleasantries. Surely prosperity would be wasted on a person so gifted with optimism. I felt it to be kind and proper, however, to express the hope that he had reached the end of his adversity, and to assure him that I would do anything I could in the world to help him.

"Tom Wattles, I believe you would."

Before the close of that day Mrs. Wattles, who is a lady that does not allow any species of vegetation to accumulate under her feet, had secured a furnished room for our kinsman in a street branching off from Clinton Place, and at a moderate additional expense contracted to have him served with breakfasts on the premises. Previous to this I had dined down town, returning home in the evening to a rather heavy tea, which was really my wife's dinner—Sheridan and Ulysses (such were the heroic names under which the two little Wattleses were staggering) had their principal meal at midday. It was, of course, not desirable that the colonel should share this meal with them and Mrs. Wattles in my absence. So we decided to have a six-o'clock dinner; a temporary disarrangement of our domestic economy, for my cousin Flagg would doubtless find some acceptable employment before long, and leave the household free to slip back into its regular grooves.

An outline of the physical aspects of the exotic kinsman who had so unexpectedly added himself to the figures at our happy fireside seems not out of place here. The portrait, being the result of many sittings, does not in some points convey the exact impression he made upon us in the earlier moments of our intimacy; but that is not important.

Though Washington Flagg had first opened his eyes on the banks of the Penobscot, he appeared to have been planned by nature to adorn the banks of the Rappahannock. There was nothing of the New-Englander about him. The sallowness of his complexion and the blackness of his straight hair, which he wore long, were those of the typical Southerner. He was of medium height and loosely built, with a kind of elastic grace in his disjointedness. When he smiled he was positively handsome; in repose his features were nearly plain, the lips too indecisive, and the eyes lacking in lustre. A sparse tuft of beard at his chin—he was otherwise smoothly shaven—lengthened the face. There was, when he willed it, something very ingratiating in his manner—even Mrs. Wattles admitted that—a courteous and unconventional sort of ease. In all these surface characteristics he was a geographical anomaly. In the cast of his mind he was more Southern than the South, as a Northern

convert is apt to be. Even his speech, like the dyer's arm, had taken tints from his environment. One might say that his pronunciation had literally been colored by his long association with the colored race. He invariably said *flo'* for floor, and *djew* for dew; but I do not anywhere attempt a phonetic reproduction of his dialect; in its finer qualities it was too elusive to be snared in a network of letters. In spite of his displacements, for my cousin had lived all over the South in his boyhood, he had contrived to pick up a very decent education. As to his other attributes, he shall be left to reveal them himself.

III.

Mrs. Wattles kindly assumed the charge of establishing Washington Flagg in his headquarters, as he termed the snug hall bedroom in Macdougal Street. There were numberless details to be looked to. His wardrobe, among the rest, needed replenishing down to the most unconsidered button, for Flagg had dropped into our little world with as few impedimenta as if he had been a newly born infant. Though my condition, like that desired by Agur, the son of Jakeh, was one of neither poverty nor riches, greenbacks in those days were greenbacks. I mention the fact in order to say that my satisfaction in coming to the rescue of my kinsman would have been greatly lessened if it had involved no self-denial whatever.

The day following his installation I was partly annoyed, partly amused, to find that Flagg had purchased a rather expensive meerschaum pipe and a pound or two of Latakia tobacco.

"I cannot afford to smoke cigars," he explained. "I must economize until I get on my feet."

Perhaps it would have been wiser if I had personally attended to his expenditures, minor as well as major, but it did not seem practicable to leave him without a cent in his pocket. His pilgrimage down town that forenoon had apparently had no purpose beyond this purchase, though on the previous evening I had directed his notice to two or three commercial advertisements which struck me as worth looking into. I hesitated to ask him if he had looked into them. A collateral feeling of delicacy prevented me from breathing a word to Clara about the pipe.

Our reconstructed household, with its

unreconstructed member, now moved forward on the lines laid down. Punctually at a quarter to six P.M. my cousin appeared at the front door, hung his hat on the rack, and passed into the sitting-room, sometimes humming in the hall a bar or two of "The Bonny Blue Flag that bears a Single Star," to the infinite distaste of Mrs. Wattles, who was usually at that moment giving the finishing touches to the dinner table. After dinner, during which I was in a state of unrelaxed anxiety lest the colonel should get himself on too delicate ground, I took him into my small snuggery at the foot of the hall, where coffee was served to us, Mrs. Wattles being left to her own devices.

For several days everything went smoothly, beyond my hope. I found it so easy, when desirable, to switch the colonel on to one of my carefully constructed side tracks that I began to be proud of my skill and to enjoy the exercise of it. But one evening, just as we were in the middle of the dessert, he suddenly broke out with,

"We were conquered by mere brute force, you know!"

"That is very true," I replied. "It is brute force that tells in war. Wasn't it Napoleon who said that he had remarked that God was generally on the side which had the heaviest artillery?"

"The North had that, fast enough, and crushed a free people with it."

"A free people with four millions of slaves?" observed Mrs. Wattles, quietly.

"Slavery was a patriarchal institution, my dear lady. But I reckon it is exploded now. The Emancipation Proclamation was a dastardly war measure."

"It did something more and better than free the blacks," said Mrs. Wattles; "it freed the whites. Dear me!" she added, glancing at Sheridan and Ulysses, who, in a brief reprieve from bed, were over in one corner of the room dissecting a small wooden camel, "I cannot be thankful enough that the children are too young to understand such sentiments."

The colonel, to my great relief, made no reply; but as soon as Clara had closed the dining-room door behind her, he said, "Tom Wattles, I reckon your wife doesn't wholly like me."

"She likes you immensely," I cried, silently begging to be forgiven. "But she is a firm believer in the justice of the Northern cause."

"Maybe she lost a brother, or something."

"No; she never had a brother. If she had had one, he would have been killed in the first battle of the war. She sent me to the front to be killed, and I went willingly; but I wasn't good enough; the enemy wouldn't have me at any price after a year's trial. Mrs. Wattles feels very strongly on this subject, and I wish you would try, like a good fellow, not to bring the question up at dinner-time. I am squarely opposed to your views myself, but I don't mind what you say as she does. So talk to me as much as you want to, but don't talk in Clara's presence. When persons disagree as you two do, argument is useless. Besides, the whole thing has been settled on the battle-field, and it isn't worth while to fight it all over again on a table-cloth."

"I suppose it isn't," he assented, good-naturedly. "But you people up at the North here don't suspicion what we have been through. You caught only the edge of the hurricane. The most of you, I take it, weren't in it at all."

"Our dearest were in it."

"Well, we got whipped, Wattles, I acknowledge it; but we deserved to win, if ever bravery deserved it."

"The South was brave, nobody contests that; but 'tis not enough to be brave'—

"'The angry valor dashed
On the awful shield of God,'

as one of our poets says."

"Blast one of your poets! Our people were right, too."

"Come, now, Flagg, when you talk about your people, you ought to mean Northerners, for you were born in the North."

"That was just the kind of luck that has followed me all my life. My body belongs to Bangor, Maine, and my soul to Charleston, South Carolina."

"You've got a problem there that ought to bother you."

"It does," said the colonel, with a laugh.

"Meanwhile, my dear boy, don't distress Mrs. Wattles with it. She is ready to be very fond of you, if you will let her. It would be altogether sad and shameful if a family so contracted as ours couldn't get along without internal dissensions."

My cousin instantly professed the greatest regard for Mrs. Wattles, and declared that both of us were good enough to be

Southrons. He promised that in future he would take all the care he could not to run against her prejudices, which merely grew out of her confused conception of State rights and the right of self-government. Women never understood anything about political economy and government, anyhow.

Having accomplished thus much with the colonel, I turned my attention, on his departure, to smoothing Clara. I reminded her that nearly everybody North and South had kinsmen or friends in both armies. To be sure, it was unfortunate that we, having only one kinsman, should have had him on the wrong side. That was better than having no kinsman at all. (Clara was inclined to demur at this.) It had not been practicable for him to divide himself; if it had been, he would probably have done it, and the two halves would doubtless have arrayed themselves against each other. They would, in a manner, have been bound to do so. However, the war was over, we were victorious, and could afford to be magnanimous.

"But he doesn't seem to have discovered that the war is over," returned Mrs. Wattles. "He 'still waves.'"

"It is likely that certain obstinate persons on both sides of Mason and Dixon's Line will be a long time making the discovery. Some will never make it—so much the worse for them and the country."

Mrs. Wattles meditated and said nothing, but I saw that so far as she and the colonel were concerned the war was not over.

IV.

This slight breeze cleared the atmosphere for the time being at least. My cousin Flagg took pains to avoid all but the most indirect allusions to the war, except when we were alone, and in several small ways endeavored—with not too dazzling success—to be agreeable to Clara. The transparency of the effort was perhaps the partial cause of its failure. And then, too, the nature of his little attentions was not always carefully considered on his part. For example, Mrs. Wattles could scarcely be expected to lend herself with any grace at all to the proposal he made one sultry June evening to "knock her up" a mint-julep, "the most refreshing beverage on earth, madam, in hot weather, I can assure you." Judge Ashburton Todhunter, of Fauquier County, had taught him to prepare this pungent elixir from a private receipt for which the judge had once refused the sum of fifty dollars, offered to him by Colonel Stanly Bluegrass, of Chattanooga, and this was at a moment, too, when the judge had been losing very heavily at draw poker.

"All quiet along the Potomac," whispered the colonel, with a momentary pride in the pacific relations he had established between himself and Mrs. Wattles.

As the mint and one or two other necessary ingredients were lacking to our family stores, the idea of julep was dismissed as a vain dream, and its place supplied by iced Apollinaris, a liquid which my cousin characterized, in a hasty aside to me, as being a drink fit only for imbecile infants of a tender age.

Washington Flagg's frequent and familiar mention of governors, judges, colonels, and majors clearly indicated that he had moved in aristocratic latitudes in the South, and threw light on his disinclination to consider any of the humbler employments which might have been open to him. He had so far conceded to the exigency of the case as to inquire if there were a possible chance for him in the Savonarola Fire-insurance Company. He had learned of my secretaryship. There was no vacancy in the office, and if there had been, I would have taken no steps to fill it with my cousin. He knew nothing of the business. Besides, however deeply I had his interests at heart, I should have hesitated to risk my own situation by becoming sponsor for so unmanageable an element as he appeared to be.

At odd times in my snuggery after dinner Flagg glanced over the "wants" columns of the evening journal, but never found anything he wanted. He found many amusing advertisements that served him as pegs on which to hang witty comment, but nothing to be taken seriously. I ventured to suggest that he should advertise. He received the idea with little warmth.

"No, my dear boy, I can't join the long procession of scullions, cooks, butlers, valets, and bottle-washers which seems to make up so large a part of your population. I couldn't keep step with them. It is altogether impossible for me to conduct myself in this matter like a menial-of-all-work out of place. 'Wanted, a situation, by a respectable young person of temperate habits; understands the care of horses; is willing to go into the country and milk the cow with the crumpled horn.' No; many thanks."

"State your own requirements, Flagg. I didn't propose that you should offer yourself as coachman."

"It would amount to the same thing, Wattles. I should at once be relegated to his level. Some large opportunity is dead sure to present itself to me if I wait. I believe the office should seek the man."

"I have noticed that a man has to meet his opportunities more than half way, or he doesn't get acquainted with them. Mohammed was obliged to go to the mountain, after waiting for the mountain to come to him."

"Mohammed's mistake was that he didn't wait long enough. He was too impatient. But don't you fret. I have come to Yankeedom to make my fortune. The despot's heel is on your shore, and it means to remain there until he hears of something greatly to his advantage."

A few days following this conversation, Mr. Nelson, of Files and Nelson, wholesale grocers on Front Street, mentioned to me incidentally that he was looking for a shipping clerk. Before the war the firm had done an extensive Southern trade, which they purposed to build up again now that the ports of the South were thrown open. The place in question involved a great deal of out-door work—the loading and unloading of spicy cargoes, a life among the piers—all which seemed to me just suited to my cousin's woodland nature. I could not picture him nailed to a desk in a counting-room. The salary was not bewildering, but the sum was to be elastic, if ability were shown. Here was an excellent chance, a stepping-stone, at all events; perhaps the large opportunity itself, slightly disguised as fifteen dollars a week. I spoke of Flagg to Mr. Nelson, and arranged a meeting between them for the next day.

I said nothing of the matter at the dinner table that evening; but an encouraging thing always makes a lantern of me, and Mrs. Wattles saw the light in my face. As soon as dinner was over I drew my cousin into the little side room, and laid the affair before him.

"And I have made an appointment for you to meet Mr. Nelson to-morrow at one o'clock," I said, in conclusion.

"My dear Wattles" he had listened to me in silence, and now spoke without enthusiasm—"I don't know what you were thinking of to do anything of the sort. I will not keep the appointment with that person. The only possible intercourse I could have with him would be to order groceries at his shop. The idea of a man who has moved in the best society of the South, who has been engaged in great if unsuccessful enterprises, who has led the picked chivalry of his oppressed land against the Northern hordes—the idea of a gentleman of this kidney meekly simmering down into a factotum to a Yankee dealer in canned goods! No, sir; I reckon I can do better than that."

The lantern went out.

I resolved that moment to let my cousin shape his own destiny—a task which in no way appeared to trouble him. And, indeed, now that I look back to it, why should he have troubled himself? He had a comfortable if not luxurious apartment in Macdougal Street; a daily dinner that asked only to be eaten; a wardrobe that was replenished when it needed replenishing; a weekly allowance that made up for its modesty by its punctuality. If ever a man was in a position patiently to await the obsequious approach of large opportunities, that man was Washington Flagg. He was not insensible to the fact. He passed his time serenely. He walked the streets—Flagg was a great walker—sometimes wandering for hours in the Central Park. His Southern life, passed partly among plantations, had given him a relish for trees and rocks and waters. He was also a hungry reader of novels. When he had devoured our slender store of fiction, which was soon done, he took books from a small circulating library on Sixth Avenue. That he gave no thought whatever to the future was clear. He simply drifted down the gentle stream of the present. Sufficient to the day was the sunshine thereof.

In spite of his unforgivable inertia, and the egotism that enveloped him like an atmosphere, there was a charm to the man that put my impatience to sleep. I tried to think that this indifference and sunny idleness were perhaps the natural reaction of that larger life of emotion and activity from which he had just emerged. I reflected a great deal on that life, and, though I lamented the fact that he had drawn his sword on the wrong side, there was, down deep in my heart, an involuntary sympathetic throb for the valor that had not availed. I suppose the inexplicable ties of kinship had something to do with all this.

Washington Flagg had now been with us five weeks. He usually lingered awhile after dinner; sometimes spent the entire evening with the family, or, rather, with me, for Mrs. Wattles preferred the sitting-room to my den when I had company. Besides, there were Sheridan and Ulysses to be looked to. Toward the close of the sixth week I noticed that Flagg had fallen into a way of leaving immediately after dinner. He had also fallen into another way not so open to pleasant criticism.

By degrees—by degrees so subtle as almost to escape measurement—he had glided back to the forbidden and dangerous ground of the war. At first it was an intangible reference to something that occurred on such and such a date, the date, in question being that of some sanguinary battle; then a swift sarcasm, veiled and softly shod; then a sarcasm that dropped its veil for an instant, and showed its sharp features. At last his thought wore no disguise. Possibly the man couldn't help it; possibly there was something in the atmosphere of the house that impelled him to say things which he would have been unlikely to say elsewhere. Whatever was the explanation, my cousin Flagg began to make himself disagreeable again at meal-times.

He had never much regarded my disapproval, and now his early ill-defined fear of Mrs. Wattles was evaporated. He no longer hesitated to indulge in his war reminiscences, which necessarily brought his personal exploits under a calcium-light. These exploits usually emphasized his intimacy with some of the more dashing Southern leaders, such as Stonewall Jackson and Jeb Stuart and Mosby. We found ourselves practically conscripted into the Confederate army. We were taken on long midnight rides through the passes of the Cumberland Mountains and hurled on some Federal outpost; we were made—a mere handful as we were—to assault and carry most formidable earthworks; we crossed dangerous fords, and bivouacked under boughs hung with weird gonfalons of gray moss, slit here and there by the edge of a star. Many a time we crawled stealthily through tangled vines and shrubs to the skirt of a wood, and across a fallen log sighted the

Yankee picket whose bayonet point glimmered now and then far off in the moonlight. We spent a great many hours around the camp fire counting our metaphorical scalps.

One evening the colonel was especially exasperating with anecdotes of Stonewall Jackson, and details of what he said to the general and what the general said to him. "Stonewall Jackson often used to say to me, 'George'—he always called me George, in just that off-hand way—'George, when we get to New York, you shall have quarters in the Astor House, and pasture your mare Spitfire in the park.'"

"That was very thoughtful of Stonewall Jackson," remarked Mrs. Wattles, with the faintest little whiteness gathering at the lips. "I am sorry that your late friend did not accompany you to the city, and personally superintend your settlement here. He would have been able to surround you with so many more comforts than you have in Macdougal Street."

The colonel smiled upon Clara, and made a deprecating gesture with his left hand. Nothing seemed to pierce his iron-clad composure. A moment afterward he returned to the theme, and recited some verses called "Stonewall Jackson's Way." He recited them very well. One stanza lingers in my memory:

"We see him now—the old slouched hat
  Cocked o'er his brow askew,
The shrewd, dry smile, the speech so pat,
  So calm, so blunt, so true.
The Blue-light Elder knows 'em well.
Says he: 'That's Banks; he's fond of shell.
Lord save his soul! we'll give him—' Well,
  That's Stonewall Jackson's way."

"His ways must have been far from agreeable," observed my wife, "if that is a specimen of them."

After the colonel had taken himself off, Mrs. Wattles, sinking wearily upon the sofa, said, "I think I am getting rather tired of Stonewall Jackson."

"We both are, my dear; and some of our corps commanders used to find him rather tiresome now and then. He was really a great soldier, Clara; perhaps the greatest on the other side."

"I suppose he was; but Flagg comes next—according to his own report. Why, Tom, if your cousin had been in all the battles he says he has, the man would have been killed ten times over. He'd have had at least an arm or a leg shot off."

That Washington Flagg had all his limbs on was actually becoming a grievance to Mrs. Wattles.

The situation filled me with anxiety. Between my cousin's deplorable attitude and my wife's justifiable irritation, I was extremely perplexed. If I had had a dozen cousins, the solution of the difficulty would have been simple. But to close our door on our only kinsman was an intolerable alternative.

If any word of mine has caused the impression that Mrs. Wattles was not gentle and sympathetic and altogether feminine, I have wronged her. The reserve which strangers mistook for coldness was a shell that melted at the slightest kind touch, her masterful air the merest seeming. But whatever latent antagonism lay in her nature the colonel had the faculty of bringing to the surface. It must be conceded that the circumstances in which she was placed were trying, and Clara was without that strong, perhaps abnormal, sense of relationship which sustained me in the ordeal. Later on, when matters grew more complicated, I could but admire her resignation—if it were not helpless despair. Sometimes, indeed, she was unable to obliterate herself, and not only stood by her guns, but carried the war into the enemy's country. I very frequently found myself between two fires, and was glad to drag what small fragments were left of me from the scene of action. In brief, the little house in Clinton Place was rapidly transforming itself into a ghastly caricature of home.

Up to the present state of affairs the colonel had never once failed to appear at dinner-time. We had become so accustomed to his ring at the prescribed hour, and to hearing him, outside in the hall, softly humming "The Bonny Blue Flag," or "I wish I was in Dixie's Land" (a wish which he did not wholly monopolize)— we had, I repeat, become so accustomed to these details that one night when he absented himself we experienced a kind of alarm. It was not until the clock struck ten that we gave over expecting him. Then, fearing that possibly he was ill, I put on my hat and stepped round to Macdougal Street. Mr. Flagg had gone out late in the afternoon, and had not returned. No, he had left no word in case any one called. What had happened? I smile to myself now, and I have smiled a great many times, at the remembrance of

how worried I was that night as I walked slowly back to Clinton Place.

The next evening my cousin explained his absence. He had made the acquaintance of some distinguished literary gentlemen, who had invited him to dine with them at a certain German café, which at an earlier date had been rather famous as the rendezvous of a group of young journalists, wits, and unblossomed poets, known as "The Bohemians." The war had caused sad havoc with these light-hearted Knights of the Long Table, and it was only upon a scattered remnant of the goodly company that the colonel had fallen. How it came about, I do not know. I know that the acquaintance presently flowered into intimacy, and that at frequent intervals after this we had a vacant chair at table. My cousin did not give himself the pains to advise us of his engagements, so these absences were not as pleasant as they would have been if we had not expected him every minute.

Recently, too, our expectation of his coming was tinged with a dread which neither I nor Mrs. Wattles had named to each other. A change was gradually taking place in my cousin. Hitherto his amiability, even when he was most unendurable, had been a part of him. Obviously he was losing that lightness of spirit which we once disliked and now began to regret. He was inclined to be excitable and sullen by turns, and often of late I had been obliged to go to the bottom of my diplomacy in preventing some painful scene. As I have said, neither my wife nor I had spoken definitely of this alteration; but the cause and nature of it could not long be ignored between us.

"How patient you are with him, dear!" said Mrs. Wattles, as I was turning out the gas after one of our grim and grotesque little dinners: the colonel had not dined with us before for a week. "I don't see how you can be so patient with the man."

"Blood is thicker than water, Clara."

"But it isn't thicker than whiskey and water, is it?"

She had said it. The colonel was drinking. It was not a question of that light elixir the precious receipt for which had been confided to him by Judge Ashburton Todhunter of Fauquier County; it was a question of a heavier and more immediate poison. The fact that Flagg might in some desperate state drop in on us at any moment stared us in the face. That was a very serious contingency, and it was one I could not guard against. I had no illusions touching my influence over Washington Flagg. I did not dream of attempting to influence him; I was powerless. I could do nothing but wait, and wonder what would happen. There was nothing the man might not be capable of in some insane moment.

In the mean while I was afraid to go out of an evening and leave Clara alone. It was impossible for us to ask a friend to dinner, though, indeed, we had not done that since my cousin dropped down on us. It was no relief that his visits grew rarer and rarer; the apprehension remained. It was no relief when they ceased altogether, for it came to that at last.

A month had elapsed since he had called at the house. I had caught a glimpse of him once on Broadway as I was riding up town in an omnibus. He was standing at the top of the steep flight of steps that led to Herr Pfaff's saloon in the basement. It was probably Flagg's dinner hour. Mrs. Morgan, the landlady in Macdougal Street, a melancholy little soul, was now the only link between me and my kinsman. I had a weekly interview with her. I learned that Mr. Flagg slept late, was seldom in through the day, and usually returned after midnight. A person with this eccentric scheme of life was not likely to be at home at such hours as I might find it convenient to call. Nevertheless, from time to time I knocked at the door of his empty room. The two notes I had written to him he left unanswered.

All this was very grievous. He had been a trouble to me when I had him, and he was a trouble to me now I had lost him. My trouble had merely changed its color. On what downward way were his footsteps? What was to be the end of it? Sometimes I lay awake at night thinking of him. Of course, if he went to the dogs, he had nobody to blame but himself. I was not responsible for his wrong-going; nevertheless, I could not throw off my anxiety in the matter. That Flagg was leading a wild life in these days was presumable. Indeed, certain rumors to that effect were indirectly blown to me from the caves of Gambrinus. Not that I believe the bohemians demoralized him. He probably demoralized the bohemians. I began to reflect whether fate

had not behaved rather handsomely, after all, in not giving me a great many relatives.

If I remember rightly, it was two months since I had laid eyes on my cousin, when, on returning home one evening, I noticed that the front door stood wide open, and had apparently been left to take care of itself. As I mounted the steps, a little annoyed at Mary's carelessness, I heard voices in the hall. Washington Flagg was standing at the foot of the staircase, with his hand on the newel-post, and Mrs. Wattles was half-way up the stairs, as if in the act of descending. I learned later that she had occupied this position for about three-quarters of an hour. She was extremely pale and much agitated. Flagg's flushed face and tilted hat told his part of the story. He was not in one of his saturnine moods. He was amiably and, if I may say it, gracefully drunk, and evidently had all his wits about him.

"I've been telling Mrs. Wattles," he began at once, as if I had been present all the while, and he was politely taking me into the conversation—"I've been telling Mrs. Wattles that I'm a Lost Cause."

"A lost soul," was Mrs. Wattles's amendment from the staircase. "Oh, Tom, I am so glad you have come! I thought you never would! I let him in an hour or two ago, and he has kept me here ever since."

"You were so entertaining," said my cousin, with a courteous sweep of his disengaged hand, and speaking with that correctness of enunciation which sometimes survives everything.

"Flagg," I said, stepping to his side, "you will oblige me by returning to your lodgings."

"You think I'm not all right?"

"I am sure of it."

"And you don't want me here, dear old boy?"

"No, I don't want you here. The time has come for me to be very frank with you, Flagg, and I see that your mind is clear enough to enable you to understand what I say."

"I reckon I can follow you, Thomas."

"My stock of romantic nonsense about kinship and family duties, and all that, has given out, and will not be renewed."

"Won't do business any more at the old stand?"

"Exactly so. I have done everything

I could to help you, and you have done nothing whatever for yourself. You have not even done yourself the scant justice of treating Clara and me decently. In future you will be obliged to look after your own affairs, financial as well as social. Your best plan now is to go to work. I shall no longer concern myself with your comings and goings, except so far as to prevent you from coming here and disturbing Clara. Have you put that down?"

"Wattles, my boy, I'll pay you for this."

"If you do, it will be the first thing you have paid for since you came North."

My statement, however accurate, was not wholly delicate, and I subsequently regretted it, but when a patient man loses his patience he goes to extremes. Washington Flagg straightened himself for an instant, and then smiled upon me in an amused, patronizing way quite indescribable.

"Thomas, that was neat, very neat—for you. When I see Judge Ashburton Todhunter, I'll tell him about it. It's the sort of mild joke he likes."

"I should be proud to have Judge Ashburton Todhunter's approval of any remark of mine, but in the mean while it would be a greater pleasure to me to have you return at once to Macdougal Street, where, no doubt, Mrs. Morgan is delaying dinner for you."

"Say no more, Wattles. I'll never set foot in your house again, as sure as my name is Flagg—and long may I wave o'er the land of the free and the home of the brave."

"He is a kind of Flagg that I don't wish to have wave over *my* home," said Mrs. Wattles, descending the stairs as my cousin with painful care closed the door softly behind him.

So the end was come. It had come with less unpleasantness than I should have predicted. The ties of kindred, too tightly stretched, had snapped; but they had snapped very gently, so to speak.

V.

Washington Flagg was as good as his word, which is perhaps not a strong endorsement. He never set foot in my house again. A week afterward I found that he had quitted Macdougal Street.

"He has gone South," said Mrs. Morgan.

"Did he leave no message for me?"

"He didn't leave a message for nobody."

"Did he happen to say to what part of the South he was bound?"

"He said he was going back to Dixie's Land, and didn't say no more."

That was all. His departure had been as abrupt and unlooked-for as his arrival. I wondered if he would turn up again at the end of another twenty years, and I wondered how he had paid his travelling expenses to the land of the magnolia and the persimmon. That mystery was solved a few days subsequently when a draft (for so reasonable a sum as not to be worth mentioning to Mrs. Wattles) was presented to me for payment at my office.

Washington Flagg was gone, but his shadow was to linger for a while longer on our household. It was difficult to realize that the weight which had oppressed us had been removed. We were scarcely conscious of how heavy it had been until it was lifted. I was now and then forced to make an effort not to expect the colonel to dinner.

A month or two after his disappearance an incident occurred which brought him back very vividly and in a somewhat sinister shape to our imaginations. Quite late one night there was a sharp ring at the door. Mary having gone to bed, I answered the bell. On the door-step stood a tall pale girl, rather shabbily dressed, but with a kind of beauty about her; it seemed to flash from her eyelashes, which I noticed were very long and very black. The hall light fell full upon this slight figure, standing there wrapped in an insufficient shawl, against a dense background of whirling snow-flakes. She asked if I could give her Colonel Flagg's address. On receiving my reply, the girl swiftly descended the steps, and vanished into the darkness. There was a tantalizing point of romance and mystery to all this. As I slowly closed the front door, I felt that perhaps I was closing it on a tragedy—one of those piteous, unwritten tragedies of the great city. I have wondered a thousand times who that girl was and what became of her.

Before the end of the year another incident—this time with a touch of comedy—lighted up the past of my kinsman. Among the travelling agents for the Savonarola Fire-insurance Company was a young man by the name of Brett, Charles

"ON THE DOOR-STEP STOOD A TALL PALE GIRL."

Brett, a new employé. His family had been ruined by the war, and he had wandered North, as the son of many a Southern gentleman had been obliged to do, to earn his living. We became friends, and frequently lunched together when his business brought him to the city. Brett had been in the Confederate army, and

it occurred to me one day to ask him if he had ever known my cousin the colonel. Brett was acquainted with a George W. Flagg; had known him somewhat intimately, in fact; but it was probably not the same man. We compared notes, and my Flagg was his Flagg.

"But he wasn't a colonel," said Brett.

"Why, Flagg wasn't in the war at all. I don't fancy he heard a gun fired, unless it went off by accident in some training-camp for recruits. He got himself exempt from service in the field by working in the government saltworks. A heap of the boys escaped conscription that way."

In the saltworks! That connected my cousin with the navy rather than with the army!

I would have liked not to believe Brett's statement, but it was so circumstantial and precise as not to be doubted. Brett was far from suspecting how deeply his information had cut me. In spite of my loyalty, the discovery that my kinsman had not been a full-blown rebel was vastly humiliating. How that once curiously regarded flower of chivalry had withered! What about those reckless moonlight raids? What had become of Prince Rupert, at the head of his plumed cavaliers, sweeping through the valley of the Shenandoah, and dealing merited destruction to the boys in blue? In view of Brett's startling revelation, my kinsman's personal anecdotes of Stonewall Jackson took on an amusing quality which they had not possessed for us in the original telling.

I was disappointed that Mrs. Wattles's astonishment was much more moderate than mine.

"He was too brave, Tom dear. He always seemed to be overdoing it just a grain, don't you think?"

I didn't think so at the time; I was afraid he was telling the truth. And now, by one of those contradictions inseparable from weak humanity, I regretted that he was not. A hero had tumbled from the family pedestal—a misguided hero, to be sure, but still a hero. My vanity, which in this case was of a complex kind, had received a shock.

I did not recover from it for nearly three months, when I received a second shock of a more serious nature. It came in the shape of a letter, dated at Pensacola, Florida, and written by one Sylvester K. Matthews, advising me that George Flagg had died of the yellow-fever in that city on the previous month. I gathered from the letter that the writer had been with my cousin through his illness, and was probably an intimate friend; at all events, the details of the funeral had fallen to the charge of Mr. Matthews, who enclosed the receipted bills with the remark that he had paid them, but supposed

that I would prefer to do so, leaving it, in a way, at my option.

The news of my cousin's death grieved me more than I should have imagined beforehand. He had not appreciated my kindness; he had not added to my happiness while I was endeavoring to secure his; he had been flagrantly ungrateful, and in one or two minor matters had deceived me. Yet, after all said and done, he was my cousin, my only cousin—and he was dead. Let us criticise the living, but spare the dead.

I put the ghastly memoranda back into the envelope; they consisted of a bill for medical attendance, a board bill, the nurse's account, and an undertaker's bill, with its pathetic and, to me, happily, unfamiliar items. For the rest of the day I was unable to fix my thought on my work, or to compose myself sufficiently to write to Mr. Matthews. I quitted the office that evening an hour earlier than was my habit.

Whether Clara was deeply affected by what had happened, or whether she disapproved of my taking upon myself expenses which, under the peculiar circumstances, might properly be borne by Flagg's intimate friend and comrade, was something I could not determine. She made no comments. If she considered that I had already done all that my duty demanded of me to do for my cousin, she was wise enough not to say so; for she must have seen that I took a different and unalterable view of it. Clara has her own way fifty-nine minutes out of the hour, but the sixtieth minute is mine.

She was plainly not disposed to talk on the subject; but I wanted to talk with some one on the subject; so when dinner was through, I put the Matthews papers into my pocket, and went up to my friend Bleeker's in Seventeenth Street. Though a little cynical at times, he was a man whose judgment I thought well of.

After reading the letter and glancing over the memoranda, Bleeker turned to me and said, "You want to know how it strikes me—is that it?"

"Well—yes."

"The man is dead?"

"Yes."

"And buried?"

"Assuredly."

"And the bills are paid?"

"You see yourself they are receipted."

"Well, then," said Bleeker, "considering all things, I should let well enough alone."

"You mean you would do nothing in the matter?"

"I should 'let the dead past bury its dead,' as Longfellow says." Bleeker was always quoting Longfellow.

"Then pay them. You have come to me for advice after making up your mind to follow your own course. That's just the way people do when they really want to be advised. I've done it myself, Wattles—I've done it myself."

The result was I sent Mr. Matthews a

THE COLONEL REDIVIVUS.

"But it isn't the dead past, it's the living present that has attended to the business; and he has sent in his account with all the items. I can't have this Matthews going about the country telling everybody that I allowed him to pay my cousin's funeral expenses."

check, after which I impulsively threw those dreadful bills into the office grate. I had no right to do it, for the vouchers really belonged to Mr. Matthews, and might be wanted some day; but they had haunted me like so many ghosts until I destroyed them. I fell asleep that night trying to recollect whether the items included a headstone for my cousin's grave. I couldn't for the life of me remember, and it troubled me not a little. There were enough nameless graves in the South, without his being added to the number.

One day, a fortnight later, as Clara and I were finishing dinner, young Brett called at the house. I had supposed him to be in Omaha. He had, in effect, just come from there and elsewhere on one of his long business tours, and had arrived in the city too late in the afternoon to report himself at the office. He now dropped in merely for a moment, but we persuaded him to remain and share the dessert with us. I purposed to keep him until Mrs. Wattles left us to our cigars. I wished to tell him of my cousin's death, which I did not care to do while she was at the table. We were talking of this and that, when Brett looked up, and said, rather abruptly: "By-the-way, I saw Flagg on the street the other day in Mobile. He was looking well."

The bit of melon I had in my mouth refused to be swallowed. I fancy that my face was a study. A dead silence followed; and then my wife reached across the table, and pressing my hand, said, very gently,

"Wattles, you were not brilliant, but you were good."

All this was longer ago than I care to remember. I heard no more from Mr. Matthews. Last week, oddly enough, while glancing over a file of recent Southern newspapers, I came across the announcement of the death of George W. Flagg. It was yellow-fever this time also. If later on I receive any bills in connection with that event, I shall let my friend Bleeker pay them.

TOM SAWYER, DETECTIVE
(PART 1)
by Mark Twain
(As told by Huck Finn)

CHAPTER I.

WELL, it was the next spring after me and Tom Sawyer set our old nigger Jim free, the time he was chained up for a runaway slave down there on Tom's uncle Silas's farm in Arkansaw. The frost was working out of the ground, and out of the air too, and it was getting closer and closer onto barefoot time every day; and next it would be marble time, and next mumbletypeg, and next tops and hoops, and next kites, and then right away it would be summer and going in a-swimming. It just makes a boy homesick to look ahead like that and see how far off summer is. Yes, and it sets him to sighing and saddening around, and there's something the matter with him, he don't know what. But anyway, he gets out by himself and mopes and thinks; and mostly he hunts for a lonesome place high up on the hill in the edge of the woods, and sets there and looks away off on the big Mississippi down there a-reaching miles and miles around the points where the timber looks smoky and dim it's so far off and still, and everything's so solemn it seems like everybody you've loved is dead and gone, and you 'most wish you was dead and gone too, and done with it all.

Don't you know what that is? It's spring fever. That is what the name of it is. And when you've got it, you want —oh, you don't quite know what it is you *do* want, but it just fairly makes your heart ache, you want it so! It seems to you that mainly what you want is to get away; get away from the same old tedious things you're so used to seeing and so tired of, and see something new. That is the idea; you want to go and be a wanderer; you want to go wandering far away to strange countries where everything is mysterious and wonderful and romantic. And if you can't do that, you'll put up with considerable less; you'll go anywhere you *can* go, just so as to get away, and be thankful of the chance, too.

Well, me and Tom Sawyer had the spring-fever, and had it bad, too; but it warn't any use to think about Tom trying to get away, because, as he said, his aunt Polly wouldn't let him quit school and go traipsing off somers wasting time; so we was pretty blue. We was setting on the front steps one day about sundown talking this way, when out comes his aunt Polly with a letter in her hand and says—

"Tom, I reckon you've got to pack up and go down to Arkansaw—your aunt Sally wants you."

I 'most jumped out of my skin for joy. I reckoned Tom would fly at his aunt and hug her head off; but if you believe me he set there like a rock, and never said a word. It made me fit to cry to see him act so foolish, with such a noble chance as this opening up. Why, we might lose it if he didn't speak up and show he was thankful and grateful. But he set there and studied and studied till I was that distressed I didn't know what to do; then he says, very ca'm, and I could a shot him for it:

"Well," he says, "I'm right down sorry, Aunt Polly, but I reckon I got to be excused—for the present."

His aunt Polly was knocked so stupid and so mad at the cold impudence of it that she couldn't say a word for as much as a half a minute, and this give me a chance to nudge Tom and whisper:

"Ain't you got any sense? Sp'iling such a noble chance as this and throwing it away?"

But he warn't disturbed. He mumbled back:

"Huck Finn, do you want me to let her *see* how bad I want to go? Why, she'd begin to doubt, right away, and imagine a lot of sicknesses and dangers and objections, and first you know she'd take

Strange as the incidents of this story are, they are not inventions, but facts—even to the public confession of the accused. I take them from an old-time Swedish criminal trial, change the actors, and transfer the scene to America. I have added some details, but only a couple of them are important ones.—M. T.

it all back. You lemme alone; I reckon I know how to work her."

Now I never would a thought of that. But he was right. Tom Sawyer was always right—the levelest head I ever see, and always *at* himself and ready for anything you might spring on him. By this time his aunt Polly was all straight again, and she let fly. She says:

"You'll be excused! *You* will! Well, I never heard the like of it in all my days! The idea of you talking like that to *me!* Now take yourself off and pack your traps; and if I hear another word out of you about what you'll be excused from and what you won't, I lay *I'll* excuse you—with a hickory!"

She hit his head a thump with her thimble as we dodged by, and he let on to be whimpering as we struck for the stairs. Up in his room he hugged me, he was so out of his head for gladness because he was going travelling. And he says:

"Before we get away she'll wish she hadn't let me go, but she won't know any way to get around it now. After what she's said, her pride won't let her take it back."

Tom was packed in ten minutes, all except what his aunt and Mary would finish up for him; then we waited ten more for her to get cooled down and sweet and gentle again; for Tom said it took her ten minutes to unruffle in times when half of her feathers was up, but twenty when they was all up, and this was one of the times when they was all up. Then we went down, being in a sweat to know what the letter said.

She was setting there in a brown study, with it laying in her lap. We set down, and she says:

"They're in considerable trouble down there, and they think you and Huck 'll be a kind of a diversion for them—'comfort,' they say. Much of that they'll get out of you and Huck Finn, I reckon. There's a neighbor named Brace Dunlap that's been wanting to marry their Benny for three months, and at last they told him pine blank and once for all, he *couldn't;* so he has soured on them, and they're worried about it. I reckon he's somebody they think they better be on the good side of, for they've tried to please him by hiring his no-account brother to help on the farm when they can't hardly afford it, and don't want him around anyhow. Who are the Dunlaps?"

"They live about a mile from Uncle Silas's place, Aunt Polly—all the farmers live about a mile apart down there—and Brace Dunlap is a long sight richer than any of the others, and owns a whole grist of niggers. He's a widower, thirty-six years old, without any children, and is proud of his money and overbearing, and everybody is a little afraid of him. I judge he thought he could have any girl he wanted, just for the asking, and it must have set him back a good deal when he found he couldn't get Benny. Why, Benny's only half as old as he is, and just as sweet and lovely as—well, you've seen her. Poor old Uncle Silas—why, it's pitiful, him trying to curry favor that way—so hard pushed and poor, and yet hiring that useless Jubiter Dunlap to please his ornery brother."

"What a name—Jubiter! Where'd he get it?"

"It's only just a nickname. I reckon they've forgot his real name long before this. He's twenty-seven, now, and has had it ever since the first time he ever went in swimming. The school-teacher seen a round brown mole the size of a dime on his left leg above his knee, and four little bits of moles around it, when he was naked, and he said it minded him of Jubiter and his moons; and the children thought it was funny, and so they got to calling him Jubiter, and he's Jubiter yet. He's tall, and lazy, and sly, and sneaky, and ruther cowardly, too, but kind of good-natured, and wears long brown hair and no beard, and hasn't got a cent, and Brace boards him for nothing, and gives him his old clothes to wear, and despises him. Jubiter is a twin."

"What's t'other twin like?"

"Just exactly like Jubiter—so they say; used to was, anyway, but he hain't been seen for seven years. He got to robbing when he was nineteen or twenty, and they jailed him; but he broke jail and got away—up North here, somers. They used to hear about him robbing and burglaring now and then, but that was years ago. He's dead, now. At least that's what they say. They don't hear about him any more."

"What was his name?"

"Jake."

There wasn't anything more said for a considerable while; the old lady was thinking. At last she says:

"The thing that is mostly worrying

your aunt Sally is the tempers that that man Jubiter gets your uncle into."

Tom was astonished, and so was I. Tom says:

"Tempers? Uncle Silas? Land, you must be joking! I didn't know he *had* any temper."

"Works him up into perfect rages, your aunt Sally says; says he acts as if he would really hit the man, sometimes."

"Aunt Polly, it beats anything I ever heard of. Why, he's just as gentle as mush."

"Well, she's worried, anyway. Says your uncle Silas is like a changed man, on account of all this quarrelling. And the neighbors talk about it, and lay all the blame on your uncle, of course, because he's a preacher and hain't got any business to quarrel. Your aunt Sally says he hates to go into the pulpit he's so ashamed; and the people have begun to cool towards him, and he ain't as popular now as he used to was."

"Well, ain't it strange? Why, Aunt Polly, he was always so good and kind and moony and absent-minded and chuckle-headed and lovable—why, he was just an angel! What *can* be the matter of him, do you reckon?"

CHAPTER II.

WE had powerful good luck; because we got a chance in a stern-wheeler from away North which was bound for one of them bayous or one-horse rivers away down Louisiana way, and so we could go all the way down the Upper Mississippi and all the way down the Lower Mississippi to that farm in Arkansaw without having to change steamboats at St. Louis: not so very much short of a thousand miles at one pull.

A pretty lonesome boat; there warn't but few passengers, and all old folks, that set around, wide apart, dozing, and was very quiet. We was four days getting out of the "upper river," because we got aground so much. But it warn't dull—couldn't be for boys that was travelling, of course.

From the very start me and Tom allowed that there was somebody sick in the state-room next to ourn, because the meals was always toted in there by the waiters. By-and-by we asked about it—Tom did—and the waiter said it was a man, but he didn't look sick.

"Well, but *ain't* he sick?"

"I don't know; maybe he is, but 'pears to me he's just letting on."

"What makes you think that?"

"Because if he was sick he would pull his clothes off *some* time or other—don't you reckon he would? Well, this one don't. At least he don't ever pull off his boots, anyway."

"The mischief he don't! Not even when he goes to bed?"

"No."

It was always nuts for Tom Sawyer—a mystery was. If you'd lay out a mystery and a pie before me and him, you wouldn't have to say take your choice; it was a thing that would regulate itself. Because in my nature I have always run to pie, whilst in his nature he has always run to mystery. People are made different. And it is the best way. Tom says to the waiter:

"What's the man's name?"

"Phillips."

"Where'd he come aboard?"

"I think he got aboard at Elexandria, up on the Iowa line."

"What do you reckon he's a-playing?"

"I hain't any notion—I never thought of it."

I says to myself, here's another one that runs to pie.

"Anything peculiar about him?—the way he acts or talks?"

"No — nothing, except he seems so scary, and keeps his doors locked night and day both, and when you knock he won't let you in till he opens the door a crack and sees who it is."

"By jimminy, it's int'resting! I'd like to get a look at him. Say—the next time you're going in there, don't you reckon you could spread the door and—"

"No, indeedy! He's always behind it. He would block that game."

Tom studied over it, and then he says:

"Looky-here. You lend me your apern and let me take him his breakfast in the morning. I'll give you a quarter."

The boy was plenty willing enough, if the head steward wouldn't mind. Tom says that's all right, he reckoned he could fix it with the head steward; and he done it. He fixed it so as we could both go in with aperns on and toting vittles.

He didn't sleep much, he was in such a sweat to get in there and find out the mystery about Phillips; and moreover he done a lot of guessing about it all night, which warn't no use, for if you are going to find out the facts of a thing, what's the sense in guessing out what ain't the facts and wasting ammunition? I didn't lose no sleep. I wouldn't give a dern to know what's the matter of Phillips, I says to myself.

Well, in the morning we put on the aperns and got a couple of trays of truck, and Tom he knocked on the door. The man opened it a crack, and then he let us in and shut it quick. By Jackson, when we got a sight of him, we most dropped the trays! and Tom says:

"Why, Jubiter Dunlap, where'd *you* come from!"

Well, the man was astonished, of course; and first off he looked like he didn't know whether to be scared, or glad, or both, or which, but finally he settled down to being glad; and then his color come back, though at first his face had turned pretty white. So we got to talking together while he et his breakfast. And he says:

"But I ain't Jubiter Dunlap. I'd just as soon tell you who I am, though, if you'll swear to keep mum, for I ain't no Phillips, either."

Tom says:

"We'll keep mum, but there ain't any need to tell who you are if you ain't Jubiter Dunlap."

"Why?"

"Because if you ain't him you're t'other twin, Jake. You're the spit'n image of Jubiter."

"Well, I *am* Jake. But looky-here, how do you come to know us Dunlaps?"

Tom told about the adventures we'd had down there at his uncle Silas's last summer, and when he see that there warn't anything about his folks — or him either, for that matter — that we didn't know, he opened out and talked perfectly free and candid. He never made any bones about his own case; said he'd been a hard lot, was a hard lot yet, and reckoned he'd *be* a hard lot plumb to the end. He said of course it was a dangerous life, and—

He give a kind of gasp, and set his head like a person that's listening. We didn't say anything, and so it was very still for a second or so, and there warn't no sounds but the screaking of the wood-work and

"I RECKON I GOT TO BE EXCUSED."

the chug-chugging of the machinery down below.

Then we got him comfortable again, telling him about his people, and how Brace's wife had been dead three years, and Brace wanted to marry Benny and she shook him, and Jubiter was working

"SWEAR YOU'LL BE GOOD TO ME AND HELP ME SAVE MY LIFE."

for Uncle Silas, and him and Uncle Silas quarrelling all the time—and then he let go and laughed.

"Land!" he says, "it's like old times to hear all this tittle-tattle, and does me good. It's been seven years and more since I heard any. How do they talk about me these days?"

"Who?"

"The farmers—and the family."

"Why, they don't talk about you at all—at least only just a mention, once in a long time."

"The nation!" he says, surprised; "why is that?"

"Because they think you are dead long ago."

"No! Are you speaking true?—honor bright, now." He jumped up, excited.

"Honor bright. There ain't anybody thinks you are alive."

"Then I'm saved, I'm saved, sure! I'll

go home. They'll hide me and save my life. You keep mum. Swear you'll keep mum—swear you'll never, never tell on me. Oh, boys, be good to a poor devil that's being hunted day and night, and dasn't show his face! I've never done you any harm; I'll never do you any, as God is in the heavens; swear you'll be good to me and help me save my life."

We'd a swore it if he'd been a dog; and so we done it. Well, he couldn't love us enough for it or be grateful enough, poor cuss; it was all he could do to keep from hugging us.

We talked along, and he got out a little hand-bag and begun to open it, and told us to turn our backs. We done it, and when he told us to turn again he was perfectly different to what he was before. He had on blue goggles and the naturalest-looking long brown whiskers and mustashes you ever see. His own mother wouldn't a knowed him. He asked us if he looked like his brother Jubiter, now.

"No," Tom said; "there ain't anything left that's like him except the long hair."

"All right, I'll get that cropped close to my head before I get there; then him and Brace will keep my secret, and I'll live with them as being a stranger, and the neighbors won't ever guess me out. What do you think?"

Tom he studied awhile, then he says:

"Well, of course me and Huck are going to keep mum there, but if you don't keep mum yourself there's going to be a little bit of a risk—it ain't much, maybe, but it's a little. I mean, if you talk, won't people notice that your voice is just like Jubiter's; and mightn't it make them think of the twin they reckoned was dead, but maybe after all was hid all this time under another name?"

"By George," he says, "you're a sharp one! You're perfectly right. I've got to play deef and dumb when there's a neighbor around. If I'd a struck for home and forgot that little detail— However, I wasn't striking for home. I was breaking for any place where I could get away from these fellows that are after me; then I was going to put on this disguise and get some different clothes, and—"

He jumped for the outside door and laid his ear against it and listened, pale and kind of panting. Presently he whispers:

"Sounded like cocking a gun! Lord, what a life to lead!"

Then he sunk down in a chair all limp and sick like, and wiped the sweat off of his face.

CHAPTER III.

FROM that time out, we was with him 'most all the time, and one or t'other of us slept in his upper berth. He said he had been so lonesome, and it was such a comfort to him to have company, and somebody to talk to in his troubles. We was in a sweat to find out what his secret was, but Tom said the best way was not to seem anxious, then likely he would drop into it himself in one of his talks, but if we got to asking questions he would get suspicious and shet up his shell. It turned out just so. It warn't no trouble to see that he *wanted* to talk about it, but always along at first he would scare away from it when he got on the very edge of it, and go to talking about something else.

The way it come about was this: He got to asking us, kind of indifferent like, about the passengers down on deck. We told him about them. But he warn't satisfied; we warn't particular enough. He told us to describe them better. Tom done it. At last, when Tom was describing one of the roughest and raggedest ones, he gave a shiver and a gasp and says:

"Oh, lordy, that's one of them! They're aboard sure—I just knowed it. I sort of hoped I had got away, but I never believed it. Go on."

Presently when Tom was describing another mangy rough deck passenger, he give that shiver again and says—

"That's him!—that's the other one. If it would only come a good black stormy night and I could get ashore! You see, they've got spies on me. They've got a right to come up and buy drinks at the bar yonder forrard, and they take that chance to bribe somebody to keep watch on me—porter or boots or somebody. If I was to slip ashore without anybody seeing me, they would know it inside of an hour."

So then he got to wandering along, and pretty soon, sure enough, he was telling! He was poking along through his ups and downs, and when he come to that place he went right along. He says:

"It was a confidence game. We played it on a julery-shop in St. Louis. What we was after was a couple of noble big

"SOUNDED LIKE COCKING A GUN!"

di'monds as big as hazelnuts, which everybody was running to see. We was dressed up fine, and we played it on them in broad daylight. We ordered the di'-monds sent to the hotel for us to see if we wanted to buy, and when we was examining them we had paste counterfeits all ready, and *them* was the things that went back to the shop when we said the water wasn't quite fine enough for twelve thousand dollars."

"Twelve — thousand — dollars !" Tom says. "Was they really worth all that money, do you reckon?"

"Every cent of it."

"And you fellows got away with them?"

"As easy as nothing. I don't reckon the julery people know they've been robbed yet. But it wouldn't be good sense to stay around St. Louis, of course, so we considered where we'd go. One was for going one way, one another, so we throwed up, heads or tails, and the Upper Mississippi won. We done up the di'monds in a paper and put our names on it and put it in the keep of the hotel clerk, and told him not to ever let either of us have it again without the others was on hand to see it done; then we went down town, each by his own self — because I reckon maybe we all had the same notion. I don't know for certain, but I reckon maybe we had."

"What notion?" Tom says.

"To rob the others."

"What—one take everything, after all of you had helped to get it?"

"Cert'nly."

It disgusted Tom Sawyer, and he said it was the orneriest, low-downest thing he ever heard of. But Jake Dunlap said it warn't unusual in the profession. Said when a person was in that line of business he'd got to look out for his own intrust, there warn't nobody else going to do it for him. And then he went on. He says:

"You see, the trouble was, you couldn't divide up two di'monds amongst three. If there'd been three— But never mind about that, there *warn't* three. I loafed along the back streets studying and studying. And I says to myself, I'll hog them di'monds the first chance I get, and I'll have a disguise all ready, and I'll give the boys the slip, and when I'm safe away I'll put it on, and then let them find me if they can. So I got the false whiskers and the goggles and this countrified suit of clothes, and fetched them along back in a hand-bag; and when I was passing a shop where they sell all sorts of things, I got a glimpse of one of my pals through the window. It was Bud Dixon. I was

glad, you bet. I says to myself, I'll see what he buys. So I kept shady, and watched. Now what do you reckon it was he bought?"

"Whiskers?" said I.

"No."

"Goggles?"

"No."

"Oh, keep still, Huck Finn, can't you, you're only just hendering all you can. What *was* it he bought, Jake?"

"You'd never guess in the world. It was only just a screw-driver—just a wee little bit of a screw-driver."

"Well, I declare! What did he want with that?"

"That's what *I* thought. It was curious. It clean stumped me. I says to myself, what can he want with that thing? Well, when he come out I stood back out of sight, and then tracked him to a second-hand slop-shop and see him buy a red flannel shirt and some old ragged clothes —just the ones he's got on now, as you've described. Then I went down to the wharf and hid my things aboard the up-river boat that we had picked out, and then started back and had another streak of luck. I seen our other pal lay in *his* stock of old rusty second-handers. We got the di'monds and went aboard the boat.

"But now we was up a stump, for we couldn't go to bed. We had to set up and watch one another. Pity, that was; pity to put that kind of a strain on us, because there was bad blood between us from a couple of weeks back, and we was only friends in the way of business. Bad anyway, seeing there was only two di'monds betwixt three men. First we had supper, and then tramped up and down the deck together smoking till most midnight; then we went and set down in my state-room and locked the doors and looked in the piece of paper to see if the di'monds was all right, then laid it on the lower berth right in full sight; and there we set, and set, and by-and-by it got to be dreadful hard to keep awake. At last Bud Dixon he dropped off. As soon as he was snoring a good regular gait that was likely to last, and had his chin on his breast and looked permanent, Hal Clayton nodded towards the di'monds and then towards the outside door, and I understood. I reached and got the paper, and then we stood up and waited perfectly still; Bud never stirred; I turned the

"WE STOOD UP AND WAITED PERFECTLY STILL."

key of the outside door very soft and slow, then turned the knob the same way, and we went tiptoeing out onto the guard, and shut the door very soft and gentle.

"There warn't nobody stirring anywhere, and the boat was slipping along, swift and steady, through the big water in the smoky moonlight. We never said a word, but went straight up onto the hurricane-deck and plumb back aft, and set down on the end of the skylight. Both of us knowed what that meant, without having to explain to one another. Bud Dixon would wake up and miss the swag, and would come straight for us, for he ain't afeard of anything or anybody, that man ain't. He would come, and we would heave him overboard, or get killed trying. It made me shiver, because I ain't as brave as some people, but if I showed the white feather—well, I knowed better than do that. I kind of hoped the boat would land somers, and we could skip ashore and not have to run the risk of this row, I was so scared of Bud Dixon, but she was an upper-river tub and there warn't no real chance of that.

"Well, the time strung along and along, and that fellow never come! Why, it strung along till dawn begun to break, and still he never come. 'Thunder,' I says, 'what do you make out of this?—ain't it suspicious?' 'Land!' Hal says, 'do you reckon he's playing us?—open the paper!' I done it, and by gracious there warn't anything in it but a couple of little pieces of loaf-sugar! That's the reason he could set there and snooze all night so comfortable. Smart? Well, I reckon! He had had them two papers all fixed and ready, and he had put one of them in place of t'other right under our noses.

"We felt pretty cheap. But the thing to do, straight off, was to make a plan; and we done it. We would do up the paper again, just as it was, and slip in, very elaborate and soft, and lay it on the bunk again, and let on *we* didn't know about any trick, and hadn't any idea he was a-laughing at us behind them bogus snores of his'n; and we would stick by him, and the first night we was ashore we would get him drunk and search him, and get the di'monds; and *do* for him, too, if it warn't too risky. If we got the swag, we'd *got* to do for him, or he would hunt us down and do for us, sure. But I didn't have no real hope. I knowed we could get him drunk—he was always ready for that—but what's the good of it? You might search him a year and never find—

"Well, right there I catched my breath and broke off my thought! For an idea went ripping through my head that tore my brains to rags—and land, but I felt gay and good! You see, I had had my boots off, to unswell my feet, and just then I took up one of them to put it on, and I catched a glimpse of the heel-bottom, and it just took my breath away. You remember about that puzzlesome little screw-driver?"

"You bet I do," says Tom, all excited.

"Well, when I catched that glimpse of that boot heel, the idea that went smashing through my head was, *I* know where he's hid the di'monds! You look at this boot heel, now. See, it's bottomed with a steel plate, and the plate is fastened on with little screws. Now there wasn't a screw about that feller anywhere but in his boot heels; so, if he needed a screw-driver, I reckoned I knowed why."

"Huck, ain't it bully!" says Tom.

"Well, I got my boots on, and we went down and slipped in and laid the paper of sugar on the berth, and sat down soft and sheepish and went to listening to Bud Dixon snore. Hal Clayton dropped off pretty soon, but I didn't; I wasn't ever so wide-awake in my life. I was spying out from under the shade of my hat brim, searching the floor for leather. It took me a long time, and I begun to think maybe my guess was wrong, but at last

I struck it. It laid over by the bulkhead, and was nearly the color of the carpet. It was a little round plug about as thick as the end of your little finger, and I says to myself there's a di'mond in the nest you've come from. Before long I spied out the plug's mate.

"Think of the smartness and coolness of that blatherskite! He put up that scheme on us and reasoned out what we would do, and we went ahead and done it perfectly exact, like a couple of pudd'n-heads. He set there and took his own time to unscrew his heel-plates and cut out his plugs and stick in the di'monds and screw on his plates again. He allowed we would steal the bogus swag and wait all night for him to come up and get drownded, and by George it's just what we done! *I* think it was powerful smart."

"You bet your life it was!" says Tom, just full of admiration.

CHAPTER IV.

"WELL, all day we went through the humbug of watching one another, and it was pretty sickly business for two of us and hard to act out, I can tell you. About night we landed at one of them little Missouri towns high up towards Iowa, and had supper at the tavern, and got a room upstairs with a cot and a double bed in it, but I dumped my bag under a deal table in the dark hall whilst we was moving along it to bed, single file, me last, and the landlord in the lead with a tallow candle. We had up a lot of whiskey, and went to playing high-low-jack for dimes, and as soon as the whiskey begun to take hold of Bud we stopped drinking, but we didn't let him stop. We loaded him till he fell out of his chair and laid there snoring.

"We was ready for business now. I said we better pull our boots off, and his'n too, and not make any noise, then we could pull him and haul him around and ransack him without any trouble. So we done it. I set my boots and Bud's side by side, where they'd be handy. Then we stripped him and searched his seams and his pockets and his socks and the inside of his boots, and everything, and searched his bundle. Never found any di'monds. We found the screw-driver, and Hal says, 'What do you reckon he wanted with that?' I said I didn't know; but when he wasn't looking I hooked it.

At last Hal he looked beat and discouraged, and said we'd got to give it up. That was what I was waiting for. I says:

"'There's one place we hain't searched.'

"'What place is that?' he says.

"'His stomach.'

"'By gracious, I never thought of that! *Now* we're on the homestretch, to a dead moral certainty. How'll we manage?'

"'Well,' I says, 'just stay by him till I turn out and hunt up a drug-store, and I reckon I'll fetch something that'll make them di'monds tired of the company they're keeping.'

"He said that's the ticket, and with him looking straight at me I slid myself into Bud's boots instead of my own, and he never noticed. They was just a shade large for me, but that was considerable better than being too small. I got my bag as I went a-groping through the hall, and in about a minute I was out the back way and stretching up the river road at a five-mile gait.

"And not feeling so very bad, neither—walking on di'monds don't have no such effect. When I had gone fifteen minutes I says to myself, there's more'n a mile behind me, and everything quiet. Another five minutes and I says there's considerable more land behind me now, and there's a man back there that's begun to wonder what's the trouble. Another five and I says to myself he's getting real uneasy—he's walking the floor now. Another five, and I says to myself, there's two mile and a half behind me, and he's *awful* uneasy—beginning to cuss, I reckon. Pretty soon I says to myself, forty minutes gone—he *knows* there's something up! Fifty minutes—the truth's a-busting on him now! he is reckoning I found the di'monds whilst we was searching, and shoved them in my pocket and never let on—yes, and he's starting out

"SEARCHED HIS SEAMS AND HIS POCKETS AND HIS SOCKS."

to hunt for me. He'll hunt for new tracks in the dust, and they'll as likely send him down the river as up.

"Just then I see a man coming down on a mule, and before I thought I jumped into the bush. It was stupid! When he got abreast he stopped and waited a little for me to come out; then he rode on again. But I didn't feel gay any more. I says to myself I've botched my chances by that; I surely have, if he meets up with Hal Clayton.

"Well, about three in the morning I fetched Elexandria and see this stern-wheeler laying there, and was very glad, because I felt perfectly safe, now, you know. It was just daybreak. I went aboard and got this state-room and put on these clothes and went up in the pilot-house—to watch, though I didn't

"WALKED ASHORE."

reckon there was any need of it. I set there and played with my di'monds and waited and waited for the boat to start, but she didn't. You see, they was mending her machinery, but I didn't know anything about it, not being very much used to steamboats.

"Well, to cut the tale short, we never left there till plumb noon; and long before that I was hid in this state-room; for before breakfast I see a man coming, away off, that had a gait like Hal Clayton's, and it made me just sick. I says to myself, if he finds out I'm aboard this boat, he's got me like a rat in a trap. All he's got to do is to have me watched, and wait —wait till I slip ashore, thinking he is a thousand miles away, then slip after me and dog me to a good place and make me give up the di'monds, and then he'll—oh, I know what he'll do! Ain't it awful—

awful! And now to think the *other* one's aboard, too! Oh, ain't it hard luck, boys —ain't it hard! But you'll help save me, *won't* you?—oh, boys, be good to a poor devil that's being hunted to death, and save me—I'll worship the very ground you walk on!"

We turned in and soothed him down and told him we would plan for him and help him, and he needn't be so afeard; and so by-and-by he got to feeling kind of comfortable again, and unscrewed his heel-plates and held up his di'monds this way and that, admiring them and loving them; and when the light struck into them they *was* beautiful, sure; why, they seemed to kind of bust, and snap fire out all around. But all the same I judged he was a fool. If I had been him I would a handed the di'monds to them pals and got them to go ashore and leave me alone. But he was made different. He said it was a whole fortune and he couldn't bear the idea.

Twice we stopped to fix the machinery and laid a good while, once in the night; but it wasn't dark enough, and he was afeard to skip. But the third time we had to fix it there was a better chance. We laid up at a country wood-yard about forty mile above Uncle Silas's place a little after one at night, and it was thickening up and going to storm. So Jake he laid for a chance to slide. We begun to take in wood. Pretty soon the rain come a-drenching down, and the wind blowed hard. Of course every boat-hand fixed a gunny sack and put it on like a bonnet, the way they do when they are toting wood, and we got one for Jake, and he slipped down aft with his hand-bag and come tramping forrard just like the rest, and walked ashore with them, and when we see him pass out of the light of the torch-basket and get swallowed up in the dark, we got our breath again and just felt grateful and splendid. But it wasn't for long. Somebody told, I reck-on; for in about eight or ten minutes them two pals come tearing forrard as tight as they could jump and darted ashore and was gone. We waited plumb till dawn for them to come back, and kept hoping they would, but they never did. We was awful sorry and low-spirited. All the hope we had was that Jake had got such a start that they couldn't get on his track, and he would get to his brother's and hide there and be safe.

He was going to take the river road, and told us to find out if Brace and Jubiter was to home and no strangers there, and then slip out about sundown and tell him. Said he would wait for us in a little bunch of sycamores right back of Tom's uncle Silas's tobacker-field on the river road, a lonesome place.

We set and talked a long time about his chances, and Tom said he was all right if the pals struck up the river instead of down, but it wasn't likely, because maybe they knowed where he was from; more likely they would go right, and dog him all day, him not suspecting, and kill him when it come dark, and take the boots. So we was pretty sorrowful.

CHAPTER V.

WE didn't get done tinkering the machinery till away late in the afternoon, and so it was so close to sundown when we got home that we never stopped on our road, but made a break for the sycamores as tight as we could go, to tell Jake what the delay was, and have him wait till we could go to Brace's and find out how things was there. It was getting pretty dim by the time we turned the corner of the woods, sweating and panting with that long run, and see the sycamores thirty yards ahead of us; and just then we see a couple of men run into the bunch and heard two or three terrible screams for help. "Poor Jake is killed, sure," we says. We was scared through and through, and broke for the tobacker-field and hid there, trembling so our clothes would hardly stay on; and just as we skipped in there, a couple of men went tearing by, and into the bunch they went, and in a second out jumps four men and took out up the road as tight as they could go, two chasing two.

We laid down, kind of weak and sick, and listened for more sounds, but didn't hear none for a good while but just our hearts. We was thinking of that awful thing laying yonder in the sycamores, and it seemed like being that close to a ghost, and it give me the cold shudders. The moon come a-swelling up out of the ground, now, powerful big and round and bright, behind a comb of trees, like a face looking through prison bars, and the black shadders and white places begun to creep around, and it was miserable quiet and still and night-breezy and graveyardy and scary. All of a sudden Tom whispers:

"Look!—what's that?"

"Don't!" I says. "Don't take a person by surprise that way. I'm 'most ready to die, anyway, without you doing that."

"Look, I tell you. It's something coming out of the sycamores."

"Don't, Tom!"

"It's terrible tall!"

"Oh, lordy-lordy! let's—"

"Keep still—it's a-coming this way."

He was so excited he could hardly get breath enough to whisper. I had to look. I couldn't help it. So now we was both on our knees with our chins on a fence-rail and gazing—yes, and gasping, too. It was coming down the road—coming

"IT WAS JAKE DUNLAP'S GHOST."

in the shadder of the trees, and you couldn't see it good; not till it was pretty close to us; then it stepped into a bright splotch of moonlight and we sunk right down in our tracks—it was Jake Dunlap's ghost! That was what we said to ourselves.

We couldn't stir for a minute or two;

then it was gone. We talked about it in low voices. Tom says:

"They're mostly dim and smoky, or like they're made out of fog, but this one wasn't."

"No," I says; "I seen the goggles and the whiskers perfectly plain."

"Yes, and the very colors in them loud countrified Sunday clothes—plaid breeches, green and black—"

"Cotton - velvet westcot, fire - red and yaller squares—"

"Leather straps to the bottoms of the breeches legs and one of them hanging unbuttoned—"

"Yes, and that hat—"

"What a hat for a ghost to wear!"

You see it was the first season anybody wore that kind—a black stiff-brim stovepipe, very high, and not smooth, with a round top—just like a sugar-loaf.

"Did you notice if its hair was the same, Huck?"

"No—seems to me I did, then again it seems to me I didn't."

"I didn't either; but it had its bag along, I noticed that."

"So did I. How can there be a ghost-bag, Tom?"

"Sho! I wouldn't be as ignorant as that if I was you, Huck Finn. Whatever a ghost has, turns to ghost-stuff. They've got to have their things, like anybody else. You see, yourself, that its clothes was turned to ghost-stuff. Well, then, what's to hender its bag from turning, too? Of course it done it."

That was reasonable. I couldn't find no fault with it. Bill Withers and his brother Jack come along by, talking, and Jack says:

"What do you reckon he was toting?"

"I dunno; but it was pretty heavy."

"Yes, all he could lug. Nigger stealing corn from old Parson Silas, I judged."

"So did I. And so I allowed I wouldn't let on to see him."

"That's me, too!"

Then they both laughed, and went on out of hearing. It showed how unpopular old Uncle Silas had got to be, now. They wouldn't a let a nigger steal anybody else's corn and never done anything to him.

We heard some more voices mumbling along towards us and getting louder, and sometimes a cackle of a laugh. It was Lem Beebe and Jim Lane. Jim Lane says:

"Who?—Jubiter Dunlap?"

"Yes."

"Oh, I don't know. I reckon so. I seen him spading up some ground along about an hour ago, just before sundown—him and the parson. Said he guessed he wouldn't go to-night, but we could have his dog if we wanted him."

"Too tired, I reckon."

"Yes—works so hard!"

"Oh, you bet!"

They cackled at that, and went on by. Tom said we better jump out and tag along after them, because they was going our way and it wouldn't be comfortable to run across the ghost all by ourselves. So we done it, and got home all right.

That night was the second of September—a Saturday. I sha'n't ever forget it. You'll see why, pretty soon.

CHAPTER VI

WE tramped along behind Jim and Lem till we come to the back stile where old Jim's cabin was that he was captivated in, the time we set him free, and here come the dogs piling around us to say howdy, and there was the lights of the house, too; so we warn't afeard any more, and was going to climb over, but Tom says:

"Hold on; set down here a minute. By George!"

"What's the matter?" says I.

"Matter enough!" he says. "Wasn't you expecting we would be the first to tell the family who it is that's been killed yonder in the sycamores, and all about them rapscallions that done it, and about the di'monds they've smouched off of the corpse, and paint it up fine, and have the glory of being the ones that knows a lot more about it than anybody else?"

"Why, of course. It wouldn't be you, Tom Sawyer, if you was to let such a chance go by. I reckon it ain't going to suffer none for lack of paint," I says, "when you start in to scollop the facts."

"Well, now," he says, perfectly ca'm, "what would you say if I was to tell you I ain't going to start in at all?"

I was astonished to hear him talk so. I says:

"I'd say it's a lie. You ain't in earnest, Tom Sawyer."

"You'll soon see. Was the ghost barefooted?"

"No, it wasn't. What of it?"

"You wait—I'll show you what. Did it have its boots on?"

"Yes. I seen them plain."

"Swear it?"

"Yes, I swear it."

"So do I. Now do you know what that means?"

"No. What does it mean?"

"Means that them thieves *didn't get the di'monds?*"

"Jimminy! What makes you think that?"

"I don't only think it, I know it. Didn't the breeches and goggles and whiskers and hand-bag and every blessed thing turn to ghost-stuff? Everything it had on turned, didn't it? It shows that the reason its boots turned too was because it still had them on after it started to go ha'nting around, and if that ain't proof that them blatherskites didn't get the boots, I'd like to know what you'd *call* proof."

Think of that, now. I never see such a head as that boy had. Why, *I* had eyes and I could see things, but they never meant nothing to me. But Tom Sawyer was different. When Tom Sawyer seen a thing it just got up on its hind legs and *talked* to him—told him everything it knowed. *I* never see such a head.

"Tom Sawyer," I says, "I'll say it again as I've said it a many a time before: I ain't fitten to black your boots. But that's all right—that's neither here nor there. God Almighty made us all, and some He gives eyes that's blind, and some He gives eyes that can see, and I reckon it ain't none of our lookout what He done it for; it's all right, or He'd a fixed it some other way. Go on—I see plenty plain enough, now, that them thieves didn't get away with the di'monds. Why didn't they, do you reckon?"

"Because they got chased away by them other two men before they could pull the boots off of the corpse."

"That's so! I see it now. But looky-here, Tom, why ain't we to go and tell about it?"

"Oh, shucks, Huck Finn, can't you see? Look at it. What's a-going to happen? There's going to be an inquest in the morning. Them two men will tell how they heard the yells and rushed there just in time to not save the stranger. Then the jury'll twaddle and twaddle and twaddle, and finally they'll fetch in a verdict that he got shot or stuck or busted over the head with something, and come to his death by the inspiration of God. And

after they've buried him they'll auction off his things for to pay the expenses, and then's *our* chance."

"How, Tom?"

"Buy the boots for two dollars!"

Well, it 'most took my breath.

"WAS THE GHOST BAREFOOTED?"

"My land! Why, Tom, *we'll* get the di'monds!"

"You bet. Some day there'll be a big reward offered for them—a thousand dollars, sure. That's our money! Now we'll trot in and see the folks. And mind you we don't know anything about any murder, or any di'monds, or any thieves—don't you forget that."

I had to sigh a little over the way he had got it fixed. *I'd* a *sold* them di'monds—yes, sir—for twelve thousand dollars; but I didn't say anything. It wouldn't done any good. I says:

"But what are we going to tell your aunt Sally has made us so long getting down here from the village, Tom?"

"Oh, I'll leave that to you," he says. "I reckon you can explain it somehow."

He was always just that strict and delicate. He never would tell a lie himself.

We struck across the big yard, noticing this, that, and t'other thing that was so familiar, and we so glad to see it again, and when we got to the roofed big passageway betwixt the double log house and the kitchen part, there was everything hanging on the wall just as it used to was, even to Uncle Silas's old faded green baize working-gown with the hood to it, and raggedy white patch between the shoulders that always looked like somebody had hit him with a snowball; and then we lifted the latch and walked in. Aunt Sally she was just a-ripping and a-tearing around, and the children was huddled in one corner, and the old man he was huddled in the other and praying for help in time of need. She jumped for us with joy and tears running down her face and give us a whacking box on the ear, and then hugged us and kissed us and boxed us again, and just couldn't seem to get enough of it, she was so glad to see us; and she says:

"Where *have* you been a-loafing to, you good-for-nothing trash! I've been that worried about you I didn't know what to do. Your traps has been here *ever* so long, and I've had supper cooked fresh about four times so as to have it hot and good when you come, till at last my patience is just plumb wore out, and I declare I—I—why I could skin you alive! You must be starving, poor things!—set down, set down, everybody; don't lose no more time."

It was good to be there again behind all that noble corn pone and spareribs, and everything that you could ever want in this world. Old Uncle Silas he peeled off one of his bulliest old-time blessings, with as many layers to it as an onion, and whilst the angels was hauling in the slack of it I was trying to study up what to say about what kept us so long. When our plates was all loadened and we'd got agoing, she asked me, and I says:

"Well, you see,—er—Mizzes—"

"Huck Finn! Since when am I Mizzes to you? Have I ever been stingy of cuffs or kisses for you since the day you stood in this room and I took you for Tom Sawyer and blessed God for sending you to me, though you told me four thousand lies and I believed every one of them like a simpleton? Call me Aunt Sally—like you always done."

So I done it. And I says:

"Well, me and Tom allowed we would come along afoot and take a smell of the woods, and we run across Lem Beebe and Jim Lane, and they asked us to go with them blackberrying to-night, and said they could borrow Jubiter Dunlap's dog, because he had told them just that minute—"

"Where did they see him?" says the old man; and when I looked up to see how *he* come to take an intrust in a little thing like that, his eyes was just burning into me, he was that eager. It surprised me so it kind of throwed me off, but I pulled myself together again and says:

"It was when he was spading up some ground along with you, towards sundown or along there."

He only said, "Um," in a kind of a disappointed way, and didn't take no more intrust. So I went on. I says:

"Well, then, as I was a-saying—"

"That 'll do, you needn't go no furder." It was Aunt Sally. She was boring right into me with her eyes, and very indignant. "Huck Finn," she says, "how'd them men come to talk about going a-blackberrying in September—in *this* region?"

I see I had slipped up, and I couldn't say a word. She waited, still a-gazing at me, then she says:

"And how'd they come to strike that idiot idea of going a-blackberrying in the night?"

"Well, m'm, they—er—they told us they had a lantern, and—"

"Oh, *shet* up—do! Looky-here; what was they going to do with a dog?—hunt blackberries with it?"

"I think, m'm, they—"

"Now, Tom Sawyer, what kind of a lie are you fixing *your* mouth to contribit to this mess of rubbage? Speak out—and I warn you before you begin, that I don't believe a word of it. You and Huck's been up to something you no business to —*I* know it perfectly well; *I* know you, *both* of you. Now you explain that dog, and them blackberries, and the lantern, and the rest of that rot—and mind you talk as straight as a string—do you hear?"

Tom he looked considerable hurt, and says, very dignified:

"It is a pity if Huck is to be talked to that away, just for making a little bit of a mistake that anybody could make."

"What mistake has he made?"

"Why, only the mistake of saying blackberries when of course he meant strawberries."

"Tom Sawyer, I lay if you aggravate me a little more, I'll—"

"Aunt Sally, without knowing it—and of course without intending it—you are in the wrong. If you'd a studied natural history the way you ought, you would know that all over the world except just here in Arkansaw they *always* hunt straw-berries with a dog—and a lantern—"

But she busted in on him there and just piled into him and snowed him under. She was so mad she couldn't get the words out fast enough, and she gushed them out in one everlasting freshet. That was what Tom Sawyer was after. He allowed to work her up and get her started and then leave her alone and let her burn herself out. Then she would be so aggravated with that subject that she wouldn't say another word about it, nor let anybody else. Well, it happened just so. When she was tuckered out and had to hold up, he says, quite ca'm:

"And yet, all the same, Aunt Sally—"

"Shet up!" she says, "I don't want to hear another word out of you."

So we was perfectly safe, then, and didn't have no more trouble about that delay. Tom done it elegant.

CHAPTER VII.

BENNY she was looking pretty sober, and she sighed some, now and then; but pretty soon she got to asking about Mary, and Sid, and Tom's aunt Polly, and then Aunt Sally's clouds cleared off and she got in a good humor and joined in on the questions and was her lovingest best self, and so the rest of the supper went along gay and pleasant. But the old man he didn't take any hand hardly, and was absent-minded and restless, and done a considerable amount of sighing; and it was kind of heart-breaking to see him so sad and troubled and worried.

By-and-by, a spell after supper, come a nigger and knocked on the door and put his head in with his old straw hat in his hand bowing and scraping, and said his Marse Brace was out at the stile and wanted his brother, and was getting tired waiting supper for him, and would Marse Silas please tell him where he was? I never see Uncle Silas speak up so sharp and fractious before. He says:

"Am *I* his brother's keeper?" And then he kind of wilted together, and looked like he wished he hadn't spoken so, and then he says, very gentle: "But

you needn't say that, Billy; I was took sudden and irritable, and I ain't very well these days, and not hardly responsible. Tell him he ain't here."

And when the nigger was gone he got up and walked the floor, backwards and forwards, mumbling and muttering to himself and ploughing his hands through his hair. It was real pitiful to see him. Aunt Sally she whispered to us and told us not to take notice of him, it embarrassed him. She said he was always thinking and thinking, since these troubles come on, and she allowed he didn't more'n about half know what he was about when the thinking spells was on him; and she said he walked in his sleep considerable more now than he used to, and sometimes wandered around over the house and even out-doors in his sleep, and if we catched him at it we must let him alone and not disturb him. She said she reckoned it didn't do him no harm, and maybe it done him good. She said Benny was the only one that was much help to him these days. Said Benny appeared to know just when to try to soothe him and when to leave him alone.

So he kept on tramping up and down the floor and muttering, till by-and-by he begun to look pretty tired; then Benny she went and snuggled up to his side and put one hand in his and one arm around his waist and walked with him; and he smiled down on her, and reached down and kissed her; and so, little by little the trouble went out of his face and she persuaded him off to his room. They had very petting ways together, and it was uncommon pretty to see.

Aunt Sally she was busy getting the children ready for bed; so by-and-by it got dull and tedious, and me and Tom took a turn in the moonlight, and fetched up in the watermelon-patch and et one, and had a good deal of talk. And Tom said he'd bet the quarrelling was all Jubiter's fault, and he was going to be on hand the first time he got a chance, and see; and if it was so, he was going to do his level best to get Uncle Silas to turn him off.

And so we talked and smoked and stuffed watermelon as much as two hours, and then it was pretty late, and when we got back the house was quiet and dark, and everybody gone to bed.

Tom he always seen everything, and now he see that the old green baize work-

"SMOKED AND STUFFED WATERMELON."

down by the tobacker-field. Out of sight now. It's a dreadful pity he can't rest no better."

We waited a long time, but he didn't come back any more, or if he did he come around the other way; so at last we was tuckered out and went to sleep and had nightmares, a million of them. But before dawn we was awake again, because meantime a storm had come up and been raging, and the thunder and lightning was awful, and the wind was a-thrashing the trees around, and the rain was driving down in slanting sheets, and the gullies was running rivers. Tom says:

"Looky-here, Huck, I'll tell you one thing that's mighty curious. Up to the time we went out, last night, the family hadn't heard about Jake Dunlap being murdered. Now the men that chased Hal Clayton and Bud Dixon away would spread the thing around in a half an hour, and every neighbor that heard it would shin out and fly around from one farm to t'other and try to be the first to tell the news. Land, they don't have such a big thing as that to tell twice in thirty year! Huck, it's mighty strange; I don't understand it."

So then he was in a fidget for the rain to let up, so we could turn out and run across some of the people and see if they would say anything about it to us. And he said if they did we must be horribly surprised and shocked.

We was out and gone the minute the rain stopped. It was just broad day, then. We loafed along up the road, and now and then met a person and stopped and said howdy, and told them when we come, and how we left the folks at home, and how long we was going to stay, and all that, but none of them said a word about that thing; which was just astonishing, and no mistake. Tom said he believed if we went to the sycamores we would find that body laying there solitary and alone, and not a soul around. Said he believed the men chased the thieves so far into the woods that the thieves prob'ly

gown was gone, and said it wasn't gone when we went out; and so we allowed it was curious, and then we went up to bed.

We could hear Benny stirring around in her room, which was next to ourn, and judged she was worried a good deal about her father and couldn't sleep. We found we couldn't, neither. So we set up a long time, and smoked and talked in a low voice, and felt pretty dull and downhearted. We talked the murder and the ghost over and over again, and got so creepy and crawly we couldn't get sleepy nohow and noway.

By-and-by, when it was away late in the night and all the sounds was late sounds and solemn, Tom nudged me and whispers to me to look, and I done it, and there we see a man poking around in the yard like he didn't know just what he wanted to do, but it was pretty dim and we couldn't see him good. Then he started for the stile, and as he went over it the moon came out strong, and he had a long-handled shovel over his shoulder, and we see the white patch on the old work-gown. So Tom says:

"He's a-walking in his sleep. I wish we was allowed to follow him and see where he's going to. There, he's turned seen a good chance and turned on them at last, and maybe they all killed each other, and so there wasn't anybody left to tell.

First we knowed, gabbling along that away, we was right at the sycamores. The cold chills trickled down my back and I wouldn't budge another step, for all Tom's persuading. But he couldn't hold in; he'd *got* to see if the boots was safe on that body yet. So he crope in—and the next minute out he come again with his eyes bulging he was so excited, and says:

"Huck, it's gone!"

I *was* astonished! I says:

"Tom, you don't mean it."

"It's gone, sure. There ain't a sign of it. The ground is trampled some, but if there was any blood it's all washed away by the storm, for it's all puddles and slush in there."

At last I give in, and went and took a look myself; and it was just as Tom said—there wasn't a sign of a corpse.

"Dern it," I says, "the di'monds is gone. Don't you reckon the thieves slunk back and lugged him off, Tom?"

"Looks like it. It just does. Now where'd they hide him, do you reckon?"

"I don't know," I says, disgusted, "and what's more I don't care. They've got the boots, and that's all *I* cared about. He'll lay around these woods a long time before *I* hunt him up."

Tom didn't feel no more intrust in him neither, only curiosity to know what come of him; but he said we'd lay low and keep dark and it wouldn't be long till the dogs or somebody rousted him out.

We went back home to breakfast ever so bothered and put out and disappointed and swindled. I warn't ever so down on a corpse before.

[TO BE CONTINUED.]

"HUCK, IT'S GONE!"

TOM SAWYER, DETECTIVE
(PART 2)
by Mark Twain
(As told by Huck Finn)

CHAPTER VIII.

IT warn't very cheerful at breakfast. Aunt Sally she looked old and tired, and let the children snarl and fuss at one another and didn't seem to notice it was going on, which wasn't her usual style; me and Tom had a plenty to think about without talking; Benny she looked like she hadn't much sleep, and whenever she'd lift her head a little and steal a look towards her father you could see there was tears in her eyes; and as for the old man, his things staid on his plate and got cold without him knowing they was there, I reckon, for he was thinking and thinking all the time, and never said a word and never et a bite.

By-and-by when it was stillest, that nigger's head was poked in at the door again, and he said his Marse Brace was getting powerful uneasy about Marse Jubiter, which hadn't come home yet, and would Marse Silas please—

He was looking at Uncle Silas, and he stopped there, like the rest of his words was froze; for Uncle Silas he rose up shaky and steadied himself leaning his fingers on the table, and he was panting, and his eyes was set on the nigger, and he kept swallowing, and put his other hand up to his throat a couple of times, and at last he got his words started, and says:

"Does he—does he—think—*what* does he think! Tell him—tell him—" Then he sunk down in his chair limp and weak, and says, so as you could hardly hear him: "Go away—go away!"

The nigger looked scared, and cleared out, and we all felt—well, I don't know how we felt, but it was awful, with the old man panting there, and his eyes set and looking like a person that was dying. None of us could budge; but Benny she slid around soft, with her tears running down, and stood by his side, and nestled his old gray head up against her and begun to stroke it and pet it with her hands, and nodded to us to go away, and we done it, going out very quiet, like the dead was there.

Me and Tom struck out for the woods mighty solemn, and saying how different it was now to what it was last summer when we was here, and everything was so peaceful and happy and everybody thought so much of Uncle Silas, and he was so cheerful and simple-hearted and pudd'nheaded and good—and now look at him. If he hadn't lost his mind he wasn't much short of it. That was what we allowed.

It was a most lovely day, now, and bright and sunshiny; and the further and further we went over the hill towards the prairie the lovelier and lovelier the trees and flowers got to be, and the more it seemed strange and somehow wrong that there had to be trouble in such a world as this. And then all of a sudden I catched my breath and grabbed Tom's arm, and all my livers and lungs and things fell down into my legs.

"There it is!" I says. We jumped back behind a bush, shivering, and Tom says:

"'Sh!—don't make a noise."

It was setting on a log right in the edge of the little prairie, thinking. I tried to get Tom to come away, but he wouldn't, and I dasn't budge by myself. He said we mightn't ever get another chance to see one, and he was going to look his fill at this one if he died for it. So I looked too, though it give me the fantods to do it. Tom he *had* to talk, but he talked low. He says:

"Poor Jakey, it's got all its things on, just as he said he would. *Now* you see what we wasn't certain about—its hair. It's not long, now, the way it was; it's got it cropped close to its head, the way he said he would. Huck, I never see anything look any more naturaler than what *it* does."

"Nor I neither," I says; "I'd recognize it anywheres."

"So would I. It looks perfectly solid and genuwyne, just the way it done before it died."

So we kept a-gazing. Pretty soon Tom says:

"Huck, there's something mighty curious about this one, don't you know? *It* oughtn't to be going around in the daytime."

"That's so, Tom—I never heard the like of it before."

"No, sir, they don't ever come out only at night—and then not till after twelve. There's something wrong about this one, now you mark my words. I don't believe it's got any right to be around in the daytime. But don't it look natural! Jake was going to play deef and dumb here, so the neighbors wouldn't know his voice. Do you reckon it would do that if we was to holler at it?"

"Lordy, Tom, don't talk so! If you was to holler at it I'd die in my tracks."

"Don't you worry, I ain't going to holler at it. Look, Huck, it's a-scratching its head—don't you see?"

"Well, what of it?"

"Why, this: What's the sense of it scratching its head? There ain't anything there to itch; its head is made out of fog or something like that, and *can't* itch. A fog can't itch; any fool knows that."

"Well, then, if it don't itch and can't itch, what in the nation is it scratching it for? Ain't it just habit, don't you reckon?"

"No, sir, I don't. I ain't a bit satisfied about the way this one acts. I've a blame good notion it's a bogus one—I have, as sure as I'm a-setting here. Because, if it— Huck!"

"Well, what's the matter now?"

"*You can't see the bushes through it !*"

"Why, Tom, it's so, sure! It's as solid as a cow. I sort of begin to think—"

"Huck, it's biting off a chaw of tobacker! By George, *they* don't chaw—they hain't got anything to chaw *with*. Huck!"

"I'm a-listening."

"It ain't a ghost at all. It's Jake Dunlap his own self!"

"Oh, your granny !" I says.

"Huck Finn, did we find any corpse in the sycamores?"

"No."

"Or any sign of one?"

"No."

"Mighty good reason. Hadn't ever been any corpse there."

"Why, Tom, you know we heard—"

"Yes, we did—heard a howl or two. Does that prove anybody was killed? Course it don't. And we soon four men run, then this one come walking out, and we took it for a ghost. No more ghost

than you are. It was Jake Dunlap his own self, and it's Jake Dunlap now. He's been and got his hair cropped, the way he said he would, and he's playing himself for a stranger, just the same as he said he would. Ghost! Hum?— he's as sound as a nut."

Then I see it all, and how we had took too much for granted. I was powerful glad he didn't get killed, and so was Tom, and we wondered which he would like the best—for us to never let on to know him, or how? Tom reckoned the best way would be to go and ask him. So he started; but I kept a little behind, because I didn't know but it might be a ghost, after all. When Tom got to where he was, he says:

"Me and Huck's mighty glad to see you again, and you needn't be afeard we'll tell. And if you think it 'll be safer for you if we don't let on to know you when we run across you, say the word, and you'll see you can depend on us, and would rather cut our hands off than get you into the least little bit of danger."

First off he looked surprised to see us, and not very glad, either; but as Tom went on he looked pleasanter, and when he was done he smiled, and nodded his head several times, and made signs with his hands, and says:

"Goo-goo—goo-goo," the way deef and dummies does.

Just then we see some of Steve Nickerson's people coming that lived t'other side of the prairie, so Tom says:

"You do it elegant; I never seen anybody do it better. You're right; play it on us, too; play it on us same as the others; it 'll keep you in practice and prevent you making blunders. We'll keep away from you and let on we don't know you, but any time we can be any help, you just let us know."

Then we loafed along past the Nickersons, and of course they asked if that was the new stranger yonder, and where'd he come from, and what was his name, and which communion was he, Babtis' or Methodis', and which politics, Whig or Democrat, and how long is he staying, and all them other questions that humans always asks when a stranger comes, and animals does too. But Tom said he warn't able to make anything out of deef and dumb signs, and the same with goo-gooing. Then we watched them go and bullyrag Jake; because we was pretty uneasy for him. Tom said it would take him

"WHAT DOES HE THINK?"

days to get so he wouldn't forget he was a deef and dummy sometimes, and speak out before he thought. When we had watched long enough to see that Jake was getting along all right and working his signs very good, we loafed along again, allowing to strike the school-house about recess time, which was a three-mile tramp.

I was so disappointed not to hear Jake tell about the row in the sycamores, and how near he come to getting killed, that I couldn't seem to get over it, and Tom he felt the same, but said if we was in Jake's fix we would want to go careful and keep still, and not take any chances.

The boys and girls was all glad to see us again, and we had a real good time all through recess. Coming to school the Henderson boys had come across the new deef and dummy and told the rest; so all the scholars was chuck-full of him and couldn't talk about anything else,

and was in a sweat to get a sight of him because they hadn't ever seen a deef and dummy in their lives, and it made a powerful excitement.

Tom said it was tough to have to keep mum now; said we would be heroes if we could come out and tell all we knowed; but, after all, it was still more heroic to keep mum; there warn't two boys in a million could do it. That was Tom Sawyer's idea about it, and I reckoned there warn't anybody could better it.

CHAPTER IX.

IN the next two or three days Dummy he got to be powerful popular. He went associating around with the neighbors, and they made much of him and was proud to have such a rattling curiosity amongst them. They had him to breakfast, they had him to dinner, they had him to supper; they kept him loaded up with hog and hominy, and warn't ever tired staring at him and wondering over him, and wishing they knowed more about him, he was so uncommon and romantic. His signs warn't no good; people couldn't understand them, and he prob'ly couldn't himself, but he done a sight of goo-gooing, and so everybody was satisfied, and admired to hear him go it. He toted a piece of slate around, and a pencil; and people wrote questions on it and he wrote answers; but there warn't anybody could read his writing but Brace Dunlap. Brace said he couldn't read it very good, but he could manage to dig out the meaning most of the time. He said Dummy said he belonged away off somers, and used to be well off, but got busted by swindlers which he had trusted, and was poor now, and hadn't any way to make a living.

Everybody praised Brace Dunlap for being so good to that stranger. He let him have a little log cabin all to himself, and had his niggers take care of it, and fetch him all the vittles he wanted.

Dummy was at our house some, because old Uncle Silas was so afflicted himself, these days, that anybody else that was afflicted was a comfort to him. Me and Tom didn't let on that we had knowed him before, and he didn't let on that he had knowed us before. The family talked their troubles out before him the same as if he wasn't there, but we reckoned it wasn't any harm for him to hear what they said. Gener'ly he didn't seem to notice, but sometimes he did.

Well, two or three days went along, and everybody got to getting uneasy about Jubiter Dunlap. Everybody was asking everybody if they had any idea what had become of him. No, they hadn't, they said; and they shook their heads and said there was something powerful strange about it. Another and another day went by; then there was a report got around that praps he was murdered. You bet it made a big stir! Everybody's tongue was clacking away after that. Saturday two or three gangs turned out and hunted the woods to see if they could run across his remainders. Me and Tom helped, and it was noble good times and exciting. Tom he was so brim-full of it he couldn't eat nor rest. He said if we could find that corpse we would be celebrated, and more talked about than if we got drownded.

The others got tired and give it up; but not Tom Sawyer—that warn't his style.

Saturday night he didn't sleep any, hardly, trying to think up a plan; and towards daylight in the morning he struck it. He snaked me out of bed and was all excited, and says—

"Quick, Huck, snatch on your clothes—I've got it! Blood-hound!"

In two minutes we was tearing up the river road in the dark towards the village. Old Jeff Hooker had a blood-hound, and Tom was going to borrow him. I says—

"The trail's too old, Tom—and besides, it's rained, you know."

"It don't make any difference, Huck. If the body's hid in the woods anywhere around, the hound will find it. If he's been murdered and buried, they wouldn't bury him deep, it ain't likely, and if the dog goes over the spot he'll scent him, sure. Huck, we're going to be celebrated, sure as you're born!"

He was just a-blazing; and whenever he got afire he was most likely to get afire all over. That was the way this time. In two minutes he had got it all ciphered out, and wasn't only just going to find the corpse—no, he was going to get on the track of that murderer and hunt *him* down, too; and not only that, but he was going to stick to him till—

"Well," I says, "you better find the corpse first; I reckon that's a plenty for to-day. For all we know, there *ain't* any corpse and nobody hain't been murdered. That cuss could a gone off somers and not been killed at all."

That gravelled him, and he says—

"Huck Finn, I never seen such a person as you to want to spoil everything. As long as *you* can't see anything hopeful in a thing, you won't let anybody else. What good can it do you to throw cold water on that corpse and get up that selfish theory that there hain't been any murder? None in the world. I don't see how you can act so. I wouldn't treat you like that, and you know it. Here we've got a noble good opportunity to make a ruputation, and—"

"Oh, go ahead," I says, "I'm sorry and I take it all back. I didn't mean nothing. Fix it any way you want it. *He* ain't any consequence to me. If he's killed, I'm as glad of it as you are; and if he—"

"I never said anything about being glad; I only—"

"Well, then, I'm as *sorry* as you are. Any way you druther have it, that is the way *I* druther have it. He—"

"There ain't any druthers *about* it, Huck Finn; nobody said anything about druthers. And as for—"

He forgot he was talking, and went tramping along, studying. He begun to get excited again, and pretty soon he says—

"Huck, it'll be the bulliest thing that ever happened if we find the body after everybody else has quit looking, and then go ahead and hunt up the murderer. It won't only be an honor to us, but it'll be an honor to Uncle Silas because it was us that done it. It'll set him up again, you see if it don't."

But old Jeff Hooker he throwed cold water on the whole business when we got to his blacksmith shop and told him what we come for.

"You can take the dog," he says, "but you ain't a-going to find any corpse, because there ain't any corpse to find. Everybody's quit looking, and they're right. Soon as they come to think, they knowed there warn't no corpse. And I'll tell you for why. What does a person kill another person *for*, Tom Sawyer?—answer me that."

"Why, he—er—"

"Answer up! You ain't no fool. What does he kill him *for?*"

"Well, sometimes it's for revenge, and—"

"Wait. One thing at a time. Revenge, says you; and right you are. Now who ever had anything agin that poor trifling no-account? Who do you reckon would want to kill *him?*—that rabbit!"

Tom was stuck. I reckon he hadn't thought of a person having to have a reason for killing a person before, and now he see it warn't likely anybody would have that much of a grudge against a lamb like Jubiter Dunlap. The blacksmith says, by-and-by—

" GOO-GOO—GOO-GOO."

"The revenge idea won't work, you see. Well, then, what's next? Robbery? B'gosh that must a been it, Tom! Yes, sir-ree, I reckon we've struck it this time. Some feller wanted his gallus-buckles, and so he—"

But it was so funny he busted out laughing, and just went *on* laughing and laughing and laughing till he was 'most dead, and Tom looked so put out and cheap that I knowed he was ashamed he had come, and wished he hadn't. But old Hooker never let up on him. He raked up everything a person ever could want to kill another person about, and any fool could see they didn't any of them fit this case, and he just made no end of fun of the whole business, and of the people that had been hunting the body; and he said—

"If they'd had any sense they'd a knowed the lazy cuss slid out because he wanted a loafing spell after all this work. He'll come pottering back in a couple of weeks, and then how'll you fellers feel? But, laws bless you, take the dog and go and hunt his remainders. Do, Tom."

Then he busted out and had another of them forty-rod laughs of his'n. Tom couldn't back down after all this, so he said, "All right, unchain him," and the blacksmith done it, and we started home, and left that old man laughing yet.

It was a lovely dog. There ain't any dog that's got a lovelier disposition than a blood-hound, and this one knowed us and liked us. He capered and raced around ever so friendly, and was powerful glad to be free and have a holiday; but Tom was so cut up he couldn't take any intrust in him, and said he wished he'd stopped and thought a minute before he ever started on such a fool errand. He said old Jeff Hooker would tell everybody, and we'd never hear the last of it.

So we loafed along home down the back lanes, feeling pretty glum and not talking. When we was passing the far corner of our tobacker-field we heard the dog set up a long howl in there, and we went to the place, and he was scratching the ground with all his might, and every now and then canting up his head sideways and fetching another howl.

It was a long square the shape of a grave; the rain had made it sink down and show the shape. The minute we come and stood there we looked at one another and never said a word. When the dog had dug down only a few inches he

grabbed something and pulled it up, and it was an arm and a sleeve. Tom kind of gasped out and says—

"Come away, Huck—it's found."

I just felt awful. We struck for the road and fetched the first men that come along. They got a spade at the crib and dug out the body, and you never see such an excitement. You couldn't make anything out of the face, but you didn't need to. Everybody said—

"Poor Jubiter; it's his clothes, to the last rag!"

Some rushed off to spread the news and tell the justice of the peace and have an inquest, and me and Tom lit out for the house. Tom was all afire and 'most out of breath when we come tearing in where Uncle Silas and Aunt Sally and Benny was. Tom sung out—

"Me and Huck's found Jubiter Dunlap's corpse all by ourselves with a blood-hound after everybody else had quit hunting and given it up; and if it hadn't a been for us it never *would* a been found; and he *was* murdered, too—they done it with a club or something like that; and I'm going to start in and find the murderer, next, and I bet I'll do it!"

Aunt Sally and Benny sprung up pale and astonished, but Uncle Silas fell right forward out of his chair onto the floor, and groans out—

"Oh, my God, you've found him *now!*"

CHAPTER X.

THEM awful words froze us solid. We couldn't move hand or foot for as much as a half a minute. Then we kind of come to, and lifted the old man up and got him into his chair, and Benny petted him and kissed him and tried to comfort him, and poor old Aunt Sally she done the same; but, poor things, they was so broke up and scared and knocked out of their right minds that they didn't hardly know what they was about. With Tom it was awful; it 'most petrified him to think maybe he had got his uncle into a thousand times more trouble than ever, and maybe it wouldn't ever happened if he hadn't been so ambitious to get celebrated, and let the corpse alone the way the others done. But pretty soon he sort of come to himself again and says—

"Uncle Silas, don't you say another word like that. It's dangerous, and there ain't a shadder of truth in it."

Aunt Sally and Benny was thankful to

"FETCHING ANOTHER HOWL."

hear him say that, and they said the same; but the old man he wagged his head sorrowful and hopeless, and the tears run down his face, and he says—

"No—I done it; poor Jubiter, I done it!"

It was dreadful to hear him say it. Then he went on and told about it, and said it happened the day me and Tom come—along about sundown. He said Jubiter pestered him and aggravated him till he was so mad he just sort of lost his mind and grabbed up a stick and hit him over the head with all his might, and Jubiter dropped in his tracks. Then he was scared and sorry, and got down on his knees and lifted his head up, and begged him to speak and say he wasn't dead; and before long he come to, and when he see

who it was holding his head, he jumped like he was 'most scared to death, and cleared the fence and tore into the woods, and was gone. So he hoped he wasn't hurt bad.

"But laws," he says, "it was only just fear that give him that last little spurt of strength, and of course it soon played out, and he laid down in the bush, and there wasn't anybody to help him, and he died."

Then the old man cried and grieved, and said he was a murderer and the mark of Cain was on him, and he had disgraced his family and was going to be found out and hung. Tom said—

"No, you ain't going to be found out. You *didn't* kill him. *One* lick wouldn't kill him. Somebody else done it."

"Oh, yes," he says. "I done it—nobody else. Who else had anything against him? Who else *could* have anything against him?"

He looked up kind of like he hoped some of us could mention somebody that could have a grudge against that harmless no-account, but of course it warn't no use —he *had* us; we couldn't say a word. He noticed that, and he saddened down again, and I never see a face so miserable and so pitiful to see. Tom had a sudden idea, and says -

"But hold on!—somebody *buried* him. Now who—"

He shut off sudden. I knowed the reason. It give me the cold shudders when he said them words, because right away I remembered about us seeing Uncle Silas prowling around with a long-handled shovel away in the night that night. And I knowed Benny seen him too, because she was talking about it one day. The minute Tom shut off he changed the subject and we..t to begging Uncle Silas to keep mum, and the rest of us done the same, and said he *must*, and said it wasn't his business to tell on .imself, and if he kept mum nobody would ever know, but if it was found out and any harm come to him it would break the family's hearts and kill them, and yet never do anybody any good. So at last he promised. We was all of us more comfortable then, and went to work to cheer up the old man. We told him all he'd got to do was to keep still and it wouldn't be long till the whole thing would blow over and be forgot. We all said there wouldn't anybody ever suspect Uncle Silas, nor ever dream of such a thing, he being so good and kind and having such a good character; and Tom says, cordial and hearty, he says—

"Why, just look at it a minute; just consider. Here is Uncle Silas, all these years a preacher—at his own expense; all these years doing good with all his might and every way he can think of— at his own expense, all the time; always been loved by everybody, and respected; always been peaceable and minding his own business, the very last man in this whole deestrict to touch a person, and everybody knows it. Suspect *him*? Why, it ain't any more possible than—"

"By authority of the State of Arkansaw—I arrest you for the murder of Jubiter Dunlap!" shouts the sheriff at the door.

It was awful. Aunt Sally and Benny flung themselves at Uncle Silas, screaming and crying, and hugged him and hung to him, and Aunt Sally said go away, she wouldn't ever give him up, they shouldn't have him, and the niggers they come crowding and crying to the door, and—well, I couldn't stand it; it was enough to break a person's heart; so I got out.

They took him up to the little one-horse jail in the village, and we all went along to tell him good-by, and Tom was feeling elegant, and says to me, "We'll have a most noble good time and heaps of danger some dark night, getting him out of there, Huck, and it 'll be talked about everywheres and we will be celebrated"; but the old man busted that scheme up the minute he whispered to him about it. He said no, it was his duty to stand whatever the law done, and he would stick to the jail plumb through to the end, even if there warn't no door to it. It disappointed Tom, and gravelled him a good deal, but he had to put up with it.

But he felt responsible and bound to get his uncle Silas free; and he told Aunt Sally, the last thing, not to worry, because he was going to turn in and work night and day and beat this game and fetch Uncle Silas out innocent; and she was very loving to him and thanked him and said she knowed he would do his very best. And she told us to help Benny take care of the house and the children, and then we had a good-by cry all around and went back to the farm, and left her there to live with the jailer's wife a month till the trial in October.

CHAPTER XI.

WELL, that was a hard month on us all. Poor Benny, she kept up the best she could, and me and Tom tried to keep things cheerful there at the house, but it kind of went for nothing, as you may say. It was the same up at the jail. We went up every day to see the old people, but it was awful dreary, because the old man warn't sleeping much, and was walking in his sleep considerable, and so he got to looking fagged and miserable, and his mind got shaky, and we all got afraid his troubles would break him down and kill him. And whenever we tried to persuade him to feel cheerfuler, he only shook his head and said if we only knowed what it was to carry around a

murderer's load on your
heart we wouldn't talk
that way. Tom and all
of us kept telling him it
wasn't murder, but just
accidental killing, but it
never made any differ-
ence — it was murder,
and he wouldn't have
it any other way. He
actuly begun to come
out plain and square
towards trial-time and
acknowledge that he
tried to kill the man.
Why, that was awful,
you know. It made
things seem fifty times
as dreadful, and there
warn't no more com-
fort for Aunt Sally and
Benny. But he prom-
ised he wouldn't say a
word about his murder
when others was around,
and we was glad of that.

"KEPT ME UP 'MOST ALL NIGHT."

Tom Sawyer racked
the head off of himself
all that month trying
to plan some way out for Uncle Silas, and
many's the night he kept me up 'most all
night with this kind of tiresome work, but
he couldn't seem to get on the right track
no way. As for me, I reckoned a body
might as well give it up, it all looked
so blue and I was so downhearted; but
he wouldn't. He stuck to the business
right along, and went on planning and
thinking and ransacking his head.

So at last the trial come on, towards
the middle of October, and we was all in
the court. The place was jammed, of
course. Poor old Uncle Silas, he looked
more like a dead person than a live one,
his eyes was so hollow and he looked so
thin and so mournful. Benny she set
on one side of him and Aunt Sally on
the other, and they had veils on, and
was full of trouble. But Tom he set by
our lawyer, and had his finger in everywheres, of course. The lawyer let him,
and the judge let him. He 'most took
the business out of the lawyer's hands
sometimes; which was well enough, because that was only a mud-turtle of a
back-settlement lawyer, and didn't know
enough to come in when it rains, as the
saying is.

They swore in the jury, and then the
lawyer for the prostitution got up and
begun. He made a terrible speech against
the old man, that made him moan and
groan, and made Benny and Aunt Sally
cry. The way *he* told about the murder
kind of knocked us all stupid, it was so different from the old man's tale. He said
he was going to prove that Uncle Silas was
seen to kill Jubiter Dunlap, by two good
witnesses, and done it deliberate, and
said he was going to kill him the very
minute he hit him with the club; and
they seen him hide Jubiter in the bushes,
and they seen that Jubiter was stone-
dead. And said Uncle Silas come later
and lugged Jubiter down into the tobacker-field, and two men seen him do it.
And said Uncle Silas turned out, away in
the night, and buried Jubiter, and a man
seen him at it.

I says to myself, poor old Uncle Silas
has been lying about it because he reckoned nobody seen him and he couldn't
bear to break Aunt Sally's heart and
Benny's; and right he was: as for me, I
would a lied the same way, and so would
anybody that had any feeling, to save
them such misery and sorrow which *they*
warn't no ways responsible for. Well, it
made our lawyer look pretty sick; and it

knocked Tom silly too, for a little spell; but then he braced up and let on that he warn't worried—but I knowed he *was*, all the same. And the people—my, but it made a stir amongst them!

And when that lawyer was done telling the jury what he was going to prove, he set down and begun to work his witnesses.

First, he called a lot of them to show that there was bad blood betwixt Uncle Silas and the diseased; and they told how they had heard Uncle Silas threaten the diseased, at one time and another, and how it got worse and worse, and everybody was talking about it, and how diseased got afraid of his life, and told two or three of them he was certain Uncle Silas would up and kill him some time or another.

Tom and our lawyer asked them some questions, but it warn't no use, they stuck to what they said.

Next, they called up Lem Beebe, and he took the stand. It come into my mind, then, how Lem and Jim Lane had come along talking, that time, about borrowing a dog or something from Jubiter Dunlap; and that brought up the blackberries and the lantern; and that brought up Bill and Jack Withers, and how *they* passed by, talking about a nigger stealing Uncle Silas's corn; and that fetched up our old ghost that come along about the same time and scared us so—and here *he* was, too, and a privileged character, on accounts of his being deef and dumb and a stranger, and they had fixed him a chair inside the railing, where he could cross his legs and be comfortable, whilst the other people was all in a jam so they couldn't hardly breathe. So it all come back to me just the way it was that day; and it made me mournful to think how pleasant it was up to then, and how miserable ever since.

Lem Beebe sworn, said: "I was a-coming along, that day, second of September, and Jim Lane was with me, and it was towards sundown, and we heard loud talk, like quarrelling, and we was very close, only the hazel bushes between (that's along the fence); and we heard a voice say: 'I've told you more'n once I'd kill you,' and knowed it was this prisoner's voice, and then we see a club come up above the bushes and down out of sight again, and heard a smashing thump, and then a groan or two; and then we crope soft to where we could see, and there laid Jubiter Dunlap dead, and this prisoner standing over him with the club; and the next he hauled the dead man into a clump of bushes and hid him, and then we stooped low, to be out of sight, and got away."

Well, it was awful. It kind of froze everybody's blood to hear it, and the house was 'most as still whilst he was telling it as if there warn't nobody in it. And when he was done, you could hear them gasp and sigh, all over the house, and look at one another the same as to say, "Ain't it perfectly terrible—ain't it awful!"

Now happened a thing that astonished me. All the time the first witnesses was proving the bad blood and the threats and all that, Tom Sawyer was alive and laying for them; and the minute they was through, he went for them, and done his level best to catch them in lies and spile their testimony. But now, how different! When Lem first begun to talk, and never said anything about speaking to Jubiter or trying to borrow a dog off of him, he was all alive and laying for Lem, and you could see he was getting ready to cross-question him to death pretty soon, and then I judged him and me would go on the stand by-and-by and tell what we heard him and Jim Lane say. But the next time I looked at Tom I got the cold shivers. Why, he was in the brownest study you ever see—miles and miles away. He warn't hearing a word Lem Beebe was saying; and when he got through he was still in that brown study, just the same. Our lawyer joggled him, and then he looked up startled, and says, "Take the witness if you want him. Lemme alone —I want to think."

Well, that beat me. I couldn't understand it. And Benny and her mother— oh, they looked sick, they was so troubled. They shoved their veils to one side and tried to get his eye, but it warn't any use, and I couldn't get his eye either. So the mud-turtle he tackled the witness, but it didn't amount to nothing; and he made a mess of it.

Then they called up Jim Lane, and he told the very same story over again, exact. Tom never listened to this one at all, but set there thinking and thinking, miles and miles away. So the mud-turtle went in alone again, and come out just as flat as he done before. The lawyer for the prostitution looked very comfortable, but the judge looked disgusted. You see, Tom was just the same as a regular lawyer, nearly, because it was Arkansaw law for a prisoner to choose anybody he wanted to help his lawyer, and Tom had had Uncle Silas shove him into the case, and now he was botching it, and you could see the judge didn't like it much.

All that the mud-turtle got out of Lem and Jim was this: he asked them—

"Why didn't you go and tell what you saw?"

"We was afraid we would get mixed up in it ourselves. And we was just starting down the river a-hunting for all the week besides; but as soon as we come back we found out they'd been searching for the body, so then we went and told Brace Dunlap all about it."

"When was that?"

"Saturday night, September 9th."

The judge he spoke up and says—

"Mr. Sheriff, arrest these two witnesses on suspicions of being accessionary after the fact to the murder."

The lawyer for the prostitution jumps up all excited, and says—

"Your Honor! I protest against this extraordi—"

"Set down!" says the judge, pulling his bowie and laying it on his pulpit. "I beg you to respect the Court."

So he done it. Then he called Bill Withers.

Bill Withers, sworn, said: "I was coming along about sundown, Saturday, September 2d, by the prisoner's field, and my brother Jack was with me, and we seen a man toting off something heavy on his back, and allowed it was a nigger stealing corn; we couldn't see distinct; next we made out that it was one man carrying another; and the way it hung, so kind of limp, we judged it was somebody that was drunk; and by the man's walk we said it was Parson Silas, and we judged he had found Sam Cooper drunk in the road, which he was always trying to reform him, and was toting him out of danger."

It made the people shiver to think of poor old Uncle Silas toting off the diseased down to the place in his tobacker-field where the dog dug up the body, but there warn't much sympathy around amongst the faces, and I heard one cuss say, "'Tis the coldest-blooded work I ever struck, lugging a murdered man around like that, and going to bury him like a animal, and him a preacher at that."

"'SET DOWN!' SAYS THE JUDGE."

Tom he went on thinking, and never took no notice; so our lawyer took the witness and done the best he could, and it was plenty poor enough.

Then Jack Withers he come on the stand and told the same tale, just like Bill done.

And after him comes Brace Dunlap, and he was looking very mournful, and 'most crying; and there was a rustle and a stir all around, and everybody got ready to listen, and lots of the women folks said "Poor cretur, poor cretur," and you could see a many of them wiping their eyes.

Brace Dunlap, sworn, said: "I was in considerable trouble a long time about my poor brother, but I reckoned things warn't near so bad as he made out, and I couldn't make myself believe anybody would have the heart to hurt a poor harmless cretur like that"—(by jings, I was sure I seen Tom give a kind of a faint little start, and then look disappointed again)—"and you know I *couldn't* think a preacher would hurt him—it warn't natural to think such an onlikely thing—so I never paid much attention, and now I sha'n't ever, ever forgive myself; for if I had a-done different, my poor brother would be with me this day, and not laying yonder murdered, and him so harmless." He kind of broke down there and choked up, and waited to get his voice; and people all around said the most pitiful things, and women cried; and it was very still in there, and solemn, and old Uncle Silas, poor thing, he give a groan right out so everybody heard him. Then Brace he went on: "Saturday, September 2d, he didn't come home to supper. By-and-by I got a little uneasy, and one of my niggers went over to this prisoner's place, but come back and said he warn't there. So I got uneasier and uneasier, and couldn't rest. I went to bed, but I couldn't sleep; and turned out, away late in the night, and went wandering over to this prisoner's place and all around about there a good while, hoping I would run across my poor brother, and never knowing he was out of his troubles and gone to a better shore—" So he broke down and choked up again, and most all the women was crying now. Pretty soon he got another start and says: "But it warn't no use; so at last I went home and tried to get some sleep, but

"OUR LAWYER."

couldn't. Well, in a day or two everybody was uneasy, and they got to talking about this prisoner's threats, and took to the idea, which I didn't take no stock in, that my brother was murdered; so they hunted around and tried to find his body, but couldn't, and give it up. And so I reckoned he was gone off somers to have a little peace, and would come back to us when his troubles was kind of healed. But late Saturday night, the 9th, Lem Beebe and Jim Lane come to my house and told me all—told me the whole awful 'sassination, and my heart was broke. And *then* I remembered something that hadn't took no hold of me at the time, be-

cause reports said this prisoner had took to walking in his sleep and doing all kind of things of no consequence, not knowing what he was about. I will tell you what that thing was that come back into my memory. Away late that awful Saturday night when I was wandering around about this prisoner's place, grieving and troubled, I was down by the corner of the tobacker-field and I heard a sound like digging in a gritty soil; and I crope nearer and peeped through the vines that hung on the rail fence and seen this prisoner *shorelling*—shovelling with a long-handled shovel—heaving earth into a big hole that was most filled up; his back was to me, but it was bright moonlight and I knowed him by his old green baize work-gown with a splattery white patch in the middle of the back like somebody had hit him with a snowball. *He was burying the man he'd murdered!*"

And he slumped down in his chair crying and sobbing, and 'most everybody in the house busted out wailing, and crying, and saying "Oh, it's awful—awful—horrible!" and there was a most tremenduous excitement, and you couldn't hear yourself think; and right in the midst of it up jumps old Uncle Silas, white as a sheet, and sings out—

"*It's true every word—I murdered him in cold blood!*"

By Jackson, it petrified them! People rose up wild all over the house, straining and staring for a better look at him, and the judge was hammering with his mallet, and the sheriff yelling "Order—order in the court—order!"

And all the while the old man stood there a-quaking and his eyes a-burning, and not looking at his wife and daughter, which was clinging to him and begging him to keep still, but pawing them off with his hands and saying he *would* clear his black soul from crime, he *would* heave off this load that was more than he could bear, and he *wouldn't* bear it another hour! And then he raged right along with his awful tale, everybody a-staring and gasping, judge, jury, lawyers, and everybody, and Benny and Aunt Sally crying their hearts out. And by George, Tom Sawyer never looked at him once! Never once—just set there gazing with all his eyes at something else, I couldn't tell what. And so the old man raged right along, pouring his words out like a stream of fire:

"I killed him! I am guilty! But I never had the notion in my life to hurt him or harm him, spite of all them lies

"I STRUCK TO KILL."

about my threatening him, till the very minute I raised the club—then my heart went cold!—then the pity all went out of it, and I struck to kill! In that one moment all my wrongs come into my mind; all the insults that that man and the scoundrel his brother, there, had put upon me, and how they had laid in together to ruin me with the people, and take away my good name, and *drive* me to some deed that would destroy me and my family that hadn't ever done *them* no harm, so help me God! And they done it in a mean revenge—for why? Because my innocent pure girl here at my side wouldn't marry that rich, insolent, ignorant coward, Brace Dunlap, who's been snivelling here over a brother he never cared a brass farthing for"—(I see Tom give a jump

and look glad *this* time, to a dead certainty)—"and in that moment I've told you about, I forgot my God and remembered only my heart's bitterness—God forgive me!—and I struck to kill. In one second I was miserably sorry—oh, filled with remorse; but I thought of my poor family, and I *must* hide what I'd done for their sakes; and I did hide that corpse in the bushes; and presently I carried it to the to-backer-field; and in the deep night I went with my shovel and buried it where—"

Up jumps Tom and shouts—

"*Now*, I've got it!" and waves his hand, oh, ever so fine and starchy, towards the old man, and says—

"Set down! A murder *was* done, but you never had no hand in it!"

Well, sir, you could a heard a pin

drop. And the old man he sunk down kind of bewildered in his seat, and Aunt Sally and Benny didn't know it, because they was so astonished and staring at Tom with their mouths open and not knowing what they was about. And the whole house the same. *I* never seen people look so helpless and tangled up, and I hain't ever seen eyes bug out and gaze without a blink the way theirn did. Tom says, perfectly ca'm—

"Your Honor, may I speak?"

"For God's sake, yes—go on !" says the judge, so astonished and mixed up he didn't know what he was about hardly.

Then Tom he stood there and waited a second or two—that was for to work up an "effect," as he calls it—then he started in just as ca'm as ever, and says:

"For about two weeks, now, there's been a little bill sticking on the front .of this court-house offering two thousand dollars reward for a couple of big di'monds —stole at St. Louis. Them di'monds is worth twelve thousand dollars. But never mind about that till I get to it. Now about this murder. I will tell you all about it—how it happened—who done it —every *detail*."

You could see everybody nestle, now, and begin to listen for all they was worth.

"This man here, Brace Dunlap, that's been snivelling so about his dead brother that *you* know he never cared a straw for, wanted to marry that young girl there, and she wouldn't have him. So he told Uncle Silas he would make him sorry. Uncle Silas knowed how powerful he was, and how little chance he had against such a man, and he was scared and worried, and done everything he could think of to smooth him over and get him to be good to him; he even took his no-account brother Jubiter on the farm and give him wages, and stinted his own family to pay them; and Jubiter done everything his brother could contrive to insult Uncle Silas, and fret and worry him, and try to drive Uncle Silas into doing him a hurt, so as to injure Uncle Silas with the people. And it done it. Everybody turned against him and said the meanest kind of things about him, and it gradual broke his heart—yes, and he was so worried and distressed that often he warn't hardly in his right mind.

"Well, on that Saturday that we've had so much trouble about, two of these witnesses here, Lem Beebe and Jim Lane, come along by where Uncle Silas and Jubiter Dunlap was at work—and that much of what they've said is true, the rest is lies. They didn't hear Uncle Silas say he would kill Jubiter; they didn't hear no blow struck; they didn't see no dead man, and they didn't see Uncle Silas hide anything in the bushes. Look at them now—how they set there, wishing they hadn't been so handy with their tongues; anyway, they'll wish it before I get done.

"That same Saturday evening, Bill and Jack Withers *did* see one man lugging off another one. That much of what they said is true, and the rest is lies. First off they thought it was a nigger stealing Uncle Silas's corn—you notice it makes them look silly, now, to find out somebody overheard them say that. That's because they found out by-and-by who it was that was doing the lugging, and *they* know best why they swore here that they took it for Uncle Silas by the gait—which it *wasn't*, and they knowed it when they swore to that lie.

"A man out in the moonlight *did* see a murdered person put underground in the tobacker-field—but it wasn't Uncle Silas that done the burying. He was in his bed at that very time.

"Now, then, before I go on, I want to ask you if you've ever noticed this: that people, when they're thinking deep, or when they're worried, are most always doing something with their hands, and they don't know it and don't notice what it is their hands are doing. Some stroke their chins; some stroke their noses; some stroke up *under* their chin with their hand; some twirl a chain, some fumble a button, then there's some that draws a figure or a letter with their finger on their cheek, or under their chin, or on their under lip. That's *my* way. When I'm restless, or worried, or thinking hard, I draw capital V's on my cheek or on my under lip or under my chin, and never anything *but* capital V's—and half the time I don't notice it and don't know I'm doing it."

That was odd. That is just what I do; only I make an O. And I could see people nodding to one another, same as they do when they mean "*that's* so."

"Now, then, I'll go on. That same Saturday—no it was the night before— there was a steamboat laying at Flagler's Landing, forty miles above here, and it was raining and storming like the nation. And there was a thief aboard, and he had them two big di'monds that's advertised out here on this court-house door; and he slipped ashore with his hand-bag and struck out into the dark and the storm, and he was a-hoping he could get to this town all right and be safe. But he had two pals aboard the boat, hiding, and he knowed they was going to kill him the first chance they got and take the di'monds; because all three stole them and then this fellow he got hold of them and skipped.

"Well, he hadn't been gone more'n ten minutes before his pals found it out, and they jumped ashore and lit out after him. Prob'ly they burnt matches and found his tracks. Anyway, they dogged along after him all day Saturday and kept out of his sight; and towards sundown he come to the bunch of sycamores down by Uncle Silas's field, and he went in there to get a disguise out of his hand-bag and put it on before he showed himself here in the town—and mind you he done that just a little after the time that Uncle Silas was hitting Jubiter Dunlap over the head with a club—for he *did* hit him.

"But the minute the pals see that thief slide into the bunch of sycamores, they jumped out of the bushes and slid in after him.

"They fell on him and clubbed him to death.

"Yes, for all he screamed and howled so, they never had no mercy on him, but clubbed him to death. And two men that was running along the road heard him yelling that way, and they made a rush into the sycamore bunch—which was where they was bound for, anyway—and when the pals saw them they lit out, and the two new men after them a-chasing them as tight as they could go. But only a minute or two—then these two new men slipped back very quiet into the sycamores.

"*Then* what did they do? I will tell

"A MURDER WAS DONE."

you what they done. They found where the thief had got his disguise out of his carpet-sack to put on; so one of them strips and puts on that disguise."

Tom waited a little here, for some more "effect"—then he says, very deliberate—

"The man that put on that dead man's disguise was—*Jubiter Dunlap!*"

"Great Scott!" everybody shouted, all over the house, and old Uncle Silas he looked perfectly astonished.

"Yes, it was Jubiter Dunlap. Not dead, you see. Then they pulled off the dead man's boots and put Jubiter Dunlap's old ragged shoes on the corpse and put the corpse's boots on Jubiter Dunlap. Then Jubiter Dunlap staid where he was, and the other man lugged the dead body off in the twilight; and after midnight he went to Uncle Silas's house, and took his old green work-robe off of the peg where it always hangs in the passage betwixt the house and the kitchen and put it on, and stole the long-handled shovel and went off down into the tobacker-field and buried the murdered man."

He stopped, and stood a half a minute. Then—

"And who do you reckon the murdered

man *was?* It was—*Jake* Dunlap, the long-lost burglar!"

"Great Scott!"

"And the man that buried him was—*Brace* Dunlap, his brother!"

"Great Scott!"

"And who do you reckon is this mowing idiot here that's letting on all these weeks to be a deef and dumb stranger? It's—*Jubiter* Dunlap!"

My land, they all busted out in a howl, and you never see the like of that excitement since the day you was born. And Tom he made a jump for Jubiter, and snaked off his goggles and his false whiskers, and there was the murdered man, sure enough, just as alive as anybody! And Aunt Sally and Benny they went to hugging and crying and kissing and smothering old Uncle Silas to that degree he was more muddled and confused and mushed up in his mind than he ever was before, and that is saying considerable. And next, people begun to yell—

"Tom Sawyer! Tom Sawyer! Shut up everybody, and let him go on! Go on, Tom Sawyer!"

Which made him feel uncommon bully, for it was nuts for Tom Sawyer to be a public character thataway, and a hero, as he calls it. So when it was all quiet, he says—

"There ain't much left, only this: When that man there, Brace Dunlap, had most worried the life and sense out of Uncle Silas till at last he plumb lost his mind and hit this other blatherskite his brother with a club, I reckon he seen his chance. Jubiter broke for the woods to hide, and I reckon the game was for him to slide out in the night and leave the country. Then Brace would make everybody believe Uncle Silas killed him and hid his body somers; and that would ruin Uncle Silas and drive *him* out of the country — hang him, maybe; I dunno. But when they found their dead brother in the sycamores without knowing him, because he was so battered up, they see they had a better thing: disguise *both* and bury Jake and dig him up presently all dressed up in Jubiter's clothes, and hire Jim Lane and Bill Withers and the others to swear to some handy lies—which they done. And there they set, now, and I told them they would be looking sick before I got done, and that is the way they're looking now.

"Well, me and Huck Finn here, we come down on the boat with the thieves, and the dead one told us all about the di'monds, and said the others would murder him if they got the chance; and we was going to help him all we could. We was bound for the sycamores when we heard them killing him in there; but we was in there in the early morning after the storm and allowed nobody hadn't been killed, after all. And when we see Jubiter Dunlap here spreading around in the very same disguise Jake told us *he* was going to wear, we thought it was Jake his own self and he was goo-gooing deef and dumb, and *that* was according to agreement.

"Well, me and Huck went on hunting for the corpse after

"WHICH MADE HIM FEEL UNCOMMON BULLY."

the others quit, and we found it. And was proud, too; but Uncle Silas he knocked us crazy by telling us *he* killed the man. So we was mighty sorry we found the body, and was bound to save Uncle Silas's neck if we could; and it was going to be tough work, too, because he wouldn't let us break him out of prison the way we done with our old nigger Jim.

"I done everything I could the whole month to think up some way to save Uncle Silas, but I couldn't strike a thing. So when we come into court to-day I come empty, and couldn't see no chance anywheres. But by-and-by I had a glimpse of something that set me thinking—just a little wee glimpse—only that, and not enough to make sure; but it set me thinking hard—and *watching*, when I was only letting on to think; and by-and-by, sure enough, when Uncle Silas was piling out that stuff about *him* killing Jubiter Dunlap, I catched that glimpse again, and this time I jumped up and shut down the proceedings, because I *knowed* Jubiter Dunlap was a-setting here before me. I knowed him by a thing which I seen him do—and I remembered it. I'd seen him do it when I was here a year ago."

He stopped then, and studied a minute —laying for an "effect"—I knowed it perfectly well. Then he turned off like he was going to leave the platform, and says, kind of lazy and indifferent—

"Well, I believe that is all."

Why, you never heard such a howl!— and it come from the whole house:

"What *was* it you seen him do? Stay where you are, you little devil! You think you are going to work a body up till his mouth's a-watering and stop there? What *was* it he done?"

That was it, you see—he just done it to get an "effect"; you couldn't a pulled him off of that platform with a yoke of oxen.

"AND THERE WAS THE MURDERED MAN."

"Oh, it wasn't anything much," he says. "I seen him looking a little excited when he found Uncle Silas was actuly fixing to hang himself for a murder that warn't ever done; and he got more and more nervous and worried, I a-watching him sharp but not seeming to look at him—and all of a sudden his hands begun to work and fidget, and pretty soon his left crept up and *his finger drawed a cross on his cheek*, and then I *had* him!"

Well, then they ripped and howled and stomped and clapped their hands till Tom Sawyer was that proud and happy he didn't know what to do with himself. And then the judge he looked down over his pulpit and says—

"My boy, did you *see* all the various details of this strange conspiracy and tragedy that you've been describing?"

"No, your Honor, I didn't see any of them."

"Didn't see any of them! Why, you've told the whole history straight through, just the same as if you'd seen it with your eyes. How did you manage that?"

"TOM GIVE HALF OF IT TO ME."

Tom says, kind of easy and comfortable—

"Oh, just noticing the evidence and piecing this and that together, your Honor; just an ordinary little bit of detective work; anybody could a done it."

"Nothing of the kind! Not two in a million could a done it. You are a very remarkable boy."

Then they let go and give Tom another smashing round, and he—well, he wouldn't a sold out for a silver-mine. Then the judge says—

"But are you certain you've got this curious history straight?"

"Perfectly, your Honor. Here is Brace Dunlap—let him deny his share of it if he wants to take the chance; I'll engage to make him wish he hadn't said anything. . . . Well, you see he's pretty quiet. And his brother's pretty quiet; and them four witnesses that lied so and got paid for it, they're pretty quiet. And as for Uncle Silas, it ain't any use for him to put in his oar, I wouldn't believe him under oath!"

Well, sir, that fairly made them shout; and even the judge he let go and laughed. Tom he was just feeling like a rainbow. When they was done laughing he looks up at the judge and says—

"Your Honor, there's a thief in this house."

"A thief?"

"Yes, sir. And he's got them twelve-thousand-dollar di'monds on him."

By gracious, but it made a stir! Everybody went shouting—

"Which is him? which is him? pint him out!" And the judge says—

"Point him out, my lad. Sheriff, you will arrest him. Which one is it?"

Tom says—

"This late dead man here—Jubiter Dunlap."

Then there was another thundering let-go of astonishment and excitement; but Jubiter, which was astonished enough before, was just fairly putrefied with astonishment this time. And he spoke up, about half crying, and says—

"Now that's a lie! Your Honor, it ain't fair; I'm plenty bad enough, without that. I done the other things—Brace he put me up to it, and persuaded me, and promised he'd make me rich, some day, and I done it, and I'm sorry I done it, and I wish't I hadn't; but I hain't stole no di'monds, and I hain't got no di'monds; I wish't I may never stir if it ain't so. The sheriff can search me and see."

Tom says—

"Your Honor, it wasn't right to call him a thief, and I'll let up on that a little. He did steal the di'monds, but he didn't know it. He stole them from his brother Jake when he was laying dead, after Jake had stole them from the other thieves; but Jubiter didn't know he was stealing them; and he's been swelling around here with them a month; yes, sir, twelve thousand dollars' worth of di'monds on him—all that riches, and going around here every day just like a poor man. Yes, your Honor, he's got them on him now."

The judge spoke up and says—

"Search him, sheriff."

Well, sir, the sheriff he ransacked him high and low, and everywhere; searched his hat, socks, seams, boots, everything— and Tom he stood there quiet, laying for another of them effects of his'n. Finally the sheriff he give it up, and everybody looked disappointed, and Jubiter says—

"There, now! what 'd I tell you?"

And the judge says—

"It appears you were mistaken this time, my boy."

Then Tom he took an attitude and let on to be studying with all his might, and scratching his head. Then all of a sudden he glanced up chipper and says—

"Oh, now I've got it! I'd forgot."

Which was a lie, and I knowed it. Then he says—

"Will somebody be good enough to lend me a little small screw-driver? There was one in your brother's hand-bag that you smouched, Jubiter, but I reckon you didn't fetch it with you."

"No, I didn't. I didn't want it, and I give it away."

"That was because you didn't know what it was for."

Jubiter had his boots on again by now, and when the thing Tom wanted was passed over the people's heads till it got to him, he says to Jubiter—

"Put up your foot on this chair;" and he kneeled down and begun to unscrew the heel-plate, everybody watching; and when he got that big di'mond out of that boot heel and held it up and let it flash and blaze and squirt sunlight everwhichaway, it just took everybody's breath; and Jubiter he looked so sick and sorry you never see the like of it. And when Tom held up the other di'mond he looked sorrier than ever. Land! he was

thinking how he would a skipped out and been rich and independent in a foreign land if he'd only had the luck to guess what the screw-driver was in the carpetbag for. Well, it was a most exciting time, take it all around, and Tom got cords of glory. The judge took the di'monds, and stood up in his pulpit, and shoved his spectacles back on his head, and cleared his throat, and says—

"I'll keep them and notify the owners; and when they send for them it will be a real pleasure to me to hand you the two thousand dollars, for you've earned the money—yes, and you've earned the deepest and most sincerest thanks of this community besides, for lifting a wronged and innocent family out of ruin and shame, and saving a good and honorable man from a felon's death, and for exposing to infamy and the punishment of the law a cruel and odious scoundrel and his miserable creatures!"

Well, sir, if there'd been a brass band to bust out some music, then, it would a been just the perfectest thing I ever see, and Tom Sawyer he said the same.

Then the sheriff he nabbed Brace Dunlap and his crowd, and by-and-by next month the judge had them up for trial and jailed the whole lot. And everybody crowded back to Uncle Silas's little old church, and was ever so loving and kind to him and the family, and couldn't do enough for them; and Uncle Silas he preached them the blamedest, jambledest, idiotic sermons you ever struck, and would tangle you up so you couldn't find your way home in daylight; but the people never let on but what they thought it was the clearest and brightest and elegantest sermons that ever was; and they would set there and cry, for love and pity; but, by George, they give me the jimjams and the fantods and caked up what brains I had, and turned them solid; but by-and-by they loved the old man's intellects back into him again and he was as sound in his skull as ever he was, which ain't no flattery, I reckon. And so the whole family was as happy as birds, and nobody could be gratefuler and lovinger than what they was to Tom Sawyer; and the same to me, though I hadn't done nothing. And when the two thousand dollars come, Tom give half of it to me, and never told anybody so, which didn't surprise me, because I knowed him.

THE END.

TWO COUNTRIES
by Henry James

I.

WHEN he reached the hotel, Macarthy Grice was apprised, to his great disappointment, of the fact that his mother and sister were absent for the day, and he reproached himself with not having been more definite in announcing his arrival to them in advance. It was a little his nature to expect people to know things about himself that he had not told them, and to be vexed when he found they didn't know them. I will not go so far as to say that he was inordinately conceited, but he had a general sense that he himself knew most things without having them pumped into him. He had been uncertain about his arrival, and since he disembarked at Liverpool had communicated his movements to the two ladies who, after spending the winter in Rome, were awaiting him at Cadenabbia, only by notes as brief as telegrams, and on several occasions by telegrams simply. It struck his mother that he spent a great deal of money on these latter missives—which were mainly negative— to say that he couldn't yet say when he should be able to start for the Continent. He had had business in London, and had been apparently a good deal vexed by the discovery that, most of the people it was necessary for him to see being out of town, the middle of August was a bad time for transacting it. Mrs. Grice gathered that he had had annoyances and disappointments, but she hoped that by the time he should join them his serenity would have been restored. She had not seen him for a year, and her heart hungered for her boy. Family feeling was strong among these three (though Macarthy's manner of showing it was sometimes peculiar), and her affection for her son was jealous and passionate; but she and Agatha made no secret between themselves of the fact that the privilege of being his mother and his sister was mainly sensible when things were going well with him. They were a little afraid they were not going well just now, and they asked each other why he couldn't leave his affairs alone for a few weeks anyway, and treat his journey to Europe as a complete holiday—a course which would do him infinitely more good.

He took life too hard, and was overworked and overstrained. It was only to each other, however, that the anxious and affectionate women made these reflections, for they knew it was of no use to say such things to Macarthy. It was not that he answered them angrily; on the contrary, he never noticed them at all. The answer was in the very essence of his nature: he was indomitably ambitious.

They had gone on the steamboat to the other end of the lake, and couldn't possibly be back for several hours. There was a *festa* going on at one of the villages —in the hills, a little way from the lake —and several ladies and gentlemen had gone from the hotel to be present at it. They would find carriages at the landing, and they would drive to the village, after which the same vehicles would bring them back to the boat. This information was given to Macarthy Grice by the secretary of the hotel, a young man with a very low shirt collar, whose nationality puzzled and even defied him by its indefiniteness (he liked to know whom he was talking to, even when he couldn't have the satisfaction of feeling that it was an American), and who suggested to him that he might follow and overtake his friends in the next steamer. As, however, there appeared to be some danger that in this case he should cross them on their way back, he determined simply to lounge about the lake-side and the grounds of the hotel. The place was lovely, the view magnificent, and there was a coming and going of little boats, of travellers of every nationality, of itinerant venders of small superfluities. Macarthy observed these things as patiently as his native restlessness allowed—and indeed that quality was re-enforced to-day by an inexplicable tendency to fidget. He changed his place twenty times; he lighted a cigar and threw it away; he ordered some luncheon, and when it came didn't care to eat it. He felt nervous, and he wondered what he was nervous about; whether he were afraid that during their excursion an accident had occurred to his mother or to Agatha. He was not usually a prey to small timidities, and indeed it cost him a certain effort to admit that a little Italian lake could be deep enough to drown a pair of Americans, or that Italian horses could have the high spirit to run away with them. He talked with no one, for the Americans seemed to him all taken up with each other, and the English all taken up with themselves. He had a few elementary principles for use in travelling (he had travelled little, but he had an abundant supply of theory on the subject), and one of them was that with Englishmen an American should never open the conversation. It was his belief that in doing so an American was exposed to be snubbed, or even insulted, and this belief was unshaken by the fact that Englishmen very often spoke to him, Macarthy, first.

The afternoon passed, little by little, and at last, as he stood there, with his hands in his pockets, and his hat pulled over his nose to keep the western sun out of his eyes, he saw the boat that he was waiting for round a distant point. At this stage the little annoyance he had felt at the trick his relations had unwittingly played him passed completely away, and there was nothing in his mind but the eagerness of affection, the joy of reunion—of the prospective embrace. This feeling was in his face, in the fixed smile with which he watched the boat grow larger and larger. If we watch the young man himself as he does so we shall perceive him to be a tallish, lean personage, with an excessive slope of the shoulders, a very thin neck, a short light beard, and a bright, sharp, expressive eye. He almost always wore his hat too much behind or too much in front; in the former case it showed a very fine high forehead. He looked like a man of intellect whose body was not much to him, and its senses and appetites not importunate. His feet were small, and he always wore a double-breasted frock-coat, which he never buttoned. His mother and sister thought him very handsome. He had this appearance especially, of course, when, making them out on the deck of the steamer, he began to wave his hat and his hand to them. They responded in the most demonstrative manner, and when they got near enough, his mother called out to him over the water that she couldn't forgive herself for having lost so much of his visit. This was a bold proceeding for Mrs. Grice, who usually held back. Only she had been uncertain—she hadn't expected him that day in particular. "It's

my fault!—it's my fault!" exclaimed a gentleman beside her, whom our young man had not yet noticed, raising his hat slightly as he spoke. Agatha, on the other side, said nothing, but only smiled at her brother. He had not seen her for so many months that he had almost forgotten how pretty she was. She looked lovely, under the shadow of her hat and of the awning of the steamer, as she stood there, with happiness in her face and a big bunch of familiar flowers in her hand. Macarthy-was proud of many things, but on this occasion he was proudest of having such a charming sister. Before they all disembarked he had time to observe the gentleman who had spoken to him — an extraordinarily fair, clean-looking man, with a white waistcoat, a white hat, a glass in one eye, and a flower in his button-hole. Macarthy wondered who he was, but only vaguely, as it explained him sufficiently to suppose that he was a gentleman staying at the hotel, who had made acquaintance with his mother and sister, and taken part in the excursion. The only thing Grice had against him was that he had the air of an American who tried to look like an Englishman—a definite and conspicuous class to the young man's sense, and one in regard to which he entertained a peculiar abhorrence. He was sorry his relatives should associate themselves with persons of that stamp; he would almost have preferred that they should become acquainted with the genuine English. He happened to perceive that the individual in question looked a good deal at him; but he disappeared, instantly and discreetly, when the boat drew up at the landing, and the three Grices—I had almost written the three Graces—pressed each other in their arms.

Half an hour later Macarthy sat between the two ladies at the *table d'hôte*, where he had a hundred questions to answer and to ask. He was still more struck with Agatha's improvement; she was older, handsomer, brighter: she had turned completely into a young lady, and into a very accomplished one. It seemed to him that there had been a change for the better in his mother as well, the only change of that sort of which the good lady was susceptible, an amelioration of health, a fresher color, and a less frequent cough. Mrs. Grice was a gentle, sallow, serious little woman, the main principle of whose being was the habit of insisting that no-

"SHE LOOKED LOVELY AS SHE STOOD THERE, WITH HAPPINESS IN HER FACE."

thing that concerned herself was of the least consequence. She thought it indelicate to be ill, and obtrusive even to be better, and discouraged all conversation of which she herself was in any degree the subject. Fortunately she had not been able to prevent her children from discussing her condition sufficiently to agree —it took but few words, for they agreed easily, that is, Agatha always agreed with her brother—that she must have a change of climate, and spend a winter or two in the south of Europe. Mrs. Grice kept her son's birthday all the year, and knew an extraordinary number of stitches in knitting. Her friends constantly received from her, by post, offerings of little mats for the table, done up in an envelop, usually without any writing. She could make little mats in forty or fifty different ways. Toward the end of the dinner, Macarthy, who up to this moment had been wholly occupied with his companions, began to look about him, and to ask questions about the people opposite. Then he leaned forward a little, and turned his eye up and down the row of their fellow-tourists on the same side. It was in this way that he perceived the gentleman who had said from the steamer that it was *his* fault that Mrs. Grice and her daughter had gone away for so many hours, and who now was seated at some distance below the younger lady. At the moment Macarthy leaned forward, this personage happened to be looking toward him, so that he caught his eye. The stranger smiled at him and nodded, as if an acquaintance might be considered to have been established between them, rather to Macarthy's surprise. He drew back and asked his sister who he was—the fellow who had been with them on the boat.

"He's an Englishman—Sir Rufus Chasemore," said the girl. Then she added, "Such a nice man."

"Oh, I thought he was an American making a fool of himself!" Macarthy rejoined.

"There's nothing of the fool about him," Agatha declared, laughing; and in a moment she added that Sir Rufus's usual place was beside hers, on her left hand. On this occasion he had moved away.

"What do you mean by this occasion?" her brother inquired.

"Oh, because you are here."

"And is he afraid of me?"

"Yes, I think he is."

"He doesn't behave so, anyway."

"Oh, he has very good manners," said the girl.

"Well, I suppose he's bound to do that. Isn't he a kind of nobleman?" Macarthy asked.

"Well, no, not exactly a nobleman."

"Well, some kind of a panjandarum. Hasn't he got one of their titles?"

"Yes, but not a very high one," Agatha explained. "He's only a K.C.B. And also an M.P."

"A K.C.B. and an M.P.? What the deuce is all that?" And when Agatha had elucidated these mystic signs, as to which the young man's ignorance was partly simulated, he remarked that the Post-office ought to charge her friend double for his letters—for requiring that amount of stuff in his address. He also said that he owed him one for leading them astray at a time when they were bound to be on hand to receive one who was so dear to them; to which Agatha replied:

"Ah, you see, Englishmen are like that. They expect women to be so much honored by their wanting them to do anything. And it must always be what *they* like, of course."

"What the men like? Well, that's all right, only they mustn't be Englishmen," said Macarthy Grice.

"Oh, if one is going to be a slave, I don't know that the nationality of one's master matters!" his sister exclaimed. After which his mother began to ask him if he had seen anything during the previous months of their Philadelphia cousins— some cousins who wrote their name Gryce, and for whom Macarthy had but a small affection.

After dinner the three sat out on the terrace of the hotel, in the delicious warmth of the September night. There were boats on the water, decked with colored lanterns; music and song proceeded from several of them, and every influence was harmonious. Nevertheless, by the time Macarthy had finished a cigar it was judged best that the old lady should withdraw herself from the evening air. She went into the *salon* of the hotel, and her children accompanied her, against her protests, so that she might not be alone. Macarthy liked better to sit with his mother in a drawing-room which the lamps made hot than without her under the stars. At the end of a quarter of an hour he became aware that his sister had disappeared, and as some time elapsed without her returning, he asked his mother what had become of her.

"I guess she has gone to walk with Sir Rufus," said the old lady, candidly.

"Why, you seem to do everything Sir Rufus wants, down here!" her son exclaimed. "How did he get such a grip on you?"

"Well, he has been most kind, Macarthy," Mrs. Grice returned, not appearing to deny that the Englishman's influence was considerable.

"I have heard it stated that it's not the custom, down here, for young girls to walk round—at night—with foreign lords."

"Oh, he's not foreign, and he's most reliable," said the old lady, very earnestly. It was not in her nature to treat such a question, or indeed any question, as unimportant.

"Well, that's all right," her son remarked, in a tone which implied that he was in good-humor, and didn't wish to have his equanimity ruffled. Such accidents, with Macarthy Grice, were not light things. All the same, at the end of five minutes more, as Agatha did not reappear, he expressed the hope that nothing of any kind had sprung up between her and the K.C.B.

"Oh, I guess they are just conversing by the lake. I'll go and find them if you like," said Mrs. Grice.

"Well, haven't they been conversing by the lake—and on the lake—all day?" asked the young man, without taking up her proposal.

"Yes, of course we had a great deal of bright talk while we were out. It was quite enough for me to listen to it. But he is most kind—and he knows everything, Macarthy."

"Well, that's all right!" exclaimed the young man again. But a few moments later he returned to the charge, and asked his mother if the Englishman were paying any serious attention—she knew what he meant—to Agatha. "Italian lakes, and summer evenings, and glittering titles, and all that sort of thing—of course you know what they may lead to."

Mrs. Grice looked anxious and veracious, as she always did, and appeared to consider a little. "Well, Macarthy, the truth is just this. Your sister is so attractive and so admired that it seems as if, wherever she went, there was a great interest taken in her. Sir Rufus certainly does like to converse with her, but so have many others—and so would any one in their place. And Agatha is full of conscience. For me that's her highest attraction."

"I'm very much pleased with her—she's a lovely creature," Macarthy remarked.

"Well, there's no one whose appreciation could gratify her more than yours. She has praised you up to Sir Rufus," added the old lady, simply.

"Dear mother, what has *he* got to do with it?" her son demanded, staring. "I don't care what Sir Rufus thinks of me."

Fortunately the good lady was left only for a moment confronted with this inquiry, for Agatha now re-entered the room, passing in from the terrace by one of the long windows, and accompanied precisely by the gentleman whom her relatives had been discussing. She came toward them smiling, and perhaps even blushing a little, but with an air of considerable resolution, and she said to Macarthy, "Brother, I want to make you acquainted with a good friend of ours, Sir Rufus Chasemore."

"Oh, I asked Miss Grice to be so good." The Englishman laughed, looking easy and genial.

Macarthy got up and extended his hand, with a "Very happy to know you, sir," and the two men stood a moment looking at each other, while Agatha, beside them, bent her regard upon both. I shall not attempt to translate the reflections which rose in the young lady's mind as she did so, for they were complicated and subtle, and it is quite difficult enough to reproduce our own more casual impression of the contrast between her companions. This contrast was extreme and complete, and it was not weakened by the fact that both the men had the signs of character and ability. The American was thin, dry, fine, with something in his face which seemed to say that there was more in him of the spirit than of the letter. He looked unfinished, and yet somehow he looked mature, though he was not advanced in life. The Englishman had more detail about him, something stippled and retouched, an air of having been more artfully fashioned in conformity with traditions and models. He wore old clothes which looked new, while his transatlantic brother wore new clothes which looked old. He thought he had never heard the American tone so marked as on the lips of Mr. Macarthy Grice, who on his side found in the accent of his sister's friend a strange, exaggerated, even affected, variation of the tongue in which he supposed himself to have been brought up. In general he was much irritated by the tricks which the English played with the English language, and he deprecated especially their use of familiar slang.

"Miss Grice tells me that you have just crossed the ditch, but I'm afraid you are not going to stay with us long," Sir Rufus remarked, with much pleasantness.

"Well, no, I shall return as soon as I have transacted my business," Macarthy replied. "That's all I came for."

"You don't do us justice; you ought to follow the example of your mother and sister, and take a look round," Sir Rufus went on, with another laugh. He was evidently of a mirthful nature.

"Oh, I have been here before; I've seen the principal curiosities."

"He has seen everything thoroughly," Mrs. Grice murmured over her crochet.

"Ah, I dare say you have seen much more than we poor natives. And your own country is so interesting. I have an immense desire to see that."

"Well, it certainly repays observation," said Macarthy Grice.

"You wouldn't like it at all; you would find it awful," his sister remarked, sportively, to Sir Rufus.

"Gracious, daughter!" the old lady exclaimed, trying to catch Agatha's eye.

"That's what she's always telling me, as if she were trying to keep me from going. I don't know what she has been doing over there that she wants to prevent me from finding out." Sir Rufus's eyes, while he made this observation, rested on the young lady in the most respectful yet at the same time the most complacent manner.

She smiled back at him, and said, with a laugh still clearer than his own, "I know the kind of people who will like America and the kind of people who won't."

"Do you know the kind who will like *you*, and the kind who won't?" Sir Rufus Chasemore inquired.

"I don't know that in some cases it particularly matters what people like,"

Macarthy interposed, with a certain severity.

"Well, I must say I like people to like my country," said Agatha.

"You certainly take the best way to make them, Miss Grice!" Sir Rufus exclaimed.

"Do you mean by dissuading them from visiting it, sir?" Macarthy asked.

"Oh dear no; by being so charming a representative of it. But I shall most positively go on the first opportunity."

"I hope it won't be while we are on this side," said Mrs. Grice, very civilly.

"You will need us over there to explain everything," her daughter added.

The Englishman looked at her a moment with his glass in his eye. "I shall certainly pretend to be very stupid." Then he went on, addressing himself to Macarthy: "I have an idea that you have some rocks ahead, but that doesn't diminish—in fact it increases—my curiosity to see the country."

"Oh, I suspect we'll scratch along all right," Macarthy replied, with rather a grim smile, in a tone which conveyed that the success of American institutions might not altogether depend on Sir Rufus's judgment of them. He was on the point of expressing his belief, further, that there were European countries which would be glad enough to exchange their "rocks" for those of the United States; but he kept back this reflection, as it might appear too pointed, and he didn't wish to be rude to a man who seemed on such sociable terms with his mother and sister. In the course of a quarter of an hour the ladies took their departure for the upper regions, and Macarthy Grice went off with them. The Englishman looked for him again, however, as something had been said about their smoking a cigar together before they went to bed; but he didn't turn up, and Sir Rufus puffed his own weed in solitude, strolling up and down the terrace without mingling with the groups that remained, and looking much at the starlit lake and mountains.

II.

The next morning, after breakfast, Mrs. Grice had a conversation with her son in her own room. Agatha had not yet appeared, and she explained that the girl was sleeping late, having been much fatigued by her excursion the day before, as well as by the excitement of her brother's arrival. Macarthy thought it a little singular that she should bear her fatigue so much less well than her mother, but he understood everything in a moment, as soon as the old lady drew him toward her, with her little conscious, cautious face, taking his hand in hers. She had a long and important talk with Agatha the previous evening after they went upstairs, and she had extracted from the girl some information which she had within a day or two begun very much to desire.

"It's about Sir Rufus Chasemore. I couldn't but think you would wonder—just as I was wondering myself," said Mrs. Grice. "I felt as if I couldn't be satisfied till I had asked. I don't know how you will feel about it. I am afraid it will upset you a little; but anything that you may think—well, yes, it is the case."

"Do you mean she is engaged to be married to your Englishman?" Macarthy demanded, with a face that suddenly flushed.

"No, she's not engaged. I presume she wouldn't take that step without finding out how you'd feel. In fact that's what she said last night."

"I feel like—well, I feel like thunder!" Macarthy exclaimed, "and I hope you'll tell her so."

Mrs. Grice looked frightened and pained. "Well, my son, I'm glad you've come, if there is going to be any trouble."

"Trouble—what trouble should there be? He can't marry her if she won't have him."

"Well, she didn't say she wouldn't have him; she said the question hadn't come up. But she thinks it would come up if she were to give him any sort of opening. That's what I thought, and that's what I wanted to make sure of."

Macarthy looked at his mother for some moments in extreme seriousness; then he took out his watch and looked at that. "What time is the first boat?" he asked.

"I don't know — there are a good many."

"Well, we'll take the first—we'll quit this." And the young man put back his watch and got up with decision.

His mother sat looking at him rather ruefully. "Would you feel so badly if she were to do it?"

"She may do it without my consent, she shall never do it with," said Macarthy Grice.

"Well, I could see last evening, by the way you acted—" his mother murmured, as if she thought it her duty to try and enter into his opposition.

"How did I act, ma'am?"

"Well, you acted as if you didn't think much of the English."

"Well, I don't," said the young man.

"Agatha noticed it, and she thought Sir Rufus noticed it too."

"They have such thick hides in general that they don't notice anything. But if he is more sensitive than the others, perhaps it will keep him away."

"Would you like to wound him, Macarthy?" his mother inquired, with an accent of timid reproach.

"Wound him? I should like to kill him! Please to let Agatha know that we'll move on," the young man added.

Mrs. Grice got up as if she were about to comply with this injunction, but she stopped in the middle of the room, and asked of her son, with a quaint effort of conscientious impartiality which would have made him smile if he had been capable of smiling in such a connection, "Don't you think that in some respects the English are a fine nation?"

"Well, yes; I like them for pale ale, and note-paper, and umbrellas; and I got a first-rate trunk there the other day. But I want my sister to marry one of her own people."

"Yes, I presume it would be better," Mrs. Grice remarked. "But Sir Rufus has occupied very high positions in his own country."

"I know the kind of positions he has occupied; I can tell what they were by looking at him. The more he has done of that, the more intensely he represents what I don't like."

"Of course he would stand up for England," Mrs. Grice felt herself compelled to admit.

"Then why the mischief doesn't he do so, instead of running round after Americans?" Macarthy demanded.

"He doesn't run round after us; but we knew his sister, Lady Bolitho, in Rome. She is a most sweet woman, and we saw a great deal of her; she took a great fancy to Agatha. I surmise she mentioned us to him pretty often when she went back to England, and when he came abroad for his autumn holiday, as he calls it—he met us first in the Engadine, three or four weeks ago, and came down here with us—it seemed as if we already knew him and he knew us. He is very talented, and he is quite well off."

"Mother," said Macarthy Grice, going close to the old lady, and speaking very gravely, "why do you know so much about him? Why have you gone into it so?"

"I haven't gone into it; I only know what he has told us."

"But why have you given him the right to tell you? How does it concern you whether he is well off?"

The poor woman began to look flurried and scared. "My son, I have given him no right; I don't know what you mean. Besides, it wasn't he who told us he is well off; it was his sister."

"It would have been better if you hadn't known his sister," said the young man, gloomily.

"Gracious, Macarthy, we must know some one!" Mrs. Grice rejoined, with a flicker of spirit.

"I don't see the necessity of your knowing the English."

"Why, Macarthy, can't we even *know* them?" pleaded his mother.

"You see the sort of thing it gets you into."

"It hasn't got us into anything. Nothing has been done."

"So much the better, mother darling," said the young man. "In that case we will go on to Venice. Where is he going?"

"I don't know, but I suppose he won't come on to Venice if we don't ask him."

"I don't believe any delicacy would prevent him," Macarthy rejoined. "But he loathes me; that's an advantage."

"He *loathes* you—when he wanted so to know you?"

"Oh yes, I understand. Well, now he knows me! He knows he hates everything I like, and I hate everything he likes."

"He doesn't imagine you hate your sister, I suppose!" said the old lady, with a little vague laugh.

"Mother," said Macarthy, still in front of her, with his hands in his pockets, "I verily believe I should hate her if she were to marry him."

"Oh, gracious! my son! don't! don't," cried Mrs. Grice, throwing herself into his arms with a shudder of horror, and burying her face on his shoulder.

Her son held her close, and as he bent over her he went on: "Dearest mother, don't you see that we must remain together—that at any rate we mustn't be separated by different ideas, different associations and institutions? I don't believe any family has ever had more of the feeling that holds people closely together than we have had; therefore, for Heaven's sake, let us keep it, let us find our happiness in it, as we always have done. Of course Agatha will marry some day, but why need she marry in such a way as to make a gulf? You and she are all I have, and—I may be selfish—I should like very much to keep you."

"Of course I will let her know the way you feel," said the old lady, a moment later, rearranging her cap and her shawl, and putting away her pocket-handkerchief.

"It's a matter she certainly ought to understand. She would wish to, unless she is very much changed," Macarthy added, as if he saw all this with high lucidity.

"Oh, she isn't changed—she'll never change!" his mother exclaimed, with rebounding optimism. She thought it wicked not to take cheerful views.

"She wouldn't if she were to marry an Englishman," he declared, as Mrs. Grice left him to go to her daughter.

She told him an hour later that Agatha would be quite ready to start for Venice on the morrow, and that she said he need have no fear that Sir Rufus Chasemore would follow them. He was naturally anxious to know from her what had passed between her and the girl, but the only very definite information he extracted was to the effect that Agatha had declared, with infinite feeling, that she would never marry an enemy of her country. When he saw her, later in the day, he thought she had been crying; but there was nothing in her manner to show that she resented any pressure her mother might have represented to her that he had put upon her, or that she was making a reluctant sacrifice. Agatha Grice was very fond of her brother, whom she knew to be upright, distinguished, and exceedingly mindful of the protection and support that he owed her mother and herself. He was perverse and obstinate, but she was aware that in essentials he was supremely tender, and he had always been very much the most eminent figure in her horizon.

No allusion was made between them to Sir Rufus Chasemore, though the silence on either side was rather a conscious one, and they talked of the prospective pleasures of Venice, and of the arrangements Macarthy would be able to make in regard to his mother's spending another winter in Rome. He was to accompany them to Venice and spend a fortnight with them there, after which he was to return to London, to terminate his business, and then take his way back to New York. There was a plan of his coming to see them again later in the winter, in Rome, if he should succeed in getting six weeks off. As a man of energy and decision, though indeed of a somewhat irritable stomach, he made light of the Atlantic voyage; it was a rest and a relief, alternating with his close attention to business. That the disunion produced by the state of Mrs. Grice's health was a source of constant regret, and even of much depression to him, was well known to his mother and sister, who would not have broken up his home by coming to live in Europe if he had not insisted upon it. Macarthy was in the highest degree conscientious, and capable of suffering the extremity of discomfort in a cause which he held to be right. But his mother and sister *were* his home, all the same, and in their absence he was perceptibly desolate. Fortunately it had been hoped that a couple of southern winters would quite set Mrs. Grice up again, and that then everything, in America, would be as it had been before. Agatha's affection for her brother was very nearly as great as his affection for herself; but it took the form of wishing that his loneliness might be the cause of his marrying some thoroughly nice girl, inasmuch as, after all, her mother and she might not always be there. Fraternal tenderness in Macarthy's bosom followed a different logic. He was so fond of his sister that he had a secret hope that she would never marry at all. He had spoken otherwise to his mother, because that was the only way not to seem offensively selfish; but the bottom of his thought, as the French say, was that on the day Agatha should marry she would throw him over. On the day she should marry an Englishman she would not throw him over—she would betray him. That is, she would betray her country, and it came to the same thing. Macarthy's patriotism was of so intense a hue that, to his own sense, the

national life and his own life flowed in an indistinguishable current.

The particular Englishman he had his eye upon now was not, as a general thing, visible before luncheon. He had told Agatha, who mentioned it to her brother, that in the morning he was immersed in work—in letter-writing. Macarthy wondered what his work might be, but did not condescend to inquire. He was enlightened, however, by happening by an odd chance to observe an allusion to Sir Rufus in a copy of the London *Times* which he took up in the reading-room of the hotel. This occurred in a letter to the editor of the newspaper, the writer of which accused Agatha's friend of having withheld from the public some information to which the public was entitled. The information had respect to "the situation in South Africa," and Sir Rufus was plainly an agent of the British government, the head of some kind of department or sub-department. This didn't make Macarthy like him any better. He was displeased with the idea of England's possessing colonies at all, and considered that she had acquired them by force and fraud, and held them by a frail and unnatural tenure. It appeared to him that any man who occupied a place in this unrighteous system must have false, detestable views. Sir Rufus Chasemore turned up on the terrace in the afternoon, and bore himself with the serenity of a man unconscious of the damaging inferences that had been formed about him. Macarthy neither avoided him nor sought him out—he even relented a little toward him mentally when he thought of the loss he was about to inflict on him; but when the Englishman approached him and appeared to wish to renew their conversation of the evening before, it struck him that he was wanting in delicacy. There was nothing strange in that, however, for delicacy and tact were not the strong point of one's transatlantic cousins, with whom one had always to dot one's i's. It seemed to Macarthy that Sir Rufus Chasemore ought to have guessed that he didn't desire to keep up an acquaintance with him, though indeed the young American would have been at a loss to say how he was to guess it, inasmuch as he would have resented the imputation that he himself had been rude enough to make such a fact patent. The American ladies were in their apartments, occupied in some manner connected with their intended retreat, and there was nothing for Macarthy but to stroll up and down for nearly half an hour with the personage who was so provokingly the cause of it. It had come over him now that he should have liked extremely to spend several days on the lake of Como. The place struck him as much more delicious than it had done while he chafed the day before at the absence of his relations. He was angry with the Englishman for forcing him to leave it, and still more angry with him for showing so little responsibility, or even perception, in regard to the matter. It occurred to him while he was in this humor that it might be a good plan to make himself so disagreeable that Sir Rufus would take to his heels and never reappear, fleeing before the portent of such an insufferable brother-in-law. But this plan demanded powers of execution which Macarthy did not flatter himself that he possessed; he felt that it was impossible to him to divest himself of his character of a polished American gentleman.

If he found himself dissenting from most of the judgments and opinions which Sir Rufus Chasemore happened to express in the course of their conversation, there was nothing perverse in that; it was a simple fact, apparently, that the Englishman had nothing in common with him, and was predestined to enunciate propositions to which it was impossible for him to assent. Moreover, how could he assent to propositions enunciated in that short, off-hand, clipping tone, with the words running into each other, and the voice rushing up and down the scale? Macarthy, who spoke very slowly, with great distinctness, and in general with great correctness, was annoyed not only by his companion's intonation, but by the odd and, as it seemed to him, licentious application that he made of certain words. He struck him as wanting in reverence for the language, which Macarthy had an idea, not altogether unjust, that he himself deeply cherished. He would have admitted that these things were small and not great, but in the usual relations of life the small things count more than the great, and they sufficed, at any rate, to remind him of the essential antipathy and incompatibility which he had always believed to exist between an Englishman and an American. They

were, in the very nature of things, disagreeable to each other, both mentally and physically irreconcilable. In cases where this want of correspondence had been bridged over, it was because the American had made weak concessions, had been shamefully accommodating. That was a kind of thing the Englishman, to do him justice, never did; he had at least the courage of his prejudices. It was not unknown to Macarthy that the repugnance in question appeared to be confined to the American male, as was shown by a thousand international marriages, which had transplanted as many of his countrywomen to unnatural British homes. That variation had to be allowed for, and the young man felt that he was allowing for it when he reflected that very likely his own sister liked the way Sir Rufus Chasemore spoke. In fact he was intimately convinced she liked it, which was a reason the more for their quitting Cadenabbia the next morning.

Sir Rufus took the opposite point of view quite as much as himself, only he took it gayly and familiarly and laughed about it, as if he were amused at the preferences his companion betrayed, and especially amused that he should hold them so gravely, so almost gloomily. This sociable jocosity, as if they had known each other for three months, was what appeared to Macarthy so indelicate. They talked no politics, and Sir Rufus said nothing more about America; but it stuck out of the Englishman at every pore that he was a resolute and consistent conservative, a prosperous, accomplished, professional, official Tory. It gave Macarthy a kind of palpitation to think that his sister had been in danger of associating herself with such arrogant theories; not that a woman's political creed mattered, but that of her husband did. He had an impression that he himself was a passionate democrat, an unshrinking radical. It was a proof of how far Sir Rufus's manner was from being satisfactory to his companion that the latter was unable to guess whether he already knew of the sudden determination of his American friends to leave Cadenabbia, or whether their intention was first revealed to him in Macarthy's casual mention of it, which apparently didn't put him out at all, eliciting nothing more than a frank, cheerful expression of regret. Macarthy somehow mistrusted a man who could conceal his emotions like that. How could he have known they were going unless Agatha had told him, and how could Agatha have told him, since she couldn't as yet have seen him? It did not even occur to the young man to suspect that she might have conveyed the unwelcome news to him by a letter. And if he hadn't known it, why wasn't he more startled and discomfited when Macarthy dealt the blow? The young American made up his mind at last that the reason why Sir Rufus was not startled was that he had thought in advance it would be no more than natural that the newly arrived brother should wish to spoil his game. But in that case why wasn't he angry with him for such a disposition? Why did he come after him and insist on talking with him? There seemed to Macarthy something impudent in this incongruity—as if to the mind of an English statesman the animosity of a Yankee lawyer were really of too little account.

III.

It may be intimated to the reader that Agatha Grice had written no note to her English friend, and she held no communication with him of any sort, till after she had left the *table d'hôte* with her mother and brother in the evening. Sir Rufus had seated himself at dinner in the same place as the night before; he was already occupying it, and he simply bowed to her, with a smile, from a distance, when she came into the room. As she passed out to the terrace, later, with her companions, he overtook her, and said to her, in a lower tone of voice than usual, that he had been exceedingly sorry to hear that she was leaving Cadenabbia so soon. Was it really true? couldn't they put it off a little? shouldn't they find the weather too hot in Venice, and the mosquitoes too numerous? Agatha saw that Sir Rufus asked these questions with the intention of drawing her away, engaging her in a walk, in some talk to which they should have no listeners, and she resisted him at first a little, keeping near the others, because she had made up her mind that morning, in deep and solitary meditation, that she would force him to understand that further acquaintance could lead to nothing profitable for either party. It presently came over her, however, that it would take some little time to explain this truth, and that the time might

be obtained by their walking a certain distance along the charming shore of the lake together. The windows of the hotel and of the little water-side houses and villas projected long shafts of lamp-light over the place, which shimmered on the water, broken by the slow-moving barges, laden with musicians, and gave the whole region the air of an illuminated garden surrounding a magnificent pond. Agatha made the further reflection that it would be only common kindness to give Sir Rufus an opportunity to say anything he wished to say, that is, within the limits she was prepared to allow; they had been too good friends to separate without some of the forms of regret, without a backward look at least, since they might not enjoy a forward one. In short, she had taken in the morning a resolution so virtuous, founded on so high and large a view of the whole situation, that she felt herself entitled to some reward, some present liberty of action. She turned away from her relatives with Sir Rufus—she observed that they paid no attention to her—and in a few moments she was strolling by his side at a certain distance from the hotel.

"I will tell you what I should like to do," he said, as they went; "I should like to turn up in Venice—about a week hence."

"I don't recommend you to do that," the girl replied, promptly enough, though as soon as she had spoken she bethought herself that she could give him no definite reason why he should not follow her; she could give him no reason at all that would not be singularly wanting in delicacy. She had a movement of vexation with her brother for having put her in a false position; it was the first, for in the morning, when her mother repeated to her what Macarthy had said, and she perceived all that it implied, she had not been in the least angry with him—she sometimes, indeed, wondered why she was not—and she didn't propose to become so for Sir Rufus Chasemore. What she had been was sad, and touched, too, with a sense of horror—horror at the idea that she might be in danger of denying, under the influence of an insinuating alien, the pieties and sanctities in which she had been brought up. Sir Rufus *was* a tremendous conservative, though perhaps that didn't matter so much, and he had let her know at an early stage of their acquaintance that he had never liked Americans in the least as a people. As it was apparent that he liked her—all American, and very American, as she was —she had regarded this shortcoming only in its minor bearings, and it had even entertained her to form a private project of converting him to a friendlier view. If she hadn't found him a charming man, she wouldn't have cared what he thought about her country people; but, as it happened, she did find him a charming man, and it grieved her to see a mind that was really worthy of the finest initiations (as regarded the American question) wasting itself on poor prejudices. Somehow, by showing him how nice she was herself, she could make him like the people better with whom she had so much in common, and as he admitted that his observation of them had, after all, been very restricted, she would also make him know them better. This prospect drew her on till suddenly her brother sounded the note of warning. When it came she understood it perfectly; she couldn't pretend that she didn't. If she didn't look out, she would give her country away: and in the privacy of her own room she had colored up to her hair at the thought. She had a lurid vision in which the chance seemed to be greater that Sir Rufus Chasemore would bring her over to his side than that she should make him like anything he had begun by disliking; so that she resisted, with the conviction that the complications which might arise from allowing a prejudiced Englishman to possess himself, as he evidently desired to do, of her affections, would be much greater than a sensitive girl with other loyalties to observe might be able to manage. A moment after she had said to her companion that she didn't recommend him to come to Venice she added that of course he was free to do as he liked; only why should he come if he was sure the place was so uncomfortable? To this Sir Rufus replied that he didn't care how uncomfortable it was if she should be there, and that there was nothing he wouldn't put up with for the sake of a few days more of her society.

"Oh, if it's for that you are coming," the girl replied, laughing and feeling nervous—feeling that something was in the air which she had wished precisely to keep out of it—"Oh, if it's for that you are coming, you had very much better not take

the trouble; you would have very little of my society. While my brother is with us, all my time will be given up to him."

"Confound your brother!" Sir Rufus exclaimed. Then he went on: "You told me yourself he wouldn't be with you long. After he's gone you will be free again, and you will still be in Venice, sha'n't you? I do want to float in a gondola with you."

"It's very possible my brother may be with us for weeks."

Sir Rufus hesitated a moment. "I see what you mean—that he won't leave you so long as I am about the place. In that case, if you are so fond of him, you ought to take it as a kindness of me to hover about." Before the girl had time to make a rejoinder to this ingenious proposition he added, "Why in the world has he taken such a dislike to me?"

"I know nothing of any dislike," Agatha said, not very honestly. "He has expressed none to me."

"He has to me, then. He quite loathes me."

She was silent a little. Then she inquired, "And do you like him very much?"

"I think he's immense fun! He's very clever, like most of the Americans I have seen, including yourself. I should like to show him I like him, and I have salaamed and kowtowed to him whenever I had a chance; but he won't let me get near him. Hang it, it's cruel!"

"It's not directed to you, in particular, any dislike he may have. I have told you before that he doesn't like the English," Agatha remarked.

"Bless me! no more do I! But my best friends have been among them."

"I don't say I agree with my brother, and I don't say I disagree with him," Sir Rufus's companion went on. "I have told you before that we are of Irish descent, on my mother's side. Her mother was a Macarthy. We have kept up the name, and we have kept up the feeling."

"I see—so that even if the Yankee were to let me off, the Paddy would come down! That's a most unholy combination. But you remember, I hope, what I have also told you—that I am quite as Irish as you can ever be. I had an Irish grandmother—a beauty of beauties, a certain Lady Laura Fitzgibbon, *qui vaut bien la vôtre*. A charming old woman she was."

"Oh, well, she wasn't of our kind," the girl exclaimed, laughing.

"You mean that yours wasn't charming? In the presence of her granddaughter permit me to doubt it."

"Well, I suppose that those hostilities of race—transmitted and hereditary, as it were—are the greatest of all." Agatha Grice uttered this sage reflection by no means in the tone of successful controversy, and with the faintest possible tremor in her voice.

"Good God! do you mean to say that a hostility of race, a legendary feud, is to prevent you and me from meeting again?" The Englishman stopped short as he made this inquiry, but Agatha continued to walk, as if that might help her to elude it. She had come out with a perfectly sincere determination to prevent Sir Rufus from saying what she believed he wanted to say, and if her voice had trembled just now, it was because it began to come over her that her preventive measures would fail. The only tolerably efficacious one would be to turn straight round and go home. But there would be a rudeness in this course, and even a want of dignity; and besides, she didn't wish to go home. She compromised by not answering her companion's question, and though she couldn't see him, she was aware that he was looking after her with an expression in his face of high impatience momentarily baffled. She knew that expression, and thought it handsome; she knew all his expressions, and thought them all handsome. He overtook her in a few moments, and then she was surprised that he should be laughing, as he exclaimed, "It's too absurd!—it's too absurd!" It was not long, however, before she understood the nature of his laughter, as she understood everything else. If she was nervous, he was scarcely less so; his whole manner now expressed the temper of a man wishing to ascertain rapidly whether he may enjoy or must miss great happiness. Before she knew it he had spoken the words which she had flattered herself he should not speak; he had said that since there appeared to be a doubt whether they should soon meet again, it was important he should seize the present occasion. He was very glad, after all, because for several days he had been wanting to speak. He loved her as he had never loved any woman, and he be-

sought her earnestly to believe it. What was this crude stuff about disliking the English and disliking the Americans? what had questions of nationality to do with it any more than questions of ornithology? It was a question simply of being his wife, and that was rather between themselves, wasn't it? He besought her to consider it, as *he* had been turning it over from almost the first hour he met her. It was not in Agatha's power to go her way now, because he had laid his hand upon her in a manner that kept her motionless, and while he talked to her in low, kind tones, touching her face with the breath of supplication, she stood there in the warm darkness, very pale, looking as if she were listening to a threat of injury rather than to a declaration of love. "Of course I ought to speak to your mother," he said; "I ought to have spoken to her first. But your leaving at an hour's notice, and apparently wishing to shake me off, has given me no time. For God's sake, give me your permission, and I will do it to-night."

"Don't—don't speak to my mother," said Agatha, mournfully.

"Don't tell me to-morrow, then, that she won't hear of it!"

"She likes you, Sir Rufus," the girl rejoined, in the same singular, hopeless tone.

"I hope you don't mean to imply by that that you don't!"

"No; I like you, of course; otherwise I should never have allowed myself to be in this position, because I hate it." The girl uttered these last words with a sudden burst of emotion, and an equally sudden failure of sequence, and turning round quickly, began to walk in the direction from which they had come. Her companion, however, was again beside her, close to her, and he found means to prevent her from going as fast as she wished. History has lost the record of what at that moment he said to her; it was something that made her exclaim, in a tone which seemed on the point of breaking into tears: "Please don't say that, or anything like it, again, Sir Rufus, or I shall have to take leave of you forever, this instant, on the spot." He strove to be obedient, and they walked on a little in silence; after which she resumed, with a slightly different manner: "I am very sorry you have said this to-night. You have troubled and distressed me; it isn't a good time."

"1 wonder if you would favor me with your idea of what might be a good time?"

"I don't know. Perhaps never. I am greatly obliged to you for the honor you have done me. I beg you to believe me when I say this. But I don't think I shall ever marry. I have other duties. I can't do what I like with my life."

At this Sir Rufus made her stop again, to tell him what she meant by such an extraordinary speech. What overwhelming duties had she, pray, and what restrictions upon her life that made her so different from other women? He couldn't, for his part, imagine a woman more free. She explained that she had her mother, who was terribly delicate, and who must be her first thought and her first care. Nothing would induce her to leave her mother. She was all her mother had except Macarthy, who was absorbed in his profession.

"What possible question need there be of your leaving her?" the Englishman demanded. "What could be more delightful than that she should live with us, and that we should take care of her together? You say she is so good as to like me, and I assure you I like her—most uncommonly."

"It would be impossible that we should take her away from my brother," said the girl, after a hesitation.

"Take her away?" And Sir Rufus Chasemore stood staring. "Well, if he won't look after her himself—you say he is so taken up with his work—he has no earthly right to prevent other people from doing so."

"It's not a man's business—it's mine—it's her daughter's."

"That's exactly what I think, and what in the world do I wish but to help you? If she requires a mild climate, we will find some lovely place in the south of England, and be as happy there as the day is long."

"So that Macarthy would have to come *there* to see his mother? Fancy Macarthy in the south of England—especially as happy as the day is long! He would find the day very long," Agatha Grice continued, with the strange little laugh which expressed—or rather which disguised—the mixture of her feelings. "He would never consent."

"Never consent to what? Is what you mean to say that he would never consent to your marriage? I certainly never

dreamed that you would have to ask him. Haven't you defended to me again and again the freedom, the independence, with which American girls marry? Where is the independence when it comes to your own case?" Sir Rufus Chasemore paused a moment, and then he went on, with bitterness: "Why don't you say outright that you are afraid of your brother? Miss Grice, I never dreamed that that would be your answer to an offer of everything that a man—and a man of some distinction, I may say, for it would be affectation in me to pretend that I consider myself a nonentity—can lay at the feet of a woman."

The girl did not reply immediately; she appeared to think over intently what he had said to her, and while she did so she turned her white face and her charming serious eyes upon him. When at last she spoke it was in a very gentle, considerate tone. "You are wrong in supposing that I am afraid of my brother. How can I be afraid of a person of whom I am so exceedingly fond?"

"Oh, the two things are quite consistent," said Sir Rufus Chasemore, impatiently. "And is it impossible that I should ever inspire you with a sentiment which you would consent to place in the balance with this intense fraternal affection?" He had no sooner spoken those somewhat sarcastic words than he broke out, in a different tone, "Oh, Agatha, for pity's sake, don't make difficulties where there are no difficulties!"

"I don't make them; I assure you they exist. It is difficult to explain them, but I can see them, I can feel them. Therefore we mustn't talk this way any more. Please, please don't," the girl pursued, imploringly. "Nothing is possible to-day. Some day or other very likely there will be changes. Then we shall meet; then we shall talk again."

"I like the way you ask me to wait ten years. What do you mean by 'changes'? Before Heaven, I shall never change," Sir Rufus declared.

Agatha Grice hesitated. "Well, perhaps you will like us better."

"Us? Whom do you mean by 'us'? Are you coming back to that beastly question of one's feelings—real or supposed it doesn't matter—about your great and glorious country? Good God, it's too monstrous! One tells a girl one adores her, and she replies that she doesn't care so long as one doesn't adore her compatriots. What do you want me to do to them? What do you want me to say? I will say anything in the English language, or in the American, that you like. I'll say that they're the greatest of the great, and have every charm and virtue under heaven. I'll go down on my stomach before them, and remain there forever. I can't do more than that."

Whether this extravagant profession had the effect of making Agatha Grice ashamed of having struck that note in regard to her companion's international attitude, or whether her nerves were simply upset by his vehemence, his insistence, is more than I can say: what is certain is that her rejoinder to this last speech was a sudden burst of tears. They fell for a moment rapidly, soundlessly, but she was quicker still in brushing them away. "You may laugh at me, or you may despise me," she said, when she could speak, "and I dare say my state of mind is deplorably narrow, but I couldn't be happy with you if you hated my country."

"You would hate mine back, and we should pass the liveliest, jolliest days!" returned the Englishman, gratified, softened, enchanted, by her tears. "My dear girl, what is a woman's country? It's her house and her garden, her children, and her social world. You exaggerate immensely the difference which that part of the business makes. I assure you that if you were to marry me, it would be the last thing you would find yourself thinking of. However, to prove how little I hate your country, I am perfectly willing to go there and live with you."

"Oh, Sir Rufus Chasemore!" murmured Agatha Grice, protestingly.

"You don't believe me?"

She didn't believe him, and yet to hear him make such an offer was sweet to her, for it gave her a sense of the reality of his passion. "I shouldn't ask that — I shouldn't even like it," she said; and then he wished to know what she would like. "I should like you to let me go—not to press me, not to distress me any more now. I shall think of everything—of course you know that. But it will take me a long time. That's all I can tell you now, but I think you ought to be content." He was obliged to say that he was content, and they resumed their walk, in the direction of the hotel. Shortly before

they reached it Agatha exclaimed, with a certain irrelevance, "You ought to go there first; then you would know."

"Then I should know what?"

"Whether you would like it."

"Like your great country? Good Lord! what difference does it make whether I like it or not?"

"No—that's just it—you don't care," said Agatha; "yet you said to my brother that you wanted immensely to go."

"So I do; I am ashamed not to have been; that's an immense drawback to-day in England to a man in public life. Something has always stopped me off, tiresomely, from year to year. Of course I shall go the very first moment I can take the time."

"It's a pity you didn't go this year, instead of coming down here," the girl observed, rather sententiously.

"I thank my stars I didn't!" he responded, in a very different tone.

"Well, I should try to make you like it," she went on. "I think it very probable I should succeed."

"I think it very probable you could do with me exactly whatever you might attempt."

"Oh, you hypocrite!" the girl exclaimed; and it was on this that she separated from him and went into the house. It soothed him to see her do so, instead of rejoining her mother and brother, whom he distinguished at a distance sitting on the terrace. She had perceived them there as well, but she would go straight to her room; she preferred the company of her thoughts. It suited Sir Rufus Chasemore to believe that those thoughts would plead for him and eventually win his suit. He gave a melancholy, lover-like sigh, however, as he walked toward Mrs. Grice and her son. He couldn't keep away from them, though he was so interested in being and appearing discreet. The girl had told him that her mother liked him, and he desired both to stimulate and to reward that inclination. Whatever he desired he desired with extreme definiteness and energy. He would go and sit down beside the little old lady (with whom hitherto he had no very direct conversation), and talk to her and be kind to her and amuse her. It must be added that he rather despaired of the success of these arts as he saw Macarthy Grice, on becoming aware of his approach, get up and walk away.

IV.

"It sometimes seems to me as if he didn't marry on purpose to make me feel badly." That was the only fashion, as yet, in which Lady Chasemore had given away her brother to her husband. The words fell from her lips some five years after Macarthy's visit to the lake of Como —two years after her mother's death—a twelvemonth after her marriage. The same idea came into her mind—a trifle whimsically, perhaps, only this time she didn't express it—as she stood by her husband's side on the deck of the steamer, half an hour before they reached the wharf at New York. Six years had elapsed between the scenes at Cadenabbia and their disembarkation in that city. Agatha knew that Macarthy would be on the wharf to meet them, and that he should be there alone was natural enough. But she had a prevision of their return with him—she also knew he expected that —to the house, so narrow, but fortunately rather deep, in Thirty-seventh Street, in which such a happy trio had lived in the old days, before this unexpressed but none the less perceptible estrangement. As her marriage had taken place in Europe (Sir Rufus coming to her at Bologna, in the very midst of the Parliamentary session, the moment he heard, by his sister, of her mother's death: this was really the sign of devotion that had won her)— as the ceremony of her nuptials, I say (it was a very quiet one), had been performed in Paris, so that her absence from her native land had had no intermission, she had not seen the house since she left it with her mother for that remedial pilgrimage in the course of which poor Mrs. Grice, travelling up from Rome in the spring, after her third winter there (two had been so far from sufficing), was to succumb, from one day to the other, to inflammation of the lungs. She saw it over again now, even before she left the ship, and felt in advance all that it would imply to find Macarthy living there as a bachelor, struggling with New York servants, unaided and unrelieved by the sister whose natural place might by many people have been thought to be the care of his establishment, as her natural reward would have been the honors of such a position. Lady Chasemore was prepared to feel pang upon pang when she should perceive how much less comfortably he lived than he would have lived if she had not quitted him. She

knew that their second cousins in Boston, whose sense of duty was so terrible (even her poor mother, who never had a thought for herself, used to try as much as possible to conceal her life from them), considered that she had, in a manner almost immoral, deserted him for the sake of an English title. When they went ashore and drove home with Macarthy, Agatha received exactly the impression she had expected: her brother's life struck her as bare, ungarnished, helpless, socially and domestically speaking. He didn't know how to keep house, naturally, and in New York, unless one had a larger fortune than his, it was very difficult to do that sort of thing by deputy. But Lady Chasemore made to her husband no further allusion to the idea that he remained single out of perversity. The situation was too serious for that or for any other flippant speech.

It was a delicate matter for the brothers-in-law to spend two or three weeks together, not, however, because, when the moment for her own real decision came, Macarthy had protested in vivid words against her marriage. By the time he arrived from America, after his mother's death, the Englishman was in possession of the field, and it was too late to save her. He had had the opportunity to show her kindness, for which her situation made her extremely grateful—he had, indeed, rendered her services which Macarthy himself, though he knew they were the result of an interested purpose, could not but appreciate. When her brother met her in Paris he saw that she was already lost to him, she had ceased to struggle, she had accepted the fate of a Briton's bride. It appeared that she was much in love with her Briton, and that was the end of it. Macarthy offered no opposition, and she would have liked it better if he had, as it would have given her a chance to put him in the wrong a little more than, formally at least, she had been able to do. He knew that she knew what he thought and how he felt, and there was no need of saying any more about it. No doubt he would not have accepted a sacrifice from her, even if she had been capable of making it (there were moments when it seemed to her that even at the last, if he had appealed to her directly and with tenderness, she would have renounced); but it was none the less clear to her that he was deeply disappointed at her having found it in her heart to separate herself so utterly. And there was something in his whole attitude which seemed to say that it was not only from him that she separated herself, but from all her fellow-countrymen besides, and from everything that was best and finest in American life. He regarded her marriage as an abjuration, an apostasy, a kind of moral treachery. It was of no use to say to him that she was doing nothing original or extraordinary, to ask him if he didn't know that in England, at the point things had come to, American wives were as thick as blackberries, so that if she were doing wrong she was doing wrong with—well, almost the majority; for he had an answer to such cheap arguments, an answer according to which it appeared that the American girls who had done what she was about to do were notoriously poor specimens, the most frivolous and rattle-brained young persons in the country. They had no conception of the great meaning of American institutions, no appreciation of their birthright, and they were doubtless very worthy recruits to a debauched and stultified aristocracy. The pity of Agatha's desertion was that *she* had been meant for better things, she had appreciated her birthright, or, if she hadn't, it had not been the fault of a brother who had taken so much pains to form her mind and character. The sentiment of her nationality had been cultivated in her; it was not a mere brute instinct or customary prejudice, but a responsibility, a faith, a religion. She was not a poor specimen, but a remarkably fine one; she was intelligent, she was clever, she was sensitive, she could understand difficult things and feel great ones.

Of course, in those days of trouble, in Paris, when it was arranged that she should be married immediately (as if there had really been an engagement to Sir Rufus from the night before their flight from Cadenabbia), of course she had had a certain amount of talk with Macarthy about the matter, and at those moments she had almost wished to drive him to protest articulately, so that she might as explicitly reassure him, endeavor to bring him round. But he had never said to her personally what he had said to her mother at Cadenabbia — what her mother, frightened and distressed, had immediately repeated to her. The most he said was that he hoped she was conscious

of all the perfectly different and opposed things she and her husband would represent when they should find themselves face to face. He hoped she had measured in advance the strain that might arise from the fact that in so many ways her good would be his evil, her white his black, and *vice versa*—the fact, in a word, that by birth, tradition, convictions, she was the product of a democratic society, while the very breath of Sir Rufus's nostrils was the denial of human equality. She had replied, "Oh yes, I have thought of everything"; but in reality she had not thought that she was, in any very aggressive manner, a democrat, or even that she had a representative function. She had not thought that Macarthy, in his innermost soul, was a democrat either; and she had even wondered what would happen if, in regard to some of those levelling theories, he had suddenly been taken at his word. She knew, however, that nothing would have made him more angry than to hint that anything could happen which would find him unprepared, and she was ashamed to repudiate the opinions, the general character, her brother attributed to her, to fall below the high standard he had set up for her. She had, moreover, no wish to do so. She was well aware that there were many things in English life that she shouldn't like, and she was never a more passionate American than the day she married Sir Rufus Chasemore.

To what extent she remained one, an observer of the deportment of this young lady would at first have had considerable difficulty in judging. The question of the respective merits of the institutions of the two countries came up very little in her life. Her husband had other things to think of than the great republic beyond the sea, and her horizon, social and political, became for the time exclusively English. Sir Rufus was immersed in politics and in administrative questions; but these things belonged wholly to the domestic field; they were embodied in big blue-books with terrible dry titles (Agatha had tried conscientiously to acquaint herself with the contents of some of them), which piled themselves up on the table of his library. The Conservatives had come into power just after his marriage, and he had held honorable, though not supereminent, office. His duties had nothing to do with foreign relations; they were altogether of an economical and statistical kind. He performed them in a manner which showed, perhaps, that he was conscious of some justice in the reproach usually addressed to the Tories—the taunt that they always came to grief in the department of industry and finance. His wife was sufficiently in his confidence to know how much he had it at heart to prove that a Conservative administration could be strong on that side. He never spoke to her of her own country—they had so many other things to talk about—but if there was nothing in his behavior to betray the assumption that she had given it up, so, on the other hand, there was nothing to show that he doubted of her having done so. What he had said about a woman's country being her husband and children, her house and garden and visiting list, was very considerably verified; for it was certain that her ladyship's new career gave her, though she had no children, plenty of occupation. Even if it had not, however, she would have found a good deal of work to her hand in loving her husband, which she continued to do with the most commendable zeal. He seemed to her a very magnificent person, and he didn't bully her half so much as she expected. There were times when it even occurred to her that he really didn't bully her enough, for she had always had an idea that it would be agreeable to be subjected to this probation by some one she should be very fond of.

After they had been married a year he became a permanent official, in succession to a gentleman who was made a peer on his retirement from the post to which Sir Rufus was appointed. This gave Lady Chasemore an opportunity to reflect that she might some day be a peeress, it being reasonable to suppose that the same reward would be meted out to her husband on the day on which, in the fulness of time and of credit, he also should retire. She was obliged to admit to herself that the reflection was unattended with any sense of horror; it exhilarated her indeed to the point of making her smile at the contingency of Macarthy's finding himself the brother of a member of the aristocracy. As a permanent official, her husband was supposed to have no active political opinions; but she could not flatter herself that she perceived any diminution of his Conservative zeal. Even if

she had, it would have made little difference, for it had not taken her long to discover that she had married into a tremendous Tory "set"—a set in which people took for granted she had feelings that she was not prepared to publish on the house-tops. It was scarcely worth while, however, to explain at length that she had not been brought up in that way, partly because the people wouldn't have understood, and partly because really, after all, they didn't care. Of how little it was possible, in general, to care, her career in England helped her gradually to discover. The people who cared least appeared to be those who were most convinced that everything in the national life was going to the dogs. Lady Chasemore was not struck with this tendency herself; but if she had been, the belief would have worried her more than it seemed to worry her friends. She liked most of them extremely, and thought them very kind, very easy to live with; but she liked London much better than the country, rejoiced much when her husband's new post added to the number of months he would have annually to spend there (they ended by being there as much as any one), and had grave doubts as to whether she would have been able to " stand" it if her lot had been cast among those members of her new circle who lived mainly on their acres. All the same, though what she had to bear she bore very easily, she indulged in a good deal of private meditation on some of the things that displeased and distressed her. She didn't always mention them to her husband, but she always intended to. She desired he should not think that she swallowed his country whole, that she was stupidly undiscriminating. Of course he knew that she was not stupid, and of course, also, he knew that she could not fail to be painfully impressed by the misery and brutality of the British populace. She had never, anywhere else, seen anything like that. Of course, furthermore, she knew that Sir Rufus had given, and would give in the future, a great deal of thought to legislative measures directed to elevating gradually the condition of the lower orders. It came over Lady Chasemore at times that it would be well if some of these measures might arrive at maturity with as little delay as possible.

The night before she quitted England with her husband they slept at a hotel at Liverpool, in order to embark early on the morrow. Sir Rufus went out to attend to some business, and the evening being very close, she sat at the window of their sitting-room, looking out on a kind of square which stretched in front of the hotel. The night was muggy, the window was open, and she was held there by a horrible fascination. Dusky forms of vice and wretchedness moved about in the stuffy darkness, visions of grimy, half-naked, whining beggary hovered before her, curses and the sound of blows came to her ears; there were young girls, frowzy and violent, who evidently were drunk, as every one seemed to be, more or less, which was little wonder, as four public-houses flared into the impure night, visible from where Lady Chasemore sat, and they appeared to be gorged with customers, half of whom were women. The impression came back to her that the horrible place had made upon her and upon her mother when they landed in England years before, and as she turned from the window she liked to think that she was going to a country where, at any rate, there would be less of that sort of thing. When her husband came in he said it was of course a beastly place, but much better than it used to be—which she was glad to hear. She made some allusion to the confidence they might have that they should be treated to no such scenes as that in her country; whereupon he remonstrated, jocosely expressing a hope that they should not be deprived of a glimpse of the celebrated American drinks and bar-room fights.

It must be added that in New York he made of his brother-in-law no inquiry about these phenomena—a reserve, a magnanimity even, keenly appreciated by his wife. She appreciated altogether the manner in which he conducted himself during their visit to the United States, and felt that if she had not already known that she had married a perfect gentleman, the fact would now have been revealed to her. For she had to make up her mind to this, that after all (it was vain to shut one's eyes to it) Sir Rufus personally didn't like the United States: he didn't like them, yet he made an immense effort to behave as if he did. She was grateful to him for that; it assuaged her nervousness (she was afraid there might be "scenes" if he should break out with some of his displeasures)—so grateful that

she almost forgot to be disappointed at the failure of her own original intent, to be distressed at seeing, or rather at guessing (for he was reserved about it even to her), that a nearer view of American institutions had not had the effect which she once promised herself a nearer view should have. She had married him partly to bring him over to an admiration of her country (she had never told any one this, for she was too proud to make the confidence to an English person, and if she had made it to an American, the answer would have been so prompt, "What on earth does it signify what he thinks of it?" no one, of course, being obliged to understand that it might signify to her); she had united herself to Sir Rufus in this missionary spirit, and now not only did her proselyte prove unamenable, but the vanity of her enterprise became a fact of secondary importance. She wondered a little that she didn't suffer more from it, and this is partly why she rejoiced that her husband kept most of his observations to himself: it gave her a pretext for not being ashamed. She had flattered herself before that in general he had the manners of a diplomatist (she did not suspect that this was not the opinion of all his contemporaries), and his behavior during the first few weeks at least of their stay in the Western world struck her as a triumph of diplomacy. She had really passed from caring whether he disliked American manners to caring primarily whether he showed he disliked them—a transition which, on her own side, she was very sensible it was important to conceal from Macarthy. To love a man who could feel no tenderness for the order of things which had encompassed her early years, and had been intimately mixed with her growth, which was a part of the conscience, the piety, of many who had been most dear to her, and whose memory would be dear to her always—that was an irregularity which was, after all, shut up in her own breast, where she could trust her dignity to get, some way or other, the upper hand of it. But to be pointed at as having such a problem as that on one's back was quite another affair: it was a kind of exposure of one's sanctities, a surrender of private judgment. Lady Chasemore had by this time known her husband long enough to enter into the logic of his preferences; if he disliked or disapproved of what he saw in America, his reasons for doing so had ceased to be a mystery. They were the very elements of his character, the joints and vertebration of his general creed. All the while she was absent from England with him (it was not very long, their whole tour, including the two voyages, being included in ten weeks) she knew more or less the impression that things would have made upon him; she knew that both in the generals and in the particulars American life would have gone against his grain, contradicted his traditions, violated his taste.

V.

All the same, he was determined to see it thoroughly, and this is doubtless one of the reasons why, after the first few days, she cherished the hope that they should be able to get off at the end without any collision with Macarthy. Of course it was to be taken into account that Macarthy's own behavior was much more that of a man of the world than she had ventured to hope. He appeared for the time almost to have smothered his national consciousness, which had always been so acute, and to have accepted his sister's perfidious alliance. She could see that he was delighted that she should be near him again—so delighted that he neglected to look for the signs of corruption in her, or to manifest any suspicion that in fact, now that she was immersed in them again, she regarded her old associations with changed eyes. So, also, if she had not already been aware of how much Macarthy was a gentleman, she would have seen it from the way he rose to the occasion. Accordingly they were all superior people, and all was for the best, in Lady Chasemore's simple creed. Her brother asked her no questions whatever about her life in England, but his letters had already enlightened her as to his determination to avoid that topic. They had hitherto not contained a single inquiry on the subject of her occupations and pursuits, and if she had been domiciled in the moon he could not have indulged in less reference to public or private events in the British Islands. It was a tacit form of disapprobation of her being connected with that impertinent corner of the globe; but it had never prevented her from giving him the fullest information on everything he didn't ask about. He never took up her allusions, and when she poured forth infor-

mation to him now, in regard to matters concerning her in her new home (on these points she was wilfully copious and appealing), he listened with a sort of exaggerated dumb deference, as if she were reciting a lesson, and he must sit quiet till she should come to the end. Usually, when she stopped, he simply sighed, then directed the conversation to something as different as possible. It evidently pleased him, however, to see that she enjoyed her native air and her temporary reunion with some of her old familiars. This was a graceful inconsistency on his part: it showed that he had not completely given her up. Perhaps he thought Sir Rufus would die, and that in this case she would come back and live in New York. She was careful not to tell him that such a calculation was baseless, that with or without Sir Rufus she should never be able to settle in her native city as Lady Chasemore. He was scrupulously polite to Sir Rufus, and this personage asked Agatha why he never by any chance addressed him save by his title. She could see what her husband meant, but even in the privacy of the conjugal chamber she was loyal enough to Macarthy not to reply, "Oh, it's a mercy he doesn't say simply 'Sir.'"

The English visitor was immensely active; he desired to leave nothing unexplored, unattempted; his purpose was to inspect institutions, to collect statistics, to talk with the principal people, to see the workings of the political machine, and Macarthy acquitted himself scrupulously, even zealously, in the way of giving him introductions and facilities. Lady Chasemore reflected with pleasure that it was in her brother's power to do the honors of his native land very completely. She suspected, indeed, that as he didn't like her husband (he *couldn't* like him, in spite of Sir Rufus's now demeaning himself so sweetly), it was a relief to him to pass him on to others—to work him off, as it were, into penitentiaries and chambers of commerce. Sir Rufus's frequent expeditions to these establishments, and long interviews with local worthies of every kind, kept him constantly out of the house, and removed him from contact with his host, so that as Macarthy was extremely busy with his own profession (Sir Rufus was greatly struck with the way he worked; he had never seen a gentleman work so hard, without any shooting or hunting or fishing), it may be said, though it sounds odd, that the two men met very little directly—met scarcely more than in the evening, or, in other words, always in company. During the twenty days the Chasemores spent together in New York they either dined out or were members of a party given at home by Macarthy, and on these occasions Sir Rufus found plenty to talk about with his new acquaintance. His wife flattered herself he was liked, he was so hilarious and so easy. He had a most appreciative manner, but she really wished sometimes that he might have subdued his hilarity a little; there were moments when perhaps it looked as if he took everything in the United States as if it were more than all else amusing. She knew exactly how it must privately affect Macarthy, this implication that it was merely a comical country; but, after all, it was not very easy to say how Macarthy would have preferred that a stranger, or that Sir Rufus in particular, should take the great republic. A cheerful view, yet untinged by the sense of drollery—that would have been the right thing if it could have been arrived at. At all events (and this was something gained), if Sir Rufus was in his heart a pessimist in regard to things he didn't like, he was not superficially sardonic. And then he asked questions by the million; and what was curiosity but a homage?

It will be inferred, and most correctly, that Macarthy Grice was not personally in any degree, for his brother-in-law, the showman of the exhibition. He caused him to be conducted, but he didn't conduct him. He listened to his reports of what he had seen (it was at breakfast mainly that these fresh intimations dropped from Sir Rufus's lips), with very much the same cold patience (as if he were civilly forcing his attention) with which he listened to Agatha's persistent anecdotes of things that had happened to her in England. Of course, with Sir Rufus, there could be no question of persistence; he didn't care whether Macarthy cared or not, and he didn't stick to this everlasting subject of American institutions either to entertain him or to entertain himself—all he wanted was to lead on to further researches and discoveries. Macarthy always met him with the same response: "Oh, So-and-So is the man to tell you all about that. If you wish, I will give you a letter to him." Sir Rufus always wished, and certainly Macarthy wrote, a prodigious number of letters. The inquiries and conclusions of his visitor (so far as Sir Rufus indulged in the latter) all bore special points; he was careful to commit himself to no crude generalizations. He had to remember that he had still the rest of the country to see, and after a little discussion (which was confined to Lady Chasemore and her husband) it was decided that he should see it without his wife, who would await his return among her friends in New York. This arrangement was much to her taste, but it gives again the measure of the degree to which she had renounced her early dream of interpreting the Western world to Sir Rufus. If she was not to be at his side at the moment, on the spot, of course she couldn't interpret—he would get a tremendous start of her. In short, by staying quietly with Macarthy during his absence she almost gave up the great advantage she had hitherto had of knowing more about America than her husband could. She liked, however, to feel that she was making a sacrifice—making one, indeed, both to Sir Rufus and to her brother. The idea of giving up something for Macarthy (she only wished it had been something more) did her great good—sweetened the period of her husband's absence.

The whole season had been splendid, but at this moment the golden days of the Indian summer descended upon the shining city, and steeped it in a kind of fragrant haze. For two or three weeks New York seemed to Lady Chasemore poetical; the marble buildings looked yellow in the sleeping sunshine, and her native land exhibited, for the occasion, an atmosphere; vague memories came back to her of her younger years, of things that had to do, somehow, with the blurred brightness of the late autumn in the country. She walked about, she walked irresponsibly for hours; she didn't care, as she had to care in London. She met friends in the streets and turned and walked with them; and pleasures as simple as this acquired an exaggerated charm for her. She liked walking, and as an American girl had indulged the taste freely; but in London she had no time but to drive—besides which, there were other tiresome considerations. Macarthy came home from his office earlier, and she went to meet him in

Washington Square, and walked up the Fifth Avenue with him in the rich afternoon. It was many years since she had been in New York, and she found herself taking a kind of personal interest in changes and improvements. There were houses she used to know, where friends had lived in the old days, and where they lived no more (no one in New York seemed to her to live where they used to live), which reminded her of incidents she had long ago forgotten, which it pleased and touched her now to recall. Macarthy became very easy and sociable; he even asked her a few questions about her arrangements and habits in England, and struck her (though she had never been particularly aware of it before) as having had an immense deal of American humor. On one occasion he staid away from work altogether and took her up the Hudson, on the steamer, to West Point—an excursion in which she found a peculiar charm. Every day she lunched intimately with a dozen ladies at the house of one or other of them.

In due time Sir Rufus returned from Canada, the Mississippi, the Rocky Mountains, and California; he had achieved marvels in the way of traversing distances and seeing manners and men with rapidity and facility. Everything had been settled in regard to their sailing for England almost directly after his return; there were only to be two more days in New York, then a rush to Boston, followed by another rush to Philadelphia and Washington. Macarthy made no inquiry whatever of his brother-in-law touching his impression of the great West; he didn't even ask him if he had been favorably impressed with Canada. There would not have been much opportunity, however, for Sir Rufus, on his side, was extremely occupied with the last things he had to do. He had not even time, as yet, to impart his impressions to his wife, and she forbore to interrogate him, feeling that the voyage close at hand would afford abundant leisure for the history of his adventures. For the moment almost the only light that he threw upon them was by saying to Agatha (not before Macarthy) that it was a pleasure to him to see a handsome woman again, as he had not had that satisfaction in the course of his travels. Lady Chasemore wondered, exclaimed, protested, and elicited the declaration that, to his sense, and in the in-

terior at least, the beauty of the women was, like a great many other things, a gigantic American fraud. Sir Rufus had looked for it in vain—he went so far as to say that he had, in the course of extensive wanderings about the world, seen no female type on the whole less to his taste than that of the ladies in whose society, in hundreds (there was no paucity of specimens), in the long, hot, heaving trains, he had traversed a large part of the American continent. His wife inquired whether by chance he preferred the young persons they had (or at least she had) observed at Liverpool the night before their departure; to which he replied that they were no doubt sad creatures, but that the looks of the woman mattered only so long as one lived with her, and he didn't live, and never should live, with the daughters of that grimy seaport. With the women in the American cars he had been living—oh, tremendously! and they were deucedly plain. Thereupon Lady Chasemore wished to know whether he didn't think Mrs. Eugene had beauty, and Mrs. Ripley, and her sister Mrs. Redwood, and Mrs. Long, and several other ornaments of the society in which they had mingled during their stay in New York. "Mrs. Eugene is Mrs. Eugene, and Mrs. Redwood is Mrs. Redwood," Sir Rufus retorted; "but the women in the cars weren't either, and all the women I saw were like the women in the cars." "Well, there may be something in the cars," said Lady Chasemore, pensively; and she mentioned that it was very odd that during her husband's absence, as she roamed about New York, she should have made precisely the opposite reflection, and been struck with the number of pretty faces. "Oh, pretty faces, pretty faces, I dare say!" But Sir Rufus had no time to develop this vague rejoinder.

When they came back from Washington to sail, Agatha told her brother that he was going to write a book about America; it was for this he had made so many inquiries and taken so many notes. She hadn't known it before; it was only while they were in Washington that he told her he had made up his mind to it. Something he saw or heard in Washington appeared to have brought this resolution to a point. Lady Chasemore privately thought it rather a formidable fact: her husband had startled her a good deal in

announcing his intention. She had said,
"Of course it will be friendly—you'll say
nice things?" And he had replied, "My
poor child, they will abuse me like a
pickpocket." This had scarcely been reassuring, and she had had it at heart to
probe the question further, in the train,
after they left Washington. But as it
happened, in the train, all the way, Sir
Rufus was engaged in conversation with
a Democratic Representative, whom he
had picked up she didn't know how—very
certain he hadn't met him at any respectable house in Washington. They sat in
front of her in the car, with their heads
almost touching, and although she was a
better American than her husband, she
shouldn't have liked hers to be so close
to that of the Democratic Representative.
Now of course she knew that Sir Rufus
was taking in material for his book. This
idea made her uncomfortable, and she
would have liked immensely to separate
him from his companion—she scarcely
knew why, after all, except that she
couldn't believe the Representative represented anything very nice. She promised
herself to ascertain thoroughly, after they
should be comfortably settled in the ship,
the animus with which the book was to be
written. She was a very good sailor, and
she liked to talk at sea; there her husband
would not be able to escape from her, and
she foresaw the manner in which she
should catechise him. It exercised her
greatly in advance, and she was more agitated than she could easily have expressed by the whole question of the book.
Meanwhile, however, she was careful not
to show her agitation to Macarthy. She
referred to her husband's project as casually as possible, and the reason she referred
to it was that this seemed more loyal—
more loyal to Macarthy. If the book,
when written, should attract attention by
the severity of its criticism (and that by
many qualities it would attract attention
of the widest character Lady Chasemore
could not doubt), she should feel more
easy not to have had the air of concealing
from her brother that such a work was in
preparation, which would also be the air
of having a bad conscience about it. It
was to prove (both to herself and Macarthy) that she had a good conscience that
she told him of Sir Rufus's design. The
habit of detachment from matters connected with his brother-in-law's activity
was strong in him, nevertheless he was

not able to repress some sign of emotion
—he flushed very perceptibly. Quickly,
however, he recovered his appearance of
considering that the circumstance was one
in which he could not hope to interest
himself much; though the next moment
he observed, with a certain inconsequence,
"I am rather sorry to hear it."

"Why are you sorry?" asked Agatha.
She was surprised, and indeed gratified,
that he should commit himself even so
far as to express regret. What she had
supposed he would say, if he should say
anything, was that he was obliged to her
for the information, but that if it was
given him with any expectation that he
might be induced to read the book, he
must really let her know that such an expectation was positively vain. Sir Rufus's printed ideas could have no more
value for him than his spoken ones.

"Well, it will be rather disagreeable
for you," he said, in answer to her question. "Unless, indeed, you don't care
what he says."

"But I do care. The book will be sure
to be very able. Do you mean if it should
be severe—that would be disagreeable for
me? Very certainly it would; it would
put me in a false, in a ridiculous, position,
and I don't see how I should bear it,"
Lady Chasemore went on, feeling that her
candor was generous, and wishing it to
be. "But I sha'n't allow it to be severe.
To prevent that, if it's necessary, I will
write every word of it myself."

She laughed as she made this declaration, but there was nothing in Macarthy's
face to show that he could lend himself to
a mirthful treatment of the question. "I
think an Englishman had better look at
home," he said, "and if he does so I don't
easily see how the occupation should leave
him any leisure or any assurance for
reading lectures to other nations. The
self-complacency of your husband's countrymen is colossal and imperturbable.
Still, with the tight place they find themselves in to-day, and with the judgment
of the rest of the world upon them being
what it is, it's grotesque to see them still
sitting in their old judgment-seat, and
pronouncing upon the shortcomings of
people who are full of the life that has
so long since left them." Macarthy Grice
spoke slowly, mildly, with a certain dry-
ness, as if he were delivering himself once
for all, and would not return to the subject. The quietness of his manner made

the words solemn for his sister, and she
stared at him a moment, wondering, as if
they pointed to strange things, which she
had hitherto but imperfectly apprehended.

"The judgment of the rest of the world
—what is that?"

"Why, that they are simply finished;
that they don't count."

"Oh, a nation must count which pro-
duces such men as my husband," Agatha
rejoined, with another laugh. Macarthy
was on the point of retorting that it counted as the laughing-stock of the world (that,
of course, was something), but he checked himself, and she, moreover, checked
him by going on: "Why, Macarthy, you
ought to come out with a book yourself
about the English. You would steal my
husband's thunder."

"Nothing would induce me to do anything of the sort: I pity them too much."

"You pity them!" Lady Chasemore
exclaimed. "It would amuse my husband to hear that."

"Very likely, and it would be exactly
a proof of what is so pitiable—the contrast
between their gross pretensions and the
real facts of their condition. They have
pressing upon them at once every problem, every source of weakness, every danger, that can threaten the life of a people,
and they have nothing to meet the situation with but their classic stupidity."

"Well, that has been useful to them
before," said Lady Chasemore, smiling.
Her smile was a little forced, and she colored, as her brother had done when she
first spoke to him. She found it impossible not to be impressed by what he said,
and yet she was vexed that she was, because she didn't wish to be.

He looked at her as if he saw some
warning in her face, and continued:
"Excuse my going so far. In this last
month that we have spent together, so
happily for me, I had almost forgotten
that you are one of them."

Lady Chasemore said nothing, and she
didn't deny that she was one of them. If
her husband's country was denounced—
after all, he hadn't written his book yet—
she felt as if this would be a repudiation of
one of the responsibilities she had taken in
marrying him.

VI.

The postman was at the door in Grosvenor Crescent when she came back from
her drive; the servant took the letters
from his hand as she passed into the
house. In the hall she stopped to see
which of the letters were for her; the butler gave her two, and retained those that
were for Sir Rufus. She asked him what
orders Sir Rufus had given about his letters, and he replied that they were to be
forwarded up to the following night.
This applied only to letters, not to parcels,
pamphlets, and books. "But would he
wish this to go, my lady?" the man asked,
holding up a small packet; he added that
it appeared to be a kind of document.
She took it from him; her eye had caught
a name printed on the wrapper, and
though she made no great profession of
literature she recognized the name as that
of a distinguished publisher, and the packet as a roll of proof-sheets. She turned
it up and down while the servant waited;
it had quite a different look from the
bundles of printed official papers which
the postman was perpetually leaving, and
which, when she scanned the array on the
hall table in her own interest, she recognized even at a distance. They were certainly the sheets, at least the first, of her
husband's book—those of which he had
said to her, on the steamer, on the way
back from New York a year before, "My
dear child, when I tell you that you shall
see them—every page of them—that you
shall have complete control of them!"
Since she was to have complete control of
them, she began with telling the butler not
to forward them—to lay them on the hall
table. She went upstairs to dress—she
was dining out in her husband's absence
—and when she came down to re-enter
her carriage, she saw the packet lying
where it had been placed. So many
months had passed that she had ended by
forgetting that the book was on the stocks;
nothing had happened to remind her of
it. She had believed, indeed, that it was
not on the stocks, and even that the project would die a natural death. Sir Rufus
would have no time to carry it out—he
had returned from America to find himself more than ever immersed in official
work—and if he didn't put his hand to it
within two or three years, at the very
most, he would never do so at all, for he
would have lost the freshness of his impressions, on which the success of the
whole thing would depend. He had his
notes, of course, but none the less a delay
would be fatal to the production of the
volume (it was to be only a volume, and
not a big one), inasmuch as by the time it

should be published it would have to encounter the objection that everything changed in America in two or three years, and no one wanted to know anything about a dead past.

Such had been the reflections with which Lady Chasemore consoled herself for the results of those inquiries she had promised herself in New York to make when once she should be ensconced in a sea chair by her husband's side, and which she had in fact made, to her no small discomposure. Meanwhile, apparently, he had stolen a march upon her, he had put his hand to *The Modern Warning* (that was to be the title, as she had learned on the ship), he had worked at it in his odd hours, he had sent it to the printers, and here were the first-fruits of it. Had he had a bad conscience about it—was that the reason he had been so quiet? She didn't believe much in his bad conscience, for he had been tremendously, formidably explicit when they talked the matter over; had let her know as fully as possible what he intended to do. Then it was that he relieved himself, that in the long, unoccupied hours of their fine voyage (he was in wonderful "form" at sea) he took her into the confidence of his real impressions —made her understand how things had struck him in the United States. They had not struck him well; oh no, they had not struck him well at all! But at least he had prepared her, and therefore, since then, he had nothing to hide. It was doubtless an accident that he appeared to have kept his work away from her, for sometimes, in other cases, he had paid her intelligence the compliment (was it not for that, in part, he had married her?) of supposing that she could enter into it. It was probable that in this case he had wanted first to see for himself how his chapters would look in print. Very likely, even, he had not written the whole book, nor even half of it; he had only written the opening pages, and had them "set up": she remembered to have heard him speak of that as a very convenient system. It would be very convenient for her as well, and she should also be made interested in seeing how they looked. On the table, in their neat little packet, they seemed half to solicit her, half to warn her off.

They were still there, of course, when she came back from her dinner, and this time she took possession of them. She

carried them upstairs, and in her dressing-room, when she had been left alone, in her wrapper, she sat down with them under the lamp. The packet lay in her lap a long time, however, before she decided to detach the envelop. Her hesitation came not from her feeling in any degree that this roll of printed sheets had the sanctity of a letter, a seal that she might not discreetly break, but from an insurmountable nervousness as to what she might find within. She sat there for an hour, with her head resting on the back of her chair, and her eyes closed; but she had not fallen asleep; Lady Chasemore was very wide-awake indeed. She was living for the moment in a kind of concentration of memory, thinking over everything that had fallen from her husband's lips after he began, as I have said, to relieve himself. It turned out that the opinion he had formed of the order of society in the United States was even less favorable than she had reason to fear. There were not many things of which he had thought well, and the few exceptions related to the matters that were the most characteristic of the country, not idiosyncrasies of American life. The idiosyncrasies he had held to be one and all detestable. The whole spectacle was a colossal warning, a consummate illustration of the horrors of democracy. The only thing that had saved the misbegotten republic as yet was its margin, its geographical vastness; but that was now discounted and exhausted. For the rest, every democratic vice was in the ascendant, and could be studied there *sur le vif;* he couldn't be too thankful that he had not delayed longer to go over and study it. He had come back with a head full of lessons and a heart fired with the resolve to enforce them upon his own people, who, as Agatha knew, had begun to move in the same lamentable direction. As she listened to him she perceived the mistake she had made in not going to the West with him, for it was from that part of the country that he had drawn his most formidable anecdotes and examples. Of these he produced a terrific array; he spoke by book, he overflowed with facts and figures, and his wife felt herself submerged by the deep, bitter waters. She even felt what a pity it was that she had not dragged him away from that common little Congressman whom he had stuck to so in the train coming from Washington; yet it didn't matter—a little more or a little less—the whole affair had rubbed him so the wrong way, exasperated his taste, confounded his traditions. He proved to have disliked quite unspeakably things that she supposed he liked, to have suffered acutely on occasions when she thought he was really pleased. It would appear that there had been no occasion, except once, sitting at dinner between Mrs. Redwood and Mrs. Eugene, when he was really pleased. Even his long chat with the Pennsylvania Congressman had made him almost ill at the time. His wife could be none the less struck with the ability which had enabled him to master so much knowledge in so short a time; he had not only gobbled up facts, he had arranged them in a magnificent order, and she was proud of his being so clever, even when he made her bleed by the way he talked. He had had no intention whatever of this, and he was as much surprised as touched when she broke out into a passionate appeal to him not to publish such horrible misrepresentations. She defended her country with exaltation, and so far as was possible in the face of his own flood of statistics, of anecdotes of "lobbying," of the corruption of public life, for which she was unprepared, endeavoring to gainsay him in the particulars as well as in the generals. She maintained that he had seen everything wrong, seen it through the distortion of prejudice, of a hostile temperament, in the light—or rather in the darkness—of wishing to find weapons to worry in England the opposite party. Of course America had its faults, but on the whole it was a much finer country than any other, finer even than his clumsy, congested old England, where there was plenty to do to sweep the house clean, if he would give a little more of his time to that. Scandals for scandals she had heard more since she came to England than all the years she had lived at home. She didn't quote Macarthy to him (she had reasons for not doing so), but something of the spirit of Macarthy flamed up in her as she spoke.

Sir Rufus smiled at her vehemence; he took it in perfectly good part, though it evidently left him not a little astonished. He had forgotten that America was hers—that she had any allegiance but the allegiance of her marriage. He had made her his own, and being the intense Englishman that he was, it had never occurred to him to doubt that she now partook of his quality in the same degree as himself. He had assimilated her, as it were, completely, and he had assumed that she had also assimilated him, and his country with him—a process which would have for its consequence that the other country, the ugly, vulgar, superfluous one, would be, as he mentally phrased it to himself, "shunted." That it hadn't been was the proof of a rather morbid sensibility, which tenderness and time would still assuage. Sir Rufus was tender, he reassured his wife on the spot, in the first place by telling her that she knew nothing whatever about the United States (it was astonishing how little many of the people in the country itself knew about them), and in the second by promising her that he would not print a word to which her approval should not be expressly given. She should countersign every page before it went to press, and none should leave the house without her *visé*. She wished to know if he possibly could have forgotten—so strange would it be—that she had told him long ago at Cadenabbia how horrible it would be to her to find herself married to a man harboring evil thoughts of her father-land. He remembered this declaration perfectly, and others that had followed it, but was prepared to ask if she, on her side, recollected giving him notice that she should convert him into an admirer of transatlantic peculiarities. She had had an excellent opportunity, but she had not carried out her plan. He had been passive in her hands, she could have done what she liked with him (hadn't he offered, that night by the lake of Como, to throw up his career and go and live with her in some beastly American town? and he had really meant it—upon his honor he had!), so that if the conversion hadn't come off, whose fault was it but hers? She hadn't gone to work with any sort of earnestness. At all events, now it was too late; he had seen for himself—the impression was made. Two points were vivid beyond the others in Lady Chasemore's evocation of the scene on the ship; one was her husband's insistence on the fact that he had not the smallest animosity to the American people, but had only his own English brothers in view, wished only to protect and save them, to point a certain moral as it never had been pointed before; the other was his pledge that nothing should be made public without

"MY DEAR GIRL, DO YOU THINK ME AN AWFUL BRUTE?"

her assent. As at last she broke the envelop of the packet in her lap she wondered how much she should find to assent to. More, perhaps, than a third person, judging the case, would have expected; for after what had passed between them, Sir Rufus must have taken great pains to tone down his opinions—or at least the expression of them.

VII.

He came back to Grosvenor Place the next evening, very late, and on asking for his wife, was told that she was in her apartments. He was furthermore informed that she was to have dined out, but had given it up, countermanding the carriage at the last moment, and despatching a note instead. On Sir Rufus asking if she were ill, it was added that she had seemed rather poorly, and had not left the house since the day before. A minute later he found her in her own sitting-room, where she appeared to have been walking up and down. She stopped when he entered, and stood there, looking at him; she was in her dressing-gown, very pale, and she received him without a smile. He went up to her, kissed her, saw something strange in her eyes, and asked, with eagerness, if she had been suffering. "Yes, yes," she said, "but I have not been ill," and the next moment flung herself upon his neck and buried her face there, sobbing, yet at the same time stifling her sobs. Inarticulate words were mingled with them, and it was not till after a moment he understood that she was saying, "How could you? ah, how *could* you?" He failed to understand her allusion, and while he was still in the dark, she recovered herself and broke away from him. She went quickly to a drawer and possessed herself of some papers, which she held out to him, this time without meeting his eyes. "Please take them away—take them away forever. It's your book—the things from the printers. I saw them on the table—I guessed what they were—I opened them to see. I read them—I read them. Please take them away."

He had by this time become aware that, even though she had flung herself upon his breast, his wife was animated by a spirit of the deepest reproach, an exquisite sense of injury. When he first saw the papers he did not recognize his book: it had not been in his mind. He took them from her with an exclamation of wonder, accompanied by a laugh which was meant in kindness, and turned them over, glancing at page after page. Disconcerted as he was at the condition in which Agatha presented herself, he was still accessible to that agreeable titillation which a man feels on seeing his prose, and still more his verse, "set up." Sir Rufus had been quoted and reported by the newspapers, and had put into circulation several little pamphlets, but this was his first contribution to the regular literature of his country, and his publishers had given him a very handsome page. Its striking beauty held him a moment, then his eyes passed back to his wife, who, with her grand, cold, wounded air, was also very handsome. "My dear girl, do you think me an awful brute? have I made you ill?" he asked. He declared that he had no idea that he had gone so far as to shock her; he had left out such a lot; he had tried to keep the sting out of everything; he had made it all butter and honey. But he begged her not to get into a state; he would go over the whole thing with her if she liked—make any changes she should require. It would spoil the book, but he would rather do that than spoil her love-

ly temper. It was in a highly jocular manner that he made this allusion to her temper, and it was impressed upon her that he was not too much discomposed by her discomposure to be able to joke. She took notice of two things: the first of which was that he had a perfectly good conscience, and that no accusing eye that might have been turned upon him would have made him change color. He had no sense that he had broken faith with her, and he really thought his horrible book was very mild. He spoke the simple truth in saying that for her sake he had endeavored to qualify his strictures, and strange as it might appear, he honestly believed he had succeeded. Later, at other times, Agatha wondered what he would have written if he had felt himself free. What she observed in the second place was that though he saw she was much upset, he didn't in the least sound the depth of her distress, or, as she herself would have said, of her shame. He never would—he never would; he couldn't enter into her feelings, because he couldn't believe in them; they could only strike him as exaggerated and factitious. He had given her a country, a magnificent one, and why in the name of commonsense was she making him a scene about another? With the simplest form of the national consciousness a woman had more than the tenor of the feminine existence and the scope of her responsibilities demanded: what, therefore, was this morbid fancy of his wife's to give it in her own case an indefinite extension?

When he accused her of being morbid, it was very simple for her to deny it utterly, and to express her astonishment at his being able to allow so little for her just susceptibility. He couldn't take it seriously that she had American feelings; he couldn't believe that it would make a terrible difference in her happiness to go about the world as the wife, the cynical, consenting wife, of the author of a blow dealt with that brutality at a breast to which she owed filial honor. She didn't say to him that she should never hold her head up before Macarthy again (her strength had been that hitherto, as against Macarthy, she was perfectly straight); but it was in a great degree the prefigurement of her brother's cold, life-long scorn that had kindled in her, while she awaited her husband's return, the passion with which she now protested. He would never read

The Modern Warning, but he would hear all about it, he would meet it in the newspapers, in every one's talk; the very voices of the air would distil the worst pages into his ear, and make the scandal of the participation even greater than—as Heaven knew—it would deserve to be. She thought of the month of renewed tenderness, of happy, pure impressions, that she had spent a year before in the midst of American kindness and memories more innocent than her visions of to-day, and the effect of this retrospect was galling in the face of her possible shame. Shame—shame. She repeated that word to Sir Rufus in a tone which made him stare, as if it dawned upon him that her reason was perhaps deserting her. That shame should attach itself to his wife in consequence of any behavior of *his* was an idea that he had to make a very considerable effort to embrace, and while his candor betrayed it, his wife was touched, even through her resentment, by seeing that she had not made him angry. He thought she was strangely unreasonable, but he was determined not, on his own side, to fall into that vice. She was silent about Macarthy, because Sir Rufus had accused her before her marriage of being afraid of him, and she had then resolved never again to incur such a taunt; but before things had gone much further between them she reminded her husband that she had Irish blood, the blood of the people, in her veins, and that he must take that into account in measuring the provocation he might think it safe to heap upon her. She was far from being a fanatic on this subject, as he knew, but when America was made out to be an object of holy horror to virtuous England, she could not but remember that millions of her Celtic cousins had found refuge there from the blessed English dispensation, and be struck with his recklessness in challenging comparisons which were better left to sleep.

When his wife began to represent herself as Irish, Sir Rufus evidently thought her "off her head" indeed; it was the first he had heard of it since she communicated the mystic fact to him on the lake of Como. Nevertheless he argued with her for half an hour as if she were sane, and before they separated he made her a liberal concession, such as only a perfectly lucid mind would be able to appreciate. This was a simple indulgence, at the end of their midnight discussion; it

was not dictated by any recognition of his having been unjust; for though his wife reiterated this charge, with a sacred fire in her eyes which made them more beautiful than he had ever known them, he took his stand, in his own stubborn opinion, too firmly upon piles of evidence, revelations of political fraud and corruption, and the "whole tone of the newspapers" to speak only of that. He remarked to her that, clearly, he must simply give way to her opposition. If she were going to suffer so inordinately, it settled the question. The book should not be published, and they would say no more about it. He would put it away, he would burn it up, and *The Modern Warning* should be as if it had never been. Amen! amen! Lady Chasemore accepted this sacrifice with eagerness, although her husband (it must be added) did not fail to place before her the exceeding greatness of it. He didn't lose his temper, he was not petulant nor spiteful, he didn't throw up his project and his vision of literary distinction in a huff; but he called her attention very vividly and solemnly to the fact that in deferring to the feelings she so uncompromisingly expressed he renounced the dream of rendering a signal service to his country. There was a certain bitterness in his smile as he told her that *her* wish was the only thing in the world that could have made him throw away such a golden opportunity. The rest of his life would never offer him such another; but patriotism might go to the dogs if only it were settled that she shouldn't have a grudge. He didn't care what became of poor old England, if once that precious result were obtained; poor old England might pursue impure delusions and rattle down hill as fast as she chose, for want of the word his voice would have spoken—really inspired, as he held it to be, by the justice of his cause.

Lady Chasemore flattered herself that they did not part that night in acrimony; there was nothing of this in the long kiss which she took from her husband's lips, with wet eyes, with a grateful, comprehensive murmur. It seemed to her that nothing could be fairer or finer than their mutual confidence; her husband's concession was gallant in the extreme; but even more than this was it impressed upon her that her own affection was perfect, since it could accept such a renunciation without a fear of the after-taste. She had been in love with Sir Rufus from the day he sought her hand at Cadenabbia, but she was never so much in love with him as during the weeks that immediately followed his withdrawal of his book. It was agreed between them that neither of them would speak of the circumstance again, but she at least, in private, devoted an immense deal of meditation to it. It gave her a tremendous reprieve, lifted a nightmare off her breast, and that, in turn, gave her freedom to reflect that probably few men would have made such a graceful surrender. She wanted him to understand, or at any rate she wanted to understand herself, that in all its particulars too she thoroughly appreciated it; if he really couldn't conceive how she could feel as she did, it was all the more generous of him to comply blindly, to take her at her word, little as he could make of it. It did not become less obvious to Lady Chasemore, but quite the contrary, as the weeks went on, that *The Modern Warning* would have been a masterpiece of its class. In her room, that evening, her husband had told her that the best of him, intellectually, had gone into it, that he believed he had uttered certain truths there as they never would be uttered again —contributed his grain of gold to the limited sum of human wisdom. He had done something to help his country, and then —to please her—he had undone it. Above all it was delightful to her that he had not been sullen or rancorous about it, that he didn't make her pay for his magnanimity. He didn't sigh or scowl, or take on the air of a domestic martyr; he came and went with his usual step and his usual smile, and remained to all appearance the same fresh-colored, decided, accomplished high official.

Therefore it is that I find it difficult to explain how it was that Lady Chasemore began to feel at the end of a few months that their difficulties had, after all, not become the mere reminiscence of a flurry, making present security more deep. What if the flurry continued, impalpably, insidiously, under the surface? She thought there had been no change, but now she suspected that there was at least a difference. She had read Tennyson, and she knew the famous phrase about the little rift within the lute. It came back to her with a larger meaning, it haunted her at last, and she asked herself whether, when she accepted her husband's relinquishment, it had been her happiness and his that she staked and threw away. In the light of this fear she struck herself as having lived in a fool's paradise—a misfortune from which she had ever prayed to be delivered. She wanted in every situation to know the worst, and in this case she had not known it; at least she knew it only now, in the shape of the formidable fact that Sir Rufus's outward good manners misrepresented his real reaction. At present she began, anxiously, broodingly, to take this reaction for granted, and to see signs of it in the very things which she had regarded at first as signs of resignation. She secretly watched his face; she privately counted his words. When she began to do this it was no very long time before she made up her mind that the latter had become much fewer, that Sir Rufus talked to her very much less than he had done of old. He took no revenge, but he was cold, and in his coldness there was something horribly inevitable. He looked at her less and less, whereas formerly his eyes had had no more agreeable occupation. She tried to teach herself that her suspicions were woven of air, and were an injury to a just man's character; she remembered that Sir Rufus had told her she was morbid, and if the charge had not been true at the time, it might very well be true now. But the effect of this reflection was only to suggest to her that Sir Rufus himself was morbid, and that her behavior had made him so. It was the last thing that would be in his nature, but she had subjected that nature to a most unnatural strain. He was feeling it now; he was feeling that he had failed in the duty of a good citizen: a good citizen being what he had ever most earnestly proposed to himself to be. Lady Chasemore pictured to herself that his cheek burned for this when it was turned away from her—that he ground his teeth with shame in the watches of the night. Then it came over her with unspeakable bitterness that there had been no real solution of their difficulty; that it was too great to be settled by so simple an arrangement as that—an arrangement too primitive for a complicated world. Nothing was less simple than to bury one's gold and live without the interest. It is a singular circumstance, and suggesting perhaps a perversion of the imagination under the influence of distress, but Lady Chasemore at this time found herself thinking with a kind of baffled pride of the merits of *The Modern Warning* as a literary composition, a political essay. It would have been dreadful for her, but at least it would have been superb, and that was what was, naturally enough, present to the defeated author as he tossed through the sleepless hours. She determined at last to question him, to confess her fears, to make him tell her whether his weakness—if he considered it a weakness—really did rankle; though when he made the sacrifice months before (nearly a year had come round), he let her know that he wished the subject buried between them for evermore. She approached it with some trepidation, and the manner in which he looked at her as she stammered out her inquiry was not such as to make the effort easier. He waited in silence till she had expressed herself as she best could, without helping her, without showing that he guessed her trouble, her need to be assured that he didn't feel her to have been cruel. Did he?—*did* he? that was what she wanted to be certain of. Sir Rufus's answer was in itself a question; he demanded what she meant by imputing to him such hypocrisy, such bad faith. What did she take him for, and what right had he given her to make a new scene, when he flattered himself the last pretext had been removed? If he had been dissatisfied, she might be very sure he would have told her so; and as he hadn't told her, she might pay him the compliment to believe he was honest. He expressed the hope—and for the first time in his life he was stern with her—that this would be the last endeavor on her part to revive an odious topic. His sternness was of no avail; it neither wounded her nor comforted her; it only had the effect of making her perfectly sure that he suffered, and that he regarded himself as a kind of traitor. He was one more in the long list of those whom a woman had ruined, who had sold themselves, sold their honor and the commonwealth, for a fair face, a quiet life, a show of tears, a bribe of caresses. The vision of this smothered pain, which he tried to carry off as a gentleman should, only ministered to the love she had ever borne him, the love that had the power originally to throw her into his arms in the face of an opposing force. As month followed month, all her nature centred itself in this feeling; she loved him more than ever,

and yet she had been the cause of the most tormenting thing that had ever happened to him. This was a tragic contradiction, impossible to bear, and she sat staring at it with tears of rage.

One day she had occasion to tell him that she had received a letter from Macarthy, who announced that he should soon sail for Europe, even intimated that he should spend two or three weeks in London. He had been overworked, it was years since he had had a proper holiday, and the doctor threatened him with nervous prostration if he didn't very soon break off everything. His sister had a vision of his reason for offering to let her see him in England; it was a piece of appreciation, on Macarthy's part, a reward for their having behaved—that is, for Sir Rufus's having behaved—apparently under her influence, better than might have been expected. He had the good taste not to bring out his insolent book, and Macarthy gave this little sign, the most mollified thing he had done as yet, that he noticed. If Lady Chasemore had not at this moment been thinking of something else, it might have occurred to her that nervous prostration in her brother's organism had already set in. The prospect of his visit held Sir Rufus's attention very briefly, and in a few minutes Agatha herself ceased to dwell upon it. Suddenly, illogically, fantastically, she could not have told why, at that moment and in that place, for she had had no such intention when she came into the room, she broke out: "My own darling, do you know what has come over me? I have changed entirely—I see it differently; I want you to publish that grand thing." And she stood there smiling at him, expressing the transformation of her feeling so well that he might have been forgiven for not doubting it.

Nevertheless he did doubt it, especially at first. But she repeated, she pressed, she insisted; once she had spoken in this sense, she abounded and overflowed. It went on for several days (he had begun by refusing to listen to her, for even in touching the question she had violated his solemn injunction), and by the end of a week she persuaded him that she had really come round. She was extremely ingenious and plausible in tracing the process by which she had done so, and she drew from him the confession (they kissed a great deal after it was made) that the manuscript of *The Modern Warning* had not been destroyed at all, but was safely locked up in a cabinet, together with the interrupted proofs. She doubtless placed her tergiversation in a more natural light than her biographer has been able to do; he, however, will spare the reader the exertion of following the impalpable clew which leads to the heart of the labyrinth. A month was still to elapse before Macarthy would show himself, and during this time she had the leisure and freedom of mind to consider the sort of face with which she should meet him, her husband having virtually promised that he would send the book back to the printers. Now, of course, she renounced all pretension of censureship; she had nothing to do with it; it might be whatever he liked; she gave him formal notice that she should not even look at it after it was printed. It was his affair altogether now—it had ceased to be hers. A hard crust had formed itself, in the course of a year, over a sensibility that was once so tender; this she admitted was very strange, but it would be stranger still if (with the value that he had originally set upon his opportunity) he should fail to feel that he might throw his weight upon it. In this case the morbidness would be on *his* side. Several times, during the period that preceded Macarthy's arrival, Lady Chasemore saw on the table in the hall little packets which reminded her of the roll of proofs she had opened that evening in her room. Her courage never failed her, and an observer of her present relations with her husband might easily have been excused for believing that the solution which at one time appeared so illusory was now substantial and complete. Sir Rufus was immensely taken up with the resumption of his task; the revision of his original pages went forward the more rapidly that in fact, though his wife was unaware of it, they had repeatedly been in his hands since he put them away. He had retouched and amended them, by the midnight lamp, disinterestedly, platonically, hypothetically, and the alterations and improvements which suggest themselves when a work is laid by to ripen, like a row of pears on a shelf, started into life and liberty. Sir Rufus was as happy as a man who, after having been obliged for a long time to entertain a passion in secret, finds it recognized and

legitimated, finds that the obstacles are removed, and he may conduct his beloved to the altar.

Nevertheless, when Macarthy Grice alighted at the door of his sister's house—he had assented at the last to her urgent request that he would make it his habitation during his stay in London—he stepped into an atmosphere of sudden alarm and dismay. It was late in the afternoon, a couple of hours before dinner, and it so happened that Sir Rufus drove up at the moment the American traveller issued from the carriage that had been sent for him. The two men exchanged greetings on the steps of the house, but in the next breath Macarthy's host asked what had become of Agatha, whether she had not gone to the station to meet him, as she had announced at noon, when Sir Rufus saw her last, that she intended.

It appeared that she had not accompanied the carriage; Macarthy had been met only by one of the servants, who had been with the Chasemores to America, and was therefore in a position to recognize him. This functionary said to Sir Rufus that her ladyship had sent him down word, an hour before the carriage started, that she had altered her intention, and he was to go on without her. By this time the door of the house had been thrown open; the butler and the other footman had come to the front. They had not, however, their usual perpendicular demeanor, and the master's eye immediately saw that there was something wrong in the house. This apprehension was confirmed by the butler on the instant, before he had time to ask a question. "We are afraid her ladyship is ill, sir; rather seriously, sir; we have but this moment discovered it, sir; her maid is with her, sir, and the other women."

Sir Rufus started; he paused but a single instant, looking from one of the men to the other. Their faces were very white; they had a strange, scared expression. "What do you mean by rather seriously? —what the devil has happened?" But he had sprung to the stairs—he was half-way up before they could answer.

"You had better go up, sir, really," said the butler, to Macarthy, who was planted there, and had turned as white as himself; "we are afraid she has taken something."

"Taken something?"

"By mistake, sir, you know, sir," quavered the footman, looking at his companion. There were tears in the footman's eyes. Macarthy felt sick.

"And there's no doctor? You don't send? You stand gaping?"

"We are going, sir—we have already gone!" cried both the men together. "He'll come from the hospital, round the corner; he'll be here by the time you're upstairs. It was but this very moment, sir, just before you rang the bell," one of them went on. The footman who had come with Macarthy from Euston dashed out of the house, and he himself followed the direction his brother-in-law had taken. The butler was with him, saying he didn't know what—that it was only while they were waiting—that it would be a stroke for Sir Rufus. He got before him, on the upper landing; he led the way to Lady Chasemore's room, the door of which was open, revealing a horrible hush, and, beyond the interior, a flurried, gasping flight of female domestics. Sir Rufus was there, he was at the bed still; he had cleared the room; two of the women had remained, they had hold of Lady Chasemore, who lay there passive, with a lifeless arm that caught Macarthy's eye—calling her, chafing her, pushing each other, saying that she would come to in a minute. Sir Rufus had apparently been staring at his wife in stupefaction and horror, but as Macarthy came to the bed he caught her up in his arms, pressing her to his bosom, and the American visitor met his face, glaring at him over her shoulder, convulsed and transformed. "She has taken something, but only by mistake;" he was conscious that the butler was saying that again, behind him, in his ears.

"My God, you have killed her! it's *your* infernal work!" cried Sir Rufus, in a voice that matched his terrible face.

"*I* have killed her?" answered Macarthy, bewildered and appalled.

"Your d——d fantastic opposition the fear of meeting you," Sir Rufus went on. But his words lost themselves, as he bent over her in violent kisses and imprecations, in demands whether nothing could be done, why the doctor wasn't there, in clumsy, passionate attempts to arouse, to revive.

"Oh, I am sure she wanted you to come. She was very well this morning, sir," the lady's-maid broke out, to Macarthy, contradicting Sir Rufus in her fright, and protesting again that it was nothing; that it

was a faint—for the very pleasure—that her ladyship would come round. The other woman had picked up a little phial. She thrust it at Macarthy with the boldness of their common distress, and as he took it from her mechanically he perceived that it was empty, and had a strange odor. He sniffed it, and with a shout of horror flung it away. He rushed at his sister, and for a moment almost had a struggle with her husband for the possession of her body, in which, as soon as he touched it, he felt the absence of life. Then she was in the bed again, beautiful, irresponsive, inanimate, and they were both beside her for an instant, after which Sir Rufus broke away, and staggered out of the room. It seemed an eternity to Macarthy while he waited, though it had already come over him that he was waiting only for something still worse. The women talked, tried to tell him things; one of them said something about the pity of his coming all the way from America on purpose. Agatha was beautiful; there was no disfigurement. The butler had gone out with Sir Rufus, and he came back with him, reappearing first, and with the doctor. Macarthy didn't even heed what the doctor said. By this time he knew it all for himself. He flung himself into a chair, overwhelmed, covering his face with the cape of his ulster. The odor of the little phial was in his nostrils. He let the doctor lead him out without resistance, scarcely with consciousness, after some minutes.

Lady Chasemore had taken something —the doctor gave it a name—but it was not by mistake. In the hall, down-stairs, he stood looking at Macarthy, kindly, soothingly, tentatively, with his hand on his shoulder. "Had she—a—had she some domestic grief?" Macarthy heard him ask. He couldn't stay in the house —not with Chasemore. The servant who had brought him from the station took him to a hotel, with his luggage, in the carriage, which was still at the door—a horrible hotel, where in a dismal, dingy back room, with chimney-pots outside, he spent a night of unsurpassable anguish. He could not understand, and he howled to himself, "Why, *why*, just now?" Sir Rufus, in the other house, had exactly such another vigil; it was plain enough that this was the case when, the next morning, he came to the hotel. He held out his hand to Macarthy—he appeared to take back his monstrous words of the evening before. He made him come back to Grosvenor Crescent; he made him spend three days there, three days during which the two men scarcely exchanged a word. But the rest of the holiday that Macarthy had undertaken for the benefit of his health was passed upon the Continent, with little present evidence that he should find what he had sought. *The Modern Warning* has not yet been published, but it may still appear. This doubtless will depend upon whether, this time, the sheets have really been destroyed — buried in Lady Chasemore's grave, or only put back into the cabinet.

OLE 'STRACTED
by Tomas Nelson Page

"AWE, little Ephum! awe, little Eph-um! ef you don' come 'long heah, boy, an' rock dis chile, I'll buss you haid open!" screamed the high-pitched voice of a woman, breaking the stillness of the summer evening. She had just come to the door of the little cabin, where she was now standing, anxiously scanning the space before her, while a baby's plaintive wail rose and fell within with wearying monotony. The log cabin, set in a gall in the middle of an old field all grown up in sassafras, was not a very inviting-looking place; a few hens loitering about the new hen-house, a brood of half-grown chickens picking in the grass and watching the door, and a runty pig tied to a "stob," were the only signs of thrift; yet the face of the woman cleared up as she gazed about her, and afar off where the gleam of green made a pleasant spot, where the corn grew in the river-bottom, for it was her home, and the best of all was she thought it belonged to them.

A rumble of distant thunder caught her ear, and she stepped down and took a well-worn garment from the clothes-line, stretched between two dogwood forks, and having, after a keen glance down the path through the bushes, satisfied herself that no one was in sight, she returned to the house, and the baby's voice rose louder than before. The mother, as she set out her ironing table, raised a dirge-like hymn, which she chanted, partly from habit and partly in self-defence. She ironed carefully the ragged shirt she had just taken from the line, and then, after some search, finding a needle and cotton, she drew a chair to the door and proceeded to mend the garment.

"Dis de on'ies' shut Ole 'Stracted got," she said, as if in apology to herself for being so careful.

The cloud slowly gathered over the pines in the direction of the path; the fowls carefully tripped up the path, and after a prudent pause at the hole, disappeared one by one within; the chickens picked in a gradually contracting circuit, and finally one or two stole furtively to the cabin door, and after a brief recognizance came in, and fluttered up the ladder to the loft, where they had been born, and yet roosted. Once more the baby's voice pre-vailed, and once more the woman went to the door, and, looking down the path, screamed, "Awe, little Ephum! awe, little Ephum!"

"Mam," came the not very distant answer from the bushes.

"Why 'n't you come 'long heah, boy, an' rock dis chile?"

"Yes, 'm, I comin'," came the answer. She waited, watching, until there emerged from the bushes a queer little caravan, headed by a small brat, who staggered under the weight of another apparently nearly as large and quite as black as himself, while several more of various degrees of diminutiveness struggled along behind.

"Ain't you heah me callin' you, boy? You better come when I call you. I'll tyah you all to pieces!" pursued the woman, in the angriest of keys, her countenance, however, appearing unruffled. The head of the caravan stooped and deposited his burden carefully on the ground; then, with a comical look of mingled alarm and penitence, he slowly approached the door, keeping his eye watchfully on his mother, and picking his opportunity, slipped in past her, dodging skilfully just enough to escape a blow which she aimed at him, and which would have "slapped him flat" had it struck him, but which, in truth, was intended merely to warn and keep him in wholesome fear, and was purposely aimed high enough to miss him, allowing for the certain dodge.

The culprit, having stifled the whimper with which he was prepared, flung himself on to the foot of the rough plank cradle, and began to rock it violently and noisily, using one leg as a lever, and singing an accompaniment, of which the only words that rose above the noise of the rockers were, "By-a-by, don't you cry; go to sleep, little baby;" and sure enough the baby stopped crying and went to sleep.

Eph watched his mammy furtively as she scraped away the ashes and laid the thick pone of dough on the hearth, and shovelled the hot ashes upon it. Supper would be ready directly, and it was time to propitiate her. He bethought himself of a message.

"Mammy, Ole 'Stracted say you must

bring he shut; he say he marster comin' to-night."

"How he say he is?" inquired the woman, with some interest.

"He ain' say—jes say he want he shut. He sutny is comical—he layin' down in de baid." Then having relieved his mind, Eph went to sleep in the cradle.

"'Layin' down in de baid?'" quoted the woman to herself as she moved about the room. "I 'ain' nuver hearn 'bout dat befo'. Dat sutny is a comical ole man anyways. He say he used to live on dis plantation, an' yit he al'ays talkin' 'bout de gret house an' de fine kerridges dee used to have, an' 'bout he marster comin' to buy him back. De 'ain' nuver been no gret house on dis place, not sence I know nuttin 'bout it, 'sep de overseer house whar dat man live. I heah Ephum say Aunt Dinah tell him de ole house whar used to be on de hill whar dat gret oak-tree is in de pines bu'nt down de year he wuz born, an' he ole marster had to live in de overseer house, an' hit break he heart, an' dee teck all he niggers, an' dat's de way *he* come to blongst to we all; but dat ole man ain' know nuttin 'bout dat house, 'cause hit bu'nt down. I wonder whar he did come from?" she pursued, "an' what he sho' 'nough name? He sholy couldn' been named 'Ole 'Stracted,' jes so; dat ain' no name 'tall. Yit ef he ain' 'stracted, 'tain' nobody is. He ain' even know he own name," she continued, presently. "Say he marster 'll know him when he come— ain' know de folks is free; say he marster gwi buy him back in de summer an' kyar him home, an' 'bout de money he gwine gi' him. Ef he got any money, I wonder he live down dyah in dat evil-sperit hole."

And the woman glanced around with great complacency on the picture-pasted walls of her own by no means sumptuously furnished house. "Money!" she repeated aloud, as she began to rake in the ashes. "He 'ain' got nuttin. I got to kyar him piece o' dis bread now," and she went off into a dream of what they would do when the big crop on their land should be all in, and the last payment made on the house; of what she would wear, and how she would dress the children, and the appearance she would make at meeting, not reflecting that the sum they had paid on the property had never, even with all their stinting, amounted in any one year to more than a few dollars over the rent charged for the place, and that the eight hundred

dollars yet due on it was more than they could make at the present rate in a lifetime.

"Ef Ephum jes had a mule, or even somebody to help him," she thought, "but he 'ain' got nuttin. De chil'n ain' big 'nough to do nuttin but eat; he 'ain' got no brurrs, an' he deddy took 'way an' sold down Souf de same time my ole marster whar dead buy him; dat's what I al'ays heah 'em say, an' I know he's dead long befo' dis, 'cause I heah em say dese Virginia niggers carn stan' hit long deah, hit so hot, hit frizzle 'em up, an' I reckon he die befo' he ole marster, whar I heah say die of a broked heart torectly after dee teck he niggers an' sell 'em befo' he face. I heah Aunt Dinah say dat, an' dat he might'ly sot on he ole servants, spressaly on Ephum deddy. whar named Little Ephum, an' whar used to wait on him. Dis mus' 'a been a gret place dem days, 'cordin' to what dee say." She went on: "Dee say he sutny live strong, wuz jes rich as cream, an' weahed he blue coat an' brass buttons, an' lived in dat ole house whar wuz up whar de pines is now, an' whar bu'nt down, like he owned de wull. An' now look at it; dat man own it all, an' cuttin' all de woods off it. He don' know nuttin 'bout black folks, ain' nuver been fotch up wid him. Who ever heah he name 'fo' he come heah an' buy de place, an' move in de overseer house, an' charge we all eight hundred dollars for dis land, jes 'cause it got little piece o' bottom on it, and forty-eight dollars rent besides, wid he ole stingy wife whar oon' even gi' 'way buttermilk!" An expression of mingled disgust and contempt concluded the reflection.

She took the ash-cake out of the ashes, slapped it first on one side, then on the other, with her hand, dusted it with her apron, and walked to the door and poured a gourd of water from the piggin over it. Then she divided it in half; one half she set up against the side of the chimney, the other she broke up into smaller pieces and distributed among the children, dragging the sleeping Eph, limp and soaked with sleep, from the cradle to receive his share. Her manner was not rough—was perhaps even tender—but she used no caresses, as a white woman would have done under the circumstances. It was only toward the baby at the breast that she exhibited any endearments. Her nearest approach to it with the others was when she told them, as she portioned out the ash-cake, "Mam-

"THEY WERE AT THE CABIN NOW, AND A BRIEF PAUSE OF DOUBT ENSUED."

my 'ain' got nuttin else; but nuver min',
she gwine have plenty o' good meat next
year, when deddy done pay for he land."

"Hi! who dat out dyah?" she said, suddenly. "Run to de do', son, an' see who
dat comin'," and the whole tribe rushed
to inspect the new-comer.

It was, as she suspected, her husband,
and as soon as he entered she saw that
something was wrong. He dropped into
a chair, and sat in moody silence, the picture of fatigue, physical and mental. After waiting for some time, she asked, indifferently, "What de matter?"

"Dat man."

"What he done do now?" The query
was sharp with suspicion.

"He say he ain' gwine let me have my
land."

"He's a half-strainer," said the woman,
with sudden anger. "How he gwine help
it? 'Ain' you got crap on it?" She felt
that there must be a defence against such
an outrage.

"He say he ain' gwine wait no longer;
dat I wuz to have tell Christmas to finish
payin' for it, an' I 'ain' do it, an' now he
done change he min'."

"Tell dis Christmas comin'," said his
wife, with the positiveness of one accustomed to expound contracts.

"Yes; but I tell you he say he done
change he min'." The man had evidently given up all hope; he was dead beat.

"De crap's yourn," said she, affected
by his surrender, but prepared only to
compromise.

"He say he gwine teck all dat for de
rent, an' dat he gwine drive Ole 'Stracted
'way too."

"He ain' nuttin but po' white trash!"
It expressed her supreme contempt.

"He say he'll gi' me jes one week mo'
to pay him all he ax for it," continued he,
forced to a correction by her intense feeling, and the instinct of a man to defend
the absent from a woman's attack, and
perhaps in the hope that she might suggest some escape.

"He ain' nuttin sep po' white trash!"
she repeated. "How you gwine raise
eight hunderd dollars at once? Dee kyarn
nobody do dat. Gord mout! He 'ain' got
good sense."

"You 'ain' see dat corn lately, is you?"
he asked. "Hit jes as rank! You can
almos' see it growin' ef you look at it
good. Dat's strong land. I know dat
when I buy it."

He knew it was gone now, but he had
been in the habit of calling it his in the
past three years, and it did him good to
claim the ownership a little longer.

"I wonder whar Marse Johnny is?"
said the woman. He was the son of her
former owner; and now, finding her proper support failing her, she instinctively
turned to him. "He wouldn' let him
turn we all out."

"He 'ain' got nuttin, an' ef he is, he
kyarn git it in a week," said Ephraim.

"Kyarn you teck it in de co't?"

"Dat's whar he say he gwine have it ef
I don' git out," said her husband, despairingly.

Her last defence was gone.

"Ain' you hongry?" she inquired.

"What you got?"

"I jes gwine kill a chicken for you."
It was her nearest approach to tenderness, and he knew it was a mark of special attention, for all the chickens and
eggs had for the past three years gone to
swell the fund which was to buy the home,
and it was only on special occasions that
one was spared for food.

The news that he was to be turned out
of his home had fallen on him like a
blow, and had stunned him; he could
make no resistance, he could form no
plans. He went into a rough estimate as
he waited.

"Le' me see: I done wuck for it three
years dis Christmas done gone; how much
does dat meck?"

"An' fo' dollars, an' five dollars, an' two
dollars an' a half last Christmas from de
chickens, an' all dem ducks I done sell he
wife, an' de washin' I been doin' for 'em;
how much is dat?" supplemented his wife.

"Dat's what I say!"

His wife endeavored vainly to remember the amount she had been told it was;
but the unaccounted-for washing changed
the sum and destroyed her reliance on the
result. And as the chicken was now approaching perfection, and required her
undivided attention, she gave up the arith-
metic and applied herself to her culinary
duties.

Ephraim also abandoned the attempt,
and waited in a reverie, in which he saw
corn stand so high and rank over his land
that he could scarcely distinguish the
balk, and a stable and barn and a mule,
or may be two—it was a possibility—and
two cows which his wife would milk, and
a green wagon driven by his boys, while

he took it easy and gave orders like a master, and a clover patch, and wheat, and he saw the yellow grain waving, and heard his sons sing the old harvest song of "Cool Water" while they swung their cradles, and—

"You say he gwine turn Ole 'Stracted out too?" inquired his wife, breaking the spell. The chicken was done now, and her mind reverted to the all-engrossing subject.

"Yes; say he tired o' ole 'stracted nigger livin' on he place an' payin' no rent."

"Good Gord A'mighty! Pay rent for dat ole pile o' logs! 'Ain't he been mendin' he shoes an' harness for rent all dese years?"

"'Twill kill dat ole man to tu'n him out dat house," said Ephraim; "he 'ain' nuver stay away from dyah a hour sence he come heah."

"Sutny 'twill," assented his wife; then she added, in reply to the rest of the remark, "Nuver min', den; we'll see what he got in dyah." To a woman, that was at least some compensation. Ephraim's thoughts had taken a new direction.

"He al'ays feared he marster 'd come for him while he 'way," he said, in mere continuance of his last remark.

"He sen' me wud he marster comin' to-night, an' he want he shut," said his wife, as she handed him his supper. Ephraim's face expressed more than interest; it was tenderness which softened the rugged lines as he sat looking into the fire. Perhaps he thought of the old man's loneliness, and of his own father torn away and sold so long ago, before he could even remember, and perhaps very dimly of the beauty of the sublime devotion of this poor old creature to his love and his trust, holding steadfast beyond memory, beyond reason, after the knowledge even of his own identity and of his very name was lost.

The woman caught the contagion of his sympathy.

"De chil'n say he mighty comical, an' he layin' down in de baid," she said.

Ephraim rose from his seat.

"Whar you gwine?"

"I mus' go to see 'bout him," he said, simply.

"Ain' you gwine finish eatin'?"

"I gwine kyar dis to him."

"Well, I kin cook you anurr when we come back," said his wife, with ready acquiescence.

In a few minutes they were on the way, going single file down the path through the sassafras, along which little Eph and his followers had come an hour before, the man in the lead and his wife following, and according to the custom of their race, carrying the bundles, one the surrendered supper, and the other the neatly folded and well patched shirt in which Ole 'Stracted hoped to meet his long-expected loved ones.

As they came in sight of the ruinous little hut which had been the old man's abode since his sudden appearance in the neighborhood a few years after the war, they observed that the bench beside the door was deserted, and that the door stood ajar—two circumstances which neither of them remembered ever to have seen before; for in all the years in which he had been their neighbor Ole 'Stracted had never admitted any one within his door, and had never been known to leave it open. In mild weather he occupied a bench outside, where he either cobbled shoes for his neighbors, accepting without question anything they paid him, or else sat perfectly quiet with the air of a person waiting for some one. He held only the briefest communication with anybody, and was believed by some to have intimate relations with the evil one, and his tumble-down hut, which he was particular to keep closely daubed, was thought by such as took this view of the matter to be the temple where he practised his unholy rites. For this reason, and because the little cabin, surrounded by dense pines and covered with vines which the popular belief held "pizonous," was the most desolate abode a human being could have selected, most of the dwellers in that section gave the place a wide berth, especially toward nightfall, and Ole 'Stracted would probably have suffered but for the charity of Ephraim and his wife, who, although often wanting the necessaries of life themselves, had long divided it with their strange neighbor. Yet even they had never been admitted inside his door, and knew no more of him than the other people about the settlement knew.

His advent in the neighborhood had been mysterious. The first that was known of him was one summer morning, when he was found sitting on the bench beside the door of this cabin, which had long been unoccupied and left to decay.

He was unable to give any account of himself, except that he always declared that he had been sold by some one other than his master from that plantation, that his wife and boy had been sold to some other person at the same time for $1200 (he was particular as to the amount), and that his master was coming in the summer to buy him back and take him home, and would bring him his wife and child when he came. Everything since that day was a blank to him, and as he could not tell the name of his master or wife, or even his own name, and as no one was left old enough to remember him, the neighborhood having been entirely deserted after the war, he simply passed as a harmless old lunatic laboring under a delusion. He was devoted to children, and Ephraim's small brood were his chief delight. They were not at all afraid of him, and whenever they got a chance they would slip off and steal down to his house, where they might be found any time squatting about his feet listening to his accounts of his expected visit from his master, and what he was going to do afterward. It was all of a great plantation, and fine carriages and horses, and a house with his wife and the boy.

This was all that was known of him, except that once a stranger, passing through the country, and hearing the name Ole 'Stracted, said that he heard a similar one once, long before the war, in one of the Louisiana parishes, where the man roamed at will, having been bought of the trader by the gentleman who owned him, for a small price, on account of his infirmity.

"Is you gwine in dyah ?" asked the woman as they approached the hut.

"Hi! yes; 'tain' nuttin gwine hu't you; an' you say Ephum say he layin' in de baid ?" he replied, his mind having evidently been busy on the subject.

"An' mighty comical," she corrected him, with exactness born of apprehension.

"Well ? I 'feared he sick."

"I 'ain' nuver been in dyah," she persisted.

"'Ain' de chil'n been in dyah ?"

"Dee say 'stracted folks oon hu't chil'n."

"Dat ole man oon hu't nobody; he jes tame as a ole tomcat."

"I wonder he ain' feared to live in dat lonesome ole house by hisself. I jes lieve stay in a graveyard at once. I ain' won-

der folks say he see sperrits in dat hanty-lookin' place." She came up by her husband's side at the suggestion. "I wonder he don' go home ?"

"Whar he got any home to go to sep heaven ?" said Ephraim.

"What was you mammy name, Ephum ?"

"Mymy," said he, simply.

They were at the cabin now, and a brief pause of doubt ensued. It was perfectly dark inside the door, and there was not a sound. The bench where they had heretofore held their only communication with their strange neighbor was lying on its side in the weeds which grew up to the very walls of the ruinous cabin, and a lizard suddenly ran over it, and with a little rustle disappeared under the rotting ground-sill. To the woman it was an ill omen. She glanced furtively behind her, and moved nearer her husband's side. She noticed that the cloud above the pines was getting a faint yellow tinge on its lower border, while it was very black above them. It filled her with dread, and she was about to call her husband's notice to it, when a voice within arrested their attention. It was very low, and they both listened in awed silence, watching the door meanwhile as if they expected to see something supernatural spring from it.

"Nem min'—jes wait—'tain' so long now—he'll be heah torectly," said the voice. "Dat's what he say—gwine come an' buy me back—den we gwine home."

In their endeavor to catch the words they moved nearer, and made a slight noise. Suddenly the low earnest tone changed to one full of eagerness.

"Who dat ?" was called in sharp inquiry.

"'Tain' nobody but me an' Polly, Ole 'Stracted," said Ephraim, pushing the door slightly wider open and stepping in. They had an indistinct idea that the poor deluded creature had fancied them his longed-for loved ones, yet it was a relief to see him bodily.

"Who you say you is ?" inquired the old man, feebly.

"Me an' Polly."

"I done bring you shut home," said the woman, as if supplementing her husband's reply. "Hit all bran' clean, an' I done patch it."

"Oh, I thought—" said the voice, sadly. They knew what he thought. Their eyes were now accustomed to the darkness, and they saw that the only article of furniture which the room contained was the wretched bed or bench on which the old man was stretched. The light sifting through the chinks in the roof enabled them to see his face, and that it had changed much in the last twenty-four hours, and an instinct told them that he was near the end of his long waiting.

"How is you, Ole 'Stracted?" asked the woman.

"Dat ain' my name," answered the old man, promptly. It was the first time he had ever disowned the name.

"Well, how is you, Ole— What I gwine call you?" asked she, with feeble finesse.

"I don' know—he kin tell you."

"Who?"

"Who? Marster. He know it. Ole 'Stracted ain' know it; but dat ain' nuttin. *He* know it—got it set down in de book. I jes waitin' for em now."

A hush fell on the little audience—they were in full sympathy with him, and knowing no way of expressing it, kept silence. Only the breathing of the old man was audible in the room. He was evidently nearing the end. "I mighty tired of waitin'," he said, pathetically. "Look out dyah and see ef you see anybody," he added, suddenly.

Both of them obeyed, and then returned and stood silent; they could not tell him no.

Presently the woman said, "Don' you warn put you' shut on?"

"What did you say my name was?" he said.

"Ole 'Str—" She paused at the look of pain on his face, shifted uneasily from one foot to the other, and relapsed into embarrassed silence.

"Nem min'! dee'll know it—dee'll know me 'dout any name, oon dee?" He appealed wistfully to them both. The woman for answer unfolded the shirt. He moved feebly as if in assent.

"I so tired waitin'," he whispered—"done 'mos' gin out, an' he oon come; but I thought I heah little Eph to-day?" There was a faint inquiry in his voice.

"Yes, he wuz heah,"

"Wuz he?" The languid form became instantly alert, the tired face took on a look of eager expectancy. "Heah, gi' m'y shut quick. I knowed it. Wait; go over dyah, son, and git me dat money. He'll be heah torectly." They thought his mind wandered, and merely followed the direction of his eyes with theirs. "Go over dyah quick—don't you heah me?"

And to humor him Ephraim went over to the corner indicated.

"Retch up dyah, an' run you' hand in onder de second jice. It's all in dyah," he said to the woman—"twelve hunderd dollars—dat's whad dee went for. I wucked night an' day forty year to save dat money for marster: you know dee teck all he land an' all he niggers an' tu'n him out in de ole fiel'? I put 'tin dyah 'ginst he come. You ain' know he comin' dis evenin' is you? Heah, help me on wid dat shut, gal—I stan'in' heah talkin' an' maybe ole marster waitin'. Push de do' open so you kin see. Forty year ago," he murmured, as Polly jambed the door back and returned to his side—"forty year ago dee come an' lovelled on me: marster sutny did cry. 'Nem min',' he say, 'I comin' right down in de summer to buy you back an' bring you home. He's comin', too—nuver tol' me a lie in he life —comin' dis evenin'. Make 'aste." This in tremulous eagerness to the woman, who had involuntarily caught the feeling, and was now with eager and ineffectual haste trying to button his shirt.

An exclamation from her husband caused her to turn around, as he stepped into the light and held up an old sock filled with something.

"Heah, hol' you' apron," said the old man to Polly, who gathered up the lower corners of her apron and stood nearer the bed.

"Po' it in dyah." This to Ephraim, who mechanically obeyed. He pulled off the string, and poured into his wife's lap the heap of glittering coin—gold and silver more than their eyes had ever seen before.

"Hit's all dyah," said the old man, confidentially, as if he were rendering an account. "I been savin' it ever sence dee took me 'way. I so busy savin' it I 'ain' had time to eat, but I ain' hongry now; have plenty when I git home." He sank back exhausted. "Oon marster be glad to see me?" he asked, presently, in pathetic simplicity. "You know we growed up togerr? I been waitin' so long I 'feared dee 'mos' done forgit me. You reckon dee is?" he asked the woman, appealingly.

"No, suh, dee 'ain' forgit you," she said, comfortingly.

"I know dee 'ain'," he said, reassured. "Dat's what he tell me—he ain' nuver gwine forgit me." The reaction had set in, and his voice was so feeble now it was scarcely audible. He was talking rather to himself than to them, and finally he sank into a doze. A painful silence reigned in the little hut, in which the only sound was the breathing of the dying man. A single shaft of light stole down under the edge of the slowly passing cloud and slipped up to the door. Suddenly the sleeper waked with a start, and gazed around.

"Hit gittin' mighty dark," he whispered, faintly. "You reckon dee'll git heah 'fo' dark?"

The light was dying from his eyes.

"Ephum," said the woman, softly, to her husband.

The effect was electrical.

"Heish! you heah dat?" exclaimed the dying man, eagerly.

"Ephum"—she repeated. The rest was drowned by Ole 'Stracted's joyous exclamation.

"Gord! I knowed it!" he cried, suddenly rising upright, and, with beaming face, stretching both arms toward the door. "Dyah dee come! Now watch 'em smile. All y'all jes stand back. Heah de one you lookin' for. Marster—Mymy—heah's little Ephum!" And with a smile on his face he sank back into his son's arms.

The evening sun, dropping on the instant to his setting, flooded the room with light; but as Ephraim gently eased him down and drew his arm from around him, it was the light of the unending morning that was on his face. His Master had at last come for him, and after his long waiting, Ole 'Stracted had indeed gone home.

SISTER PEACHAM'S TURN
by Sarah Orne Jewett

I

THE wind had gone down suddenly after blowing hard until the middle of the afternoon, and Mrs. Pamela Fellows went to the sitting-room closet, where she kept her every-day bonnet and black woollen shawl, and then stood before the little mirror in the clock front to put them straight. The glass was so small that she had to inspect her broad shoulders by sections, but by ducking to see the top of her head, and standing on tiptoe and dodging from side to side, she reassured herself of proper adjustment and equipment, and stepped out to the sidewalk, after locking the door carefully and putting the key deep into her accessible pocket. Then she struck a steady rolling gait and went away down the street with fine energy.

Once she stopped and turned about to look at the western sky. There was a heavy bank of clouds just lifting, and below it all the west was clear, but the cold greenish-blue of its color gave no promise of warmth. "Winter's come," grumbled Mrs. Fellows, half aloud, as she resumed her eastward course. "Looks like the sky at sea this time o' year, crossin' from English ports; goin' to be cold and clear for a day or two, and then look out for snow! I for one like to have some snow for Thanksgivin' time; I ain't like Lyddy Ann; she sets right down an' weeps when the first flakes come."

Half-way down the long street of the straggling town Mrs. Fellows met a familiar friend, Mrs. Peters, who stopped with a frank smile of interest.

"Where be you goin' this cold afternoon? Ain't you settin' forth rather late?"

Mrs. Peters asked the question, with an air of expecting to hear all about the errand.

"I thought I'd go over and see Lyddy Ann before dark," answered the adventurer. "Yes, I thought I'd make haste and get ahead of her and see if I can't make her invite me over to Thanksgivin'. She needs to make a break; I've asked her to my house six or seven years now, and I thought I should lead up to the subject gradual and ask her what she intended to do; that's the way she always catches me with my mind unprepared, and I've gone an' invited her before I stop to think."

Mrs. Peters laughed; they were very close friends; there was a droll twinkle in the complaining sister's eyes.

"'Twould be a grand thing for her if she could feel that havin' company wouldn't hurt her; she needs more occupation, and not to settle right down expecting to be always done for," said Mrs. Peters, gravely.

"Oh, yes'm, you're quite right," answered Mrs. Fellows, soberly, and the twinkle in her eyes disappeared. "Here we are both of us widows, and own sisters; we're all that's left out of a large family, and she makes use of as much ceremony in asking me over to stop to tea with her as if I was the minister. She's always amiable, but she's fallin' into a way of being plaintive, and oh, so dreadful set! I lost my husband an' his ship with him, but, although bereaved, Lyddy Ann's left in the best o' circumstances. Yes'm, she's dreadful set, an' gettin' more so year by year. Well, I'm goin' to see what I can do to persuade her; if I don't beat, why, she *will!*"

Mrs. Fellows tossed her head gallantly and waved her hand as she departed.

Mrs. Peters laughed aloud. "If I was goin' to bet on who's likely to come out ahead, I'd bet on Lyddy Ann," she exclaimed, with an air of certainty. "Mrs. Fellows is the best-natured heart o' the two; 'tis the biggest heart that always gives up easiest. I guess I'll remember to call over to-morrow and see who gets the invitation. I'm afeard it won't be Pamela, for all her boast and bravery."

II

Mrs. Lydia Ann Peacham was as thin and precise as her sister was round and easy-going. She inclined by nature toward the economies and excuses of life, and even sighed over being left alone, when no mortal soul could have prevailed upon her to accept permanent companionship. She was sitting alone this very afternoon, rocking gently, and worrying because she was again fearful that something would be expected of her on Thanksgiving day.

"I do hope that sister Fellows 'll feel she can ask me there again, I've got such a habit now o' goin' there to keep Thanksgivin'," she said, mournfully. "I'll offer to make one o' my nice apple pies and carry over, and any little thing she may suggest. I know 'twas the custom o' our family to take turn an' turn about, but it's so much easier for her than 'tis for me. This anxiety's very tryin'. I'm all worked up an' I want things settled, but she didn't speak till 'most the last minute last year; she's so dilatory, Pamely is!"

The sun came down from the gray cloud at this moment, and shone out cheerfully over a cold world. Its startling splendor dazzled Mrs. Peacham's short-sighted eyes. The dull little room where she sat, the plain gabled houses and thick-boughed maple-trees in the street, were all transfigured with sudden glory. There was even a touch of the old reddish gold of her youth on Mrs. Peacham's faded hair. She had once been the prettiest of her family, and this pleasing fact Mrs. Fellows, the eldest and plainest, could never forget.

"I'll be sort of easy with poor Lyddy Ann," Mrs. Fellows was saying to herself at that moment as she toiled up the long hill. "She never was so strong as I be, and I ain't goin' to let no Thanksgivin' day fall a burden on her."

Mrs. Peacham started in dismay at the harsh sound of the door-latch, and looked apprehensive as her sister entered the room.

"Well, Lyddy Ann, what be you goin' to do for Thanksgivin'?" demanded sister Fellows, without forethought or preface, and then sat down quite out of breath. Her first intention had prevailed almost against her conscience; there was no leading up to the great subject; it exploded in the timid sitting-room like a Fourth-of-July cannon.

There was no answer for a moment, and Mrs. Fellows unpinned her black woollen shawl and seated herself on a common chair as if it had been a throne; having spoken, she did not mean to be a coward, but she did not fail to look kind and sisterly.

"I don't know, I'm sure," replied Mrs. Peacham, with dignity. She was provoked as well as startled by the sudden question, and even a little excited. "I may invite the minister," she proclaimed. It was no use to sit there and be browbeaten in your own house, and Pamela Fellows had taken the advantage.

"Why, there he goes now; there's Mr. Downer now. You'd better speak if you want to; you'll lose him if you wait till Sunday!" exclaimed sister Fellows before Mrs. Peacham could get breath enough to protest. Sister Fellows was always a creature of impulse; she caught up the big thimble on the window-sill and rapped sharply on the glass, so that the minister waved his hand in instant response and turned in at the gate. Pamela Fellows loved a minister; her heart beat fast, and she opened the door to receive him. Sister Peacham looked like one in deep affliction; she half rose from her rocking-chair and sank back again; then she sprang up with fine spirit. There was a color on her cheeks such as nobody had seen in years.

"I hope you weren't in a hurry, sir; you must excuse my sister Pamela for knocking so," she said, politely, to the Reverend Mr. Downer; but the tired little man looked pleased and amiable.

"Of course, of course," he answered, looking for a proper place to lay his hat. "I felt it to be very neighborly; I had intended to call this afternoon, but I feared you might think it too late. I was just dreading the long cold stretch of road between me and the fire at home." The good man was conscious of something unusual, and looked from the round sister to the thin one and back again to Mrs. Fellows before he meekly sat down. "It has been a beautiful winter sunset. I suppose you have been enjoying it together?" he added, with some formality.

Mrs. Peacham did not speak, so somebody else must. It was Mrs. Fellows who continued the conversation, gayly; it seemed as if the very spirit of mischief possessed her. Sister Lyddy Ann could not believe her own ears.

"My sister Peacham was just sayin' that she'd thought to invite you an' Mrs. Downer to keep Thanksgivin' with us. I hope you ain't promised to nobody else?" The words were out; she did not dare to look her sister's way. After all, she could transfer the invitation to her own house if the skies really fell upon her; besides, the minister might be already engaged. Mrs. Peacham was heard to make a queer clucking noise in her throat as she turned to receive the minister's answer, but whatever her real thoughts may have been, they were not articulate.

"Why, Mrs. Peacham, how more than kind of you to think of us! My wife will be perfectly delighted; but are you sure that it will not be too much for you to undertake in your frail condition of health?" exclaimed the minister, with joyful surprise, and a perfectly beautiful considerateness. "What time shall we come—right after church? You know I am to conduct the union services this year. To tell the truth, Mrs. Downer expressed two wishes this very morning at breakfast; one was that she could get to see you oftener, and the other that we might have some pleasant invitation for Thanksgiving day from some of our own people. Having her old home broken up by her mother's death makes a great change for her. She will feel very grateful to you, as I do."

There was something so sincere and so affectionate in the good man's voice and manner that it lifted even such a sinking heart as Mrs. Peacham's, and her courage began to rise. She did not deign to look at her sister, but promptly accepted all the honors of the situation.

"It is a number of years since I have felt equal to entertaining my friends," she said, prettily, and with less than usual of her sad affectation of voice. "You and Mrs. Downer will be very welcome. I have been with Sister Pamela for several of these sad anniversaries. But this year—"

"You are planning to be together here?" suggested the minister, at a happier moment than he could guess. "I shall look forward with great pleasure to the day. We must try to forget sad changes, and I am sure we shall make a cheerful company together. I cannot express half my gratitude to you on my wife's account."

Mrs. Downer was a great favorite with both the sisters, and Mrs. Peacham, the unexpected hostess, looked more resigned than ever. The Reverend Mr. Downer made himself so entertaining and friendly that he left no looks of deprecation or dismay behind him. He little knew upon what dangerous ground he had innocently and unexpectedly trodden.

The early darkness of that late November day had quite fallen when the guest took leave. He inquired politely if he might not have the pleasure of Sister Fellows's company as far as their ways lay together, and this boon was generously granted. In fact, though Mrs. Peacham seemed to be in her most reasonable and even affectionate mood, the minister's invitation made a welcome avenue of escape. Her sister said at parting that she might be expected over again within a day or two, since they should have one or two things to talk over.

"Yes, you'd better come, Sister Pamela," rejoined Mrs. Peacham, with decision, "or else you'll have me coming after you!" There was an astonishing absence of the spirit of revenge in her tone; on the contrary, she met Pamela's timid glance with a funny little shake of the head, and they both laughed aloud right before the minister. Mr. Downer had never seen Mrs. Peacham in such a cheerful, awakened frame of mind, or thought her such a good-looking person before. She had usually worn a die-away look on the occasions of his pastoral visits, and had only given expression to laments and fears.

"I hope she won't go and lay awake all night worryin'," thought the guilty instigator of such a dark Thanksgiving plot, as she tried to keep pace with the minister's longer steps along the frozen road. "She did carry it off splendid, I must say. Well, I'll help Lyddy Ann all I can, and not let the day sag too heavy. She's got everything pretty to set her table with; there ain't a richer-lookin' parlor closet in this town."

When the sisters met again it was in the presence of witnesses. Mrs. Peters and another sister of the church were calling upon Mrs. Peacham when Mrs. Pamela Fellows came in. To her great relief, she was received as anything but a culprit; Mrs. Peacham was proudly relating her plans, and taking all the glory of these unforeseen Thanksgiving hospitalities to herself.

"Yes'm," she said, with no attempt at either meekness or apology, "I don't deny that it costs me some effort. I have had little health or spirit for entertaining, these late years, but I have long desired to show our pastor and his wife some proper attention. As long as I was going to invite Sister Pamela anyway, it seemed a very good time. I never saw such a parish as this is; everybody hangs back! Mr. Downer said they had received no other invitation, and I did feel provoked even if I was the gainer. Poor man, he really did appear gratified! I have been downtown this morning—there's nobody, not even my sister Fellows, that I wanted to trust in the matter of a turkey."

"Oh no, I can't boast of my own judgment beside yours," protested Mrs. Fellows, warmly; but Mrs. Peters, who had a great sense of humor, caught her eye, and they both feigned the sudden discovery of a pin on the carpet, and startled their companions by bobbing down together to pick up, not the pin, but a little plain composure.

III

The next day after Thanksgiving Mrs. Peters found time to leave home and a cheerful party of children and grandchildren and go over to Mrs. Fellows's for a friendly call.

"I saw the minister this morning," she said, eagerly. "He came to our house to speak with Mr. Peters about something, and I took occasion to remark that I expected he'd had a pleasant time yesterday."

"What did he say?" asked Mrs. Fellows. "He was the life of it all, I thought. Lyddy Ann laughed as I haven't seen her laugh for years, at some o' the stories he told about awkward couples

coming to be married. Oh yes, he was certainly very entertainin', Mr. Downer was!"

"He told me 'twas one of the pleasantest occasions he had ever enjoyed, or Mis' Downer, either," announced Mrs. Peters, with triumph. "He'd never tasted no such a turkey since he'd been in this parish; 'twas like the best he ever saw down Rhode Island way, where he came from when he was a boy. He said you an' your sister was so cordial and made them both feel so welcome, and Mrs. Downer was all heartened up; he told me she said you couldn't be no kinder if you'd been her own sisters. She'd always admired Lyddy Ann very much, but hadn't felt so free with her before. She thought everything of her showing such sympathy, and remembering that this would be the first Thanksgiving she'd spent without any of her own folks. Those was his very words. Now do tell me, Pamely, what on earth set Lyddy Ann out? You know how we joked that day on the street, and—"

Mrs. Fellows struggled between a natural desire to give the full particulars and an obligation to maintain the dignity of her house. "Why, I went over this morning myself," she answered. "I expected to find her with her face tied up from the neuralgy, or all used up some way or 'nother with some o' her usual complaints, and instead o' that she come right to the door and stood there waitin' when she saw me coming, pleased as a child. We sat down together and talked it all over same's we used to when we were girls. 'Now let it be a lesson not to think you can't do the things you *can* do, Lyddy Ann!' says I once, but she took no heed and went right on talkin'. There was one minute that day, when Mr. Downer was assurin' her they'd be delighted to come, when I was so scared I saw stars all over the room, and my heart did thump like an old-fashioned churn," continued Mrs. Fellows, in a hushed voice. "'Twas worth venturin', I must say. The minister's wife wore her best black silk, and Lyddy Ann wore hers, and her little red Injy shawl with the narrow border, as her dress felt thin about the shoulders. Why, she was in great spirits, Mis' Peters! I declare I kept looking at her as we set at the table, and she was laughin' more'n I was, and looked as young and pretty as a girl."

"There! we all of us need a little encouragin' sometimes," confessed neighbor Peters. "Pamely, I don't seem to understand yet how she came to invite the minister."

"Why, he said right off that he should be very happy to come," answered Mrs. Fellows, a little vaguely, after a moment's reflection. "I shall be very glad to have Lyddy Ann know how much he enjoyed himself," she added, for Mrs. Peters still looked so expectant. "I want them all to come and have dinner with me next year, though. The house looked kind o' lonesome when I got back, as if it sort of resented bein' left. I can't set so handsome a table as Sister can, but I love to have company. I'm the oldest o' the family that's left; but when I gave them the invitation, Lyddy Ann spoke right up and said no: we'd all three got to promise to come again next year. Oh, she's made a break now, I can tell you!"

"You and me might catch up our work and go over some afternoon to take tea with her!" suggested Mrs. Peters, with ready enthusiasm.

"I don't know as it's best to let her overdo too much!" answered sister Fellows, smiling, and so they parted.

The very next Sunday the minister was moved to preach an excellent sermon on the beauties of hospitality, and Mrs. Lydia Ann Peacham was at church and heard it in her front pew. Her thin cheeks flushed a little now and then with pleased self-consciousness. At first she hoped that her neighbors in the pew behind would derive some benefit from their appropriate lesson. Then the honesty of her own heart prevailed.

"'Twas time I made amends," she said to herself. "Pamely was in the right; I'd got way down to livin' for myself alone, an' there's nothin' makes life so dull an' wearin', let alone the shame to a Christian person!"

THE GREAT MEDICINE-HORSE
by *Frederic Remington*

"ITSONEORRATSEAHOOS," or Paint, as the white men called him, had the story, and had agreed to tell it to me. His tepee was not far, so "Sun-Down La Flare" said he would go down and interpret.

Sun-Down was cross-bred, red and white, so he never got mentally in sympathy with either strain of his progenitors. He knew about half as much concerning Indians as they did themselves, while his knowledge of white men was in the same proportion. I felt little confidence that I should get Paint's mysterious musings transferred to my head without an undue proportion of dregs filtered in from Sun-Down's lack of appreciation. While the latter had his special interest for me, the problem in this case was how to eliminate "Sun-Down" from "Paint." So much for interpreters.

We trudged on through the soft gray-blues of the moonlight, while drawing near to some tepees grouped in the creek bottom. The dogs came yelling; but a charge of Indian dogs always splits before an enemy which does not recoil, and recovers itself in their rear. There they may become dangerous. Sun-Down lifted the little tepee flap, and I crawled through. A little fire of five or six split sticks burned brightly in the centre, illumining old Paint as he lay back on his resting-mat. He grunted, but did not move; he was smoking. We shook hands, and Sun-Down made our peace-offering to the squaw, who sat at her beading. We reclined about the tepee and rolled cigarettes. There is a solemnity about the social intercourse of old Indian warriors which reminds me of a stroll through a winter forest. Every one knows by this how the interior of an Indian tepee looks, though every one cannot necessarily know how it feels; but most people who have wandered much have met with fleas. Talk came slow; but that is the Indian of it: they think more than they talk. Sun-Down explained something at length to Paint, and back came the heavy guttural clicking of the old warrior's words, accompanied by much subtle sign language.

"He sais he will tell you 'bout de horse. Now you got for keep still and wait; he'll talk a heap, but you'll get de story eef you don' get oneasy."

"Now, Sun-Down, remember to tell me just what Paint says. I don't care what you think Paint means," I admonished.

"I step right in hees tracks."

Paint loaded his long red sandstone pipe with the utmost deliberation, sat up on his back-rest, and puffed with an exhaust like a small stationary engine. The squaw put two more sticks on the fire, which spitted and fluttered, lighting up the broad brown face of the old Indian, while it put a dot of light in his fierce little left eye. He spoke slowly, with clicking and harsh gutturals, as though he had an ounce of quicksilver in his mouth which he did not want to swallow. After a time Sun-Down raised his hand to enjoin silence.

"He sais dat God—not God, but dat is bess word I know for white man; I have been school, and I know what he want for say ees what you say medicin', but dat ees not right. What he want for say ees de ding what direct heem un hees people what is best for do; et ees de speret what tell de ole men who can see best when dey sleep. Well—anyhow, it was long, long time ago, when hees fader was young man, and 'twas hees fader's fader what it all happened to. The Absarokees deedn't have ponies 'nough—de horses ware new in de country—dey used for get 'em out of a lac,* 'way off somewhere—dey come out of de water, and dese Enjun† lay in the bulrush for rope 'em, but dey couldn't get 'nough; besides, de Enjun from up north she use steal 'em from Absarokee. Well—anyhow, de medicin' tole hees fader's fader dat he would get plenty horses eef he go 'way south. So small party went 'long wid heem—dey was on foot—dey was

"HE JUMP FROM HEES PONY TO DEES RED HORSE."

travel for long time, keepin' in de foot-hill. Dey was use for travel nights un lay by daytime, 'cept when dey was hunt for de grub. De country was full up wid deir enemies, but de medicin' hit was strong, and de luck was wid 'em. De medicin' hit keep tellin' 'em for go 'long —go on—on—on—keep goin' long, long time. He's been tellin' me de names of revers dey cross, but you wouldn't know dem plass by what he call 'em. Dey keep spyin' camps, but de medicin' he keep tellin' 'em for go on, go on, un not bodder dem camp, un so dey keep goin'."

Here Sun-Down motioned Paint, and he started his strange high-pitched voice —winking and moving his hands at Sun-Down, who was rolling a cigarette, though keeping his eyes on the old Indian. Presently the talking ceased.

"He sais—dey went on—what he is tryin' for say ees dey went on so far hit was heap hot, un de Enjun dey was deef-erent from what dees Enjun is. He's tryin' for to get so far off dat I don' know for tell you how far he ees."

"Never mind, Sun-Down; you stick to Paint's story," I demanded.

"Well—anyhow—he's got dees outfit hell of a long way from home, un dey met up wid a camp un heap of pony. He was try tell how many pony — like de buffalo use be—more pony dan you see ober, by Gar. Den de medicin' say dey was for tac dose pony eef dey can. Well, den de outfit lay roun' camp wid de wolf-skin on—de white wolf. De En-jun he do jus' same as wolf, un fool de oder Enjun, you see; well, den come one night dey got de herds whar dey wanted 'em, un cut out all dey could drive. Et was terrible big bunch, 'cording as Paint say. Dey drive 'em all night un all nex' day, wid de horse-guides ahead, un de oders behin', floppin' de wolf-robe, un Paint say de grass will nevar grow where dey pass 'long; but I dink, by Gar, Paint ees talk t'ro' hees hat."

"Never mind — I don't want you to think — you jus' freeze to old Paint's talk, Mr. Sun-Down," I interlarded.

"Well, den—damn 'em, after dey had spoil de grass for 'bout night un day de people what dey had stole from come a-runnin'. Et was hard for drive such beeg bunch fas'—dey ought for have tac whole outfit un put 'em foot; but Paint say—un he's been horse-tief too hisself,

by Gar — he say dey natu'lly couldn't; but I say—"

"Never mind what you say."

"Well, anyhow, I say—"

"Never mind, Sun-Down!"

"Well, ole Paint he say same t'ing. De oder fellers kim up wid 'em, so just natu'lly dey went fightin'; but dey had extra horses, un de oder fellers dey didn't, 'cep' what was fall out of bunch, dem be-in' slow horses, un horses what was no 'count, noway. Dey went runnin' un fightin' 'way in de night; but de herd split on 'em, un hees fader's fader went wid one bunch, un de oder fellers went wid de 'split,' which no one neber heard of no more. De men what had loss de horses all went after de oder bunch. Hees fader's fader rode all dat night, all nex' day, un den stopped for res'. Dar was only 'bout ten men for look after de herd, which was more horses dan you kin see een dees valley to-day; what ees more horses dan ten men kin wrangle, 'cordin' to me."

"Never mind, Sun-Down."

"Let 'er roll, Paint," said La Flare, be-ginning a new cigarette.

"He sais," interrupted Sun-Down, "dey was go 'long slowly, slowly—goin' tow-ard de villages—when one day dey was jump by Cheyenne. Dey went runnin' and fightin' till come night, un couldn't drive de herd rightly. Dey loss heap of horses, but as dey come onto divide, dey saw camp right in front of dem. It was 'mos' night, so four or five of hees fader's fader's men dey cut out a beeg bunch, un split hit off down a coulie. De Enjun foller de oder bunch, which ram right eento de village, whar de 'hole outfit went for fight lac hell. Paint's fader's fader she saw dees as she rode ober de hill. Dey was loss heap of men dat day by bein' kill un by run eento dose camp— lesewise none of dem ever show up no more. Well, den, Paint say dey was keep travellin' on up dees way—hit was tac heem d—— long story for geet hees fader's fader's outfit back here, wheech ees hall right, seein' he got 'em so far 'way for begin wid."

Then Paint continued his story:

"He sais de Sioux struck 'em one day, un dey was have hell of a fight—runnin' deir pony, shootin' deir arrow. One man he was try mount fresh horse, she stan' steel un buck, buck, buck, un dees man he was not able for geet on; de Sioux dey

come run, run, un dey kiell* heem. You
see, when one man he catch fresh horse,
he alway' stab hees played-out horse,
'cause he do not want eet for fall eento
hand of de Enjun follerin'. Den White
Bull's horse she run slow; he 'quirt'
heem, but eet was do no good—ze horse
was done; de Sioux dey was shoot de
horse, un no one know whatever becom'
of heem, but I dink he was kiell all right
'nough. Den 'noder man's horse she was
stick hees foot in dog-hole, un de Sioux
dey shoot las' man 'cept hees fader's fader.
Den he was notice a beeg red horse what
had alway' led de horse ban' since dey was
stole. Dese Enjun had try for rope dees
horse plenty times, but dey was never
been able, but hees fader's fader was ride
up to de head of de ban', un jus' happen
for rope de red horse. He jump from hees
pony to dees red horse jus' as Sioux was
'bout to run heem down. De big red
horse was run—run lac† hell—ah! He
was run, by Gar, un de Sioux dey was—
aah!—de Sioux dey couldn't run wid de
big red horse nohow.

"He was gone now half-year, un he
deed not know where he find hees people.
He was see coyote runnin' 'head, un he
was say 'good medicin'.' He foller after
leetle wolf—he was find two buffalo what
was kiell by lightnin', what show coyote
was good medicin'. He was give coyote
some meat, un nex' day he was run on
some Absarokee, who was tell him whar
hees people was, wheech was show how
good de coyote was. When he got camp
de Enjun was terrible broke up, un dey
had nevar before see red horse. All of
deir horses was black, gray, spotted, roan,
but none of dem was red—so dees horse
was tac to de big medicin' in de medicin'-
lodge, un he was paint up. He got be
strong wid Absarokee, un hees fader's
fader was loss horse because he was keep
in medicin'-tepee, un look after by big
medicin'-chiefs. Dey was give out eef he
was loss eet would be bad, bad for Absarokee, un dey was watch out mighty close
—by Gar, dey was watch all time dees red
horse. When he go out for graze, t'ree
warriors was hole hees rope un t'ree was
sit on deir pony 'longside. No one was
ride heem."

Then, talking alternately, the story
came: "He sais de horse of de Absarokee
was increase—plenty pony—un de mare he
was all red colts; de big horse was strong.

De buffalo dey was come right to de
camp—by Gar, de horse was good. De
Sioux sent Peace Commission for try buy
de horse—dey was do beesness for Enjun
down whar de summer come from, what
want for geet heem back—for he was a
medicin'-horse. De Absarokee dey was
not sell heem. Den a big band of de Oga-
lalas, Brulés, Minneconjous, Sans Arcs,
Cheyennes, was come for tac de red horse,
dey was kiell one village, but dare was
one man 'scape, what was come to red
horse, un de Absarokee dey was put de red
paint on deir forehead. Ah! de Sioux
dey was not get de red horse—dey was
haf to go 'way. Den some time de beeg
medicin'-horse was have hell of a trouble
wid de bigges' medicin'-chief, right in de
big medicin'-lodge. Dees word medicin'
don't mean what de Enjun mean; de tent
whar de sperets come for tell de people
what for do, ees what dey mean; all same
as Fader Lacomb he prance 'roun' when
he not speak de French—dat's what dey
mean. All right, he have dees trouble wid
de head chief, un he keek heem een de
head, un he kiell him dead. After dat
he was get for be head medicin'-chief hisself, un he tole all de oder medicin'-chief
what for do. He was once run 'way from
de men what was hol' hees rope when he
was graze—dey was scared out of deir
life of heem eef dey was mak' heem mad,
un he was go out een herd un kiell some
horse. No one was dare go after heem.
De medicin'-men dey was go out wid de
big medicin'—dey was talk come back to
heem; but he wouldn't come. Den de virgin woman of de tribe—she was kind of
medicin'-man herself—she was go out un
make a talk; she was tell red horse to go
off—dat's de way for talk to people when
deir minds not lac oder people's minds—
un de horse she was let heem bring heem
back. After dat all de Absarokee women
had for behave preety well, or de medicin'-
men kiell dem, 'cause dey say de medicin'-
horse she was want de woman for be better in de tribe. Be d—— good t'ing eef
dat horse she 'roun' here now."

"Oh, you reptile! will you never mind
this thinking—it is fatal," I sighed.

"Well, anyhow, he sais de woman dey
was have many pappoose, un de colts was
red, un was not curly hair, un de 'yellow
eyes'* was come wid de gun for trade
skin. De buffalo she was stay late; de
winter was mile; de enemy no steal de

* Kill. † Like.

* White men.

THE GOING OF THE MEDICINE-HORSE.

pony, un de Absarokee he tac heap scalp—all dese was medicin'-horse work. But in de moon een which de geese lay deir eggs de great horse he was rise up een de curl of de smoke of dé big lodge—he was go plum' t'ro' de smoke-hole. De chief ask him for not go, but he was say he was go to fight de T'under-Bird. He say he would come back. Dey could keep his ghost. So he went 'way, un since den he has nevar come back no more. But Paint say lots of ole men use for see heem go t'ro' air wid de lightnin' comin' out of his nose, de T'under-Bird always runnin' out of hees way; he was always lick de t'under. Paint say dese Enjun have not see de medicin'-horse nowday; eef dey was see heem more, dey see no 'yellow eyes' een dees country. He sais he has seen de medicin'-horse once. He was hunt over een de mountain, but he was not have no luck; he was hungry, un was lay down by leetle fire een cañon. He was see de beeg medicin'-horse go 'long de ridge of de hill 'gainst de moon—he was beeg lac de new school-house. Paint got up un talked loud to de horse, askin' heem eef he was nevar come back. De horse stop un sais—muffled, lac man talk t'ro' blanket—'Yes, he was come back from speret-land, when he was bring de buffalo plenty; was roll de lan' over de white men; was fight de north wind. He sais he was come back when de Absarokee was not wear pants, was ride widout de saddle; when de women was on de square—un, by Gar, I t'ink he not come varrie soon."

"What does Paint say?"

"Ah, Paint he sais hit weel all come some day."

"Is that all?"

"Yes—dat ees all," said Sun-Down.

To be sure, there is quite as much Sun-Down in this as Paint—but if you would have more Paint, it will be necessary to acquire the Crow language, and then you might not find Paint's story just as I have told it.

A FABLE FOR YOUTHS
by Alice Duer

MANY years since there was a country by the sea where the fields were always green and the sky was always blue, and only the water varied from blue to green. Once countless shepherds and shepherdesses had tended their flocks on the gentle slopes, but gradually they had grown fewer and fewer, for, like every other, this country had one serious objection.

A short distance from the shore there was a rock, and here, whenever the moon shone, a mermaid sat and sang. So charming was she that almost all the shepherds, sooner or later, wished to visit the rock. Many were drowned in the attempt, while those who reached it seldom cared to return, so the shepherdesses thought very little of the beautiful pastures, but urged the men away, until only two of all the host were left—a shepherd and a shepherdess.

She staid because she loved him, and he because he was the victim of one absorbing idea — to find the woman who could make him happy.

It was all very well in his youth to spend the evenings playing upon pipes with the other shepherds on the hill, but he worried a great deal about his old age, and he felt he ought to settle down. For this reason he was seeking the woman who could make him happy.

He had been so much occupied in searching for her among the shepherdesses that he had had no time to think about the mermaid; but now, although he was almost convinced that the shepherdess who loved him was in every way suited to him, he thought it would be safer to interview the mermaid once before he made up his mind definitely.

Perhaps he would never have gone to the rock at all, for he found himself growing very fond of the little shepherdess when he was left alone with her, if she had not had the misfortune to lose one of her sheep. She was a careful little soul, and the loss preyed upon her mind. All the day she went about looking very sad, and described in detail again and again exactly where she had last seen the woolly wanderer.

In the evening they were idling by the shore. The moon was full, and made a wide white way straight to the rock where the mermaid was sitting singing; and this is the song that she sang:

> Pleasant to sit and sing
>   In the midst of a rippling sea,
> To a tune that the breezes bring,
>   To a time that the waves decree.
> 'Tis a song that the fish approve,
>   And the sea-birds take a part,
> But therein is never a word of love,
>   For a mermaid has no heart.

The swing of the song was still in his ears when he heard the little shepherdess saying:

"I should know it anywhere. It had a blue ribbon round its neck, and I saw it where the woods meet the fields, and . . ."

With an exclamation he sprang to his feet and plunged into the sea, swimming straight and strong up the moonlight.

"May I sit on the rock too?" he asked, shaking the water out of his hair.

The mermaid looked at him and smiled.

"I don't think you may," she said. "You look as if you would be troublesome and want me to love you."

"Indeed you need not be afraid of that," answered the shepherd, with some asperity. "I don't think you even so marvellously pretty."

"That's such an old, old game," said the mermaid; and then, seeing that he looked annoyed, she added, insinuatingly, "but you play it better than most people."

"Perhaps because I care about it less," returned the shepherd, whose methods, though crude, had a certain ability.

"You will care more by-and-by," said the mermaid, who was evidently a bold person.

"I don't think I shall," said he. "I love a little shepherdess who lives on the shore."

"Then why did you leave her to come here?" asked the mermaid.

He felt that the lady had the best of the argument, but he answered: "I am fond of swimming. I am going back to her now."

"Good-night!" said the mermaid. "I hope for your sake she has found her sheep."

He had scarcely slid into the water when she called him back. She made him swim round the rock until his back was to the moon, and the light shone full on her face. Then she looked at him for a whole minute.

"Don't you think me at all pretty?" she said, plaintively.

The shepherd's answer is not recorded.

He went back and told the little shepherdess all about it. He said that the mermaid was an amusing person, but not calculated to make any man happy. Yet the next evening found him at the rock.

And now followed a period of great anxiety for him. With the exception of making up his mind, nothing was so distressing to him as to unmake it; yet when he was with the shepherdess he found she had ceased to enthrall him, and when he was with the mermaid he could not but feel that she was lacking in those qualities likely to soothe his declining years. Besides this, he had continual and disagreeable scenes with the little shepherdess, who seemed to feel that he was treating her badly, and was apparently incapable of understanding that he was acting from the highest motives.

At last one day she burst into tears.

"This can't go on any longer," she said.

"No one can feel it more than I do," he returned; for he was very much harassed.

"You love the mermaid better than me."

He feared she was right, but not being quite sure, he answered nothing.

"I sha'n't stay here any longer," sobbed the shepherdess. "I shall go and join the others beyond the woods."

The shepherd sighed. "I believe it would be the best thing you could do," he said. "I really am not worth your affection," which speech was a combination of a noble sentiment and a short-cut to freedom that he may have been the first, but certainly was not the last, to make use of.

He went with her as far as the woods, and kissed her good-by with real regret. He felt so depressed after she had gone that he said to himself that he had no heart to go to the rock. Yet he went.

As he approached, the mermaid called out to him: "You have come just in time to say good-by to me. I am going off for a frolic with the dolphins."

"Oh, you must not do that," said he, climbing up on the rock. "I want you to settle down with me. I think you could make me happy."

"You must be mad, you pretty boy," cried the mermaid, laughing. She was in high spirits. "As if I could settle down with any one! The shepherdess is the person for you."

"She has gone away," he answered, sadly; "and, anyhow, I love you."

"Why could not you have said so that first evening? I liked you then," she said, plaintively. "Ah, there are the dolphins! Good-by!"

"But what shall I do when I'm old?" cried the shepherd, almost frenzied.

"When you get old enough you'll die," laughed the mermaid, springing into the sea. "I never grow old."

And so, the dolphins leaping round her, she swam away.

THE COCK LANE GHOST
by *Howard Pyle*

I.

THE world that reads is the grand high court of appeal to which we all of us may at any time apply for a reversion of sentence. For its judgments are never final; they are always tentative, and open to amendment or revision. So, though the verdict rendered a hundred and thirty years ago against the Cock Lane ghost has so far stood almost without appeal, it cannot even yet be said to be closed, for only one side of this case has been heard; and there is no truism truer than the old adage, "There are two sides to every question."

In the early part of the year 1762 a first little spark of news was dropped that by-and-by set all London in a blaze of talk. It began first to be whispered and then to be talked of that a ghost of a strange and unusual sort had made its appearance in Cock Lane.

Cock Lane was until that time almost unknown to the great world of London, being a most obscure little vein in the great arterial system of the metropolis; a narrow, dirty little street back of St. Sepulchre's Church, and running between Snow Hill and Giltspur Street. Upon the one side of it, and almost adjoining, was West Smithfield, where was held all the gaudy, tawdry splendor of St. Bartholomew's Fair. Upon the other side, and not further distant, was the Old Bailey, and the accompanying gloomy, frowning, forbidding face of Newgate Prison, black, dirty, squalid.

Cock Lane was almost a connecting link between these two extremes of squalid misery and squalid gayety; and more than once in those days, had you stood at the opening of some of its crooked courts or alleyways, you might have heard upon the one side the shouting and the laughing at the fair, the piping of fifes and the drubbing of drums, the squealing of pigs and the rattling and clattering of the pork-pie dishes, the creaking of swings and merry-go-rounds, and the confused cackle and hum and grumble of the motley crowd trying to enjoy itself; while at the same time, upon the other side, you might have heard the creaking and rattling of the hangman's cart, carrying the victims of Moloch law to the sacrificial tree at Tyburn.

In the old time, and before the days of modern spirit-rappings, a good, honest, old-fashioned ghost was generally thought to haunt either some old, mossy, mildewed country house, or else the gloomy recesses of a crumbling castle—the scene, perhaps, of some mysterious legendary crime or other. But this particular ghost of Cock Lane was one of a more modern fancy. It was of the spiritualistic order of our days, and was in advance of its

town at large took up the matter of the famous ghost, the presence of something mysterious in the house of the clerk in Cock Lane was known of in the neighborhood for some time before. To take a step still further backward, in 1759 a young widower (known in the annals of the Cock Lane ghost indifferently as Mr. Kempe or Kent), who was at that time living at Greenwich—then a semi-rural suburb of London—"employed," says a record in the case, "an agent to carry a letter to a young gentlewoman of reputable family in Norfolk." It was his deceased wife's sister, and the letter contained a final plea that, in spite of the

times. So, instead of preferring any such out-of-the-way scene for its doings, it chose this place—the heart of the metropolis, and the midst of a busy, jostling, noisy, tatterdemalion crowd—to make its intangible presence heard. The chosen place of its manifestation was the house of Mr. Parsons, the clerk of the neighboring church of St. Sepulchre's; and its chosen medium was the clerk's daughter, a girl of twelve years of age—a little, mischievous, spiteful, impish creature, if we may trust the faint, evanescent image that stands dimly out from the mists of the past.

Though it was not until 1762 that the

law against their legal union, they should live together as man and wife. By way of answer, the young gentlewoman came up in person to Greenwich in a post-chaise, "and was received most affectionately by Mr. Kent." No attempt at any sort of marriage ceremony was gone through with, but each of the two made a will in favor of the other of all he or she possessed.

One morning Mr. Parsons, who, as was said, was the officiating clerk of St. Sepulchre's, observed at early prayers a lady and gentleman of very genteel appearance standing in the aisle, and seeing them to be strangers, ordered them to a

convenient pew.   It was Mr.
Kent and the young gentlewoman from Norfolk. After
prayers the gentleman took
occasion to thank the clerk
for his courtesy, and entering into conversation with
him, asked him if he knew of
any convenient house in the
neighborhood where he and
his lady might find lodgings.
Mr. Parsons offered lodgings
in his own house, which the
other very gladly accepted,
and very soon he and the
young lady removed thither.
For some time the couple
lived pleasantly and intimately at the clerk's house,
and constant visits and friendly offices were exchanged.
The young lady—Miss Fanny
she was called by the family
—seemed to take a particular
liking to the little daughter of
her landlord, and once, when
Mr. Kent was away in the
country to attend a wedding,
she had the child to bed with
her for companionship.

It was upon this occasion
that the ghost for the first
time made itself audible.   In
the morning Miss Fanny complained to
the family that both she and the little girl had been very greatly disturbed
throughout the night by loud and continuous noises.   She described it as an alter-
nate rapping and scratching of a peculiar
kind (afterward described as being like
the sound of a cat clawing a cane-bottom
chair), which seemed to proceed now from
the bedstead, and now from the wainscot
of the adjoining wall.

After a great many speculations and
surmises, Mr. Parsons advanced the theory that the noise must have been occa-
sioned by a neighboring shoemaker, an
industrious fellow, who used sometimes
to work far into the small hours of the
night, and for the time no more was
thought of the matter.   But a few days
later the young lady said,

"Pray, Mr. Parsons, does your industrious shoemaker work upon Sundays as
well as upon other days?"

"No," said Mr. Parsons.   "Why do
you ask?"

"Because," said she, "that noise that

we heard was greater last night than ever
before."

From that time the noises continued
intermittently, becoming now more violent, and now ceasing altogether, but oc-
curring always in the room where the
child lay.   The matter became the talk
of the neighborhood, but for the time no
investigation seems to have been made.

Some little time after these manifesta-
tions had first occurred Mr. Kent quarrelled with his landlord, and he and the
young lady removed to other lodgings in
the neighborhood of Clerkenwell.   Within a few months after this last removal of
the couple the young gentlewoman died
rather suddenly, and was interred in the
crypt at St. John's.

After their removal the mysterious
noises that had disturbed the clerk's house
ceased entirely.   Nearly two years passed,
and then, suddenly and without warning,
the same scratching and the same rapping
began again—this time with more persistence and violence—and, as before, always
haunted the bedroom of the child.

At the time of their first coming she seems to have given little or no thought to them; now it appears to have occurred to her that there was something maybe supernatural connected with them. At their recurrence she was thrown into such violent fits of agitation that a woman of the neighborhood—one Mary Fraser—was called in to stay with her. It seemed to be chiefly through her ingenuity that the idea originated of putting queries to the ghost—as the manifestation was now generally called—to be answered yes or no by a series of taps negative or affirmative, after the manner of our modern spirit-rappings.

This was, perhaps, the first record of any such communication being held with the unseen world, and the result was amazing. By means of affirmative or negative taps or scratchings, the people on this side of the veil of life were informed by the people on the other side that Mr. Kent had poisoned his sister-in-law with red arsenic (a substance perhaps never before heard of, unless it was known in the great unseen world that lies beyond), which he had administered in a mug of purl. Upon being further questioned, the spirit proclaimed itself as being none other than Miss Fanny herself, who took this means of coming back to the world that she might bring justice upon her murderer.

II.

It is impossible to conceive of the blaze of excitement that the news of this manifestation caused in the neighborhood—a blaze that in the end spread to all the extremities of London—nay, the country at large—to Scotland, to Ireland, and even to the Continent. No doubt if Mr. Parsons and the others concerned in the matter had realized the hubbub that his ghost was destined to raise about his ears, he would have been chary enough in spreading the report of its doings. But as it was, the little spark was dropped, and instantly the wildfire spread far beyond his power to circumscribe. Maybe the excitement would have died out as quickly as it had flashed up, extending no further than Cock Lane, had not other and confirmatory circumstances added fuel to the blaze. The child herself, when questioned by the neighbors, asserted again and again that she had seen the figure of a woman surrounded by a blazing light; and the story of this miraculous vision was further confirmed by a publican in the neighborhood, who asserted that he also had seen the bright figure of a woman upon the stairs one night, presumably in the house of Parsons. The figure, he said, had beckoned him to follow her, when, in his agitation, he had (a delicious circumstantial detail) dropped his pot of beer, and had run all the way home.

Then the further circumstance of Miss Fanny's having made her will at Greenwich in favor of Mr. Kent was remembered, and finally it became known that at the time of the funeral of the poor young gentlewoman in the crypt of St. John's, her sister, who had come from the country for the purpose of attending the ceremony, was much surprised at not seeing Fanny's name upon the coffin plate. She had questioned "Mr. Browne" concerning the matter after the funeral was over, and had lamented that she had not been permitted to see her sister's face, the lid having been screwed down before she came. It was also known that this sister had spoken very bitterly of Mr. Kent, saying that by means of the Greenwich will he had availed himself of the young lady's fortune, "to the prejudice of her brother and sisters, who had all lived in perfect harmony until this unhappy affair happened."

It was, no doubt, the coincidence of these circumstances that first gave a color of plausibility to the tale of the ghost. Anyhow, the curiosity of London itself began to stir and awaken.

The Methodists, under the lead of the benevolent Lord Dartmouth, seem to have been the first to thrust their fingers into the clerk's private ghostly affairs. At that time a considerable faction of this sect were rather inclined to spiritualism. There was not only a deal of talk and questioning concerning the—to say at least—curiously strange phenomena that Mr. John Wesley had experienced, but a deal of belief in these phenomena, and to those who thus believed

it seemed quite possible that spirits could come back from the other world to manifest themselves for more or less rational causes to men in this world. To such it would have been indeed a triumphant vindication of what Mr. Wesley had asserted as to his own experiences, if a soul from the unseen world should come to bring the vengeance of God upon a murderer, and they were ready to give credence to the tale.

Upon the other hand, though the regular clergy were much more disposed to stand aloof, yet among them also were a number, chiefly in the purlieus of St. Sepulchre's, who were not disinclined to listen seriously. One of the accounts of the affair tells us that one night between eleven and twelve, the noises being particularly violent, a "respectable clergyman" (probably the Mr. Moore, curate of St. Sepulchre's, who afterward figured so prominently in the case) was sent for by Mr. Parsons to investigate into the matter. He himself not caring to render an immediate decision, two other clergymen and some twenty others were called in, and a regular series of questions was put to the ghost. There is something so solemnly and so grotesquely funny in this examination of the supernatural visitant that the temptation to repeat it in full is not to be resisted. They began by ask-

ing: Q. "In what was the poison administered—beer or purl?" A. "Purl." Q. "How long before your death?" A. "Three hours." Q. "Is the person called Carrots able to give any information about the poison?" A. "Yes." Q. "Are you Kent's wife's sister?" A. "Yes." Q. "Were you married to Kent?" A. "No." Q. "Was any other person beside Kent engaged in the poisoning?" A. "No." Q. "Can you appear visibly to any one?" A. "Yes." Q. "Will you do so?" A. "Yes." Q. "Can you go out of this house?" A. "Yes." Q. "Can you follow this child everywhere?" A. "Yes." Q. "Are you pleased at being asked questions?" A. "Yes." Q. "Does it ease your mind?" A. "Yes." (Here a mysterious noise, compared to the fluttering of wings round the room, was heard.) Q. "How long before your death did you tell Carrots that you were poisoned?" A. "One hour." Carrots admitted that this was so. Q. "How long did Carrots live with you?" A. "Three or four days." Carrots attested the truth of this. Q. "If the accused shall be taken up, will he confess?" A. "Yes." Q. "Will it ease your mind if the man be hanged?" A. "Yes." Q. "How long will it be before he is executed?" A. "Three years." Q. "How many clergymen are there in the room?" A. "Three." Q. "How many negroes?" A. "Two." One of the clergymen, holding up a watch, asked whether it was white, yellow, blue, or black; to which he was answered black. The watch was in a black shagreen case. Q. "At what time in the morning will you depart?"

A. "At four o'clock;" *which, strange to say, was the case.*

The mysterious rustling of wings appears to have been a great card in the ghostly programme, and subsequently the additional evidence of two other clergymen, who also heard the same mysterious sounds, was added to what had already been published. It was, they said, repeated several times, and was taken as a sign that the spirit was pleased.

London had now become thoroughly aroused. The newspapers were full of the affair, the coffee-houses buzzed with it, and a dozen different pamphlet accounts burst into an ephemeral life in Grub Street garrets, and fluttered out into the light of the reading world.

It became the fashion of the day. Horace Walpole interlards it in a letter written to Mann—a letter relating chiefly to the death of the Czarina and the complicated state of European politics. "I am ashamed to tell you," says he, "that we are again dipping into an egregious scene of folly. The reigning fashion is a ghost!—a ghost that would not pass muster in the paltriest convent in the Apennines. It only knocks and scratches; does not pretend to appear or to speak. The clergy give it their benediction; and all the

world, whether believers or infidels, go to hear it. I, in which number you may guess, go to-morrow; for it is as much the mode to visit the ghost as the Prince of Mecklenburg, who is just arrived."

Cock Lane and the surrounding courts and alleyways were crowded not only with the motley masses from the mazy wilderness of courts and alleys in the surrounding of St. Paul's, but also with high-stepping, rustling beaux and dames from the neighborhood of St. James's, where coaches and chairs fairly blocked the adjoining way.

We can only see a reflected picture of nether London and its excitement in records of the time; of the manner in which it affected high life we have several accounts, among the most amusing and clever of which is another letter from the ubiquitous Walpole, written in the intervals of his busy gossip of politics, the court, the opera, recapitulation of the droll bric-à-brac which he collected at his still droller mansion at Strawberry Hill, to Montague, then in Ireland. " I could," says he, " send you volumes on the ghost, and I believe if I were to stay a little I might send its life, dedicated to my Lord Dartmouth, by the ordinary of Newgate, its two great patrons. A drunken parish clerk set it on foot out of revenge, the Methodists have adopted it, and the whole town of London think of nothing else. Elizabeth Canning and the rabbit woman were modest impostors in comparison of this, which goes on without saving the least appearances. The Archbishop, who

would not suffer the *Minor* to be acted in ridicule of the Methodists, permits this farce to be played every night, and I shall not be surprised if they perform in the great hall at Lambeth. I went to hear it, for it is not an apparition, but an audition. We set out from the opera, changed our clothes at Northumberland House—the Duke of York, Lady Northumberland, Lady Mary Coke, Lord Hertford, and I, all in one hackney-coach—and drove to the spot. It rained torrents, yet the lane was full of mob, and the house so full we could not get in. At last they discovered it was the Duke of York, and the company squeezed themselves into one another's pockets to make room for us. The house, which is borrowed, and to which the ghost has adjourned, is wretchedly small and miserable. When we opened the chamber, in which were fifty people, with no light but one tallow candle at the end, we tumbled over the bed of the child to whom the ghost comes, and whom they are murdering by inches in such insufferable heat and stench. At the top of the room are ropes to dry clothes. I asked if we were to have rope-dancing between the acts? We had nothing. They told us, as they would at a puppet-show, that it would not come that night till seven in the morning—that is, when there are only 'prentices and old women. We staid, however, till half an hour after one. The Methodists have promised them contributions; provisions are sent in like forage; and all the taverns and ale-houses in the neighborhood make fortunes. The most diverting part is to hear people wondering when it will be found out; as if there were anything to find out; as if the actors would make their noises when they can be discovered. However, as this pantomime cannot last much longer, I hope Lady Fanny Shirley will set up a ghost of her own at Twickenham, and then you shall hear one. The Methodists, as Lord Aylesford assured Mr. Chute two nights ago at Lord Dacre's, have attempted ghosts three times in Warwickshire."

Nor were the fingers even of intellectual and literary London entirely clean of the dabbling in this squalid supernaturalism. Some years later, when Mr. Boswell ventured to question Doctor Johnson, he received a rebuff from his idol even more boorish and bearish than usual. The subject of the Cock Lane ghost was evidently a sore one with the worthy lexicographer, and the snub royal was administered with more than ordinary of the bludgeon stroke. But though the good doctor then took pains to intimate that, so far from his having been partial to the spirit of Miss Fanny, it was very largely owing to his particular pen strokes administered through the newspapers that the props of superstition which boosted up the ghost were knocked from under it, it is nevertheless almost certain that he was one of a party that went down into the crypt of St. John's, Clerkenwell, to hear the "audition" rap upon its own coffin lid. There is hardly a doubt but that it was his pen that wrote the deliciously funny account published in the *Gentleman's Magazine* at the time. "The supposed spirit," says that account, "had publicly promised by an affirmative knock that it would attend one of the gentlemen into the vault under the church of St. John's, Clerkenwell, where the body is deposited, and give a token of her presence there by a knock upon her coffin. It was therefore determined to make this trial of the existence or veracity of the supposed spirit.

"While they were inquiring and deliberating, they were summoned into the girl's chamber by some ladies who were near her bed, and who had heard knocks and scratches. When the gentlemen entered, the girl declared that *she felt the spirit like a mouse upon her back.*

"The spirit was then very seriously advertised that the person to whom the promise was made of striking upon the coffin was then about to visit the vault, and that the performance of the promise was then claimed. The company at one o'clock went into the church, and the gentleman to whom the promise was made went, with one more, into the vault. The spirit was solemnly required to perform its promise, but nothing more than silence ensued. The person supposed to be accused by the spirit then went down with several others, but no effect was perceived."

Churchill wrote a now unreadable poem strung upon the theme of the ghost, in which he tells how

"Thrice each the pond'rous key apply'd,
And thrice to turn it vainly try'd;

and then how

"Silent All Three went In, about,
All three turn'd Silent, and Came Out."

Elsewhere in the poem the author thus describes the Pomposo of this scene:

"Pomposo, insolent and loud;
Vain idol of a scribbling crowd,
Whose very name inspires an awe,
Whose ev'ry word is Sense and Law,
Who, proudly seiz'd of Learning's throne,
Now damns all Learning but his own;
But makes each sentence current pass
With Puppy, Coxcomb, Scoundrel, Ass;
For 'tis with him a certain rule,
The Folly's prov'd when he calls Fool."

There can be no doubt as to whom that likeness fits; so, in spite of the worthy doctor's assurance to his friend Boswell, one cannot help but believe that he himself really was, as reported, one of those poor funny gulls that went down into the crypt of St. John's, Clerkenwell, to hear Miss Fanny rap on her own coffin lid.

III.

For some months the ghost and her chosen medium seemed to have carried everything their own way. The voice of those who would have called for a reasonable examination into the matter was drowned on the one hand by the clamor of those who believed, on the other hand by the laughter and jeers of those who disbelieved. But at last the voice of cooler common-sense began to make itself heard, as it is, in the long-run, always sure to do. First it became publicly known that Miss Fanny's fortune, for which her husband was supposed to have murdered her, amounted to only £100; then, that the physician who attended her in her last sickness had declared that, so far from Miss Fanny's having been murdered, she had died of confluent smallpox; and finally that Mr. Kent had loaned his landlord a considerable sum, for the recovery of which he had brought suit against him.

The finding, as a possible root of the whole affair, such a palpable motive as revenge against an overpressing and clamorous creditor tipped the balance, perhaps, with the greatest weight of all; it shook the faith of those who believed most firmly. The child from whom the whole scandal originated was now (by order of the Lord Mayor, it appears) removed from her father's house, and subjected to a strict and rigorous examination.

At first the result was not very promising. The noises seemed rather to increase than to diminish in violence. Nevertheless, the steady drift of the current was now set full against the ghost and its abetters. Numberless little circumstances seemed of a more and more suspicious nature. One account says: "About twenty persons sat up in the room, but it was not until about six o'clock in the morning that the first alarm was given, which, coming spontaneously as well as suddenly, a good deal struck the imagination of those present. The scratching was compared with that of a cat on a cane chair. The child appeared to be in a sound sleep, and nothing further could be obtained. Those who sat around discussed the matter in low tones, questioning what would be likely to happen to the child and her father should the trick be discovered. About seven o'clock the girl seemed to awake in a violent fit of crying and tears. On being asked the occasion and assured that no harm should happen to her, she declared that her tears were the effect of her imagining what would become of her father, who must be ruined and undone if the matter should be supposed to be an imposture.

"'But,' said they who were present, 'who told you anything about an imposture? We supposed you to be sound asleep.'

"To which she answered, 'But not so sound but what I could hear all you said.'"

So, the tide having turned fully against the marvellous rapping and scratching, the world of London demanded imperatively that the mystery should at once be solved. So one day, as a final test, the girl's bed was swung up in the manner of a hammock, about a yard and a half from the ground, and her hands and feet were tied as far apart as might be without hurting her, and fastened with fillets. This was repeated for two or three nights successively, and during that time no noises were heard. It was now felt to be almost a matter of certainty that those noises, whatever they were, had emanated from the child herself, and it was not long before the *dénouement* happened which all the disbelievers had looked forward to with the most perfect confidence — a *dénouement* which forever wrecked the lives of the unfortunate clerk of St. Sepulchre's and his family, and nearly drove him to madness. Feeling now sure that the poor wretched little creature had some means by which she produced the mysterious noises, the examiners began, with an almost inquisitorial severity, to press her to confess; but, in spite of all, she still persisted in the denial of any trickery. She was then told that if she did not make the ghost heard within half an hour, she herself and her father and mother would be sent to Newgate. At that the miserable little hussy began crying, and asked that she might be put to bed to try if the noises would come.

"She lay in bed," says one of the accounts, "much longer than usual, but no noises; this was on Saturday.

"Being told on Sunday that the ensuing night only would be allowed for trial, she concealed a board about four inches long and six inches wide under her stays. Having got into bed, she told the gentlemen that she would bring Fanny at six the next morning.

"The master of the house, however, and a friend of his, being informed by the maids that the girl had taken a board to bed with her, impatiently waited for the appointed hour, when she began to knock and scratch upon the board, remarking, however, what they themselves were convinced of, *that these noises were not like those that used to be made.*

"She was then told that she had taken a board to bed with her, and on denying it, searched, and caught in a lie.

"The two gentlemen who, with the maids, were the only persons present at this scene, sent to a third gentleman to acquaint him that the whole affair was detected, and to desire his immediate attendance; but he brought another along with him.

"Their concurrent opinion was that the child had been frightened into this attempt by the threats which had been made the two preceding nights; and the master of the house also and his friends both declared that *the noises the girl had made that morning had not the least likeness to the former noises.* Probably the organs with which she performed these strange noises were not always in a proper tone for that purpose, and she imagined she might be able to supply the place of them by a piece of board."

The next morning all the newspapers and coffee-houses buzzed with the news that the trick of the ghost had at last been found out. And that, af-

ter all, it was nothing but a little imp of a girl scratching upon a piece of a board.

IV.

One can faintly imagine what must have been the feelings of poor Mr. Kent, the butt and victim of it, while all this had been going on. At first he seems to have brought evidence in rebuttal of the same grotesque sort as the accusations fulminated against him. He was one of those, as has been said, who paid that midnight visit to the crypt of St. John's. He employed a pamphleteer to write a somewhat elaborate defence, in which many of his most private and sacred affairs were set forth at length, especially his relations with "Miss Fanny," the manner of her death, etc., etc. An accusation had been brought forward by the believers in the ghost that Mr. Kent, fearing the detection of his guilt, had had the body secretly removed from the vault. Whereupon Mr. Kent, together with a clergyman, the undertaker, the clerk and sexton of the parish, and two or three gentlemen, went down into the crypt, overhauled the coffins piled up therein, and identified the particular one in which "Scratching Fanny" lay.

At last, upon the final supposed detection of the fraud, he instituted a civil suit for libel against all those concerned in the affair in which his credit had suffered so severely. We read in the *Gentleman's Magazine*, July 10, 1762: "Come on before Lord Mansfield in the Court of the King's Bench, Guildhall, a trial by a special jury, on an indictment against William Parsons and Elizabeth his wife, Mary Fraser, a clergyman [Mr. Moore, curate of St. Sepulchre's], and a reputable tradesman [one Mr. James], for a conspiracy in the Cock Lane ghost affair to injure the character, etc., of Mr. William Kent; when they were all found guilty. The trial lasted above twelve hours."

Richard Parsons was ordered to be set on the pillory three times in one month, and imprisoned two years, his wife one year, and Mary Fraser six months in Bridewell, to be kept to hard labor. Mr. Brown, for publishing some matters relating to that foolish affair, was fined £50 and discharged.

Mr. Moore, the curate, and Mr. James, the tradesman, were sentenced to pay Mr. Kent a round sum of money as indemnity; some say between £500 and £600.

Such was the verdict of the court. The verdict of the great, many-headed was given as undoubtedly and as emphatically in favor of the defendant. Among the riffraff and the ragtag of the neighborhood of Cock Lane, faith in the ghost had neither weakened nor waned. They believed in it still, and as heartily as ever. In one of the journals of the day we read, under date March 16, 1763: "Parsons, the fellow who was principally concerned in the Cock Lane ghost, stood on the pillory at the end of Cock Lane, and instead of being pelted, had money given him." Elsewhere we read of the unusual sympathy of the mob, and of a drunken fellow, who jeered at the unfortunate man whilst he stood in the pillory, being knocked into a kennel by some indignant neighbor of the whilom clerk.

As for that poor Miss Fanny, her bones seem destined to lie very uneasily. In the earlier part of this century we hear of her again from her restless resting-place. "While drawing the crypt of St. John's, Clerkenwell," says Mr. J. W. Archer, "in a narrow cloister on the north side, there being at that time coffins, fragments of shrouds, and human remains lying about in disorder, the sexton's boy pointed to one of the coffins and said that it was 'Scratching Fanny.' This reminded me of the Cock Lane ghost. I removed the lid of the coffin, which was loose, and saw the body of a woman, which had become adipocere. The face was perfect, handsome, oval, with an aquiline nose. Will not arsenic produce adipocere? She is said to have been poisoned, although the charge is understood to have been disproved. I inquired of one of the church-wardens of the time, Mr. Bird, who said the coffin had always been understood to contain the body of the woman whose spirit was said to have haunted the house in Cock Lane."

Such is the true story of the Cock Lane ghost. Since its time the great high court of appeal—the world that reads—has been in a general way satisfied that it was then finally settled. But was it settled?

Undoubtedly the little girl was caught in a trick, but does that prove that the noises heard before were made by a like trick? Even those adverse witnesses, with all their bias against the ghostly nature of the phenomena, acknowledged that the noises she then made "were not like those which used to be made"; and even went so far as to suggest that the poor little wretch, terrified by the threats fulminated against her, resorted to this last shift to imitate a sound which she had at one time made somehow else. Before, when she had been examined and had been put to bed by the committee of ladies, the record as given says: "They first thoroughly examined the bed, bedclothes, etc., and being satisfied that there was no visible appearance of deceit," etc., "yet when the child with its sister was put into bed," it "was found to shake extremely by the gentleman who had placed himself at the foot of it." Apart from the strange shaking of the bed, is it not likely that if she had concealed about her a piece of board four inches long and six broad, those ladies would have found it upon her?

Again, there is a palpable incongruity about the whole affair that has never been explained. If the child were merely a mischievous, cunning, tricky little imp, and her father the low, drunken, vulgar cheat we have been taught to believe, is it likely that they would have been so very short-sighted, so very stupid and dull of wits, as to pretend that the ghost that haunted their house was the ghost of that very Miss Fanny who had one time heard these sounds with her living ears?

Now, unless it was all planned for the sake of revenge, is it possible to conceive what was to be gained by the whole affair, the sinister result of which, to their own undoing and ruin, seems to have been very plain to the whole Parsons family long before its final collapse?

So maybe, in view of all the evidence, it is not safe to say positively that the secret of the Cock Lane ghost was finally discovered, Lord Mansfield and his verdict to the contrary notwithstanding.

THE SPORT OF FORTUNE
by Melville Davisson Post

MOST of the congregation had gone when David Talbott came out of the church. There had been a little business to transact on this Wednesday afternoon, and he had remained to speak with the class-leader. He got on his horse and began to descend the country road winding through a wood into the valley below. It was a day of early autumn. The sun lay warm on the many-colored foliage. There was silence. Nature seemed gently sinking into slumber.

Talbott was sixty-five years old. About him was every physical evidence of a never-ceasing, rigorous conflict with the soil; his shoulders were stooped, his joints big, his hands flattened and covered with a callous like bony plates. The man bore also the aspect of a rigid economy—the economy that cannot permit the tiniest detritus.

Everything about him spoke to the very slightest expenditure of money. His clothes were of jeans—that material which is country woven and wears like a skin. His boots were of cowhide, and hand-made by the village shoemaker. His shirt had been purchased at the country store, and was of that tough material called in the South "hickory." Usually he wore these shirts without a collar, but to-day, out of respect for the religious service, he had added a paper one, fastened with a detachable button, the head of which was some bright-colored composition enclosed in a brass band.

This man represented life maintained against a mean soil that would hardly support it. But industry, a painful economy, and an exact, accurate knowledge of conditions had enabled him to advance. He owned a little farm of some fifty acres, and he was out of debt. His habit of purchasing only those things which he actually required, and paying for them in cash, and his extreme care in contracting about what he would do, had in the end established his reputation for integrity.

When a man advances against difficulties that beset him, in whatever avenue of life, he takes on a certain feeling of security. In him, in spite of the humility engendered by religion, there develops a deep and abiding belief that the human mind is master over the mysterious and unknown agencies with which it is forced to contend. And in his aspect the man will come to carry this egotism. Talbott rode with his legs thrust out, his chin depressed, and his face in repose. Those things which he had wrung from the soil, and the esteem in which he was held by his neighbors, had endowed him with a feeling of security.

When Talbott turned out of the wood at the foot of the hill, he saw a man standing in the road, and beside him, drawn up on the sod, was a horse and wagon. The wagon was covered with a tarpaulin drawn over wooden bows, and within sat a woman, wrapped in a bed-quilt. Talbott knew these persons for gipsies. It was their custom in the autumn to follow this road over the mountains into the South, and to return North upon it when the winter had passed.

Talbott nodded as he approached. The gipsy stopped him.

"I would trade horses, mister," he said; "it is a good colt, but I travel, and I require an old horse."

Talbott glanced over the horse which the gipsy indicated. It was a big, iron-gray gelding; evidently young, compactly built, with short, flat, bony legs, and a deep chest. Talbott's horse was nearly fifteen years old. He saw the possibilities of this young animal, and he got down out of his saddle.

"I'll look at your horse," he said.

He went over to the wagon and began that careful examination which those who cannot afford to be mistaken are accustomed to make—that examination which scrutinizes everything, and by its sheer care eliminates the element of chance. Without the knowledge of anatomy taught in veterinary schools, this man was a judge of a horse. By long experience and by the closest observation he knew every point of the animal.

Talbott was profoundly puzzled. The horse appeared to be sound. And yet there must be some reason why this man wished to exchange a young animal for an old one. And he began again to apply those tests upon which he was accustomed to rely. Finally he discovered the trouble; the horse was "graveled" —that is, a tiny pebble had entered the hoof under the shoe. This was not a serious thing, but it would cause the horse to go lame until it gradually worked out through the top of the hoof.

Talbott rose and turned to the gipsy.

"Your horse is lame," he said.

The gipsy began profuse explanations. He ran to the horse and pointed out the small hole in the hoof which Talbott had already discovered. It was nothing; the gravel would presently work out; the horse required only to be turned to pasture for a week. But for him that was impossible; he must go on; therefore he would trade—he would trade at a sacrifice—this young horse for an old one.

TALBOTT RODE WITH HIS LEGS THRUST OUT AND HIS CHIN DEPRESSED

A certain thing pressed him; he could not stop.

What the gipsy said of the horse, Talbott knew to be true, and he would have willingly exchanged his old horse for the young one. But the evident anxiety of the man moved him to ask a bonus. And after the manner of those among whom he was accustomed to barter, he named a sum very greatly in excess of what he could hope to receive.

"I'll take twenty dollars to boot," he said.

To his astonishment, the gipsy seemed to consider this absurd demand. He began to talk, to gesticulate, to complain of the hard terms, and the situation in which he was placed, and as he talked, in his excitement he began to speak in Romany. He pointed to the woman. Talbott did not understand, but he saw that the gipsy was exceedingly anxious for this trade, and he remained firm. The man went over to the woman, they talked in Romany, excitedly and with gesticulations. Finally they got a twenty-dollar bill out of a greasy wallet; the woman held it in her hand and spoke for some time in a low voice, then the man came out into the road and handed the money to Talbott.

Talbott took his saddle on his arm, and, leading the young horse, returned to his home.

His little farm, with its thin, inhospitable soil, lay beside the river. Here in the early autumn there was some pasture, and he turned the horse into the field. That night, before the fire, alone in his house, he began to review the incidents of the trade. Why had the gipsy been so willing to give him this twenty-dollar bonus? These men were proverbially excellent judges of a horse; this one must have known that the young animal was superior to the older one for which he had exchanged it. And he became fearful lest this horse had some obscure defect which he had not discovered.

He was uneasy. And very early in the morning he caught the horse and began again with that thorough, painstaking examination that excludes error. It was the eye of which he was especially fearful. And with care and with patience he made every test, and created every condition in which a hidden defect would appear, but discovered nothing. Nevertheless, he was not wholly convinced, and throughout the day, as some further experiment occurred to him, he would return, and again verify the examination which he had made. But no defect appeared. And in spite of the abiding conviction that some potent reason must exist for this extraordinary trade, he was at last convinced that the horse was sound.

By one accustomed closely to consider the trivialities of life, no problem is abandoned. Such a one does not dismiss a puzzle that touches him at any point. His margin of gain is so slight that he dare not be involved with a thing which he does not understand, and the habit is established to remain before the enigma until its meaning appears.

Talbott continued to consider this extraordinary trade. All day in the field, about his labors, he subjected it to a certain method of exclusion after the manner in which he had examined the horse for a defect. And one by one he dismissed those theories which seemed the less likely to contain the truth. By virtue of this proceeding he finally arrived before the suggestion that probably

"I'LL TAKE TWENTY DOLLARS TO BOOT"

the twenty-dollar bill which the gipsy had so easily paid over was not good money.

He stopped before this possibility, and certain evidences advanced to support it. Counterfeit money was associated, in this country, with the stranger, the circus, the traveling salesman, the gipsy. Moreover, the man and his wife had discussed this bill, and they had easily paid it over. Having reached this point in his consideration, Talbott's mind remained there.

That evening when he went in from the field he got the bill from his leather wallet and scrutinized it carefully before the candle. It appeared not precisely the proper color. He laid it aside until morning, and examined it in the daylight. It seemed faded. He replaced it in the wallet, which he kept concealed in the mattress of his bed, and sat down to consider what he should do. He did not permit himself to decide upon the validity of this bill. He had the right to the security of the doubt. He had received it in the course of trade for valid money, and he had the right to so dispose of it. Moreover, the discoloration was slight, and had he not been seeking for the gipsy's motive he knew that he should not have marked it.

The storekeeper in the neighboring village had been urging him to purchase a certain fertilizer for his field. He had refused because he had not the money and could not afford the debt. He determined now to make this purchase, and he went in the afternoon to the village. The storekeeper was pleased to agree to Talbott's proposition. He would purchase twenty dollars' worth of the fertilizer, provided the storekeeper would undertake to sell at the store those extra bags which Talbott would not require for his field.

"When will you be goin' into town?"

"I'm expecting to go Saturday," replied the storekeeper.

And Talbott promised to bring him the money before that day.

On Friday evening Talbott went with the twenty-dollar bill to the village. The evenings were a bit chill, and there was a crowd about the stove when he entered the store. It was baiting the storekeeper. The topic of conversation was a traveling circus, advertised to visit the village, and some one was saying:

"You've got to look out for that set, Andy; they always leave their plugged half-dollars with the country storekeeper."

The crowd laughed.

"They won't leave any with me," replied the storekeeper. "I always examine silver when I take it in."

"S'pose it's a greenback?" some one said; "you can't always tell about a greenback."

"I can't," replied the storekeeper, "but the bank can. The cashier always examines your money when you deposit it, an' if you had a bad bill he'd stamp it 'counterfeit.' Now, I always remember who I get a bill from, an' if a man give me a bad one, I'd go after him an' I'd make him fork over good money for it."

Talbott stopped. He remained a moment in the door, then he spoke to the storekeeper.

"I guess I won't buy that fertilizer, Andy."

The storekeeper was surprised and annoyed. He received a good commission on this article.

"You've already bought it," he said; "I've ordered it."

Talbott was now alarmed.

"Well," he said, "I've been thinkin' it over, an' I find that I ain't just exactly in a position to take it."

The storekeeper was insistent.

"You said you'd take it."

"Yes," Talbott replied, "I thought I could manage, but things have turned out a little different from what I expected."

"You mean you haven't the money?"

Talbott hesitated. "Well, yes, . . . that's about it."

The storekeeper did not continue. He went around the counter to his desk and began to write a note countermanding his order. He knew that if Talbott had not the money, it was useless to insist; such a man could not be persuaded to incur a debt. But he was angry, and when Talbott was gone out he said:

"Now, who'd a-thought that ol' Talbott would back out of a trade?"

And he began to relate the incident, and to explain how definitely the transaction had been concluded. The crowd about the store, with the exception of the blacksmith, were inclined to take the side of the storekeeper. The blacksmith said:

"A man's sometimes disappointed about layin' his hands on money to pay for a thing, an' that's excusable. If he's got the money an' he won't stand up to his bargain, that's different. Now, I'd say that, if Talbott had the money on him, he'd be no man to back out."

This sound comment silenced the crowd. But the chagrin of the storekeeper over the loss of his commission remained. And that night he related the story to his wife. She said:

"If there's a yellow streak in a man, it 'll come out when he gets old."

Talbott returned to his home. He was annoyed over this incident. In order to extricate himself from a purchase which he now feared to make he had in a manner repudiated his word, and he had drawn perilously near to a statement that, from one point of view, was not precisely the truth. He had not the money for this purchase unless the bill was valid. And the certain test indicated by the storekeeper had alarmed him. In that moment in the door he had seen the danger. If the bank stamped this bill, he would have to find other money in its stead. And on the instant, without reflection, he had been forced to withdraw from the difficulty in the best way that he could manage.

HE GOT THE BILL FROM HIS LEATHER WALLET, AND SCRUTINIZED IT CAREFULLY

That night he reflected. He had done no wrong. He had received this money innocently and in the course of trade. He had taken it in good faith, and he was entitled to the benefit of any doubt. But deliberately to make a test such as the storekeeper indicated was neither prudent nor necessary. And it seemed to him that if the bill quietly entered the avenues of trade, other than through the doors of a bank, no one would suspect it and no one would suffer loss.

On Monday, at work in his field, he saw a young man approaching along the road. When he drew nearer, Talbott recognized him for one who had come into the community and established a summer subscription school. This man was from a distant State; his school had closed, and Talbott was curious to know why he remained. He went down to the fence and engaged the school-teacher in conversation. He learned that the man was going about to collect certain subscriptions that were due him; when these were secured, he would set out for his home. The man complained that the persons in his debt were able to pay, and in the end would do so, but they required him to await their pleasure.

Talbott had an inspiration. "How much do the people owe you?" he said.

"About twenty-five dollars," replied the school-teacher.

Talbott appeared to reflect. "I might be able to help you out a little," he said.

And he explained that to accommodate the school-teacher he would advance him twenty dollars and take an assignment of these subscriptions.

The school-teacher was pleased; this arrangement would enable him to set out on his journey without further delay. "If you have the idle money, Mr. Talbott," he said, "and if it won't inconvenience you, I would be very much obliged."

Talbott assured him that he had the money in cash; that for the present he had no use for it, and that it would gratify him to do this favor. And it was arranged that on Friday the school-teacher should come with an assignment of the subscriptions and receive the money.

In a small country community everything is known. A few days later, when Talbott entered the village on his way to the post-office, the storekeeper stopped him.

"I thought you was short of money," he said.

Talbott, who divined some reference to the fertilizer, sought refuge in an ambiguity.

"Well, yes," he said, "I've been a little hard up this fall."

The storekeeper nodded his head. "I knew it wasn't so," he said.

Talbott saw that the man referred to some other incident. "What wasn't so?"

"That you was goin' to advance the school-teacher twenty dollars."

Then Talbott realized the position into which he had unwittingly entered. He made some equivocal reply and went on to the post-office. He was greatly disturbed. He saw no way out of this dilemma except to say that he found himself unable to carry out his suggestion. And, obtaining a sheet of paper and a stamped envelop from the postmaster, he wrote a letter to the school-teacher.

There is this disadvantage in a life of integrity, that an indiscretion is all the more conspicuously marked. One does not observe a stain upon that which is already stained; it is the white background that proclaims it.

A few days later the school-teacher came into the village with the letter which he had received; he was disappointed, and he went about showing the letter, and explaining that Talbott had agreed to advance him the money, and had then repudiated that agreement. He had made his arrangements to depart, depending on what Talbott had said, and he complained.

When the gossip came to the storekeeper's wife, she said, "I always knew that ol' Talbott was crooked."

These two contracts from which Talbott had withdrawn after his word had been given, his conflicting statements about the possession of money, and his disingenuous excuses were discussed. Such conduct in one hitherto beyond reproach aggravated the obliquity of it, and public opinion began to reform itself upon this data.

Without hearing it directly, Talbott became aware of this change. Such a thing is intangible, like the air, but, like the air, perceptible. He felt it moving around him, extending itself, gaining with every day.

This change in public opinion presently became indicated in certain acts which Talbott understood, but could not resent. When, in the course of his petty trades, an element was his promise to do certain things on his part, it was suggested that the agreement be reduced to writing. And when an element was his promise to pay money, he was asked for an earnest upon the bargain. He recognized these requests as the ones which he himself had been accustomed to exact when dealing with persons not entirely to be trusted. And he recognized the excuses with which they were suggested as the very ones which he had made to the tricky and unreliable—namely, the uncertainty of life and the custom and usage of trade.

Deeply smitten by this evident distrust, he strove to discover in what esteem he was held; and he endeavored in every way that he could to surprise this secret out of those with whom he conversed and with whom he associated. But in this he never succeeded.

In such old, isolated communities, public opinion insinuates itself behind the amenities of life. By the word and by the manner of his neighbors one cannot learn that he has fallen. The liar will be no longer believed, and the thief no longer trusted, but he will not hear it from his neighbor's mouth. In the multitude of excuses, and in the safeguards with which his neighbor hedges himself about, it will sufficiently appear. Nevertheless, like one ill of some desperate malady, who suspects the physician of having warned his family while offering to himself consoling words, Talbott, in his manner and by the subtleties of speech, probed for the truth. But it was by accident that he found it.

One evening in the village he passed some children at play; they spoke to him pleasantly, but when he had gone by he heard the storekeeper's little girl remark to a companion, " You'd think ol' Talbott would be ashamed to show his face after my pap caught him in a lie."

Talbott went on, but the truth was now naked before him. He walked past the blacksmith's shop, out to the little house by the roadside where the shoemaker kept the village post-office. There he stopped and reflected; this matter must be somehow cleared up. It was unjust that he should be so regarded. But how could he clear it up? How could he explain? What could he say? The incidents going to establish this conclusion were all incontrovertible. And yet this opinion of him was unjust. He had been caught in a certain conjunction of events and carried forward, whither he had not willed. His theory of life had been very simple—that one received here what his acts deserved. Virtue had its reward, and its negation its reward. And over the affairs of men a Judge presided who dealt according to this rule of thumb. One controlled events. One's agency was free. What one did and what one did not were wholly matters of one's own selection. Or how else could the scheme of things be just? He had depended on this theory, and now, somehow, it had failed him.

That night alone in his house, he sat for a long time before the fire. He was perplexed. He was like a litigant who has got an unjust decision from a judge whose integrity he cannot doubt. Such a one reviews each detail in his case with painful recurrence, seeking that aspect of it which could have influenced the court against him. And Talbott, like that litigant, believed himself the victim of some error. Certain injustices were,

in this case, too clearly indicated. His conscience was not against him; he had intended no injury to any man, and he had, in fact, done no man an injury; and yet as a result of certain trivial events he would be ruined.

And after he had gone to bed he lay a long time staring at the whitewashed ceiling. How could it happen that one questionable thing outweighed all those blameless acts that heretofore had made up the sum total of his life? He had told the truth innumerable times; he had dealt fairly innumerable times; and yet the force and virtue of this mass yielded before a single disingenuous incident, and that incident of the most trifling moment. How did it happen that such a hideous virility lay in those events that are hostile to us?

He could not sleep, and he got up and went out onto the porch of his house. A fog was rising from the river and creeping across the field slowly toward him, and he thought how this heavy mist symbolized that sinister influence which had been let loose against him, and which he could neither seize nor resist. And the oldest explanation in the world to account for the evil potentiality of incidents otherwise slight and trifling occurred to him—that by virtue of supernal powers, and through the agency of vicious persons, petty things were sometimes charged with an influence that compelled one to an evil destiny. And he recalled all the housewives' tales and all the scraps of legend that in every community lie incrusted on this ancient belief.

The hard common sense of the man dismissed this testimony. But that vague fear which lay at the root of this belief he could not dismiss. And, in spite of the sane conclusions of his reason, he began to associate his ill fortune with the possession of this twenty-dollar bill. Here were incidents of the family of those tales: the thing was a piece of money, and he had got it from a gipsy.

He returned to his bed, but he did not sleep. The suggestion remained, and he continued to regard it. The man's austere religion, rooted in the Hebrew Scriptures, accepted certain ancient legends that comprehended this idea. The ruin of men, innocent of wrong, of women, of children, of whole tribes and cities, had followed the possession of articles in themselves harmless, but charged with an evil influence. And here a suggestion presented itself, namely, that of some expiatory act. And vaguely, through the half-sleep into which he presently entered, this idea moved with the problem that disturbed him.

The following day this suggestion took on the habiliments of fancy and withdrew. Talbott went about his labors. The health of the sun and of the air encouraged him, and he endeavored to believe that the change in public opinion had not been so great or of so wide an influence. But an event of the afternoon eviscerated this hope.

When he came in from the field he saw a man sitting on his porch and a horse tied at the gate. The man was the Superintendent of Free Schools, and, as Talbott was a member of the district board, this call did not disturb him. The man remained during the entire afternoon. He talked with Talbott on every conceivable subject except that one which had moved him to this visit. As the hours passed, and the man's conversation remained general, Talbott became uneasy. He knew what this subterfuge portended; when one had a disagreeable thing to say he remained for a long time, and always approached it after an interminable discussion of subjects in no way related to it. Talbott's anxiety was presently justified.

When the Superintendent of Schools had finished his visit and gone out to his horse, he finally said the word:

" By-the-way, Mr. Talbott, the people think that the school board ought to be made up of men who have children to educate—naturally a man with a family could afford to give more of his time to school matters; so, if you have no objection, the people would like to have Henry Lightwood on the board."

Talbott was forced to express himself as satisfied with this successor, and the Superintendent of Schools rode away.

Talbott was not deceived by these excuses. And that night the idea of some sinister influence attached to the piece of money assailed and possessed him. The reputation which during a lifetime he had laboriously established seem-

ed now to be attacked by a deadly and insidious erosion. He was like one forced to observe a bronze which he cherished, eaten by some invisible agencies lying in the very odors of his garden. And on every occasion and at every hour he could see the metal that once had been so hard and bright scaling from the figure, and he could see this figure, that once had been a thing of beauty, changing perceptibly into something formless.

And the suggestion of an expiatory act returned to him with a greater force. Those visited by misfortune have in all ages believed that the authority moving events could be appeased. One brought an offering to the temple, or cast a gift into the sea. And, under forms and subterfuges, the custom remains. This man, possessed by fear, and prepared by the precedents abounding in the sacred books of his religion, moved toward this idea.

The following Sunday an itinerant minister preached at the church. This man was a sort of celebrity, who on occasion traveled through the country. The unrestraint of his speech and his violent and erratic manner assured him an audience. On this day the grove before the church was filled with horses; every seat in the church was occupied, and persons stood along the wall. Talbott sat on the first bench before the pulpit. He had made up his mind about what he intended to do, and when the man called upon him to take up the collection, he put the twenty-dollar bill into his hat.

The minister rose and began to speak to the congregation while the collection went forward. In order to prick this man to some intemperate speech, it had been the custom of certain mischievous persons to put mutilated coins, tokens, and the like into his collection, and it was against this habit that he now uttered his invective. He threatened such offenders with the law. Such acts were comprehended by the criminal statutes against counterfeit money; they were felonies, punishable by imprisonment in the penitentiary. He had consulted with the authorities. He would put up with it no longer. And with gestures and with violence he presented the terrors and the severities of the law.

The dense crowd forced Talbott to move slowly, and as the minister spoke he was seized with terror. He had not thought of the law, and the fear of it chilled him. If this bill were counterfeit, he was on the point of committing a crime. This man would denounce him, and he would be wholly and inextricably ruined. And as the minister continued, and as he went forward with the collection, the thing which he was about to do seemed to be the very refinement of madness. Finally appalled by the danger, as he turned the collection out onto the table he slipped the bill into his hand, and, returning to his seat, got it into his pocket. He was cold and his body was sprayed with sweat. He sat on the bench breathing deeply, like one who, with his foot extended, is plucked backward from an abyss.

When the minister announced the result of the collection, some eighteen dollars, there was a whispering about the congregation, and when the service was concluded some persons went forward to speak with the minister. This was usual, and without giving it any attention Talbott went out with the crowd. He had got his horse, when some one came to the door and called him; when he entered there was a little crowd in discussion before the pulpit. The minister came forward.

"Brother Talbott," he said, "I wish you'd look under the band of your hat; some of the congregation thought they saw a twenty-dollar bill in the collection." And he began to explain how, when the hat was turned over, money sometimes slipped under the band and remained there.

Talbott was appalled. He presented his hat and began to turn up the band. But nothing appeared.

The persons standing around the minister made no comment while Talbott remained. But when he had gone out somebody said:

"An' he's a thief, too!"

On an afternoon of early March, Talbott rode again down the wooded hill from the country church. Beyond him the great road ran over the mountains into the South. He was on his way into some new country. He had sold his little farm, and about him, on the horse, he carried all that he possessed. At the turn of the wood he saw several covered wagons moving along the great road from the direction of the mountains. He continued to observe them now and then through the openings of the trees. Finally, at the foot of the hill, he met these wagons. As he approached, in the last team he saw his old horse that he had traded to the gipsy. He stopped. The man walking beside the wagon ran over, and, lifting the foot of Talbott's horse, began to examine it.

"He's got well," he said, "the young horse. I have sorrow to trade him." Then he rose. "But a child was to be born and I must get to my own people then."

He drew back a corner of the tarpaulin and revealed a woman holding a baby in her arms.

Talbott was not listening to this speech; he had been getting out his wallet.

"I want you to take back this counterfeit money," he said.

The gipsy looked puzzled.

"What is that you say, mister?"

Talbott presented the twenty-dollar bill.

"I want you to take back this counterfeit money that you gave me."

The gipsy came over to Talbott; he looked at the faded bill, then his face brightened with comprehension.

"That money, mister, it have been wet with water, but bad! no, it is good. I will give you gold."

And he handed Talbott two eagles.

THE MOVING FINGER
by Edith Wharton

"SHE WAS THE MOST BEAUTIFUL . . . OF EXPLANATIONS"

HE news of Mrs. Grancy's death came to me with the shock of an immense blunder — one of fate's most irretrievable acts of vandalism. It was as though all sorts of renovating forces had been checked by the clogging of that one wheel. Not that Mrs. Grancy contributed any perceptible momentum to the social machine: her unique distinction was that of filling to perfection her special place in the world. There are so many people like badly composed statues, overlapping their niches at one point and leaving them vacant at another. Mrs. Grancy's niche was her husband's life; and if it be argued that the space was not large enough for its vacancy to leave a very big gap, I can only say that, at the last resort, such dimensions must be determined by finer instruments than any ready-made standard of utility. Ralph Grancy's was, in short, a kind of disembodied usefulness— one of those constructive influences that, instead of crystallizing into definite forms, remain as it were a medium for the development of clear thinking and fine feeling. He faithfully irrigated his own dusty patch of life, and the fruitful moisture stole far beyond his boundaries. If, to carry on the metaphor, Grancy's life was a sedulously cultivated enclosure, his wife was the flower he had planted in its midst—the embowering tree, rather, which gave him rest and shade at its foot and the wind of dreams in its upper branches.

We had all—his small but devoted band of followers—known a moment when it seemed likely that Grancy would fail us. We had watched him pitted against one stupid obstacle after another—ill health, poverty, misunderstanding and, worst of all for a man of his texture, his first wife's soft insidious egotism. We had seen him sinking under the leaden embrace of her affection like a swimmer in a drowning clutch; but just as we despaired he had always come to the surface again, blinded, panting, but striking out fiercely for the shore. When at last her death released him, it became a question as to how much of the man she had carried with her. Left alone, he revealed numb withered patches, like a tree from which a parasite has been stripped. But gradually he began to put out new leaves; and when he met the lady who was to become his second wife—his one *real* wife, as his friends reckoned—the whole man burst into flower.

The second Mrs. Grancy was past thirty when he married her, and it was clear that she had harvested that crop of middle joy which is rooted in young despair. But if she had lost the surface of eighteen, she had kept its inner light; if her cheek lacked the gloss of immaturity, her eyes were young with the stored youth of half a lifetime. Grancy had first known her somewhere in the East—I believe she was the sister of one of our consuls out there—and when he brought her home to New York she came among us as a stranger. The idea of Grancy's remarriage had been a shock to us all. After one such calcining most men would have kept out of the fire; but we agreed that he was predestined to sentimental blunders and we awaited with resignation the embodiment of his latest mistake. Then Mrs. Grancy came—and we understood. She was the most beautiful and the most complete of explanations. We shuffled our defeated omniscience out of sight, and gave it hasty burial under a prodigality of welcome. For the first time in years we had Grancy off our minds. "He'll do something great now!" the least sanguine of us prophesied; and our sentimentalist emended, "He *has* done it—in marrying her!"

It was Claydon, the portrait-painter, who risked this hyperbole, and who soon afterward, at the happy husband's request, prepared to defend it in a portrait of Mrs. Grancy. We were all—even Claydon—ready to concede that Mrs. Grancy's unwontedness was in some degree a matter of environment. Her graces were complementary and it needed the mate's call to reveal the flash of color beneath her neutral-tinted wings. But if she needed Grancy to interpret her, how much greater was the service she rendered him! Claydon professionally described her as the right frame for him; but if she defined, she also enlarged; if she threw the whole into perspective, she also cleared new ground, opened fresh vistas, reclaimed whole areas of activity that had run to waste under the harsh husbandry of privation. This interaction of sympathies was not without its visible expression. Claydon was not alone in maintaining that Grancy's presence—or indeed the mere mention of his name—had a perceptible effect on his wife's appearance. It was as though a light were shifted, a curtain drawn back; as though, to borrow another of Claydon's metaphors, Love, the indefatigable artist, were perpetually seeking a happier "pose" for his model. In this interpretative light Mrs. Grancy acquired the charm which makes some women's faces like a book of which the last page is never turned. There was always something new to read in her eyes. What Claydon read there—or at least such scattered hints of the ritual as reached him through the sanctuary doors—his portrait in due course declared to us. When the picture was exhibited, it was at once acclaimed as his masterpiece; but the people who knew Mrs. Grancy smiled and said it was flattered. Claydon, however, had not set out to paint *their* Mrs. Grancy—or ours, even—but Ralph's; and Ralph knew his own at a glance. At the first confrontation he saw that Claydon had understood. As for Mrs. Grancy, when the finished picture was shown to her she turned to the painter and said simply, " Ah, you've done me facing the east!"

The picture, then, for all its value, seemed a mere incident in the unfolding of their double destiny a foot-note to the illuminated text of their lives. It was not till afterward that it acquired the significance of last words spoken on a threshold never to be recrossed. Grancy, a year after his marriage, had given up his town house and carried his bliss an hour's journey away, to a little place among the hills. His various duties and interests brought him frequently to New York, but we necessarily saw him less often than when his house had served as the rallying-point of kindred enthusiasms. It seemed a pity that such an influence should be withdrawn, but we all felt that his long arrears of happiness should be paid in whatever coin he chose. The distance from which the fortunate couple radiated warmth on us was not too great for friendship to traverse; and our conception of a glorified leisure took the form of Sundays spent in the Grancys' library, with its sedative rural outlook, and the portrait of Mrs. Grancy illuminating its studious walls. The picture was at its best in that setting; and we used to accuse Claydon of visiting Mrs. Grancy in order to see her portrait. He met this by declaring that the portrait *was* Mrs. Grancy; and there were moments when the statement seemed unanswerable. One of us, indeed—I think it must have been the novelist—said that Claydon had been saved from falling in love with Mrs. Grancy only by falling in love with his picture of her; and it was noticeable that he, to whom his finished work was no more than the shed husk of future effort, showed a perennial tenderness for this one achievement. We smiled afterward to think how often, when Mrs. Grancy was in the room, her presence reflecting itself in our talk like a gleam of sky in a hurrying current, Claydon, averted from the real woman, would sit as it were listening to the picture. His attitude, at the time, seemed only a part of the unusualness of those picturesque afternoons, when the most familiar combinations of life underwent a magical

change. Some human happiness is a landlocked lake; but the Grancys' was an open sea, stretching a buoyant and illimitable surface to the voyaging interests of life. There was room and to spare on those waters for all our separate ventures; and always, beyond the sunset, a mirage of the fortunate isles toward which our prows were bent.

II

It was in Rome that, three years later, I heard of her death. The notice said " suddenly "; I was glad of that. I was glad, too—basely, perhaps—to be away from Grancy at a time when silence must have seemed obtuse and speech derisive.

I was still in Rome when, a few months afterward, he suddenly arrived there. He had been appointed secretary of legation at Constantinople, and was on the way to his post. He had taken the place, he said frankly, " to get away." Our relations with the Porte held out a prospect of hard work, and that, he explained, was what he needed. He could never be satisfied to sit down among the ruins. I saw that, like most of us in moments of extreme moral tension, he was playing a part, behaving as he thought it became a man to behave in the eye of disaster. The instinctive posture of grief is a shuffling compromise between defiance and prostration; and pride feels the need of striking a worthier attitude in face of such a foe. Grancy, by nature musing and retrospective, had chosen the rôle of the man of action, who answers blow for blow and opposes a mailed front to the thrusts of destiny; and the completeness of the equipment testified to his inner weakness. We talked only of what we were not thinking of, and parted, after a few days, with a sense of relief that proved the inadequacy of friendship to perform in such cases the office assigned to it by tradition.

Soon afterward my own work called me home, but Grancy remained several years in Europe. International diplomacy kept its promise of giving him work to do, and during the year in which he acted as *chargé d'affaires* he acquitted himself, under trying conditions, with conspicuous zeal and discretion. A political redistribution of matter removed him from office just as he had proved his usefulness to the government; and the following summer I heard that he had come home and was down at his place in the country.

On my return to town I wrote him, and his reply came by the next post. He answered as it were in his natural voice, urging me to spend the following Sunday with him and suggesting that I should bring down any of the old set who could be persuaded to join me. I thought this a good sign, and yet—shall I own it?—I was vaguely disappointed. Perhaps we are apt to feel that our friends' sorrows should be kept like those historic monuments from which the encroaching ivy is periodically removed.

That very evening at the club I ran across Claydon. I told him of Grancy's invitation and proposed that we should go down together; but he pleaded an engagement. I was sorry, for I had always felt that he and I stood nearer Ralph than the others, and if the old Sundays were to be renewed, I should have preferred that we two should spend the first alone with him. I said as much to Claydon, and offered to fit my time to his; but he met this by a general refusal.

" I don't want to go to Grancy's," he said bluntly.

I waited a moment, but he appended no qualifying clause.

" You've seen him since he came back?" I finally ventured.

Claydon nodded.

" And is he so awfully bad?"

" Bad? No; he's all right."

" All right? How can he be, unless he's changed beyond all recognition?"

" Oh, you'll recognize *him*," said Claydon, with a puzzling deflection of emphasis.

His ambiguity was beginning to exasperate me, and I felt myself shut out from some knowledge to which I had as good a right as he.

" You've been down there already, I suppose?"

" Yes, I've been down there."

" And you've done with each other— the partnership is dissolved?"

" Done with each other? I wish to God we had!" He rose nervously and tossed aside the review from which my approach had diverted him. " Look here," he said, standing before me, " Ralph's the best fellow going and there's nothing un-

der heaven I wouldn't do for him—short of going down there again." And with that he walked out of the room.

Claydon was incalculable enough for me to read a dozen different meanings into his words; but none of my interpretations satisfied me. I determined, at any rate, to seek no farther for a companion; and the next Sunday I travelled down to Grancy's alone. He met me at the station and I saw at once that he had changed since our last meeting. Then he had been in fighting array, but now if he and grief still housed together it was no longer as enemies. Physically the transformation was as marked, but less reassuring. If the spirit triumphed, the body showed its scars. At five-and-forty he was gray and stooping, with the tired gait of an old man. His serenity, however, was not the resignation of age. I saw that he did not mean to drop out of the game. Almost immediately he began to speak of our old interests, not with an effort, as at our former meeting, but simply and naturally, in the tone of a man whose life has flowed back into its normal channels. I remembered, with a touch of self-reproach, how I had distrusted his reconstructive powers; but my admiration for his reserved force was now tinged by the sense that, after all, such happiness as his ought to have been paid with his last coin. The feeling grew as we neared the house, and I found how inextricably his wife was interwoven with my remembrance of the place; how the whole scene was but an extension of that vivid presence.

Within-doors nothing was changed, and my hand would have dropped without surprise into her welcoming clasp. It was luncheon-time, and Grancy led me at once to the dining-room, where the walls, the furniture, the very plate and porcelain, seemed a mirror in which a moment since her face had been reflected. I wondered whether Grancy, under the recovered tranquillity of his smile, concealed the same sense of her nearness, saw perpetually between himself and the actual her bright unappeasable ghost. He spoke of her once or twice in an easy incidental way, and her name seemed to hang in the air after he had uttered it, like a chord that continues to vibrate. If he felt her presence it was evidently as an enveloping medium, the moral atmosphere in which he breathed. I had never before known how completely the dead may survive.

After luncheon we went for a long walk through the autumnal fields and woods, and dusk was falling when we reentered the house. Grancy led the way to the library, where at this hour his wife had always welcomed us back to a bright fire and a cup of tea. The room faced the west and held a clear light of its own after the rest of the house had grown dark. I remembered how young she had looked in this pale gold light, which irradiated her eyes and hair, or silhouetted her girlish outline as she passed before the windows. Of all the rooms in the library was most peculiarly hers; and here I felt that her nearness might take visible shape. Then, all in a moment, as Grancy opened the door, the feeling vanished, and a kind of resistance met me on the threshold. I looked about me. Was the room changed? Had some desecrating hand effaced the traces of her presence? No; here too the setting was undisturbed. My feet sank into the same deep-piled Daghestan; the bookshelves took the firelight on the same rows of rich subdued bindings; her arm-chair stood in its old place near the tea-table; and from the opposite wall her face confronted me.

Her face—but *was* it hers? I moved nearer and stood looking up at the portrait. Grancy's glance had followed mine and I heard him move to my side.

"You see a change in it?" he said.

"What does it mean?" I asked.

"It means—that five years have passed."

"Over *her?*"

"Why not? Look at me!" He pointed to his gray hair and furrowed temples. "What do you think kept *her* so young? It was happiness! But now—" he looked up at her with infinite tenderness. "I like her better so," he said. "It's what she would have wished."

"Have wished?"

"That we should grow old together. Do you think she would have wanted to be left behind?"

I stood speechless, my gaze travelling from his worn grief-beaten features to the painted face above. It was not fur-

rowed like his; but a veil of years seemed to have descended on it. The bright hair had lost its elasticity, the cheek its clearness, the brow its light—the whole woman had waned.

Grancy laid his hand on my arm. "You don't like it?" he said sadly.

"Like it? I—I've lost her!" I burst out.

"And I've found her," he answered.

"In *that?*" I cried, with a reproachful gesture.

"Yes, in that." He swung round on me almost defiantly. "The other had become a sham, a lie! This is the way she would have looked—does look, I mean. Claydon ought to know, oughtn't he?"

I turned suddenly. "Did Claydon do this for you?"

Grancy nodded.

"Since your return?"

"Yes; I sent for him after I'd been back a week—"

He turned away and gave a thrust to the smouldering fire. I followed, glad to leave the picture behind me. Grancy threw himself into a chair near the hearth, so that the light fell on his sensitive variable face. He leaned his head back, shading his eyes with his hand, and began to speak.

III

"You fellows knew enough of my early history to guess what my second marriage meant to me. I say guess, because no one could understand—really. I've always had a feminine streak in me, I suppose—the need of a pair of eyes that should see with me, of a pulse that should keep time with mine. Life is a big thing, of course; a magnificent spectacle; but I got so tired of looking at it alone! Still, it's always good to live, and I had plenty of happiness—of the evolved kind. What I'd never had a taste of was the simple inconscient sort that one breathes in like the air. . . .

"Well—I met her. It was like finding the climate in which I was meant to live. You know what she was—how indefinitely she multiplied one's points of contact with life, how she lit up the caverns and bridged the abysses. Well, I swear to you (though I suppose the sense of all that was latent in me) that what I used to think of on my way home at the end of the day was simply that when I opened this door she'd be sitting over there, with the lamp-light falling in a particular way on one little curl in her neck. . . . When Claydon painted her he caught just the look she used to lift to mine when I came in—I've wondered, sometimes, at his knowing how she looked when she and I were alone. How I rejoiced in that picture! I used to say to her: 'You're my prisoner now—I shall never lose you. If you grew tired of me and left me, you'd leave your real self there on the wall!' It was always one of our jokes that she was going to grow tired of me—

"Three years of it—and then she died. It was so sudden that there was no change, no diminution. It was as if she had suddenly become fixed, immovable, like her own portrait; as if Time had ceased at its happiest hour, just as Claydon had thrown down his brush one day and said, 'I can't do better than that.'

"I went away, as you know, and staid over there five years. I worked as hard as I knew how, and after the first black months a little light stole in on me. From thinking that she would have been interested in what I was doing, I came to feel that she *was* interested—that she was there and that she knew. I'm not talking any psychical jargon—I'm simply trying to express the sense I had that an influence so full, so abounding as hers couldn't pass like a spring shower. We had so lived into each other's hearts and

"I HAD THE FEELING THAT SHE DIDN'T EVEN RECOGNIZE ME"

minds that the consciousness of what she would have thought and felt illuminated all I did. At first she used to come back shyly, tentatively, as though not sure of finding me; then she staid longer and longer, till at last she became again the very air I breathed.... There were bad moments, of course, when her nearness mocked me with the loss of the real woman; but gradually the distinction between the two was effaced and the mere thought of her grew warm as flesh and blood.

"Then I came home. I landed in the morning and came straight down here. The thought of seeing her portrait possessed me, and my heart beat like a lover's as I opened the library door. It was in the afternoon and the room was full of light. It fell on her picture—the picture of a young and radiant woman. She smiled at me coldly across the distance that divided us. I had the feeling that she didn't even recognize me. And then I caught sight of myself in the mirror over there—a gray-haired broken man whom she had never known!

"For a week we two lived together—the strange woman and the strange man. I used to sit night after night and question her smiling face; but no answer ever came. What did she know of me, after all? We were irrevocably separated by the five years of life that lay between us. At times, as I sat here, I almost grew to hate her; for her presence had driven away my gentle ghost—the real wife who had wept, aged, struggled with me during those awful years.... It was the worst loneliness I've ever known. Then, gradually, I began to notice a look of sadness in the picture's eyes; a look that seemed to say, 'Don't you see that *I* am lonely too?' And all at once it came over me how she would have hated to be left behind! I remembered her comparing life to a heavy book that could not be read with ease unless two people held it together; and I thought how impatiently her hand would have turned the pages that divided us! So the idea came to me: 'It's the picture that stands between us; the picture that is dead, and not my wife. To sit in this room is to keep watch beside a corpse.' As this feeling grew on me the portrait became like a beautiful mausoleum in which she had

been buried alive; I could hear her beating against the painted walls and crying to me faintly for help....

"One day I found I couldn't stand it any longer and I sent for Claydon. He came down, and I told him what I'd been through and what I wanted him to do. At first he refused point-blank to touch the picture. The next morning I went off for a long tramp and when I came home I found him sitting here alone. He looked at me sharply for a moment and then he said, 'I've changed my mind; I'll do it.' I arranged one of the north rooms as a studio and he shut himself up there for a day; then he sent for me. The picture stood there as you see it now—it was as though she'd met me on the threshold and taken me in her arms! I tried to thank him, to tell him what it meant to me, but he cut me short.

"'There's an up train at five, isn't there?' he asked. 'I'm booked for a dinner to-night. I shall just have time to make a bolt for the station and you can send my traps after me.' I haven't seen him since....

"I can guess what it cost him to lay hands on his masterpiece; but, after all, to him it was only a picture lost; to me it was my wife regained!"

IV

After that, for ten years or more, I watched the strange spectacle of a life of hopeful and productive effort based on the structure of a dream. There could be no doubt to those who saw Grancy during this period that he drew his strength and courage from the sense of his wife's mystic participation in his task. When I went back to see him a few months later I found the portrait had been removed from the library and placed in a small study upstairs, to which he had transferred his desk and a few books. He told me he always sat there when he was alone, keeping the library for his Sunday visitors. Those who missed the portrait of course made no comment on its absence, and the few who were in his secret respected it. Gradually all his old friends had gathered about him and our Sunday afternoons regained something of their former character; but Claydon never reappeared among us.

As I look back now I see that Grancy must have been failing from the time of his return home. His invincible spirit belied and disguised the signs of weakness that afterward asserted themselves in my remembrance of him. He seemed to have an inexhaustible fund of life to draw on, and more than one of us was a pensioner on his superfluity.

Nevertheless, when I came back one summer from my European holiday and heard that he had been at the point of death, I understood at once that we had believed him well only because he wished us to.

I hastened down to the country and found him midway in a slow convalescence. I felt then that he was lost to us and he read my thought at a glance.

"Ah," he said, "I'm an old man now and no mistake. I suppose we shall have to go half-speed after this; but we sha'n't need towing just yet!"

The plural pronoun struck me, and involuntarily I locked up at Mrs. Grancy's portrait. Line by line I saw my fear reflected in it. It was the face of a woman *who knows that her husband is dying.*

My heart stood still at the thought of what Claydon had done.

Grancy had followed my glance. "Yes, it's changed her," he said quietly. "For months, you know, it was touch and go with me—we had a long fight of it and it was worse for her than for me." After a pause he added "Claydon has been very kind; he's so busy nowadays that I seldom see him, but when I sent for him the other day he came down at once."

I was silent, and we spoke no more of Grancy's illness; but when I took leave it seemed like shutting him in alone with his death-warrant.

The next time I went down to see him he looked much better. It was a Sunday and he received me in the library, so that I did not see the portrait again. He continued to improve and toward spring we began to feel that, as he had said, he might yet travel a long way without being towed.

One evening, on returning to town after a visit which had confirmed my sense of reassurance, I found Claydon dining alone at the club. He asked me to join

him, and over the coffee our talk turned to his work.

"If you're not too busy," I said at length, "you ought to make time to go down to Grancy's again."

He looked up quickly. "Why?" he asked.

"Because he's quite well again," I returned with a touch of cruelty. "His wife's prognostications were mistaken."

Claydon stared at me a moment. "Oh, *she* knows," he affirmed with a smile that chilled me.

"You mean to leave the portrait as it is, then?" I persisted.

He shrugged his shoulders. "He hasn't sent for me yet!" A waiter came up with the cigars, and Claydon rose and joined another group.

It was just a fortnight later that Grancy's housekeeper telegraphed for me. She met me at the station with the news that he had been "taken bad" and that the doctors were with him.

I had to wait for some time in the deserted library before the medical men appeared. They had the baffled manner of empirics who have been superseded by the great Healer, and I lingered only long enough to hear that Grancy was not suffering and that my presence could do him no harm.

I found him seated in his arm-chair in the little study. He held out his hand with a smile.

"You see she was right, after all," he said.

"She?" I repeated, perplexed for the moment.

"My wife." He indicated the picture. "Of course I knew she had no hope from the first. I saw that"—he lowered his voice — "after Claydon had been here. But I wouldn't believe it at first!"

I caught his hands in mine. "For God's sake don't believe it now!" I adjured him.

He shook his head gently. "It's too late," he said. "I might have known that she knew."

"But, Grancy, listen to me," I began; and then I stopped. What could I say that would convince him? There was no common ground of argument on which we could meet; and after all it would be easier for him to die feeling that she *had* known. Strangely enough, I saw that Claydon had missed his mark....

V

Grancy's will named me as one of his executors; and my associate, having other duties on his hands, begged me to assume the task of carrying out our friend's wishes. This placed me under the necessity of informing Claydon that the portrait of Mrs. Grancy had been bequeathed to him; and he replied by the next post that he would send for the picture at once. I was staying in the deserted house when the portrait was taken away; and as the door closed on it I felt that Grancy's presence had vanished too. Was it his turn to follow her now, and could one ghost haunt another?

After that, for a year or two, I heard nothing more of the picture, and though I met Claydon from time to time we had little to say to each other. I had no definable grievance against the man and I tried to remember that he had done a fine thing in sacrificing his best picture to a friend; but my resentment had all the tenacity of unreason.

One day, however, a lady whose portrait he had just finished begged me to go with her to see it. To refuse was impossible, and I went with the less reluctance that I knew I was not the only person invited. The others were all grouped around the easel when I entered, and after contributing my share to the chorus of approval I turned away and began to stroll about the studio. Claydon was something of a collector and his things were generally worth looking at. The studio was a long tapestried room with a curtained archway at one end. The curtains were looped back, showing a smaller apartment, with books and flowers and a few fine bits of bronze and porcelain. The tea-table standing in this inner room proclaimed that it was open to inspection, and I wandered in. A *bleu poudré* vase first attracted me; then I turned to examine a slender bronze Ganymede, and in so doing found myself face to face with Mrs. Grancy's portrait. I stared up at it blankly and the face smiled back at me in all the recovered radiance of youth. The artist had effaced every trace of his later touches and the original picture had reappeared. It throned alone on the

panelled wall, asserting a brilliant supremacy over its carefully chosen surroundings. I felt in an instant that the whole room was tributary to it — that Claydon had heaped his treasures at the feet of the woman he loved. Yes—it was the woman he had loved, and not the picture; and my instinctive resentment was explained.

Suddenly I felt a hand on my shoulder. "Ah, how could you?" I cried, turning on him.

"How could I?" he retorted. "How could I *not*? Doesn't she belong to me now?"

I moved away impatiently.

"Wait a moment," he said with a detaining gesture. "The others have gone and I want to say a word to you— Oh, I know what you've thought of me—I can guess! You think I killed Grancy, I suppose?"

I was startled by his sudden vehemence. "I think you tried to do a cruel thing," I said slowly.

"Ah—what a little way you others see into life!" he murmured. "Sit down a moment—here, where we can look at her—and I'll tell you."

He threw himself on the ottoman beside me and sat gazing up at the picture, with his hands clasped about his knee.

"Pygmalion," he began slowly, "turned his statue into a real woman; *I* turned my real woman into a picture. Small compensation, you think—but you don't know how much of a woman belongs to you after you've painted her! Well, I made the best of it, at any rate— I gave her the best I had in me; and she gave me in return what such a woman gives by merely being. And after all she rewarded me enough by making me paint as I shall never paint again. There was one side of her, though that was mine alone, and that was her beauty; for no one else understood it. To Grancy, even, it was the mere expression of herself—what language is to thought. Even when he saw the picture he didn't guess my secret—he was so sure she was all his! As though a man should think he owned the moon because it was reflected in the pool at his door—

"Well—when he came home and sent for me to change the picture, it was like asking me to commit murder. He wanted me to make an old woman of her—of her who had been so divinely, unchangeably young! As if any man who really loved a woman would ask her to sacrifice her youth and beauty for his sake! At first I told him I couldn't do it—but afterward, when he left me alone with the picture, something queer happened. I suppose it was because I was always so confoundedly fond of Grancy that it went against me to refuse what he asked. .... Anyhow, as I sat looking up at her, she seemed to say, 'I'm not yours, but his, and I want you to make me what he wishes.' And so I did it. I could have cut my hand off when the work was done —I dare say he told you I never would go back and look at it. He thought I was too busy—he never understood....

"Well—and then last year he sent for me again—you remember. It was after his illness, and he told me he'd grown twenty years older and that he wanted her to grow older too—he didn't want her to be left behind. The doctors all thought he was going to get well at that time, and

he thought so too; and so did I when I first looked at him. But when I turned to the picture—ah! now I don't ask you to believe me, but I swear it was *her* face that told me he was dying, and that she wanted him to know it! She had a message for him and she made me deliver it."

He rose abruptly and walked toward the portrait; then he sat down beside me again.

"Cruel? Yes, it seemed so to me at first; and this time, if I resisted, it was for *his* sake and not for mine. But all the while I felt her eyes drawing me, and gradually she made me understand. If she'd been there in the flesh (she seemed to say) wouldn't she have seen before any of us that he was dying? Wouldn't he have read the news first in her face? And wouldn't it be horrible if now he should discover it instead in strange eyes? Well—that was what she wanted of me and I did it. I kept them together to the last!" He looked up at the picture again. "But now she belongs to me," he repeated.

THE FROG THAT PLAYED
THE TROMBONE
by Brander Matthews

ON a corner of my desk there stands a china shell; its flat and oval basin is about as broad as the palm of my hand; it is a spotted brownish-yellow on the outside, and a purply-pinkish white on the inside; and on the crinkled edge of one end there sits a green frog with his china mouth wide open, thus revealing the ruddy hollow of his interior. At the opposite end of the shell there is a page of china music, purporting to be the first four bars of a song by Schubert. Time was when the frog held in his long greenish-yellow arms a still longer trombone made of bright brass wire, bent into shape, and tipped with a flaring disk of gilded porcelain. In the days when the china frog was young he pretended to be playing on the brass trombone. Despite its musical assertiveness, the function of the frog that played the trombone was humble enough: the shell was designed to serve as a receiver for the ashes of cigars and cigarettes. But it is a score of years at least since the china frog has held the brass trombone to its open lips. Only a few months after he gave his first mute concert on the corner of my table the carelessness of a chance visitor toppled him over on the floor, and broke off both his arms and so bent the trombone that even the barren pretence of his solo became an impossibility. A week or two later the battered musical instrument disappeared; and ever since then the gaping mouth of the frog has seemed to suggest that he was trying to sing Schubert's song. His open countenance, I am sorry to say, has often tempted my friends to make sport of him. They have filled the red emptiness of his body with the gray ashes of their cigars; they have even gone so far as to put the stump of a half-smoked cigarette between his lips, as though he were solacing himself thus for the loss of his voice.

Although the frog is no longer playing an inaudible tune on an immovable instrument, I keep it on a corner of my desk, where it has been for nearly twenty years. Sometimes of a winter's night, when I take my seat at the desk before the crackling and cheerful hickory fire, the frog that played the trombone catches my eye, and I go back in memory to the evening when it performed its first solo in my presence, and I see again the beautiful liquid eyes of the friend who brought it to me. We were very young then, both of us, that night before Christmas, and our hearts kept time with the lilt of the tune that the frog played silently on his trombone. Now I am young no longer, I am even getting old, and my friend has been dead this many a year. Sometimes, as I look at the gaping frog, I know that if I could hear the song he is trying to sing I should hate it for the memories it would recall.

He who gave it to me was not a school-fellow, a companion of my boyhood, but he was the friend of my youth and a classmate in college. It was in our Junior year that he joined us, bringing a good report from the fresh-water college where he had been for two years. I can recall his shy attitude the first morning in chapel when we were wondering what sort of a fellow the tall, dark, handsome new-comer might be. The accidents of the alphabet put us side by side in certain class-rooms, and I soon learned to know him, and to like him more and more with increasing knowledge. He was courte-ous, gentle, kindly, ever ready to do a favor, ever grateful for help given him, and if he had a fault it was this, that he was jealous of his friends. Although his nature was healthy and manly, he had a feminine craving for affection, and an almost womanly unreason in the exac-tions he made on his friends. Yet he was ever ready to spend himself for oth-ers, and to do to all as he would be done by.

Although fond of out-door sports, his health was not robust. He lacked stam-ina. There was more than a hint of consumption in the brightness of his eye, in the spot of color on his cheek, in the hollowness of his chest, and in the cough which sometimes seized him in the mid-dle of a recitation. Toward the end of our Senior year he broke down once, and was kept from college a week; but the spring came early, and with the return-ing warmth of the sunshine he made an effort and took his place with us again. He was a good scholar, but not one of the best in the class. He did his work faith-fully in the main, having no relish for science, but enjoying the flavor of the classics. He studied German that year, and he used to come to me reciting Heine's poems with enthusiasm, carried away by the sentiment, but shocked by the witty cynicism which serves as its corrective. He wrote a little verse now and then, as young men do, immature, of course, and individual only in so far as it was morbid. I think that he would have liked to devote himself to literature as a career, but it had been decided that he was to study law.

After class day and Commencement the class scattered forever. In September, when I returned to New York and settled down to my profession, I found my friend at the Columbia Law School. His fa-ther had died during the summer, leaving nothing but a life-insurance policy, on the income of which the mother and son could live modestly until he could get into a law office and begin to make his way in the world. They had taken a floor in a little boarding-house in a side street, and they were very comfortable; their money had been invested for them by one of his father's business associates, who had so arranged matters that their income was much larger than they had expected. In this modest home he and his mother lived happily. I guessed that the father had been hard and unbending, and that my friend and his mother had been drawn closer together. Of a cer-tainty I never saw a man more devoted than he was to her, or more tender, and she was worthy of the affection he lav-ished on her.

In those days the Law School course extended over two years only, and it did not call for very hard work on the part of the student, so he was free to pass fre-quent evenings in my library. I used to go and see him often, for I liked his mo-ther, and I liked to see them sitting side by side, he holding her hand often as he debated vehemently with me the insol-uble questions which interested us then. During the second winter I sometimes saw there a brown-eyed girl of perhaps twenty, pretty enough, but with a sharp, nervous manner I did not care for. This was the daughter of the lady who kept the boarding-house; and my friend was polite to her, as he was to all women; he was attentive even, as a young man is wont to be toward a quick-witted girl. But nothing in the manner led me to suppose that he was interested in her more than in any other woman. I did not like her myself, for she struck me as sharp-tongued.

It is true that I saw less of my friend that second winter, being hard at work myself. It was in the spring, two years after our graduation, that I received a letter from him announcing his engage-ment to the young lady I had seen him with, his landlady's daughter. My first thought, I remember, was to wonder how his mother would feel at the prospect of another woman's coming between them.

"I WENT TO SEE THE WOMAN MY FRIEND LOVED."

His letter was a long dithyramb, and it declared that never had there been a man so happy, and that great as was his present joy, it was as nothing compared with the delight in store for him. He wrote me that each had loved the other from the first, and each had thought the other did not care, until at last he could bear it no longer; so he had asked her, and got his answer. "You cannot know," he wrote, "what this is to me. It is my life—it is the making of my life; and if I should die to-night, I should not have lived in vain, for I have tasted joy, and death cannot rob me of that."

Of course the engagement must needs be long, because he was as yet in no position to support a wife; but he had been admitted to the bar, and he could soon make his way, with the stimulus he had now.

I was called out of town suddenly about that time, and I saw him for a few minutes only before I left New York. He was overflowing with happiness, and he could talk about nothing but the woman he loved — how beautiful she was! how clever! how accomplished! how devoted to his mother! In the midst of his rhapsody he was seized by a fit of violent coughing, and I saw the same danger signal in his cheeks which had preceded the breakdown in his Senior year. I begged him to take care of himself. With a light laugh he answered that he intended to do so—it was his duty to do so, now that he did not belong to himself.

In the fall, when I came back to the city, I found him in the office of a law firm the head of which had been an intimate of his father's. The girl he was to marry went one night a week to dine with her grandmother, and he came to me that evening and talked about her. As the cold weather stiffened his cough became more frequent, and long before Christmas I was greatly alarmed by it. He consulted a distinguished doctor, who told him that he ought to spend the winter in a drier climate—in Colorado, for example.

It was on Christmas eve that year that he brought me the frog that played the trombone. Ever since the first Christmas of our friendship we had made each other little presents.

"This is hardly worth giving," he said, as he placed the china shell on the corner of my desk, where it stands to this day. "But it is quaint and it caught my fancy.

Besides, I've a notion that it is the tune of one of Heine's lyrics set by Schubert that the fellow is trying to play. And then I've a certain satisfaction in thinking that I shall be represented here by a performer of marvellous force of lung, since you seem to think my lungs are weak."

A severe cough seized him then, but when he had recovered his breath he laughed lightly, and said: "That's the worst one I've had this week. However, when the spring warms me up again I shall be all right once more. It wasn't on me that the spring poet wrote the epitaph:

"It was a cough
That carried him off;
It was a coffin
They carried him off in."

"You ought to go away for a month at least," I urged. "Take a run down South and fill your lungs with the balsam of the pines."

"That's what my mother wants me to do," he admitted; "and I've half promised to do it. If I go to Florida for January, can you go with me?"

I knew how needful it was for him to escape from the bleakness of our New York winter, so I made a hasty mental review of my engagements. "Yes," I said, "I will go with you."

He held out his hand and clasped mine firmly. "We'll have a good time," he responded, "just we two. But you must promise not to object if I insist on talking about her all the time."

As it turned out, I was able to keep all my engagements, for we never went away together. Before the new year came there was a change in my friend's fortunes. The man who had pretended to invest for them the proceeds of his father's life-insurance policy absconded, leaving nothing behind but debts. For the support of his mother and himself my friend had only his own small salary. A vacation, however necessary, became impossible, and the marriage, which had been fixed for the spring, was postponed indefinitely. He offered to release the girl, but she refused.

Through a classmate of ours I was able to get my friend a place in the law department of the Denver office of a great insurance company. In the elevated air of Colorado he might regain his strength, and in a new city like Denver he might find a way to mend his fortunes. His mother went with him, of course; and it was beautiful to see her devotion to him. I saw them off.

"She bore the parting very bravely," he said to me. "She is braver than I am, and better in every way. I wish I were more worthy of her. You will go and see her, won't you? There's a good fellow, and a good friend. Go and see her now and then, and write and tell me all about her—how she looks and what she says."

I promised, of course, and about once a month I went to see the woman my friend loved. He wrote me every fortnight, but it was often from her that I got the latest news. His health was improving; his cough had gone; Denver agreed with him, and he liked it. He was working hard, and he saw the prospect of advancement close before him. Within two years he hoped to take a month off, and return to New York and marry her, and bear his bride back to Colorado with him.

When I returned to town the next October I expected to find two or three letters from my friend awaiting me. I found only one, a brief note, telling me that he had been too busy to write the month before, and that he was now too tired with overwork to be able to do more than say how glad he was that I was back again in America, adding that a friend at hand might be farther away than one who was on the other side of the Atlantic. The letter seemed to me not a little constrained in manner. I did not understand it; and with the hope of getting some light by which to interpret its strangeness, I went to call on her. She refused to see me, pleading a headache.

It was a month before I had a reply to my answer to his note, and the reply was as short as the note, and quite as constrained. He told me that he was well enough himself, but that his mother's health worried him, since Denver did not agree with her, and she was pining to be back in New York. He added a postscript in which he told me that he had dined a few nights before with the local manager of the insurance company, and that he had met the manager's sister, a wealthy widow from California, a most attractive woman, indeed. With needless emphasis he declared that he liked a woman of the world old enough to talk sensibly.

Another month passed before I heard from him again, and Christmas had gone and the New Year had almost come. The contents of this letter, written on Christmas eve, when the frog that played the trombone had been sitting on the corner of my desk for just a year, was as startling as its manner was strange. He told me that his engagement was broken off irrevocably.

If my own affairs had permitted it I should have taken the first train to Denver to discover what had happened. As it was I went again to call on the landlady's daughter. But she refused to see me again. Word was brought me that she was engaged, and begged to be excused.

About a fortnight later I chanced to meet on a street corner the classmate who had got my friend the Denver appointment. I asked if there was any news.

"Isn't there!" was the response. "I should think there was, and lots of it! You know our friend in Denver? Well, we have a telegram this morning: his health is shaky, and so he has resigned his position."

"Resigned his position!" I echoed. "What does that mean?"

"That's what we wanted to know," replied my classmate, "so we telegraphed to our local manager, and he gave us an explanation right off the reel. The manager has a sister who is the widow of a California millionaire, and she has been in Denver for the winter, and she has met our friend; and for all she is a good ten years older than he is, she has been fascinated by him—you know what a handsome fellow he is—and she's going to marry him next week, and take him to Egypt for his health."

"He's going to marry the California widow?" I asked, in astonishment. "Why, he's enga—" Then I suddenly held my peace.

"He's going to marry the California widow," was the answer,—"or she's going to marry him; it's all the same, I suppose."

Two days later I had a letter from Denver confirming this report. He wrote that he was to be married in ten days to a most estimable lady, and that they were to leave his mother in New York as they passed through. Fortunately he had been able to make arrangements whereby his mother would be able to live hereafter where she pleased, and in comfort. He invited me to come out to Colorado for the wedding, but hardly hoped to persuade me, he said, knowing how pressing my engagements were. But as their steamer sailed on Saturday week they would be at a New York hotel on the Friday night, and he counted on seeing me then.

I went to see him then, and I was shocked by his appearance. He was thin, and his chest was hollower than ever. There were dark lines below his liquid eyes, brighter then than I had ever seen them before. There were two blazing spots on his high cheek-bones. He coughed oftener than I had ever known him, and the spasms were longer and more violent. His hand was feverishly hot. His manner, too, was restless. To my surprise, he seemed to try to avoid being alone with me. He introduced me to his wife, a dignified, matronly woman with a full figure and a cheerful smile. She had a most motherly manner of looking after him and of anticipating his wants; twice she jumped up to close a door which had been left open behind him. He accepted her devotion as a matter of course, apparently. Once, when she was telling me of their projects, how they were going direct to Egypt to remain till late in the spring, and then to return to Paris for the summer, with a possible run over to London before the season was over, he interrupted her to say that it mattered little where he went or what he did—one place was as good as another.

When I rose to go he came with me out into the hotel corridor, despite his wife's suggestion that there was sure to be a draught there.

He thrust into my hand a note-book. "There," he said, "take that; it's a journal I started to keep, and never did. Of course you can read it if you like. In the pocket you will find a check. I want you to get some things for me after I've gone; I've written down everything. You will do that for me, I know."

I promised to carry out his instructions to the letter.

"Then that's all right," he answered.

At that moment his wife came to the door of their parlor. "I know it must be chilly out in the hall there," she said.

"Oh, I'm coming," he responded.

Then he grasped my fingers firmly in his hot hand. "Good-by, old man," he whispered. "You remember how I used to think the frog that played the trombone was trying to execute a Heine-Schubert song? Well, perhaps it is—I don't know; but what I do know is that it has played a wedding march, after all. And now good-by. God bless you! Go and see my mother as often as you can."

He gave my hand a hearty shake, and went back into the parlor, and his wife shut the door after him.

I had intended to go down to the boat and see him off the next morning, but at breakfast I received a letter from his wife saying that he had passed a very restless night, and that she thought it would excite him still more if I saw him again, and begging me, therefore, not to come to the steamer if such had been my intention. And so it was that he sailed away and I never saw him again.

In the note-book I found a check for five hundred dollars, and a list of the things he wished me to get and to pay for. They were for his mother mostly, but one was a seal-ring for myself. And there was with the check a jeweller's bill, "To articles sent as directed," which I was also requested to pay.

The note-book itself I guarded with care. It was a pocket-journal, and my friend had tried to make it a record of his life for the preceding year. There were entries of letters received and sent, of money earned and spent, of acquaintances made, of business appointments, of dinner engagements, and of visits to the doctor. Evidently his health had been failing fast, and he had been struggling hard to keep the knowledge not only from his mother, but even from himself. While he had set down these outward facts of his life, he had also used the note-book as the record of his inward feelings. To an extent that he little understood, that journal, with its fragmentary entries and its stray thoughts, told the story of his spiritual experience.

Many of the entries were personal, but many were not; they were merely condensations of the thought of the moment as it passed through his mind. Here are two specimens:

"We judge others by the facts of life—by what we hear them say and see them do. We judge ourselves rather by our own feelings—by what we intend and desire and hope to do some day in the future. Thus a poor man may glow with inward satisfaction at the thought of the hospital he is going to build when he gets rich. And a wealthy man can at least pride himself on the fortitude with which he would, if need be, bear the deprivations of poverty."

"To pardon is the best and the bitterest vengeance."

Toward the end of the year the business entries became fewer and fewer, as though he had tired of keeping the record of his doings. But the later pages were far fuller than the earlier of his reflections—sometimes a true thought happily expressed, sometimes, more often than not perhaps, a mere verbal antithesis, such as have furnished forth many an aphorism long before my friend was born. And these later sentiments had a tinge of bitterness lacking in the earlier.

"There are few houses," he wrote, in October, apparently, "where happiness is a permanent boarder; generally it is but a transient guest; and sometimes, indeed, it is only a tramp that knocks at the side door and is refused admittance."

"Many a man forgets his evil deeds so swiftly that he is honestly surprised when any one else recalls them."

Except the directions to me for the expenditure of the five hundred dollars, the last two entries in the book were written on Christmas morning. One of these was the passage which smote me most when I first read it, for it struck me as sadness itself when written by a young man not yet twenty-five:

"If we had nothing else to wish, we should at least wish to die."

At the time I did not seize the full significance of the other passage, longer than this, and far sadder when its meaning was finally grasped.

"The love our parents gave us we do not pay back, nor a tithe of it even. We may bestow it to our own children, but we never render it again to our father and our mother. And what can equal the love of a woman for the son she has borne? No peak is as lofty, and no ocean is as wide; it is fathomless, boundless, immeasurable; it is poured without stint, unceasing and unfailing. And how do we men meet it? We do not even make a pretence of repaying it, most of us. Now and again there may be a son here and there who does what he can for his mother, little as it is, and much as he may despise himself for doing it: and why not? Are there not seven swords in the heart of the Mater Dolorosa? And what sort of a son is he who would add another?"

Although I had already begun to guess at the secret of my friend's conduct, a mystery to all others, it was the first of these two final entries in his note-book which came flashing back into my memory one evening toward the end of March, ten weeks or so after he had bidden me good-by and had gone away to Egypt. I was seated in my library, smoking, when there came a ring at the door, and a telegram was handed to me. I laid my cigar down on the brownish-yellow shell, at the crinkled edge of which the green frog was sitting, reaching out his broken arms for the trombone whereon he had played in happier days. I saw that the despatch had come by the cable under the ocean, and I wondered who on the other side of the Atlantic had news for me that would not keep till a letter could reach me.

I tore open the envelope. The message was dated Alexandria, Egypt, and it was signed by my friend's widow. He had died that morning, and I was asked to break the news to his mother.

JESSEKIAH BROWN'S COURTSHIP
by Ruth McEnry Stuart

JESSEKIAH BROWN, a fat, bow-legged fellow of forty years or thereabouts, enjoyed the double distinction of being the fattest man as well as the oldest bachelor of his color on the plantation.

He had been a general beau in colored circles ever since he had begun to wear shoes to church, about twenty-five years ago. The "young ladies" he had "gone with" and "had feelin's about" were now staid matrons, mothers of grown sons and daughters, and yet Jessekiah had never been known to speak a serious word of love to any woman.

It was a common thing for the old wives on the place to say, as they sat together on the levee and laughed to see him still playing the beau, "Po' Ki! I don't b'lieve pos'tive he know how ter out an' cote a gal!"

And this was true, or at least it was half the truth. The other half was that Jessekiah had never been able to make up his mind decidedly as to the identical woman he wished to marry.

His was a case of ultra all-round susceptibility resulting in an embarrassment of emotions. It is probable that a certain indecision amounting to a psychological idiosyncrasy had descended to Ki by direct maternal inheritance, as it is related on reliable authority that his good mother had been utterly unable, even while she stood at the baptismal font with her babe, to decide whether his name should be Jesse or Hezekiah, and an embarrassed effort to change it at the last moment resulted in the unique cognomen which distinguished him through life.

There had been times in Jessekiah's life when he had *almost decided* that some special woman was the undisputed possessor of his affections, but they were fleeting moments.

On the old levee just opposite his present cabin he had once been sitting with Diana Forbes, a copper-skinned lass of seventeen years, for whom he had long confessed a soft spot in his soft heart, and the moonlight and a white gown she wore on that occasion had settled the question —for the moment.

He had even gotten as far as "Roses" in his avowal of love, when a silvery laugh, descending all the way from high C to inaudibility, had floated to him from the quarters.

Jessekiah could never propose to another girl while he heard Silv'y Simms laugh, and so, instead of saying "Roses is red an' vi'lets blue," and becoming hopelessly involved on the second line, he had coughed and remarked:

"Roses smells a heap mo' sweeter, ter my min', 'n honeysuckles does. Which you lak de moes', Miss Diana?"

And so the crisis had passed.

The only distinction Ki had attained as a person of superior years among the youth of the plantation was the title of brother.

"Brer Brown" had long ago "professed," and while never attaining any celebrity either as a speaker or worker in the fold, neither had he introduced shame in any shape, which was saying a good deal.

Ki's life, as care-free as that of the humming-bird that flits at will from flower to flower, and apparently as sunny and bright, was yet not without its trials. For years a certain single woman on the place, as huge as himself, hence familiarly known as "Fat Ann," had been his *bête noire*.

It was not enough that every one took special delight in teasing him about her, but the woman herself, in spite of years of avoidance on his part, seemed to have a fancy for him.

The bitterest hours of Ki's life had been on account of Fat Ann.

Any joke that threw their names together, any premeditated pairing off of couples that left him as her escort, was regarded as great fun. And it was one of those jokes that never wear out.

So it happened that on a certain memorable occasion Ki, suddenly finding himself allotted to walk with her at a cake walk, actually disgraced his manhood by genuine tears.

Happily, however, they were not shed in Ann's presence, and when she met him with a smiling salutation, and took his arm with her best effort at a flourish, there was something within him that felt challenged to a best effort—for in his heart poor Jessekiah was something of a gentleman—and the result was that,

THE CAKE WALK.

amidst uproarious cheering, Ki and Ann, fat, bow-legs, and all notwithstanding, took the cake.

This teased Ki even more than the walking had done. Nor was this all: it brought him suddenly up to the point of revolt.

When he went home that night his frame of mind was altogether unbecoming a Christian, not to say a Methodist.

Instead of going quietly to his cabin and to bed, as he should have done, he walked out upon the levee alone, and with head uncovered in the moonlight, while he mopped off his forehead, he swore that he wouldn't, so help him, "stan' one speck mo' o' dis cornfounded, doggorned, plague-taked nornsense!"

He had wept before he had stepped out into the arena with Ann to walk for the cake, and now, having done his duty fully, manfully, having amiably served as her "pardner" for the remainder of the evening, and courteously escorted her home, having deposited his own portion of the hated cake in the river, he wept again.

When Ki joined his companions in the field next day there was something in his face which forbade any allusion to the incident of the night before. It was a new dignity, the dignity of a fixed resolve.

As he had walked alone at midnight on the levee after spending his emotion in tears, he had reviewed the situation with a calm scrutiny, and he saw clearly that there were but two honorable ways out of his dilemma.

He could not run away. The world beyond the community of the coast meant little more to Ki than the planet Mars. An open revolt would be a personal insult to the lady in question. To be forever freed from all association with this hated, detested woman, he must either marry—or die.

Life was sweet to Ki. Death, even palliated with the consolations of religion, had never lost its terror to him. Marriage, on the other hand—Ki actually giggled foolishly to himself as he contemplated it as an actual probability—had always been an inviting prospect, and so tonight, sitting alone beneath the stars, he registered a vow—a sacred vow *to marry*.

The resolution had no sooner possessed him, however, than he began to question himself as to whom, of all the girls he knew, he should select.

For one thing, she must be slim. If there was one thing that in his present state of mind he hated more than anything else in creation, it was fat. He ran over in his mind the names of the several slender girls of his acquaintance, hesitating and chuckling afresh over each at the idea of her actually becoming Mrs. Brown.

The enumeration complete, he found himself sadly lapsing into his old state of indecision. He would to-night, at the toss of a penny—or perhaps it would be better to say at the toss of her head—have been happy to wed any one of seven sweet dusky maidens, varying as to complexion, temper, and general character, but all willowy and slender.

A realization of his irresolution even now, in the extremity of his woe, filled him with dismay, but his desperation had carried him for once safely beyond the possibility of retreat.

If he could not in a moment make up his mind whom he most desired, he could at least resolve that he would not put his foot out of his cabin, excepting to go to the field, until he should decide.

Calmed with this resolution, Ki finally repaired to his cabin, and found forgetfulness in sleep.

A week passed, and another. In the evenings, seated alone upon his door-step, or within the broad crotch of a log of drift-wood that lay embedded in the outer levee beyond his gate, Ki still agonized in indecision.

The threatened failure of the old embankment had last year sent a new levee into the heart of the plantation, and for a considerable distance here it ran close against a nest of negro quarters. Ki's cabin, sitting somewhat apart from the others, at the point of divergence of the two banks, commanded an easy approach to both. The low land between the two levees, a safe play-ground for the children when the river was low, was now covered with shallow water.

After a third week of painful indecision, Ki made a little progress. *He decided that he could never decide*—and of this decision was born a plan of relief.

"Look lak I mus' be one o' deze heah reg'lar Mormondizers, an' want 'em all," he had been moaning to himself, when suddenly his reverie began to take shape in this fashion: "Ef a man go a-huntin' all day, an' can't meck up 'is min' what bird he want ter shoot, he gwine come home wid a empty game-bag ev'y time."

Then something within him had seemed to answer. "Yas, an' de bes' thing he k'n do is ter stay home an' set a trap, an' pray Gord ter sen' de right bird ter 'im."

It was an inspiration. Ki was so pleased with the idea that he answered it aloud: "Dat's hit! Dat's hit! Dat's des what I gwine do. I gwine buil' me a—gwine buil' me a—gwine buil'—" and he fell to meditating again. "Gwine buil' me a fine fancified seat, right out heah on dis ol' levee, side o' dis lorg, an'—an' de fus' gal dat sets in it— My Gord! whyn't I thunk about dis befo'? De fus' gal what set down in it gwine be Mrs. Jessekiah Brown—*ef she do lak I say!*"

He was happier than he had been since the cake walk. Throwing himself down upon the grass, he rolled over and over, chuckling aloud. The chair, a quaint affair made of pine saplings, and finished with arms of gnarled twigs, was the work of several mornings, and when at last it was finished, even to the not inartistic braiding of cross-twigs into an easy head-rest, Ki was as happy over it as a child with a new toy.

"Come 'long, Mis' Brown, honey. Teck yo' seat, my love, an' set down," he exclaimed, giggling foolishly as he moved back to his notch in the log, and glanced up at the imaginary occupant of the seat.

He felt almost as if his wedding invitations were already out; and yet no sooner did he picture any special one enthroned beside him than his mind reverted with a pang to half a dozen others. His only safety lay in the sacredness of his oath. He had sworn, and called on God to witness his pledge, that he would ask the first woman who sat here to marry him, and he would do it.

For the first week after its completion Ki watched the chair from his window with a timorous nervousness, expecting, hoping, and yet fearing at any time to look out upon the future Mrs. Brown.

But a month passed, and she did not come, and although Ki managed to preserve a calm exterior, and had replied to all inquiries as to his retirement that he "had done got tired out o' s'ciety an' had done settled down," he was growing desperately weary of it.

The "settling down" had, however, by slow degrees resulted in a decidedly improved state of affairs at Ki's cabin.

When the little one-roomed hut had been only a place to keep his garden tools, to hang up his saddle, and to "turn in" himself as a last resort to sleep at night, it had been a small matter that the front yard was overrun with cockle-burs and "jimsonweed"; that the rank, malodorous gourd vine that straggled over the remains of last year's bean poles to embrace his mud chimney was a harbor for wasps, lizards, and the brilliant spiders that spun their filmy wheels in every available space. It hadn't mattered that the corners of his room and his mosquito-netting were decorated with this same delicate tracery, and that the high-water mark from the last crevasse had supplied the walls of his apartment with a unique dado of decay—a dado done in low brown tones, with strong stucco effects in green close-clinging mosses.

It is possibly not exceptional that a very startling apparent incongruity should sometimes exist between a bachelor's apartment and the gorgeously attired gentleman who goes forth from the same to enter the most exclusive inwardness of most exclusive society. A finely feathered he bird has been known to take daily flight, joining a flock of very high fliers, from a roofless nest of mud and straw and unwashed rags.

It had been enough for Ki to know that the pine press in the corner of his hovel held in safe preservation his silk hat, dress suit, and the various delicate appointments of a gentleman's toilet; that a cake of very strongly scented sweet soap of a marbleized reddish color lay wrapped in tin-foil beside a boot-shaped bottle of "hair-ile" that for potency of perfume put both gourd-vine and jimson-weed to shame; and that his varied assortment of scarfs, scarf-pins, handkerchiefs, and the like was safe from wind or weather in a shell-covered box made by one of his earliest sweethearts.

Here also were a little folding-comb with a mirror within its handle—a vest-pocket convenience for last toilet touches at church doors and front gates—a gorgeous walking-cane, and cotton umbrella. In fact, as to the matter of toilet furnishings, Ki was quite up to the requirements of a finished society man, and he had, besides, what he would probably have called an "innard" grace of manner. It would have come outward and manifested itself in *mannerisms* if there had been any chance for it, but, as he himself lamented, "How kin a feather-bed teck orn manners?"

Ki was too hopelessly fat to cultivate anything more than the negations, so to speak, of manners polite. His strength lay rather in the avoidance of inelegancies than in the attempt to assume impossible graces.

A genial amiability is ofttimes a surer guarantee of social success than a figure of artistic proportions, and yet Ki would have given all he owned or hoped to possess of personal attractiveness for the power to bend at the waist when he lifted his stove-pipe hat.

We have said that during the period of his retreat he had improved the condition of his home. Indeed, when two months had passed, the freshly whitewashed little cabin that sat smiling through a cool green garment of butter-bean and morning-glory vines, in the midst of a riotous mass of sunflowers, hollyhocks, and zinnias, was in no way recognizable as the recent neglected hovel.

While the trap to catch his bird was out upon the levee, Ki, with loving care, was getting the nest in order, and although he was eager at times for his mate, there were moments when the tortures of indecision were distinctly sharpened with a dread that her coming would involve a life-long regret.

While he had chopped down the mud crawfish chimneys along his garden walk and strewed it with white shells, somehow he had been unable to think with any pleasure of any other girl than Hannah Frierson, a willowy yellow maid, tripping up and down the walk; and yet, within the cozy corner of his porch, where he had placed a bench just broad enough for two among the vines, the brown piquant face of another insistently and bewitchingly met his eye. She who seemed naturally to stand on the little stepladder to gather butter-beans was a third. And yet another, by a strange persistency, struck his fancy as the dainty creature who should occupy the chair upon the levee. Her delicate, shapely wrist seemed in his imagination just fitted to lie over its rustic arm, and her slender foot would, he was sure, just about rest on the log where he sat.

He somehow had a feeling that maybe —he wasn't quite sure, but maybe—it would be pleasant to lay his hand upon her foot and pat it. Would that be lover-like? He doubted that it was exactly the correct thing to do; and yet, while he sat and looked at the end of the log, the impulse to reach out and touch the imaginary foot resting upon it always came so irresistibly that he chuckled over the very thought.

Notwithstanding the fact that Ki was distinctly in a courting frame of mind, there were times when he would in desperation have retreated from his vow and started out again, hoping to make his choice, had it not been for his dread of meeting Fat Ann, and *that* he was resolved, with all the hitherto dormant decision of his tardy manhood, he would not do—*no, not if he died*. He hated, despised, abhorred the very thought of her with a morbid intensity heightened by solitude and long-suffering. Even yet, when he recalled the picture he and she must have made as they promenaded before the company arm in arm for the cake, cold chills ran down his back, and he talked bitterly to himself.

"De idee o' dat great big apple flitter, what 'ain't got no mo' shape 'n a spinnin'-turtle, a-waddlin' by my side—matchin' fatness wid fatness! My Lord! De mo' I ponders on it, de mo' madder an' pervokeder I gits! De idee! A gal what 'ain't got no mo' wais'-line 'n a—'n a—'n *I is!*"

The summer was waning. Ki was now an acknowledged recluse. And though his little home grew prettier and more attractive; though his wages, untaxed by the demands of society, lay for the first time in his life a growing account to his credit; though his chair sat, clover-scented and picturesque, on the brow of the levee at his door, waiting to hold in its open arms the future mistress of the manse; though the nest grew daily more attractive and the waiting mate within it more eligible, never a bird had perched upon the limb prepared to entrap it.

A few of the settled married folk and some of the boys had strolled out, partly from curiosity and a desire for a friendly chat, but as Ki was rather taciturn they had been satisfied to consider this a last idiosyncrasy confirming his bachelorhood, and had not returned.

The girls missed him in an impersonal sort of way; but beaux, real marrying fellows, full to overflowing of direct sentiment, were plentiful, and so were skiffs and fishing-lines and blackberry patches. They hadn't time to think seriously of Ki.

At last it was an evening near the end of September. Ki, dispirited and sad, oppressed with that worst vacancy of the heart, a sense of having no one to care for him, had strolled out, following the old levee to the most distant point of its outward curve, and here he sat down.

He had seen several rowing parties start out in skiffs, and even now, though they were but floating black lines in the distance, he caught occasionally in a breath of wind the sound of laughter mingled with the witching notes of a harmonicon. He was desperately lonely and blue.

The sun was nearly down when at last he rose wearily to go in. He had proceeded some distance when the rustic chair came within range of his vision. The recent sunlight reflected from the river into his eyes embarrassed his sight somewhat, and bright spots were dancing before them, yet in a flash came the impression that there was something unusual in the appearance of the chair. The very idea startled him so that some moments passed before he dared confirm the suspicion by a second glance, and he was so maddened with a sort of stage-fright that he staggered a little when he did finally look again.

It was true. Some one was comfortably seated in the chair beside the log, taking the evening breeze. He could see the flutter of a flounce in the wind as he slowly and falteringly approached, his heart in his throat, breathing hard. Suddenly he stopped, leaned forward, ducked his head down, looked intently for a moment, and falling like a log, rolled down the inside of the levee.

It was Fat Ann. Let us hope that his recording angel took note of the poor fellow's anguish of soul as, when he reached the bottom, he ejaculated, with a groan, "Good Gord!" If he did, the exclamation was surely not registered as profanity, but was rather entered as a prayer on the credit side of his account.

Ann, conscious only of unsuspicious friendly feeling, seeing him fall, hurried to the spot.

"Fo' Gord sake, Brer Brown, huccome you twissen so sudd'nt orf de aidge o' de levee?" she exclaimed, breathlessly.

Ki lay still where he had fallen, at the water's edge.

"Po' Brer Brown done tooken wid a fit! Wait tell I come an' he'p you up," she continued, measuring the difficult descent with her eye.

This was a stimulant. Ki groaned aloud to show that he still lived. If she should come to him, he felt that he would die outright.

The girl, misinterpreting the groan as an indication of serious disaster, hurried to his aid. Somehow, in attempting the steep declivity, her foot slipped.

Whether, sliding like an irresistible avalanche, she carried Ki into the water with her, or whether she rolled clear over him, and he afterward fell in in his effort to rescue her, it is hard to say. Certain it is, however, that when after some time they reappeared arm in arm over the brow of the levee, both bore marks of a recent baptism.

That Ki was passing through another baptism of fire was evinced by the expression of dull despair that had settled over his face, as well as by a suspicion of incoherency in his speech.

Through it all, however, he had never quite forgotten that he was a gentleman and that Ann was a lady. Neither had he forgotten his oath, nor that he was a Christian—and a Methodist.

Now that it was, so far as she knew, all over, Ann, overcome with a sense of the ludicrous, shook with suppressed laughter. Her own effort at control fortunately kept her from realizing that Ki had several times distinctly sobbed, even while he made such polite remarks as he could command to the lady upon his arm.

"I 'clare, Miss—ur—a—Miss Ann, seem lak I los' my ekalubium. Dishere levee ain't fitt'n' fur no plump lady—ur—a—I means hit ain't ter say fitt'n' fur nothin' but—but goats. I trus' you 'ain't frac tioned none o' yo' dislocutioms, Miss Ann."

Ann had not yet found her voice. Still trembling somewhat from the shock, chilled with her wet skirts, and a bit hysterical withal, she shook so that when they reached the chair Ki felt impelled, by sheer courtesy, to steady her by laying his hand upon her shoulder as he bade her be seated. Then, moving off, he took his seat, not within the notch at her side, but astride the most distant end of the log.

"I 'clare, Brer Brown," said his guest, finally, "I sholy is glad ter set down an' wring out my frock." And after a pause:

"Umh! Dishere cheer des fits me, lak you done had tooken my measure fur it. Was you studyin' 'bout me, Brer Brown, when you made it?"

Ki, looking dazed, only blinked, and fortunately she did not wait for an answer. He sat wiping off his clothing with his handkerchief, while great drops of perspiration trickled down his face, and an occasional quiver like summer lightning played about the corners of his mouth.

Long after there was any need for it he continued to rub his trousers legs and the sleeve of the one arm that had been submerged. He was trying, with all the strength of a resolve grown strong by patient waiting, to bring himself to accept the conditions of his oath. He had prayed over this matter. He had trustingly begged the Lord in His infinite wisdom to send the right woman to him. And there sat Ann—the answer to his prayers—Ann, whom all his manœuvre had been planned to avoid.

After he had wiped his coat and she had wrung her gown until both acts were growing palpably absurd, and the silence was becoming momentarily more painful, Ki ventured to look up at the woman whom he must ask to be his wife. For a moment he was tempted to throw himself backward and roll into the outer depths of the Mississippi. The chill of its waters was still upon him, however, and shivering at the thought, he turned from it to glance once more at his bride-elect. Of course she would accept him. Who ever doubts the descent of a dreaded and evidently impending evil?

Ki's proposal scene had been arranged for years, and he knew it all by heart from beginning to end; but that old formula beginning with "Roses red" would never do now. He had fancied that when he should come to the "Sugar is sweet, an' so is you," the dainty little miss might be a trifle coy, and he should have to insist upon it. She might even protest, "I ain't no sweeter'n you is." But if Ann should say so silly a thing to him, he would scream—he felt it.

The moments were passing. He had several times taken off his hat and wiped it, only to be reminded that it had never been wet, and now he did so again.

Finally Ann spoke. "Yo' cabin do look mighty sweet, Brer Brown," she said. "Settin' whar it do, hit mus' ketch all de breezes an' be mighty cool. Ain't it?"

Ki breathed fiercely. "No, Miss—ur—a—Miss Ann," he replied, swallowing a lump in his throat. "Hit's pow'ful hot; an'—an' yit"—he could hardly control his agitation enough to speak—"an' yit I's afeerd ter leave de winders open of nights, 'caze de lizards an' scorpions an' snakes is awful bad roun' my cabin—an'—an' rats; deze heah grea' big fox-rats. Dey—dey des runs roun' my room at night lak squir'ls in de woods; an'—an' skunks, too. Dey comes roun' reg'lar, a whole passel ob 'em, an'—an'—ur—a—bats, an'—an'—ur—a—squinch-owls, an'—an'—"

"De laws-a-mussy, Brer Brown, you ain't sesso! An' does you sleep heavy wid all sech varmints a-swarmin' roun' of nights?"

"Sleep heavy? Who, me? I—ur—a—I—" He was gaining time. "I nuver sleeps heavy, Miss Ann. No, ma'am, I—I nuver sleeps heavy. Yer see, mos'ly ev'y night I has de nightmares, an'—an' sometimes I gits up in de middle o' de night, an' seem lak I 'magine I hears robbers, an' I des teck a stick an' whup ev'y-thing in de room. I taken my bolster one night, an'—an' I beat it all ter pieces 'gins' de side o' de bed in one o' deze heah nightmares. I tell yer, I's—I's a dange'ous sleeper, Miss Ann!"

"Umh! Look ter me lak you oughter have some light sleeper ter stay wid you, Brer Brown, an' teck cyar you."

Ki swallowed again. "B-b-but, yer see, Miss Ann, I's afeerd I mought kill 'em 'fo' dey'd weck up, don't yer see. Dat's de onies' trouble. I des tecks de load out'n my gun 'fo' I goes ter bed, an' hides all de knives an' forks—'caze, yer know, a pusson could job a pusson's eyes out wid a fork—an' den I des lays down an' goes ter sleep. Dey does say how sometime' a pusson do load a gun in his sleep."

"Whee! You all but scares me, Brer Brown. Don't you never git lonesome by yo' lone se'f, Brer Brown?"

Here was a real opening. His heart thumped so that he heard it. He could hardly speak.

"Y-y-yas, 'm. I—I gits—I gits lonesome some nights—some nights when—when de—de dorgs comes onder my cabin an' howl—an'—"

"Dat's a mighty bad sign, Brer Brown. Is dey cry two times an' stop?"

Ki coughed. "N-no, Miss Ann. Dat what meck me fin' it so strange. Dey say ef a dorg howl two times an' stop, hit's fur a man ter die; but—but deze heah dorgs dey keep a-cryin' three times an' stop—three times an' stop; dat's a sho call fur a ooman ter die. Ef—ef I had air mammy—ur—a—any ooman pusson stayin' wid me, I'd—I'd look fur ter lose 'er, sho."

"Umh! Dat's mighty strange. How long is dey been comin', Brer Brown?"

"Des—des deze las' few nights—an' I done tried ev'y way I kin ter get shet of 'em—but dey won't go."

"My Lord! You done got me 'mos' too skeer'd ter go home, Brer Brown. But I mus' travel; hit's gitt'n' late." She rose.

"D-don't—don't go yit, Miss Ann." He began to gasp again. "S-set down. I—I des berginnin' ter talk ter yer good. I—I was des a-sayin'—"

She sat down again. Ki mopped his forehead.

"What was you sayin', Brer Brown? I 'clare, seem lak I kin see dorgs' shadders runnin' 'long de levee. I mus' be gitt'n' home. You done got me rattled."

"I des say—I say, don't hurry yo'se'f— I des—I des a-sayin'—"

He mopped his forehead again, and his ears, and the back of his neck.

"I was des a-sayin', Miss Ann, it's—it's awful hot heah ter-night—des lis'n at me, 'awful hot!'—I 'ain't got no manners. Hit's pretty toler'ble warm heah, Miss Ann, ain't it? I—I des a-pusfirin' lak rain."

"Hit's cool an' winny ter me, Brer Brown. Look how de win' blowin' my hat strings. I 'clare I mus' go. Hit's gitt'n' plumb dark."

"B-b-but I gwine tell yer, Miss Ann, dat of co'se I—I does feel lonesome heah some nights—an' I—ur—a—I feels—"

If he could only bring in the "Roses red" and be done with it!

"An'—of co'se—sometimes I craves fur com—fur company."

"I knows how you feels, Brer Brown, dat I does! I done been lonesome my-se'f, an' I knows de mizry! I often 'low-ed I'd come over heah an' see yo' fanci-fied cheer, what I done heerd de chillen all talkin' 'bout, an' talk wid you, but I 'ain't had de cour'ge ter do so, tell dis evenin' I was a-passin' by, an' I seen Betty Taylor a-settin' heah lak a queen, a-fannin' herse'f—"

"Wh-wh-wh-what—what you say, Miss Ann?"

"I say, of co'se, when I seen Betty Taylor a-settin' heah in yo' high-back cheer, big as life—howsomever she ain't no thicker'n a stick o' sugar-cane—I 'low-ed I could come too."

Ki never knew how he kept from fall-ing at this juncture.

"Wh-when—when is you see Miss— Miss Betty heah, Miss—ur—a Miss Ann?"

"She was heah when I come—when you was settin' orn de aidge o' de levee. When she got up, I sot down, an' I had des sca'cely tooken my seat when you was tooken wid—wid a some'h'n' 'nother an' done so cuyus. What was you sayin', Brer Brown, 'bout bein' so lone-some?"

Ki was grinning so he could hardly speak. "Who, me? I was des a-sayin'— I 'clare, Miss Ann, what was I sayin'?"

"You sayin' some'h'n' 'bout lonesome-ness—"

"Is I? I 'clare I forgits. Who-who-who I say was lonesome?"

"You, yo'se'f. You say sometimes you feels lak— You ain't say what you feels lak."

"I—I 'clare, Miss Ann! Hit's so hot— ur—a—so col'—ur—a—I means ter say hit's so warm up heah ter-night— Look lak I done los' de thread o' my speech, Miss Ann—I—" And he actually giggled outright.

Ann was seized with a sudden panic. She felt sure that a spell of some dreadful kind was coming upon him.

She was afraid to stay, and yet she feared that if she started to go he might seize her, and beat her as he had beaten the things in the nightmare.

She was sure he would presently do something sudden. If he would only tumble down the levee again, she would be relieved, for then she could run and call for help.

It was quite dark now, and growing really chill.

Suddenly Ki sneezed. Starting as if she were shot, poor Ann sprang with sur-prising agility from her chair, and facing round, started in a steady trot toward the quarters.

It seems too much that she should have rolled off the edge of the levee a second time, and really it would not have hap-pened but for the darkness and the fright, which blinded her utterly.

Even after she realized that Ki was not madly pursuing her, she had fled in unabated terror from an imaginary pack of howling dogs, rats, and reptiles, fearing at each step the flapping into her face of the wings of owl or bat.

Her second tumble was perhaps a happy accident, for while for a moment it was as if the end of all things had come, she soon rallied, unhurt, to find herself safely in the road leading to her own door.

When Ki realized that he was alone, he threw himself on the grass again, and laughed until he cried, verily.

It was perhaps two hours later, when, gorgeously attired in his dress suit, a zinnia and a sprig of mint in his button-hole, equally polished as to boots and beaver, and redolent of sundry perfumes of the toilet, he emerged from his embowered cottage, and started, clearing his throat and giggling ever and anon as he went, to the cabin where lived, with her mother, the umber lass Betty Taylor. Never once did his courage fail him, never did he falter, never look back. The string of Cupid's bow had been drawn nearly to the point of snapping, but now that it had sprung, the arrow sped without a waver straight to the mark. Looking neither to right nor left, nor behind him, nor yet within, fluttering and giggling only as the arrow whizzed from the very speed and directness of its flight, Ki proceeded to make his first unequivocal declaration of love.

There have been more graceful suitors perhaps than our poor hero. Others there have been more fluent of thought, more gifted in speech, but it is doubtful whether upon the ear of woman ever fell a more ardent avowal than that which greeted the surprised but not offended ear of the nut-brown mayde with the slender slender waist who was seen in the tender moonlight that night to walk arm in arm with Ki up the levee and take her seat by his side in the rustic chair. And Ki sat in the crotch of the log.

And when he saw that her slim foot rested just where he fancied it would on the end of the branch beside him, he clasped his hands tightly behind his head until he could steady himself.

The announcement of the engagement created a tremendous sensation on the plantation. The first one to whom Ki personally confided it was Ann. Somehow since his happiness his heart had gone out to her to a degree that was distinctly brotherly.

"I wanted ter be de fus one ter tell yer, Miss Ann," he said, in a tone mellow with friendly feeling, as they returned from the field together, "'caze you an' me's been des, as yer mought say, lak brother an' sister together fur so long—"

Ann laughed. "Dat's des de way I felt, Brer Brown, an' dat's huccome I went up an' sot in yo' cheer las' week ter tell you 'bout I gwine marry, but look lak you sort o' sca'ed me orf."

"How you say dat, Miss Ann? You gwine marry! Who—who you 'low ter marry, Miss Ann?"

"Is you tooken notice ter dat little slim yaller musicianer what play de bones at de cake walk? He come f'om de Teche. He an' me been keepin' comp'ny ever sence."

"What! Hursh! You don't say!"

"Yas, I does say. You been stayin' home so clost fixin' up fur Betty you 'ain't kep' up wid de news. But look heah, Brer Brown"—she lowered her voice—"co'se I knows you's a perfessin' man, an' you gwine do what's right, but—but is you tol' Betty 'bout—'bout dem nightmares?"

Ki hesitated, and there was a twinkle in his eye when he said: "I nuver has 'em on'y in de summer, Miss Ann, an' we don't 'low ter marry tell nex' month; but tell de trufe, I 'ain't kep' nothin' back f'om Miss Betty. But look heah! I's mo' tooken up wid yo' marryin' 'n I is wid me an' Miss Betty's. An' you say ever sence de cake walk?"

"Yassir. He say when he seed me step out so mannerly an' taken yo' arm— But co'se he des run orn ter me dat way."

"Well done! An' Miss Betty say dat same word ter me."

Both laughed.

"Is she? But Betty allus is liked de fat style; but fur me, gi' me de slim style! Hones', Brer Brown, I'd o' give all I owned de night o' dat cake walk ef you er me, one, had o' been slim. I des dashed out reckless ter hide my feelin's. Ef air one of us had o' moped ur stepped heavy, dey'd o' had de laugh on us!"

"Dat's so; an' look lak de laugh on our side now. Well, Miss Ann, I wishes you joy, an' I shek yo' han'."

"An' I shek yo' han', Brer Brown."

SILENCE
by Mary E. Wilkins

AT ENSIGN SHELDON'S HOUSE THE MORNING AFTER THE MASSACRE.

AT dusk Silence went down the Deerfield street to Ensign John Sheldon's house. She wore her red blanket over her head, pinned closely under her chin, and her white profile showed whiter between the scarlet folds. She had been spinning all day, and shreds of wool still clung to her indigo petticoat; now and then one floated off on the north wind. It was bitterly cold, and the snow was four feet deep. Silence's breath went before her in a cloud; the snow creaked under her feet. All over the village the crust was so firm that men could walk upon it. The houses were half sunken in sharp, rigid drifts of snow; their roofs were laden with it; icicles hung from the eaves. All the elms were white on their windward sides, and the snow was so nearly ice and frozen to them so strong-

ly that it was not shaken off when they were lashed by the fierce wind.

There was an odor of boiling meal in the air: the housewives were preparing supper. Silence had eaten hers: she and her aunt, Widow Eunice Bishop, supped early. She had not far to go to Ensign Sheldon's. She was nearly there when she heard quick footsteps on the creaking snow behind her. Her heart beat quickly, but she did not look around. "Silence," said a voice. Then she paused, and waited, with her eyes cast down and her mouth grave, until David Walcott reached her. "What do you out this cold night, sweetheart?" he said.

"I am going down to Goodwife Sheldon's," replied Silence. Then suddenly she cried out, wildly: "Oh, David, what is that on your cloak? What is it?"

David looked curiously at his cloak. "I see naught on my cloak save old weather stains," said he. "What mean you, Silence?"

Silence quieted down suddenly. "It is gone now," said she, in a subdued voice.

"What did you see, Silence?"

Silence turned toward him; her face quivered convulsively. "I saw a blotch of blood," she cried. "I have been seeing them everywhere all day. I have seen them on the snow as I came along."

David Walcott looked down at her in a bewildered way. He carried his musket over his shoulder, and was shrugged up in his cloak; his heavy flaxen mustache was stiff and white with frost. He had just been relieved from his post as sentry, and it was no child's play to patrol Deerfield village on a day like that, nor had it been for many previous days. The weather had been so severe that even the French and Indians, lurking like hungry wolves in the neighborhood, had hesitated to descend upon the town, and had staid in camp.

"What mean you, Silence?" he said.

"What I say," returned Silence, in a strained voice. "I have seen blotches of blood everywhere all day. The enemy will be upon us."

David laughed loudly, and Silence caught his arm. "Don't laugh so loud," she whispered. Then David laughed again. "You be all overwrought, sweetheart," said he. "I have kept guard all the afternoon by the northern palisades, and I have seen not so much as a red fox on the meadow. I tell thee the French and Indians have gone back to Canada. There is no more need of fear."

"I have started all day and all last night at the sound of war-whoops," said Silence.

"Thy head is nigh turned with these troublous times, poor lass. We must cross the road now to Ensign Sheldon's house. Come quickly, or you will perish in this cold."

"Nay, my head is not turned," said Silence, as they hurried on over the crust; "the enemy be hiding in the forests beyond the meadows. David, they be not gone."

"And I tell thee they be gone, sweetheart. Think you not we should have seen their camp smoke had they been there? And we have had trusty scouts out. Come in, and my aunt Hannah Sheldon shall talk thee out of this folly."

The front windows of John Sheldon's house were all flickering red from the hearth fire. David flung open the door, and they entered. There was such a goodly blaze from the great logs in the wide fireplace that even the shadows in the remote corners of the large keeping-room were dusky red, and the faces of all the people in the room had a clear red glow upon them.

Goodwife Hannah Sheldon stood before the fire, stirring some porridge in a great pot that hung on the crane; some fair-haired children sat around a basket shelling corn, a slight young girl in a snuff-yellow gown was spinning, and an old woman in a great quilted hood crouched in a corner of the fireplace, holding out her lean hands to the heat.

Goodwife Sheldon turned around when the door opened. "Good-day, Mistress Silence Hoit," she called out, and her voice was sweet, but deep like a man's. "Draw near to the fire, for in truth you must be near perishing with the cold."

"There'll be fire enough ere morning, I trow, to warm the whole township," said the old woman in the corner. Her small black eyes gleamed sharply out of the gloom of her great hood; her yellow face was all drawn and puckered toward the centre of her shrewdly leering mouth.

"Now you hush your croaking, Goody Crane," cried Hannah Sheldon. "Draw the stool near to the fire for Silence, David. I cannot stop stirring, or the porridge will burn. How fares your aunt this cold weather, Silence?"

"Well, except for her rheumatism," replied Silence. She sat down on the stool that David placed for her, and slipped her blanket back from her head. Her beautiful face, full of a grave and delicate stateliness, drooped toward the fire, her smooth fair hair was folded in clear curves like the leaves of a lily around her ears, and she wore a high, transparent, tortoise-shell comb like a coronet in the knot at the back of her head.

David Walcott had pulled off his cap and cloak, and stood looking down at her. "Silence is all overwrought by this talk of Indians," he remarked, presently, and a blush came over his weather-beaten blond face at the tenderness in his own tone.

"The Indians have gone back to Canada," said Goodwife Sheldon, in a magisterial voice. She stirred the porridge faster; it was smoking fiercely.

"So I tell her," said David.

Silence looked up in Hannah Sheldon's sober, masterly face. "Goodwife, may I have a word in private with you?" she asked, in a half-whisper.

"As soon as I take the porridge off," replied Goodwife Sheldon.

"God grant it be not the last time she takes the porridge off!" said the old woman.

Hannah Sheldon laughed. "Here be Goody Crane in a sorry mind to-night," said she. "Wait till she have a sup of this good porridge, and I trow she'll pack off the Indians to Canada in a half-hour!"

Hannah began dipping out the porridge. When she had placed smoking dishes of it on the table and bidden everybody draw up, she motioned to Silence. "Now, Mistress Silence," said she, "come into the bedroom if you would have a word with me."

Silence followed her into the little north room opening out of the keeping-room, where Ensign John Sheldon and his wife Hannah had slept for many years. It was icy cold, and the thick fur of frost on the little window-panes sent out sparkles in the candle-light. The two women stood beside the great chintz draped and canopied bed, Hannah holding the flaring candle. "Now, what is it?" said she.

"Oh, Goodwife Sheldon!" said Silence. Her face remained quite still, but it was as if one could see her soul fluttering beneath it.

"You be all overwrought, as David saith," cried Goodwife Sheldon, and her voice had a motherly harshness in it. Silence had no mother, and her lover, David Walcott, had none. Hannah was his aunt, and loved him like her son, so she felt toward Silence as toward her son's betrothed.

"In truth I know not what it is," said Silence, in a kind of reserved terror, "but there has been all day a great heaviness of spirit upon me, and last night I dreamed. All day I have fancied I saw blood here and there. Sometimes, when I have looked out of the window, the whole snow hath suddenly glared with red. Goodwife Sheldon, think you the

Indians and the French have in truth gone back to Canada?"

Goodwife Sheldon hesitated a moment, then she spoke up cheerily. "In truth have they!" cried she. "John said but this noon that naught of them had been seen for some time."

"So David said," returned Silence; "but this heaviness will not be driven away. You know how Parson Williams hath spoken in warning in the pulpit and elsewhere, and besought us to be vigilant. He holdeth that the savages be not gone."

Hannah Sheldon smiled. "Parson Williams be a godly man, but prone ever to look upon the dark side," said she.

"If the Indians should come to-night—" said Silence.

"I tell ye they will not come, child. I shall lay me down in that bed a-trusting in the Lord, and having no fear against the time I shall arise from it."

"If the Indians should come— Goodwife Sheldon, be not angered, hear me. If they should come, I pray you keep David here to defend you in this house, and let him not out to seek me. You know well that our house be musket-proof as well as this, and it has long been agreed that they who live nearest, whose houses have not thick walls, shall come to ours and help us make defence. I pray you let not David out of the house to seek me, should there be a surprise to-night. I pray you give me your promise for this, Goodwife Sheldon."

Hannah Sheldon laughed. "In truth will I give thee the promise, if it make thee easier, child," said she. "At the very first war-screech will I tie David in the chimney-corner with my apron-string, unless you lend me yours. But there will be no war-screech to-night, nor to-morrow night, nor the night after that. The Lord will preserve His people that trust in Him. To-day have I set a web of linen in the loom, and I have candles ready to dip to-morrow, and the day after that I have a quilting. I look not for Indians. If they come I will set them to work. Fear not for David, sweetheart. In truth you should have a bolder heart, an you look to be a soldier's wife some day."

"I would I had never been aught to him, that he might not be put in jeopardy to defend me!" said Silence, and her words seemed visible in a white cloud at her mouth.

"We must not stay here in the cold," said Goodwife Sheldon. "Out with ye, Silence, and have a sup of hot porridge, and then David shall see ye home."

Silence sipped a cup of the hot porridge obediently, then she pinned her red blanket over her head. Hannah Sheldon assisted her, bringing it warmly over her face. "'Tis bitter cold," she said. "Now have no more fear, Mistress Silence; the Indians will not come to-night; but do you come over to-morrow, and keep me company while I dip the candles."

"There'll be company enough—there'll be a whole houseful," muttered the old woman in the corner, but nobody heeded her. She was a lonely and wretched old creature whom people sheltered from pity, although she was somewhat feared and held in ill repute. There were rumors that she was well versed in all the dark lore of witchcraft, and held commerce with unlawful beings. The children of Deerfield village looked askance at her, and clung to their mothers if they met her on the street, for they whispered among themselves that old Goody Crane rode through the air on a broom in the night-time.

Silence and David passed out into the keen night. "If you meet my goodman, hasten him home, for the porridge is cooling," Hannah Sheldon called after them.

But they met not a soul on Deerfield street. They parted at Silence's door. David would have entered had she bidden him, but she said peremptorily that she had a hard task of spinning that evening, and then she wished him goodnight, and without a kiss, for Silence Hoit was chary of caresses. But to-night she called him back ere he was fairly in the street. "David," she called, and he ran back.

"What is it, Silence?" he asked.

She put back her blanket, threw her arms around his neck, and clung to him trembling.

"Why, sweetheart," he whispered, "what has come over thee?"

"You know—this house is made like a fort," she said, bringing out her words in gasps, "and—there are muskets, and—powder stored in it, and—Captain Moulton, and his sons, and—John Carson will come, and make—a stand in it. I have—no fear should—the Indians come. Re-member that I have no fear, and shall be safe here, David."

David laughed, and patted her clinging shoulders. "Yes, I will remember, Silence," he said; "but the Indians will not come."

"Remember that I am safe here, and have no fear," she repeated. Then she kissed him of her own accord, as if she had been his wife, and entered the house, and he went away, wondering.

Silence's aunt, Widow Eunice Bishop, did not look up when the door opened; she was knitting by the fire, sitting erect with her mouth pursed. She had a hostile expression, as if she were listening to some opposite argument. Silence hung her blanket on a peg; she stood irresolute a minute, then she breathed on the frosty window and cleared a little space through which she could look out. Her aunt gave a quick fierce glance at her, then she tossed back her head and knitted. Silence stood staring out of the little peephole in the frosty pane. Her aunt glanced at her again, then she spoke.

"I should think if you had been out gossiping and gadding for two hours, you had better get yourself at some work now," she said, "unless your heart be set on idling. A pretty housewife you'll make!"

"Come here quick, quick!" Silence cried out.

Her aunt started, but she would not get up; she knitted, scowling. "I cannot afford to idle if other folk can," said she. "I have no desire to keep running to windows and standing there gaping, as you have done all this day."

"Oh, aunt, I pray you to come," said Silence, and she turned her white face over her shoulder toward her aunt; "there is somewhat wrong surely."

Widow Bishop got up, still scowling, and went over to the window. Silence stood aside and pointed to the little clear circle in the midst of the frost. "Over there to the north," she said, in a quick, low voice.

Her aunt adjusted her horn spectacles and bent her head stiffly. "I see naught," said she.

"A red glare in the north!"

"A red glare in the north! Be ye out of your mind, wench! There be no red glare in the north. Everything be quiet in the town. Get ye away from the window and to your work. I have no more patience with such doings. Here have I left my knitting for nothing, and I just about setting the heel. You'd best keep to your spinning instead of spying out of the window at your own nightmares, and gadding about the town after David Walcott. Pretty doings for a modest maid, I call it, following after young men in this fashion!"

Silence turned on her aunt, and her blue eyes gleamed dark; she held up her head like a queen. "I follow not after young men," she said.

"Heard I not David Walcott's voice at the door? Went you not to Goody Sheldon's, where he lives? Was it not his voice—hey?"

"Yes, 'twas, an' I had a right to go there an I chose, an' 'twas naught unmaidenly," said Silence.

"'Twas unmaidenly in my day," retorted her aunt; "perhaps 'tis different now." She had returned to her seat, and was clashing her knitting-needles like two swords in a duel.

Silence pulled a spinning-wheel before the fire and fell to work. The wheel turned so rapidly that the spokes were a revolving shadow; there was a sound as if a bee had entered the room.

"I staid at home, and your uncle did the courting," Widow Eunice Bishop continued, in a voice that demanded response.

But Silence made none. She went on spinning. Her aunt eyed her maliciously. "I never went after nightfall to his house that he might see me home," said she. "I trow my mother would have locked me up in the garret, and kept me on meal and water for a week, had I done aught so bold."

Silence spun on. Her aunt threw her head back, and knitted, jerking out her elbows. Neither of them spoke again until the clock struck nine. Then Widow Bishop wound her ball of yarn closer, and stuck in the knitting-needles, and rose. "'Tis time to put out the candle," she said, "and I have done a good day's work, and feel need of rest. They that have idled cannot make it up by wasting tallow." She threw open the door that led to her bedroom, and a blast of icy confined air rushed in. She untied the black cap that framed her nervous face austerely, and her gray head, with its tight rosette of hair on the crown, appeared. Silence set her spinning-wheel

back, and raked the ashes over the hearth fire. Then she took the candle and climbed the stairs to her own chamber. Her aunt was already in bed, her pale, white-frilled face sunk in the icy feather pillow. But she did not bid her good-night: not on account of her anger; there was seldom any such formal courtesy exchanged between the women. Silence's chamber had one side sloping with the slope of the roof, and in it were two dormer-windows looking toward the north. She set her candle on the table, breathed on one of these windows, as she had on the one downstairs, and looked out. She stood there several minutes, then she turned away, shaking her head. The room was very cold. She let down her smooth fair hair, and her fingers began to redden; she took off her kerchief; then she stopped, and looked hesitatingly at her bed, with its blue curtains. She set her mouth hard, and put on her kerchief. Then she sat down on the edge of her bed and waited. After a while she pulled a quilt from the bed and wrapped it around her. Still she did not shiver. She had blown out the candle, and the room was very dark. All her nerves seemed screwed tight like fiddle-strings, and her thoughts beat upon them and made terrific waves of sound in her ears. She saw sparks and flashes like diamond fire in the darkness. She had her hands clinched tight, but she did not feel her hands nor her feet—she did not feel her whole body. She sat so until two o'clock in the morning. When the clock down in the keeping-room struck the hours, the peals shocked her back for a minute to her old sense of herself; then she lost it again. Just after the clock struck two, while the silvery reverberation of the bell tone was still in her ears, and she was breathing a little freer, a great rosy glow suffused the frosty windows. A horrible discord of sound arose without. Above everything else came something like a peal of laughter from wild beasts or fiends.

Silence arose and went down stairs. Her aunt rushed out of her bedroom, shrieking, and caught hold of her. "Oh, Silence, what is it, what is it?" she cried.

"Get away till I light a candle," said Silence. She fairly pushed her aunt off, shovelled the ashes from the coals in the fireplace, and lighted a candle. Then she threw some wood on the smouldering fire.

Her aunt was running around the room screaming. There came a great pound on the door.

"It's the Indians! it's the Indians! don't let 'em in!" shrieked her aunt. "Don't let them in! don't let them!" She placed her lean shoulder in her white bed-gown against the door. "Go away! go away!" she yelled. "You can't come in! O Lord Almighty, save us!"

"You stand off," said Silence. She took hold of her aunt's shoulders. "Be quiet," she commanded. Then she called out, in a firm voice, "Who is there?"

At the shout in response she drew the great iron bolts quickly and flung open the heavy nail-studded door. There was a press of frantic white-faced people into the room; then the door was slammed to and the bolts shot. It was very still in the room, except for the shuffling rush of the men's feet and now and then a stern gasping order. The children did not cry; all the noise was without. The house might have stood in the midst of some awful wilderness peopled with fiendish beasts, from the noise without. The cries seemed actually in the room. The children's eyes glared white over their mothers' shoulders.

The men hurriedly strengthened the window-shutters with props of logs, and fitted the muskets into the loop-holes. Suddenly there was a great crash at the door and a wilder yell outside. The muskets opened fire, and some of the women rushed to the door and pressed fiercely against it with their delicate shoulders, their white desperate faces turning back dumbly, like a spiritual phalanx of defence. Silence and her aunt were among them.

Suddenly Widow Eunice Bishop, at a fresh onslaught upon the door and a fiercer yell, lifted up her voice and shrieked back in a rage as mad as theirs. Her speech, too, was almost inarticulate, and the sense of it lost in a savage frenzy; her tongue stuttered over abusive epithets; but for a second she prevailed over the terrible chorus without. It was like the solo of a fury. Then louder yells drowned her out; the muskets cracked faster; the men rammed in the charges; the savages fell back somewhat; the blows on the door ceased.

Silence ran up the stairs to her chamber, and peeped cautiously out of a little dormer window. Deerfield village was roaring with flames, the sky and snow were red, and leaping through the glare came the painted savages, a savage white face and the waving sword of a French officer in their midst. The awful war-whoops and the death-cries of her friends and neighbors sounded in her ears. She saw, close under her window, the dark sweep of the tomahawk, the quick glance of the scalping-knife, and the red starting of caps of blood. She saw infants dashed through the air, and the backward-straining forms of shrieking women dragged down the street; but she saw not David Walcott anywhere.

She eyed in an agony some dark bodies lying like logs in the snow. A wild impulse seized her to run out, turn their dead faces, and see that none of them was her lover's. Her room was full of red light; everything in it showed distinctly. The roof of the next house crashed in, and the sparks and cinders shot up like a volcano. There was a great outcry of terror from below, and Silence hurried down. The Indians were trying to fire the house from the west side. They had piled a bank of brush against it, and the men had hacked new loop-holes and were beating them back.

John Carson's wife clutched Silence as she entered the keeping-room. "They are trying to set the house on fire," she gasped, "and—the bullets are giving out!" The woman held a little child hugged close to her breast; she strained him closer. "They shall not have him, anyway," she said. Her mouth looked white and stiff.

"Put him down and help, then," said Silence. She began pulling the pewter plates off the dresser.

"What be you doing with my pewter plates?" screamed her aunt at her elbow.

Silence said nothing. She went on piling the plates under her arm.

"Think you I will have the pewter plates I have had ever since I was wed melted to make bullets for those limbs of Satan?"

Silence carried the plates to the fire; the women piled on wood and made it hotter. John Carson's wife laid her baby on the settle and helped, and Widow Bishop brought out her pewter spoons, and her silver cream-jug when the pewter ran low, and finally her dead husband's knee-buckles from the cedar chest. All the pewter and silver in Widow Eunice

Bishop's house was melted down on that night. The women worked with desperate zeal to supply the men with bullets, and just before the ammunition failed, the Indians left Deerfield village, with their captives in their train.

The men had stopped firing at last. Everything was quiet outside, except for the flurry of musket-shots down on the meadow, where the skirmish was going on between the Hatfield men and the retreating French and Indians. The dawn was breaking, but not a shutter had been stirred in the Bishop house; the inmates were clustered together, their ears straining for another outburst of slaughter.

Suddenly there was a strange crackling sound overhead; a puff of hot smoke came into the room from the stairway. The roof had caught fire from the shower of sparks, and the stanch house that had withstood all the fury of the savages was going the way of its neighbors.

The men rushed up the stair, and fell back. "We can't save it!" Captain Isaac Moulton said, hoarsely. He was an old man, and his white hair tossed wildly around his powder-blackened face.

Widow Eunice Bishop scuttled into her bedroom, and got her best silk pelisse and her gilt-framed looking-glass. "Silence, get out the feather bed!" she shrieked.

The keeping-room was stifling with smoke. Captain Moulton' loosened a window-shutter cautiously and peered out. "I see no sign of the savages," he said. They unbolted the door, and opened it inch by inch, but there was no exultant shout in response. The crack of muskets on the meadow sounded louder ; that was all.

Widow Eunice Bishop pushed forward before the others; the danger by fire to her household goods had driven her own danger from her mind, which could compass but one terror at a time. "Let me forth!" she cried; and she laid the looking-glass and silk pelisse on the snow, and pelted back into the smoke for her feather bed and the best andirons.

Silence carried out the spinning-wheel, and the others caught up various articles which they had wit to see in the panic. They piled them up on the snow outside, and huddled together, staring fearfully down the village street. They saw, amid the smouldering ruins, Ensign John Sheldon's house standing.

"We must make for that," said Captain Isaac Moulton, and they started. The men went before and behind, with their muskets in readiness, and the women and children walked between. Widow Bishop carried the pelisse and looking-glass; somebody had helped her to bring out her feather bed, and she had dragged it to a clean place well away from the burning house.

The dawnlight lay pale and cold in the east; it was steadily overcoming the fireglow from the ruins. Nobody would have known Deerfield village. The night before the sun had gone down upon the snowy slants of humble roofs and the peaceful rise of smoke from pleasant hearth fires. The curtained windows had gleamed out one by one with mild candle-light, and serene faces of white-capped matrons preparing supper had passed them. Now, on both sides of Deerfield street were beds of glowing red coals; grotesque ruins of door-posts and chimneys in the semblances of blackened martyrs stood crumbling in the midst of them, and twisted charred heaps, which the people eyed trembling, lay in the old doorways. The snow showed great red patches in the gathering light, and in them lay still bodies that seemed to move.

Silence Hoit sprang out from the hurrying throng, and turned the head of one dead man whose face she could not see. The horror of his red crown did not move her. She only saw that he was not David Walcott. She stooped and wiped off her hands in some snow.

"That is Israel Bennett," the others groaned.

John Carson's wife had been the dead man's sister. She hugged her baby tighter, and pressed more closely to her husband's back. There was no longer any sound of musketry on the meadows. There was not a sound to be heard except the wind in the dry trees and the panting breaths of the knot of people.

A dead baby lay directly in the path, and a woman caught it up, and tried to warm it at her breast. She wrapped her cloak around it, and wiped its little bloody face with her apron. "'Tis not dead," she declared, frantically; "the child is not dead!" She had not shed a tear nor uttered a wail before, but now she began sobbing aloud over the dead child. It was Goodwife Barnard's, and no kin to her. She was a single woman. The others were looking right and left for lurking savages. She looked only at the little cold face on her bosom. "The child breathes," she said, and hurried on faster that she might get succor for it.

The party halted before Ensign John Sheldon's house. The stout door was fast, but there was a hole in it, as if hacked by a tomahawk. The men tried it and shook it. "Open, open, Goodwife Sheldon!" they hallooed. "Friends! friends! Open the door!" But there was no response.

Silence Hoit left the throng at the door, and began clambering up on a slant of icy snow to a window which was flung wide open. The window-sill was stained with blood, and so was the snow.

One of the men caught Silence and tried to hold her back. "There may be Indians in there," he whispered, hoarsely.

But Silence broke away from him, and was in through the window, and the men followed her, and unbolted the door for the women, who pressed in wildly, and flung it to again. And a child who was among them, little Comfort Arms, stationed herself directly with her tiny back against the door, with her mouth set like a soldier's, and her blue eyes gleaming fierce under her flaxen locks. "They shall not get in," said she. Somehow she had gotten hold of a great horse-pistol, which she carried like a doll.

Nobody heeded her, Silence least of all. She stared about the room, with her lips parted. Right before her on the hearth lay a little three-year-old girl, Mercy Sheldon, her pretty head in a pool of blood, but Silence cast only an indifferent glance when the others gathered about her, groaning and sighing.

Suddenly Silence sprang toward a dark heap near the pantry door, but it was only a woman's quilted petticoat.

The spinning-wheel lay broken on the floor, and all the simple furniture was strewn about wildly. Silence went into Goodwife Sheldon's bedroom, and the others followed her, trembling, all except little Comfort Arms, who stood unflinchingly with her back pressed against the door, and the single woman, Grace Mather; she staid behind, and put wood on the fire after she had picked up the quilted petticoat, and laid the dead baby tenderly wrapped in it on the settle. Then she pulled the settle forward before the fire, and knelt before it, and fell to cha-

fing the little limbs of the dead baby, weeping as she did so.

Goodwife Sheldon's bedroom was in wild disorder. A candle still burned, although it was very low, on the table, whose linen cover had great red fingerprints on it. Goodwife Sheldon's decent clothes were tossed about on the floor; the curtains of the bed were half torn away. Silence pressed forward unshrinkingly toward the bed; the others, even the men, hung back. There lay Goodwife Sheldon dead in her bed. All the light in the room, the candle-light and the low daylight, seemed to focus upon her white frozen profile propped stiffly on the pillow, where she had fallen back when the bullet came through that hole in the door.

Silence looked at her. "Where is David, Goodwife Sheldon?" said she.

Eunice Bishop sprang forward. "Be you clean out of your mind, Silence Hoit?" she cried. "Know you not she's dead? She's dead! Oh, she's dead, she's dead! An' here's her best silk hood trampled underfoot on the floor!" Eunice snatched up the hood, and seized Silence by the arm, but she pushed her back.

"Where is David? Where is he gone?" she demanded again of the dead woman.

The other women came crowding around Silence then, and tried to soothe her and reason with her, while their own faces were white with horror and woe. Goodwife Sarah Spear, an old woman whose sons lay dead in the street outside, put an arm around the girl, and tried to draw her head to her broad bosom.

"Mayhap thou'lt find him, sweetheart," she said. "He's not among the dead out there."

But Silence broke away from the motherly arm, and sped wildly through the other rooms, with the people at her heels, and her aunt crying vainly after her. They found no more dead in the house; naught but ruin and disorder, and bloody footprints and handprints of savages.

When they returned to the keeping-room, Silence seated herself on a stool by the fire, and held out her hands toward the blaze to warm them. The daylight was broad now, and the great clock that had come from overseas ticked; the Indians had not touched that.

Captain Isaac Moulton lifted little Mercy Sheldon from the hearth and carried her to her dead mother in the bedroom, and two of the older women went in there and shut the door. Little Comfort Arms still stood with her back against the outer door, and Grace Mather tended the dead baby on the settle.

"What do ye with that dead child?" a woman called out roughly to her.

"I tell ye 'tis not dead; it breathes," returned Grace Mather; and she never turned her harsh plain face from the dead child.

"An' I tell ye 'tis dead."

"An' I tell ye 'tis not dead. I need but some hot posset for it."

Goodwife Carson began to weep. She hugged her own living baby tighter. "Let her alone!" she sobbed. "I wonder our wits be not all gone." She went sobbing over to little Comfort Arms at the door. "Come away, sweetheart, and draw near the fire," she pleaded, brokenly.

The little girl looked obstinately up at her. "They shall not come in," she said. "The wicked savages shall not come in again."

"No more shall they, an the Lord be willing, sweet. But, I pray you, come away from the door now."

Comfort shook her head, and she looked like her father as he fought on the Deerfield meadows.

"The savages be gone, sweet."

But Comfort answered not a word, and Goodwife Carson sat down and began to nurse her baby. One of the women hung the porridge-kettle over the fire; another put some potatoes in the ashes to bake. Presently the two women came out of Goodwife Sheldon's bedroom with grave, strained faces, and held their stiff blue fingers out to the hearth fire.

Eunice Bishop, who was stirring the porridge, looked at them with sharp curiosity. "How look they?" she whispered.

"As peaceful as if they slept," replied Goodwife Spear, who was one of the women.

"And the child's head?"

"We put on her little white cap with the lace frills."

Eunice stirred the bubbling porridge, scowling in the heat and steam; some of the women laid the table with Hannah Sheldon's linen cloth and pewter dishes, and presently the breakfast was dished up.

Little Comfort Arms had sunk at the foot of the nail studded door in a deep slumber. She slept at her post like the faithless sentry whose slumbers the night

before had brought about the destruction of Deerfield village. Goodwife Spear raised her up, but her curly head drooped helplessly.

"Wake up, Comfort, and have a sup of hot porridge," she called in her ear.

She led her over to the table, Comfort stumbling weakly at arm's-length, and set her on a stool with a dish of porridge before her, which she ate uncertainly in a dazed fashion, with her eyes filming and her head nodding.

They all gathered gravely around the table except Silence Hoit and Grace Mather. Silence sat still, staring at the fire, and Grace had dipped out a little cup of the hot porridge, and was trying to feed it to the dead baby, with crooning words.

"Silence, why come you not to the table?" her aunt called out.

"I want nothing," answered Silence.

"I see not why you should so set yourself up before the others, as having so much more to bear," said Eunice, sharply. "There be Goodwife Spear, with her sons unburied on the road yonder, and she doth eat her porridge with good relish."

John Carson's wife set her baby on her husband's knee, and carried a dish of porridge to Silence.

"Try and eat it, sweet," she whispered. She was near Silence's age.

Silence looked up at her. "I want it not," said she.

"But he may not be dead, sweet. He may presently be home. You would not he should find you spent and fainting. Perchance he may have wounds for you to tend."

Silence seized the dish and began to eat the porridge in great spoonfuls, gulping it down fast.

The people at the table eyed her sadly and whispered, and they also cast frequent glances at Grace Mather bending over the dead baby. Once Captain Isaac Moulton called out to her in his gruff old voice, which he tried to soften, and she answered back, sharply: "Think ye I will leave this child while it breathes, Captain Isaac Moulton? In faith I be the only one of ye all that hath regard to it."

But suddenly, when the meal was half over, Grace Mather arose, and gathered up the little dead baby, carried it into Goodwife Sheldon's bedroom, and was gone some time.

"She has lost her wits," said Eunice Bishop. "Think you not we should follow her? She may do some harm."

"Nay, let her be," said Goodwife Spear.

When at last Grace Mather came out of the bedroom, and they all turned to look at her, her face was stern but quite composed. "I found a little clean linen shift in the chest," she said to Goodwife Spear, who nodded gravely. Then she sat down at the table and ate.

The people, as they ate, cast frequent glances at the barred door and the shuttered windows. The daylight was broad outside, but there was no glimmer of it in the room, and the candles were lighted. They dared not yet remove the barricades, and the muskets were in readiness: the Indians might return.

All at once there was a shrill clamor at the door, and men sprang to their muskets. The women clutched each other, panting.

"Unbar the door!" shrieked a quavering old voice. "I tell ye, unbar the door! I be nigh frozen a-standing here. Unbar the door! The Indians be gone hours ago."

"'Tis Goody Crane," cried Eunice Bishop.

Captain Isaac Moulton shot back the bolts and opened the door a little way, while the men stood close at his back, and Goody Crane slid in like a swift black shadow out of the daylight.

She crouched down close to the fire, trembling and groaning, and the women gave her some hot porridge.

"Where have ye been?" demanded Eunice Bishop.

"Where they found me not," replied the old woman, and there was a sudden leer like a light in the gloom of her great hood. She motioned toward the bedroom door.

"Goody Sheldon sleeps late this morning, and so doth Mercy," said she. "I trow she will not dip her candles to-day."

The people looked at each other; a subtler horror than that of the night before shook their spirits.

Captain Isaac Moulton towered over the old woman on the hearth. "How knew you Goodwife Sheldon and Mercy were dead?" he asked, sternly.

The old woman leered up at him undauntedly; her head bobbed. There was a curious, grotesqueness about her blanketed and hooded figure when in motion.

There was so little of the old woman herself visible that motion surprised, as it would have done in a puppet. "Told I not Goody Sheldon last night she would never stir porridge again?" said she. "Who stirred the porridge this morning? I trow Goody Sheldon's hands be too stiff and too cold, though they have stirred well in their day. Hath she dipped her candles yet? Hath she begun on her weaving? I trow 'twill be a long day ere Mary Sheldon's linen-chest be filled, if she herself go a-gadding to Canada and her mother sleep so late."

"Eat this hot porridge and stop your croaking," said Goodwife Spear, stooping over her.

The old woman extended her two shaking hands for the dish. "That was what she said last night," she returned. "The living echo the dead, and that be enough wisdom for a witch."

"You'll be burned for a witch yet, Goody Crane, an you be not careful," cried Eunice Bishop.

"There be fire enough outside to burn all the witches in the land," muttered the old woman, sipping her porridge. Suddenly she eyed Silence sitting motionless opposite. "Where be your sweetheart this fine morning, Silence Hoit?" she inquired.

Silence looked at her. There was a strange likeness between the glitter in her blue eyes and that in Goody Crane's black ones.

The old woman's great hood nodded over the porridge-dish. "I can tell ye, Mistress Silence," she said, thickly, as she ate. "He be gone to Canada on a moose-hunt, and unless I be far wrong, he hath taken thy wits with him."

"How know you David Walcott is gone to Canada?" cried Eunice Bishop; and Silence stared at her with her hard blue eyes.

Silence's soft fair hair hung all matted like uncombed flax over her pale cheeks. There was a rigid, dead look about her girlish forehead and her sweet mouth.

"I know," returned Goody Crane, nodding her head.

The women washed the pewter dishes, set them back on the dresser, and swept the floor. Little Comfort Arms had been carried upstairs and laid in the bed whence poor Mary Sheldon had been dragged and haled to Canada. The men stood talking near their stacked muskets. One of the shutters had been opened and the candles put out. The winter sun shone in the window as it had shone before, but the poor folk in Ensign Sheldon's keeping-room saw it with a certain shock, as if it were a stranger. That morning their own hearts had in them such strangeness that they transferred it like motion to all familiar objects. The very iron dogs in the Sheldon fireplace seemed on the leap with tragedy, and the porridge-kettle swung darkly out of some former age.

Now and then one of the men opened the door cautiously and peered out and listened. The reek of the smouldering village came in at the door, but there was not a sound except the whistling howl of the savage north wind, which still swept over the valley. There was not a shot to be heard from the meadows. The men discussed the wisdom of leaving the women for a short space and going forth to explore, but Widow Eunice Bishop interposed, thrusting in her sharp face among them.

"Here we be," scolded she, "a passel of women and children, and Hannah Sheldon and Mercy a-lying dead, and me with my house burnt down, and nothing saved except my silk pelisse and my looking-glass and my feather bed, and it's a mercy if that's not all smooched, and you talk of going off and leaving us!"

The men looked doubtfully at each other; then there was the hissing creak of footsteps on the snow outside, and Widow Bishop screamed. "Oh, the Indians have come back!" she proclaimed.

Silence looked up.

The door was tried from without.

"Who's there?" cried out Captain Moulton.

"John Sheldon," responded a hoarse voice. "Who's inside?"

Captain Moulton threw open the door, and John Sheldon stood there. His severe and sober face was painted like an Indian's with blood and powder grime; he stood staring in at the company.

"Come in, quick, and let us bar the door!" screamed Eunice Bishop.

John Sheldon came in hesitatingly, and stood looking around the room.

"Have you but just come from the meadows?" inquired Captain Moulton. But John Sheldon did not seem to hear him. He stared at the company, who all stood still staring back at him; then he looked hard and long at the doors, as if

expecting some one to enter. The eyes of the others followed his, but no one spoke.

"Where's Hannah?" asked John Sheldon.

Then the women began to weep.

"She's in there," sobbed John Carson's wife, pointing to the bedroom door—"in there with little Mercy, Goodman Sheldon."

"Is—the child hurt, and—Hannah a-tending her?"

The women wept, and pushed each other forward to tell him, but Captain Isaac Moulton spoke out, and drove the knife home like an honest soldier, who will kill if he must, but not mangle.

"Goodwife Sheldon lies yonder, shot dead in her bed, and we found the child dead on the hearth-stone," said Isaac Moulton.

John Sheldon turned his gaze on him.

"The judgments of the Lord are just and righteous altogether," said Isaac Moulton, confronting him with stern defiance.

"Amen," returned John Sheldon. He took off his cloak, and hung it up on the peg where he was used.

"Where is David Walcott?" asked Silence, standing before him.

"David, he be gone with the Indians to Canada, and the boys, Ebenezer and Remembrance."

"Where is David?"

"I tell ye, lass, he be gone with the French and Indians to Canada; and you need be thankful he was but your sweetheart, and ye not wed, with a half-score of babes to be taken too. The curse that was upon the women of Jerusalem is upon the women of Deerfield." John Sheldon looked sternly into Silence's white wild face; then his voice softened. "Take heart, lass," said he. "Erelong I shall go to Governor Dudley and get help, and then after them to Canada, and fetch them back. Take heart; I will fetch thee thy sweetheart presently."

Silence returned to her seat in the fireplace. Goody Crane looked across at her. "He will come back over the north meadow," she whispered. "Keep watch over the north meadow; but 'twill be a long day ere ye see him."

Silence paid seemingly little heed. She paid little heed to Ensign John Sheldon relating how the French and Indians, with Hertel de Rouville at their head, were on the road to Canada with their captives; of the fight on the meadow between the retreating foe and the brave band of Deerfield and Hatfield men, who had made a stand there to intercept them; how they had been obliged to cease firing because the captives were threatened; and the pitiful tale of Parson John Williams, with two children dead, dragged through the wilderness with the others, and his sick wife.

"Had folk listened to him, we had all been safe in our good houses with our belongings," cried Eunice Bishop.

"They will not drag Goodwife Williams far," said Goody Crane, "nor the babe at her breast. I trow well it hath stopped wailing ere now."

"How know you that?" questioned Eunice Bishop, turning sharply on her.

But the old woman only nodded her head, and Silence paid no heed, for she was not there. Her slender girlish shape sat by the hearth fire in John Sheldon's house in Deerfield, her fair head showed like a delicate flower, but Silence Hoit was following her lover to Canada. Every step that he took painfully through pathless forests, on treacherous ice, and desolate snow fields, she took more painfully still; every knife gleaming over his head she saw. She bore his every qualm of hunger and pain and cold, and it was all the harder because they struck on her bare heart with no flesh between, for she sat in the flesh in Deerfield, and her heart went with her lover to Canada.

The sun stood higher, but it was still bitter cold; the blue frost on the windows did not melt, and the icicles on the eaves, which nearly touched the sharp snow-drifts underneath, did not drip. The desolate survivors of the terrible night began work among the black ruins of their homes. They cared as well as they might for the dead in Deerfield street, and the dead on the meadow where the fight had been. Their muscles were all tense with the cold, their faces seamed and blue with it, but their hearts were strained with a fiercer cold than that. Not one man of them but had one or more slain, with dead face upturned seeking his in the morning light or on that awful road to Canada. Ever as the men worked they turned their eyes northward, and met grimly the icy blast of the north wind, and sometimes to their excited fancies it seemed to bring to their ears the cries of their friends who were facing it also, and they stood still and listened.

Silence Hoit crept out of the house and down the road a little way, and then stood looking over the meadow toward the north. Her fair hair tossed in the wind, her pale cheeks turned pink, the wind struck full upon her delicate figure. She had come out without her blanket.

"David!" she called. "David! David! David!" The north wind bore down upon her, shrieking with a wild fury like a savage of the air; the dry branches of a small tree near her struck her in the face. "David!" she called again. "David! David!" She swelled out her white throat like a bird, and her voice was shrill and sweet and far-reaching. The men moving about on the meadow below, and stooping over the dead, looked up at her, but she did not heed them. She had come through a break in the palisades; on each side of her the frozen snow-drifts slanted sharply to their tops; over the drifts the enemy had passed the night before, and they glittered with blue lights like glaciers in the morning sun.

The men on the meadow saw Silence's hair blowing like a yellow banner between the drifts of snow.

"The poor lass has come out bareheaded," said Ensign Sheldon. "She is near out of her mind for David Walcott."

"A man should have no sweetheart in these times, unless he would her heart be broke," said a young man beside him. He was hardly more than a boy, and his face was as rosy as a girl's in the wind. He kept close to Ensign Sheldon, and his mind was full of young Mary Sheldon travelling to Canada on her weary little feet. He had often, on a Sabbath day, looked across the meeting-house at her, and thought that there was no maiden like her in Deerfield.

Ensign John Sheldon thought of his sweetheart lying with her heart still in her freezing bedroom, and stooped over a dead Hatfield man whose face was frozen into the snow.

The young man, whose name was Freedom Wells, bent over to help him. Then he started. "What's that?" he cried.

"'Tis only Silence Hoit calling David Walcott again," replied Ensign Sheldon.

The voice had sounded like Mary Sheldon's to Freedom. The tears rolled over his boyish cheeks as he put his hands into the snow and tried to dig it away from the dead man's face.

"'DAVID!' SHE CALLED. 'DAVID! DAVID! DAVID!'"

"David! David! David!" called Silence.

Suddenly her aunt threw a wiry arm around her. "Be you gone clean daft," she shrieked against the wind, "standing here calling David Walcott? Know you not he is a half-day's journey toward Canada, an the savages have not scalped him and left him by the way? Standing here with your hair blowing and no blanket! Into the house with ye!"

Silence followed her aunt unresistingly. The women in Ensign Sheldon's house were hard at work. They were baking in the great brick oven, spinning, and even dipping poor Goodwife Sheldon's candles.

"Bind up your hair, like an honest maid, and go to spinning," said Eunice, and she pointed to the spinning-wheel which had been saved from her own house. "We that be spared have to work, and not sit down and trot our own hearts on our knees. There be scarce a yard of linen left in Deerfield, to say naught of woollen cloth. Bind up your hair!"

And Silence bound up her hair, and sat down by her wheel meekly, and yet with a certain dignity. Indeed, through all the disorder of her mind, that delicate maiden dignity never forsook her, and there was never aught but respect shown her.

As time went on, it became quite evident that although the fair semblance of Silence Hoit still walked the Deerfield street, sat in the meeting-house, and toiled at the spinning-wheel and the loom, yet she was as surely not all there as though she had been haled to Canada with the other captives on that terrible February night. And it became the general opinion that Silence Hoit would never be quite her old self again and walk in the goodly company of all her fair wits unless David Walcott should be redeemed from captivity and restored to her. Then, it was accounted possible, the mending of the calamity which brought her disorder upon her might remove it.

"Ye wait," Widow Eunice Bishop would say, hetchelling flax the while as though it were the scalp-locks of the enemy—"ye wait. If once David Walcott show his face, ye'll see Silence Hoit be not so lacking. She hath a tenderer heart than some I could mention, who go about smiling when their nearest of kin lay in torment in Indian lodges. She cares naught for picking up a new sweetheart.

She hath a steady heart that be not so easy turned as some. Silence was never a light hussy, a-dancing hither and thither off the bridle-path for a new flower on the bushes. An', for all ye call her lacking now, there be not a maid in Deerfield does such a day's task as she."

And that last statement was quite true. All the Deerfield women, the matrons and maidens, toiled unceasingly, with a kind of stern patience like that which served their husbands and lovers in the frontier corn fields, and which served all the dauntless border settlers, who were forced continually to rebuild after destruction, like way-side ants whose nests are always being trampled underfoot. There was need of unflinching toil at wheel and loom, for there was great scarcity of household linen in Deerfield, and Silence Hoit's shapely white maiden hands flinched less than any.

Nevertheless, many a day, in the morning when the snowy meadows were full of blue lights, at sunset when all the snow levels were rosy, but more particularly in wintry moonlight when the country was like a waste of silver, would Silence Hoit leave suddenly her household task, and hasten to the terrace overlooking the north meadow, and shriek out: "David! David! David Walcott!"

The village children never jeered at her, as they would sometimes jeer at Goody Crane if not restrained by their elders. They eyed with a mixture of wonder and admiration Silence's beautiful bewildered face, with the curves of gold hair around the pink cheeks, and the fret-work of tortoise-shell surmounting it. David Walcott had given Silence her shell comb, and she was never seen without it.

Many a time when Silence called to David from the terrace of the north meadow, some of the little village maids in their homespun pinafores would join her and call with her. They had no fear of her, as they had of Goody Crane.

Indeed, Goody Crane, after the massacre, was in worse repute than ever in Deerfield. There were dark rumors concerning her whereabouts upon that awful night. Some among the devout and godly were fain to believe that the old woman had been in league with the powers of darkness and their allies the savages, and had so escaped harm. Some even whispered that in the thickest of the slaughter, when Deerfield was in the midst of that storm of fire, old Goody Crane's laugh had been heard, and one, looking up, had spied her high overhead riding her broomstick, her face red with the glare of the fire. The old woman was sheltered under protest, and had Deerfield not been a frontier town, and graver matters continually in mind, she might have come to harm in consequence of the gloomy suspicions concerning her.

Many a night after the massacre would the windows fly up and anxious faces peer out. It was as if the ears of the people were tuned up to the pitch of the Indian war-whoops, and their very thoughts made the nights ring with them.

The palisades were well looked to; there was never a slope of frozen snow again to form foothold for the enemy, and the sentry never slept at his post. But the anxious women listened all winter for the war-whoops, and many a time it seemed they heard them. In the midst of their nervous terror it was often a sore temptation to consult old Goody Crane, since she was held to have occult knowledge.

"I'll warrant old Goody Crane could tell us in a twinkling whether or no the Indians would come before morning," Eunice Bishop said one fierce windy night that called to mind the one of the massacre.

"Knowledge got in unlawful ways would avail us naught," returned Goodwife Spear. "I trow the Lord be yet able to protect His people."

"I doubt not that," said Eunice Bishop, "but I would like well to know if I had best bury my pelisse and my spinning-wheel and looking-glass in a snow-drift to-night. I have no mind the Indians shall get them. I warrant she knoweth well."

But Eunice Bishop did not consult Goody Crane, although she watched her narrowly and had a sharp ear to her mutterings as she sat in the chimney-corner. Eunice and Silence were living in John Sheldon's house, as did many of the survivors for some time after the massacre. It was the largest house in the village, and most of its original inhabitants were dead or gone into captivity. The people all huddled together fearfully in the few houses that were left, and the women's spinning-wheels and looms jostled each other.

As soon as the weather moderated, the work of building new dwellings commenced, and went on bravely with the advance of the spring. The air was full of the calls of spring birds and the strokes of axes and hammers. A little house was built on the site of their old one for Widow Bishop and Silence Hoit. Widow Sarah Spear also lived with them, and Goody Crane took shelter at their fireside for the most part. So they were a household of women, with loaded muskets at hand, and spinning-wheels and looms at full hum. They had but a scanty household store, although Widow Bishop tried in every way to increase it. Several times during the summer she took perilous journeys to Hatfield and Squakheak, for the sake of bartering skeins of yarn or rolls of wool for household articles. In December, when Ensign Sheldon with young Freedom Wells went down to Boston to consult with Governor Dudley concerning an expedition to Canada to redeem the captives, Widow Eunice Bishop, having saved a few shillings, burdened him with a commission to purchase for her a new cap and a pair of bellows. She was much angered when he returned without them, having clean forgotten them in his press of business.

On the day when John Sheldon and Freedom Wells started upon their terrible journey of three hundred miles to redeem the captives, Eunice Bishop scolded well as she spun by her hearth fire. "I trow they will bring back nobody," said she, her nose high in air, and her voice shrilling over the drone of the wheel; "an they could not do the bidding of a poor lone widow-woman, and fetch her not the cap and bellows from Boston, they'll fetch nobody home from Canada. I would I had ear of Governor Dudley. I trow men with minds upon their task would be sent." Eunice kept jerking her head as she scolded, and spun like a bee angry with its own humming.

Silence sat knitting, and paid no heed. She had paid no heed to any of the talk about Ensign Sheldon's and Freedom Wells's journey to Canada. She had not seemed to listen when Widow Spear had tried to explain the matter to her. "It may be, sweetheart, if it be the will of the Lord, that they will bring David back to thee," she had said over and over, and Silence had knitted and made no response.

She was the only one in Deerfield who

was not torn with excitement and suspense as the months went by, and the only one unmoved by joy or disappointment when in May John Sheldon and Freedom Wells returned with five of the captives. But David Walcott was not among them.

"Said I not 'twould be so?" scolded Eunice Bishop. "Knew I not 'twould be so when they forgot to get the cap and the bellows in Boston? The one of all the captives that could have saved a poor maid's wits they leave behind. There's Mary Sheldon come home, and she a-coloring red before Freedom Wells, and everybody in the room a-seeing it. I trow they might have done somewhat for poor Silence," and Eunice broke down and wailed and wept, but Silence shed not a tear. Before long she stole out to the terrace and called "David! David! David!" over the north meadow, and strained her blue eyes toward Canada, and held out her fair arms, but it was with no new disappointment and desolation.

There was never a day nor a night that Silence called not over the north meadow like a spring bird from the bush to her absent mate, and people heard her and sighed and shuddered. One afternoon in the last of the month of June, as Silence was thrusting her face between the leaves of a wild cherry-tree and calling "David! David! David!" David himself broke through the thicket and stood before her. He and three other young men had escaped from their captivity and come home, and the four, crawling half dead across the meadow, had heard Silence's voice from the terrace above, and David, leaving the others, had made his way to her.

"Silence!" he said, and held out his poor arms, panting.

But Silence looked past him. "David! David! David Walcott!" she called.

David could scarcely stand for trembling, and he grasped a branch of the cherry-tree to steady himself, and swayed with it.

"Know—you not—who I am, Silence?" he said.

But she made as though she did not hear, and called again, always looking past him. And David Walcott, being near spent with fatigue and starvation, wound himself feebly around the trunk of the tree, and the tears dropped over his cheeks as he looked at her; and she called past him, until some women came and led him away and tried to comfort him, telling him how it was with her, and that she would soon know him when he looked more like himself.

But the summer wore away and she did not know him, although he constantly followed her beseechingly. His elders even reproved him for paying so little heed to his work in the colony. "It is not meet for a young man to be so weaned from usefulness by grief for a maid," said they. But David Walcott would at any time leave his reaping-hook in the corn and his axe in the tree, leave aught but his post as sentry, when he heard Silence calling him over the north meadow. He would stand at her elbow and say, in his voice that broke like a woman's: "Here I be, sweetheart, at thy side. I pray thee turn thy head." But she would not let her eyes rest upon him for more than a second's space, but turned them ever past him toward Canada, and called in his very ears with a sad longing that tore his heart: "David! David! David!" It was as if her mind, reaching out ever and speeding fast in search of him, had gotten such impetus that she passed the very object of her search and knew it not.

Now and then would David Walcott grow desperate, fling his arms around her, and kiss her upon her cold delicate lips and cheeks as if he would make her recognize him by force; but she would free herself from him with a passionless resentment that left him helpless.

One day in autumn, when the borders of the Deerfield meadows were a smoky purple with wild asters, and golden-rods flashed out like golden flames in the midst of them, David Walcott had been pleading vainly with Silence as she stood calling on the north terrace. Suddenly he turned and rushed away, and his face was all convulsed like a weeping boy's. As he came out of the thicket he met the old woman Goody Crane, and would fain have hidden his face from her, but she stopped him.

"Prithee stop a moment's space, Master David Walcott," said she.

"What would you?" David cried out in a surly tone, and he dashed the back of his hand across his eyes.

"'Tis full moon to-night," said the old woman, in a whisper. "Come out here to-night when the moon shall be an hour high, and I promise ye she shall know ye."

The young man stared at her.

"I tell ye Mistress Silence Hoit shall know ye to-night," repeated the old woman. Her voice sounded hollow in the depths of her great hood, which she donned early in the fall. Her eyes in the gloom of it gleamed with a small dark brightness.

"I'll have no witch-work tried on her," said David, roughly.

"I'll try no witch-work but mine own wits," said Goody Crane. "If they would hang me for a witch for that, then they may. None but I can cure her. I tell ye, come out here to-night when the moon is an hour high; and mind ye wear a white sheep's fleece over your shoulders. I'll harm her not so much with my witch-work as ye'll do with your love, for all your prating."

The old woman pushed past him to where Silence stood calling, and waited there, standing in the shadow cast by the wild cherry-tree until she ceased and turned away. Then she caught hold of the skirt of her gown, and David stood, hidden by the thicket, listening.

"I prithee, Mistress Silence Hoit, listen but a moment," said Goody Crane.

Silence paused, and smiled at her gently and wearily.

"Give me your hand," demanded the old woman.

And Silence held out her hand, flashing white in the green gloom, as if she cared not.

The old woman turned the palm, bending her hooded head low over it. "He draweth near!" she cried out suddenly; "he draweth near, with a white sheep's fleece over his shoulders! He cometh through the woods from Canada. He will cross the meadow when the moon is an hour high to-night. He will wear a white sheep's fleece over his shoulders, and ye'll know him by that."

Silence's wandering eyes fastened upon her face.

The old woman caught hold of her shoulders and shook her to and fro. "David! David! David Walcott!" she screamed. "David Walcott with a white sheep's fleece on his back! On the meadow! To-night when the moon's an hour high! Be ye out here to-night, Silence Hoit, if ye'd see him a-coming down from the north!"

Silence gasped faintly when the old woman released her and went muttering away. Presently she crept home, and sat down with her knitting-work in the chimney-place.

When Eunice Bishop hung on the porridge-kettle, Goody Crane lifted the latch-string and came in. It was growing dusky, but the moon would not rise for an hour yet. Goody Crane sat opposite Silence, with her eyes fixed upon her, and Silence, in spite of herself, kept looking at her. A gold brooch at the old woman's throat glittered in the firelight, and that seemed to catch Silence's eyes. She finally knitted with them fixed upon it.

She scarcely took her eyes away when she ate her supper; then she sat down to her knitting and knitted, and gazed, in spite of herself, at the gold spot on the old woman's throat.

The moon arose; the tree branches before the windows tossed half in silver light; the air was shrill with crickets. Silence stirred uneasily, and dropped stitches in her knitting-work. "He draweth near," muttered Goody Crane, and Silence quivered.

The moon was a half-hour high. Widow Bishop was spinning. Widow Spear was winding quills, and Silence knitted. "He draweth near," muttered Goody Crane.

"I'll have no witchcraft!" Silence cried out, suddenly and sharply. Her aunt stopped spinning, and Widow Spear started.

"What's that?" said her aunt. But Silence was knitting again.

"What meant you by that?" asked her aunt, sharply.

"I have dropped a stitch," said Silence.

Her aunt spun again, with occasional wary glances. The moon was three-quarters of an hour high. Silence gazed steadily at the gold brooch at Goody Crane's throat.

"The moon is near an hour high; you had best be going," said the old woman, in a low monotone.

Silence arose directly.

"Where go you at this time of night?" grumbled her aunt. But Silence glided past her.

"You'll lose your good name as well as your wits," cried Eunice. But she did not try to stop Silence, for she knew it was useless.

"A white sheep's fleece over his shoulders," muttered Goody Crane as Silence went out of the door; and the other women marvelled what she meant.

Silence Hoit went swiftly and softly down Deerfield street to her old haunt on the north meadow terrace. She pushed in among the wild cherry-trees, which waved, white with the moonlight, like ghostly arms in her face. Then she called, setting her face toward Canada and the north: "David! David! David!" But her voice had a different tone in it, and it broke with her heart-beats.

David Walcott came slowly across the meadow below; a white fleece of a sheep thrown over his back caught the moonlight. He came on, and on, and on; then he went up the terrace to Silence. Her face, white like a white flower in the moonlight, shone out suddenly close be-

fore him. He waited a second, then he spoke. "Silence!" he said.

Then Silence gave a great cry, and threw out her arms around his neck, and pressed softly and wildly against him with her wet cheek to his.

"Know you who 'tis, sweetheart?"

"Oh, David, David, 'tis thou, 'tis thou, 'tis thou!"

The trees arched like arbors with the weight of the wild grapes, which made the air sweet; the night insects called from the bushes; Deerfield village and the whole valley lay in the moonlight like a landscape of silver. The lovers stood in each other's arms, motionless, and seemingly fixed as the New England flora around them, as if they too might reappear hundreds of spring-times hence, with their loves as fairly in blossom.

THE PROMISED LAND
by Owen Wister

PERHAPS there were ten of them—these galloping dots were hard to count—down in the distant bottom across the river. Their swiftly moving dust hung with them close, thinning to a yellow veil when they halted short. They clustered a moment, then parted like beads, and went wide asunder on the plain. They veered singly over the level, merged in twos and threes, apparently racing, shrank together like elastic, and broke ranks again to swerve over the stretching waste. From this visioned pantomime presently came a sound, a tiny shot. The figures were too far for discerning which fired it. It evidently did no harm, and was repeated at once. A babel of diminutive explosions followed, while the horsemen galloped on in unexpected circles. Soon, for no visible reason, the dots ran together, bunching compactly. The shooting stopped, the dust rose thick again from the crowded hoofs, cloaking the group, and so passed back and was lost among the silent barren hills.

Four emigrants had watched this from the high bleak rim of the Big Bend. They stood where the flat of the desert broke and tilted down in grooves and bulges deep to the lurking Columbia. Empty levels lay opposite, narrowing up into the high country.

"That's the Colville Reservation across the river from us," said the man.

"Another!" sighed his wife.

"The last Indians we'll strike. Our trail to the Okanagon goes over a corner of it."

"We're going to those hills?" The mother looked at her little girl and back where the cloud had gone.

"Only a corner, Liza. The ferry puts us over on it, and we've got to go by the ferry or stay this side of the Columbia. You wouldn't want to start a home here?"

They had driven twenty-one hundred miles at a walk. Standing by them were the six horses with the wagon, and its tunnelled roof of canvas shone duskily on the empty verge of the wilderness. A dry windless air hung over the table-land of the Big Bend, but a sound rose from somewhere, floating voluminous upon the silence, and sank again.

"Rapids!" The man pointed far up the giant rut of the stream to where a streak of white water twinkled at the foot of the hills. "We've struck the river too high." he added.

"Then we don't cross here?" said the woman, quickly.

"No. By what they told me the cabin and the ferry ought to be five miles down."

Her face fell. "Only five miles! I was wondering, John— Wouldn't there be a way round for the children to—"

"Now, mother," interrupted the husband, "that ain't like you. We've crossed plenty Indian reservations this trip a'ready."

"I don't want to go round," the little girl said. "Father, don't make me go round."

Mart, the boy, with a loose hook of hair

hanging down to his eyes from his hat, did not trouble to speak. He had been disappointed in the westward journey to find all the Indians peaceful. He knew which way he should go now, and he went to the wagon to look once again down the clean barrel of his rifle.

"Why, Nancy, you don't like Indians?" said her mother.

"Yes, I do. I like chiefs."

Mrs. Clallam looked across the river. "It was so strange, John, the way they acted. It seems to get stranger, thinking about it."

"They didn't see us. They didn't have a notion—"

"But if we're going right over?"

"We're not going over there, Liza. That quick water's the Mahkin Rapids, and our ferry's clear down below from this place."

"What could they have been after, do you think?"

"Those chaps? Oh, nothing, I guess. They weren't killing anybody."

"Playing cross-tag," said Mart.

"I'd like to know, John, how you know they weren't killing anybody. They might have been trying to."

"Then we're perfectly safe, Liza. We can set and let 'em kill us all day."

"Well, I don't think it's any kind of way to behave, running around shooting right off your horse."

"And Fourth of July over too," said Mart from the wagon. He was putting cartridges into the magazine of his Winchester. His common-sense told him that those horsemen would not cross the river, but the notion of a night attack pleased the imagination of sixteen.

"It was the children," said Mrs. Clallam. "And nobody's getting me any wood. How am I going to cook supper? Stir yourselves!"

They had carried water in the wagon, and father and son went for wood. Some way down the hill they came upon a gully with some dead brush, and climbed back with this. Supper was eaten on the ground, the horses were watered, given grain, and turned loose to find what pickings they might in the lean growth, and dusk had not turned to dark when the emigrants were in their beds on the soft dust. The noise of the rapids dominated the air with distant sonority, and the children slept at once, the boy with his rifle along his blanket's edge. John

Clallam lay till the moon rose hard and brilliant, and then quietly, lest his wife should hear from her bed by the wagon, went to look across the river. Where the downward slope began he came upon her. She had been watching for some time. They were the only objects in that bald moonlight. No shrub grew anywhere that reached to the waist, and the two figures drew together on the lonely hill. They stood hand in hand and motionless, except that the man bent over the woman and kissed her. When she spoke of Iowa they had left, he talked of the new region of their hopes, the country that lay behind the void hills opposite, where it would not be a struggle to live. He dwelt on the home they would make, and her mood followed his at last, till husband and wife were building distant plans together. The Dipper had swung low when he remarked that they were a couple of fools, and they went back to their beds. Cold came over the ground, and their musings turned to dreams. Next morning both were ashamed of their fears.

By four the wagon was on the move. Inside, Nancy's voice was heard discussing with her mother whether the schoolteacher where they were going to live now would have a black dog with a white tail, that could swim with a basket in his mouth. They crawled along the edge of the vast descent, making slow progress, for at times the valley widened and they receded far from the river, and then circuitously drew close again where the slant sank abruptly. When the ferryman's cabin came in sight, the canvas interior of the wagon was hot in the long-risen sun. The lay of the land had brought them close above the stream, but no one seemed to be at the cabin on the other side, nor was there any sign of a ferry. Groves of trees lay in the narrow folds of the valley, and the water swept black between untenanted shores. Nothing living could be seen along the scant levels of the bottom-land. Yet there stood the cabin as they had been told, the only one between the rapids and the Okanagon; and bright in the sun the Colville Reservation confronted them. They came upon tracks going down over the hill, marks of wagons and horses, plain in the soil, and charred sticks, with empty cans, lying where camps had been. Heartened by this proof that they were on

the right road, John Clallam turned his
horses over the brink. The slant steep-
ened suddenly in a hundred yards, tilting the wagon so no brake or shoe would
hold it if it moved further.

"All out!" said Clallam. "Either
folks travel light in this country or they
unpack." He went down a little way.
"That's the trail too," he said. "Wheel
marks down there and the little bushes
snapped off."

Nancy slipped out. "I'm unpacked,"
said she. "Oh, what a splendid hill to
go down! We'll go like anything."

"Yes, that surely is the trail," Clallam
pursued. "I can see away down where
somebody's left a wheel among them
big stones. But where does he keep his
ferry-boat? And where does he keep
himself?"

"Now, John, if it's here we're to go
down, don't you get to studying over
something else. It 'll be time enough
after we're at the bottom. Nancy, here's
your chair." Mrs. Clallam began lifting
the lighter things from the wagon.

"Mart," said her husband, "we'll have
to chain-lock the wheels after we're empty. I guess we'll start with the worst.
You and me 'll take the stove apart and
get her down somehow. We're in luck
to have open country and no timber
to work through. Drop that bedding,
mother! Yourself is all you're going to
carry. We'll pack that truck on the
horses."

"Then pack it now and let me start
first. I'll make two trips while you're at
the stove."

"There's the man!" said Nancy.

A man—a white man—was riding up
the other side of the river. Near the
cabin he leaned to see something on the
ground. Ten yards more and he was off
the horse and picked up something and
threw it away. He loitered along, picking up and throwing till he was at the
door. He pushed it open and took a survey of the interior. Then he went to his
horse, and when they saw him going
away on the road he had come, they set
up a shouting, and Mart fired a signal.
The rider dived from his saddle and
made headlong into the cabin, where the
door clapped to like a trap. Nothing
happened further, and the horse stood
on the bank.

"That's the funniest man I ever saw,"
said Nancy.

"They're all funny over there," said
Mart. "I'll signal him again." But
the cabin remained shut, and the deserted horse turned, took a few first steps of
freedom, then trotted briskly down the
river.

"Why, then, he don't belong there at
all," said Nancy.

"Wait, child, till we know something
about it."

"She's liable to be right, Liza. The
horse, anyway, don't belong, or he'd not
run off. That's good judgment, Nancy.
Right good for a little girl."

"I am six years old," said Nancy, "and
I know lots more than that."

"Well, let's get mother and the bedding started down. It 'll be noon before
we know it."

There were two pack-saddles in the
wagon, ready against such straits as this.
The rolls were made, balanced as side
packs, and circled with the swing-ropes,
loose cloths, clothes, frying-pans, the lantern, and the axe tossed in to fill the gap
in the middle, canvas flung over the
whole, and the diamond-hitch hauled
taut on the first pack, when a second
rider appeared across the river. He came
out of a space between the opposite hills,
into which the trail seemed to turn, and
he was leading the first man's horse. The
heavy work before them was forgotten,
and the Clallams sat down in a row to
watch.

"He's stealing it," said Mrs. Clallam.

"Then the other man will come out
and catch him," said Nancy.

Mart corrected them. "A man never
steals horses that way. He drives them
up in the mountains, where the owner
don't travel much."

The new rider had arrived at the bank
and came steadily along till opposite the
door, where he paused and looked up and
down the river.

"See him stoop," said Clallam the father. "He's seen the tracks don't go
further."

"I guess he's after the other one," added Clallam the son.

"Which of them is the ferry-man?"
said Mrs. Clallam.

The man had got off and gone straight
inside the cabin. In the black of the
doorway appeared immediately the first
man, dangling in the grip of the other,
who kicked him along to the horse.
There the victim mounted his own ani-

mal and rode back down the river. The chastiser was returning to the cabin, when Mart fired his rifle. The man stopped short, saw the emigrants, and waved his hand. He dismounted and came to the edge of the water. They could hear he was shouting to them, but it was too far for the words to carry. From a certain reiterated cadence, he seemed to be saying one thing. John and Mart tried to show they did not understand, and indicated their wagon, walking to it and getting aboard. On that the stranger redoubled his signs and shoutings, ran to the cabin, where he opened and shut the door several times, came back, and pointed to the hills.

"He's going away, and can't ferry us over," said Mrs. Clallam.

"And the other man thought he'd gone," said Nancy, "and he came and caught him in his house."

"This don't suit me," Clallam remarked. "Mart, we'll go to the shore and talk to him."

When the man saw them descending the hill, he got on his horse and swam the stream. It carried him below, but he was waiting for them when they reached the level. He was tall, shambling, and bony, and roved over them a pleasant, restless eye.

"Good - morning," said he. "Fine weather. I was baptized Edward Wilson, but you inquire for Wild - Goose Jake. Them other names are retired and pensioned. I expect you seen me kick him?"

"Couldn't help seeing."

"Oh, I ain't blamin' you, son, not a bit, I ain't. He can't bile water without burnin' it, and his toes turns in, and he's blurry round the finger-nails. He's jest kultus, he is. Hev some?" With a furtive smile that often ran across his lips, he pulled out a flat bottle, and all took an acquaintanceship swallow, while the Clallams explained their journey. "How many air there of yu' slidin' down the hill?" he inquired, shifting his eye to the wagon.

"I've got my wife and little girl up there. That's all of us."

"Ladies along! Then I'll step behind this bush." He was dragging his feet from his waterlogged boots. "Hear them suck, now?" he commented. "Didn't hev to think about a wetting onced. There, I guess I 'ain't caught a chill." He had whipped his breeches off and spread them on the sand. "Now you arrive down this here hill from Ioway, and says you: 'Where's that ferry? 'Ain't we hit the right spot?' Well, that's what you hev hit. You're all right, and the spot is hunky-dory, and it's the durned old boat hez made the mistake, begosh! A cloud busted in this country, and she tore out fer the coast, and the joke's on her! You'd ought to hev heerd her cable snap! Whoosh, if that wire didn't screech! Jest last week it was, and the river come round the corner on us in a wave four feet high, same as a wall. I was up here on business, and seen the whole thing. So the ferry she up and bid us good-by, and lit out for Astoria with her cargo. Beggin' pardon, hev you tobacco, for mine's in my wet pants? Twenty-four hogs and the driver, and two Sheeny drummers bound to the mines with brass jew'lry, all gone to hell, for they didn't near git to Astoria. They sank in the sight of all, as we run along the bank. I seen their arms wave, and them hogs rolling over like 'taters bilin' round in the kettle." Wild-Goose Jake's words came slow and went more slowly as he looked at the river and spoke, but rather to himself. "It warn't long, though. I expect it warn't three minutes till the water was all there was left there. My stars, what a lot of it! And I might hev been part of that cargo, easy as not. Freight behind time was all that come between me and them that went. So, we'd hev gone bobbin' down that flood, me and my piah-chuck."

"Your piah-chuck?" Mart inquired.

The man faced the boy like a rat, but the alertness faded instantly from his eye, and his lip slacked into a slipshod smile. "Why yes, sonny, me and my grub-stake. You've been to school, I'll bet, but they didn't learn yu' Chinook, now, did they? Chinook's the lingo us white folks trade in with the Siwashes, and we kinder falls into it, talking along. I was thinkin' how but for delay me and my grub-stake—provisions, ye know—that was consigned to me clear away at Spokane, might hev been drownded along with them hogs and Hebrews. That's what the good folks calls a dispensation of the Sauklee Tyee! 'One shall be taken and the other left.' And that's what beats me—they got left; and I'm a bigger sinner than them drummers, for I'm ten

WILD-GOOSE JAKE.

years older than they was. And the poor hogs was better than any of us. That can't be gainsaid. Oh no! oh no!"

Mart laughed.

"I mean it, son. Some day such thoughts will come to you." He stared at the river unsteadily with his light gray eyes.

"Well, if the ferry's gone," said John Clallam, getting on his legs, "we'll go on down to the next one."

"Hold on! hold on! Did you never hear tell of a raft? I'll put you folks over this river. Wait till I git my pants on," said he, stalking nimbly to where they lay.

"It's just this way," Clallam continued; "we're bound for the upper Okanagon country, and we must get in there to build our cabin before cold weather."

"Don't you worry about that. It 'll take you three days to the next ferry, while you and me and the boy kin build a raft right here by to-morrow noon. You hev an axe, I expect? Well, here is timber close, and your trail takes over to my place on the Okanagon, where

you've got another crossin' to make. And all this time we're keeping the ladies waitin' up the hill! We'll talk business as we go along; and, see here, if I don't suit yu', or fail in my bargain, you needn't to pay me a cent."

He began climbing, and on the way they came to an agreement. Wild-Goose Jake bowed low to Mrs. Clallam, and as low to Nancy, who held her mother's dress and said nothing, keeping one finger in her mouth. All began emptying the wagon quickly, and tins of baking-powder, with rocking-chairs and flowered quilts, lay on the hill. Wild-Goose Jake worked hard, and sustained a pleasant talk by himself. His fluency was of an eagerness that parried interruption or inquiry.

"So you've come acrosst the Big Bend! Ain't it a cozy place? Reminds me of them medicine pictures, 'Before and After Using.' The Big Bend's the way this world looked before. Ever seen specimens of Big Bend produce, ma'am? They send 'em East. Grain and plums and such. The feller that gathered them curiosities hed to hunt forty square miles apiece for 'em. But it's good-payin' policy, and it fetches lots of settlers to the Territory. They come here hummin' and walks around the wilderness, and ' Where's the plums?' says they. ' Can't you see I'm busy?' says the land agent; and out they goes. But you needn' to worry, ma'am. The country where you're goin' ain't like that. There's water and timber and rich soil and mines. Billy Moon has gone there—he's the man run the ferry. When she wrecked, he pulled his freight for the new mines at Loop Loop."

" Did the man live in the little house?" said Nancy.

" Right there, miss. And nobody lives there any more, so you take it if you're wantin' a place of your own."

" What made you kick the other man if it wasn't your house?"

" Well, now, if it ain't a good one on him to hev you see that! I'll tell him a little girl seen that, and maybe he'll feel the disgrace. Only he's no account, and don't take any experience the reg'lar way. He's nigh onto thirty, and you'll not believe me, I know, but he 'ain't never learned to spit right."

" Is he yours?" inquired Nancy.

" Gosh! no, miss — beggin' pardon. He's jest workin' for me."

" Did he know you were coming to kick him when he hid?"

" Hid? What's that?" The man's eyes narrowed again into points. " You folks seen him hide?" he said to Clallam.

" Why, of course; didn't he say anything?"

" He didn't get much chance," muttered Jake. " What did he hide at?"

" Us."

" You, begosh!"

" I guess so," said Mart. " We took him for the ferry-man, and when he couldn't hear us—"

" What was he doin'?"

" Just riding along. And so I fired to signal him, and he flew into the door."

" So you fired, and he flew into the door. Oh, h'm." Jake continued to pack the second horse, attending carefully to the ropes. " I never knowed he was that weak in the upper story," he said, in about five minutes. " Knew his brains was tenas, but didn't suspect he were that weak in the upper story. You're sure he didn't go in till he heerd your gun?"

" He'd taken a look and was going away," said Mart.

" Now ain't some people jest odd! Now you follow me, and I'll tell you folks what I figured he'd been at. Billy Moon he lived in that cabin, yu' see. And he had his stuff there, yu' see, and run the ferry, and a kind of a store. He kept coffee and canned goods and star-plug and this and that to supply the prospectin' outfits that come acrosst on his ferry on the trail to the mines. Then a cloud-bust hits his boat and his job's sp'iled on the river, and he quits for the mines, takin' his stuff along—do you follow me? But he hed to leave some, and he give me the key, and I was to send the balance after him next freight team that come along my way. Leander—that's him I was kickin'—he knowed about it, and he'll steal a hot stove he's that dumb. He knowed there was stuff here of Billy Moon's. Well, last night we hed some horses stray, and I says to him, ' Andy, you git up by daylight and find them.' And he gits. But by seven the horses come in all right of theirselves, and Mr. Leander he was missin'; and says I to myself, ' I'll ketch you, yu' blamed hobo.' And I thought I had ketched him, yu' see. Weren't that reasonable of me? Wouldn't any of you folks hev drawed that conclusion?" The man had fallen into a wheedling tone as he studied their faces. " Jest put yourselves in my place," he said.

" Then what was he after?" said Mart.

" Stealin'. But he figured he'd come again."

" He didn't like my gun much."

" They always skeers him when he don't know the parties shootin'. That's his dumbness. Maybe he thought I was after him; he's jest that distrustful. Begosh! we'll hev the laugh on him when he finds he run from a little girl."

" He didn't wait to see who he was running from," said Mart.

" Of course he didn't. Andy hears your gun and he don't inquire further, but hits the first hole he kin crawl into. That's Andy! That's the kind of boy I hev to work for me. All the good ones goes where you're goin', where the grain grows without irrigation and the black-tail deer comes out on the hill and asks yu' to shoot 'em for dinner. Who's ready for the bottom? If I stay talkin' the sun 'll go down on us. Don't yu' let me get

LEANDER.

started agin. Jest you shet me off twiced anyway each twenty-four hours."

He began to descend with his pack-horse and the first load. All afternoon they went up and down over the hot bare face of the hill, until the baggage, heavy and light, was transported and dropped piecemeal on the shore. The torn-out insides of their home littered the stones with familiar shapes and colors, and Nancy played among them, visiting each parcel and folded thing.

"There's the red table cover!" she exclaimed, "and the big coffee-grinder. And there's our table, and the hole Mart burned in it." She took a long look at this. "Oh, how I wish I could see our pump!" she said, and began to cry.

"You talk to her, mother," said Clallam. "She's tuckered out."

The men returned to bring the wagon.

With chain-locked wheels, and tilted half over by the cross slant of the mountain, it came heavily down, reeling and sliding on the slippery yellow weeds, and grinding deep ruts across the faces of the shelving beds of gravel. Jake guided it as he could, straining back on the bits of the two hunched horses when their hoofs glanced from the stones that rolled to the bottom; and the others leaned their weight on a pole lodged between the spokes, making a balance to the wagon, for it leaned the other way so far that at any jolt the two wheels left the ground. When it was safe on the level of the stream, dusk had come and a white flat of mist lay along the river, striping its course among the gaunt hills. They slept without moving, and rose early to cut logs, which the horses dragged to the shore. The outside trunks were nailed and lashed with ropes, and sank almost below the surface with the weight of the wood fastened crosswise on top. But the whole floated dry with its cargo, and crossed clumsily on the quick wrinkled current. Then it brought the wagon; and the six horses swam. The force of the river had landed them below the cabin, and when they had repacked there was too little left of day to go on. Clallam suggested it was a good time to take Moon's leavings over to the Okanagon, but Wild-Goose Jake said at once that their load was heavy enough; and about this they could not change his mind. He made a journey to the cabin by himself, and returned saying that he had managed to lock the door.

"Father," said Mart, as they were harnessing next day, "I've been up there. I went awful early. There's no lock to the door, and the cabin's empty."

"I guessed that might be."

"There has been a lock pried off pretty lately. There was a lot of broken bottles around everywheres, inside and out."

"Part of what he says is all right," said Clallam. "You can see where the ferry's cable used to be fastened on this side. And yonder goes the trail."

"What do you make out of it?" said Mart.

"Nothing yet. He wants to get us away, and I'm with him there. I want to get up the Okanagon as soon as we can."

"Well, I'm takin' yu' the soonest way," said Wild-Goose Jake, behind them. From his casual smile there was no telling

"SET UP A WAILING LIKE VULTURES"

what he had heard. "I'll put your stuff acrosst the Okanagon to-morrow mornin'. But to-night yourselves 'll all be over, and the ladies kin sleep in my room."

The wagon made good time. The trail crossed easy valleys and over the yellow grass of the hills, while now and then their guide took a short-cut. He wished to get home, he said, since there could be no estimating what Leander might be doing. While the sun was still well up in the sky they came over a round knob and saw the Okanagon, blue in the bright afternoon, and the cabin on its further bank. This was a roomier building to see than common, and a hay-field was by it, and a bit of green pasture, fenced in. Saddle-horses were tied in front, heads hanging and feet knuckled askew with long waiting, and from inside an uneven, riotous din whiffled lightly across the river and intervening meadow to the hill.

"If you'll excuse me," said Jake, "I'll jest git along ahead, and see what game them folks is puttin' up on Andy. Likely as not he's weighin' 'em out flour at two cents, with it costin' me two and a half on freightin' alone. I'll hev supper ready time you ketch up."

He was gone at once, getting away at a sharp pace, till presently they could see him swimming the stream. When he was in the cabin the sounds changed, dropping off to one at a time, and expired. But when the riders came out into the air, they leaned and collided at random, whirled their arms, and screaming till they gathered heart, charged with wavering menace at the door. The foremost was flung from the sill, and he shot along toppling and scraped his length in the dust, while the owner of the cabin stood in the entrance. The Indian picked himself up, and at some word of Jake's which the emigrants could half follow by the fierce lift of his arm, all got on their horses and set up a wailing, like vultures driven off. They went up the river a little and crossed, and Mrs. Clallam was thankful when their evil noise had died away up the valley. They had seen the wagon coming, but gave it no attention. A man soon came over the river from the cabin, and was lounging against a tree when the emigrants drew up at the margin.

"I don't know what you know," he whined defiantly from the tree, "but I'm goin' to Cornwall, Connecticut, and

I don't care who knows it." He sent a cowed look across the river.

"Get out of the wagon, Nancy," said Clallam. "Mart, help her down."

"I'm going back," said the man, blinking like a scolded dog. "I ain't stayin' here for nobody. You can tell him I said so, too." Again his eye slunk sidewise toward the cabin, and instantly back.

"While you're staying," said Mart, "you might as well give a hand here."

He came with alacrity, and made a shift of unhitching the horses. "I was better off coupling freight cars on the Housatonic," he soon remarked. His voice came shallow, from no deeper than his throat, and a peevish apprehension rattled through it. "That was a good job. And I've had better, too; forty, fifty, sixty dollars better."

"Shall we unpack the wagon?" Clallam inquired.

"I don't know. You ever been to New Milford? I sold shoes there. Thirty-five dollars and board."

The emigrants attended to their affairs, watering the horses and driving picket stakes. Leander uselessly followed behind them with conversation, blinking and with lower lip sagged, showing a couple of teeth. "My brother's in business in Pittsfield, Massachusetts," said he, "and I can get a salary in Bridgeport any day I say so. That a Marlin?"

"No," said Mart. "It's a Winchester."

"I had a Marlin. He's took it from me. I'll bet you never got shot at."

"Anybody want to shoot you?" Mart inquired.

"Well and I guess you'll believe they did day before yesterday."

"If you're talking about up at that cabin, it was me."

Leander gave Mart a leer. "That won't do," said he. "He's put you up to telling me that, and I'm going to Cornwall, Connecticut. I know what's good for me, I guess."

"I tell you we were looking for the ferry, and I signalled you across the river."

"No, no," said Leander. "I never seen you in my life. Don't you be like him and take me for a fool."

"All right. Why did they want to murder you?"

"Why?" said the man, shrilly. "Why? Hadn't they broke in and filled themselves up on his piah-chuck till they were crazy-

drunk? And when I came along didn't
they—"

"When you came along they were nowhere near there," said Mart.

"Now you're going to claim it was me
drunk it and scattered all them bottles of
his," screamed Leander, backing away.
"I tell you I didn't. I told him I didn't,
and he knowed it well, too. But he's just
that mean when he's mad he likes to put
a thing on me whether or no, when he
never seen me touch a drop of whiskey,
nor any one else, neither. They were riding and shooting loose over the country
like they always do on a drunk. And I'm
glad they stole his stuff. What business
had he to keep it at Billy Moon's old cabin and send me away up there to see it
was all right? Let him do his own dirty
work. I ain't going to break the laws on
the salary he pays me."

The Clallam family had gathered round
Leander, who was stricken with volubility. "It ain't once in a while, but it's
every day and every week," he went on,
always in a woolly scream. "And the
longer he ain't caught the bolder he gets,
and puts everything that goes wrong on
to me. Was it me traded them for that
liquor this afternoon? It was his squaw,
Big Tracks, and he knowed it well. He
lets that mud-faced baboon run the house
when he's off, and I don't have the keys
nor nothing, and never did have. But of
course he had to come in and say it was
me just because he was mad about having
you see them Siwashes hollering around.
And he come and shook me where I was
sittin', and oh, my, he knowed well the lie
he was acting. I bet I've got the marks
on my neck now. See any red marks?"
Leander exhibited the back of his head,
but the violence done him had evidently
been fleeting. "He'll be awful good to
you, for he's that scared—"

Leander stood tremulously straight in
silence, his lip sagging, as Wild-Goose
Jake called pleasantly from the other
bank. "Come to supper, you folks," said
he. "Why, Andy, I told you to bring
them acrosst, and you've let them picket
their horses. Was you expectin' Mrs.
Clallam to take your arm and ford six
feet of water?" For some reason his voice
sounded kind as he spoke to his assistant.

"Well, mother?" said Clallam.

"If it was not for Nancy, John—"

"I know, I know. Out on the shore
here would be a pleasanter bedroom for

you, but" (he looked up the valley) "I
guess our friend's plan is more sensible
to-night."

The horses put them with not much
wetting to the other bank, where Jake,
most eager and friendly, hovered to meet
his party, and when they were safe ashore
pervaded his premises in their behalf.

"Turn them horses into the pasture,
Andy," said he, "and first feed 'em a
couple of quarts." It may have been
hearing himself say this, but tone and
voice dropped to the confidential and his
sentences came with a chuckle. "Quarts
to the horses and quarts to the Siwashes
and a skookum peck of trouble all round,
Mrs. Clallam! If I hedn't a-came to stop
it a while ago, why about all the spirits
that's in stock jest now was bein' traded
off for some blamed ponies the bears hev
let hobble on the range unswallered ever
since I settled here. A store on a trail
like this here, ye see, it hez to keep spirits,
of course; and—well, well! here's my
room; you ladies 'll excuse, and make
yourselves at home as well as you can."

It was of a surprising neatness, due all
to him, they presently saw; the log walls
covered with a sort of bunting that was
also stretched across to make a ceiling below the shingles of the roof; fresh soap
and towels, china service, a clean floor
and bed, on the wall a print of some
white and red village among elms, with
a covered bridge and the water running
over an apron-dam just above; and a rich
smell of whiskey everywhere. "Fix up
as comfortable as yu' can," the host repeated, "and I'll see how Mrs. Jake's
tossin' the flapjacks. She's Injun, yu'
know, and five years of married life
hain't learned her to toss flapjacks. Now
if I was you" (he was lingering in the
doorway) "I wouldn't shet that winder so
quick. It don't smell nice yet for ladies
in here, and I'd hev like to git the time
to do better for ye; but them Siwashes—
well, of course, you folks see how it is.
Maybe it ain't always and only white men
that patronizes our goods. Uncle Sam is
a long way off, and I don't say we'd ought
to, but when the cat's away, why the
mice *will*, ye know—they most always
will!"

There was a rattle of boards outside, at
which he shut the door quickly, and they
heard him run. A light muttering came
in at the window, and the mother, peeping out, saw Andy fallen among a rub-

bish of crates and empty cans, where he lay staring, and his two fists beat up and down like a disordered toy. Wild-Goose Jake came, and having lifted him with great tenderness, was laying him flat as Elizabeth Clallam hurried to his help.

"No, ma'am," he sighed, "you can't do nothing, I guess."

"Just let me go over and get our medicines."

"Thank you, ma'am," said Jake, and the pain on his face was miserable to see; "there ain't no medicine. We're kind o' used to this, Andy and me. Maybe, if you wouldn't mind stayin' till he comes to— Why, a sick man takes comfort at the sight of a lady."

When the fit had passed they helped him to his feet, and Jake led him away.

Mrs. Jake made her first appearance upon the guests sitting down to their meal, when she waited on table, passing forth and back from the kitchen with her dishes. She had but three or four English words, and her best years were plainly behind her; but her cooking was good, fried and boiled with sticks of her own chopping, and she served with industry. Indeed, a squaw is one of the few species of the domestic wife that survive to-day upon our continent. Andy seemed now to keep all his dislike for her, and followed her with a scowling eye, while he frequented Jake, drawing a chair to sit next him when he smoked by the wall after supper, and sometimes watching him with a sort of clouded affection upon his face. He did not talk, and the seizure had evidently jarred his mind as well as his frame. When the squaw was about lighting a lamp he brushed her arm in a childish way so the match went out, and set him laughing. She poured out a harangue in Chinook, showing the dead match to Jake, who rose and gravely lighted the lamp himself, Andy laughing more than ever. When Mrs. Clallam had taken Nancy with her to bed, Jake walked John Clallam to the river-bank, and looking up and down, spoke a little of his real mind.

"I guess you see how it is with me. Anyway, I don't commonly hev use for stranger-folks in this house. But that little girl of yourn started cryin' about not havin' the pump along that she'd been used to seein' in the yard at home. And I says to myself, 'Look a-here, Jake, I don't care if they do ketch on to you

and yer blamed whiskey business. They're not the sort to tell on you.' Gee! but that about the pump got me! And I says, 'Jake, you're goin' to give them the best you hev got.' Why, that Big Bend desert and lonesome valley of the Columbia hez chilled my heart in the days that are gone when I weren't used to things; and the little girl hed came so fur! And I knowed how she was a-feelin'."

He stopped, and seemed to be turning matters over.

"I'm much obliged to you," said Clallam.

"And your wife was jest beautiful about Andy. You've saw me wicked to Andy. I am, and often, for I rile turruble quick, and God forgive me! But when that boy gits at his meanness—yu've seen jest a touch of it—there's scarcely livin' with him. It seems like he got reg'lar inspired. Some days he'll lie—make up big lies to the fust man comes in at the door. They ain't harmless, his lies ain't. Then he'll trick my woman, that's real good to him; and I believe he'd lick whiskey up off the dirt. And every drop is poison for him with his complaint. But I'd ought to remember. You'd surely think I could remember, and forbear. Most likely he made a big talk to you about that cabin."

John Clallam told him.

"Well, that's all true, for onced. I did think he'd been up to stealin' that whiskey gradual, 'stead of fishin', the times he was out all day. And the salary I give him"—Jake laughed a little—"ain't enough to justify a man's breaking the law. I did take his rifle away when he tried to shoot my woman. I guess it was Siwashes bruck into that cabin."

"I'm pretty certain of it," said Clallam.

"You? What makes yu'?"

John began the tale of the galloping dots, and Jake stopped walking to listen the harder. "Yes," he said; "that's bad. That's jest bad. They hev carried a lot off to drink. That's the worst."

He had little to say after this, but talked under his tongue as they went to the house, where he offered a bed to Clallam and Mart. They would not turn him out, so he showed them over to a haystack, where they crawled in and went to sleep.

Most white men know when they have had enough whiskey. Most Indians do not. This is a difference between the races of which government has taken notice. Government says that "no ardent spirits shall be introduced under any pretence into the Indian country." It also says that the white man who attempts to break this law "shall be punished by imprisonment for not more than two years and by a fine of not more than three hundred dollars." It further says that if any superintendent of Indian affairs has reason to suspect a man, he may cause the "boats, stores, packages, wagons, sleds, and places of deposit" of such person to be searched, and if ardent spirits be found it shall be forfeit, together with the boats and all other substances with it connected, one half to the informer and the other half to the use of the United States. The courts and all legal machines necessary for trial and punishment of offenders are oiled and ready; two years is a long while in jail; three hundred dollars and confiscation sounds heavy; altogether the penalty looks severe on the printed page—and all the while there's no brisker success in our far West than selling whiskey to Indians. Very few people know what the whiskey is made of, and the Indian does not care. He drinks till he drops senseless. If he has killed nobody and nobody him during the process, it is a good thing, for then the matter ends with his getting sober and going home to his tent till such happy time when he can put his hand on some further possession to trade away. The white offender is caught now and then; but Okanagon County lies pretty snug from the arm of the law. It's against Canada to the north, and the empty county of Stevens to the east; south of it rushes the Columbia, with the naked horrible Big Bend beyond, and to its west rises a domain of unfooted mountains. There is law up in the top of it at Conconully sometimes, but not much even to-day, for that is still a new country, where flow the Methow, the Ashinola, and the Similikameen.

Consequently a cabin like Wild-Goose Jake's was a holiday place. The blanketed denizens of the reservation crossed to it, and the citizens who had neighboring cabins along the trail repaired here to spend what money they had. As Mrs. Clallam lay in her bed she heard customers arrive. Two or three loud voices spoke in English, and several Indians and squaws seemed to be with the party, bantering in Chinook. The visitors were in too strong force for Jake's word about coming some other night to be of any avail.

"Open your cellar and quit your talk," Elizabeth heard, and next she heard some door that stuck pulled open with a shriek of the warped timber. Next they were gambling, and made not much noise over it at first; but the Indians in due time began to lose to the soberer whites, becoming quarrelsome, and raising a clumsy disturbance, though it was plain the whites had their own way and were feared. The voices rose, and soon there was no moment that several were not shouting curses at once, till Mrs. Clallam stopped her ears. She was still for a time, hearing only in a muffled way, when all at once the smell of drink and tobacco, that had sifted only a little through the cracks, grew heavy in the room, and she felt Nancy shrink close to her side.

"Mother, mother," the child whispered, "what's that?"

It had gone beyond card-playing with the company in the saloon; they seemed now to be having a savage horse-play, those on their feet tramping in their scuffles upon others on the floor, who bellowed incoherently. Elizabeth Clallam took Nancy in her arms and told her that nobody would come where they were.

But the child was shaking. "Yes they will," she whispered, in terror. "They are!" And she began a tearless sobbing, holding her mother with her whole strength.

A little sound came close by the bed, and Elizabeth's senses stopped so that for half a minute she could not stir. She staid rigid beneath the quilt, and Nancy clung to her. Something was moving over the floor. It came quite near, but turned, and its slight rustle crawled away towards the window.

"Who is that?" demanded Mrs. Clallam, sitting up.

There was no answer, but the slow creeping continued, always close along the floor, like the folds of stuff rubbing, and hands feeling their way in short slides against the boards. She had no way to find where her husband was sleeping, and while she thought of this and whether or not to rush out at the door, the table was gently shaken, there was a drawer opened, and some object fell.

"Only a thief," she said to herself, and in a sort of sharp joy cried out her question again.

The singular broken voice of a woman answered, seemingly in fear. "Match-es," it said; and "Match-es" said a second voice, pronouncing with difficulty like the first. She knew it was some of the squaws, and sprang from the bed, asking what they were doing there. "Match-es," they murmured; and when she had struck a light she saw how the two were cringing, their blankets huddled round them. Their motionless black eyes looked up at her from the floor where they lay sprawled, making no offer to get up. It was clear to her from the pleading fear in the one word they answered to whatever she said that they had come here to hide from the fury of the next room; and as she stood listening to that she would have let them remain, but their escape had been noticed. A man burst into the room, and at sight of her and Nancy stopped, and was blundering excuses, when Jake caught his arm and had dragged him almost out, but he saw the two on the floor; at this, getting himself free, he half swept the crouching figures with his boot as they fled out of the room, and the door was swung shut. Mrs. Clallam heard his violent words to the squaws for daring to disturb the strangers, and there followed the heavy lashing of a quirt, with screams and lamenting. No trouble came from the Indian husbands, for they were stupefied on the ground, and when their intelligences quickened enough for them to move, the punishment was long over and no one in the house awake but Elizabeth and Nancy, seated together in their bed, watching for the day. Mother and daughter heard them rise and go out one by one, and the horses grew distant up and down the river. As the rustling trees lighted and turned transparent in the rising sun, Jake roused those that remained and got them away. Later he knocked at the door.

"I hev a little raft fixed this morning," said he, "and I guess we can swim the wagon."

"Whatever's quickest to take us from this place," Elizabeth answered.

"Breakfast 'll be ready, ma'am, whenever you say."

"I am ready now. I shall want to start ferrying our things— Where's Mr. Clallam? Tell him to come here."

"I will, ma'am. I'm sorry—"

"Tell Mr. Clallam to come here, please."

John had slept sound in his haystack, and heard nothing. "Well," he said, after comforting his wife and Nancy, "you were better off in the room, anyway. I'd not blame him so, Liza. How was he going to help it?"

But Elizabeth was a woman, and just now saw one thing alone: if selling whiskey led to such things in this country, the man who sold it was much worse than any mere law-breaker. John Clallam, being now a long time married, made no argument. He was looking absently at the open drawer of a table. "That's queer," he said, and picked up a tintype.

She had no curiosity for anything in that room, and he laid it in the drawer again, his thoughts being taken up with the next step of their journey, and what might be coming to them all.

During breakfast Jake was humble about the fright the ladies had received in his house, explaining how he thought he had acted for the best; at which Clallam and Mart said that in a rough country folks must look for rough doings, and get along as well as they can; but Elizabeth said nothing. The little raft took all but Nancy over the river to the wagon, where they set about dividing their belongings in loads that could be floated over, one at a time, and Jake returned to repair some of the disorder that remained from the night at the cabin. John and Mart poled the first cargo across, and while they were on the other side, Elizabeth looked out of the wagon, where she was working alone, and saw five Indian riders coming down the valley. The dust hung in the air they had rushed through, and they swung apart and closed again as she had seen before; so she looked for a rifle; but the fire-arms had gone over the Okanagon with the first load. She got down and stood at the front wheel of the wagon, confronting the riders when they pulled up their horses. One climbed unsteadily from his saddle and swayed towards her.

"Drink!" said he, half friendly, and held out a bottle.

Elizabeth shook her head.

"Drink," he grunted again, pushing the bottle at her. "Piah-chuck! Skookum!" He had a sluggish animal grin, and when she drew back, tipped the bottle into his mouth, and directly choked, so that his friends on their horses laughed loud as he stood coughing. "Heap good," he remarked, looking at Elizabeth, who watched his eyes swim with the glut of the drink. "Where you come back?" he inquired, touching the wagon. "You cross Okanagon? Me cross you; cross horses; cross all. Heap cheap. What yes?"

The others nodded. "Heap cheap," they said.

"We don't want you," said Elizabeth. "No cross? Maybe he going cross you? What yes?"

Again Elizabeth nodded.

"Maybe he Jake?" pursued the Indian.

"Yes, he is. We don't want you."

"We cross you all same. He not."

The Indian spoke loud and thick, and Elizabeth looked over the river where her husband was running with a rifle, and Jake behind him, holding a warning hand on his arm. Jake spoke to the Indians, who listened sullenly, but got on their horses and went up the river.

"Now," said Jake to Clallam, "they ain't gone. Get your wife over so she kin set in my room till I see what kin be done."

She was stepping on the raft that John had taken over at once, when the noise and flight of riders descended along the other bank. They went in a circle, with hoarse shouts, round the cabin as Mart with Nancy came from the pasture. The boy no sooner saw them than he caught his sister up and carried her quickly away among the corrals and sheds, where the two went out of sight.

"You stay here, Liza," her husband said. "I'll go back over."

But Mrs. Clallam laughed.

"Get ashore," he cried to her. "Quick!"

"Where you go, I go, John."

"What good, what good, in the name—"

"Then I'll get myself over," said she. And he seized her as she would have jumped into the stream.

While they crossed, the Indians had tied their horses and rambled into the cabin. Jake came from it to stop the Clallams.

"They're after your contract," said he, quietly. "They say they're going to have the job of takin' your stuff acrosst the Okanagon."

"What did you say?" asked Mrs. Clallam.

"I set 'em up drinks to gain time."

"Do you want me there?" said Clallam.

"Begosh, no! That would mix things worse."

"Can't you make them go away?" Elizabeth inquired.

"Me and them, ye see, ma'am, we her a sort of bargain they're to git certain ferryin'. I can't make 'em savvy how I took charge of you. If you want them—" He paused.

"We want them!" exclaimed Elizabeth. "If you're joking, it's a poor joke."

"It ain't no joke at all, ma'am." Jake's face grew brooding. "Of course folks kin say who they'll be ferried by. And you may believe I'd rather do it. I didn't look for jest this complication; but maybe I kin steer through; and it's myself I've got to thank. Of course, if them Siwashes did git your job, they'd sober up gittin' ready. And—"

The emigrants waited, but he did not go on with what was in his mind. "It's all right," said he, in a brisk tone. "Whatever's a-comin's a-comin'." He turned abruptly towards the door. "Keep yerselves away jest now," he added, and went inside.

The parents sought their children, finding Mart had concealed Nancy in the haystack. They put Mrs. Clallam also in a protected place, as a loud altercation seemed to be rising at the cabin; this grew as they listened, and Jake's squaw came running to hide herself. She could tell them nothing, nor make them understand more than they knew; but she touched John's rifle, signing to know if it were loaded, and was greatly relieved when he showed her the magazine full of cartridges. The quarrelling had fallen silent, but rose in a new gust of fierceness, sounding as if in the open air and coming their way. No Indian appeared, however, and the noise passed to the river, where the emigrants soon could hear wood being split in pieces.

John risked a survey. "It's the raft," he said. "They're smashing it. Now they're going back. Stay with the children, Liza."

"You're never going to that cabin?" she said.

"He's in a scrape, mother."

John started away, heedless of his wife's despair. At his coming the Indians shouted and surrounded him, while he heard Jake say, "Drop your gun and drink with them."

"Drink!" said Andy, laughing with the screech he had made at the match going out. "We're all going to Canaan, Connecticut."

Each Indian held a tin cup, and at the instant these were emptied they were thrust towards Jake, who filled them again, going and coming through a door that led a step or two down into a dark place which was half underground. Once he was not quick, or was imagined to be refusing, for an Indian raised his cup and drunkenly dashed it on Jake's head. Jake laughed good-humoredly, and filled the cup.

"It's our one chance," said he to John as the Indian, propping himself by a hand on the wall, offered the whiskey to Clallam.

"We cross you Okanagon," he said. "What yes?"

"Maybe you say no?" said another, pressing the emigrant to the wall.

A third interfered, saying something in their language, at which the other two disagreed. They talked a moment with threatening rage till suddenly all drew pistols. At this the two remaining stumbled among the group, and a shot went into the roof. Jake was there in one step with a keg, that they no sooner saw than they fell upon it, and the liquor jetted out as they clinched, wrestling over the room till one lay on his back with his mouth at the open bung. It was wrenched from him, and directly there was not a drop more in it. They tilted it, and when none ran out, flung the keg out of doors and crowded to the door of the dark place, where Jake barred the way. "Don't take to that yet!" he said to Clallam, for John was lifting his rifle.

"Piah-chuck!" yelled the Indians, scarcely able to stand. All other thought had left them, and a new thought came to Jake. He reached for a fresh keg, while they held their tin cups in the left hand and pistols in the right, pushing so it was a slow matter to get the keg opened. They were fast nearing the sodden stage, and one sank on the floor. Jake glanced in at the door behind him, and filled the cups once again. While all were drinking he went in the store-room and set more liquor open, beckoning them to come as they looked up from the rims where their lips had been glued. They moved round behind the table, grasping it to keep on their feet, with the one on the floor crawling among the legs

of the rest. When they were all inside, Jake leaped out and locked the door.

"They kin sleep now," said he. "Gunpowder won't be needed. Keep wide away from in front."

There was a minute of stillness within, and then a grovelling noise and struggle. A couple of bullets came harmless through the door. Those inside fought together as well as they could, while those outside listened as it grew less, the bodies falling stupefied without further sound of rising. One or two, still active, began striking at the boards with what heavy thing they could find, until suddenly the blade of an axe crashed through.

"Keep away!" cried Jake. But Andy had leaped insanely in front of the door, and fell dead with a bullet through him. With a terrible scream, Jake flung himself at the place, and poured six shots through the panel; then, as Clallam caught him, wrenched at the lock, and they saw inside. Whiskey and blood dripped together, and no one was moving there. It was liquor with some, and death with others, and all of it lay upon the guilty soul of Jake.

"You deserve killing yourself," said Clallam.

"That's been attended to," replied Jake, and he reeled, for during his fire the Indian shot once more.

Clallam supported him to the room where his wife and Nancy had passed the night, and laid him on the bed. "I'll get Mrs. Clallam," said he.

"If she'll be willin' to see me," said the wounded man, humbly.

She came, dazed beyond feeling any horror, or even any joy, and she did what she could.

"It was seein' 'em hit Andy," said Jake. "Is Andy gone? Yes, I kin tell he's gone from your face." He shut his eyes, and lay still so long a time that they thought he might be dying now; but he moved at length, and looked slowly round the wall till he saw the print of the village among the elms and the covered bridge. His hand lifted to show them this. "That's the road," said he. "Andy and me used to go fishin' acrosst that bridge. Did you ever see the Housatonic River? I've fished a lot there. Cornwall, Connecticut. The hills are pretty there. Then Andy got worse. You look in that drawer." John remembered, and when he got out the tintype, Jake stretched for it eagerly. "His mother and him, age ten," he explained to Elizabeth, and held it for her to see, then studied the faces in silence. "You kin tell it's Andy, can't yu'?" She told him yes. "That was before we knowed he weren't—weren't goin' to grow up like the other boys he played with. So after a while, when she was gone, I got ashamed seein' Andy's friends makin' their way when he couldn't seem to, and so I took him away where nobody hed ever been acquainted with us. I was layin' money by to git him the best doctor in Europe. I 'ain't been a good man."

A faintness mastered him, and Elizabeth would have put the picture on the table, but his hand closed round it. They let him lie so, and Elizabeth sat there, while John, with Mart, kept Nancy away till the horror in the outer room was made invisible. They came and went quietly, and Jake seemed in a deepening torpor, once only rousing suddenly to call his son's name, and then, upon looking from one to the other, he recollected, and his eyes closed again. His mind wandered, but very little, for torpor seemed to be overcoming him. The squaw had stolen in, and sat cowering and useless. Towards sundown John's heart sickened at the sound of more horsemen; but it was only two white men, a sheriff and his deputy.

"Go easy," said John. "He's not going to resist."

"What's up here, anyway? Who are you?"

Clallam explained, and was evidently not so much as half believed.

"If there are Indians killed," said the sheriff, "there's still another matter for the law to settle with him. We're sent to search for whiskey. The county's about tired of him."

"You'll find him pretty sick," said John.

"People I find always are pretty sick," said the sheriff, and pushed his way in, stopping at sight of Mrs. Clallam and the figure on the bed. "I'm arresting that man, madam," he said, with a shade of apology. "The county court wants him."

Jake sat up and knew the sheriff. "You're a little late, Proctor," said he. "The Supreme Court's a-goin' to call my case." Then he fell back, for his case had been called.

THE RECOVERY
by Edith Wharton

I

TO the visiting stranger Hillbridge's
first question was, " Have you seen
Keniston's things?"
Keniston took precedence of the Colonial State House, the Gilbert Stuart
Washington, and the Ethnological Museum; nay, he ran neck and neck with
the President of the University, a pre-
historic relic who had known Emerson,
and who was still sent about the country
in cotton-wool to open educational institutions with a toothless oration on Brook
Farm.

Keniston was sent about the country
too; he opened art exhibitions, laid the
foundations of academies, and acted, in a
general sense, as the spokesman and apolo-
gist of art. Hillbridge was proud of him
in his peripatetic character, but his fel-
low-townsmen let it be understood that to
" know " Keniston one must come to Hillbridge. Never was work more dependent
for its effect on " atmosphere," on *milieu*.
Hillbridge was Keniston's *milieu,* and
there was one lady, a devotee of his art,
who went so far as to assert that once,
at an exhibition in New York, she had
passed a Keniston without recognizing it.
" It simply didn't want to be seen in such
surroundings; it was hiding itself under
an incognito," she declared.

It was a source of special pride to Hillbridge that it contained all the artist's
best works. Strangers were told that
Hillbridge had discovered him. The discovery had come about in the simplest
manner. Professor Driffert, who had a
reputation for " collecting," had one day
hung a sketch on his drawing-room wall,
and thereafter Mrs. Driffert's visitors (always a little flurried by the sense that it
was the kind of house in which one might
be suddenly called upon to distinguish
between a dry-point and an etching, or
between Raphael Mengs and Raphael
Sanzio) were not infrequently subjected
to the Professor's off - hand inquiry,

" By-the-way, have you seen my Keniston?" The visitors, perceptibly awed,
would retreat to a critical distance and
murmur the usual guarded generalities,
while they tried to keep the name in mind
long enough to look it up in the Encyclo-
pædia. The name was not in the En-
cyclopædia; but, as a compensating fact,
it became known that the man himself
was in Hillbridge. Hillbridge, then, owned an artist whose celebrity it was the
proper thing to take for granted! Some
one else, emboldened by the thought,
bought a Keniston; and the next year, on
the occasion of the President's golden
jubilee, the Faculty, by unanimous consent, presented him with a Keniston.
Two years later there was a Keniston exhibition, to which the art-critics came
from New York and Boston; and not
long afterward a well-known Chicago
collector vainly attempted to buy Professor Driffert's sketch, which the art
journals cited as a rare example of the
painter's first or silvery manner. Thus
there gradually grew up a small circle of
connoisseurs known in artistic circles as
men who collected Kenistons.

Professor Wildmarsh, of the chair of
Fine Arts and Archæology, was the first
critic to publish a detailed analysis of
the master's methods and purpose. The
article was illustrated by engravings
which (though they had cost the magazine a fortune) were declared by Professor
Wildmarsh to give but an imperfect suggestion of the esoteric significance of the
originals. The Professor, with a tact
that contrived to make each reader feel
himself included among the exceptions,
went on to say that Keniston's work
would never appeal to any but exceptional
natures; and he closed with the usual
assertion that to apprehend the full meaning of the master's " message " it was
necessary to see him in the surroundings
of his own home at Hillbridge.

Professor Wildmarsh's article was read

one spring afternoon by a young lady just speeding eastward on her first visit to Hillbridge, and already flushed with anticipation of the intellectual opportunities awaiting her. In East Onondaigua, where she lived, Hillbridge was looked on as an Oxford. Magazine writers, with the easy American use of the superlative, designated it as " the venerable Alma Mater," the " antique seat of learning," and Claudia Day had been brought up to regard it as the fountainhead of knowledge, and of that mental distinction which is so much rarer than knowledge. An innate passion for all that was thus distinguished and exceptional made her revere Hillbridge as the native soil of those intellectual amenities that were of such difficult growth in the thin air of East Onondaigua. At the first suggestion of a visit to Hillbridge—whither she went at the invitation of a girl - friend who (incredible apotheosis!) had married one of the University professors—Claudia's spirit dilated with the sense of new possibilities. The vision of herself walking under the " historic elms " toward the Memorial Library, standing rapt before the Stuart Washington, or drinking in, from some obscure corner of an academic drawing-room, the President's reminiscences of the Concord group—this vividness of self-projection into the emotions awaiting her made her glad of any delay that prolonged so exquisite a moment.

It was in this mood that she opened the article on Keniston. She knew about him, of course; she was wonderfully " well up," even for East Onondaigua. She had read of him in the magazines; she had met, on a visit to New York, a man who collected Kenistons, and a photogravure of a Keniston, in an " artistic " frame, hung above her writing-table at home. But Professor Wildmarsh's article made her feel how little she really knew of the master; and she trembled to think of the state of relative ignorance in which, but for the timely purchase of the magazine, she might have entered Hillbridge. She had, for instance, been densely unaware that Keniston had already had three " manners," and was showing symptoms of a fourth. She was equally ignorant of the fact that he had founded a school and " created a

formula "; and she learned with a thrill that no one could hope to understand him who had not seen him in his studio at Hillbridge, surrounded by his own works. " The man and the art interpret each other," their exponent declared; and Claudia Day, bending a brilliant eye on the future, wondered if she would ever be admitted to the privilege of that double initiation.

Keniston to his other claims to distinction added that of being hard to know. His friends always hastened to announce the fact to strangers—adding after a pause of suspense that they " would see what they could do." Visitors in whose favor he was induced to make an exception were further warned that he never spoke unless he was interested—so that they mustn't mind if he remained silent. It was under these reassuring conditions that, some ten days after her arrival at Hillbridge, Miss Day was introduced to the master's studio. She found him a tall listless - looking man, who appeared middle-aged to her youth, and who stood before his own pictures with a vaguely interrogative gaze, leaving the task of their interpretation to the lady who had courageously contrived the visit. The studio, to Claudia's surprise, was bare and shabby. It formed a rambling addition to the small cheerless house in which the artist lived with his mother and a widowed sister. For Claudia it added the last touch to his distinction to learn that he was poor, and that what he earned was devoted to the maintenance of the two limp women who formed a sort of neutral-tinted background to his impressive outline. His pictures of course fetched high prices; but he worked slowly—" painfully," as his devotees preferred to phrase it—with frequent intervals of ill health and inactivity, and the circle of Keniston connoisseurs was still as small as it was distinguished. The girl's fancy instantly hailed in him that favorite figure of imaginative youth, the artist who would rather starve than paint a pot-boiler. It is known to comparatively few that the production of successful pot-boilers is an art in itself, and that such heroic abstentions as Keniston's are not always purely voluntary.

On the occasion of her first visit the

artist said so little that Claudia was able to indulge to the full the harrowing sense of her inadequacy. No wonder she had not been one of the few that he cared to talk to; every word she uttered must so obviously have diminished the inducement! She had been cheap, trivial, conventional; at once gushing and inexpressive, eager and constrained. She could feel him counting the minutes till the visit was over, and as the door finally closed on the scene of her discomfiture she almost shared the hope with which she confidently credited him—that they might never meet again.

II

Mrs. Davant glanced reverentially about the studio. " I have always said," she murmured, " that they ought to be seen in Europe."

Mrs. Davant was young, credulous, and emotionally extravagant; she reminded Claudia of her earlier self—the self that, ten years before, had first set an awestruck foot on that very threshold.

" Not for *his* sake," Mrs. Davant continued, " but for Europe's."

Claudia smiled. She was glad that her husband's pictures were to be exhibited in Paris. She concurred in Mrs. Davant's view of the importance of the event; but she thought her visitor's way of putting the case a little overcharged. Ten years spent in an atmosphere of Keniston-worship had insensibly developed in Claudia a preference for moderation of speech. She believed in her husband, of course; to believe in him, with an increasing abandonment and tenacity, had become one of the necessary laws of being; but she did not believe in his admirers. Their faith in him was perhaps as genuine as her own; but it seemed to her less able to give an account of itself. Some few of his appreciators doubtless measured him by their own standards; but it was difficult not to feel that in the Hillbridge circle, where rapture ran the highest, he was accepted on what was at best but an indirect valuation; and now and then she had a frightened doubt as to the independence of her own convictions. That innate sense of relativity which even East Onondaigua had not been able to check in Claudia Day had been fostered in Mrs. Keniston by the artistic absolutism of

Hillbridge, and she often wondered that her husband remained so uncritical of the quality of admiration accorded him. Her husband's uncritical attitude toward himself and his admirers had in fact been one of the surprises of her marriage. That an artist should believe in his potential powers seemed to her at once the incentive and the pledge of excellence: she knew there was no future for a hesitating talent. What perplexed her was Keniston's satisfaction in his achievement. She had always imagined that the true artist must regard himself as the imperfect vehicle of the cosmic emotion—that beneath every difficulty overcome a new one lurked, the vision widening as the scope enlarged. To be initiated into these creative struggles, to shed on the toiler's path the consolatory ray of faith and encouragement, had seemed the chief privilege of her marriage. But there is something supererogatory in believing in a man obviously disposed to perform that service for himself; and Claudia's ardor gradually spent itself against the dense surface of her husband's complacency. She could smile now at her ignorant vision of an intellectual communion which should admit her to the inmost precincts of his inspiration. She had learned that the creative processes are seldom self-explanatory, and Keniston's inarticulateness no longer discouraged her; but she could not reconcile her sense of the continuity of all high effort to his unperturbed air of finishing each picture as though he had despatched a masterpiece to posterity. In the first recoil from her disillusionment she even allowed herself to perceive that if he worked slowly it was not because he mistrusted his powers of expression, but because he had so little to express.

" It's for Europe," Mrs. Davant vaguely repeated; and Claudia noticed that she was blushingly intent on tracing with the tip of her elaborate sunshade the pattern of the shabby carpet.

" It will be a revelation to them," she went on, provisionally, as though Claudia had missed her cue and left an awkward interval to fill.

Claudia had in fact a sudden sense of deficient intuition. She felt that her visitor had something to communicate which required, on her own part, an intelligent co-operation; but what it was her insight failed to suggest. She was, in truth, a little tired of Mrs. Davant, who was Keniston's latest worshipper, who ordered pictures recklessly, who paid for them regally in advance, and whose gallery was, figuratively speaking, crowded with the artist's unpainted masterpieces. Claudia's impatience was perhaps complicated by the uneasy sense that Mrs. Davant was too young, too rich, too inexperienced; that somehow she ought to be warned. Warned of what? That some of the pictures might never be painted? Scarcely that, since Keniston, who was scrupulous in business transactions, might be trusted not to take any material advantage of such evidence of faith. Claudia's impulse remained undefined. She merely felt that she would have liked to help Mrs. Davant, and that she did not know how.

"You'll be there to see them?" she asked, as her visitor lingered.

"In Paris?" Mrs. Davant's blush deepened. "We must all be there together."

Claudia smiled. "My husband and I mean to go abroad some day—but I don't see any chance of it at present."

"But he *ought* to go—you ought both to go this summer!" Mrs. Davant persisted. "I know Professor Wildmarsh and Professor Driffert and all the other critics think that Mr. Keniston's never having been to Europe has given his work much of its wonderful individuality, its peculiar flavor and meaning—but now that his talent is formed, that he has full command of his means of expression" (Claudia recognized one of Professor Driffert's favorite formulas), "they all think he ought to see the work of the *other* great masters—that he ought to visit the home of his ancestors, as Professor Wildmarsh says!" She stretched an impulsive hand to Claudia. "You ought to let him go, Mrs. Keniston!"

Claudia accepted the admonition with the philosophy of the wife who is used to being advised on the management of her husband. "I sha'n't interfere with him," she declared; and Mrs. Davant instantly caught her up with a sudden cry of, "Oh, it's too lovely of you to say that!" With this exclamation she left Claudia to a silent renewal of wonder.

A moment later Keniston entered; to a mind curious in combinations it might have occurred that he had met Mrs. Davant on the door-step. In one sense he might, for all his wife cared, have met fifty Mrs. Davants on the door-step: it was long since Claudia had enjoyed the solace of resenting such coincidences. Her only thought now was that her husband's first words might not improbably explain Mrs. Davant's last; and she waited for him to speak.

He paused with his hands in his pockets before an unfinished picture on the easel; then, as his habit was, he began to stroll touristlike from canvas to canvas, standing before each in a musing ecstasy of contemplation that no readjustment of view ever seemed to disturb. Her eye instinctively joined his in its inspection; it was the one point where their natures merged. Thank God, there was no doubt about the pictures! She was what she had always dreamed of being— the wife of a great artist. Keniston dropped into an arm-chair and filled his pipe. "How should you like to go to Europe?" he asked.

His wife looked up quickly. "When?"

"Now—this spring, I mean." He paused to light the pipe. "I should like to be over there while these things are being exhibited."

Claudia was silent.

"Well?" he repeated after a moment.

"How can we afford it?" she asked.

Keniston had always scrupulously fulfilled his duty to the mother and sister whom his marriage had dislodged; and Claudia, who had the atoning temperament which seeks to pay for every happiness by making it a source of fresh obligations, had from the outset accepted his ties with an exaggerated devotion. Any disregard of such a claim would have vulgarized her most delicate pleasures; and her husband's sensitiveness to it in great measure extenuated the artistic obtuseness that often seemed to her like a failure of the moral sense. His loyalty to the dull women who depended on him was, after all, compounded of finer tissues than any mere sensibility to ideal demands.

"Oh, I don't see why we shouldn't," he rejoined. "I think we might manage it."

"At Mrs. Davant's expense?" leaped from Claudia. She could not tell why she had said it; some inner barrier seemed to have given way under a confused pressure of emotions.

He looked up at her with frank surprise. "Well, she *has* been very jolly about it—why not? She has a tremendous feeling for art—the keenest I ever knew in a woman." Claudia imperceptibly smiled. "She wants me to let her pay in advance for the four panels she has ordered for the Memorial Library. That would give us plenty of money for the trip, and my having the panels to do is another reason for my wanting to go abroad just now."

"Another reason?"

"Yes; I've never worked on such a big scale. I want to see how those old chaps did the trick; I want to measure myself with the big fellows over there. An artist ought to, once in his life."

She gave him a wondering look. The words implied a dawning sense of possible limitation; but his easy tone seemed to retract what they conceded. What he really wanted was fresh food for his self-satisfaction: he was like an army that moves on after exhausting the resources of the country.

Womanlike, she abandoned the general survey of the case for the consideration of a minor point.

"Are you sure you can do that kind of thing?" she asked.

"What kind of thing?"

"The panels."

He glanced at her indulgently: his self-confidence was too impenetrable to feel the pin-prick of such a doubt.

"Immensely sure," he said, smiling.

"And you don't mind taking so much money from her in advance?"

He stared. "Why should I? She'll get it back — with interest!" He laughed and drew at his pipe. "It will be an uncommonly interesting experience. I shouldn't wonder if it freshened me up a bit."

She looked at him again. This second hint of potential self-distrust struck her as the sign of a quickened sensibility. What if, after all, he was beginning to be dissatisfied with his work? The thought filled her with a renovating sense of his sufficiency.

III

They stopped in London to see the National Gallery. It was thus that, in their inexperience, they had narrowly put it; but in reality every stone of the streets, every trick of the atmosphere, had its message of surprise for their virgin sensibilities. The pictures were simply the summing up, the final interpretation, of the cumulative pressure of an unimagined world; and it seemed to Claudia that long before they reached the doors of the gallery she had some intuitive revelation of what awaited them within.

They moved about from room to room without exchanging a word. The vast noiseless spaces seemed full of sound, like the roar of a distant multitude heard only by the inner ear. Had their speech been articulate their language would have been incomprehensible; and even that far-off murmur of meaning pressed intolerably on Claudia's throbbing nerves. Keniston took the onset without outward sign of disturbance. Now and then he paused before a canvas, or prolonged from one of the benches his silent communion with some miracle of line or color; but he neither looked at his wife nor spoke to her. He seemed to have forgotten her presence.

Claudia was conscious of keeping a furtive watch on him; but the sum total of her impressions was negative. She remembered thinking when she first met him that his face was rather expressionless; and he had the habit of self-engrossed silences.

All that evening, at the hotel, they talked about London, and he surprised her by an acuteness of observation that she had sometimes inwardly accused him of lacking. He seemed to have seen everything, to have examined, felt, compared, with nerves as finely adjusted as her own; but he said nothing of the pictures. The next day they returned to the National Gallery, and he began to examine the paintings in detail, pointing out differences of technique, analyzing and criticising, but still without summing up his conclusions. He seemed to have a sort of provincial dread of showing himself too much impressed. Claudia's own sensations were too complex, too overwhelming, to be readily classified. Lacking the craftsman's instinct to steady her, she felt herself carried off her feet by the rush of incoherent impressions. One point she consciously avoided, and that was the comparison of her husband's work with what they were daily seeing. Art, she inwardly argued, was too various, too complex, dependent on too many inter-relations of feeling and environment, to allow of its being judged by any provisional standard. Even the subtleties of technique must be modified by the artist's changing purpose, as this in turn is acted on by influences of which he is himself unconscious. How, then, was an unprepared imagination to distinguish between such varied reflections of the elusive vision? She took refuge in a passionate exaggeration of her own ignorance and insufficiency.

After a week in London they went to Paris. The exhibition of Keniston's pictures had been opened a few days earlier; and as they drove through the streets on the way to the station an "impressionist" poster here and there invited them to the display of the American artist's work. Mrs. Davant, who had been in Paris for the opening, had already written rapturously of the impression produced, enclosing commendatory notices from one or two papers. She reported that there had been a great crowd on the first day, and that the critics had been "immensely struck."

The Kenistons arrived in the evening, and the next morning Claudia, as a matter of course, asked her husband at what time he meant to go and see the pictures.

He looked up absently from his guide-book.

"What pictures?"

"Why—yours," she said, surprised.

"Oh, they'll keep," he answered; adding, with a slightly embarrassed laugh, "We'll give the other chaps a show first." Presently he laid down his book and proposed that they should go to the Louvre.

They spent the morning there, lunched at a restaurant near by, and returned to the gallery in the afternoon. Keniston had passed from inarticulateness to an eager volubility. It was clear that he was beginning to co-ordinate his impressions, to find his way about in a corner of the great imaginative universe. He

seemed extraordinarily ready to impart his discoveries; and Claudia was conscious that her ignorance served him as a convenient buffer against the terrific impact of new sensations.

On the way home she asked when he meant to see Mrs. Davant.

His answer surprised her. "Does she know we're here?"

"Not unless you've sent her word," said Claudia, with a touch of harmless irony.

"That's all right, then," he returned simply. "I want to wait and look about a day or two longer. She'd want us to go sight-seeing with her; and I'd rather get my impressions alone."

The next two days were hampered by the necessity of eluding Mrs. Davant. Claudia, under different circumstances, would have scrupled to share in this somewhat shabby conspiracy; but she found herself in a state of suspended judgment, wherein her husband's treatment of Mrs. Davant became for the moment merely a clue to larger meanings.

They had been four days in Paris when Claudia, returning one afternoon from a parenthetical excursion to the Rue de la Paix, was confronted on her threshold by the reproachful figure of their benefactress. It was not to her, however, that Mrs. Davant's reproaches were addressed. Keniston, it appeared, had borne the brunt of them; for he stood leaning against the mantel-piece of their modest *salon* in that attitude of convicted negligence when, if ever, a man is glad to take refuge behind his wife.

Claudia had, however, no immediate intention of affording him such shelter. She wanted to observe and wait.

"He's too impossible!" cried Mrs. Davant, sweeping her at once into the central current of her grievance.

Claudia looked from one to the other.

"For not going to see you?"

"For not going to see his pictures!" cried the other, nobly.

Claudia colored, and Keniston shifted his position uneasily.

"I can't make her understand," he said, turning to his wife.

"I don't care about myself!" Mrs. Davant interjected.

"*I* do, then; it's the only thing I do care about," he hurriedly protested. "I meant to go at once—to write—Claudia wanted to go, but I wouldn't let her." He looked helplessly about the pleasant red-curtained room, which was rapidly burning itself into Claudia's consciousness as a visible extension of Mrs. Davant's claims.

"I can't explain," he broke off.

Mrs. Davant in turn addressed herself to Claudia.

"People think it's so odd," she complained. "So many of the artists here are anxious to meet him; they've all been so charming about the pictures; and several of our American friends have come over from London expressly for the exhibition. I told every one that he would be here for the opening—there was a private view, you know—and they were so disappointed—they wanted to give him an ovation; and I didn't know what to say. What *am* I to say?" she abruptly ended.

"There's nothing to say," said Keniston, slowly.

"But the exhibition closes the day after to-morrow."

"Well, *I* sha'n't close—I shall be here," he declared with an effort at playfulness. "If they want to see me—all these people you're kind enough to mention—won't there be other chances?"

"But I wanted them to see you *among* your pictures—to hear you talk about them, explain them in that wonderful way. I wanted you to interpret each other, as Professor Wildmarsh says!"

"Oh, hang Professor Wildmarsh!" said Keniston, softening the commination with a smile. "If my pictures are good for anything they oughtn't to need explaining."

Mrs. Davant stared. "But I thought that was what made them so interesting!" she exclaimed.

Keniston looked down. "Perhaps it was," he murmured.

There was an awkward silence, which Claudia broke by saying, with a glance at her husband: "But if the exhibition is to remain open to-morrow, could we not meet you there? And perhaps you could send word to some of our friends."

Mrs. Davant brightened like a child whose broken toy is glued together. "Oh, *do* make him!" she implored. "I'll ask them to come in the afternoon—we'll make it into a little tea—a *five o'clock*. I'll send word at once to everybody!" She gathered up her beruffled boa and sunshade, settling her plumage like a reassured bird. "It will be too lovely!" she ended in a self-consoling murmur.

But in the doorway a new doubt assailed her. "You won't fail me?" she said, turning plaintively to Keniston. "You'll make him come, Mrs. Keniston?"

"I'll bring him!" Claudia promised.

IV

When, the next morning, she appeared equipped for their customary ramble, her husband surprised her by announcing that he meant to stay at home.

"The fact is I'm rather surfeited," he said, smiling. "I suppose my appetite isn't equal to such a plethora. I think I'll write some letters and join you somewhere later."

She detected the wish to be alone, and responded to it with her usual readiness.

"I shall sink to my proper level and buy a bonnet, then," she said. "I haven't had time to take the edge off that appetite."

They agreed to meet at the Hôtel Cluny at mid-day, and she set out alone with a vague sense of relief. Neither she nor Keniston had made any direct reference to Mrs. Davant's visit; but its effect was implicit in their eagerness to avoid each other.

Claudia accomplished some shopping in the spirit of perfunctoriness that robs even new bonnets of their bloom; and this business despatched, she turned aimlessly into the wide inviting brightness of the streets. Never had she felt more isolated amid that ordered beauty which gives a social quality to the very stones and mortar of Paris. All about her were evidences of an artistic sensibility pervading every form of life like the nervous structure of the huge frame — a sensibility so delicate, alert, and universal that it seemed to leave no room for obtuseness or error. In such a medium the faculty of plastic expression must develop as unconsciously as any organ in its normal surroundings; to be "artistic" must cease to be an attitude and become a natural function. To Claudia the significance of the whole vast revelation was centred in the light it shed on one tiny spot of consciousness—the value of her husband's work. There are moments when to the groping soul the world's accumulated experiences are but stepping-stones across a private difficulty.

She stood hesitating on a street corner. It was barely eleven, and she had an hour to spare before going to the Hôtel Cluny. She seemed to be letting her inclination float as it would on the cross-currents of suggestion emanating from the brilliant complex scene before her; but suddenly, in obedience to an impulse that she became aware of only in acting on it, she called a cab and drove to the gallery where her husband's pictures were exhibited.

A magnificent official in gold braid sold her a ticket and pointed the way up the empty crimson-carpeted stairs. His duplicate, on the upper landing, offered her a catalogue with an air of recognizing the futility of the offer; and a moment later she found herself in the long noiseless impressive room full of velvet-covered ottomans and exotic plants. It was clear that the public ardor on which Mrs. Davant had expatiated had spent itself earlier in the week; for Claudia had this luxurious apartment to herself. Something about its air of rich privacy, its diffusion of that sympathetic quality in other countries so conspicuously absent from the public show-room, seemed to emphasize its present emptiness. It was as though the flowers, the carpet, the lounges, surrounded their visitor's solitary advance with the mute assurance that they had done all they could toward making the thing "go off," and that if they had failed it was simply for lack of efficient co-operation. She stood still and looked about her. The pictures struck her instantly as odd gaps in the general harmony: it was self-evident that they had not co-operated. They had not been pushing, aggressive, discordant: they had merely effaced themselves. She swept a startled eye from one familiar painting to another. The canvases were all there—and the frames—but the miracle, the mirage of life and meaning, had vanished like some atmospheric illusion. What was it that had happened? And had it happened to *her* or to the pictures? She tried to rally her frightened thoughts; to push or coax them into a

semblance of resistance; but argument was swept off its feet by the huge rush of a single conviction—the conviction that the pictures were bad. There was no standing up against that: she felt herself submerged.

The stealthy fear that had been following her all these days had her by the throat now. The great vision of beauty through which she had been moving as one enchanted turned to a phantasmagoria of evil mocking shapes. She hated the past; she hated its splendor, its power, its wicked magical vitality. She dropped into a seat and continued to stare at the wall before her. Gradually, as she stared, there stole out to her from the dimmed humbled canvases a reminder of what she had once seen in them, a spectral appeal to her faith to call them back to life. What proof had she that her present estimate of them was less subjective than the other? The confused impressions of the last few days were hardly to be pleaded as a valid theory of art. How, after all, did she know that the pictures were bad? On what suddenly acquired technical standard had she thus decided the case against them? It seemed as though it were a standard outside of herself, as though some unheeded inner sense were gradually making her aware of the presence, in that empty room, of a critical intelligence that was giving out a subtle effluence of disapproval. The fancy was so vivid that, to shake it off, she rose and began to move about again. In the middle of the room stood a monumental divan surmounted by a *massif* of palms and azaleas. As Claudia's muffled wanderings carried her around the angle of this seat, she saw that its farther side was occupied by the figure of a man, who sat with his hands resting on his stick and his head bowed upon them. She gave a little cry and her husband rose and faced her.

Instantly the live point of consciousness was shifted, and she became aware that the quality of the pictures no longer mattered. It was what *he* thought of them that counted: her life hung on that.

They looked at each other a moment in silence; such concussions are not apt to flash into immediate speech. At length he said simply, "I didn't know you were coming here."

She colored as though he had charged her with something underhand.

"I didn't mean to," she stammered; "but I was too early for our appointment—"

Her blundering words cast a revealing glare on the situation. Neither of them looked at the pictures; but to Claudia those unobtruding presences seemed suddenly to press upon them and force them apart.

Keniston glanced at his watch. "It's twelve o'clock," he said. "Shall we go on?"

V

At the door he called a cab and put her in it; then, drawing out his watch again, he said, abruptly: "I believe I'll let you go alone. I'll join you at the hotel in time for luncheon." She wondered for a moment if he meant to return to the gallery; but, looking back as she drove off, she saw him walk rapidly away in the opposite direction.

The cabman had carried her half-way to the Hôtel Cluny before she realized where she was going, and cried out to him to turn home. There was an acute irony in this mechanical prolongation of the quest of beauty. She had had enough of it, too much of it; her one longing was to escape, to hide herself away from its all-suffusing implacable light.

At the hotel, alone in her room, a few tears came to soften her seared vision; but her mood was too tense to be eased by weeping. Her whole being was centred in the longing to know what her husband thought. Their short exchange of words had, after all, told her nothing. She had guessed a faint resentment at her unexpected appearance; but that might merely imply a dawning sense, on his part, of being furtively watched and criticised. She had sometimes wondered if he was never conscious of her observation; there were moments when it seemed to radiate from her in visible waves. Perhaps, after all, he was aware of it, on his guard against it, as a lurking knife behind the thick curtain of his complacency; and to-day he must have caught the gleam of the blade.

Claudia had not reached the age when pity is the first chord to vibrate in contact with any revelation of failure. Her one hope had been that Keniston should be clear-eyed enough to face the truth. Whatever it turned out to be, she wanted him to measure himself with it. But as his image rose before her she felt a sudden half-maternal longing to thrust herself between him and disaster. Her eagerness to see him tested by circumstances seemed now like a cruel scientific curiosity. She saw in a flash of sympathy that he would need her most if he fell beneath his fate.

He did not, after all, return for luncheon; and when she came up stairs from her solitary meal their *salon* was still untenanted. She permitted herself no sensational fears; for she could not, at the height of apprehension, figure Keniston as yielding to any tragic impulse; but the lengthening hours brought an uneasiness that was fuel to her pity. Suddenly she heard the clock strike five. It was the hour at which they had promised to meet Mrs. Davant at the gallery—the hour of the "ovation." Claudia rose and went to the window, straining for a glimpse of her husband in the crowded street. Could it be that he had forgotten her, had gone to the gallery without her? Or had something happened—that veiled "something" which, for the last hour, had grimly hovered on the outskirts of her mind?

She heard a hand on the door and Keniston entered. As she turned to meet him her whole being was swept forward on a great wave of pity: she was so sure, now, that he must know.

But he confronted her with a glance of preoccupied brightness; her first impression was that she had never seen him so vividly, so expressively pleased. If he needed her, it was not to bind up his wounds.

He gave her a smile which was clearly the lingering reflection of some inner light. "I didn't mean to be so late," he said, tossing aside his hat and the little red volume that served as a clue to his explorations. "I turned in to the Louvre for a minute after I left you this morning, and the place fairly swallowed me up—I couldn't get away from it. I've been there ever since." He threw himself into a chair and glanced about for his pipe.

"It takes time," he continued musingly, "to get at them, to make out what they're saying—the big fellows, I mean. They're not a communicative lot. At first I couldn't make much out of their lingo— it was too different from mine! But gradually, by picking up a hint here and there, and piecing them together, I've begun to understand; and to-day, by Jove, I got one or two of the old chaps by the throat and fairly turned them inside out —made them deliver up their last drop." He lifted a brilliant eye to her. "Lord, it was tremendous!" he declared.

He had found his pipe and was musingly filling it. Claudia waited in silence.

"At first," he began again, "I was afraid their language was too hard for me—that I should never quite know what they were driving at; they seemed to cold-shoulder me, to be bent on shutting me out. But I was bound I wouldn't be beaten, and now, to-day "—he paused a moment to strike a match—"when I went to look at those things of mine it all came over me in a flash. By Jove! it was as if I'd made them all into a big bonfire to light up my road!"

His wife was trembling with a kind of sacred terror. She had been afraid to pray for light for him, and here he was joyfully casting his whole past upon the pyre!

"Is there nothing left?" she faltered.

"Nothing left? There's everything!" he exulted. "Why, here I am, not much over forty, and I've found out already— already!" He stood up and began to move excitedly about the room. "My God! Suppose I'd never known! Suppose I'd gone on painting things like that forever! Why, I feel like those chaps at revivalist meetings when they get up and say they're saved! Won't somebody please start a hymn?"

Claudia, with a tremulous joy, was letting herself go on the strong current of his emotion; but it had not yet carried her beyond her depth, and suddenly she felt hard ground underfoot.

"Mrs. Davant—" she exclaimed.

He stared, as though suddenly recalled from a long distance.

"Mrs. Davant?"

"We were to have met her—this afternoon—now—"

"At the gallery? Oh, that's all right. I put a stop to that; I went to see her after I left you; I explained it all to her."

"All?"

"I told her I was going to begin all over again."

Claudia's heart gave a forward bound and then sank back hopelessly.

"But the panels—?"

"That's all right too. I told her about the panels," he reassured her.

"You told her—?"

"That I can't paint them now. She doesn't understand, of course; but she's the best little woman and she trusts me."

She could have wept for joy at his exquisite obtuseness. "But that isn't all," she wailed. "It doesn't matter how much you've explained to her. It doesn't do away with the fact that we're living on those panels!"

"Living on them?"

"On the money that she paid you to paint them. Isn't that what brought us here? And—if you mean to do as you say—to begin all over again—how in the world are we ever to pay her back?"

Her husband turned on her an inspired eye.

"There's only one way that I know of," he imperturbably declared; "and that's to stay out here till I learn how to paint them."

A THANKSGIVING BREAKFAST
by Harriet Prescott Spofford

PERHAPS you remember the house, a little remote from the avenue and its approaches, in that part of the town which is now the fashionable centre, but was then on the edge of a wood, a house sitting high on its terraces, half covered with honeysuckles green all winter, and half hidden by its hedges.

Here Miss Veronica and her sister lived, intrenched not only behind their hedges, but behind a respectability that took small note of new people and affairs; and as some trees find sustenance in the decay of their roots, they nourished themselves upon past grandeur. Administrations came and administrations went; they passed like ephemera before Miss Veronica and Miss Sedley. In forty years they had not thought it worth while to attend a President's levee, or to enter the White House at all. The Capitol had blown up the bubble of its mighty dome unvisited by them. The civil war had surged over the country, scarcely causing them a heart-throb. When Early made his raid upon the borders of the town they only smiled to hear of it; they were Southern ladies and safe in any event. Soldiers marched and countermarched in street and avenue; they only bowed their blinds and sat further back in their parlors. Milly and Hark became free people, and the country rocked with jubilation and blazed with banners; so far as they were conscious of it they regarded it as a part of the latter-day ruin. A President was impeached; it did not signify; the new Presidents were like children playing with crowns and sceptres. As nearly as possible time and the march of nations stood still that Miss Veronica Sidney and her sister Sedley might pass, pausing if not with the President who had been an uncle-in-law of some long-dead aunt of theirs, yet with his immediate successors.

The income of these old gentlewomen was very small, consisting of the rents of certain houses, sometimes paid and sometimes not, and it was now smaller than ever, since under the new system of street improvement some of the houses had simply been swallowed in the abyss of the betterments. But their needs were very small also. They changed the fashion of their garments but little; one wax candle burned a long while; and the best part of the table was its thin old silver. The Easter ham, stuffed with chives and shallots, lasted them almost to Ascension; and there was some of the Christmas pudding left for Twelfth-night. They paid wages now to Milly, small ones, but none at all to Hark, who waited at table and on the door, and had his satisfaction in it; and the two old slaves, beaming and content, said nothing about the fact that they were much better off than their mistresses, having long ago squatted on some vacant lots, and having now sold out for an independence. Milly went home every evening, and came back every morning as Miss Veronica opened the door to go out to six-o'clock mass, for the sisters were devout Catholics. And with Milly came half a dozen little pickaninnies in every size and shade, who played all day on the brick floor of the great kitchen or in the area behind it, and who were fed at no particular cost on potatoes and gravy. Hark did the marketing and whatever might become a man; and if now and then dainties in the shape of an early radish or a crisp lettuce, a shaddock dressed with sherry, a deviled crab, a bird, appeared on the table, the ladies only thought how apt Hark was at getting the money's worth, and never dreamed that it was Hark's money.

So Miss Veronica's and Miss Sedley's days went by in a great quiet. They had a few friends somewhat like themselves, with whom they exchanged visits. They occasionally went over to the convent and got the news of the world. They now and then read a newspaper, but with the air of holding it with a pair of tongs. They regarded a woman who wrote for the papers as false to her sex; an interviewer was something less reprehensible than a house-breaker perhaps; and they associated suffrage in their minds with divorce, and regarded them both as scandals, for mention of which, were it necessary to allude to them, you lowered your voice. Their contempt for the North, its fasts and feasts and people, was inbred, but was not active, the subject being too remote to concern them. They looked askance at the employment of women in the Treasury; and they took almost as much care not to brush their skirts against a Treasury girl as against a play-actress, as they called it—a person who represented to them an unknown quantity, not exactly human, but allied to the powers of evil. And as for modern science, so far as they knew anything about it, it was a fairy story, or a lure of the devil, and they regarded mention of protoplasm or germs or evolution as uncomfortably near profanity. They did endless cross-stitch with crewels on canvas, and some beautiful tambour-work on muslin. They had a week of dissipation when one of the fairs of their church took place, and they would revel in half the bad passions of the race over the countless raffles for a picture, an India shawl, a lace mantle, there. When Miss Sedley broke her arm, Miss Veronica kept the bandages wet with holy water, and was confident that the dressing did more good than the surgeon's splints. And Miss Sedley had for some time been putting by a secret hoard, if by possibility it might reach such proportions that Miss Veronica could make the pilgrimage to Lourdes, not very long known then, and wash away the little knobs that were coming on the joints of her long white slender fingers.

So, neither of the world nor in the world, they sat one summer morning, now and then murmuring a sentence or two, wearing their old sheer muslin gowns, a little open at the ruffled throat, a faint color from the heat upon their withered cheeks, the slightly loose and thin gray hair having the fine curl about the brow which belongs alike to age and infancy, as beautiful, alas! as it is given to old women to be. And they slowly waved their great feather fans, more with a sense of the terrible heat that struck up from the blazing concrete pavements outside, than with any actual experience of it here where the south wind blew in the windows and brought with it the sweetness of the roses that bent their long stems and swung damask and maroon and blush and white, such heavy hundred-leaved roses as summer seldom gives the North. Miss Sedley had yawned and yawned again. "Dear, dear," she said. "It does seem as if life were too empty to live. One day just like another, and nothing ever happening."

"Sometimes it seems to me," said Miss Veronica, "as if we were our own ghosts," and then she stopped, overcome with the irreverence of the fancy. "I

mean we are really so dead, not merely dead and alive, but dead. There is nothing that could happen."

"Oh, sister!"

"There is no one to come. And no one to go. Nothing to hope for. Nothing to wish. There are old people who amount to something. But I reckon they married, or their sisters did—"

"Yes, oh, yes!"

"If we only had some one to love, Sedley, I would not care how worthless—it would be better than stagnation."

"Oh, sister!"

"I've always been tolerably content, you know," said Miss Veronica, taking the little powder-puff from the reticule on her arm and cooling her face with it, "but lately I have thought we might as well be dead and done with as done with and not dead!"

"I'm afraid it is very irreligious. I feel so, too. I'm afraid perhaps we've been living too well. It has puffed us up and made us discontented. I'm afraid I had better tell Milly," said Miss Sedley, "not to put caraway into the next seed-cakes."

Perhaps the sisters were dozing then, the briefest moment possible, when a blow from the knocker resounded through the hall, and resounded again with determination, before Hark could loiter up from the kitchen and shuffle along to the door.

"Oh, my goodness!" cried Miss Sedley. "To think of any one out in this heat! Who do you suppose it can be? Perhaps it is Mrs. Entwisle's Polly about the gooseberries. You don't think it can be Father Walter? I wish the sherbet—Oh—ah—yes—no—I'm sure—" For Hark was taking an impression of his thumb on a visiting-card, and Miss Veronica had slowly adjusted her lorgnon and read

MISS CELESTE DREER.

The Graphic.
The Free Press.

without, however, observing the lower left-hand corner, and had passed the card to her sister.

"Dreer?" she said. "Dreer? There were the Yardley Dreers, and the Queen Anne County Dreers—well, well— Yes, Hark, of course we shall be pleased." And then a young lady in a frou-frou of light summer silk and a hat of corn-flowers and poppies was in the room and bending with a pretty grace to the old ladies, opening a fan that swung at her waist, taking the seat they both indicated at the same moment, a pair of keen quick eyes busying themselves with the environment.

"No," she said, in bright crisp tones. "I'm so sorry. But I'm neither the Yardley nor the Queen Anne Dreers. I'm just a no-account Dreer. But when I was quite a little girl old Chancellor Babb used to tell me of you—"

"The Chancellor! Indeed! It is so long since—"

"And my kind friend, General Fitz Hardee—"

"Oh, certainly, any friend of General Fitz Hardee's!"

"And so I am venturing, although it is so unceremonious, and I am awfully afraid a thunder-gust is coming up."

And by this time the lively eyes had taken in the lofty old-fashioned room, where the Canton mattings diffused their odor of dates; where Windsor chairs stood between white dimity-covered sofas; bright Lowestoft china illuminated dark wall-cabinets; spidery tables held jars of pot-pourri and great bowls of fresh roses and one or two faded silken-bound Souvenirs and Annuals; a spindle-legged piano, whose ivory inlay was yellow as old paper, companioned a harp over whose strings and tarnished gilding she could in an instant see Miss Sedley drooping the flaxen ringlets and curving the round white arms of long ago; and half-guessed in the shadow and the dimness the portraits of gentlemen in gold lace, and of ladies in long corsets and scarfs and feathers, looked down from the walls among century-old engravings framed in black and bearing long-descended stains.

"Oh, we do not mind the thundergusts," said Miss Veronica.

"I do, then," said the visitor. "I grow stone-cold, and have to have something warm to drink, and nearly die with fright anyway. But I had to come. You know, after Congress is gone and there's nothing doing at the departments or in society, there's so little to write about, and—"

"You want to tell them at home that you have seen their old friends," said Miss Sedley.

"Oh, dear, no! nothing of the sort. You must excuse my saying so, but what a perfectly charming room this is! Who would think down in our stuffy little boarding-house that such a cool bowery place of seclusion could be found in the same town? You can never know anything about the heat here. Why, some nights I just gasp for breath. We take our chairs out on the sidewalk after dark and simply suffer. I went to sleep last summer for six weeks with the thermometer at a hundred and two, and it was ninety-eight when I woke up. In the daytime it is hotter after a shower than it was before. I held my parasol down coming up here, for the heat from the pavement was worse than the heat from the sky. Oh, it is so deliciously cool in here!" And she stopped talking long enough to use her fan vigorously.

"We were thinking it was warm," said Miss Veronica.

"In this place! Why. it belongs to the Dwelling of Delightful Days! It is ages ago here, but without the dust of ages. Oh, it is fine to have your grandmothers' old low-boys when you don't have to have your grandmothers' old cobwebs too! And will you really let me see the things you have that belonged to the President? What treasures! oh, what treasures!"

And Miss Veronica and Miss Sedley were as wax in the hands of this young business woman; and the gold-embroidered waistcoat, and the Malines lace ruffles, and the gold snuff-box, and the order given by the King of Spain, and the diary kept at sea, and the sleeve-links and the mourning-ring and the paste knee-buckles, and the lock of his hair, passed processionally before her.

"And this work-box," said Miss Veronica at last, "was once the property of Queen Marie Antoinette."

"That!"

Miss Sedley bridled. "Perhaps you have not examined it," she said. "It is ebony and niello-work."

"I beg your pardon. I'm right glad you told me. I thought it was just bits of wood-cuts, you know, laid on the black wood and varnished over, like mamma used to do."

"The i-dea!" said Miss Sedley. "It came from the Little Trianon. There is her thimble with the topaz top; there is the bit of lace and lawn she was beginning—see where the needle was stuck in hurriedly as she laid it down. There is a tiny blood-spot where she pricked her finger—"

"Oh, the poor lovely creature! the

poor, great, sweet martyr! Oh, Miss Sidney, if you would let me touch it!" And she lifted it over the tip of her finger, and suddenly pressed her lips upon the tiny spot and held it to her glowing cheek.

"You dear child! You dear girl!" cried Miss Veronica. "How susceptible you are! We should not have shown it to you. We—"

"Oh, yes, yes! You have given me such a pleasure! It has been such an experience!"

And at that Miss Sedley had gone upstairs and brought down a gown in which some one had danced with Aaron Burr, two breadths and a gore of a brocade whose delicate rose tints and multitudinous yellowing ribbons would not have been unbecoming to either of the gentle ladies then. "Now," said Miss Sedley, when this also had been sufficiently admired, "I think we really must have some sherbet, sister. Shall I speak to Hark?" And while Miss Veronica was telling the adventures of that dance, Celeste was eating cherry ice with a little thin gold apostle-spoon, and wondering how these people lived cut off from the present; and if they really were alive; and were she once outside could she ever find the house again; and if she could remember half that she had seen and heard. And she walked home almost as well pleased with herself as she was when, some ten days afterward, she again stood at the door with the slip of newspaper containing the letter in which she had described the place, the house, the treasures, and themselves.

She received, as she expected, the most cordial welcome. The sweet old ladies—Miss Veronica tall and slender, Miss Sedley not so tall and not so slender, in their soft muslin gowns, with their great feather fans, and the faint flush of the heat on their cheeks—seemed to have been sitting in the same spot since she left them. "I declare," she said afterwards, "I wanted to pinch myself to make sure it wasn't some absurd enchantment, or I wasn't dreaming, or something." But she only waved her own fan and unfolded the newspaper.

"Now," she said, gayly, "it is my turn. I have brought you something. And I do hope it will give you the pleasure to read it that it did me to write it!"

Miss Veronica and Miss Sedley Sidney bent their heads together over the slip of paper she handed them. She had cut off the scare-heads because she had not been responsible for them, and would not have had them—"Two Ancient Beauties of the District," "Butterflies in Amber," "Links with Aaron Burr"—and the letter itself she knew was not half bad. She had taken off her hat at their request, they a little flattered that youth had found them pleasant enough to come back so soon, and she sat with a smile on her face expectant of the smile on theirs.

"Oh!" she suddenly heard Miss Veronica exclaim, like a cry of pain; "it is impossible!"

"Oh!" Miss Sedley echoed her sister. "I cannot believe it."

The faint blush on their faces grew a deep scarlet, their eyes were staring wide and frightened, their lips trembled, their hands trembled.

"I cannot read it," stammered Miss Veronica. "I—I—have never been so insulted in my life."

"So outraged," whispered Miss Sedley. "So humiliated!"

"I don't know what you mean!" cried Celeste, her cheeks blazing. "Do you—"

"Oh!" exclaimed Miss Veronica, looking at her a moment with burning eyes. "We do not mean anything. Only please to go away."

"But I don't understand," urged Celeste. "Haven't I said enough? Have I made a mistake? Is there anything wrong?"

"Oh, it is all wrong!" cried Miss Sedley.

"All wrong?" Celeste repeated, tremulously.

"Oh, cruel! Wrong and cruel!"

"Wrong and cruel! Why, there must be— You can't— I don't see—"

"You don't see," exclaimed Miss Veronica, "that you have come into our quiet lives and stripped them bare, and let in the glare as if I threw that blind open to the sun? That you have violated our hospitality—"

"Our welcome."

"Our friendliness," the slip of paper shaking in the knobby fingers.

"Our confidence."

"That you have betrayed us, exposed us. Oh, we shall not dare to be seen upon the street—"

"To show our faces."

"I—I thought you would be pleased," faltered Celeste.

"Pleased! Pleased to be held up as a show; to be bandied about the crowd; to be vulgarized; to be in the mouth of people as if we were criminals; to be—to be profaned—"

"And we have lived such quiet lives, so respectable," said Miss Sedley, her lips quivering again. "And now our modesty, our decency—"

"Oh, don't, don't, don't!" cried Celeste, springing up with her hands upon her eyes, from which the tears were spurting. "How could I tell? Every one else has liked it. People have offered me money to do it. It is my livelihood. I got enough to pay a week's board for the letter—"

"A reporter!"

"But, oh! I would never, never have done it if I had thought you felt this way. I don't understand now. I don't see why. Oh, I liked you so! You were so sweet to me. I never saw any one I felt so near to all at once. And now— Oh, you are breaking my heart!" And her voice had risen almost to a scream, and she had thrown herself on her knees beside Miss Veronica, and buried her face in the lady's lap, sobbing bitterly.

"I am glad you feel so," said Miss Sedley. "It is something to have you see what you have done."

"Oh, oh!" she cried, lifting her hot wet face. "It isn't any matter about me. Oh, I am so sorry I did it, when you feel so! I couldn't know—I never dreamed— oh! oh! oh!" And she cried so that Miss Veronica, who at first had shrunk away, put out her hand and laid it on her hair. But the sobs only grew wilder, more uncontrollable, and convulsive.

"Really," said Miss Veronica, "you mustn't. Indeed you mustn't. I—I didn't know you were so sensitive—I am sure—"

"Please don't feel so," prayed Miss Sedley. "Oh, please! I forgive you. We forgive you. Oh, do get up! You will make yourself sick!" And then it became evident that they had something more on their hands than they could manage. The thunder that had been growling in the sky for some minutes burst in a sudden clap. Miss Veronica reached for her smelling-salts; and Miss Sedley remembered and hastened for something warm to drink; and Celeste, vainly trying to swallow her sobs and stay her tears, toppled over white and stiff; and Hark and Milly came and carried her up stairs, and Miss Sedley herself put her to bed in the room in the wing with the southern exposure and the gal-

lery, and sent for Dr. John. "I don't know but we have killed her," she whispered over and over to Miss Veronica.

"The fact is," said Dr. John on taking leave, "that she is about used up. And this was bound to come. She's the most hard-working little thing in town. Up at the Capitol, into the Departments, over at the White House, down to the printing-offices, every morning, every afternoon at the receptions, and every night reporting a dinner or a ball, and hunting out new facts to write about betweenwhiles."

"Oh, my goodness, doctor! What for?"

"For the news of the world. And she has a high standard for the honor of her profession, and will run all over town to verify an item, about a ribbon, maybe. I told her she would break down the last time she had one of these attacks. It would wear out a man of brass, to say nothing of a little Southern girl brought up on eider-down. And just now she seems to have had a shock. How in the world came she here?" And he looked about him quizzically.

"Oh, she has! she has had a shock!" cried Miss Sedley. "And it's our fault! I don't know but we have killed her. You must, you must bring her round, doctor. Your father could, and you can"—with the implicit confidence that every one had in Dr. John as the dispenser of life and death—"and we will spare no pains." And the two poor ladies forgot all about the sin of the sufferer, forgot the heat and their delicate old toilettes, and bathed the girl, and rubbed her, and fed her, and watched over her day and night.

"It is quite worth the pains," said Miss Sedley, coming down into the drawing-room, where, after three or four days of anxiety, Miss Veronica was drawing a free breath. "The beautiful young creature— so finely bred! How she came to be working like she does—that sort of work— I reckon she hasn't any mother. You can see she's a lady to the tips of her fingers. You can see it," said Miss Sedley, in a whisper, "by her under-clothes."

"How pretty she is, lying there so white in all the heat! Oh, how I should like a daughter like that—"

"Veronica!"

"I should! Indeed, indeed! But, there—"

"The indelicacy!"

"I don't care anything about the indelicacy," said Miss Veronica, recklessly.

"I should have liked the daughter. I would have taken better care of her, too, I reckon—"

"She told me she was in the Treasury once, sister." Veronica deserved some reproof, and should have the undiluted fact. "In the Treasury."

"Sedley!"

"And she seemed to think it a misfortune to have lost the place."

"Oh!" shuddered Miss Veronica. "Do not let us think of it any more." And she went out to the pantry and poured a little rose-water into the palms of her hands, as if she were cleansing herself, and Celeste too, of a stain. Then they took up their great feather fans again with fresh enjoyment, for Celeste was resting sweetly upstairs, watched by the young friend for whom she had begged them to send, saying Jinny had no engagement now, and would be glad to come and relieve them.

"It is dreadful, my giving you such trouble," Celeste had sighed. "And bringing two people in upon you! It only shows what saints and angels you are."

"Oh, we have grown so fond of you, my child!"

"Then you will call me Celeste. I sha'n't think you've forgiven me till you call me Celeste."

"We have forgotten all about forgiving. It was an accident, a misunderstanding. You will forget it too, dear —I mean—Celeste."

They had scarcely composed themselves with their fans when there came a series of resounding blows of the knocker, and they heard the prancing of horses down at the gate.

"Why doesn't Hark hurry?" exclaimed Miss Sedley, with the consciousness that such a summons should be answered at once, and slipping down the hall herself. "Hark, where's this you're at? Don't you hear the door?" she cried. And then Hark brought in the cards of the Russian Minister and the inquiries of Madame the Princess for Miss Dreer. And directly afterward there came another boom of the knocker, and there was a basket of flowers from the White House. And the news of Miss Dreer's sickness having spread, as news spreads nowhere else with more rapidity, cards from the British embassy and from the German, and the personal inquiry of more than one of the

South American Ministers, followed all the week, with flowers and fruits and wine from these just leaving for the summer in Europe, and those for Newport and the North.

"I feel like I had changed my identity," said Miss Sedley.

"Because some foreign officials have left cards on our guests?" said Miss Veronica, with dignity.

"We have been out of the world so long."

"We never were in it personally, except by family tradition."

"I hope it won't keep Mrs. Entwisle away."

"It seems absurd, when we hardly know where next month's dinners are coming from," replacing in its envelope the bill she had just received. "We shall have to sell the G Street house now; this charge for the betterments is more than it is worth. It is perfectly infamous. But," with a helpless sigh, "they have everything their own way. There is only the place across the Avenue left."

"Sister—why couldn't we keep Celeste here? She has to pay her board elsewhere, and she may as well pay it to us—"

"Pay us board!" said Miss Veronica.

"She wouldn't stay if she didn't, you know. And that dear little creature that is taking care of her—I don't know why I call her little; she's taller than I am, but she's a dear. She's so sweet and bright. I really don't know which I love the best. And that engaging girl that comes to see them, Mattie Tillinghurst—"

"She certainly is refinement and grace itself. I wonder—"

"And just see what a difference it makes with us already! When I heard them all three laughing together this morning, oh, I felt forty years younger!"

"If we were only able to keep open house—"

And then there was a rustle in the hall where two pairs of slippered feet had been creeping down the stairs.

"I heard you!" cried Celeste, gayly. "I heard you! Oh, if you only would! We would be so well behaved—"

"Celeste! You down! Oh, my dear, isn't this imprudent? That is right, Miss Jinny, the pillows. There, dear, lie right down," said the two ladies together, bustling about one of the sofas.

"I feel so nicely," said Celeste, "I couldn't have the face to stay upstairs any more. It's been an imposition anyway. And I really think we must go home, unless you were in earnest just now and would let us stay that way. You know we couldn't stay and be a burden—if we didn't do just as we do down in E Street. And it would be the kindest, loveliest, and most Christian act, giving homes to two homeless girls, which the most they could pay wouldn't half pay for—"

"Oh, sister," cried Miss Sedley, "it seems too good to be true—to keep these dear things all the time! You will say Yes?"

"Sedley, if you will promise not to shed a tear. We can't have Celeste excited one atom. Yes. You shall send for your trunks, my dears. And if you like the home it shall be yours while it is ours." And Celeste, who could not be excited, tottered up from the sofa and fell upon their necks, with an arm round each, in a passion of tears and kisses.

"To think of having a home!" she cried. "And such a home! And with you! Oh, Jinny, doesn't it seem as if we had gone to heaven! And, oh, it is really—really too hot for heroics!"

It was several days after Jinny had brought up and disposed their worldly belongings, and a feeling of peace and bliss, a sense of youth and cheer, had settled over the household, that Miss Sedley brought to Celeste's sofa a number of the cards that had been left during her illness. They had been sitting in the moonlight, while the ineffable fragrance of the great grandiflora magnolia tree, a half-mile away, rolled in softly all about them, and the candles had been but a little while lighted.

"'Señor and Madame Castilla,'" read Celeste. "Yes. I've been a very good friend of theirs. And they know it."

"You!" said Miss Veronica, as if she had heard the mouse boast in relation to the lion.

"Oh yes. You know, I have written a good deal about both of them. In Europe the censorship of the press gives importance to every item; and if anything really is in the paper they feel there that it means something. And so all I have said about them — they cut out every scrap and sent it home—counted for more than it was worth. And when they were going away—you know they were promoted to another mission, and he was

made a Grand Panjandrum or something —she sent for me and told me all this, and gave me that," and she held out her hand with its ring of sapphires and diamonds.

"It—it seems impossible," murmured Miss Sedley, under her breath.

"But, my love," said Miss Veronica, "because they like flattery, it doesn't make the business—the dealing in personality—any less reprehensible."

"Sister!"

"Well, dear, perhaps not," said Celeste, "when you show me that it is reprehensible. People want it, at any rate; and people will have what they want; and if I don't give it to them another will."

"You might say that of any disgraceful business."

"But it isn't disgraceful," said Celeste, coaxingly. "You need a great deal of enlightenment. I describe the inside of a beautiful home; it shows them far in the wilderness how to have a beautiful home. I describe a fine lady; women all over the country can be fine ladies on that model. I tell the social happenings; and I don't know that they are not as much to the purpose really as the political happenings. I'm sure they're a great deal pleasanter. Just look at this place before they had telegraphs and reporters and correspondents and interviewers—"

"Oh yes, how perfect, how lovely it was!"

"You dear little innocent angels! Well, we let a flood of light in. And men can't do now as they did then—without being found out, you know. Oh yes, and here are the Russian embassy cards again. How good it was to send their carriage for us to take the air!"

"It made me feel like an adventuress, driving out in state with imperial arms on the carriage door," said Miss Veronica.

"I don't know," said Miss Sedley. "I reckon I enjoyed it. Although I was a little afraid of the men on the box."

"Well, you saw what a splendid city they are making of it—"

"At our expense."

"And there never was a sweeter sight in that carriage," said Miss Jinny, "than your two dear aristocratic faces."

"Oh, but the Princess herself is beautiful," said Celeste. "I wish you had seen her leaving her box, with her velvet and ermine cloak falling about her, and the long thick braid of her fair hair down one side to her knee. 'A daughter of the gods, divinely tall, and most divinely fair.' Don't you remember, Jinny dear? It was the night you made your hit in *Cinderella Afterwards*, and the house came down, and you thought they were applauding the beautiful Princess, and that made them go wild with applauding you again, and all the diplomats and the little attachés stood up and shouted, and the stage was half covered with flowers for you—"

"The stage!" exclaimed two startled voices.

"Why, yes; the stage of the National. Where she had her last engagement. And she had an offer of an engagement from a New York manager the very next day but one, and she refused it, the little goose, so that she might stay on at the National till it closed, and be with me, and get her things ready to marry Jerome, when, if she'd kept on, she might be one of the great actresses—"

"An actress!"

"She's a very good one as it is. Oh, she can make you laugh, and she can make you cry, and her dancing is—"

"A dancer!"

Miss Veronica was as white as death. Miss Sedley was secretly, but involuntarily, crossing herself.

"Oh, that I should live to see the day!" one murmured.

"Merciful mother!" moaned the other.

"Miss Veronica! Dear Miss Sedley! What is it?" cried the girls, springing toward them. "What is the matter?"

"Oh!" Miss Sedley was whispering. "I must see Father Walter."

But Miss Veronica waved them off, gathering her skirts away. "In our house!" she exclaimed. "In our mother's drawing-room! The pollution of it!"

"What, what, Miss Sidney!"

"An actress!" and Miss Veronica's tones were unmistakable.

"Oh!" And both the girls fell back. But in a moment Celeste had thrown her arms round Jinny, who had begun to cry.

"Didn't you know she was an actress?" she exclaimed to the two horrified ladies. "I thought every one knew it. And what of it? Most of the people here would think it an honor to have her in their houses. An actress, indeed! Virginia Cantrell is just as good as I am,

and a great deal better, for she is a genius, too, and she is the soul of honor and uprightness. She is just as good as you are! She is better!" cried the infuriated Celeste. "For she doesn't keep out of the way of the world for fear of being contaminated, but she is in the world, doing her duty with the talent God gave her, and not contaminated by it. And you had better ask Father White about her, and he'll tell you she's as true a Catholic as you are. You run right up stairs and pack your trunk, Jinny, and I'll pack mine. I wouldn't stay another night in this house for money! I thought it was too good to be true—our having such a pleasant home," and here Celeste began to cry, "with two angels—narrow-minded angels—but angels all the same. Live creatures sweeping by on the current—couldn't live with barnacles—"

Was Jinny acting? It crossed Miss Veronica's mind that here was more desecration of the drawing-room with its portraits and spider-legged tables and jars of pot-pourri packed by dear fingers a half-hundred years ago and more. And then she felt as if her heart were a millstone that would sink her into a bottomless pit. She instinctively put her hand in her reticule for the companionship of her little rosary.

For Jinny had left Celeste, and was approaching her with outstretched arms. "Miss Sidney," she said, "you're not going to send me away for that? You *don't* think there is any harm in me? You can't tell what it has been to me to think I had this resting-place. I should have played so much better if I had always had such a support behind me. And, indeed, I can't think what you mean. I never did anything you need be ashamed of if you were my own mother."

The candles only made darkness visible in the long room round the little spot near Celeste. But the moonlight streamed through the window and bathed the girl in a white glow—so tender, so appealing, so innocent— No, no, only a play-actress! Miss Veronica lifted her open hand as if warding off a great terror or a bitter draught, and turned her head aside. "It is very late," she said, hoarsely. "We will not talk any more. Please go to bed." And as she stood up there was an air of gentle authority about her that was not to be disobeyed.

"Oh!" cried Celeste, as she swept by

her, following Jinny. "I've no doubt you will go to heaven, you are so good. But how surprised you will be when you get there to find Jinny nearer to God than you are!"

Miss Veronica put out the candles, and looked round for her sister. But Miss Sedley had gone too. She sank into the arm-chair by the hearth that Celeste had filled with ferns from Kalorama, forgetting to close the windows through which the summer night breeze still rolled heavy with perfumes into the moonlighted place. She was entirely bewildered, weak and faint with her mental confusion. She did not know whether she had suffered a degradation, her mother's parlor a desecration, or whether she must reverse the opinions, the prejudices of a lifetime. Why had all this oversetting come to her? Why had she been suffered to grow fond of this young actress — the word made her shiver; why had it not been that pretty Mattie Tillinghurst, Celeste's other friend, who ran in every day and made the house gay with laughter? She had a warm feeling for that child the moment she saw her—old General Tillinghurst's daughter they called her. There had been a time when Tom Tillinghurst— However, all that was in the golden age. And these were dark days. She was cold in all the warm night, filled with a sort of vague horror of she knew not what. Perhaps she fell asleep; she did not know; but certainly the broad moonbeam had come round and fallen full upon her mother's portrait, lighting the wistful eyes and the sweet mouth there; had slowly shifted and lain across the picture in the panel and silvered it with a glory—an old print of the Shepherd with the stray lamb in His arms, and with the gaze of unspeakable tenderness in His eyes, the gaze bent full on her and seeming to search her soul. If she were in the body or out of it, Miss Veronica could not have told, only for an instant her soul was bared to her own gaze. And then the moonlight passed, and she was shivering like one alone in a wide black desert, and felt suddenly, with a sense of infinite relief, the warmth of two young arms about her neck, and heard Jinny saying: "Oh, you mustn't be afraid of me. I truly am not bad. Dear, I can't have you sitting up down here alone. Don't you fret—I am going away of my own accord. Poor Miss Veronica, you must go to bed or

you'll be ill." And she had reached up her arms and drawn the girl down into her lap and hidden her old face in her breast.

And directly afterward there was a swish of drapery and patter of feet on the matting. "Oh, sister! sister!" sobbed Miss Sedley. "You know the world moves, and we must move with it. And our mother used to say we weren't here to judge, but to help. And if we love our Lord, we must do the work of our Lord. And Celeste feels so badly that she spoke so! And if they're not good, we must make them good. And they are—oh, they're every whit as good as we are!" Just then the mocking-birds hanging in their cages outside the windows of the next street suddenly burst into their wild night-song, and with their arms round one another the four happy people had a beautiful time crying together.

The air next morning was like air purified by a thunder-storm passing through it. When Mattie Tillinghurst stopped to ask if Celeste had a letter for her to post on her way to work, Miss Veronica's prepossessions gave their last flicker.

"It's too bad to be bound to a desk in the Treasury when you would like to be flying down the Potomac on the *Arrow*," said Mattie.

"Tom Tillinghurst's daughter in the Treasury!" exclaimed Miss Veronica.

"And mighty glad to be there," said Mattie. "At least in general, you know. Just for this moment, perhaps, I would prefer being a bird out in the Rock Creek woods, or a young colt rolling on the flowers of the high-field up where we used to live in the Virginia hills."

"I wish you would take me down to the Treasury some day, Mattie," said Miss Veronica, meekly. "I should like to see—"

"Oh, come now!" cried Mattie, "before it is any warmer. I will show you all over it—the beautiful cash-room and the great vaults full of gold. And you shall see them printing new greenbacks upstairs and counting old ones downstairs —enough to make you despise money, though I don't know how you could despise it any more than you do."

"I've had such a delightful morning," said Miss Veronica, when she came home, and Jinny had taken her bonnet and parasol, and she sat sipping the iced buttermilk that Celeste brought her, while

Miss Sedley had her clabber and cream. "And it seems to me as if the Treasury were fairly peopled with ghosts. I've seen the sisters and wives and widows and daughters of half the people we used to know in the old days, that had dropped out of the great world—"

"Into the greater world," said Celeste.

"Why, it's our Faubourg St. Germain! And, Sedley, you must go down yourself. We really must make a business of acquainting ourselves with affairs—"

"I don't know how Father Walter—"

"No one would like it better than that great, noble, comforting spirit. I feel as if we had been asleep while things were growing. You've no idea what a country it is! I am going to the Patent Office to-morrow, and then— Who is that?" For a young man was mounting the terrace steps two at a time.

"I must break it to you gently," said Celeste, laughing, but catching her disengaged hand, with its little thready rings. "It is Jinny's Jerome. And he is a New-Englander!"

But Miss Veronica rose to the occasion. "I suppose he is also an American," she said.

"He is a scientific man. And he has —discovered a germ."

"Perhaps it wasn't his fault," said Miss Veronica.

"I hope it isn't unfeminine," said Miss Sedley to her sister one night some weeks afterward, when Celeste had gone up stairs to finish her *Graphic* letter, and Jinny had gone down to the gate with her lover, "but I must say it is pleasant to have a man going and coming about the house. It—it makes you feel as if you were alive, and not shut off from the world. It makes you feel as if you belonged to the race. It really makes you feel as if, after all, you weren't set away on a shelf to mould. It's natural to have a man about the house. We've been living an unnatural life."

"I don't know how we could have helped it," said Miss Veronica.

"Well, it can't last long," said Miss Sedley, pensively. "He'll take her away presently. But there's this about it: he'll be coming back to attend to that bill of his in the winter. It's a serious matter with him, Celeste says, to carry that bill."

"Then he must carry it," said Miss Veronica. "Let me see. Isn't there a Senator by the name of Sumner? I

thought there was. He was very wrong on the slavery question, wasn't he? Well, bygones are bygones. And he is interested in old prints and medals, some one said. And "—here she lowered her voice—"isn't—isn't—isn't Butler in the House? I shall go to see him. Oh yes, oh yes, I shall. I shall present the case. He must be a power. And—let me see," she said again, with her finger on her lips, "who are our own Senators?"

"We haven't any, you know," said Miss Sedley, bitterly. "They are all— what is it they call them?—carpet-baggers."

"Very well. Carpet-baggers will want the countenance of the old gentility. I shall see them all." And although her heart was shaking and her voice was trembling, the gentle old lady, who had never yet dared to stop a street car by herself, was already lobbying Jerome's bill through Congress for all she was worth.

Miss Sedley glanced at the portraits on the wall with an air of apprehension. But the personage in knee-breeches and a powdered wig, with the sword at his side, the roll of parchment in his hand, and the red curtain and the thunder-storm behind him, continued looking over her head in sublime unconcern; and as for the wax medallions in their tarnished frames, the lady there in low relief, with a high comb and an eye askew, and the gentleman with a stiff stock and a bang, went on gazing at each other with stolid indifference to the affairs of a lesser world than theirs. But the glance somehow reassured Miss Sedley. Whatever new scenes shifted across the view, the world still moved on the same axis.

It was in the mild and beautiful November weather, when all the blue river distances were swathed with sun-gilded hazes, the late roses were still blooming, and the flag floating from the top of the unfinished monument looked like a flower itself against the sky, and the bland Indian summer was sweeter than ever real summer was, that Miss Veronica sat at the head of her table one morning ready to carve a Potomac swan. "My dears," she said to the bride and groom on her either hand—when, after a nuptial mass, they had come home to a Thanksgiving breakfast, where Celeste and Mattie and Miss Sedley assisted, the latter resplendent in an adaptation of the Aaron Burr brocade which Jinny had made without injuring it—"my dears, it is not especially a festival of our Church, and it is not a festival of our part of the country, at least it used not to be—I don't know that we ever kept the day before, Sedley? But I feel as if I could not sufficiently honor it and express my thanks to-day for the goodness which, against our will, has taken us out of the clefts of the rock and into the living currents by overturning our prejudices and enlightening our ignorance—"

"You mean by giving us all these young people, sister," regardless of the spot made by every falling tear.

"Yes, these poor young people who never can know any such pleasure as ours, unless when they shall be old and sad and lonely and—"

"And tired to death of life as it was, sister."

"They shall have young blood poured into their veins as we have had, young eyes given them to see the world, young voices to put them in tune with it—"

"And young hearts to make them love it!" cried Celeste.

And as they all fell on Miss Veronica and Miss Sedley in turn, the latter, struggling and blushing and rearranging herself, exclaimed: "It's a sort of new mission field, isn't it? The mission of Youth to Age. But, oh, Veronica!" she said, "don't you remember Bettie Brierley, who declared there were four men she would never marry—a preacher, or a Protestant, or a Frenchman, or a widower?"

"And she is the third wife of a French Protestant preacher," said Miss Veronica, examining her carving-knife. "I dare say she knows a good deal more now than she did then. I suppose you mean how scandalized we should have been a year ago at this Thanksgiving Breakfast."

A DESERTION
by Stephen Crane

THE gas-light that came with an effect of difficulty through the dust-stained windows on either side of the door gave strange hues to the faces and forms of the three women who stood gabbling in the hallway of the tenement. They made rapid gestures, and in the background their enormous shadows mingled in terrific effect.

"Aye, she ain't so good as he thinks she is, I'll bet. He can watch over 'er an' take care of 'er all he pleases, but when she wants t' fool 'im, she'll fool 'im. An' how does he know she ain't foolin' 'im now?"

"Oh, he thinks he's keepin' 'er from goin' t' th' bad, he does. Oh yes. He says she's too purty t' let run 'round alone. Too purty! Huh! My Sadie—"

"Well, he keeps a clost watch on 'er, you bet. On'y las' week she met my boy Tim on th' stairs, an' Tim hadn't said two words to 'er b'fore th' ol' man begun t' holler, 'Dorter, dorter, come here; come here!'"

At this moment a young girl entered from the street, and it was evident from the injured expressions suddenly assumed by the three gossipers that she had been the object of their discussion. She passed them with a slight nod, and they swung about in a row to stare after her.

On her way up the long flights the girl unfastened her veil. One could then clearly see the beauty of her eyes, but there was in them a certain furtiveness that came near to marring the effect. It was a peculiar fixture of gaze, brought from the street, as of one who there saw a succession of passing dangers, with menaces aligned at every corner.

On the top floor she pushed open a door, and then paused on the threshold, confronting an interior that appeared black and flat like a curtain. Perhaps some girlish ideas of hobgoblins assailed her then, for she called, in a little breathless voice, "Daddie!"

There was no reply. The fire in the cooking-stove in the room crackled at spasmodic intervals. One lid was misplaced, and the girl could now see that this fact created a little flushed crescent upon the ceiling. Also a series of tiny windows in the stove caused patches of red upon the floor. Otherwise the room was heavily draped with shadows.

The girl called again, "Daddie!"

Yet there was no reply. "Oh, daddie!"

Presently she laughed, as one familiar with the humors of an old man. "Oh, I guess yer cussin'-mad about yer supper, dad," she said, and she almost entered the room, but suddenly faltered, overcome by a feminine instinct to fly from this black interior, peopled with imagined dangers. Again she called, "Daddie!" Her voice had an accent of appeal. It was as if she knew she was foolish, but yet felt obliged to insist upon being reassured. "Oh, daddie!"

Of a sudden a cry of relief, a feminine announcement that the stars still hung, burst from her. For, according to some mystic process, the smouldering coals of the fire went aflame with sudden fierce brilliance, splashing parts of the walls, the floor, the crude furniture, with a hue of blood-red. And in this dramatic outburst of light the girl saw her father seated at a table, with his back turned toward her.

She entered the room then with an aggrieved air, her logic evidently concluding that somebody was to blame for her nervous fright. "Oh, yer on'y sulkin' 'bout yer supper! I thought mebbe ye'd gone somewheres."

Her father made no reply. She went over to a shelf in the corner, and taking a little lamp, she lit it, and put it where it would give her light as she took off her hat and jacket in front of a tiny mirror. Presently she began to bustle among the cooking utensils that were crowded into the sink, and as she worked she rattled talk at her father, apparently disdaining his mood.

"I'd 'a' come earlier t' night, dad, on'y that fly foreman he kep' me in th' shop till half past six. What a fool! He came t' me, yeh know, an' he ses, 'Nell, I wanter give yeh some brotherly advice '—oh, I know him an' his brotherly advice—' I wanter give yeh some brotherly advice. Yeh too purty, Nell,' he ses, 't' be workin' in this shop an' paradin' through th' streets alone, without somebody t' give yeh good brotherly advice, an' I wanter warn yeh, Nell. I'm a bad man, but I ain't as bad as some, an' I wanter warn yeh!' 'Oh, g'long 'bout yer business,' I ses. I know 'im. He's like all of 'em, on'y he's a little slyer. I know 'im. 'You g'long 'bout yer business,' I ses. Well, he sed after a while that he guessed some evenin' he come up an' see me. 'Oh, yeh will!' I ses. 'Yeh will? Well, you jest let my ol' man ketch yeh comin' foolin' 'round our place. Yeh'll wish yeh went t' some other girl t' give brotherly advice.' 'What th'ell do I care fer yer father?' he ses. 'What's he t' me?' 'If he throws yeh down stairs yeh'll care for 'im,' I ses. 'Well,' he ses, 'I'll come when 'e ain't in.' 'Oh, he's allus in when it means takin' care o' me,' I ses. 'Don't yeh fergit it, either. When it comes t' takin' care o' his dorter, he's right on deck every single possible time.'" After a time she turned and addressed cheery words to the old man. "Hurry up th' fire, daddie! We'll have supper pretty soon."

But still her father was silent, and his form in its sullen posture was motionless.

At this the girl seemed to see the need of the inauguration of a feminine war against a man out of temper. She approached him, breathing soft coaxing syllables.

"Daddie! Oh, daddie! O-o-oh, daddie!" It was apparent from a subtle quality of valor in her tones that this manner of onslaught upon his moods had usually been successful, but to-night it had no quick effect.

The words, coming from her lips, were like the refrain of an old ballad, but the man remained stolid.

"Daddie! My daddie! Oh, daddie, are yeh *mad* at me—really, truly *mad* at me?" She touched him lightly upon the arm. Should he have turned then, he would have seen the fresh laughing face, with dew-sparkling eyes, close to his own.

"Oh, daddie! My daddie! Pretty daddie!" She stole her arm about his neck, and then slowly bended her face towards his. It was the action of a queen who knows she reigns notwithstanding irritations, trials, tempests.

But suddenly from this position she leaped backward with the mad energy of a frightened colt. Her face was in this instant turned to a gray, featureless thing of horror. A yell, wild and hoarse as a brute cry, burst from her. "Daddie!" She flung herself to a place near the door, where she remained crouching, her eyes staring at the motionless figure, splattered by the quivering flashes from the fire, her arms extended, and her frantic fingers at once besought and repelled. There was in them an expression of eagerness to caress and an expression of the most intense loathing. And the girl's hair, that had been a splendor, was in these moments changed to a disordered mass that hung and swayed in witchlike fashion. Again a cry burst from her. It was more than the shriek of agony; it was direct, personal, addressed to him in the chair, the first word of a tragic conversation with the dead.

It seemed that when she had put her arm about its neck she had jostled the body in such a way that now she and it were face to face. The attitude expressed an intention of rising from the table. The eyes, fixed upon her, were filled with an unspeakable hatred.

The cries of the girl aroused thunders in the tenement. There was a loud slamming of doors, and presently there was a roar of feet upon the boards of the stairway. Voices rang out sharply.

"What is it?"

"What's th' matter?"

"He's killin' her."

"Slug 'im with anything yeh kin lay hold of, Jack."

But over all this came the shrill, shrewish tones of a woman: "Ah, th' ol' fool, he's drivin' 'er inteh th' street—that's what he's doin.' He's drivin' 'er inteh th' street."

THE BEDQUILT
by Dorothy Canfield

OF all the Elwell family Aunt Mehetabel was certainly the most unimportant member. It was in the New England days, when an unmarried woman was an old maid at twenty, at forty was every one's servant, and at sixty had gone through so much discipline that she could need no more in the next world. Aunt Mehetabel was sixty-eight.

She had never for a moment known the pleasure of being important to any one. Not that she was useless in her brother's family; she was expected, as a matter of course, to take upon herself the most tedious and uninteresting part of the household labors. On Mondays she accepted as her share the washing of the men's shirts, heavy with sweat and stiff with dirt from the fields and from their own hard-working bodies. Tuesdays she never dreamed of being allowed to iron anything pretty or even interesting, like the baby's white dresses, or the fancy aprons of her young lady nieces. She stood all day pressing out a tiresome. monotonous succession of dish-cloths and towels and sheets.

In preserving-time she was allowed to have none of the pleasant responsibility of deciding when the fruit had cooked long enough, nor did she share in the little excitement of pouring the sweet-smelling stuff into the stone jars. She sat in a corner with the children and stoned cherries incessantly, or hulled strawberries until her fingers were dyed red to the bone.

The Elwells were not consciously unkind to their aunt, they were even in a vague way fond of her; but she was so utterly insignificant a figure in their lives that they bestowed no thought whatever on her. Aunt Mehetabel did not resent this treatment; she took it quite as unconsciously as they gave it. It was to be expected when one was an old-maid dependent in a busy family. She gathered what crumbs of comfort she could from

their occasional careless kindnesses and tried to hide the hurt which even yet pierced her at her brother's rough joking. In the winter when they all sat before the big hearth, roasted apples, drank mulled cider, and teased the girls about their beaux and the boys about their sweethearts, she shrank into a dusky corner with her knitting, happy if the evening passed without her brother saying, with a crude sarcasm, "Ask your aunt Mehetabel about the beaux that used to come a-sparkin' her!" or, "Mehetabel, how was't when you was in love with Abel Cummings." As a matter of fact she had been the same at twenty as at sixty, a quiet, mouselike little creature, too timid and shy for any one to notice, or to raise her eyes for a moment and wish for a life of her own.

Her sister-in-law, a big hearty housewife, who ruled indoors with as autocratic a sway as did her husband on the farm, was rather kind in an absent, off-hand way to the shrunken little old woman, and it was through her that Mehetabel was able to enjoy the one pleasure of her life. Even as a girl she had been clever with her needle in the way of patching bedquilts. More than that she could never learn to do. The garments which she made for herself were the most lamentable affairs, and she was humbly grateful for any help in the bewildering business of putting them together. But in patchwork she enjoyed a mild, tepid importance. She could really do that as well as any one else. During years of devotion to this one art she had accumulated a considerable store of quilting patterns. Sometimes the neighbors would send over and ask "Miss Mehetabel" for such and such a design. It was with an agreeable flutter at being able to help some one that she went to the dresser, in her bare little room under the eaves, and extracted from her crowded portfolio the pattern desired.

She never knew how her great idea came to her. Sometimes she thought she must have dreamed it, sometimes she even wondered reverently, in the phraseology of the weekly prayer-meeting, if it had not been "sent" to her. She never admitted to herself that she could have thought of it without other help; it was too great, too ambitious, too lofty a project for her humble mind to have conceived. Even when she finished drawing the design with her own fingers, she gazed at it incredulously, not daring to believe that it could indeed be her handiwork. At first it seemed to her only like a lovely but quite unreal dream. She did not think of putting it into execution — so elaborate, so complicated, so beautifully difficult a pattern could be only for the angels in heaven to quilt. But so curiously does familiarity accustom us even to very wonderful things, that as she lived with this astonishing creation of her mind, the longing grew stronger and stronger to give it material life with her nimble old fingers.

She gasped at her daring when this idea first swept over her and put it away as one does a sinfully selfish notion, but she kept coming back to it again and again. Finally she said compromisingly to herself that she would make one "square," just one part of her design, to see how it would look. Accustomed to the most complete dependence on her brother and his wife, she dared not do even this without asking Sophia's permission. With a heart full of hope and fear thumping furiously against her old ribs, she approached the mistress of the house on churning-day, knowing with the innocent guile of a child that the country woman was apt to be in a good temper while working over the fragrant butter in the cool cellar.

Sophia listened absently to her sister-in-law's halting, hesitating petition. "Why yes, Mehetabel," she said, leaning far down into the huge churn for the last golden morsels—"why yes, start another quilt if you want to. I've got a lot of pieces from the spring sewing that will work in real good." Mehetabel tried honestly to make her see that this would be no common quilt, but her limited vocabulary and her emotion stood between her and expression. At last

Sophia said, with a kindly impatience: "Oh, there! Don't bother me. I never could keep track of your quiltin' patterns anyhow. I don't care what pattern you go by."

With this overwhelmingly, although unconsciously, generous permission Mehetabel rushed back up the steep attic stairs to her room, and in a joyful agitation began preparations for the work of her life. It was even better than she hoped. By some heaven-sent inspiration she had invented a pattern beyond which no patchwork quilt could go.

She had but little time from her incessant round of household drudgery for this new and absorbing occupation, and she did not dare sit up late at night lest she burn too much candle. It was weeks before the little square began to take on a finished look, to show the pattern. Then Mehetabel was in a fever of impatience to bring it to completion. She was too conscientious to shirk even the smallest part of her share of the work of the house, but she rushed through it with a speed which left her panting as she climbed to the little room. This seemed like a radiant spot to her as she bent over the innumerable scraps of cloth which already in her imagination ranged themselves in the infinitely diverse pattern of her masterpiece. Finally she could wait no longer, and one evening ventured to bring her work down beside the fire where the family sat, hoping that some good fortune would give her a place near the tallow candles on the mantelpiece. She was on the last corner of the square, and her needle flew in and out with inconceivable rapidity. No one noticed her, a fact which filled her with relief, and by bedtime she had but a few more stitches to add.

As she stood up with the others, the square fluttered out of her trembling old hands and fell on the table. Sophia glanced at it carelessly. "Is that the new quilt you're beginning on?" she asked with a yawn. "It looks like a real pretty pattern. Let's see it." Up to that moment Mehetabel had labored in the purest spirit of disinterested devotion to an ideal, but as Sophia held her work towards the candle to examine it, and exclaimed in amazement and admiration, she felt an astonished joy to know

SHE HAD BUT LITTLE TIME FOR HER PATCHWORK

that her creation would stand the test of publicity.

"Land sakes!" ejaculated her sister-in-law, looking at the many-colored square. "Why, Mehetabel Elwell, where'd you git that pattern?"

"I made it up," said Mehetabel, quietly, but with unutterable pride.

"No!" exclaimed Sophia, incredulously. "*Did* you! Why, I never see such a pattern in my life. Girls, come here and see what your aunt Mehetabel is doing."

The three tall daughters turned back reluctantly from the stairs. "I don't seem to take much interest in patchwork," said one, listlessly.

"No, nor I neither!" answered Sophia; "but a stone image would take an interest in this pattern. Honest, Mehetabel, did you think of it yourself? And how under the sun and stars did you ever git your courage up to start in a-making it? Land! Look at all those tiny squinchy little seams! Why, the wrong side ain't a thing *but* seams!"

The girls echoed their mother's exclamations, and Mr. Elwell himself came over to see what they were discussing. "Well, I declare!" he said, looking at his sister with eyes more approving than she could ever remember. "That beats old Mis' Wightman's quilt that got the blue ribbon so many times at the county fair."

Mehetabel's heart swelled within her, and tears of joy moistened her old eyes as she lay that night in her narrow, hard bed, too proud and excited to sleep. The next day her sister-in-law amazed her by taking the huge pan of potatoes out of her lap and setting one of the younger children to peeling them. "Don't you want to go on with that quiltin' pattern?" she said; "I'd kind o' like to see how you're goin' to make the grape-vine design come out on the corner."

At the end of the summer the family interest had risen so high that Mehetabel was given a little stand in the sitting-room where she could keep her pieces, and work in odd minutes. She almost wept over such kindness, and resolved firmly not to take advantage of it by neglecting her work, which she performed with a fierce thoroughness. But the whole atmosphere of her world was changed. Things had a meaning now. Through the longest task of washing milk-pans there rose the rainbow of promise of her variegated work. She took her place by the little table and put the thimble on her knotted, hard finger with the solemnity of a priestess performing a sacred rite.

She was even able to bear with some degree of dignity the extreme honor of having the minister and the minister's wife comment admiringly on her great project. The family felt quite proud of Aunt Mehetabel as Minister Bowman had said it was work as fine as any he had ever seen, "and he didn't know but finer!" The remark was repeated verbatim to the neighbors in the following weeks when they dropped in and examined in a perverse silence some astonishingly difficult *tour de force* which Mehetabel had just finished.

The family especially plumed themselves on the slow progress of the quilt. "Mehetabel has been to work on that corner for six weeks, come Tuesday, and she ain't half done yet," they explained to visitors. They fell out of the way of always expecting her to be the one to run on errands, even for the children. "Don't bother your aunt Mehetabel," Sophia would call. "Can't you see she's got to a ticklish place on the quilt?" The old woman sat up straighter and looked the world in the face. She was

a part of it at last. She joined in the conversation and her remarks were listened to. The children were even told to mind her when she asked them to do some service for her, although this she did but seldom, the habit of self-effacement being too strong.

One day some strangers from the next town drove up and asked if they could inspect the wonderful quilt which they had heard of, even down in their end of the valley. After that such visitations were not uncommon, making the Elwells' house a notable object. Mehetabel's quilt came to be one of the town sights, and no one was allowed to leave the town without having paid tribute to its worth. The Elwells saw to it that their aunt was better dressed than she had ever been before, and one of the girls made her a pretty little cap to wear on her thin white hair.

A year went by and a quarter of the quilt was finished; a second year passed and half was done. The third year Mehetabel had pneumonia and lay ill for weeks and weeks, overcome with terror lest she die before her work was completed. A fourth year and one could really see the grandeur of the whole design; and in September of the fifth year, the entire family watching her with eager and admiring eyes, Mehetabel quilted the last stitches in her creation. The girls held it up by the four corners, and they all looked at it in a solemn silence. Then Mr. Elwell smote one horny hand within the other and exclaimed: "By ginger! That's goin' to the county fair!"

Mehetabel blushed a deep red at this. It was a thought which had occurred to her in a bold moment, but she had not dared to entertain it. The family acclaimed the idea, and one of the boys was forthwith despatched to the house of the neighbor who was chairman of the committee for their village. He returned with radiant face. "Of course he'll take it. Like's not it may git a prize, so he says; but he's got to have it right off, because all the things are goin' to-morrow morning."

Even in her swelling pride Mehetabel felt a pang of separation as the bulky package was carried out of the house. As the days went on she felt absolutely lost without her work. For years it had

Drawn by W. S. Potts

"WELL, I DECLARE!" HE SAID

SHE SAT STARING INTO THE FIRE

been her one preoccupation, and she could not bear even to look at the little stand, now quite bare of the litter of scraps which had lain on it so long. One of the neighbors, who took the long journey to the fair, reported that the quilt was hung in a place of honor in a glass case in "Agricultural Hall." But that meant little to Mehetabel's utter ignorance of all that lay outside of her brother's home. The family noticed the old woman's depression, and one day Sophia said kindly, "You feel sort o' lost without the quilt, don't you, Mehetabel?"

"They took it away so quick!" she said, wistfully; "I hadn't hardly had one real good look at it myself."

Mr. Elwell made no comment, but a day or two later he asked his sister how early she could get up in the morning.

"I dun'no'. Why?" she asked.

"Well, Thomas Ralston has got to drive clear to West Oldton to see a lawyer there, and that is four miles beyond the fair. He says if you can git up so's to leave here at four in the morning he'll drive you over to the fair, leave you there for the day, and bring you back again at night."

Mehetabel looked at him with incredulity. It was as though some one had offered her a ride in a golden chariot up to the gates of Heaven. "Why, you can't *mean* it!" she cried, paling with the intensity of her emotion. Her brother laughed a little uneasily. Even to his careless indifference this joy was a revelation of the narrowness of her life in his home. "Oh, 'tain't so much to go to the fair. Yes, I mean it. Go git your things ready, for he wants to start tomorrow morning."

All that night a trembling, excited old woman lay and stared at the rafters. She, who had never been more than six miles from home in her life, was going to drive thirty miles away—it was like going to another world. She who had never seen anything more exciting than a church supper was to see the county fair. To Mehetabel it was like making the tour of the world. She had never dreamed of doing it. She could not at all imagine what it would be like.

Nor did the exhortations of the family, as they bade good-by to her, throw any light on her confusion. They had all been at least once to the scene of gayety she was to visit, and as she tried to eat her breakfast they called out conflicting advice to her till her head whirled. Sophia told her to be sure and see the display of preserves. Her brother said not to miss inspecting the stock, her nieces said the fancy work was the only thing worth looking at, and her nephews said she must bring them home an account of the races. The buggy drove up to the door, she was helped in, and her wraps tucked about her. They all stood together and waved good-by to her as she drove out of the yard. She waved back, but she scarcely saw them. On her return home that evening she was very pale, and so tired and stiff that her brother had to lift her out bodily, but her lips were set in a blissful smile. They crowded around her with thronging questions, until Sophia pushed them all aside, telling them Aunt Mehetabel was too tired to speak until she had had her supper. This was eaten in an enforced silence on the part of the children, and then the old woman was helped into an easy chair before the fire. They gathered about her, eager for news of the great world, and Sophia said, "Now come, Mehetabel, tell us all about it!"

Mehetabel drew a long breath. "It was just perfect!" she said, "finer even than I thought. They've got it hanging up in the very middle of a sort o' closet made of glass, and one of the lower corners is ripped and turned back so's to show the seams on the wrong side."

"What?" asked Sophia, a little blankly.

"Why, the quilt!" said Mehetabel in surprise. "There are a whole lot of other ones in that room, but not one that can hold a candle to it, if I do say it who shouldn't. I heard lots of people say the same thing. You ought to have heard what the women said about that corner, Sophia. They said—well, I'd be ashamed to *tell* you what they said. I declare if I wouldn't!"

Mr. Elwell asked, "What did you think of that big ox we've heard so much about?"

"I didn't look at the stock," returned his sister, indifferently. "That set of pieces you give me, Maria, from your red waist, come out just lovely!" she assured one of her nieces. "I heard one woman say you could 'most smell the red silk roses."

"Did any of the horses in our town race?" asked young Thomas.

"I didn't see the races."

"How about the preserves?" asked Sophia.

"I didn't see the preserves," said Mehetabel, calmly. "You see, I went right to the room where the quilt was, and then I didn't want to leave it. It had been so long since I'd seen it, I had to look at it first real good myself, and then I looked at the others to see if there was any that could come up to it. And then the people begun comin' in and I got so interested in hearin' what they had to say I couldn't think of goin' anywheres else. I ate my lunch right there too, and I'm as glad as can be I did, too; for what do you think?"—she gazed about her with kindling eyes—"while I stood there with a sandwich in one hand didn't the head of the hull concern come in and open the glass door and pin 'First Prize' right in the middle of the quilt!"

There was a stir of congratulation and proud exclamation. Then Sophia returned again to the attack. "Didn't you go to see anything else?" she queried.

"Why, no," said Mehetabel. "Only the quilt. Why should I?"

She fell into a reverie where she saw again the glorious creation of her hand and brain hanging before all the world with the mark of highest approval on it. She longed to make her listeners see the splendid vision with her. She struggled for words; she reached blindly after unknown superlatives. "I tell you it looked like—" she said, and paused, hesitating. Vague recollections of hymn-book phraseology came into her mind, the only form of literary expression she knew; but they were dismissed as being sacrilegious, and also not sufficiently forcible. Finally, "I tell you it looked real *well!*" she assured them, and sat staring into the fire, on her tired old face the supreme content of an artist who has realized his ideal.

A PAIR OF PATIENT LOVERS
by W.D. Howells

I.

WE first met Glendenning on the Canadian steamboat which carries you down the rapids of the St. Lawrence from Kingston, and leaves you at Montreal. When we saw a handsome young clergyman across the promenade-deck looking up from his guide-book toward us, now and again, as if in default of knowing any one else he would be very willing to know us, we decided that I must make his acquaintance. He was instantly and cordially responsive to my question whether he had ever made the trip before, and he was amiably grateful when in my quality of old habitué of the route I pointed out some characteristic features of the scenery. I showed him just where we were on the long map of the river hanging over his knee, and I added, with no great relevancy, that my wife and I were renewing the fond emotion of our first trip down the St. Lawrence in the character of bridal pair which we had spurned when it was really ours. I explained that we had left our children with my wife's aunt, so as to render the travesty more lifelike, and when he said, "I suppose you miss them, though," I gave him my card. He tried to find one of his own to give me in return, but he could only find a lot of other people's cards. He wrote his name on the back of one, and handed it to me with a smile. "It won't do for me to put reverend before it, in my own chirography, but that's the way I have it engraved."

"Oh," I said, "the cut of your coat bewrayed you," and we had some laughing talk. But I felt the eye of Mrs. March dwelling upon me with growing impatience, till I suggested, "I should like to make you acquainted with my wife, Mr. Glendenning."

He said, Oh, he should be so happy; and he gathered his dangling map into the book, and came over with me to where Mrs. March sat; and like the good young American husband I was in those days, I stood aside and left the whole talk to her. She interested him so much more than I could that I presently wandered away, and amused myself elsewhere. When I came back, she clutched my arm, and bade me not speak a word; it was the most romantic thing in the world, and she would tell me about it when we were alone, but now I must go off again; he had just gone to get a book for her which he had been speaking of, and would be back the next instant, and it would not do to let him suppose we had been discussing him.

I was sometimes disappointed in Mrs. March's mysteries when I came up close to them; but I was always willing to take them on trust; and I submitted to the postponement of a solution in this case with more than my usual faith. She found time, before Mr. Glendenning reappeared, to ask me if I had noticed a mother and daughter on the boat, the mother evidently an invalid, and the daughter very devoted, and both decidedly ladies; and when I said, "No. Why?" she answered, "Oh, nothing," and that she would tell me. Then she drove me away, and we did not meet till I found her in our stateroom, just before the terrible mid-day meal they used to give you on the *Corinthian*, and called dinner.

She began at once, while she did something to her hair before the morsel of mirror: "Why I wanted to know if you had noticed those people was because they are the reason of his being here."

"Did he tell you that?"

"Of course not. But I knew it, for he asked if I had seen them, or could tell him who they were."

"It seems to me that he made pretty good time to get so far as that."

"I don't say he got so far himself, but you men never know how to take steps for any one else. You can't put two and two together. But to my mind it's as plain as the nose on his face that he's seen that girl somewhere and is taking this trip because she's on board. He said he hadn't decided to come till the last moment."

"What wild leaps of fancy!" I said.

"But the nose on his face is handsome rather than plain, and I sha'n't be satisfied till I see him with the lady."

"Yes, he's quite Greek," said Mrs. March, in assent to my opinion of his nose. "Too Greek for a clergyman, almost. But he isn't vain of it. Those beautiful people are often quite modest, and Mr. Glendenning is very modest."

"And I'm very hungry. If you don't hurry your prinking, Isabel, we shall not get any dinner."

"I'm ready," said my wife, and she continued, with her eyes still on the glass: "He's got a church out in Ohio, somewhere; but he's a New-Englander, and he's quite wild to get back. He thinks those people are from Boston: I could tell in a moment if I saw them. Well, now, I *am* ready," and with this she really ceased to do something to her hair, and came out into the long saloon with me where the table was set. Rows of passengers stood behind the rows of chairs, with a detaining grasp on nearly all of them. We gazed up and down in despair. Suddenly Mrs. March sped forward, and I found that Mr. Glendenning had made a sign to her from a distant point, where there were two vacant chairs for us next his own. We eagerly laid hands on them, and waited for the gong to sound for dinner. In this interval an elderly lady followed by a young girl came down the saloon toward us, and I saw signs, or rather emotions, of intelligence pass between Mr. Glendenning and Mrs. March concerning them.

The older of these ladies was a tall, handsome matron, who bore her fifty years with a native severity qualified by a certain air of wonder at a world which I could well fancy had not always taken her at her own estimate of her personal and social importance. She had the effect of challenging you to do less, as she advanced slowly between the wall of state-rooms and the backs of the people gripping their chairs, and eyed them with a sort of imperious surprise that they should have left no place for her. So at least I read her glance, while I read in that of the young lady coming after, and showing her beauty first over this shoulder and then over that of her mother, chiefly a present amusement, behind which lay a character of perhaps equal pride, if not equal hardness. She was very beautiful, in the dark style which I cannot help thinking has fallen into unmerited abeyance; and as she passed us I could see that she was very graceful. She was dressed in a lady's acceptance of the fashions of that day, which would be thought so grotesque in this. I have heard contemporaneous young girls laugh at the mere notion of hoops, but in 1870 we thought hoops extremely becoming; and this young lady knew how to hold hers a little on one side so as to give herself room in the narrow avenue, and not betray more than the discreetest hint of a white stocking. I believe the stockings are black now.

They both got by us, and I could see Mr. Glendenning following them with longing but irresolute eyes, until they turned, a long way down the saloon, as if to come toward us again. Then he hurried to meet them, and as he addressed himself first to one and then to the other, I knew him to be offering them his chair. So did my wife, and she said, "You must give up your place too, Basil," and I said I would if she wished to see me starve on the spot. But of course I went and joined Glendenning in his entreaties that they would deprive us of our chances of dinner (I knew what the second table was on the *Corinthian*); and I must say that the elder lady accepted my chair in the spirit which my secret grudge deserved. She made me feel as if I ought to have offered it when they first passed us; but it was some satisfaction to learn afterwards that she gave Mrs. March, for her ready sacrifice of me, as bad a half-hour as she ever had. She sat next to my wife, and the young lady took Glendenning's place, and as soon as we had left them, she began trying to find out from Mrs. March who he was, and what his relation to us was. The girl tried to check her at first, and then seemed to give it up, and devoted herself to being rather more amiable than she otherwise might have been, my wife thought, in compensation for the severity of her mother's scrutiny. Her mother appeared disposed to hold Mrs. March responsible for knowing little or nothing about Mr. Glendenning.

"He seems to be an Episcopal clergyman," she said in a haughty summing up. "From his name I should have supposed he was Scotch and a Presbyterian." She began to patronize the trip we were making, and to abuse it; she said that she did not see what could have induced them to undertake it; but one had to get back from Niagara somehow, and they had been told at the hotel there that the boats were very comfortable. She had never been more uncomfortable in her life; as for the rapids, they made her ill, and they were obviously so dangerous that she should not even look at them again. Then, from having done all the talking and most of the eating, she fell quite silent, and gave her daughter a chance to speak to my wife. She had hitherto spoken only to her mother, but now she asked Mrs. March if she had ever been down the St. Lawrence before.

When my wife explained, and asked her whether she was enjoying it, she answered with a rapture that was quite astonishing, in reference to her mother's expressions of disgust: "Oh, immensely! Every instant of it," and she went on to expatiate on its peculiar charm in terms so intelligent and sympathetic that Mrs. March confessed it had been part of our wedding journey, and that this was the reason why we were now taking the trip.

The young lady did not seem to care so much for this, and when she thanked her again in leaving the table with her mother, and begged her to thank the gentlemen who had so kindly given up their places, she made no overture to further acquaintance. In fact we had been so simply and merely made use of, that although we were rather meek people, we decided to avoid our beneficiaries for the rest of the day; and Mr. Glendenning, who could not, as a clergyman, indulge even a just resentment, could as little refuse us his sympathy. He laughed at some hints of my wife's experience, which she dropped before she left us to pick up a meal from the lukewarm leavings of the *Corinthian's* dinner, if we could. She said she was going forward to get a good place on the bow, and would keep two camp-stools for us, which she could assure us no one would get away from her.

We were somewhat surprised then to find her seated by the rail with the younger lady of the two whom she meant to avoid if she meant anything by what she said. She was laughing and talking on quite easy terms with her apparently, and "There!" she triumphed, as we came up, "I've kept your camp-stools for you," and she showed them at her side, where she was holding her hand on them. "You had better put them here."

The girl had stiffened a little at our approach, as I could see, but a young girl's stiffness is always rather amusing than otherwise, and I did not mind it.

Neither, that I could see, did Mr. Glendenning, and it soon passed. It seemed that she had left her mother lying down in her state-room, where she justly imagined that if she did not see the rapids she should suffer less alarm from them; the young lady had come frankly to the side of Mrs. March as soon as she saw her, and asked if she might sit with her. She now talked to me for a decent space of time, and then presently, without my knowing how, she was talking to Mr. Glendenning, and they were comparing notes of Niagara; he was saying that he thought he had seen her at the Cataract House, and she was owning that she and her mother had at least stopped at that hotel.

II.

I have no wish, and if I had the wish I should not have the art, to keep back the fact that these young people were evidently very much taken with each other. They showed their mutual pleasure so plainly that even I could see it. As for Mrs. March, she was as proud of it as if she had invented them and set them going in their advance toward each other, like two mechanical toys.

I confess that with reference to what my wife had told me of this young lady's behavior when she was with her mother, her submissiveness, her entire self-effacement, up to a certain point, I did not know quite what to make of her present independence, not to say freedom. I thought she might perhaps have been kept so strictly in the background, with regard to young men, that she was rather disposed to make the most of any chance at them which offered. If the young man in this case was at no pains to hide his pleasure in her society, one might say that she was almost eager to show her delight in his. If it was a case of love at first sight, the earliest glimpse had been to the girl, who was all eyes for Glendenning. It was very pretty, but it was a little alarming, and perhaps a little droll, even. She was actually making the advances, not consciously, but helplessly; fondly, ignorantly, for I have no belief, nor had my wife (a much more critical observer), that she knew how she was giving herself away.

I thought perhaps that she was in the habit from pride, or something like it, of holding herself in check, and that this blameless excess which I saw was the natural expansion from an inner constraint. But what I really knew was that the young people got on very rapidly, in an acquaintance that prospered up to the last moment I saw them together. This was just before the *Corinthian* drew up to her landing at Montreal, when Miss Bentley (we had learned her name) came to us from the point where she was standing with Glendenning and said that now she must go to her mother, and took a sweet leave of my wife. She asked where we were going to stay in Montreal and whether we were going on to Quebec; and said her mother would wish to send Mrs. March her card.

When she was gone, Glendenning explained, with rather superfluous apology, that he had offered to see the ladies to a hotel, for he was afraid that at this crowded season they might not find it easy to get rooms, and he did not wish Mrs. Bentley, who was an invalid, to have any anxieties about it. He bade us an affectionate, but not a disconsolate adieu, and when we had got into the modest conveyance (if an omnibus is modest) which was to take us to the Ottawa House, we saw him drive off to the St. Lawrence Hall (it was twenty-five years ago) in one of those vitreous and tinkling Montreal landaus, with Mrs. and Miss Bentley and Mrs. Bentley's maid.

We were still so young as to be very much absorbed in the love-affairs of other people; I believe women always remain young enough for that; and Mrs. March talked about the one we fancied we had witnessed the beginning of pretty much the whole evening. The next morning we got letters from Boston, telling us how the children were and all that they were doing and saying. We had stood it very well, as long as we did not hear anything about them, and we had lent ourselves in a sort of semi-forgetfulness of them to the associations of the past where they were not; but now to learn that they were hearty and happy, and that they sent love and kisses, was too much. With one mind we renounced the notion of going on to Quebec; we found that we could just get the ten-o'clock train that would reach Boston by eleven that night, and we made all haste and got it. We had not been really happy, we perceived, till that moment since we had bidden the children good-by.

III.

Perhaps it was because we left Montreal so abruptly that Mrs. March never received Mrs. Bentley's card. It may be at the Ottawa House to this day, for all I know. What is certain is that we saw and heard nothing more of her or her daughter. Glendenning called to see us as he passed through Boston on his way west from Quebec, but we were neither of us at home and we missed him, to my wife's vivid regret. I rather think we expected him to find some excuse for writing after he reached his place in northern Ohio; but he did not write, and he became more and more the memory of a young clergyman in the beginning of a love-affair, till one summer, while we were still disputing where we should spend the hot weather within business reach, there came a letter from him saying that he was settled at Gormanville, and wishing that he might tempt us up some afternoon before we were off to the mountains or sea-side. This revived all my wife's waning interest in him, and it was hard to keep the answer I made him from expressing in a series of crucial inquiries the excitement she felt at his being in New England and so near Boston, and in Gormanville of all places. It was one of the places we had thought of for the summer, and we were yet so far from having relinquished it that we were recurring from time to time in hope and fear to the advertisement of an old village mansion there, with ample grounds, garden, orchard, ice-house, and stables, for a very low rental to an unexceptionable tenant. We had no doubt of our own qualifications, but we had misgivings of the village mansion; and I am afraid that I rather unduly despatched the personal part of my letter, in my haste to ask what Glendenning knew and what he thought of the Conwell place. However, the letter seemed to serve all purposes. There came a reply from Glendenning, most cordial, even affectionate, saying that the Conwell place was delightful, and I must come at once and see it. He professed that he would be glad to have Mrs. March come too, and he declared that if his joy at having us did not fill his modest rectory to bursting, he was sure it could stand the physical strain of our presence, though he confessed that his guest-chamber was tiny.

"He wants *you*, Basil," my wife divined from terms which gave me no sense of any latent design of parting us in his hospitality. "But, evidently, it isn't a chance to be missed, and you must go—instantly. Can you go to-morrow? But telegraph him you're coming, and tell him to hold on to the Conwell place; it may be snapped up any moment if it's so desirable."

I did not go till the following week, when I found that no one had attempted to snap up the Conwell place. In fact, it rather snapped me up, I secured it with so little trouble. I reported it so perfect that all my wife's fears of a latent objection to it were roused again. But when I said I thought we could relinquish it, her terrors subsided; and I thought this the right moment to deliver a stroke that I had been holding in reserve.

"You know," I began, "the Bentleys have their summer place there—the old Bentley homestead. It's their ancestral town, you know."

"Bentleys? What Bentleys?" she demanded, opaquely.

"Why, those people we met on the *Corinthian*, summer before last — you thought he was in love with the girl—"

A simultaneous photograph could alone reproduce Mrs. March's tumultuous and various emotions as she seized the fact conveyed in my words. She poured out a volume of mingled conjectures, assertions, suspicions, conclusions, in which there was nothing final but the decision that we must not dream of going there; that it would look like thrusting ourselves in, and would be in the worst sort of taste; they would all hate us, and we should feel that we were spies upon the young people; for of course the Bentleys had got Glendenning there to marry him, and in effect did not want any one to witness the disgraceful spectacle.

I said, "That may be the nefarious purpose of the young lady, but, as I understood Glendenning, it is no part of her mother's design."

"What do you mean?"

"Miss Bentley may have got him there to marry him, but Mrs. Bentley seems to have meant nothing more than an engagement at the worst."

"What *do* you mean? They're not engaged, are they?"

"They're not married, at any rate, and I suppose they're engaged. I did not

have it from Miss Bentley, but I suppose Glendenning may be trusted in such a case."

"Now," said my wife, with a severity that might well have appalled me, "if you will please to explain, Basil, it will be better for you."

"Why, it is simply this. Glendenning seems to have made himself so useful to the mother and pleasing to the daughter after we left them in Montreal that he was tolerated on a pretence that there was reason for his writing back to Mrs. Bentley after he got home, and as Mrs. Bentley never writes letters, Miss Bentley had the hard task of answering him. This led to a correspondence."

"And to her moving heaven and earth to get him to Gormanville. I see! Of course she did it so that no one knew what she was about!"

"Apparently. Glendenning himself was not in the secret. The Bentleys were in Europe last summer, and he did not know that they had a place at Gormanville till he came to live there. Another proof that Miss Bentley got him there is the fact that she and her mother are Unitarians, and that they would naturally be able to select the rector of the Episcopal church."

"Go on," said Mrs. March, not the least daunted.

"Oh, there's nothing more. He is simply rector of St. Michael's at Gormanville; and there is not the slightest proof that any young lady had a hand in getting him there."

"As if I cared in the least whether she had! I suppose you will allow that she had something to do with getting engaged to him, and that is the *great* matter."

"Yes, I must allow that, if we are to suppose that young ladies have anything to do with young gentlemen getting engaged to them; it doesn't seem exactly delicate. But the novel phase of this great matter is the position of the young lady's mother in regard to it. From what I could make out she consents to the engagement of her daughter, but she don't and won't consent to her marriage." My wife glared at me with so little speculation in her eyes that I felt obliged to disclaim all responsibility for the fact I had reported. "Thou canst not say *I* did it. *They* did it, and Miss Bentley, if any one, is to blame. It seems, from what Glendenning says, that the young lady and he wrote to each other while she was abroad, and that they became engaged by letter. Then the affair was broken off because of her mother's opposition; but since they have met in Gormanville, the engagement has been renewed. So much they've managed against the old lady's will, but apparently on condition that they won't get married till she says."

"Nonsense! How could she stop them?"

"She couldn't, I dare say, by any of the old romantic methods of a convent or disinheritance; but she is an invalid; she wants to keep her daughter with her, and she avails with the girl's conscience by being simply dependent and obstructive. The young people have carried their engagement through, and now such hope as they have is fixed upon her finally yielding in the matter of their marriage, though Glendenning was obliged to confess that there was no sign of her doing so. They agree—Miss Bentley and he—that they cannot get married as they got engaged, in spite of her mother—it would be unclerical if it wouldn't be unfilial—and they simply have to bide their time."

My wife asked abruptly, "How many chambers are there in the Conwell place?"

I said, and then she asked, "Is there a windmill or a force-pump?" I answered proudly that in Gormanville there was town water, but that if this should give out there were both a windmill and a force-pump on the Conwell place.

"It is very complete," she sighed, as if this had removed all hope from her, and she added, "I suppose we had better take it."

IV.

We certainly did not take it for the sake of being near the Bentleys, neither of whom had given us particular reason to desire their further acquaintance, though the young lady had agreeably modified herself when apart from her mother. In fact we went to Gormanville because it was an exceptional chance to get a beautiful place for a very little money, where we could go early and stay late. But no sooner had we acted from this quite personal, not to say selfish, motive than we were rewarded with the sweetest overtures of neighborliness by the Bentleys. They waited, of course, till we were settled in our house before they came to call upon Mrs. March, but they had been preceded by several hospitable offerings from their garden, their dairy, and their henhouse, which were very welcome in the days of our first uncertainty as to tradespeople. We analyzed this hospitality as an effect of that sort of nature in Mrs. Bentley which can equally assert its superiority by blessing or banning. Evidently, since chance had again thrown us in her way, she would not go out of it to be offensive, but would continue in it, and make the best of us.

No doubt Glendenning had talked us into the Bentleys; and this my wife said she hated most of all; for we should have to live up to the notion of us imparted by a young man from the impressions of the moment when he saw us purple in the light of his dawning love. In justice to Glendenning, however, I must say that he did nothing, by a show of his own assiduities, to urge us upon the Bentleys after we came to Gormanville. If we had not felt so sure of him, we might have thought he was keeping his regard for us a little too modestly in the background. He made us one cool little call, the evening of our arrival, in which he had the effect of anxiety to get away as soon as possible; and after that we saw him no more until he came with Miss Bentley and her mother a week later. His forbearance was all the more remarkable because his church and his rectory were just across the street from the Conwell place, at the corner of another street, where we could see their wooden gothic in the cold shadow of the maples with which the green in front of them was planted.

During all that time Glendenning's personal elevation remained invisible to us, and we began to wonder if he were not that most lamentable of fellow-creatures, a clerical snob. I am not sure still that he might not have been so in some degree, there was such a mixture of joy that was almost abject in his genuine affection for us, when Mrs. Bentley openly approved us on her first visit. I dare say he would not have quite abandoned us in any case; but he must have felt responsible for us, and it must have been such a load off him, when she took that turn with us.

She called in the afternoon, and the young people dropped in again the same evening, and took the trouble to win back our simple hearts. That is, Miss

Bentley showed herself again as frank and sweet as she had been on the boat when she joined my wife after dinner and left her mother in her state-room. Glendenning was again the Glendenning of our first meeting, and something more. He fearlessly led the way to intimacies of feeling with an expansion uncommon even in an accepted lover, and we made our conclusions that however subject he might be to his indefinitely future mother-in-law, he would not be at all so to his wife, if she could help it. He took the lead, but because she gave it him; and she displayed an aptness for conjugal submissiveness which almost amounted to genius. Whenever she spoke to either of us, it was with one eye on him to see if he liked what she was saying. It was so perfect that I doubted if it could last; but my wife said a girl like that could keep it up till she dropped. I have never been sure that she liked us as well as he did; I think it was part of her intense loyalty to seem to like us a great deal more.

She was deeply in love, and nothing but her ladylike breeding kept her from being openly fond. I figured her in a sort of impassioned incandescence, such as only a pure and perhaps cold nature could burn into; and I amused myself a little with the sense of Glendenning's apparent inadequacy. Sweet he was, and admirably gentle and fine; he had an unfailing good sense, and a very ready wisdom, as I grew more and more to perceive. But neither my wife nor I could ignore the fact that he was an inch or so shorter than Miss Bentley, and that in his sunny blondness, with his golden red beard and hair, and his pinkish complexion, he wanted still more the effect of an emotional equality with her. He was very handsome, with features excellently regular; his smile was celestially beautiful, and innocent gay lights danced in his blue eyes, through lashes and under brows that were a little lighter blond than his beard and hair.

V.

The next morning, which was of a Saturday, when I did not go to town, he came over to us again from the shadow of his sombre maples, and fell simply and naturally into talk about his engagement. He was much fuller in my wife's presence than he had been with me alone, and told us the hopes he had of Mrs. Bentley's yielding within a reasonable time. He seemed to gather encouragement from the sort of perspective he got the affair into by putting it before us, and finding her dissent to her daughter's marriage so ridiculous in our eyes after her consent to her engagement that a woman of her great good sense evidently could not persist in it.

"There is no personal objection to myself," he said, with a modest satisfaction. "In fact, I think she really likes me, and only dislikes my engagement to Edith. But she knows that Edith is incapable of marrying against her mother's will, or I of wishing her to do so; though there is nothing else to prevent us."

My wife allowed herself to say, "Isn't it rather cruel of her?"

"Why, no, not altogether; or not so much so as it might be in different circumstances. I make every allowance for her. In the first place, she is a great sufferer."

"Yes, I know," my wife relented.

"She suffers terribly from asthma. I don't suppose she has lain down in bed for ten years. She sleeps in an easy-chair, and she's never quite free from her trouble; when there's a paroxysm of the disease, her anguish is frightful. I've never seen it, of course, but I have heard it: you hear it all through the house. Edith has the constant care of her. Her mother has to be perpetually moved and shifted in her chair, and Edith does this for her; she will let no one else come near her; Edith must look to the ventilation, and burn the pastilles which help her to breathe. She depends upon her every instant." He had grown very solemn in voice and face, and he now said, "When I think of what she endures, it seems to me that it is I who am cruel even to dream of taking her daughter from her."

"Yes," my wife assented.

"But there is really no present question of that. We are very happy as it is. We can wait, and wait willingly till Mrs. Bentley wishes us to wait no longer; or—"

He stopped, and we were both aware of something in his mind which he put from him. He became a little pale, and sat looking very grave. Then he rose. "I don't know whether to say how welcome you would be at St. Michael's tomorrow, for you may not be—"

"*We* are Unitarians, too," said Mrs. March. "But we are coming to hear *you*."

"I am glad you are coming *to church*," said Glendenning, putting away the personal tribute implied with a gentle dignity that became him.

VI.

We waited a discreet time before returning the call of the Bentley ladies, but not so long as to seem conscious. In fact we had been softened towards Mrs. Bentley by what Glendenning told us of her suffering, and we were disposed to forgive a great deal of patronage and superiority to her asthma; they were not part of the disease, but still they were somehow to be considered with reference to it in her case.

We were admitted by the maid, who came running down the hall stairway, with a preoccupied air, to the open door where we stood waiting. There were two great syringa-bushes on each hand close to the portal, which were in full flower, and which flung their sweetness through the doorway and the windows; but when we found ourselves in the dim old-fashioned parlor, we were aware of this odor meeting and mixing with another which descended from the floor above—the smell of some medicated pastille. There was a sound of anxious steps overhead, and a hurried closing of doors, with the mechanical sound of labored breathing.

"We have come at a bad time," I suggested.

"Yes; *why* did they let us in?" cried my wife in an anguish of compassion and vexation. She repeated her question to Miss Bentley, who came down almost immediately, looking pale, indeed, but steady, and making a brave show of welcome.

"My mother would have wished it," she said, "and she sent me as soon as she knew who it was. You mustn't be distressed," she entreated, with a pathetic smile. "It's really a kind of relief to her; anything is that takes her mind off herself for a moment. She will be so sorry to miss you, and you must come again as soon as you can."

"Oh, we will, we will!" cried my wife, in nothing less than a passion of meekness; and Miss Bentley went on to comfort her.

"It's dreadful, of course, but it isn't as bad as it sounds, and it isn't nearly so bad as it looks. She is used to it, and there is a great deal in that. Oh, *don't* go!" she begged, at a movement Mrs. March made to rise. "The doctor is with her just now, and I'm not needed. It will be kind if you'll stay; it's a relief to be out of the room with a good excuse!" She even laughed a little as she said this; she went on to lead the talk away from what was so intensely in our minds, and presently I heard her and my wife speaking of other things. The power to do this is from some heroic quality in women's minds that we do not credit them with; we think it their volatility, and I dare say I thought myself much better, or at least more serious in my make, because I could not follow them, and did not lose one of those hoarse gasps of the sufferer overhead. Occasionally there came a stifling cry that made me jump, inwardly if not outwardly, but those women had their drama to play, and they played it to the end.

Miss Bentley came hospitably to the door with us, and waited there till she thought we could not see her turn and run swiftly up stairs.

"Why *did* you stay, my dear?" I groaned. "I felt as if I were personally smothering Mrs. Bentley every moment we were there."

"I *had* to do it. She wished it, and, as she said, it was a relief to have us there, though she was wishing us at the ends of the earth all the time. But what a ghastly life!"

"Yes; and can you wonder that the poor woman doesn't want to give her up, to lose the help and comfort she gets from her? It's a wicked thing for that girl to think of marrying."

"What are you talking about, Basil? It's a wicked thing for her *not* to think of it! She is wearing her life out, *tearing* it out, and she isn't doing her mother a bit of good. Her mother would be just as well, and better, with a good strong nurse, who could lift her this way and that, and change her about, without feeling her heart-strings wrung at every gasp, as that poor child must. Oh, I *wish* Glendenning was man enough to make her run off with him, and get married, in spite of everything. But, of course, that's impossible—for a clergyman! And her sacrifice began so long ago that it's become part of her life, and she'll simply have to keep on."

VII.

When her attack passed off, Mrs. Bentley sent and begged my wife to come again and see her. She went without me, while I was in town, but she was so circumstantial in her report of her visit, when I came home at night, that I never felt quite sure I had not been present. What most interested us both was the extreme independence which the mother and daughter showed beyond a certain point, and the daughter's great frankness in expressing her difference of feeling. We had already had some hint of this, the first day we met her, and we were not surprised at it now, my wife at first hand, or I at second hand. Mrs. Bentley opened the way for her daughter by saying that the worst of sickness was that it made one such an affliction to others. She lived in an atmosphere of devotion, she said, but her suffering left her so little of life that she could not help clinging selfishly to everything that remained.

My wife perceived that this was meant for Miss Bentley, though it was spoken to herself; and Miss Bentley seemed to take the same view of the fact. She said: "We needn't use any circumlocution with Mrs. March, mother. She knows just how the affair stands. You can say whatever you wish, though I don't know why you should wish to say anything. You have made your own terms with us, and we are keeping them to the letter. What more can you ask? Do you want me to break with Mr. Glendenning? I will do that too, if you ask it. You have got everything *but* that, and you can have that at any time. But Arthur and I are perfectly satisfied as it is, and we can wait as long as you wish us to wait."

Her mother said, "I'm not allowed to forget that for a single hour;" and Miss Bentley said, "I never remind you of it unless you make me, mother. You may be thinking of it all the time, but it isn't because of anything I say."

"Or that you *do?*" said Mrs. Bentley; and her daughter answered, "I can't help existing, of course."

My wife broke off from the account she was giving me of her visit: "You can imagine how pleasant all this was for me, Basil, and how anxious I was to prolong my call!"

"Well," I returned, "there were compensations. It was extremely interesting; it was life. You can't deny that, my dear."

"It was more like death. Several times I was on the point of going, but you know when there's been a painful scene you feel so sorry for the people who've made it that you can't bear to leave them to themselves. I did get up to go once, in mere self-defence, but they both urged me to stay, and I couldn't help staying till they could talk of other things. But now tell mé what you think of it all. Which should your feeling be with the most? That is what I want to get at before I tell you mine."

"Which side was I on when we talked about them last?"

"Oh, when did we talk about them *last?* We are always talking about them! I am getting no good of the summer at all. I shall go home in the fall more jaded and worn out than when I came! To think that we should have this beautiful place, where we could be so happy and comfortable, if it were not for having this abnormal situation under our nose and eyes all the time!"

"Abnormal? I don't call it abnormal," I began, and I was sensible of my wife's thoughts leaving her own injuries for my point of view so swiftly that I could almost hear them whir.

"Not abnormal!" she gasped.

"No; only too natural. Isn't it perfectly natural for an invalid like that to want to keep her daughter with her; and isn't it perfectly natural for a daughter, with a New England sense of duty, to yield to her wish? You might say that she could get married and live at home, and then she and Glendenning could both devote themselves—"

"No, no," my wife broke in, "that wouldn't do. Marriage is marriage; and it puts the husband and wife with each other first; when it doesn't, it's a miserable mockery."

"Even when there's a sick mother in the case?"

"A thousand sick mothers wouldn't alter the case. And that's what they all three instinctively know, and they're doing the only thing they can do."

"Then I don't see what we're complaining of."

"Complaining of? We're complaining of its being all wrong and—romantic. Her mother has asked more than she had any right to ask, and Miss Bentley has tried to do more than she can perform, and that has made them hate each other."

"Should you say *hate*, quite?"

"It must come to that, if Mrs. Bentley lives."

"Then let us hope she—"

"My dear!" cried Mrs. March, warningly.

"Oh, come, now!" I retorted. "Do you mean to say that you haven't thought how very much it would simplify the situation if—"

"Of course I have! And that is the wicked part of it. It's that that is wearing me out. It's perfectly hideous!"

"Well, fortunately we're not actively concerned in the affair, and we needn't take any measures in regard to it. We are mere spectators, and as I see it the situation is not only inevitable for Mrs. Bentley, but it has a sort of heroic propriety for Miss Bentley."

"And Glendenning?"

"Oh, Glendenning isn't provided for in my scheme."

"Then I can tell you that your scheme, Basil, is worse than worthless."

"I didn't brag of it, my dear," I said, meekly enough. "I'm sorry for him, but I can't help him. He must provide for himself out of his religion."

VIII.

It was indeed a trying summer for our emotions, torn as we were between our pity for Mrs. Bentley and our compassion for her daughter. We had no repose, except when we centred our sympathies upon Glendenning, whom we could yearn over in tender regret without doing any one else wrong, or even criticising another. He was our great stay in that respect, and though a mere external witness might have thought that he had the easiest part, we who knew his gentle and affectionate nature could not but feel for him. We never concealed from ourselves certain foibles of his; I have hinted at one, and we should have liked it better if he had not been so sensible of the honor, from a worldly point, of being engaged to Miss Bentley. But this was a very innocent vanity, and he would have been willing to suffer for her mother and for herself, if she had let him. I have tried to insinuate how she would not let him, but freed him as much as possible from the stress of the situation, and assumed for him a mastery, a primacy which he would never have assumed for himself. We thought this very pretty of her, and in fact she was capable of pretty things. What was hard and arrogant in her, and she was not without something of the kind at times, was like her mother; but even she, poor soul, had her good points, as I have attempted to suggest. We used to dwell upon them, when our talk with Glendenning grew confidential, as it was apt to do; for it seemed to console him to realize that her daughter and he were making their sacrifice to a not wholly unamiable person.

He confided equally in my wife and myself, but there were times when I think he rather preferred the counsel of a man friend. Once when we had gone a walk into the country, which around Gormanville is of the pathetic Mid-Massachusetts loveliness and poverty, we sat down in a hill-side orchard to rest, and he began abruptly to talk of his affair. Sometimes, he said, he felt that it was all an error, and he could not rid himself of the fear that an error persisted in was a wrong, and therefore a species of sin.

"That is very interesting," I said. "I wonder if there is anything in it? At first blush it looks so logical; but is it? Or are you simply getting morbid? What is the error? What is your error?"

"You know," he said, with a gentle refusal of my willingness to make light of his trouble. "It is surely an error to allow a woman to give her word when she can promise nothing more, and to let her hold herself to it."

I could have told him that I did not think the error in this case was altogether or mainly his, or the persistence in it; for it had seemed to me from the beginning that the love between him and Miss Bentley was fully as much her affair as his, and that quite within the bounds of maidenly modesty she showed herself as passionately true to their plighted troth. But of course this would not do, and I had to be content with the ironical suggestion that he might try offering to release Miss Bentley.

"Don't laugh at me," he implored, and I confess his tone would have taken from me any heart to do so.

"My dear fellow," I said, "I see your point. But don't you think you are quite needlessly adding to your affliction by pressing it? You two are in the position which isn't at all uncommon with engaged people, of having to wait upon exterior circumstances before you get married. Suppose you were prevented by poverty, as often happens? It would be a hardship as it is now; but in that case would your engagement be any less an error than it is now? I don't think it would, and I don't believe you think so either."

"In that case we should not be opposing our wills to the will of some one else, who has a better claim to her daughter's allegiance than I have. It seems to me that our error was in letting her mother consent to our engagement if she would not or could not consent to our marriage. When it came to that we ought both to have had the strength to say that then there should be no engagement. It was my place to do that. I could have prevented the error which I can't undo."

"I don't see how it could have been easier to prevent than to undo your error. I don't admit it's an error, but I call it so because you do. After all, an engagement is nothing but an open confession between two people that they are in love with each other and wish to marry. There need be no sort of pledge or promise to make the engagement binding, if there is love. It's the love that binds."

"Yes."

"It bound you from your first acknowledgment of it, and unless you could deny your love now, or hereafter, it must always bind you. If you own that you still love each other, you are still engaged, no matter how much you release each other. Could you think of loving her and marrying some one else? Could she love you and marry another? There isn't any error, unless you've mistaken your feeling for each other. If you have, I should decidedly say you couldn't break your engagement too soon. In fact, there wouldn't be any real engagement to break."

"Of course you are right," said Glendenning, but not so strenuously as he might.

I had a feeling that he had not put forward the main cause of his unhappiness, though he had given a true cause; that he had made some lesser sense of wrong stand for a greater, as people often do in confessing themselves; and I was not surprised when he presently added: "It is not merely the fact that she is bound in that way, and that her young life is passing in this sort of hopeless patience, but

that—that— I don't know how to put the ugly and wicked thing into words, but I assure you that sometimes when I think —when I'm aware that I know— Ah, I can't say it!"

"I fancy I understand what you mean, my dear boy," I said, and in the right of my ten years' seniority I put my hand caressingly on his shoulder, "and you are no more guilty than I am in knowing that if Mrs. Bentley were not in the way, there would be no obstacle to your happiness."

"But such a cognition is of hell," he cried, and he let his face fall into his hands and sobbed heart-rendingly.

"Yes," I said, "such a cognition is of hell; you're quite right. So are all evil concepts and knowledges; but so long as they are merely things of our intelligence, they are no part of us, and we are not guilty of them."

"No; I trust not, I trust not," he returned, and I let him sob his trouble out before I spoke again; and then I began with a laugh of unfeigned gayety. Something that my wife had hinted in one of our talks about the lovers freakishly presented itself to my mind, and I said, "There is a way, and a very practical way, to put an end to the anomaly you feel in an engagement which doesn't imply a marriage."

"And what is that?" he asked, not very hopefully; but he dried his eyes and calmed himself.

"Well, speaking after the manner of men, you might run off with Miss Bentley."

All the blood in his body flushed into his face. "Don't!" he gasped, and I divined that what I had said must have been in his thoughts before, and I laughed again. "It wouldn't do," he added, piteously. "The scandal I am a clergyman, and my parish—"

I perceived that no moral scruple presented itself to him; when it came to the point, he was simply and naturally a lover, like any other man; and I persisted: "It would only be a seven days' wonder. I never heard of a clergyman's running away to be married; but they must have sometimes done it. Come, I don't believe you'd have to plead hard with Miss Bentley, and Mrs. March and I will aid and abet you to the limit of our small ability. I'm sure that if I promise to wrap up warm against the night air, she will let me go and help you hold the rope-ladder taut."

It was not very reverent to his cloth, or his recent tragical mood, but Glendenning was not offended; he laughed with a sheepish pleasure, and that evening he came with Miss Bentley to call upon us. The visit passed without unusual confidences until they rose to go, when she said abruptly to me: "I feel that we both owe you a great deal, Mr. March. Arthur has been telling me of your talk this afternoon, and I think that what you said was all so wise and true! I don't mean," she added, "your suggestion about putting an end to the anomaly!" and she and Glendenning both laughed.

My wife said, "That was very wicked, and I have scolded him for thinking of such a thing." She had indeed forgotten that she had put it in my head, and made me wholly responsible for it.

"Then you must scold me too a little, Mrs. March," said the girl, "for I've sometimes wondered if I couldn't work Arthur up to the point of making me run away with him," which was a joke that wonderfully amused us all.

I said, "I shouldn't think it would be so difficult"; and she retorted:

"Oh, you've no idea how obdurate clergymen are;" and then she went on, seriously, to thank me for talking Glendenning out of his morbid mood. With the frankness sometimes characteristic of her she said that if he had released her, it would have made no difference — she should have still have felt herself bound to him; and until he should tell her that he no longer cared for her, she should feel that he was bound to her. I saw no great originality in this reproduction of my own ideas. But when Miss Bentley added that she believed her mother herself would be shocked and disappointed if they were to give each other up, I was aware of being in the presence of a curious psychological fact. I so wholly lost myself in the inquiry it invited that I let the talk flow on round me unheeded while I questioned whether Mrs. Bentley did not derive a satisfaction from her own and her daughter's mutual opposition which she could never have enjoyed from their perfect agreement. She had made a certain concession in consenting to the engagement, and this justified her to herself in refusing her consent to the marriage, while the ingratitude of the young

people in not being content with what she had done formed a grievance of constant avail with a lady of her temperament. From what Miss Bentley let fall, half seriously, half jokingly, as well as what I observed, I divined a not unnatural effect of the strained relations between her and her mother. She concentrated whatever resentment she felt upon Miss Bentley, insomuch that it seemed as though she might altogether have withdrawn her opposition if it had been a question merely of Glendenning's marriage. So far from disliking him, she was rather fond of him, and she had no apparent objection to him except as her daughter's husband. It had not always been so; at first she had an active rancor against him; but this had gradually yielded to his invincible goodness and sweetness.

"Who could hold out against him?" his betrothed demanded, fondly, when these facts had been more or less expressed to us; and it was not the first time that her love had seemed more explicit than his. He smiled round upon her, pressing the hand she put in his arm; for she asked this when they stood on our threshold ready to go, and then he glanced at us with eyes that fell bashfully from ours.

"Oh, of course it will come right in time," said my wife when they were gone, and I agreed that they need only have patience. We had all talked ourselves into a cheerful frame concerning the affair; we had seen it in its amusing aspects, and laughed about it; and that seemed almost in itself to dispose of Mrs. Bentley's opposition. My wife and I decided that this could not long continue; that by-and-by she would become tired of it, and this would happen all the sooner if the lovers submitted absolutely, and did nothing to remind her of their submission.

IX.

The Conwells came home from Europe the next summer, and we did not go again to Gormanville. But from time to time we heard of the Bentleys, and we heard to our great amaze that there was no change in the situation, as concerned Miss Bentley and Glendenning. I think that later it would have surprised us if we had learned that there was a change. Their lives seemed to have all adjusted themselves to the conditions, and we who were mere spectators came at last to feel nothing abnormal in them.

Now and then we saw Glendenning, and now and then Miss Bentley came to call upon Mrs. March, when she was in town. Her mother had given up her Boston house, and they lived the whole year round at Gormanville, where the air was good for Mrs. Bentley without her apparently being the better for it; again, we heard in a roundabout way that their circumstances were not so fortunate as they had been, and that they had given up their Boston house partly from motives of economy.

There was no reason why our intimacy with the lovers' affair should continue, and it did not. Miss Bentley made mention of Glendenning, when my wife saw her, with what Mrs. March decided to be an abiding fealty, but without offer of confidence; and Glendenning, when we happened to meet at rare intervals, did not invite me to more than formal inquiry concerning the well-being of Mrs. Bentley and her daughter.

He was undoubtedly getting older, and he looked it. He was one of those gentle natures which put on fat, not from self-indulgence, but from want of resisting force, and the clerical waistcoat that buttoned black to his throat swayed decidedly beyond a straight line at his waist. His red-gold hair was getting thin, and though he wore it cut close all round, it showed thinner on the crown than on the temples, and his pale eyebrows were waning. He had a settled patience of look which would have been a sadness, if there had not been mixed with it an air of resolute cheerfulness. I am not sure that this kept it from being sad, either.

Miss Bentley, on her part, was no longer the young girl she was when we met on the *Corinthian*. She must then have been about twenty, and she was now twenty-six, but she looked thirty. Dark people show their age early, and she showed hers in cheeks that grew thinner if not paler, and in a purple shadow under her fine eyes. The parting of her black hair was wider than it once was, and she wore it smooth, in apparent disdain of those arts of fluffing and fringing, which give an air of vivacity, if not of youth. I should say she had always been a serious girl, and now she showed the effect of a life that could not have been gay for any one.

The lovers promised themselves, as we knew, that Mrs. Bentley would relent, and abandon what was more like a whimsical caprice than a settled wish. But as time wore on, and she gave no sign of changing, I have wondered whether some change did not come upon them, which affected them towards each other without affecting their constancy. I fancied their youthful passion taking on the sad color of patience, and contenting itself more and more with such friendly companionship as their fate afforded; it became, without marriage, that affectionate comradery which wedded love passes into with the lapse of as many years as they had been plighted. "What," I once suggested to my wife, in a very darkling mood—"what if they should gradually grow apart, and end in rejoicing that they had never been allowed to join their lives? Wouldn't that be rather Hawthornesque?"

"It wouldn't be true," said Mrs. March, "and I don't see why you should put such a notion upon Hawthorne. If you can't be more cheerful about it, Basil, I wish you wouldn't talk of the affair at all."

"Oh, I'm quite willing to be cheerful about it, my dear," I returned, "and, if you like, we will fancy Mrs. Bentley coming round and ardently wishing their marriage, and their gayly protesting that after having given the matter a great deal of thought they had decided it would be better not to marry, but to live on separately for their own sake, just as they have been doing for hers so long. Wouldn't that be cheerful?"

Mrs. March said that if I wished to tease it was because I had no ideas on the subject, and she would advise me to drop it. I did so, for the better part of the evening, but I could not relinquish it altogether. "Do you think," I asked, finally, "that any sort of character will stand the test of such a prolonged engagement?"

"Why not? Very indifferent character stands the test of marriage, and that's indefinitely prolonged."

"Yes, but it's not indefinite itself. Marriage is something very distinct and permanent; but such an engagement as this has no sort of future. It is a mere motionless present, without the inspiration of a common life, and with no hope of release from durance except through a chance that it will be sorrow instead of joy. I should think they would go to pieces under the strain."

"But as you see they don't, perhaps the strain isn't so great after all."

"Ah," I confessed, "there is that wonderful adaptation of the human soul to any circumstances. It's the one thing that makes me respect our fallen nature. Fallen? It seems to me that we ought to call it our risen nature; it has steadily mounted with the responsibility that Adam took for it—or Eve."

"I don't see," said my wife, pursuing her momentary advantage, "why they should not be getting as much pleasure or happiness out of life as most married people. Engagements are supposed to be very joyous, though I think they're rather exciting and restless times, as a general thing. If they've settled down to being merely engaged, I've no doubt they've decided to make the best of being merely engaged as long as her mother lives."

"There is that view of it," I assented.

X.

By the following autumn Glendenning had completed the seventh year of his engagement to Miss Bentley, and I reminded my wife that this seemed to be the scriptural length of a betrothal, as typified in the service which Jacob rendered for Rachel. "But *he* had a prospective father-in-law to deal with," I added, "and Glendenning a mother-in-law. That may make a difference."

Mrs. March did not join me in the humorous view of the affair which I took. She asked me if I had heard anything from Glendenning lately; if that were the reason why I mentioned him.

"No," I said; "but I have some office business that will take me to Gormanville to-morrow, and I did not know but you might like to go too, and look the ground over, and see how much we have been suffering for them unnecessarily." The fact was that we had now scarcely spoken of Glendenning or the Bentleys for six months, and our minds were far too full of our own affairs to be given more than very superficially to theirs at any time. "We could both go as well as not," I suggested, "and you could call upon the Bentleys while I looked after the company's business."

"Thank you, Basil, I think I will let you go alone," said my wife. "But try

to find out how it is with them. Don't be so terribly straightforward, and let it look as if that was what you came for. Don't make the slightest advance toward their confidence. But do let them open up if they will."

"My dear, you may depend upon my asking no leading questions whatever, and I shall behave with far more discretion than if you were with me. The danger is that I shall behave with too much, for I find that my interest in their affair is very much faded. There is every probability that unless Glendenning speaks of his engagement, it won't be spoken of at all."

This was putting it rather with the indifference of the past six months than with the feeling of the present moment. Since I had known that I was going to Gormanville, the interest I denied had renewed itself pretty vividly for me, and I was intending not only to get everything out of Glendenning that I decently could, but to give him as much good advice as he would bear. I was going to urge him to move upon the obstructive Mrs. Bentley with all his persuasive force, and I had formulated some arguments for him which I thought he might use with success. I did not tell my wife that this was my purpose, but all the same I cherished it, and I gathered energy for the enforcement of my views for Glendenning's happiness from the very dejection I was cast into by the outward effect of the Gormanville streets. They were all in a funeral blaze of their shade trees, which were mostly maples, but were here and there a stretch of elms meeting in arches almost consciously gothic over the roadway; the maples were crimson and gold, and the elms the paly yellow that they affect in the fall. A silence hung under their sad splendors which I found deepen when I got into what the inhabitants called the residential part. About the business centre there was some stir, and here in the transaction of my affairs I was in the thick of it for a while. Everybody remembered me in a pleasant way, and I had to stop and pass the time of day, as they would have said, with a good many whom I could not remember at once. It seemed to me that the maples in front of St. Michael's rectory were rather more depressingly gaudy than elsewhere in Gormanville; but I believe they were only thicker. I found Glendenning in his study, and he was so far from being cast down by their blazon that I thought him decidedly cheerfuler than when I saw him last. He met me with what for him was ardor, and as he had asked me most cordially about my family, I thought it fit to inquire how the ladies at the Bentley place were.

"Why, very well, very well indeed," he answered, brightly. "It's very odd, but Edith and I were talking about you all only last night, and wishing we could see you again. Edith is most uncommonly well. During the summer Mrs. Bentley had some rather severer attacks than usual, and the care and anxiety told upon Edith; but since the cooler weather has come, she has picked up wonderfully." He did not say that Mrs. Bentley had shared this gain, and I imagined that he had a reluctance to confess she had not. He went on, "You're going to stay and spend the night with me, aren't you?"

"No," I said; "I'm obliged to be off by the four-o'clock train. But if I may be allowed to name the hospitality I could accept, I should say luncheon."

"Good!" cried Glendenning, gayly. "Let us go and have it at the Bentleys'."

"Far be it from me to say where you shall lunch me," I returned. "The question isn't where, but when and how, with me."

He got his hat and stick, and as we started out of his door he began: "You'll be a little surprised at the informality, perhaps, but I'm glad you take it so easily. It makes it easier for me to explain that I'm almost domesticated at the Bentley homestead; I come and go very much as if it were my own house."

"My dear fellow," I said, "I'm not surprised at anything in your relation to the Bentley homestead, and I won't vex you with any glad inferences."

"Why," he returned, a little bashfully, "there's no explicit change. The affair is just where it has been all along. But with the gradual decline in Mrs. Bentley —I'm afraid you'll notice it—she seems rather to want me about, and at times I'm able to be of use to Edith, and so—"

He stopped, and I said, "Exactly."

He went on: "Of course it's rather anomalous, and I oughtn't to let you get the impression that she has actually conceded anything. But she shows herself much more — er, shall I say? — affectionate, and I can't help hoping that there

may be a change in her mood which will declare itself in an attitude more favorable to—"

I said again, "Exactly," and Glendenning resumed:

"In spite of Edith's not having been quite so well as usual—she's wonderfully well now—it's been a very happy summer with us, on account of this change. It seems to have come about in a very natural way with Mrs. Bentley, and out of a growing regard which I can't specifically account for, as far as anything I've done is concerned."

"I think I could account for it," said I. "She must be a stonier-hearted old lady than I imagine if she hasn't felt your goodness, all along, Glendenning."

"Why, you're very kind," said the gentle creature. "You tempt me to repeat what she said, at the only time she expressed a wish to have me oftener with them: 'You've been very patient with a contrary old woman. But I sha'n't make you wait much longer.'"

"Well, I think that was very encouraging, my dear fellow."

"Do you?" he asked, wistfully. "I thought so too, at first, but when I told Edith she could not take that view of it. She said that she did not believe her mother had changed her mind at all, and that she only meant she was growing older."

"But, at any rate," I argued, "it was pleasant to have her make an open recognition of your patience."

"Yes, that was pleasant," he said, cheerfully again. "And it was the beginning of the kind of relation that I have held ever since to her household. I am afraid I am there a good half of my time, and I believe I dine there oftener than I do at home. I am quite on the footing of a son, with her."

"There are some of the unregenerate, Glendenning," I made bold to say, "who think it is your own fault that you were not on the footing of a son-in-law with her long ago. If you'll excuse my saying so, you have been, if anything, too patient. It would have been far better for all if you had taken the bit in your teeth six or seven years back—"

He drew a deep breath. "It wouldn't have done; it wouldn't have done! Edith herself would never have consented to it."

"Did you ever ask her?"

"No," he said, innocently. "How could I?"

"And of course *she* could never ask *you*," I laughed. "My opinion is that you have lost a great deal of time unnecessarily. I haven't the least doubt that if you had brought a little pressure to bear with Mrs. Bentley herself, it would have sufficed."

He looked at me with a kind of dismay, as if my words had carried conviction, or had roused a conviction long dormant in his heart. "It wouldn't have done," he gasped.

"It isn't too late to try, yet," I suggested.

"Yes, it's too late. We must wait now." He hastened to add, "Until she yields entirely of herself."

He gave me a guilty glance when he drew near the Bentley place and we saw a buggy standing at the gate. "The doctor!" he said, and he hurried me up the walk to the door.

The door stood open and we heard the doctor saying to some one within: "No, no, nothing organic at all, I assure you. One of the commonest functional disturbances."

Miss Bentley appeared at the threshold with him, and she and Glendenning had time to exchange a glance of anxiety and of smiling reassurance, before she put out her hand in greeting to me, a very glad and cordial greeting, apparently. The doctor and I shook hands, and he got himself away with what I afterwards remembered as undue quickness, and left us to Miss Bentley.

Glendenning was quite right about her looking better. She looked even gay, and there was a vivid color in her cheeks such as I had not seen there for many years; her lips were red, her eyes brilliant. Her face was still perhaps as thin as ever, but it was indescribably younger.

I cannot say that there were the materials of a merrymaking amongst us, exactly, and yet I remember that luncheon as rather a gay one, with some laughing. I had not been till now in discovering that Miss Bentley had a certain gift of humor, so shy and proud, if I may so express it, that it would not show itself except upon long acquaintance, and I distinctly now perceived that this enabled her to make light of a burden that might otherwise have been intolerable. It qualified her to treat with cheerfulness the grimness of her mother, which had certainly not grown less since I saw her last, and

to turn into something like a joke her valetudinarian austerities of sentiment and opinion. She made a pleasant mock of the amenities which passed between her mother and Glendenning, whose gingerliness in the acceptance of the old lady's condescension would, I confess, have been notably comical without this gloss. It was perfectly evident that Mrs. Bentley's favor was bestowed with a mental reservation, and conditioned upon his forming no expectations from it, and poor Glendenning's eagerness to show that he took it upon these terms was amusing as well as touching. I do not know how to express that Miss Bentley contrived to eliminate herself from the affair, or to have the effect of doing that, and to abandon it to them. I can only say that she left them to be civil to each other, and that except when she recurred to them in playful sarcasm from time to time, she devoted herself to me.

Evidently, Mrs. Bentley was very much worse than she had been; her breathing was painfully labored. But if her daughter had any anxiety about her condition, she concealed it most effectually from us all. I decided that she had perhaps been asking the doctor as to certain symptoms that had alarmed her, and it was in the rebound from her anxiety that her spirits had risen to the height I saw. Glendenning seized the moment of her absence after luncheon, when she helped her mother up to her room, to impart to me that this was his conclusion too. He said that he had not seen her so cheerful for a long time, and when I praised her in every way, he basked in my appreciation of her as if it had all been flattery for himself. She came back directly, and then I had a chance to see what she might have been under happier stars. She could not, at any moment, help showing herself an intellectual and cultivated woman, but her opportunities to show herself a woman of rare social gifts had been scanted by circumstance and perhaps by conscience. It seemed to me that even in devoting herself to her mother as she had always done she need not have enslaved herself, and that it was in this excess her inherited puritanism came out. She might sometimes openly rebel against her mother's domination, as my wife and I had now and again seen her do; but inwardly she was almost passionately submissive. Here I thought that Glendenning, if he had been a different sort of man, might have been useful to her; he might have encouraged her in a little wholesome selfishness, and enabled her to withhold sacrifice where it was needless. But I am not sure; perhaps he would have made her more unhappy, if he had attempted this; perhaps he was the only sort of man whom, in her sense of his own utter unselfishness, she could have given her heart to in perfect peace. She now talked brilliantly and joyously to me, but all the time her eye sought his for his approval and sympathy; he for his part was content to listen in a sort of beatific pride in her which he did not, in his simple-hearted fondness, make any effort to mask.

When we came away, he made himself amends for his silence, by a long hymn in worship of her, and I listened with all the acquiescence possible. He asked me questions—whether I had noticed this thing or that about her, or remembered what she had said upon one point or another, and led up to compliments of her which I was glad to pay. In the long ordeal they had undergone they had at least kept all the young freshness of their love.

Glendenning and I went back to the rectory, and sat down in his study, or rather he made me draw a chair to the open door, and sat down himself on a step below the threshold. The day was one of autumnal warmth; the haze of Indian summer blued the still air, and the wind that now and then stirred the stiff panoply of the trees was lullingly soft. This part of Gormanville quite overlooked the busier district about the mills, where the water-power found its way, and it was something of a climb even from the business street of the old hill village, which the rival prosperity of the industrial settlement in the valley had thrown into an aristocratic aloofness. From the upper windows of the rectory one could have seen only the red and yellow of the maples, but from the study door we caught glimpses past their boles of the outlying country, as it showed between the white mansions across the way. One of these, as I have already mentioned, was the Conwell place, and after we had talked of the landscape awhile, Glendenning said: "By-the-way! Why don't you buy the Conwell place? You liked it so much, and you were all so well in Gormanville. The Conwells want to sell it, and it would

be just the thing for you, five or six months of the year!"

I explained, almost compassionately, the impossibility of a poor insurance man thinking of a summer residence like the Conwell place, and I combated as well as I could the optimistic reasons of my friend in its favor. I was not very severe with him, for I saw that his optimism was not so much from his wish to have me live in Gormanville as from the new hope that filled him. It was by a perfectly natural, if not very logical transition that we were presently talking of this greater interest again, and Glendenning was going over all the plans that it included. I encouraged him to believe, as he desired, that a sea-voyage would be the thing for Mrs. Bentley, and that it would be his duty to take her to Europe as soon as he was in authority to do so. They should always, he said, live in Gormanville, for they were greatly attached to the place, and they should keep up the old Bentley homestead in the style that he thought they owed to the region where the Bentleys had always lived. It is a comfort to a man to tell his dreams, whether of the night or of the day, and I enjoyed Glendenning's pleasure in rehearsing these fond reveries of his.

He interrupted himself to listen to the sound of hurried steps, and directly a man in his shirt sleeves came running by on the sidewalk beyond the maples. In a village like Gormanville any passer is of interest to the spectator, and a man running is of thrilling moment. Glendenning started to his feet, and moved forward for a better sight of the flying passer. He called out to the man, who shouted back something I could not understand, and ran on.

"What did he say?"

"I don't know." Glendenning's face as he turned to me again was quite white. "It is Mrs. Bentley's farmer," he added feebly, and I could see that it was with an effort he kept himself from sinking. "Something has happened."

"Oh, I guess not, or not anything serious," I answered, with an effort to throw off the weight I suddenly felt at my own heart. "People have been known to run for a plumber. But if you're anxious, let us go and see what the matter is."

I turned and got my hat; Glendenning came in for his, but seemed unable to find it, though he stood before the table where it lay. I could not help laughing, tho' I felt so little like it, as I put it in his hand.

"Don't leave me," he entreated, as we hurried out through the maples to the sidewalk. "It has come at last, and I feel, as I always knew I should, like a murderer."

"What rubbish!" I retorted. "You don't know that anything has happened. You don't know what the man's gone for."

"Yes, I do," he said. "Mrs. Bentley is— He's gone for the doctor."

As he spoke, a buggy came tearing down the street behind us; the doctor was in it, and the man in shirt sleeves beside him. We did not try to hail them, but as they whirled by the farmer put his face round, and again called something unintelligible to Glendenning.

We made what speed we could after them, but they were long out of sight in the mile that it seemed to me we were an hour in covering before we reached the Bentley place. The doctor's buggy stood at the gate, and I perceived that I was without authority to enter the house, on which some unknown calamity had fallen, no matter with what good-will I had come; I could see that Glendenning had suffered a sudden estrangement, also, which he had to make a struggle against. But he went in, leaving me without, as if he had forgotten me.

I could not go away, and I walked down the path to the gate, and waited there, in case I should be in any wise wanted. After a very long time the doctor came bolting over the walk towards me, as if he did not see me, but he brought himself up short with an "Oh!" before he actually struck against me. I had known him during our summer at the Conwell place, where we used to have him in for our little ailments, and I would never have believed that his round, optimistic face could look so worried. I read the worst in it; Glendenning was right; but I asked the doctor quite as if I did not know, whether there was anything serious the matter.

"Serious, yes," he said. "Get in with me; I have to see another patient, but I'll bring you back." We mounted into his buggy, and he went on. "She's in no immediate danger, now. The faint lasted so long I didn't know whether we should bring her out of it, at one time, but the most alarming part is over for

the present. There is some trouble with the heart, but I don't think anything organic."

"Yes, I heard you telling her daughter so, just before lunch. Isn't it a frequent complication with asthma?"

"Asthma? Her daughter? Whom are you talking about?"

"Mrs. Bentley. Isn't Mrs. Bentley—"

"No!" shouted the doctor, in disgust. "Mrs. Bentley is as well as ever. It's Miss Bentley. I wish there was a thousandth part of the chance for her that there is for her mother."

XI.

I staid over for the last train to Boston, and then I had to go home without the hope which Miss Bentley's first rally had given the doctor. My wife and I talked the affair over far into the night, and in the paucity of particulars I was almost driven to their invention. But I managed to keep a good conscience, and at the same time to satisfy the demand for facts in a measure by the indulgence of conjectures which Mrs. March continually mistook for them. The doctor had let fall, in his talk with me, that he had no doubt Miss Bentley had aggravated the affection of the heart from which she was suffering by her exertions in lifting her mother about so much; and my wife said that it needed only that touch to make the tragedy complete.

"Unless," I suggested, "you could add that her mother had just told her she would not oppose her marriage any longer, and it was the joy that brought on the access of the trouble that is killing her."

"Did the doctor say that?" Mrs. March demanded, severely.

"No. And I haven't the least notion that anything like it happened. But if it had—"

"It would have been too tawdry. I'm ashamed of you for thinking of such a thing, Basil."

Upon reflection, I was rather ashamed myself; but I plucked up courage to venture: "It would be rather fine, wouldn't it, when that poor girl is gone, if Mrs. Bentley had Glendenning come and live with her, and they devoted themselves to each other for her daughter's sake?"

"Fine! It would be ghastly. What are you thinking of, my dear? How would it be fine?"

"Oh, I mean dramatically," I apologized, and not to make bad worse, I said no more.

The next day, which was Sunday, a telegram came for me, which I decided without opening it, to be the announcement of the end. But it proved to be a message from Mrs. Bentley, begging in most urgent terms that Mrs. March and I would come to her at once, if possible. These terms left the widest latitude for surmise, but none for choice, in the sad circumstances, and we looked up the Sunday trains for Gormanville, and went.

We found the poor woman piteously grateful, but by no means so prostrated as we had expected. She was rather, as often happens, stayed and held upright by the burden that had been laid upon her, and it was with fortitude if not dignity that she appealed to us for our counsel, and if possible our help, in a matter about which she had already consulted the doctor. " The doctor says that the excitement cannot hurt Edith; it may even help her, to propose it. I should like to do it, but if you did not think well of it, I would not do it. I know it is too late now to make up to her for the past," said Mrs. Bentley, and here she gave way to the grief she had restrained hitherto.

"There is no one else," she went on, " who has been so intimately acquainted with the facts of my daughter's engagement—no one else that I can confide in or appeal to."

We both murmured that she was very good; but she put our politeness somewhat peremptorily aside.

"It is the only thing I can do now, and it is useless to do that now. It will be no reparation for the past, and it will be for myself and not for her, as all that I have done in the past has been; but I wish to know what you think of their getting married now."

I am afraid that if we had said what we thought of such a tardy and futile proof of penitence, we should have brought little comfort to the mother's heart. But we looked at each other in the disgust we both felt, and said there would be a sacred fitness in it.

She was apparently much consoled.

It was touching enough, and I at last was affected by her tears; I am not so sure my wife was. But she had instantly to consider how best to propose the matter to Miss Bentley, and to act upon her decision. After all, as she reported the

fact to me later, it was very simple to suggest her mother's wish to the girl, who listened to it with a perfect intelligence in which there was no bitterness.

"They think I am going to die," she said, quietly, "and I can understand how she feels. It seems such a mockery; but if she wishes it; and Arthur—"

It was my part to deal with Glendenning, and I did not find it so easy.

"Marriage is for life and for earth," he said, solemnly, and I thought very truly. "In the resurrection we shall be one another's without it. I don't like to go through the form of such a sacrament idly; it seems like a profanation of its mystery."

"But if Miss Bentley—"

"She will think whatever I do; I shall feel as she does," he answered, with dignity.

"Yes, I know," I urged. "It would not be for her; it would not certainly be for yourself. But if you could see it as the only form of reparation which her mother now can offer you both, and the only mode of expressing your own forgiveness— Recollect how you felt when you thought that it was Mrs. Bentley's death; try to recall something of that terrible time—"

"I don't forget that," he relented. "It was in mercy to Edith and me that our trial is what it is: we have recognized that in the face of eternity. I can forgive anything in gratitude for that."

I have often had to criticise life for a certain caprice with which she treats the elements of drama, and mars the finest conditions of tragedy with a touch of farce. No one who witnessed the marriage of Arthur Glendenning and Edith Bentley had any belief that she would survive it twenty-four hours; they themselves were wholly without hope in the moment which for happier lovers is all hope. To me it was like a funeral, but then most weddings are rather ghastly to look upon; and the stroke that life had in reserve perhaps finally restored the lost balance of gayety in this. At any rate, Mrs. Glendenning did live, and she is living yet, and in rather more happiness than comes to most people under brighter auspices. After long contention among many doctors, the original opinion that her heart trouble was functional, not organic, has been elected final, and upon these terms she bids fair to live as long as any of us.

I do not know whether she will live as long as her mother, who seems to have taken a fresh lease of years from her single act of self-sacrifice. I cannot say whether Mrs. Bentley feels herself deceived and defrauded by her daughter's recovery; but I have made my wife observe that it would be just like life if she bore the young couple a sort of grudge for unwittingly outwitting her. Certainly on the day we lately spent with them all at Gormanville, she seemed, in the slight attack of asthma from which she suffered, to come as heavily and exactingly upon both as she used to come upon her daughter alone. But I was glad to see that Glendenning eagerly bore the greater part of the common burden. He grows stouter and stouter, and will soon be the figure of a bishop.

HOPSON'S CHOICE   *by Rose Terry Cooke*

"SAY, Josiah, let's get up a fam'ly gatherin', same as other folks do."

"I'd like to see a Hopson gatherin'! Folks would say 'twas an ant-hill on a bender, Ozias. We're all too little. 'Twon't do to make our short-comin's public, as you may say."

"Well, I'd ruther be little and good than be an Irish giant. I don't never hanker after betweenness. It goes quite a ways to be somethin' nobody else is. Now there's them Schuylers, the grandees over to Newton. They do say—and I guess it's so—that they're always a-talkin' pompious about the 'Schuyler nub,' a kind of a bunion like that grows on to the outside of their hands. Why, they think the world on't, because the Schuylers all hev hed it as long as the memory of man endureth not to the con*trary*. I'd jest as lives be little as have a nub."

"Do tell! Well, Ozy, folks is folksy, ain't they? Come to think on't, there's a tribe over to Still River they call the Sandy Steeles, all of 'em red-heads. It's pop'lar to call 'em sandy, but you could warm your hands real well, the coldest day in winter, to any crop amongst 'em. Carrots a'n't nowhere; it's coals."

"Anyhow, 'Siah, if we are little, we're spry, and that's half the battle. Moreover, there haven't none of us been hanged, nor put into States-prison, nor yet see the inside of no jail."

"Not yet," said Josiah.

Ozias turned and looked at him with a twinkle in his deep-set eye.

"Expectin' on't, be ye?"

Josiah laughed.

"I don't know as I be; but life's chockfull of onexpectedness. There! there's the meetin' bell. Come over to-night, will ye, after sundown. We'll talk this here matter over deliberate then. The idee kinder takes hold of me."

"Yes, I'll drop in. 'Mandy 'll be real willin' to get rid of me for a spell. Ye see, Obed's first wife's boy's to home, and it seems as though he was a-thinkin' about sparkin' my girl. I don't know. It's pecooliar, anyway, how quick girls gets to be women-folks. I never see the beat on't. 'Tis snip, snap, so to speak. Makes me think of Priest Hawes's favoright hymn, or one line on't, that he used to come down on real sollum:

"'The creturs—look, how old they grow!'"

"Hope you don't foller that kotation out entire," said Josiah, "next line bein',

"'And wait their fiery doom.'"

Ozias looked at him with a face of the demurest fun.

"Come along," he said. "'Mandy's feller ain't one of the Still River Steeles."

Josiah tried to solemnize his face, but barely succeeded, as they entered the church door.

Hop Meadow was a little village in one of our New England States, lying in a tiny green valley shut in by low rolling hills, patched here and there with yellow grain fields, squares of waving grass, or crimson clover fragrant as the breath of Eden; and threaded by a big noisy brook that pursued its joyful way to the great river rolling but a mile or two beyond the valley, yet quite out of sight of its inhabitants. In this fertile and sunny spot, when New England was first settled, Andrew Hopson, yeoman, from Kent, Old England, had staked out his share of land, and built his hut; he had married, shortly after, his second cousin, and in due time a goodly family of ten children gathered about them. Cousins, too, came over and settled beside Andrew, and more distant relatives were gradually persuaded to find homes in the new country; so, partly for the sake of the numerous Hopsons, and partly in memory of the goodly Kentish hop fields which they hoped one day to emulate, the village was called Hop Meadow. It was a peculiarity of the Hopson family that almost without exception its members were small in body. Not a man, for years after their emigration, as for unknown years before it, reached a height of over five feet two; most of them ignored the inches; and here and there a real dwarf carried the family specialty to excess.

But if nature had given them little bodily presence, they all had keen wits, humor, good temper, and good principles—except exceptions.

Josiah and Ozias were Hopsons by name, but there were Browns among the cousinry, and here and there a Hopson girl had married "outside," and brought her tall husband home to Thanksgiving occasionally, half proud and half ashamed of him. There was a tradition in the family that the first Hopson, that Andrew who put up his log hut in the sunny intervale beside Bright Brook, had left Old England quite as much from pique as principle. He had become a Puritan, no doubt from deep conviction, but there was only the parish church for him to worship in, and the old rector was a stanch adherent of Church and King. When Parson Vivyan heard of the emigrating seceders of Leyden he felt afraid that Andrew Hopson might cast in his lot with those fanatics; and having a kindly feeling for the small yeoman, whom he had christened, and hoped to marry, he exhorted him in season and out of season on the folly of such rebellion against King and Church. Andrew resented the interference, for he had neither thought nor talked of leaving his goodly farm; and he grew tired, too, of the parson's one theme of conversation; so he evaded him everywhere, and showed all the quick wit of his race in those evasions; like a drop of mercury he departed from under Mr. Vivyan's touch and was off; so that worthy man took unworthy advantage of his position and preached a long sermon on the text, "The conies are a feeble folk, and dwell in the clefts of the rock," in which discourse he took occasion to set out with humiliating detail what would naturally be the fate of a poor little creature like the cony if it forsook its home and friends in the rocks that sheltered it, and went out to wandering and strife with wolves and foxes.

The natural history was correct, but the application was so pointed, when Parson Vivyan drew out at length the analogy, and portrayed the fate of the man unfitted by nature for wars and hardships who should leave his neighbors and his native land for the sake of a misguided and heretical opinion, that not even the proverbial good-nature of the Hopsons could abide it.

Andrew took fire at once. He made immediate preparation to sell his farm—a hereditary freehold—and having obtained Prudence's consent to follow him when he should have a home prepared for her, he gathered his household goods together and set sail for the New World, where, as he expressed himself to Parson Vivyan, "there be no prelatical priests to vex the soul, nor yet the ungodly kingdom of a carnal king."

That Sunday evening on which our story opens, a bright June moon-lit night,

Ozias, avoiding the youth who came slowly and slyly to the front door, which stood hospitably open, with evident intent of "sparking," betook himself to Josiah's house, and perfected the plan for a Hopson reunion.

There were many letters to write, for the tribe had branched far, if sparsely. There were two Browns in Ohio and three Hopsons in Illinois, and then three generations ago a certain Mark Hopson had settled on a stony piece of land in Vermont, to dig and sell iron, and called the village which sprung up about his furnace Hopyard; but so unfit was the name when that cleft in the hills became strewed with slag heaps, and overshadowed with black smoke, that a scoffing stranger had said in the tavern one night, "Better call it the Devil's Hopyard, I should say." This ill name had fastened itself firmly on the little cluster of houses, and though the Hopsons themselves swarmed therein, and looked like a troop of gnomes whenever there was a run of iron, and they skipped about the moulding beds in the lurid firelight, yet outsiders were shy of settling there, and told quaint stories of the tiny tribe who occupied the land, and delved, smelted, and hauled pig-iron with an energy that seemed to make up for strength.

It was currently reported that in the early days of the Devil's Hopyard a tin-peddler from "below" stumbled on this small village, and trying to catch some of the little people for purposes of exhibition, chased a dozen of them into the bung-hole of an empty barrel, and triumphantly proceeded to stop up the aperture and secure his prize; but while he pounded at the bung the agile creatures made their escape through the spigot-hole, and derided him with shrill laughter and mocking gestures from the top of a barn, whither they had climbed on a wild grape-vine. Peddler or not, there was plenty of Hopsons there now; and then there was Pamela Bunnell in remote parts of Iowa, who had married out of the clan; and Ozias Brown, who had settled in Pennsylvania; and Marinus Hopson, on Cape Cod; and Tertius Hopson, in Quebec; and more, whom time forbids me to chronicle, but who all received an invitation to this Hopson gathering; and almost all meant to come.

Then began a stir in Hop Meadow. There was a big tent to be hired and pitched on the green—an even bit of turf with

some fine elms about it, right in front of
the church—and there were spare rooms
to clean and dust; and the whole tavern
was engaged to afford lodgings if private
rooms overflowed; and such baking, boiling, stewing, frying, and other culinary
performances set in that one would have
thought the ten lost tribes of Israel, all in a
famished condition, were coming for a
month's stay, and needed unlimited pie,
cake, poultry, and pickles — except that
there were hams, boiled, roasted, and
chopped or sliced for sandwiches, promi-
nent in every house, and hams are pork!
In all these preparations nobody was more
busied than Prudence Hopson, Widow
Polly Hopson's daughter and only child.
Bezaleel Hopson, her father, had kept the
"store" in Hop Meadow forty years, when
he died, and having married late in life,
left behind him this little five-year-old
daughter, and plenty of "means" to console his wailing widow, who was an "outsider," and perhaps attracted her fat and
jolly husband by her extreme difference
from any of his kindred.

Paulina Flower had been pretty in a
certain way: long curling yellow hair,
limp and flabby even in its trailing ringlets, languishing blue eyes, a white skin,
narrow, low forehead, and long chin seemed to express and adorn her manners and
customs with peculiar fitness.

Nobody but the Hopsons would ever
have called her Polly; to "her folks" she
was "Pawliny," nothing less; but Bezaleel couldn't stand three syllables, so he
had followed the custom of his race, and
tried to make the best of his wife's melancholy while he lived.

"She beats all," said Ozias to Josiah,
his cousin and special crony. "I never
see a woman who likes to howl so well in
my life; she's forever a-spillin' salt-water.
She'd oughter keep clus to a pork barrel,
so's to save brine. I b'lieve she'd set down
an' cry to the heavenly gates, ef ever she
got there, to think the' wa'n't a fiery chari't
sent down to fetch her."

"Well," answered the more slow-mind-
ed Josiah, "some folks is made so; nothin'
suits 'em, never. Their eggs gets addled
second day out, and if they haven't really
got a thing to cry for, they'll do it a-pup-
pus. She's one o' them that likes to cry
jest as well as you do to larf, Ozy. It a'n't
real comfortin' to other folks to see 'em,
and I will say I've hankered some to give
Polly a hidin'; 'twould do her solid good

ter have somethin' real to cry for. But
you can't tune another man's wife nohow."

"That's so," sadly responded Ozias.

But Prudence—"little Prudy," as everybody called her, borrowing her title from
the most utterly delightful children's
books ever written—was a thorough Hopson.

When her father died she was but five
years old, and though she mourned him
heartily and sincerely, it was as children
mourn, with brief tears and tender remembrance, but a blessed incompetence of understanding what loss, death, separation,
really mean. She saw her mother no more,
if no less, tearful; she could not be more
doleful and forlorn under any loss than
she had been in the daily fashion of her
life; and Prudy was as different from Polly as was possible—a gay, sparkling, happy creature, everybody's pet and darling.
If she had lost one father, she had twenty
uncles and cousins ready to protect and
indulge her, and she grew up to woman-
hood as nearly spoiled as her sweet, honest
nature would allow. But who ever was
proof against those beautiful brown eyes,
red and saucy lips, that tossing, wavy,
shining hair, never in order, but never
anything but exquisite in its dark shadows and golden lights?

Who could resist that coaxing, caressing, beguiling voice—that voice that could
soften with pity and sparkle with mischief?
Who did not clamor for the help of those
deft and taper fingers that were always
ready and able to do whatever was asked of
them? It was Prudy who came to the front
now in all the adornments of preparation.
She made the long wreaths of ground pine
and coral pine for festooning the tent and
the church, and fastened them up under knots of golden-rod and bosses of purple aster, for the Hopson gathering was
early in September. She arranged the
baskets of fruit that adorned the table, so
that pink and purple and amber grapes
lay heaped together on vine leaves, and
the profusion of green and gold pears
was set off with the earliest scarlet foliage of the maple and deep maroon of lingering beet leaves.

She made the wonderful ornaments of
stars and roses and architectural devices
that would have adorned the countless
pies had not the oven baked them out of
all shape. And it was Prudy who manu-
factured the whitest silver cake and the

clearest jelly that made contrast of ivory and ruby beside the grosser aliments of cold ham and roast turkey.

Her mother looked on and shook her melancholy head when Prudy dragged that unwilling parent to see what had been done.

"Yes, I dare say; it's pretty, I suppose. But, oh, I can't help a-mournin' to think how that your pa would ha' relished it. This world's a fleetin' show, Prudence. Ef you'd ha' ben through what I have you wouldn't take no great of int'rest in these triflin' things."

Prudy laughed; her father had been dead a thousand years—to her; and her mother's melancholy moans had no more significance to her than the wind in the spout.

"Well, mammy, they're pretty, anyway, and I expect most of these things will be a fleetin' show when a crowd of hungry Hopsons get hold of 'em. Who's coming to our house to stay?—do you know yet?"

"I should ha' liked to have Pamely Bunnell and her boy, but she was bespoke by Ozias's folks. I used to know her some before I was married, for she married Bunnell when he lived to our place, and while she lived here a spell I come here to visit, and then I see your pa. Oh, I remember of it well, the fust time I see him; 'twas to a meetin' of the sons an' daughters of Massachusetts. Josiah he'd put it in the paper that 'all who are or were born in Massachusetts is expected to attend th' annooal meetin' in Clark Hall.' You see, Josiah's wife come from Hingham; and well do I rec'lect he got up that evenin' and said the 'highest "gaol" of his ambition hed always been to marry a Massachusetts girl.' Some didn't really understand what he meant, but Pamely she said he'd got the wrong word; Josiah's a little mixy, always an' forever was and will be; and your pa he bu'st out laughin' behind me, and I looked round and see him. He hadn't no business there, only 't he provided the provisions, and he'd jest fetched in a pot of pickles 't somebody 'd forgot, and— Oh! I've kinder run off from Pamely. Well, I can't hev her: she writ to Ozias for to have her place in his house. I s'pose 'tis more cherk up there than 'tis to a solitary widder's like me. One that's seen so much 'fliction and is so cast down into the valley of mournin' as I be a'n't

good company. And jest my luck!—me that never could abide children—they've sent Marinus's people to us—seven small children, and she's weakly. Oh land! how be I to bear it?"

Prudy laughed again; she couldn't help it; the idea of seven children secretly delighted her sunshiny soul. What romps they would have! What corn-poppings! —she would rub up the old warming-pan to-day; and there were five kittens in the barn!

Polly did not betray her own secret hopes to her daughter. Like many languid, selfish, sloppy, mournful people, she had a certain cunning or slyness, which tended to amuse her—and sometimes other people—when it did not vex them! She had purposely delayed asking Pamela Bunnell, who was a widow with one son, to her house, lest the son should take a fancy to Prudy.

Mrs. Polly did not intend to lose her girl if she could help it: no servant could or would so neatly curl her lank ringlets, that, threaded with the gray of forty-nine years, still dropped absurdly down her back; nor would any other woman wait on her so handily and cheerfully on the frequent days when she chose to keep her bed, and must be fed with the daintiest morsels that Prudy knew just how to prepare.

To be sure, Hopson Bunnell, Pamela's boy, was "well spoke of" by such of the clan as had heard of him, and had some property of his own, besides a reversion of the great prairie farm his mother superintended with all the energy and skill a bigger woman could have brought to bear on the premises; but for all this Mrs. Polly cared nothing. Her listless self-absorption would have come between Prudy and the best match possible, so she had never asked Pamela—who expected it of her—to come to her house, but had gently hinted to the Reception Committee of the occasion that she could take a large family if they were mostly children, and could be crowded two or three in a chamber. Prudy had her own intimate friend, of course, in the village, for though there were but few young girls in Hop Meadow, the Hopsons having a way of marrying young, there were a few, and Lizzy Brown was the best and prettiest, next to Prudy—a sober, steady, discreet maiden, with brown hair and blue eyes, who looked at Prudence as a robin might at an oriole, but did not treat her at all as the one bird treats the other, but held her in all adoration, and served her with earnest affection.

At last the day of the Hopson reunion arrived—one of those soft, golden, gorgeous days in autumn when the air is quiet, the heavens serene, and the earth steeped in dreams and rainbows; but the Hopsons were not still; not at all. They swarmed like troops of good-sized fairies through the wide streets, laughing, shaking hands, chattering, singing, full of welcome and cheer—slight, airy girls; rounder but still tidy matrons, with dolls of babies in their arms; fat little men, laughing and joking with every new-comer—the only woful face being Mrs. Polly's; while Prudy, in the daintiest white gown, with a big bunch of red late roses at her belt, was threading the crowd everywhere, marshalling the guests to their several lodgings, smiling at every child, coquetting with every old man, and turning a bewitching cold shoulder on the youths who buzzed about her like contending bumble-bees on a Canada thistle, prickliest and most delicate of its tribe.

But one of the race, Pamela's boy, towered far above the rest, to his own disgust and their amusement. Hopson Bunnell was all of six feet in his stockings, powerful, athletic, and handsome, with dark keen eyes, firm lips, a shock of deep brown curls, and a silky beard of darkness that showed well against the cool healthiness of his smooth if sunburned skin.

"I know he's awful tall," said Pamela, deprecatingly, to Ozias, "and I've set my heart on his marryin' one of our folks. Seems as though Providence interfered serious with my plans. The' ain't no girls anywhere near to us, and them that's nearest, Hopson don't seem to fellowship; but I never seemed to sense his tallness as I do now, 'mongst the rest of us."

"Well," answered Ozias, "'tain't always best to make no great of plans about folks's marryin'; they gener'lly do as they darn please about that, I've observed. Providence hes got sever'al other things to do, I guess, than makin' matches. I'm a free-will Baptist, so fur as that comes in, now I tell ye."

"Oh my!" exclaimed Pamela. "I don't expect to settle nothing, nor I haven't said a word to Hopson, you better believe. I was only speakin' of it to you, Ozy, out of the fullness of my heart, as you may say, accordin' to Scripter."

"Well, I sha'n't tell; and 'tain't best to put a finger into sech pies. Natur is pecooliar, Pamely; you can't never tell how it'll work; so I calc'late always to leave out the bung for fear of a bu'st. There's my 'Mandy, now. Mariar bein' dead ever sence the girl was ten year old, I've been consider'ble pestered what to do with her; but fin'lly I concluded to see 't she read the Bible right along and said her prayers punctooal, and then I let her went. She had her ups an' downs, but she's come up about as good as the average; and now she's got to keepin' company with a pretty clever feller, and she'll be off my mind afore long."

Hopson Bunnell, all unconscious of his mother's wish in his behalf, was meantime enjoying himself mightily; he recovered from his awkwardness very fast, turning the laugh on his kindred in various ways, and dangling after Prudy like an amiable giant in the toils of a fairy queen. She seemed to this tall, handsome fellow something daintier than a flower, and more bewitching than a bird; he never tired of seeing that graceful little figure waiting on the tables, coaxing the old men with dainty morsels, filling the boys with good things, hollow though they were "down to their boots," as she declared, being unused to boys; or playing with the little girls, who all adored her. But to Hopson himself Prudy was the most malicious elf! Nobody teased him as she did; nobody could.

"Cousin Hopson," she said to him, the day after the feast—for though almost all the rest had gone, a few of the more distant remained to extend a visit they had come so far to make—"Cousin Hopson, will you please to do something for me?"

"I guess I will," alertly answered Hopson, bewitched with the sweet, shy voice.

"Just hand me down one of them stars to put in my hair, will you?" and Prudy vanished with a peal of mocking mirth, echoed by a cackle of fat laughter from Tertius Hopson, the Quebec cousin, a very jolly, rosy, stout old bachelor, looking for all the world like a Sir Toby jug.

"She beats all," said Tertius. "I never see a hum-bird fuller o' buzz than little Prudy."

Hopson bit his lips. "I'll be even with her," he said to himself; so that very evening, as some of the clan gathered round a tiny open fire in Ozias's kitchen, rather for companionship than cold, the young farmer said to Prudy: "You oughter to be put to use, Prudy. I'd like to buy ye up for a mantel-shelf figure; you're just big enough."

"I a'n't for sale," snapped Prudy.

"Why, you'd do first-rate; them things are all the go, and you're the exact size."

So saying, he stooped, and before Prudy knew what had happened, two strong hands grasped her tiny waist, and she was swung up like a feather by those mighty arms, and set on the broad oaken shelf among the flat-irons, candlesticks, and other miscellaneous articles thereon; while Hopson, retreating a step, looked her in the face, and a roar of laughter from Tertius, Ozias, 'Mandy, Josiah, and the rest completed her discomfiture. Prudy colored scarlet, her eyes flashed, and one little fist clinched instinctively; the other hand held fast to the shelf.

"Cousin 'Zias, take me down," she called out, imperatively.

"Bless your soul, Prudy! I ain't big enough."

"Get a chair."

"Why, folks is settin' on 'em, every one," and Ozias looked round with an air of innocent dismay that renewed the laughter.

"I'll take ye down, Prudy, if you'll say 'please,' like a good baby," calmly remarked Hopson.

Prudy choked. "I'll stay here all night first," she snapped.

"Well, 'tis jest as I said now. You do make about as good-lookin' a figure for a mantel as ever was."

"Take me down!" shrieked Prudy.

But oh, how pretty she was up there! Dresden could not match with her costliest figurines the delicate creature in her china-blue gown (a sudden chill having come after the September heats had made woollen garments comfortable), falling in soft dim folds just to the smallest shoes that ever a Hopson even could wear, her white throat set off by carnation ribbons under the lace frill, and another bow of that tender, vivid color in her waving, shining hair, her eyes sparkling, her red lips apart, and her cheeks rosier than her ribbons. Hopson Bunnell could have looked at her forever, but he did not say so. "Say 'please' now—real pretty," was all he did say, unconsciously drawing nearer to the lovely little creature.

Prudy was quick-witted; she controlled her rage a moment. "W-e-ll"—reluctantly—"I don' know but I'd whisper it, rather'n stay up here all night."

Luckless man! He drew near to catch the precious whisper, but as he turned his ear, Prudy's hand descended on his brown cheek with a resounding slap that left a print of five little fingers impressed thereon visibly for at least an hour; but, alas! in avenging herself Prudy lost her balance, and Hopson caught her fairly in his arms, and kissed the lovely, indignant face before he really knew what he was doing.

"'A kiss for a blow, always bestow,'" cackled Tertius. And everybody roared again, except Prudy, who dropped to the floor, burst into tears, and fled.

Hopson was really ashamed of himself, but it did seem to him as if his head whirled; a sense of wild bliss ran in all his veins; he knew well that he had taken an unfair advantage of Prudy, but so reckless was his delight that he was not a bit repentant.

However, he had to repent next day. Prudy turned into a perfect snow-ball whenever he came near her. It took a week of abasement and apologies to put them on the old footing (externally) again. Could he tell, poor fellow, being only a man, how Prudy secretly exulted in the apology she professed to despise?—i. e., "You were so sweet and so pretty, I couldn't help it, Prudy."

How was he to know that these words rung in her ears like a song of joy day and night, or that in the once still depths of her heart Prudy recognized a sweet perturbation that dated from the second she was held in those powerful arms, close against a manly, throbbing heart?

But nobody could be cross in this clear autumnal weather, with gay leaves beginning to illuminate the woods, daily parties to hunt for gentian blossoms, to gather "wintergreen plums," to heap up red and golden apples under the orchard boughs, or clamber after fragrant wild grapes on the hill-sides. Hopson grew deeper in love with every new day, and Prudy fought more feebly against the chains that seemed daily to imprison her will and her thoughts. Perhaps the course of true love might for once have run smooth but for that unruly member that spoils most of our plans in this world, and brings to naught the best intentions and the sincerest good-will. Tertius Hopson still lingered in Hop Meadow, as well as Pamela Bunnell and her son. Tertius was living in Quebec "on his means," as we Yankees phrase it. He had made some money there in trade, and settled down to enjoy it in a sort of selfish fashion that was not natural to his jolly, kindly disposition.

He had never known how close and pleasant are the ties of kindred till now; he seemed at last to have got home; here was the stir, the interest, the sweetness of a daily intercourse hitherto denied him, and it seemed to warm and rejuvenate his life, to quicken his pulses, to brighten his ideas; he loved it; he could not tear himself away; and above all things he loved to "bother" Polly Hopson. Whenever she sighed, he smiled, broad and beaming as the harvest-moon; whenever she bewailed herself, he laughed; when she wept, as now and then she did weep over the departed Bezaleel, he would deliberately sit down and sing to her all the queer old songs he had learned in the "old country," as he persisted in calling Quebec, till the Meadow boys learned by heart "The Leather Bottell," "The British Grenadiers," "Hunting the Hare," "Lasses and Lads," and sundry other rollicking ditties which once delighted the ears of our forefathers across the water, and have in them still a ringing, hearty smack of country squiredom and rural sports. At first Polly was outraged; her chin fell half an inch, and her curls frayed out of curliness with the solemn shakes of her head and the dampness of her tears; but she endured from helplessness, and began at last to smile wintrily and forbearingly on the unconquerable jollity of the man whom at first she mildly contemned. It threatened to be the old story of "first endure, then pity, then embrace"; and, as usual, outsiders saw most of the game.

Ozias and Josiah, after their custom, sat in conclave upon the matter. They had just set the cider mill going, which they owned in common, and perched themselves on a cart neap, where they could "chirk up the hoss," which revolved with the beam of the press, and yet indulge in that gossip which delighted their souls, combining business with pleasure.

"Say," began Josiah, "haven't you sorter surmised, Ozy, that Tertius favors Hop Meadow for a residin'-place, so to speak?"

"Well, I hev," Ozias answered, "and I shouldn't be no more'n surprised ef that

he settled down here after a spell; he's lonesome up to Quebec, I expect. There arn't nothin' like your own folks, after all, when you're gettin' along in years; the' don't nobody else sorter seem to belong t' ye."

"It does make a sight of difference," replied the moralizing Josiah. "When one's young, and havin' their monsterious days, it don't make no great of difference where they be, nor what they're a-doin' of; but come to git rheumatiz onto a feller, and hev the grinders cease because they are few, as Scripter tells, why, you begin to be everlastin' thankful that there's a house 'n' home for ye, and a woman to cook your vittles."

"That's so, Josh, and that's why I'm a-goin' to hev 'Mandy and her feller settle down along with me when they get married. She'll hev the farm when

'The end o' my nose
An' the tips o' my toes
Is turned up to the roots of the daisies,'

as the song-book says; and she might as well stop to hum and look after me as to go further and fare worse. But seems to me kinder as if Tertius was slyin' round Polly, if you'll b'lieve it."

"Heavens to Betsey!" gasped Josiah. "That old feller?"

"Well, I never see the time, Josh, 't a man was too old to git married—nor a woman nuther, for that matter. It's everlastin' queer, surely, for him to take a likin' to Polly. I'd as lieves hang on to a wet dish-rag as her, when all's said an' done, but 'many men of many minds,' as the sayin' goes, and if she's to his'n, why, I don't make nor meddle with 'em. She's got a good place for to take him into."

"Yes; that's suthin. He's got means, I s'pose, but it's kind o' lonesome to live the way he does up to Quebec, a-lodgin', as he calls it, and to be took down with the sarcastic rheumatiz as he was, an'—"

"Land sakes! what's that?" asked Ozias.

"Well, I don't reelly know; I b'lieve it's principally confined to one leg, an' starts pretty high up, but that's what he called it, anyway; mabbe 'tis the English name on't; but it's real severe, now I tell ye; he said it made him holler like a loon."

"Polly can cry for somethin' then," dryly remarked Ozias.

"And I sorter surmise, Ozy, that Pamely's boy is a-hankerin' after little Prudy."

"Well, I've had my idees sot that way too. He's a clever feller as ever was; but I should hate to lose little Prudy. Darn the cretur! a'n't there nobody else to Hop Meadow he could set his eyes onto but her?"

"I'd like to know who else," answered Josiah. "'Mandy's spoke for, as well you know; and I have heered lately that Lizzy Brown is promised to Marinus's nevy down to Cape Cod; he's mate to a three-master, so they tell, and is off on a voyage jest now, so they don't talk on't, but it's so. Marinus has kep' his mouth shut. He's a kind of a dumb, oyster cretur." (Poor "mixy" Josiah meant "austere.")

"Nat'ral for him to keep his mouth shut," put in Ozias; "they gener'lly do."

Josiah stared, but serenely went on. "But he did allow 'twas so to Aunt Nancy, an' she up an' told my wife, so ye see the' ain't reelly nobody but little Prudy to hev."

"Hobson's choice for him, ain't it? Hullo, young feller! Speak of a donkey 'n' you see an ear direct;" for here Hopson Bunnell stalked into the cider-mill shed, his handsome face warm with exercise, and his eyes softened and deepened by his unspoken thoughts.

"We was just a-talkin' about you," explained Josiah.

"And Cousin 'Zias had to call me a donkey. Now is that friendly?" laughed Pamela's boy.

"There's worse critters than donkeys," blandly answered Ozias; "but I was only a-usin' the term proverbially, as it were, or was, or might be. Fact is, my eyes is gettin' open to your designs, sir, and I was kind of dammin' in a genteel way about your carryin' off little Prudy to Iowy, when she's the one we all set by like our eyes, and I was askin', in a general manner, ef there wasn't no other Hopson girl you could have took up with besides her; and Josiah said the' wa'n't; the rest was all bespoke; an' I said 'twas Hobson's choice with ye."

Pamely's boy flushed to his dark curls, his head was lifted as if some proud delight lay on a height that he could see, but no other, and his voice rang out in subdued yet clear cadence as he answered:

"There isn't another girl, outside of Hop Meadow neither, Ozias; there ain't in the world. There's nobody for me but little Prudy. You was right one way; she's Hopson's choice, and no other."

Unlucky mother-tongue! why are *b* and *p* so near alike in our queer old language that the distinction between them is almost inexpressible by human lips? As luck would have it, Prudy and Lizzy Brown had privately stolen up to the cider press, thinking it deserted, to indulge in the surreptitious but dear delight of sucking sweet new cider through a straw. They were old and demure enough to be ashamed of the trick if any one saw them, but the rich fruity beverage was delicious to their girlish memories, and slyly they stole out to indulge in the tipple, carrying gold-bright straws in their hands, and came up behind the shed just in time to hear Hopson's declaration.

Prudy's face flamed, the tender visions that had dwelt in her dumb heart and softened her cool brown eyes were struck by the lurid light of sudden fury, and fled away: she grasped Lizzy's arm with a vise-like grip.

"Come right away," she whispered; and fleet as a silent pair of goblins they left the green yard where the shed stood, and disappeared down a narrow lane that led to Josiah's barn.

Prudy rushed into that friendly shelter, banged the door behind her, relaxed her hold of Lizzy, and sitting down promptly on a wheelbarrow, cried with rage.

"Why, Prudy," said the gentle Elizabeth, "what in the world's the matter?"

"Didn't you he-he-hear him?—the awful, horrid, mean thing," sobbed Prudy.

"Hear who, dear?"

"Why, that great, horrid Hopson Bunnell. Didn't you hear him—I'm sure he spoke out loud enough—say that he'd got to marry me: 'twas Hobson's choice and no other?"

Prudy did extend the facts a little, it is true; she didn't mean to l—extend them, but she gave the idea as she took it in, just as the rest of us poor mortals do, without a thought that any other construction than her own could be put upon the words, or that she had confounded those confounded letters—forgive the phrase, dear reader; they continually exasperate me—*b* and *p*.

"No, I didn't hear him," condoled Lizzy. "Poor dear Prudy, did he say such a mean thing? Well, never mind, dear, that don't make it so; you know you haven't got to take him. You don't like him."

Prudy reared her dishevelled little head from the side of the wheelbarrow, like a snake about to strike.

"You goose!" she said. "I *do* like him. Oh dear! oh dear! Lizzy Brown, I'll kill you if you ever tell. But I do. I can't help it, and, oh!—and—and I thought he liked me first, or I never—oh!—oh!—"

Here a flood of tears literally drowned her voice, and in Lizzy's soft eyes tears shone with sympathetic brightness. She sat down by Prudy, and began to sob too.

"And he—oh, Liz!—he kissed me once, and now he says 'twas Hobson's choice. I'd just like to shoot him."

Prudy started suddenly, and the wheelbarrow, overloaded with grief and girls, as suddenly tipped over, leaving girls and grief in a heap on the barn floor. This was too much for Prudy. Blinded with hay seed, damp with tears, choked with hysteric laughter, it was a good hour before Lizzy could calm her or restore her to her proper aspect, and make her consent to go home quietly, though with burning vengeance in her heart.

Poor Hopson! the world was hollow now, and his doll stuffed with bran. If he didn't want to go into a convent, he did want to go back to Iowa, and yet Prudy controlled him like a Fate, and kept him miserable, abject, and longing in Hop Meadow, growing thin, pale, and silent, after the approved hang-dog fashion of unhappy lovers who are tacitly allowed to flaunt their wretchedness all abroad—probably because it is so transitory.

Polly sighed and wept; Tertius laughed and sung more than ever. Changeful as the aptest specimen of her sex, she now earnestly desired that Prudy should marry and leave her to Tertius, for Polly had at last consented to try another Hopson—"try" in more senses than one—and much she feared that Prudy would send "Pamely's boy" home in despair.

Pamela, too, was distressed to the heart with her boy's misery. She dared not try to console him, for on her feeblest attempt to break the ice he would turn on his heel and leave her. At last she brought her trouble to Ozias, with whom she had been brought up, and whom she regarded as a brother.

"Say, Ozy, what *do* you suppose ails Hopson? He don't never eat a meal of vittles; jest picks a mouthful, as you may see, not enough for a chippin'-bird. And he's a-grievin' in'ardly the whole time: I know he is, for he don't sleep nights, and he a'n't no fatter'n a hen's forehead. He's wastin' away, dyin' by inches, I do believe."

"Well, Pamely, he'll be quite a spell dyin', then, if that's a comfort to ye: there's consider'ble many inches *to* Hopson."

"Oh-zias, I b'lieve you'd laugh ef I was a-dyin'!" indignantly snapped Pamela.

"Mabbe I should. I don't love to cry before folks; but really now, Pamely, I b'lieve what ails Hopson is that little witch of a Prudy; he's most amazin' sot on her, and she won't so much as look at him. I'm free to confess I thought she liked him for a spell; but, Lord! what can a feller find out about women-folks? They're spryer, an' cuter, an' sinfuler, an' more pernickity 'n a fire-hang-bird! I don't see into it."

"Oh dear! what shall I do?" sighed Pamela, despairingly.

"Don't do nothin'! I'll see to it. It's one of them cases where somebody's got to speak in meetin', an' when there's a woman to pay, it's a sight better to ketch a-holt of her with a strong hand, same as I used ter squeeze grasshoppers when I was a boy, and hold her still till she tells. I'll tackle Miss Prudy myself, for the thing's got to be did: this hangin' on by the eyelids ain't nateral nor pleasin'. You keep still." Pamela was used to the masterful ways of Ozias, so she took to her rocker and her knitting, wiped a few mild tears from her kind old eyes, and waited for events.

Ozias, well aware of Prudy's haunts, followed the path by the side of Bright Brook down to a cluster of shag-bark walnut-trees on a meadow that belonged to Bezaleel's farm; he knew she had gone there nutting, and meeting the doleful Hopson on his way, remarked, curtly, "Young feller, I want you should happen down this road in twenty minutes: don't make it longer."

Hopson stared.

"Come, now; do as I tell you: you'll be glad on't."

"I'll come if you want me," was the listless answer.

Ozias found Prudy doing anything but nutting; her basket was on the ground empty, all about her lay husks and nuts that the keen wind of November had thrown down, but she left them to lie there. Her shawl was drawn over her head, her head leaned against a mighty tree, and she was crying fast and silently, when Ozias jumped over the fence. She tried to tie on her hat, but Ozias sat down beside her and took her two hands fast in his.

"Prudy," he said, "I've got a word to say to ye: why on the face of the airth *air* you treatin' Pamely's boy the way you be?"

"I ain't," said Prudy, irrelevantly and femininely.

Ozias went on, regardless of her futile remark: "He's a-actin' like a born fool, jest because you won't not so much as look at him. He thinks the sun rises an' sets in your face, an'—"

"He don't either," broke in Prudy, "an' you know he don't."

"I know he does. He don't nyther eat nor sleep for thinkin' of ye. The great, strong, hulkin' feller acts like a sick chicken. Now what's to pay?"

"Hm?" sniffed Prudy, her color rising and her eyes flashing. "I guess he's found out I ain't Hobson's choice for him, not noway."

"Whew!" whistled Ozias. "Who told you he thought you was?"

"Nobody. I heard him say so—and you was sittin' by and heard him too—in the cider-mill shed, that time—"

"Well, if ever I did!" and Ozias laughed till the woods about them rang again. Prudy grew furious. Ozias stopped when he heard her angry sobs, and called out,

"Hopson Bunnell, step over that air five-rail fence, and come here."

Prudy struggled to escape, but Ozias held her tight. He had reckoned well on Hopson's overpunctuality, and the tall fellow vaulted over the rails at his call.

"Say, Prudy here was behind the shed that day me an' Josiah was a-pesterin' you about sparkin' of her. Now you tell what you said."

"I? I was sort of riled at your sayin' that she was Hobson's choice, and I spoke up and said 'twa'n't so; she was Hopson's choice. And so she is, and will be for evermore, whether she cares a cent about it or not."

At the strong ring of that voice Prudy felt her very heart thrill, and Ozias, with preternatural wisdom, let go her hands, as he said: "I've always heered that two was company and three was none, and I'm a-goin' to put the hearsay into expee-r'ence direckly; but it's also a fact that two is better witness than one, and I hereby say and *declare*, a-holdin' up my right hand to wit, that this here mortal long Bunnell feller did say jest what he says he said, that the aforesaid Prudy was, out of all Hop Medder, and the hull creation besides, Hopson's choice. And I swan to man I b'lieve she is!" he added, looking abroad at the shag-barks as he saw Prudy run into Hopson's arms, and kindly left the two to their own company, whistling as he went, but not for want of thought.

FLUTE AND VIOLIN
by James Lane Allen

I.

THE PARSON'S MAGIC FLUTE.

O N one of the dim walls of Christ Church, in Lexington, Kentucky, there hangs, framed in thin black wood, an old rectangular slab of marble. A legend sets forth that the tablet is in memory of the Reverend James Moore, first minister of Christ Church and President of Transylvania University, who departed this life in the year 1814, at the age of forty-nine. Just beneath runs the brief record that he was learned, liberal, amiable, and pious.

Save this concise but not unsatisfactory summary, little is now known touching the reverend gentleman. A search through other sources of information does, indeed, result in reclaiming certain facts. Thus it appears that he was a Virginian, and that he came to Lexington in the year 1792—when Kentucky ceased to be a county of Virginia and became a State.

Virginia Episcopalians there were in and around the little wooden town; but so rampant was the spirit of the French Revolution and the influence of French infidelity that a celebrated local historian, who knew thoroughly the society of the place, though writing of it long afterward, declared that about the last thing it would have been thought possible to establish there was an Episcopal church.

Not so thought James. He beat the canebrakes and scoured the buffalo trails for his Virginia Episcopalians, huddled them into a dilapidated little frame house on the site of the present building, and there fired so deadly a volley of sermons at them free of charge that they all became living Christians. Indeed, he fired so long and so well that, several years later — under favor of Heaven and through the success of a lottery with a one-thousand-dollar prize and nine hundred and seventy-four blanks—there was built and furnished a small brick church, over which he was regularly called to officiate twice a month, at a salary of two hundred dollars a year.

Here authentic history ends, except for the additional fact that in the university he sat in the chair of logic, metaphysics, moral philosophy, and *belles-lettres*. It is said of him that he had beautiful manners.

And yet the best that may be related of him is not told in the books; and it is only when we have allowed the dust to settle once more upon the dead authentic histories, and have peered deep into the mists of oral tradition, that the parson is discovered standing there as he may have been in spirit and the flesh, but muffled and ghost-like, as a figure seen through a dense fog.

A tall, thinnish man, with silky pale brown hair, worn long and put back behind his ears, the high tops of which bent forward a little under the weight, and thus took on the most remarkable air of paying incessant attention to everybody and everything; set far out in front of these ears, as though it did not wish to be disturbed by what was heard, a white, wind-splitting face, calm, beardless, and seeming never to have been cold, or to have dropped the kindly dew of perspiration; under the serene peak of this forehead a pair of large gray eyes, patient and dreamy, being habitually turned inward upon a mind toiling with hard abstractions; having within him a conscience burning always like a planet; a bachelor —being a logician; therefore sweet-tempered, never having sipped the sour cup of experience; gazing covertly at womankind from behind the delicate veil of unfamiliarity that lends enchantment; being a bachelor and a bookworm, therefore already old at forty, and a little run down in his toilets, a little frayed out at the elbows and the knees, a little seamy along the back, a little deficient at the heels; in pocket poor always, and always the poorer because of a spendthrift habit in the matter of secret charities; kneeling down by his small hard bed every morning and praying that during the day his logical faculty might discharge its function morally, and that his moral faculty might discharge its function logically, and that over all the operations of all his other faculties he might find heavenly grace to exercise both a logical and a moral control; at night kneeling down again to ask forgiveness that, despite his prayer of the morning, one or more of

"HE HAD BEAUTIFUL MANNERS."

these same faculties—he knew and called them all familiarly by name, being a metaphysician—had gone wrong in a manner the most abnormal, shameless, and unforeseen; thus, on the whole, a man shy and dry, gentle, lovable, timid, resolute, forgetful, remorseful, eccentric, impulsive, thinking too well of every human creature but himself; an illogical logician, an erring moralist, a wool-gathering philosopher, but, humanly speaking, almost a perfect man.

But the magic flute? Ah, yes! The magic flute!

Well, the parson had a flute—a little one—and the older he grew, and the more patient and dreamy his gray eyes, always the more and more devotedly he loved this little friend.

And yet, for all the love he bore it, the parson was never known to blow his flute between the hours of sunrise and sunset— that is, never but once. Alas, that memorable day! But when the night fell and he came home—home to the two-story log house of the widow Spurlock; when the widow had given him his supper of coffee sweetened with brown sugar, hot johnny-cake, with perhaps a cold joint of venison and cabbage pickle; when he had taken from the supper table, by her permission, the solitary tallow dip in

its little brass candlestick, and climbed the rude steep stairs to his room above; when he had pulled the leathern string that lifted the latch, entered, shut the door behind him on the world, placed the candle on a little deal table covered with text-books and sermons, and seated himself beside it in a rush-bottomed chair— then— He began to play? No; then there was dead silence.

For about half an hour this silence continued. The widow Spurlock used to say that the parson was giving his supper time to settle; but, alas! it must have settled almost immediately, so heavy was the johnny-cake. Howbeit, at the close of such an interval, any one standing at the foot of the steps below, or listening beneath the window on the street outside, would have heard the silence broken.

At first the parson blew low, peculiar notes, such as a kind and faithful shepherd might blow at nightfall as an invitation for his scattered wandering sheep to gather home about him. Perhaps it was a way he had of calling in the disordered flock of his faculties—some weary, some wounded, some torn by thorns, some with their fleeces, which had been washed white in the morning prayer, now bearing many a stain. But when they had all answered, as it were, to this musical roll-call, and had taken their due places within the fold of his brain, obedient, attentive, however weary, however suffering, then the flute was laid aside, and once more there fell upon the room intense stillness; the poor student had entered upon his long nightly labors.

Hours passed. Not a sound was to be heard but the rustle of book leaves, now rapidly, now slowly turned, or the stewing of sap in the end of a log on the hearth, or the faint drumming of fingers on the table—those long fingers, the tips of which seemed not so full of particles of blood as of notes of music, circulating impatiently back and forth from his heart. At length, as midnight drew near, and the candle began to sputter in the socket, the parson closed the last book with a decisive snap, drew a deep breath, buried his face in his hands for a moment, as if asking a silent blessing on the day's work, and then, reaching for his flute, squared himself before the dying embers, and began in truth to play. This was the one brief, pure pleasure he allowed himself.

It was not a musical roll-call that he blew, but a dismissal for the night. One might say that he was playing the cradle song of his mind. And what a cradle song it was! A succession of undertone, silver-clear, simple melodies; apparently one for each faculty, as though he was having something kind to say to them all; thanking some for the manner in which they had served him during the day, the music here being brave and spirited; sympathizing with others that had been unjustly or too rudely put upon, the music here being plaintive and soothing; and finally granting his pardon to any such as had not used him quite fairly, the music here having a searching, troubled quality, though ending in the faintest breath of love and peace.

Such having been the parson's fixed habit as long as any one had known him, such being the one selfish passion and foible of his life, it is hard to believe that five years before his death he abruptly ceased to play his flute, and he never touched it again. But from this point the narrative

becomes so mysterious that it were better to have the direct testimony of witnesses.

II.

Every bachelor in this world is secretly watched by some woman. The parson was watched by several, but most closely by two. One of these was the widow Spurlock, a personage of savory countenance and wholesome figure—who was accused by the widow Babcock, living at the other end of the town, of having ro bust intentions toward her lodger. This piece of slander had no connection with the fact that she had used the point of her carving knife to enlarge in the door of

"HIS LONG NIGHTLY LABORS."

his room the hole through which the latch-string passed, in order that she might increase the ventilation. The aperture for ventilation thus formed was exactly the size of one of her innocent black eyes.

The other woman was an infirm, ill-favored beldam by the name of Arsena Furnace, who lived alone just across the street, and whose bedroom was on the second floor, on a level with the parson's. Being on terms of great intimacy with the widow Spurlock, she persuaded the latter that the parson's room was poorly lighted for one who used his eyes so much, and that the window-curtain of red calico should be taken down.

THE WIDOW SPURLOCK.

On the same principle of requiring less sun because having less use for her eyes, she hung before her own window a faded curtain, transparent only from within. Thus these two devoted, conscientious souls conspired to provide the parson unawares with a sufficiency of air and light. On Friday night, then, of August 31, 1809—for this was the exact date —the parson played his flute as usual, because the two women were sitting together below and distinctly heard him. It was unusual for them to be up at such an hour, but on that day the drawing of the lottery had come off, and they had held tickets, and were discussing their disappointment in having drawn blanks. Toward midnight the exquisite notes of the flute floated down to them from the parson's room.

"I suppose he'll keep on playing those same old tunes as long as there is a thimbleful of wind in him. I wish he'd learn some new ones," said the hag, taking her cold pipe from her cold lips, and turning her eyes toward her companion with a look of some impatience.

"He might be better employed at such an hour than playing on the flute," replied the widow, sighing audibly and smoothing a crease out of her apron.

As by-and-by the notes of the flute became intermittent, showing that the parson was beginning to fall asleep, Arsena said good-night, and crossing the street to her house, mounted to the front window. Yes, there he was; the long legs stretched out toward the hearth, head sunk sidewise on his shoulder, flute still at his lips, the sputtering candle throwing its shadowy light over his white weary face, now wearing a smile. Without doubt he played his flute that night as usual; and Arsena, tired of the sight, turned away and went to bed.

A few minutes later the widow Spurlock placed an eye at the aperture of ventilation, wishing to see whether the logs on the fire were in danger of rolling out and setting fire to the parson's bed;

but suddenly remembering that it was August, and that there was no fire, she glanced around to see whether his candle needed snuffing. Happening, however, to discover the parson in the act of shedding his coat, she withdrew her eye, and hastened precipitately down stairs, but sighing so loud that he surely must have heard her had not his faculty of external perception been already fast asleep.

At about three o'clock on the afternoon of the next day, as Arsena was sweeping the floor of her kitchen, there reached her ears a sound which caused her to listen for a moment, broom in air. It was the parson playing—playing at three o'clock in the afternoon! — and playing — she strained her ears again and again to make sure—playing a Virginia reel. Still, not believing her ears, she hastened aloft to the front window and looked across the street. At the same instant the widow Spurlock, in a state of equal excitement, hurried to the front door of her house, and threw a quick glance up at Arsena's window. The hag thrust a skinny hand through a slit in the curtain and beckoned energetically, and a moment later the two women stood with their heads close together watching the strange performance.

Some mysterious change had come over the parson and over the spirit of his musical faculty. He sat upright in his chair, looking ten years younger, his whole figure animated, his foot beating time so audibly that it could be heard across the street, a vivid bloom on his lifeless cheeks, his head rocking to and fro

OLD ARSENA.

like a ship in a storm, and his usually dreamy, patient gray eyes now rolled up toward the ceiling in sentimental perturbation. And how he played that Virginia reel! Not once, but over and over, and faster and faster, until the notes seemed to get into the particles of his blood and set them to dancing. And when he had finished that, he snatched his handkerchief from his pocket, dashed it across his lips, blew his nose with a resounding snort, and settling his figure into a more determined attitude, began another. And the way he went at that! And when he finished that, the way he went at another! Two negro boys, passing along the street with a spinning-wheel, put it down and paused to listen; then, catching the infection of the music, they began to dance. And then the widow Spurlock, catching the infection also, began to dance, and bouncing into the middle of the room, there actually did dance until her tucking-comb rolled out, and—ahem!—one of her stockings slipped down. Then the parson struck up the "Fisher's Hornpipe," and the widow, still in sympathy, against her will, sang the words:

> "Did you ever see the Devil
> With his wooden iron shovel,
> A-hoeing up coal
> For to burn your soul?"

"He's bewitched," said old Arsena, trembling and sick with terror.

"By *whom?*" cried the widow Spurlock, indignantly, laying a heavy hand on Arsena's shoulder.

"By his flute," replied Arsena, more fearfully

At length the parson, as if in for it, and possessed to go all lengths, jumped from his chair, laid the flute on the table, and disappeared in a hidden corner of the room. Here he kept closely locked a large brass-nailed hair trunk, over which hung a looking-glass. For ten minutes the two women waited for him to reappear, and then he did reappear, not in the same clothes, but wearing the ball dress of a Virginia gentleman of an older time, perhaps his grandfather's—knee-breeches, silk stockings, silver buckles, low shoes, laces at his wrists, laces at his throat and down his bosom. And to make the dress complete he had actually tied a blue ribbon around his long silky hair. Stepping airily and gallantly to the table, he seized the flute, and with a

"WITH THEIR HEADS CLOSE TOGETHER."

little wave of it through the air he began to play, and to tread the mazes of the minuet, about the room, this way and that, winding and bowing, turning and gliding, but all the time fingering and blowing for dear life.

"Who would have thought it was in him?" said Arsena, her fear changed to admiration.

"*I* would!" said the widow.

While he was in the midst of this performance the two women had their attention withdrawn from him in a rather singular way. A poor lad hobbling on a crutch made his appearance in the street below, and rapidly but timidly swung himself along to the widow Spurlock's door. There he paused a moment, as if overcome by mortification, but finally knocked. His summons not being answered, he presently knocked more loudly.

"Hist!" said the widow to him, in a half-tone, opening a narrow slit in the curtain. "What do you want, David?"

The boy wheeled and looked up, his face at once crimson with shame. "I want to see the parson," he said, in a voice scarcely audible.

"The parson's not at home," replied the widow, sharply. "He's out; studying up a sermon." And she closed the curtain.

An expression of despair came into the

boy's face, and for a moment, in physical weakness, he sat down on the door-step, but presently got up and moved away.

The women did not glance after his retreating figure, being reabsorbed by the movements of the parson. Whence had he that air of grace and high-born courtesy ? that vivacity of youth ?

"HE BEGAN TO PLAY."

"He must be in love," said Arsena. "He must be in love with the widow Babcock."

"He's no more in love with her than *I* am," replied her companion, with a toss of her head.

A few moments later the parson, whose motions had been gradually growing less animated, ceased dancing, and disappeared once more in the corner of the room, soon emerging therefrom dressed in his own clothes, but still wearing on his hair the blue ribbon, which he had forgotten to untie. Seating himself in his chair by the table, he thrust his hands into his pockets, and with his eyes on the floor seemed to pass into a trance of rather demure and dissatisfying reflections.

When he came down to supper that

night he still wore his hair in the forgotten queue, and it may have been this fact that gave him such an air of lamb-like meekness. The widow durst ask him no questions, for there was that in him which held familiarity at a distance ; but although he ate with unusual heartiness, perhaps on account of such unusual exercise, he did not lift his eyes from his plate, and thanked her for all her civilities with a gratitude that was singularly plaintive.

That night he did not play his flute. The next day being Sunday, and the new church not yet being opened, he kept his room. Early in the afternoon a messenger handed to the widow a note for him, which, being sealed, she promptly delivered. On reading it he uttered a quick, smothered cry of grief and alarm, seized his hat, and hurried from the house. The afternoon passed and he did not return. Darkness fell, supper hour came and went, the widow put a candle in his room, and then went across to commune with Arsena on these unusual proceedings.

Not long afterward they saw him enter his room carrying under his arm a violin case. This he deposited on the table, and sitting down beside it, lifted out a boy's violin.

"A *boy's* violin !" muttered Arsena.

"A *boy's* violin !" muttered the widow ; and the two women looked significantly into each other's eyes.

"Humph !"

"Humph !"

By-and-by the parson replaced the violin in the box and sat motionless beside it, one of his arms hanging listlessly at his side, the other lying on the table. The candle shone full in his face, and a storm of emotions passed over it. At length they saw him take up the violin again, go to the opposite wall of the room, mount a chair, knot the loose strings together, and hang the violin on a nail above his meagre shelf of books. Upon it he hung the bow. Then they saw him drive a nail in the wall close to the other, take his flute from the table, tie around it a piece of blue ribbon he had picked up off the floor, and hang it also on the wall. After this he went back to the table, threw himself in his chair, buried his head in his arms, and remained motionless until the candle burned out.

"What's the meaning of all this?" said one of the two women, as they separated below.

"I'll find out if it's the last act of my life," said the other.

But find out she never did. For question the parson directly she dared not; and neither to her nor any one else did he ever vouchsafe an explanation. Whenever, in the thousand ways a woman can, she would hint her desire to fathom the mystery, he would baffle her by assuming an air of complete unconsciousness, or repel her by a look of warning so cold that she hurriedly changed the subject.

As time passed on it became evident that some grave occurrence indeed had befallen him. Thenceforth, and during the five remaining years of his life, he was never quite the same. For months his faculties, long used to being soothed at midnight by the music of the flute, were like children put to bed hungry and refused to be quieted, so that sleep came to him only after hours of waiting and tossing, and his health suffered in consequence. And then in all things he lived like one who was watching himself closely as a person not to be trusted.

Certainly he was a sadder man. Often the two women would see him lift his eyes from his books at night, and turn them long and wistfully toward the wall of the room where, gathering cobwebs and dust, hung the flute and the violin.

If any one should care to learn why—if any one should feel interested in having this whole mystery cleared up, and in knowing more idle hearsay of the parson, he may read the following tale of a boy's violin.

III.

A BOY'S VIOLIN.

On Friday, the 31st of August, 1809—that being the day of the drawing of the lottery for finishing and furnishing the new Episcopal church—at about ten o'clock in the morning, there might have been seen hobbling slowly along the streets, in the direction of the public square, a little lad by the name of David. He was idle and lonesome, not wholly

HANGING THE VIOLIN.

through his fault. If there had been white bootblacks in those days, he might now have been busy around a tavern door polishing the noble toes of some old Revolutionary soldier; or if there had been newsboys, he might have been selling the *Gazette* or the *Reporter*—the two papers which the town afforded at that time. But there were enough negro slaves to polish all the boots in the town for nothing when the boots got polished at all, as was often not the case; and if people wanted to buy a newspaper, they went to the office of the editor and publisher, laid the silver down on the counter, and received a copy from the hands of that great man himself.

The lad was not even out on a joyous summer vacation, for as yet there was not a public school in the town, and his mother was too poor to send him to a private one, teaching him as best she could at home. This home was one of the rudest of the log cabins of the town, built by his father, who had been killed a few years before in a tavern brawl. His mother earned a scant livelihood, sometimes by taking in coarse sewing for the hands of the hemp factory, sometimes by her loom, on which with rare skill she wove the finest fabrics of the time.

As he hobbled on toward the public square, he came to an elm-tree which cast a thick cooling shade on the sidewalk, and sitting down, he laid his rickety crutch beside him, and drew out of the pocket of his home-made tow breeches a tangled mass of articles—pieces of violin strings, all of which had plainly seen service under the bow at many a dance; three old screws, belonging in their times to different violin heads; two lumps of rosin, one a rather large lump of dark color and common quality, the other a small lump of transparent amber wrapped sacredly to itself in a little brown paper bag labelled "Cucumber Seed"; a pair of epaulets, the brass fringes of which were tarnished and torn; and further miscellany.

These treasures he laid out one by one, first brushing the dirt off the sidewalk with the palm of one dirty hand, and then putting his mouth close down to blow away any loose particles that might remain to soil them; and when they were all displayed, he propped himself on one elbow, and stretched his figure caressingly beside them.

A pretty picture the lad made as he lay there dreaming over his earthly possessions—a pretty picture in the shade of the great elm, that sultry morning of August, three-quarters of a century ago! The presence of the crutch showed there was something sad about it; and so there was; for if you had glanced at the little bare brown foot, set toes upward on the curbstone, you would have discovered that the fellow to it was missing—cut off about two inches above the ankle. And if this had caused you to throw a look of sympathy at his face, something yet sadder must long have held your attention. Set jauntily on the back of his head was a weather-beaten dark blue cloth cap, the

DAVID.

patent-leather frontlet of which was gone, and beneath the ragged edge of this there fell down over his forehead and temples and ears a tangled mass of soft yellow hair, slightly curling. His eyes were large, and of a blue to match the depths of the calm sky above the tree-tops; the long lashes which curtained them were brown; his lips were red, his nose delicate and fine, and his cheeks tanned to the color of ripe peaches. It was a singularly winning face, intelligent, frank, not describable. On it now rested a smile, half joyous, half sad, as though his mind was for the moment full of bright hopes, the realization of which was far away. From his neck fell the wide collar of a white cotton shirt, clean but frayed at the elbows, and open and buttonless down his bosom. Over this he wore an old-fashioned satin waistcoat of a man, also frayed and buttonless. His dress was completed by a pair of baggy tow breeches, held up by a single tow suspender fastened to big brown horn buttons.

After a while he sat up, letting his foot hang down over the curb-stone, and uncoiling the longest of the treble strings, he put one end between his shining teeth, and stretched it tight by holding the other end off between his thumb and forefinger. Then, waving in the air in his other hand an imaginary bow, with his head resting a little on one side, his eyelids drooping, his mind in a state of dreamy delight, the little musician began to play —began to play the violin that he had long been working for, and hoped would some day become his own.

It was nothing to him now that his whole performance consisted of one broken string. It was nothing to him, as his body rocked gently to and fro, that he could not hear the music which ravished his soul. So real was that music to him that at intervals, with a little frown of vexation as though things were not going perfectly, he would stop, take up the small lump of costly rosin, and pretend to rub it vigorously on the hair of the fancied bow. Then he would awake that delicious music again, playing more ecstatically, more passionately than before.

At that moment there appeared in the street, about a hundred yards off, the Reverend James Moore, who was also moving in the direction of the public square, his face more cool and white than usual, although the morning was never more sultry.

He had arisen with an all but overwhelm-

ing sense of the importance of that day. Fifteen years are an immense period in a brief human life, especially fifteen years of spiritual toil, hardships, and discouragements, rebuffs, weaknesses, and burdens, and for fifteen such years he had spent himself for his Episcopalians, some of whom read too freely Tom Paine and Rousseau, some loved too well the taverns of the town, some wrangled too fiercely over their land suits. What wonder if this day, which despite all drawbacks was to witness the raising of money for equipping the first brick church, was a proud and happy one to his meek but victorious spirit! What wonder if, as he had gotten out of bed that morning, he had prayed with unusual fervor that for this day in especial all of his faculties, from the least to the greatest, and from the weakest to the strongest, might discharge their func-

tions perfectly, and that the drawing of the lottery might come off decently and in good order; and that—yes, this too was in the parson's prayer—that if it were the will of Heaven and just to the other holders of tickets, the right one of the vestrymen might draw the thousand-dollar prize; for he felt very sure that otherwise there would be little peace in the church for many a day to come, and that for him personally the pathway of life would be more slippery and thorny.

So that now as he hurried down the street he was happy; but he was anxious; and being excited for both reasons, the way was already prepared for him to lose in some degree that many-handed self-control which he had prayed so hard to retain.

He passed within the shade of the great elm, and then suddenly came to a full stop. A few yards in front of him the boy was performing his imaginary violin solo on a broken string, and the sight went straight to the heart of that musical faculty whose shy divinity was the flute. For a few moments he stood looking on in silence, with all the sympathy of a musician for a comrade in poverty and distress.

Other ties also bound him to the boy. If the divine voice had said to the Reverend James Moore: "Among all the people of this town, it will be allowed you to save but one soul. Choose you which that shall be," he would have replied: "Lord, this is a hard saying, for I wish to save them all. But if I must choose, let it be the soul of this lad."

The boy's father and he had been boyhood friends in Virginia, room-mates and classmates in college, and together they had come to Kentucky. Summoned to the tavern on the night of the fatal brawl, he had reached the scene only in time to lay his old playfellow's head on his bosom, and hear his last words:

"Be kind to my boy!... Be a better father to him than I have been!... Watch over him and help him!... Guard him from temptation!... Be kind to him in his little weaknesses!... Win his heart, and you can do everything with him!... Promise me this!"

"So help me Heaven, all that I can do for him I will do!"

From that moment he had taken upon his conscience, already toiling beneath its load of cares, the burden of this sacred responsibility. During the three years of his guardianship that had elapsed, this burden had not grown lighter; for apparently he had failed to acquire any influence over the lad, or to establish the least friendship with him. It was a difficult nature that had been bequeathed him to master — sensitive, emotional, delicate, wayward, gay, rebellious of restraint, loving freedom like the poet and the artist. The Reverend James Moore, sitting in the chair of logic, moral philosophy, metaphysics, and belles-lettres; lecturing daily to young men on all the powers and operations of the human mind, taking it to pieces and putting it together and understanding it all so perfectly, knowing by name every possible form of fallacy and root of evil—the Reverend James Moore, when he came to study the living mind of this boy, confessed to himself that he was as great a dunce as the greatest in his classes. But he loved the boy, nevertheless, with all the lonely resources of his nature, and he never lost hope that he would turn to him in the end.

How long he might have stood now looking on and absorbed with the pathos of the scene, it is impossible to say; for the lad, happening to look up and see him, instantly, with a sidelong scoop of his hand, all the treasures on the sidewalk disappeared in a cavernous pocket, and

MR. LEUBA.

the next moment he had seized his rickety crutch, and was busily fumbling at a loosened nail.

"Why, good-morning, David," cried the parson, cheerily, but with some embarrassment, stepping briskly forward, and looking down upon the little figure now hanging its head with guilt. "You've got the coolest seat in town," he continued, "and I wish I had time to sit down and enjoy it with you; but the drawing comes off at the lottery this morning, and I must hurry down to see who gets the capital prize." A shade of anxiety settled on his face as he said this. "But here's the morning paper," he added, drawing out of his coat pocket the coveted sheet of the weekly *Reporter*, which he was in the habit of sending to the lad's mother, knowing that her silver was picked up with the point of her needle. "Take it to your mother, and tell her she must be sure to go to see the wax figures." What a persuasive smile overspread his face as he said this! "And *you* must be certain to go too! They'll be fine. Good-by."

He let one hand rest gently on the lad's blue cloth cap, and looked down into the upturned face with an expression that could scarcely have been more tender.

"He looks feverish," he said to himself as he walked away, and then his thoughts turned to the lottery.

"Good-by," replied the boy, in a low voice, lifting his dark blue eyes slowly to the patient gray ones. "I'm glad he's gone!" he added to himself; but he nevertheless gazed after the disappearing figure with shy fondness. Then he also began to think of the lottery.

If Mr. Leuba should draw the prize, he might give Tom Leuba a new violin; and if he gave Tom a new violin, then he had promised to give him Tom's old one. It had been nearly a year since Mr. Leuba had said to him, laughing, in his dry hard little fashion:

"Now, David, you must be smart and run my errands while Tom's at school of mornings; and some of these days, when I get rich enough, I'll give Tom a new violin, and I'll give you his old one."

"Oh, Mr. Leuba!" David had cried, his voice quivering with excitement, and his whole countenance beaming with delight, "I'll wait on you forever, if you'll give me Tom's old violin."

Yes, nearly a whole year had passed since then—a lifetime of waiting and dis-

"EXECUTING AN INTRICATE PASSAGE."

by a beautiful female weeping over him — which makes it a most interesting scene. His Excellency Thomas Jefferson. General Buonaparte in marshal action. General Hamilton and Colonel Burr. In this interesting scene the Colonel is represented in the attitude of firing, while the General stands at his distance waiting the result of the first fire: both accurate likenesses. The death of General Braddock, who fell in Braddock's Defeat. An Indian is represented as scalping the General, while one of his men, in an attempt to rescue him out of the hands of the Indians, was overtaken by another Indian, who is ready to split him with his tomahawk. Mrs. Jerome Buonaparte, formerly Miss Patterson. The Sleeping Beauty. Eliza Wharton, or the American coquette, with her favorite gallant and her intimate friend Miss Julia Granby. The Museum will be open from ten o'clock in the morning 'til nine in the evening. Admittance fifty cents for grown persons; children half price. Profiles taken with accuracy at the Museum.

appointment. Many an errand he had run for Mr. Leuba. Many a bit of a thing Mr. Leuba had given him: pieces of violin strings, odd worn-out screws, bits of rosin, old epaulets, and a few dimes; but the day had never come when he had given him Tom's violin.

Now if Mr. Leuba would only draw the prize! As he lay on his back on the sidewalk, with the footless stump of a leg crossed over the other, he held the newspaper between his eyes and the green limbs of the elm overhead, and eagerly read for the last time the advertisement of the lottery. Then, as he finished reading it, his eyes were suddenly riveted upon a remarkable notice printed just beneath.

This notice stated that Messrs. Ollendorf and Mason respectfully acquainted the ladies and gentlemen of Lexington that they had opened at the Kentucky Hotel a new and elegant collection of wax figures, judged by connoisseurs to be equal, if not superior, to any exhibited in America. Among which are the following characters: An excellent representation of General George Washington giving orders to the Marquis de la Fayette, his aid. In another scene the General is represented as a fallen victim to death, and the tears of America, represented

The greatest attraction of the whole Museum will be a large magnificent painting of Christ in the Garden of Gethsemane.

All this for a quarter! The newspaper suddenly dropped from his hands into the dirt of the street—he had no quarter! For a moment he sat as immovable as if the thought had turned him into stone; but the next moment he had sprung from the sidewalk and was speeding home to his mother in the log cabin on the outskirts of the town. Never before had the stub of the little crutch been plied so nimbly among the stones of the rough sidewalk. Never before had he made a prettier picture, with the blue cap pushed far back from his forehead, his yellow hair blowing about his face, the old black satin waistcoat flopping like a pair of disjointed wings against his sides, the open newspaper streaming backward from his hand, and his face alive with hope.

IV.

It was perhaps two hours later when he issued from the house, and set his face in the direction of the museum. It was a face full of excitement still, but full also of pain, because he had no money, and saw no chance of getting any. It was a dull time of the year for his mother's work. Only the day before she had been paid a month's earnings, and already the money had been laid out for the frugal expenses of the household. It would be a long time before any more would come in, and in the mean time the exhibition of wax figures would have been moved to some other town. When he had told her that the parson had said that she must go to see them, she had smiled fondly at him from beside her loom, and quietly shaken her head with inward resignation; but when he told her the parson had said *he* must be sure to go too, the smile had faded into an expression of fixed sadness.

On his way down town he passed the little music store of Mr. Leuba, which was one block this side of the Kentucky Hotel. He was all eagerness to reach the museum, but his ear caught the sounds of the violin, and he forgot everything else in his desire to go in and speak with Tom, for Tom was his lord and master.

"Tom, are you going to see the wax figures?" he cried, with trembling haste, curling himself on top of the keg of nails in his accustomed corner of the little lumber-room. But Tom paid no attention to the question or the questioner, being absorbed in executing an intricate passage of "O Thou Fount of every Blessing!" For the moment David forgot his question himself, absorbed likewise in witnessing this envied performance.

When Tom had finished, he laid the violin across his knees and wiped his brow with his shirt sleeves. "Don't you know that you oughtn't to talk to me when I'm performing?" he said, loftily, still not deigning to look at his offending auditor. "Don't you know that it disturbs a fiddler to be spoken to when he's performing?"

Tom was an overgrown, rawboned lad of some fifteen years, with stubby red hair, no eyebrows, large watery blue eyes, and a long neck with a big Adam's apple.

"I didn't mean to interrupt you, Tom," said David, in a tone of the deepest penitence. "You know that I'd rather hear you play than anything."

"Father got the thousand-dollar prize," said Tom, coldly, accepting the apology for the sake of the compliment.

"Oh, *Tom!* I'm so glad! Hurrah!" shouted David, waving his old blue cap around his head, his face transfigured with joy, his heart leaping with a sudden hope, and now at last he would get the violin.

"What are *you* glad for?" said Tom, with dreadful severity. "He's *my* father; he's not *your* father;" and for the first time he bestowed a glance upon the little figure curled up on the nail keg, and bending eagerly toward him with clasped hands.

"I *know* he's *your* father, Tom, but—"

"Well, then, what are you *glad* for?" insisted Tom. "You're not going to get any of the money."

"I know *that*, Tom," said David, coloring deeply, "but—"

"Well, then, what *are* you glad for?"

"I don't think I'm so *very* glad, Tom," replied David, sorrowfully.

But Tom had taken up the bow and was rubbing the rosin on it. He used a great deal of rosin in his playing, and would often proudly call David's attention to how much of it would settle as a white dust under the bridge. David was too well used to Tom's rebuffs to mind them long, and as he now looked on at this rosining process, the sunlight came back into his face.

"Please let me try it once, Tom—just *once*." Experience had long ago taught him that this was asking too much of Tom; but with the new hope that the violin might now soon become his, his desire to handle it was ungovernable.

"Now look here, David," replied Tom, with a great show of kindness in his manner, "I'd let you try it once, but you'd spoil the tone. It's taken me a long time to get a good tone into this fiddle, and you'd take it all out of it the very first whack. As soon as you learn to get a good tone out of it, I'll let you play on it. Don't you *know* you'd spoil it, if I was to let you try it now?" he added, suddenly wheeling with tremendous energy upon his timid petitioner.

"I'm afraid I would, Tom," replied David, with a voice full of anguish.

"But just listen to me," said Tom; and taking up the violin, he rendered the opening passage of "O Thou Fount of every Blessing!" Scarcely had he finished when a customer entered the shop, and he hurried to the front, leaving the violin and the bow on the chair that he had quitted.

No sooner was he gone than the little figure slipped noiselessly from its perch, and hobbling quickly to the chair on which the violin lay, stood beside it in silent love. Touch it he durst not; but his sensitive delicate hands passed tremblingly over it, and his eyes dwelt upon it with un-

without its effect on Tom, although a suggestion from such a source was not to be respected. He merely threw his eyes up toward the heavens and said, sturdily: "You ninny! they'll not melt. Don't you see it's going to rain and turn cooler?"

"I'll bet you *I'd* not wait for it to turn

"A SMALL CROWD HAD COLLECTED AROUND THE ENTRANCE OF THE MUSEUM."

speakable longing. Then, with a sigh, he turned away, and hastened to the front of the shop. Tom had already dismissed his customer, and was standing in the door, looking down the street in the direction of the Kentucky Hotel, where a small crowd had collected around the entrance of the museum.

As David stepped out upon the sidewalk, it was the sight of this crowd that recalled him to a new sorrow.

"Tom," he cried, with longing, "are you going to see the wax figures?"

"Of course I'm going," he replied, carelessly. "We're all going."

"When, Tom?" asked David, with breathless interest.

"Whenever we want to, of course," replied Tom. "I'm not just going once; I'm going as often as I like."

"Why don't you go now, Tom? It's so hot—they might melt."

This startling view of the case was not

cooler. I'll bet you *I'd* be in there before you could say Jack Roberson, if *I* had a quarter," said David, with tremendous resolution.

V.

All that long afternoon he hung in feverish excitement around the door of the museum. There was scarce a travelling show in Kentucky in those days. It was not strange if to this idler of the streets, in whom imagination was all-powerful, and in whose heart quivered ungovernable yearnings for the heroic, the poetic, and the beautiful, this day of the first exhibition of wax figures was the most memorable of his life.

It was so easy for everybody to go in who wished; so impossible for him. Groups of gay ladies slipped their silver half-dollars through the variegated meshes of their silken purses. The men came in jolly twos and threes, and would sometimes draw out great rolls of bills. Now

"THE WIDOW DROPPED HER EYES."

a kind-faced farmer passed in, dropping into the hands of the door-keeper a half-dollar for himself, and three quarters for three sleek negroes that followed at his heels; and now a manufacturer with a couple of apprentices — lads of David's age and friends of his. Poor little fellow! at many a shop of the town he had begged to be taken as an apprentice himself, but no one would have him because he was lame.

And now the people were beginning to pour out, and he hovered about them, hoping in this way to get some idea of what was going on inside. Once, with the courage of despair, he seized the arm of a lad as he came out.

"Oh, Bobby, tell me all about it!"

But Bobby shook him off, and skipped away to tell somebody else who didn't want to hear.

After a while two sweet-faced ladies dressed in mourning appeared. As they passed down the street he was standing on the sidewalk, and there must have been something in his face to attract the attention of one of them, for she paused, and in the gentlest manner said:

"My little man, how did you like the wax figures and the picture?"

"Oh, madam," he replied, his eyes filling, "I have not seen them!"

"But you will see them, I hope," she said, moving away, but bestowing on him the lingering smile of bereft motherhood.

The twilight fell, and still he lingered, until, with a sudden remorseful thought of his mother, he turned away and passed up the dark street. His tongue was parched, there was a lump in his throat, and a numb pain about his heart. Far up the street he paused and looked back. A lantern had been swung out over the entrance of the museum, and the people were still passing in.

VI.

A happy man was the Reverend James Moore the next morning. The lottery had been a complete success, and he would henceforth have a comfortable church, in which the better to save the souls of his fellow-creatures. The leading vestry-man had drawn the capital prize, and while the other members who had drawn blanks were not exactly satisfied, on the whole the result seemed as good as providential. As he walked down town at an early hour, he was conscious of suffering from a dangerous elation of spirit; and more than once his silent prayer had been: "Lord, let me not be puffed up this day! Let me not be blinded with happiness! Keep the eyes of my soul clear, that I overlook no duty! What have I, unworthy servant, done that I should be so fortunate?"

Now and then, as he passed along, a church member would wring his hand and offer congratulations. After about fifteen years of a more or less stranded condition a magnificent incoming tide of prosperity now seemed to lift him off his very feet.

From wandering rather blindly about the streets for a while, he started for the new church, remembering that he had an engagement with a committee of ladies, who had taken in charge the furnishing of it. But when he reached there, no one had arrived but the widow Babcock. She was very beautiful; and looking at wo-

"IT WAS A VERY GAY DINNER."

mankind from behind his veil of unfamiliarity, the parson, despite his logic, had always felt a desire to lift that veil when standing in her presence. The intoxication of his mood was not now lessened by coming upon her so unexpectedly alone.

"My dear Mrs. Babcock," he said, offering her his hand in his beautiful manner, "it seems peculiarly fitting that you should be the first of the ladies to reach the spot; for it would have pained me to think you less zealous than the others. The vestry needs not only your taste in furniture, but the influence of your presence."

The widow dropped her eyes, the gallantry of the speech being so unusual. "I came early on purpose," she replied, in a voice singularly low and tremulous. "I wanted to see you alone. Oh, Mr. Moore, the ladies of this town owe you such a debt of gratitude! You have been such a comfort to those who are sad, such a support to those who needed strengthening! And who has needed these things as much as I?"

As she spoke, the parson, with a slight look of apprehension, had put his back against the wall, as was apt to be his way when talking with ladies.

"Who has needed these things as I have?" continued the widow, taking a step forward, and with increasing agitation. "Oh, Mr. Moore, I should be an ungrateful woman if I did not mingle my congratulations with the others. And I want to do this now with my whole soul. May God bless you, and crown the labors of your life with every desire of your heart!" And saying this, the widow laid the soft tips of one hand on one of the parson's shoulders, and raising herself slightly on tiptoe, kissed him.

"Oh, Mrs. Babcock!" cried the dismayed logician, "what have you done?" But the next moment, the logician giving place to the man, he grasped one of her hands, and murmuring, "May God bless *you* for *that!*" seized his hat, and hurried out into the street.

The most careless observer might have been interested in watching his movements as he walked away.

He carried his hat in his hand, forgetting to put it on. Several persons spoke to him on the street, but he did not hear them. He strode a block or two in one direction, and then a block or two in another.

"If she does it again," he muttered to himself—"if she does it again, I'll marry her!... Old?... I could run a mile in a minute!"

As he was passing the music store, the dealer called out to him:

"Come in, parson. I've got a present for you."

"A—present—for—me?" repeated the parson, blank with amazement. In his life the little music dealer had never made him a present.

"Yes, a present," repeated the fortunate vestry-man, whose dry heart, like a small seed-pod, the wind of good fortune had opened, so that a few rattling germs of generosity dropped out. Opening a drawer behind his counter, he now took out a roll of music. "Here's some new music for your flute," he said. "Accept it with my compliments."

New music for his flute! The parson turned it over dreamily, and it seemed that the last element of disorder had come to derange his faculties.

"And Mrs. Leuba sends her compliments, and would like to have you to dinner," added the shop-keeper, looking across the counter with some amusement at the expression of the parson, who now appeared as much shocked as though his whole nervous system had been suddenly put in connection with a galvanic battery of politeness.

It was a very gay dinner, having been gotten up to celebrate the drawing of the prize. The entire company were to go in the afternoon to see the waxworks, and some of the ladies wore especial toilets, with a view to having their profiles taken.

"Have you been to see the waxworks, Mr. Moore?" inquired a spinster, roguishly, wiping a drop of soup from her under-lip.

The unusual dinner, the merriment, the sense of many ladies present, mellowed the parson like old wine.

"No, madam," he replied, giddily; "but I shall go this very afternoon. I find it impossible any longer to deny myself the pleasure of beholding the great American Coquette and Sleeping Beauty. I must take my black sheep," he continued, with expanding warmth. "I must drive my entire flock of soiled lambs into the favored and refining presence of Miss Julia Granby."

Keeping to this resolution, as soon as dinner was over he made his excuses to the company, and set off to collect a certain class of boys which he had scraped together by hook and crook from the by-ways of the town, and about an hour later he might have been seen driving them before him toward the entrance of the museum. There he shouldered his way cheerfully up to the door, and shoved each of the lads good-naturedly in, finally passing in himself, with a general glance at the by-standers, as if to say, "Was there ever another man as happy in this world?"

But he soon came out, leaving his wild lambs to browse at will in those fresh pastures, and took his way up street homeward. He seemed to be under some necessity of shaking them off in order to enjoy the solitude of his thoughts.

"If she does it again!... If she does it again!... Whee! whee! whee!—whee! whee! whee!" and he began to whistle for his flute with a nameless longing.

It was soon after this that the two women heard him playing the reel, and watched him perform certain later incredible evolutions. For whether one event, or all events combined, had betrayed him into this outbreak, henceforth he was quite beside himself and hopelessly undone.

Is it possible that on this day the Reverend James Moore had driven the ancient, rusty, creaky chariot of his faculties too near the sun of love?

VII.

A sad day it had been meantime for the poor lad.

He had gotten up in the morning listless and dull and sick at the sight of his breakfast. But he had feigned to be quite well that he might have permission to set off down town. There was no chance of his being able to get into the museum, but he was drawn irresistibly thither for the mere pleasure of standing around and watching the people, and hoping that something—*something* would turn up. He was still there when his dinner hour came, but he never thought of this. Once, when the door-keeper was at leisure, he had hobbled up and said to him, with a desperate effort to smile, "Sir, if I were rich, I'd live in your museum for about five years."

But the door-keeper had pushed him rudely back, telling him to be off and not obstruct the sidewalk.

He was still standing near the entrance when the parson came down the street driving his flock of boys. Ah, if he had only joined that class, as time after time he had been asked to do! All at once his face lit up with a fortunate inspiration, and pushing his way to the very side of the door-keeper, he placed himself there that the parson might see him and take him with the others; for had he not said that *he* must be sure to go? But when the parson came up this purpose had failed him, and he had apparently shrunk to half his size behind the bulk of the door-keeper, fearing most of all things that the parson would discover him and know why he was there.

He was still lingering outside when the parson reappeared and started homeward; and he sat down and watched him out of sight. He seemed cruelly hurt, and his eyes filled with tears.

"*I'd* have taken *him* in the very first one," he said, choking down a sob; and then, as if he felt this to be unjust, he murmured over and over: "Maybe he forgot me; maybe he didn't mean it; maybe he forgot me."

Perhaps an hour later, slowly and with many pauses, he drew near the door of the parson's home. There he lifted his hand three times before he could knock.

"The parson's not at home," the widow Spurlock had called sharply down to him.

"Why don't you go in?" he said, loudly, walking up to David and jingling the silver in his pockets. "What are you standing out here for? If you want to go in, why don't you go in?"

"Oh, Tom!" cried David, in a whisper of eager confidence, his utterance choked with a sob, "I haven't got any money."

"I'd hate to be as poor as you are," said Tom, contemptuously. "I'm going this evening and to-night, and as often as I want," and he turned gayly away to join the others.

He was left alone again, and his cup of

THE PARSON CAME DOWN THE STREET DRIVING HIS FLOCK OF BOYS.

bitterness, which had been filling drop by drop, now ran over.

Several groups came up just at that moment. There was a pressure and a jostling of the throng. As Mr. Leuba, who had made his way up to the door-keeper, drew a handful of silver from his pocket, some one accidentally struck his elbow, and several pieces fell to the pavement. Then there was laughter and a scrambling as these were picked up and returned. But out through the legs of the crowd one bright silver quarter rolled unseen down the sloping sidewalk toward the spot where David was standing.

It was all done in an instant. He saw it coming; the little crutch was set forward a pace, the little body was swung silently forward, and as the quarter fell over on its shining side, the dirty sole of a brown foot covered it.

The next minute, with a sense of triumph and bounding joy, the poverty-tortured, friendless little thief had crossed

With this the last hope had died out of his bosom; for having dwelt long on the parson's kindness to him—upon all the parson's tireless efforts to befriend him—he had summoned the courage at last to go and ask him to lend him a quarter.

With little thought of whither he went, he now turned back down town, but some time later he was still standing at the entrance of the museum.

He looked up the street again. All the Leubas were coming, Tom walking, with a great air, a few feet ahead.

BEFORE THE PICTURE.

the threshold of the museum, and stood face to face with the Redeemer of the world. For the picture was so hung as to catch the eye upon entering, and it arrested his quick roving glance and held it in awe-stricken fascination. Unconscious of his own movements, he drew nearer and nearer, until he stood a few feet in front of the arc of spectators, with his breathing all but suspended, and one hand crushing the old blue cloth cap against his naked bosom.

It was a strange meeting. The large rude painting possessed no claim to art. But to him it was an overwhelming revelation, for he had never seen any pictures, and he was gifted with an untutored love of painting. Over him, therefore, it exercised an enthralling influence, and it was as though he stood in the visible presence of One whom he knew that the parson preached of and his mother worshipped.

Forgetful of all his surroundings, long he stood and gazed. Whether it may have been the thought of the stolen quarter that brought him to himself, at length he drew a deep breath, and looked quickly around with a frightened air. From across the room he saw Mr. Leuba watching him gravely, as it seemed to his guilty conscience, with fearful sternness. A burning flush dyed his face, and he shrank back, concealing himself among the crowd. The next moment, without ever having seen or so much as thought of anything else in the museum, he slipped out into the street.

There the eyes of everybody seemed turned upon him. Where should he go? Not home. Not to Mr. Leuba's music store. No; he could never look into Mr. Leuba's face again. And Tom? He could hear Tom crying out, wherever he should meet him, "You stole a quarter from father."

In utter terror and shame, he hurried away, and hobbled out to the southern end of the town, where there was an abandoned rope-walk.

It was a neglected place, damp and unhealthy. In the farthest corner of it he lay down and hid himself in a clump of iron-weeds. Slowly the moments dragged themselves along. Of what was he thinking? Of his mother? Of the parson? Of the violin that would now never be his? Of that wonderful sorrowful face which he had seen in the painting? The few noises of the little town grew very faint, the droning of the bumblebee on the purple tufts of the weed overhead very loud, and louder still the beating of his heart against the green grass as he lay on his side, with his head on his blue cap and his cheek in his hand. And then he fell asleep.

When he awoke he started up bewildered. The sun had set, and the heavy dews of twilight were falling. A chill ran through him; and then the recollection of what had happened came over him with a feeling of desolation. When it was quite dark he left his hiding-place and started back up town.

He could reach home in several ways, but a certain fear drew him into the street which led past the music store. If he could only see Mr. Leuba, he felt sure that he could tell by the expression of his face whether he had missed the quarter. At some distance off he saw by the light of the windows Mr. Leuba standing in front of his shop talking to a group of men. Noiselessly he drew near, noiselessly he was passing without the courage to look up.

"Stop, David. Come in here a moment."

As Mr. Leuba spoke, he apologized to the gentlemen for leaving, and turned back into the rear of the shop. Faint, and trembling so that he could scarcely stand, his face a deadly whiteness, the boy followed.

"David," said Mr. Leuba—in all his life he had never spoken so kindly; perhaps his heart had been touched by some late feeling, as he had studied the boy's face before the picture in the museum, and certainly it had been singularly opened by his good fortune—"David," he said, "I promised when I got rich enough I'd give Tom a new violin, and give you his old one. Well, I gave him a new one to-day; so here's yours," and going to a corner of the room, he took up the box, brought it back, and would have laid it on the boy's arm, only there was no arm extended to receive it.

"Take it! It's yours!"

"Oh, Mr. Leuba!"

It was all he could say. He had expected to be charged with stealing the quarter, and instead there was held out to him the one treasure of all the world—the violin of which he had dreamed so long, for which he had served so faithfully.

"Oh, Mr. Leuba!"

There was a pitiful note in the cry, but the dealer was not the man to hear it, or to notice the look of angelic contrition on the upturned face. He merely took the lad's arm, bent it around the violin, patted the ragged cap, and said, a little impatiently:

"Come, come! they're waiting for me at the door. To-morrow you can come down and run some more errands for me," and he led the way to the front of the shop and resumed his conversation.

Slowly along the dark street the lad toiled homeward with his treasure. At any other time he would have sat down on the first curb-stone, opened the box, and in ecstatic joy have lifted out that peerless instrument; or he would have sped home with it to his mother, flying along on his one crutch as if on the winds of heaven. But now he could not look at it, and something clogged his gait so that he loitered and faltered and sometimes stood still irresolute.

But at last he approached the log cabin which was his home. A rude fence enclosed the yard, and inside this fence there grew a hedge of lilacs. When he was within a few feet of the gate he paused, and did what he had never done before—he put his face close to the panels of the fence, and with a look of guilt and sorrow peeped through the lilacs at the face of his mother, who was sitting in the light of the open doorway.

"TOILED HOMEWARD WITH HIS TREASURE."

She was thinking of him. He knew that by the patient sweetness of her smile. All the heart went out of him at the sight, and hurrying forward, he put the violin down at her feet, and threw his arms around her neck, and buried his head on her bosom.

VIII.

After he had made his confession, a restless and feverish night he had of it, often springing up from his troubled dreams and calling to her in the darkness. But the next morning he insisted upon getting up for a while.

Toward the afternoon he grew worse again, and took to his bed, the yellow head tossing to and fro, the eyes bright and restless, and his face burning. At length he looked up and said to his mother, in the manner of one who forms

"BURIED HIS HEAD ON HER BOSOM."

a difficult resolution: "Send for the parson. Tell him I am sick and want to see him."

It was this summons that the widow Spurlock had delivered on the Sunday afternoon when the parson had quitted the house with such a cry of distress. He had not so much as thought of the boy since the Friday morning previous.

"How is it possible," he cried, as he hurried on—"how is it possible that I *could* have forgotten *him*?"

The boy's mother met him outside the house and drew him into an adjoining room, silently, for her tears were falling. He sank into the first chair.

"Is he so ill?" he asked, under his trembling breath.

"I'm afraid he's going to be very ill. And to see him in so much trouble—"

"What is the matter? In God's name, has anything happened to him?"

She turned her face away to hide her grief. "He said he would tell you himself. Oh, if I've been too hard with him! But I did it for the best. I didn't know until the doctor came that he was going to be ill, or I would have waited. Do anything you can to quiet him—anything he asks you," she implored, and pointed to the door of the room in which the boy lay.

Conscience-stricken and speechless, the parson opened it and entered.

The small white bed stood against the wall beneath an open window, and one bright-headed sunflower, growing against the house outside, leaned in and fixed its kind face anxiously upon the sufferer's.

The figure of the boy was stretched along the edge of the bed, his cheek on one hand and his eyes turned steadfastly toward the middle of the room, where, on a table, the violin lay exposed to view.

He looked quickly toward the door as the parson entered, and an expression of relief passed over his face.

"Why, David," said the parson, chidingly, and crossing to the bed with a bright smile. "Sick? This will never do;" and he sat down, imprisoning one of the burning palms in his own.

The boy said nothing, but looked at him searchingly, as though needing to lay aside all masks and disguises and penetrate at once to the bottom truth. Then he asked, "Are you mad at me?"

"My poor boy!" said the parson, his lips trembling a little as he tightened his pressure—"my poor boy! why should *I* be mad at *you*?"

"You never could do anything with me."

"Never mind that now," said the parson, soothingly, but adding, with bitterness, "it was all my fault—all my fault."

"It wasn't your fault at all," said the boy. "It was mine."

A change had come over him in his treatment of the parson. All shyness had disappeared, as is apt to be the case with the sick.

"I want to ask you something," he added, confidentially.

"Anything—anything! Ask me anything!"

"Do you remember the wax figures?"

"Oh yes, I remember them very well," said the parson, quickly, uneasily.

"I wanted to see 'em, and I didn't have any money, and I stole a quarter from Mr. Leuba."

Despite himself a cry escaped the parson's lips, and dropping the boy's hand, he started from his chair and walked rapidly to and fro across the room, with the fangs of remorse fixed deep in his conscience.

"Why didn't you come to me?" he asked at length, in a tone of helpless entreaty. "Why didn't you come to me? Oh, if you had only come to me!"

"I did come to you," replied the boy.

"When?" asked the parson, coming back to the bedside.

"About three o'clock yesterday."

About three o'clock yesterday! And what was he doing at that time? He bent his head over to his very knees, hiding his face in his hands.

"But why didn't you let me know it? Why didn't you come in?"

"Mrs. Spurlock told me you were at work on a sermon."

"God forgive me!" murmured the parson, with a groan.

"I thought you'd lend me a quarter," said the boy, simply. "I thought you liked *me*, and I like *you*, and you took the other boys, and you told me *I* must be certain to go. I thought you'd lend me a quarter till I could pay you back."

"Oh, David!" cried the parson, getting down on his knees by the bedside, and putting his arms around the boy's neck, "I would have lent you—I would have given you—anything I have in this world!"

The boy threw his arms around the parson's neck and clasped him close.

AT DAVID'S BEDSIDE.

"Can you forgive me for stealing the quarter?" he whispered.

"Oh, boy! boy! can you forgive *me*?" Sobs stifled the parson's utterance, and he went to a window on the opposite side of the room.

When he turned his face inward again, he saw the boy's gaze fixed once more intently upon the violin.

"There's something I want you to do for me," he said. "Mr. Leuba gave me a violin last night, and mamma says I ought to sell it, and pay him back." The words seemed wrung from his heart's core. "I thought I'd ask you to sell it for me. The doctor says I may be sick a long time, and it worries me." He began to grow excited, and tossed from side to side.

"Don't worry," said the parson, "I'll sell it for you."

The boy looked at the violin again. To him it was priceless, and his eyes grew heavy with love for it. Then he said, cautiously: "I thought you'd get a good price for it. I don't think I could take less than a hundred dollars. It's worth more, but if I have to sell it, I don't think I could take less than a hundred dollars," and he fixed his burning eyes on the parson's.

"Don't worry! I'll sell it for you. Oh yes, you can get a hundred dollars for it. I'll bring you a hundred dollars for it by to-morrow morning." Half a year's salary.

It was on this night that he was seen to enter his room with a boy's violin under his arm, and later to hang it, and hang his beloved flute, tied with a blue ribbon, above the meagre top shelf of books—Fuller's *Gospel*, Petrarch, Volney's *Ruins*, Zollicoffer's *Sermons*, and the *Horrors of San Domingo*. After that he remained motionless at his table, with his head bowed on his folded arms, until the candle went out, leaving him in inner and outer darkness. Moralist, logician, philosopher, he studied the boy's transgression, laying it at last solely to his own charge.

At daybreak he stood outside the house with the physician who had been with the boy during the night. "Will he die?" he asked.

The physician tapped his forehead with his forefinger. "The chances are against him. The case has peculiar complications. All night it has been nothing but the wax figures and the stolen quarter and the violin. His mother has tried to persuade him not to sell it. But he won't bear the sight of it now, and is troubled about sacrificing it."

"David," said the parson, kneeling by the bedside, and speaking in a tone pitiful enough to have recalled a soul from the other world—"David, here's the money for the violin; here's the hundred dollars," and he pressed it into one of the boy's palms. The hand closed upon it, but there was no recognition.

The first sermon that the parson preached in the new church was on the Sunday after the boy's death. It was expected that he would rise to the occasion and surpass himself, which, indeed, he did, drawing tears even from the eyes of those who knew not that they could shed them, and all through making the greatest effort to keep back his own. The subject of the sermon was, "The Temptations of the Poor." The next sermon was on the "Besetting Sin," the drift of it going to show that the besetting sin may be the one pure and exquisite pleasure of life, involving only the exercise of the loftiest faculty. And this was followed by a third sermon on "The Kiss that Betrayeth," in which innumerable illustrations were drawn from history, showing how every kind of man had been betrayed in this way. During the delivery of this sermon the parson looked so cold and even severe that it was not understood why the emotions of any one should have been touched, or why the widow Babcock should have lowered her veil and wept bitterly.

And thus being ever the more loved and revered as he grew ever the more lovable and saint-like, he passed onward to the close. But not until the end came did he once stretch forth a hand to touch his flute; and it was only in imagination then that he grasped it, to sound the final roll-call of his wandering faculties, and to blow a last good-night to his tired spirit.

"HIS HEAD BOWED ON HIS FOLDED ARMS."

THE LITTLE MAID AT THE DOOR
by Mary E. Wilkins

OSEPH BAYLEY and
his wife Ann came
riding down from
Salem village. They
had started from
their home in New-
bury the day before,
and had staid overnight with their relative, Sergeant Thomas Putnam, in Salem
village; they were on their way to the
election in Boston. The road wound
along through the woods from Salem to
Lynn; it was some time since they had
passed a house.

May was nearly gone; the pinks and
the blackberry vines were in flower. All
the woods were full of an indefinite and
composite fragrance, made up of the
breaths of myriads of green plants and
seen and unseen blossoms, like a very
bouquet of spring. The newly leaved
trees cast shadows that were as much a
part of the tender surprise of the spring
as the new flowers. They flickered delicately before Joseph Bayley and his wife
Ann on the grassy ridges of the road,
but they did not remark them. Their

own fancies cast gigantic projections
which eclipsed the sweet show of the
spring and almost their own personali-
ties. That year the leaves came out and
the flowers bloomed in vain for the people in and about Salem village. There
was an epidemic or disease of the mind
that deafened and blinded to all save its
own pains.

Ann Bayley on the pillion snuggled
closely against her husband's back; her
fearful eyes peered at the road around his
shoulder. She was a young and handsome woman; she had on her best mantle
of sad-colored silk, and a fine black hood
with a topknot, but she did not think of
that.

"Joseph, what is that in the road before us?" she whispered, timorously.

He pulled up the horse with a great
jerk. "Where?" he whispered back.

"There! there! at the right; just beyond that laurel thicket. 'Tis somewhat
black, an' it moves. There! there! Oh,
Joseph!"

Joseph Bayley sat stiff and straight in
his saddle, like a soldier; his face was

pale and stern, his eyes full of horror and defiance.

"See you it?" Ann whispered again. "There! now it moves. What is it?"

"I see it," said Joseph, in a loud, bold voice. "An' whatever it be, I will yield not to it; an' neither will you, goodwife."

Ann reached around and caught at the reins. "Let us go back," she moaned, faintly. "Oh, Joseph, let us not pass it. My spirit faints within me. I see its back among the laurel blooms. 'Tis the black beast they tell of. Let us turn back, Joseph, let us turn back!"

"Be still, woman!" returned her husband, jerking the reins from her hand. "What think ye 'twould profit us to turn back to Salem village? I trow if there be one black beast here, there be a full herd of them there. There is naught left but to ride past it as best we may. Sit fast, an' listen you not to it, whatever it promise you." Joseph looked down the road towards the laurel bushes, his muscles now as tense as a bow. Ann hid her face on his shoulder. Suddenly he shouted, with a great voice like a herald: "Away with ye, ye cursed beast! away with ye! We be not of your kind; we be gospel folk. We have naught to do with you or your master. Away with ye!"

The horse leapt forward. There was a great cracking amongst the laurel bushes at the right, a glossy black back and some white horns heaved over them, then some black flanks plunged heavily out of sight.

"Oh!" shrieked Ann, "has it gone? Goodman, has it gone?"

"The Lord hath delivered us from the snare of the enemy," answered Joseph, solemnly.

"What looked it like, Joseph, what looked it like?"

"Like no beast that was saved in the ark."

"Had it fiery eyes?" asked Ann, trembling.

"'Tis well you did not see them."

"Ride fast! oh, ride fast!" Ann pleaded, clutching hard at her husband's cloak. "It may follow on our track." The horse went down the road at a quick trot. Ann kept peering back and starting at every sound in the woods. "Do you mind the tale Samuel Endicott told last night?" she said, shuddering. "How on his voyage to Barbadoes he, sitting on the windlass on a bright moonshining night, was shook violently, and saw the appearance of that witch Goody Bradbury, with a white cap and a white neck-cloth on her? It was a dreadful tale."

"It was naught to the sight of Mercy Lewis and Sergeant Thomas Putnam's daughter Ann, when they were set upon and nigh choked to death by Goody Proctor. Know you that within a half-mile we must pass the Proctor house?"

Ann gave a shuddering sigh. "I would I were home again!" she moaned. "They said 'twas full of evil things, and that the black man himself kept tavern there since Goodman Proctor and his wife were in jail. Did you mind what Goodwife Putnam said of the black head, like a hog's, that Goodman Perley saw at the keeping-room window as he passed, and the rumbling noises, and the yellow birds that flew around the chimney and twittered in a psalm tune? Oh, Joseph, there is a yellow bird now in the birch-tree—see! see!"

They had come into a little space where the woods were thinner. Joseph urged his horse forward.

"We will not slack our pace for any black beasts nor any yellow birds," he cried, in a valiant voice.

There was a passing gleam of little yellow wings above the birch-tree.

"He has flown away," said Ann. "'Tis best to front them as you do, goodman, but I have not the courage. That looked like a common yellow-bird; his wings shone like gold. Think you it has gone forward to the Proctor house?"

"It matters not, so it but fly up before us," said Joseph Bayley.

He was somewhat older than Ann; fair-haired and fair-bearded, with blue eyes set so deeply under heavy brows that they looked black. His face was at once stern and nervous, showing not only the spirit of warfare against his foes, but the elements of strife within himself.

They rode on, and the woods grew thicker; the horse's hoofs made only a faint liquid pad on the mossy road. Suddenly he stopped and whinnied. Ann clutched her husband's arm; they sat motionless, listening; the horse whinnied again.

Suddenly Joseph started violently, and stared into the woods on the left, and Ann also. A long defile of dark evergreens stretched up the hill, with mysterious depths of blue-black shadows between them; the air had an earthy dampness.

Joseph shook the reins fiercely over the horse's back, and shouted to him in a loud voice.

"Did you see it?" gasped Ann, when they were come into a lighter place. "Was it not a black man?"

"Fear not; we have outridden him," said her husband, setting his thin intense face proudly ahead.

"I would we were safe home in Newbury," Ann moaned. "I would we had never set out. Think you not Dr. Mather will ride back from Boston with us to keep the witches off? I will bide there forever, if he will not. I will never come this dreadful road again, else. What is that? Oh, what is that? 'Tis a voice coming out of the woods like a great roar. *Joseph!* What is *that?* That was a black cat run across the road into the bushes. 'Twas a black cat. Joseph, let us turn back! No; the black man is behind us, and the beast. What shall we do? What shall we do? Oh, oh, I begin to twitch like Ann and Mercy last night! My feet move, and I cannot stop them! Now there is a pin thrust in my arm! I am pinched! There are fingers at my throat! Joseph! Joseph!"

"Go to prayer, sweetheart," shouted Joseph. "Go to prayer Be not afraid. 'Twill drive them away. Away with ye, Goody Bradbury! Away, Goody Proctor! Go to prayer, go to prayer!"

Joseph bent low in the saddle and lashed the horse, which sprang forward with a mighty bound; the green branches rushed in their faces. Joseph prayed in a loud voice. Ann clung to him convulsively, panting for breath. Suddenly they came out of the woods into a cleared space.

"The Proctor house! the Proctor house!" Ann shrieked. "Mercy Lewis said 'twas full of devils. What shall we do?" She hid her face on her husband's shoulder, sobbing and praying.

The Proctor house stood at the left of the road; there were some peach-trees in front of it, and their blossoms showed in a pink spray against the gray unpainted walls. On one side of the house was the great barn, with its doors wide open; on the other, a deep ploughed field, with the plough sticking in a furrow. John Proctor had been arrested and thrown into jail for witchcraft in April, before his spring planting was done.

Joseph Bayley reined in his horse opposite the Proctor house. "Ann," he whispered, and his whisper was full of horror.

"What is it?" she returned, wildly.

"Ann, Goodman Proctor looks forth from the chamber window, and Goody Proctor stands outside by the well, and they be both in jail in Boston." Joseph's whole frame shook in a strange rigid fashion, as if his joints were locked. "Look, Ann!" he whispered.

"I cannot."

"Look!"

Ann turned her head. "Why," she said, and her voice was quite natural and sweet, it had even a tone of glad relief in it, "I see naught but a little maid in the door."

"See you not Goodman Proctor in the window?"

"Nay," said Ann, smiling; "I see naught but the little maid in the door. She is in a blue petticoat, and she has a yellow head, but her little cheeks are pale, I trow."

"See you not Goodwife Proctor in the yard by the well?" asked Joseph.

"Nay, goodman; I see naught but the little maid in the door. She has a fair face, but now she falls a-weeping. Oh, I fear lest she be all alone in the house."

"I tell you, Goodman Proctor and Goodwife Proctor be both there," returned Joseph. "Think you I see not with my own eyes? Goodman Proctor has on a red cap, and Goodwife Proctor holds a spindle." He urged on the horse with a sudden cry. "Now the prayers do stick in my throat," he groaned. "I would we were out of this devil's nest!"

"Oh, Joseph," implored Ann, "prithee wait a minute! The little maid is calling 'mother' after me. Saw you not how she favored our little Susanna who died? Hear her! There was naught there but the little maid. Joseph, I pray you, stop."

"Nay; I'll ride till the nag drops," said Joseph Bayley, with a lash. "This last be too much. I tell ye they be there, and they be also in jail. 'Tis hellish work."

Ann said no more for a little space; a curve in the road hid the Proctor house from sight. Suddenly she raised a great cry. "Oh! oh!" she screamed, "'tis gone; 'tis gone from my foot!"

Joseph stopped. "What is gone?"

"My shoe; but now I missed it from my foot. I must alight, and go back for it."

"I SEE NAUGHT BUT A LITTLE MAID IN THE DOOR."

Joseph started the horse again.

Ann caught at the reins. "Stop, goodman," she cried, imperatively. "I tell you I must have my shoe."

"And I tell you I'll stop for no shoe in this place, were it made of gold."

"Goodman, you know not what shoe 'tis. 'Tis one of my fine shoes, in which I have never taken steps. They have the crimson silk lacings. I have even carried them in my hand to the meeting-house on a Sabbath, wearing my old ones, and only put them on at the door. Think you I will lose that shoe? Stop the nag."

But Joseph kept on grimly.

"Think you I will go barefoot or with one shoe into Boston?" said Ann. "Know you that these shoes, which were a present from my mother, cost bravely? I trow you will needs loosen your purse strings well before we pass the first shop in Boston. Well, go on, an you will, when 'tis but a matter of my slipping down from the pillion and running back a few yards."

Joseph Bayley turned his horse about; but Ann remonstrated.

"Nay," said she; "I want not to go thus. I am tired of the saddle. I would like to feel my feet for a space."

Her husband looked around at her with wonder and suspicion. Dark thoughts came into his mind.

She laughed. "Nay," said she, "make no such face at me. I go not back to meet any black man nor sign any book. I go for my fine shoe with the crimson lacing."

"'Tis but a moment since you were afraid," said Joseph. "Have you no fear now?" His blue eyes looked sharply into hers.

She looked back at him soberly and innocently. "In truth, I feel no such fear as I did," she answered. "If I mistake not, your bold front and your prayers drove away the evil ones. I will say a psalm as I go, and I trow naught will harm me."

Ann slipped lightly down from the pillion, and pulled off her one remaining shoe and her stockings; they were her fine worked silk ones, and she could not walk in them over the rough road. Then she set forth very slowly, peering here and there in the undergrowth beside the road, until she passed the curve and the reach of her husband's eyes. Then she gathered up her crimson taffeta petticoat and ran like a deer, with long graceful leaps, looking neither to right nor left, straight back to the Proctor house.

In the door of the house stood a tiny girl with a soft shock of yellow hair. She wore a little straight blue gown, and her baby feet were bare, curling over the sunny door-step. When she saw Ann coming she started as if to run; then she stood still, her soft eyes wary, her mouth quivering.

Ann Bayley ran up quickly, and threw her arms around her, kneeling down on the step. "What is your name, little maid?" said she, in a loving, agitated voice.

"Abigail Proctor," replied the little maid, shyly, in her sweet childish treble. Then she tried to free herself, but Ann held her fast.

"Nay, be not afraid. sweet," said she. "I love you. I once had a little maid like you for my own. Tell me, dear heart, are you all alone in the house?"

Then the child fell to crying again, and clung around Ann's neck.

"Is there anybody in the house, sweet?" Ann whispered, fondling her and pressing the wet baby cheek to her own.

"The constables came and took them," sobbed the little maid. "They put my poppet down the well, and they pulled mother and Sarah down the road. They took father before that, and Mary Warren did jibe and point. The constables pulled Benjamin away too. I want my mother."

"Your mother shall come again," said Ann. "Take comfort, dear little heart, they cannot have the will to keep her long away. There, there, I tell you she shall come. You watch in the door, and you will see her come down the road."

She smoothed back the little maid's yellow hair, and wiped the tears from her little face with a corner of her beautiful embroidered neckerchief. Then she saw that the face was all grimy with tears and dust, and she went over to the well, which was near the door, and drew a bucket of water swiftly with her strong young arms; then she wet the corner of the neckerchief and scrubbed the little maid's face, bidding her shut her eyes. Then she kissed her over and over.

"Now you are sweet and clean," said she. "Dear little heart, I have some sugar cakes in my bag for you, and then I must be gone."

The little maid looked at her eagerly,

her cheeks were waxen, and the blue veins showed in her full childish forehead. Ann pulled some little cakes out of a red velvet satchel she wore at her waist, and Abigail reached out for one with a hungry cry. The tears sprang to Ann's eyes; she put the rest of the cakes in a little pile on the door-stone, and watched the child eat. Then she gathered her up in her arms.

"Good-by, sweetheart," she said, kissing the soft trembling mouth, the sweet hollow under the chin, and the clinging hands. "Before long I shall come this way again, and do you stand in the door when I go past."

She put her down and hastened away, but little Abigail ran after her. Ann stopped and knelt and fondled her again. "Go back, deary," she pleaded; "go back, and eat the sugar cakes."

But this beautiful kind vision in the crimson taffeta, with the rosy cheeks and sweet black eyes looking out from the French hood, with the gleam of gold and delicate embroidery between the silken folds of her mantilla, with the ways like her mother's, was more to little deserted Abigail Proctor than the sugar cakes, although she was sorely hungry for them. She stood aloof with pitiful determined eyes until Ann's back was turned, then, as she followed, Ann looked around and saw her and caught her up again.

"My dear heart, my dear heart," she said, and she was half sobbing, "now must you go back, else I fear harm will come to you. My goodman is waiting for me yonder, and I know not what he will do or say. Nay; you must go back. I would I could keep you, my little Susanna, but you must go back." Ann Bayley put the little maid down and gave her a gentle push. "Go back," she said, smiling, with her eyes full of tears; "go back, and eat the sugar cakes."

Then she sped on swiftly: as she neared the curve in the road she thrust a hand in her pocket, and drew forth a dainty shoe with dangling lacings of crimson silk. She glanced around with a smile and a backward wave of her hand; the glowing crimson of her petticoat showed for a minute through the green mist of the undergrowth; then she disappeared.

The little maid Abigail stood still in the road, gazing after her, her soft pink mouth open, her hands clutching at her blue petticoat, as if she would thus hold herself back from following. She heard the tramp of a horse's feet beyond the curve; then it died away. She turned about and went back to the house, with the tears rolling over her cheeks; but she did not sob aloud, as she would have done had her mother been near to hear. A pitiful conviction of the hopelessness of all the appeals of grief was stealing over her childish mind. She had been alone in the house three nights and two days, ever since her sister Sarah and her brother Benjamin had been arrested for witchcraft and carried to jail. Long before that her parents, John and Elizabeth Proctor, had disappeared down the Boston road in charge of the constables. None of the family was spared save this little Abigail, who was deemed too young and insignificant to have dealings with Satan, and was therefore not thrown into prison, but was left alone in the desolate Proctor house in the midst of woods said to be full of evil spirits and witches, to die of fright or starvation as she might. There was but little mercy shown the families of those accused of witchcraft.

"Let some of Goody Proctor's familiars minister unto the brat," one of the constables had said, with a stern laugh, when Abigail had followed wailing after her brother and sister on the day of their arrest.

"Yea," said another; "she can send her yellow-bird or her black hog to keep her company. I wot her tears will be soon dried."

Then the stoutly tramping horses had borne out of sight and hearing the mocking faces of the constables; Sarah's fair agonized one turned backward toward her little deserted sister, and Benjamin's brave youthful clamor of indignation.

"Let us loose!" Abigail heard him shout; "let us loose, I tell ye! Ye be fools, rather than we be witches; ye be fools and murderers! Let us loose, I tell ye!"

And the little Abigail had waited long, thinking her brother's words would prevail; but neither he nor Sarah returned, and the sounds all died away, and she went back to the house sobbing. The damp spring night was settling down in a palpable mist, and the woods seemed full of voices. The little maid had heard enough of the terrible talk of the day to fill her innocent head with vague superstitious horror. She threw her little apron over her head and fled blindly through the woods, and now and then she fell down and bruised herself, and rose up lamenting sorely, with nobody to hear her.

As soon as she was in the house she shut the doors, and barred them with the great bars that had been made as protection against Indians, and now might wax useless against worse than savages, according to the belief of the colony.

All night long the little maid shrieked and sobbed, and called on her father and her mother and her sister and her brother. Men faring in the road betwixt Boston and Salem village heard her with horror. and fled past with psalm and prayer and blood cold in their veins, and related the next day to the raging, terror-stricken people how at midnight the accursed Proctor house was full of flitting infernal lights, and howling with devilish spirits, with mayhap a death-dealing tale of some godly woman of the village who outrode their horses on a broomstick and disappeared in the Proctor house.

The next day the little maid unbarred the door, and stood there watching up and down the road for her mother or some other to come. But they came not, although she watched all day. That night she did not sob and call out: she had become afraid of her own voice, and discovered that it had no effect to bring her help. Then, too, early in the night, she heard noises about the house which frightened her, and made her think that perchance the dreadful black beast of which she had heard them discourse was abroad.

The next morning she found that the two horses and the cow and calf were gone from the barn; also that there was left scarce anything for her to eat in the house. There had been some loaves of bread, some boiled meat, and some cakes; now it was all gone, and also all the meal from the chest, and the potatoes and pork from the cellar. But for that last she did not care, since she was not old enough to make a fire and cook. She had left for food only a little cold porridge in a blue bowl, and that she ate up at once and had no more, and a little buttermilk in a crock. which, she being not over-fond of, served her longer. But that was all she had had for a day and a night, until Goodwife Ann Bayley gave her the sugar cakes. These she ate up at once on her return to the house. Then again she stood watch-

ing in the door, but nothing passed along the road save a partridge or a squirrel. It was accounted a bold thing for any solitary traveller to come this way, save a witch, and she, it was supposed, might find many comrades in the woods beside the road and in the Proctor house, which was held to be a sort of devils' tavern. But now no witch came, nor any of her uncanny friends, unless indeed the squirrel and the partridge were familiar demons in disguise. Nothing was too harmless and simple to escape that imputation of the devil's mask.

Abigail took her little pewter porringer from the cupboard, and got herself a drink of water from the bucketful that Goodwife Bayley had drawn; then she stood on a stone, and peered into the well, leaning over the curb. Her poppet was in there, her dear rag doll that Sarah had made for her, and dressed in a beautiful silver brocade made from a piece of a wedding gown that was brought from England. One of the constables had caught sight of little Abigail Proctor's poppet, and being straightway filled with suspicion that it was an image whereby Goody Proctor afflicted her victims by proxy, had seized it and thrown it into the well. The other constables had chidden him for such rashness, saying it should have been carried to Boston, and produced as evidence at the trial; and little Abigail had shrieked out in a panic for her poppet.

She could see nothing of it now, and she went back to her watching-place in the door.

In the afternoon she felt sorely hungry again, and searched through the house for food; then she went out in the sunny fields behind the house, and found some honeysuckles on the rocks, and sucked the honey greedily from their fine horns. On her return to the house she found a corn-cob, which she snatched up and folded in her apron, and begun tending. She sat down in the doorway in her little chair, which she dragged out of the keeping-room, and hugged the poor poppet close, and crooned over it.

"Be not afraid," said she. "I'll not let the black beast harm you; I promise you I will not."

That night she formed a new plan for her solace and protection in the lonely darkness. All the garments of her lost parents and sister and brother that she could find she gathered together, and formed in a circle on the keeping-room floor; then she crept inside with her corn-cob poppet, and lay there hugging it all night. The next day she watched again in the door; but now she was weak and faint, and her little legs trembled so under her that she could not stand to watch, but sat in her little straight-backed chair, holding her poppet and peering forth wistfully.

In the course of the day she made shift to creep out into the fields again, and lying flat on the sun-heated rocks, she sucked some more honey drops from the honeysuckles. She found, too, on the edge of the woods, some young wintergreen leaves, and she even pulled some blue violets and ate them. But the delicate, sweet, and aromatic fare in the spring larder of nature was poor nourishment for a human baby.

Poor little Abigail Proctor could scarcely creep home, still clinging fast to her poppet; scarcely lift herself into her chair in the door; scarcely crawl inside her fairy-ring of her loved ones' belongings at night. She rolled herself tightly in an old cloak of her father's, and it was a sweet and harmless outcome of the dreadful superstition of the day, grafted on an innocent childish brain, that it seemed to partake of the bodily presence of her father, and protect her.

All night long, as she lay there, her mother cooked good meat and broth and sweet cakes, and she ate her fill of them; but in the morning she was too weak to turn her little body over. She could not get to her watching-place in the door, but that made little difference to her, for she did not fairly know that she was not there. It seemed to her that she sat in her little chair looking up the road and down the road; she saw the green branches weaving together, and hiding the sky to the northward and the southward; she saw the flushes of white and rose in the flowering undergrowth; she saw the people coming and going. There were her father and mother now coming with store of food and presents for her, now following the constables out of sight. There was that fine pageant passing, as she had seen it pass once before, of the two magistrates, their worshipful masters John Hathorne and Jonathan Corwin, with the marshal, constables, and aids, splendid and awe-inspiring in all their trappings

of office, to examine the accused in the Salem meeting-house. There were the ministers Parris and Noyes coming, with severe malignant faces, to question her mother as to whether she had afflicted Mary Warren, their former maid-servant, who was now bewitched. There went Benjamin, clamoring out boldly at his captors. There came Sarah with the poppet, which she had drawn out of the well, shaking the water from its silver brocade.

All this the little maid Abigail Proctor saw through her half-delirious fancy as she lay weakly on the keeping-room floor, but she saw not the reality of her sister Sarah coming about four o'clock in the afternoon.

Sarah Proctor, tall and slender, in her limp bedraggled dress, with her fair severe face set in a circle of red shawl, which she had pinned under her chin, came resolutely down the road from Boston, driving a black cow before her with a great green branch. She was nearly fainting with weariness, but she set her dusty shoes down swiftly among the road weeds, and her face was as unyielding as an Indian's.

When she came in sight of the Proctor house she stopped a second. "Abigail!" she called; "Abigail!"

There was no answer, and she went on more swiftly than before. When she reached the house she called again, "Abigail!" but did not wait except while she tied the black cow, by a rope which was around her neck, to a peach-tree. Then she ran in, and found the little maid, her sister Abigail, on the floor in the keeping-room.

She got down on her knees beside her, and Abigail smiled up in her face waveringly. She still thought herself in the door, and that she had just seen her sister come down the road.

"Abigail, what have they done to you?" asked Sarah, in a sharp voice; and the little maid only smiled.

"Abigail, Abigail, what is it?" Sarah took hold of the child's shoulders and shook her; but she got no word back, only the smile ceased, and the eyelids drooped faintly.

"Are you hungry, Abigail?"

The little maid shook her head softly.

"It cannot be that," said Sarah, as if half to herself; "there was enough in the house; but what is it? Abigail, look at me; how long is it since you have eaten? Abigail!"

"Yesterday," whispered the little maid, dreamily.

"What did you eat then?"

"Some posies and leaves out in the field."

"What became of all the bread that was baked, and the cakes, and the meat?"

"I—have forgot."

"No, you have not. Tell me, Abigail."

"The black beast came in the night and did eat it all up, and the cow, and calf, and the horses too."

"The black beast!"

"I heard him in the night, and in the morning 'twas—gone."

Sarah sprang up. "Robbers and murderers!" she cried, in a fierce voice; but the little maid on the floor did not start, she shut her eyes again, and looked up and down the road.

Sarah got a bucket quickly, and went out in the yard to the cow. Down on her knees in the grass she went and milked; then she carried in the bucket, strained the milk with trembling haste, and poured some into Abigail's little pewter porringer. "She was wont to love it warm," she whispered, with white lips.

She bent close over the little maid, and raised her on one arm, while she put the porringer to her mouth. "Drink, Abigail," she said, with tender command. "'Tis warm—the way you love it."

The little maid tried to sip, but shut her mouth, and turned her head with weak loathing, and Sarah could not compel her. She laid her back, and got a spoon and fed her a little, by dint of much pleading to make her open her mouth and swallow.

Afterwards she undressed her, and put her to bed in the south-front room, but the child was so uneasy without the ring of garments which she had arranged, that Sarah was forced to put them around her on the bed; then she fell asleep directly, and stood in her dream watching in the door.

Sarah herself stood in the door, looking up and down the road. There was the sound of a galloping horse in the distance; it came nearer and nearer. She went down to the road and stood waiting. The horse was reined in close to her, and the young man who rode him sprang off the saddle.

"It is you, Sarah; you are safe home," he cried, eagerly, and would have put his arm about her; but she stood aloof sternly.

"For what else did you take me—my apparition?" she said, in a hard voice.

"Sweetheart!"

"Know you that I have but just come from the jail in Boston, where I have lain fast chained for witchcraft? See you my fine apparel with the prison air in it? Know you that they called me a witch, and said that I did afflict Mary Warren, and the rest? I marvel not that you kept your distance, David Carr; I might perchance have hurt you, and they might have accused you, since you were in fellowship with a witch. I marvel not at that. I would have no harm come to you, though far greater than this came to me, but wherefore did you let my little sister Abigail starve? That can I not suffer, coming from you, David."

The young man took her in his arms with a decided motion; and indeed she did not repulse him, but began to weep.

"Sarah," said he, earnestly, "I was in Ipswich. I knew naught of you and Benjamin being cried out upon until within this hour, when I returned home, and my mother told me. I knew not you were acquitted, and was on my way to Boston to you when I saw you at the gate. And as for Abigail, I knew naught at all; and so 'twas with my mother, for she but now wept when she said the poor little maid had been taken with the rest. But you mean not that, sweetheart; she has not been let to starve?"

"They stole away the food in the night," said Sarah, "and the horses and the cow and calf. I found the cow straying in the woods but now, on my way home, and drove her in and milked her; but Abigail would take scarce a spoonful of the warm milk. She has had but little to eat for three days, and has been distracted with fear, being left alone. She has ever been but a delicate child, and now I fear she has a fever on her, and will die, with her mother away."

"I will go for my mother, sweetheart," said David Carr, eagerly.

"Bring her under cover of night, then," said Sarah; "else she may be suspected if she come to this witch tavern, as they call it. Oh, David, think you she will come? I am in a sore strait."

"I will bring her without fail, sweet,

and a flask of wine also, and needments for the little maid," cried David. "Only do you keep up good heart. Perchance, sweet, the child will amend soon, and the others be soon acquit. Nay, weep not, poor lass! poor lass! Thou hast me, whatever else fail thee, poor solace though that be, and I will fetch thee my mother right speedily. She has ever set great store by the little maid, and knows much about ailments; and I doubt not they will be soon acquit."

"They say my mother will," answered Sarah, tearfully; "and Benjamin is acquit now, but had best keep for a season out of Salem village. But my father will not be acquit; he has spoken his mind too boldly before them all."

"Nay, sweetheart," said David Carr, mounting, "'twill all have passed soon: 'tis but a madness. Go in to the little maid, and be of good comfort."

Sarah went sobbing into the house, but her face was quite calm when she stood over little Abigail. The child was still asleep, and she could arouse her only for a little to take a few spoonfuls of milk; then she turned her head on the pillow with weary obstinacy, and shut her eyes again. She still held the poor little corn-cob poppet fast.

Sarah washed herself, braided her hair, and changed her prison dress for a clean blue linen one; then she sat beside Abigail, and waited for David Carr and his mother, who came within an hour. Goodwife Carr was renowned through Salem village for her knowledge of medicinal herbs and her nursing. She had a gentle sobriety and decision of manner which stood her firmly in her neighbors' confidences, they seeing how she abode firmly in her own, and arguing from that. Then she had too the good fortune to have made no enemies, consequently her ability had not incurred for her the suspicion of being a witch.

Goodwife Carr brought a goodly store of healing herbs, of bread and cakes and meat, and she brewed drinks, and bent her face, pale and soberly faithful, in her close white cap, untiringly over Abigail Proctor. But the little maid never arose again. A fever, engendered by starvation and fright and grief, had seized upon her, and she lay in the bed with her little corn-cob baby a few days longer, and then died.

They made a little straight white gown for her, Sarah and Goodwife Carr, and dressed her in it, after washing her and smoothing her yellow hair; and she lay, looking longer and older than in life, all set about with flowers—pinks and lilacs and roses—from Goodwife Carr's garden, until she was buried. And they had the Ipswich minister come for the funeral, for David Carr cried out in a fury that Minister Parris, who had prosecuted this witchcraft business, was her murderer, and blood would flow from her little body if he stood beside it, and that it was the same with Minister Noyes; and Sarah Proctor's pale face had flushed up fiercely in assent.

The morning after the little maid Abigail Proctor was buried, Joseph Bayley and his wife Ann came riding down the road from Boston, and they were in brave company, and needed to have but little fear of witches; for the great minister Cotton Mather rode with them, his Excellency the Governor of the colony, two worshipful magistrates, and two other ministers—all on their way to a witch trial in Salem.

And as they neared the Proctor house there was much discourse concerning it and the inmates thereof, many strange and dreadful accounts, and much godly denunciation. And as they reached the curve in the road they came suddenly in sight of a young man and a tall fair maid standing together at the side by some white-flowering bushes. And Sarah Proctor, even with her little sister Abigail dead and her parents in danger of death, was smiling for a second's space in David Carr's face, for the love and hope in tragedy that make God possible, and the selfishness of love that makes life possible, were upon her in spite of herself.

But when she saw the cavalcade approaching, saw the gleam of rich raiment, and heard the tramp and jingling, the smile faded straightway from her face, and she stood behind David in the white alder bushes. And David stood before her, and gazed with a stern and defiant scowl at the gentry as they passed by. And the great Cotton Mather gazed back at that beautiful white face rising like another flower out of the bushes, and he speculated with himself if it were the face of a witch.

But Goodwife Ann Bayley thought only on the little maid in the door. And when they came to the Proctor house she leaned eagerly from the pillion, and she smiled and kissed her hand.

"Why do you thus, Ann?" her husband asked, looking about at her.

"See you not the little maid in the door?" she whispered low, for fear of the goodly company. "I trow she looks better than she did. The roses are in her cheeks, and they have combed her yellow hair, and put a clean white gown on her. She holds a little doll, too."

"I see nobody," said Joseph Bayley, wonderingly.

"Nay, but she stands there. I never saw aught shine like her hair and her white gown; the sunlight lies full in the door. See! see! she is smiling! I trow all her griefs be well over."

The cavalcade passed the Proctor house, but Goodwife Ann Bayley's sweet face was turned backward until it was out of sight, towards the little maid in the door.

GIFTS OF OBLIVION
by Dorothy Canfield

HIS was not one of the usual cases of failure of memory, written up picturesquely in the newspapers. After his sojourn in chaos he did not return to life as an unrecognized bit of wreckage, to be sent finally from the hospital without a label. Every one knew all the details of the accident, and knew him to be Matthew Warren. And yet when the doctor, the well-known James Farquhar, M.D., who was the closest friend of the injured man and his wife, pronounced the acute danger past and said that he might be allowed to see his family for a moment, Matthew Warren looked dully at the handsome woman and the two blooming children who, showing a frightened tendency to tears, came to the private room at the hospital to stand by his bedside. "Who are those people?" he asked his nurse, with the weak curiosity of a sick man, losing interest as he spoke. His wife drew back quickly. Dr. Farquhar motioned the visitors away. He did not seem surprised. From that time he was constantly in the sick man's room.

It was not until several days later that the slowly rising tide of Matthew Warren's vitality reached the point where he felt the significance of his condition. He woke from sleep with a scream which brought the watchful doctor to him in a bound. "Who am I? Who am I?" he called, wildly; and then, controlling himself with an effort, clutching at the doctor's arm, his teeth chattering loudly, he added, "I'm very s-s-sorry to trouble you, b-b-but I seem to have h-h-had a nightmare of some s-s-sort, and I can't—I can't remember who I am."

Two months later, when he seemed quite himself again physically, the doctor, having exhausted all other devices, resolved to try taking the sick man home. Perhaps, he argued dubiously, the utter familiarity of his surroundings might speak to his clouded brain. The experiment was tried. Matthew Warren, to all appearances restored to perfect health, went along docilely with his old friend, whom he continued to treat as a new acquaintance. He stepped into

the train with no surprise, looked about him quietly, opened a window *en route* with a practised commuter's knowledge of the catch, and talked, as he had ever since his recovery, calmly and simply of the every-day objects before him. He was especially interested in the first signs of spring in the early April landscape, pointing out to his companion with great pleasure the gray sheen of pussy willows and, as the train approached the prosperous suburban region, stretches of brilliantly green lawns.

As he walked up the well-raked gravel of the driveway toward his own expensive house he might have been the old Matthew Warren returning, as usual, after his day in the city; and coming to meet him, as usual, was Mrs. Matthew Warren, looking very picturesque in a dress he had always especially admired.

She advanced slowly, shrinking a little, very pale. She had never recovered from the shock of meeting those blankly unresponsive eyes at the hospital. It had wounded and withered something deep in her. Dr. Farquhar looked at her keenly, noting with disapproval the signs of suppressed agitation. He regretted having undertaken the risk of the experiment.

Matthew Warren lifted his hat as she drew near. "I hope you will pardon our trespassing upon your beautiful grounds," he said. She winced at the distant courtesy of the gesture and his accent. He went on, "My friend has, I believe, some errand bringing him here." He put on his hat, stepped a little to one side, to allow his wife and the doctor to walk together, and in an instant was absorbed in the green spears of the daffodils thrusting their vigorous, glistening shafts through the earth.

The woman questioned the doctor with a mute gaze in which was offended pride, as well as grief and bewilderment. She had been the handsomest girl in her set and unreservedly indulged by her husband throughout her married life. Until now she had been always a perfectly satisfied woman, and something in her heart had grown great and exacting, which now revolted angrily against this grotesque trial put upon her by fate.

"Let us try the house," said the specialist.

She walked beside him in silence. Matthew Warren followed them slowly, gazing about him at the newly green lustrous grass and at the trees swinging swollen buds in the warm, damp air. He looked curiously young, not so old, by ten years at least, as the man who, three months before, throwing a reckless wager over his shoulders to those in the, tonneau, had clamped down the brake which did not work.

"Jim, I thought best not to have the children here," whispered his wife to the doctor.

He nodded assent. "One can never tell how it will affect him. It has been an especially hard case, because the mere mention of his lost identity throws him into a fever. Otherwise he has been quite reasonable. You must remember that it is absolutely essential to keep perfectly calm yourself. He is a very, very sick man."

Mrs. Warren glanced at her husband and shivered throughout all her big, handsome, healthy body. She seemed to herself to be in a nightmare. It was all incredible. That she, of all people, should be in such a situation!

The owner of the house stepped up on the broad piazza and looked admiringly at the view of the Hudson, the view which he had discovered, and for the sake of which the house had been located where it stood.

"What a splendid stretch of the river your piazza commands!" he said, pleasantly, to his hostess, as the three stood expectantly before the door. She looked at the doctor and opened the door without speaking, motioning her guests into the big living-room, all in leather shades of brown and tan, with coals shimmering in the fireplace Matthew Warren had designed. Again he broke their silence with a pleasant comment:

"How superb those tulips are! They are more like fire than the fire itself." He glanced casually, indifferently, into his wife's face, then at the doctor, evidently with a moment's wonder that he did not introduce the object of their call, and then away, absently, out of the window. A lilac bush grew near it, and with an exclamation of delight he sprang up to examine it more closely. "Some of those buds are opening!" he announced joyfully to the two who watched him so narrowly. "I see a real little leaf—oh, and another!"

He was answered by an hysteric scream from his wife, and whirled about in astonishment to see the doctor motioning her sternly to silence. She clapped her shaking hand over her mouth, but she could not repress another scream as she met her husband's politely concerned, questioning eyes. And then suddenly she took matters in her own hands. She flung aside the doctor's detaining arm and rushed toward the sick man, crying out:

"Matt! Matt! come to yourself! Look at me! Why, I'm Molly! I'm Molly!" She threw her arms around his neck, sobbing furiously.

Almost instantly she recoiled from his rigid, unresponsive body as violently as she had flung herself upon it. Matthew Warren did not seem aware of her at all. He stood quite still, his eyes turning with a sick slowness upon the doctor.

"*Who am I?*" he asked, solemnly. His face and neck were of a dull, congested red, and the veins stood out visibly.

Dr. Farquhar, making the best of a bad turn of events, decided to risk all on a bold stroke. He advanced and said, clearly and masterfully, "You are my dear old friend Matthew Warren, and I am Jim Farquhar, and this is your home and your wife."

The other stood motionless. His eyes were fixed on a point in space incalculably distant. After a moment he turned stiffly and walked toward the door.

"There is some mistake," he said, fumbling at the latch. "I cannot for the moment remember who I am, but I have never been in this house before, and this is the first time I ever saw that lady." His trembling hands failed to open the door at once, and the trifling delay seemed the match touched to the tinder of his disordered fancies, for he began to beat on the lock and to scream: "I don't know who I am! Why doesn't somebody tell me who I am! I can't remember who—" Before the doctor could

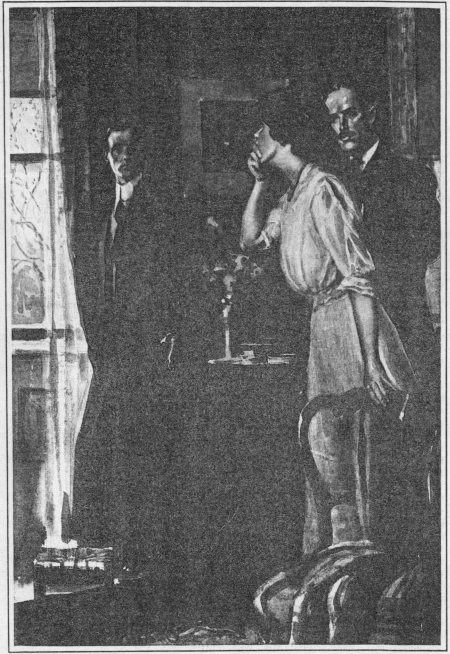

Drawn by John Alonzo Williams

SHE CLAPPED HER HAND OVER HER MOUTH AS SHE MET HIS QUESTIONING EYES

reach him he had gone down in so horridly dislocated and inhuman a heap that his wife ran shrieking from the room and from the house.

His prostration after this second shock was so great that he could not be moved back to the hospital, and he spent the slow month of collapse and utter weakness which followed in his own bed in his own room under the care of two men nurses. His wife had insisted upon men, having a panic fear of a return of his violence. The doctor advised her to keep out of the sick-room, counsel which she seemed not eager to disregard. The children she sent quite away, out of town. In her lonely and frightened days and nights she frequently asked herself with passion what wicked thing she could have done to be so unhappy now! She had a horror of her husband's presence, although she made a gallant effort to conceal this from the doctor, whom she suspected of watching her jealously for a sign of it; and as the master of the house grew stronger, so that he was reported to her up and dressed, she looked forward to the future with unspeakable dread.

And yet, on the day when, evading his nurses with an insane man's cunning, he crept from the house and disappeared, she led the search for him with unwearied faithfulness, following out every clue suggested to her, setting every possible agency in action, and going unflinchingly with the doctor to look at a corpse recovered from the river. After ten days of this sort of bad dream, Matthew Warren was discovered, not a mile from his own house. He was spading up a bed in the garden of old Timothy O'Donovan, the truck-farmer who supplied the prosperous suburb with green vegetables. As the lost man spaded, he whistled loudly, like a plowboy. The truck-farmer had not dreamed that the battered, muddy, half-witted wayfarer who had asked for work a week before, and who had set himself so vigorously and cheerfully at the tasks given him, could be the wealthy, influential Mr. Warren who owned the fine house at the other end of town.

There was a consultation of brain specialists, Dr. Farquhar, and Mrs. Warren herself. She was questioned minutely as to her husband's mental habits and tendencies, and finally succeeded in unearthing from her memory, never very vivid about other people's preferences, the fact (perhaps significant, the doctors thought) that after she and Matthew were first married, when they were quite poor, Matthew had seemed to enjoy working the bit of land about their first small home.

"But of course," she explained, "as his business grew so rapidly and took more of his time he did less and less of it. We have had a gardener ever since we lived in this house."

It was agreed that in the break-up of his higher faculties he might have returned with a blind instinct to a youthful latent inclination, and that for a while it was best to leave him where he was and trust to the slow healing influence of time and improved physical health, since all other curative means had failed. If Mrs. Warren felt an involuntary relief at this decision, she hid it deep in her heart, and throughout the discussion she showed herself loyally willing to do whatever seemed best for the man who had been her husband. And so began the anomalous situation which was to last so long that even village tongues stopped gossiping of it.

Mrs. Warren's first distracted impulse had been to take the children and go away— abroad, perhaps. That had seemed to her the only endurable future. But she gave up this plan when the doctor showed a disappointed and sternly disapproving surprise that she "abandon" a man who might be in desperate need at almost any time.

"I see, Jim—yes, of course, I see," she had submissively assented. She cared intensely that those who knew of this crisis in her life should approve her action. As a matter of fact, her acquiescence to his opinion cost her far less than she feared. The miraculous capacity of life to renew itself under any and all circumstances came brilliantly to the rescue of a nature normal above everything else. It was not long before she and the children had reorganized an existence which was tolerable at first, and then, as time slid smoothly by without change, not without its great compensations. There was plenty of money, since Matthew's business had been disposed of at a good profit, and there was very little care. The children, ten and twelve respectively, enjoyed perfect health, grew fast, were not troublesome to their vigorous mother, and had absorbing youthful interests of their own. They adapted themselves with great tact and good sense to their peculiar situation. Like their mother, they were large and comely, with a healthfully ready ability to be satisfied with life. It was hard to connect the well-groomed, trimly attired, prepossessing trio, riding and driving about the "residential portion" of the suburb, with the shabby, half-daft hired man in overalls who rarely left the truck-farm at the other end of town. In a surprisingly short time even those who knew of the unprecedented circumstances came almost involuntarily to regard Mrs. Warren as a highly ornamental widow, and the children as half-orphans.

Not that they themselves had the bad taste to make a mystery of the affair. The sad story was told with a frank sadness to their intimates, and roused among the young friends of the children a sort of romantic admiration for their extraordinary situation. From the first they had all three followed to the letter the doctor's recommendation to keep away from the region of the truck-farm. They depended for news of the sick man upon the doctor himself, who took care to go past the O'Donovan place at not infrequent intervals to inquire particulars of the new "help."

There, too, as frequently happens with busy people absorbed in their own difficult affairs, O'Donovan and his wife adjusted themselves to the singular state of things with a rapidity which astonished them. The half-fearful curiosity they had felt

AS THE LOST MAN SPADED, HE
WHISTLED LIKE A PLOW-BOY

toward the new laborer when they first learned his identity gave way little by little to an unsurprised acquiescence in his kindly, simple presence and his peculiarities. For the second shock, which had come to him during his wife's wild appeal, had, it seemed, been even more violent than the first. He had seemed only to forget his identity before. Now he had lost it. He could not now have opened automatically the window in the commuter's train. That second month of oblivion had left him with practically no memory of any kind. He not only did not know who he was, but he could not remember from one day to the next. From morning till night he was like other men; but at every dawn he rose up singing, with a mind as blank of past experiences as a little child's.

This was, of course, until a way had been invented to obviate it, the cause of the greatest practical inconvenience, since he could not remember instructions given him the day before, nor even to continue a task half completed. The trucker and his wife had several highly irritating experiences with him, as on the occasion when, having been set to plow a patch in the garden, he went on plowing because nobody told him to stop and he had forgotten orders given him the day before, until he had turned under all the sod of the O'Donovans' only meadow. Finally, applying their Celtic wits to the problem, they took advantage of the capacity of their new servant for fluent reading and writing. They gave him a standing order to carry about with him a pad of paper and a pencil, to set down in black and white every instruction given him, and to consult it at every step. He obeyed this command with a smiling, absent docility, giving, as always at this period of his life, the strange impression of one wrought upon by sweet and secret thoughts. The O'Donovans said that to see him walk across the barnyard you would know he was fey.

After this device was in working order, O'Donovan boasted that no man could wish for better help than this stalwart, cheerful, deft-handed laborer, who loved every plant in the long rows of the truck-farm, worked, whistling and singing, all day long, and never asked for a holiday. For a long time his only excursions away from the farm were on Sundays, when he went with his employer and Mrs. O'Donovan to the little Roman Catholic church set in the midst of the poorer quarter of the suburb. He could not follow the mass, but it gave him obvious pleasure to listen to the music and to look at the priest's robes and the red and white of the acolytes' garb.

Two years after his arrival at the farm he could scarcely have been recognized by his wife and children if they had seen him. Like his employer, he had allowed his beard to grow, a thick mass of brown, without a gray hair in it, although Dr. Farquhar knew him to be nearly fifty. Above this, his tanned, ruddy face and quiet eyes gave no hint of the keen animation and the piercingly satirical look which had been Matthew Warren's.

Timothy O'Donovan and his wife, childless, solitary old people, came to love the kindly "innocent," whom they regarded as a child, almost as though he had been of their own blood. Old Mrs. O'Donovan especially petted him and cherished him, and lavished on him the affection which she had been so ready to give the son Heaven had never granted her. As she and her husband grew older, and as this adopted member of their family began to seem more "like other people," read books, studied farming and trucking seriously, and recovered something of his shattered memory for every-day events, he was trusted with more and more of the farming and the business. The slow clearing of his mind brought out traces of his superior education,

and this, together with a considerable native aptitude for the business, was a great asset to the primitive older farmer. They started tentatively some hot-beds for early vegetables which later grew by degrees to a greenhouse. The younger man, after several years of experimenting, developed a new variety of tomato, especially suited to their conditions. He called it, after Mrs. O'Donovan, the "Aileen," a tribute which pleased her greatly. Not having a name of his own, the assistant took that of his employer, and the newer people of the town thought them father and son. Sometimes he drove the delivery wagon into town to the market, early in the morning, and later, so little vivid did his past seem to the O'Donovans, was sent once in a while to the Warren house to deliver at the tradesman's door their daily supply of fresh salads.

When Mrs. O'Donovan died he mourned her with sorrow so sincere that her bereaved old husband felt him to be the one link which still bound him to life, and seven years later, when old Timothy himself passed away in the arms of his faithful servitor, it was found that he had left the farm and house to the wanderer who, twelve years before, haggard and nameless, had stumbled desperately up his garden path.

The new farmer was not long to lead a solitary life. A great-nephew of O'Donovan's, a boy of fourteen, left orphaned in Ireland before his uncle's death, had already started out to the States, and four or five days after the funeral he arrived at the house, horribly frightened at everything so strange and different, horribly homesick, horribly alone, and more than willing to accept the instantly offered home thrown open to him by his uncle's successor, whom he thought his own blood relative. When he had recovered from his first panic he proved himself very useful to the solitary man. He was of the shrinking, shy, fawn-eyed type of Irish boy, very handy about the house, "as good as a girl," his dead mother had often said of him, and he took over the domestic end of the new partnership. He proved to have a taste for music, and his guardian arranged for a weekly lesson from a violinist in town. He himself sat in the evenings on the porch, smoking, reading, and listening with a pleased smile to the singing of the fiddle in the room

HE GALLOPED PAST HIS FATHER'S VEGETABLE CART

behind him. They were both always in bed by nine o'clock.

Sometimes, for an outing, he took the lad with him on his trips to town, pointing out, among other objects of interest, the fine houses of the wealthy residents and, on the rare occasions when they were detained so long as to witness the awakening of the suburb, the miraculously well-tailored people who inhabited them. His daughter, after a very successful young-ladyhood competently managed by her mother, was married now to a prosperous, hard-working, commuting banker, considerably older than herself, and lived in a house a little more expensive and very much more in accord with the latest fashions in domestic archi-

tecture than her mother's, which was now, in the swiftly advancing American town, one of the "older residences." His son still lived at home, a famous tennis-player and athlete, who occasionally, flanneled to perfection, walked past on his way to the tennis-courts, or, his smooth yellow hair tossed back from his healthy, unexcited face, galloped on his well-groomed hunter past his father's vegetable cart. Mrs. Warren too was to be seen not infrequently, as handsome, though not as slender, as formerly, the image of good comfort and good fortune, hurrying from one engagement to another, consulting her watch and tapping a well-dressed foot in impatience at the slowness of her car, as in years gone by.

She had never thought, apparently, of seeking a divorce from her husband. Among her numerous friends this constancy was much admired.

These swept by the burly, elderly gardener without a look, quite sincerely unaware of his identity. They relied on the doctor to let them know if the now quite unlooked-for "change" should ever take place, and they all of them led absorbing lives of the greatest interest to themselves.

Dr. Farquhar, whom the gardener had come to know again in his new existence through his visits to the two O'Donovans, always nodded as he passed, and received in return a respectful tradesman's salute.

Of all those concerned he alone continued to be desperately unreconciled to the state of things. His physician's pride had been stung by his professional defeat, which had, moreover, involved the ruin of his dearest friend. In spite of the friendly cordiality of Mrs. Warren, he could never rid himself of an unworthy and unfair tendency to blame her for her own untroubled good fortune. He was frequently called to the Warren house professionally and could not enter that dignified home of ease without thinking bitterly of the man exiled from it and from all his natural birthright, to poverty and obscurity, and grinding daily manual labor. He compared Mrs. Warren's smooth, aristocratic, significant hands with the work-worn claws of the ignorant old Irishwoman who had furnished so long poor Warren's only contact with the refinements of the world of women. He thought of Warren's own hands, which he had known so sensitive and nervously active, now thickened and calloused, lying half open on his knees, in the dull passivity of the laboring-man. Once or twice the doctor had been compelled to take a meal *en famille* with the Warrens, and the delicately served food had choked him. He remembered that Warren usually nowadays sat down to a single coarse dish of stew, prepared by the little Irish lout whom he had adopted. He looked about him at the tasteful elegance of the spacious interior and thought of the bare four-roomed cabin which now sheltered the master of this house. The faithful friend, feeling Warren's grotesque and tragic fate as though it were his own, had never been able to stay all through one of Mrs. Warren's evening entertainments. The well-to-do

atmosphere of expansive ease and affluence in those handsome rooms formed too embittering a contrast in his loyal mind with the imprisoning round of toil of his friend and the rustic companionship which was the only break in the solitude of his life.

Once, as the doctor fled desperately away from a cotillion, and came out shivering into the cold dawn, shrugging on his overcoat and frowning, he caught sight of the O'Donovan vegetable cart making its early start for the market. He stood still in front of the Warren house, the chilly morning air whipping streaks of red up into his pale reveler's face. The horses jogged by, Warren holding the reins loosely, his powerful body lounging on the seat, his coarse shirt open at the throat. Dr. Farquhar gazed at his weather-beaten face and raged inwardly. As the cart passed the entrance to the driveway the driver glanced up at the Warren house, saw the lighted windows yellow in the clear, blue dawn, and then caught sight of the doctor hugging his Inverness about him. He nodded cheerfully.

"It's a fine morning, Doctor," he called, and passed on.

The doctor heard him begin a moment later to whistle loudly, the sweet, shrill treble piercing the air like a bird's note.

Dr. Farquhar clenched his fists angrily. He thought of the brilliant future which had lain open before his friend, he remembered his absorbing, crowded life of varied intellectual interests, his first promising success in politics, the beginning of his reputation as an after-dinner speaker, his growing influence in financial circles, his notable social gifts, and then his beautiful, faithful wife, his creditable, highly successful children—and then— ah, what a professional triumph to effect such a cure after so long! The doctor said aloud:

"I *will* go to see that man in Vienna. There's no harm in watching him operate."

Four months later he was back again, and went straight from the station, where he landed at dusk, to the O'Donovan farmhouse. It was early autumn and, although not yet eight o'clock, the first stars were already emerging from a pure, quiet sky. He heard the singing of the violin as he went up the walk, and in answer to his knock young Tim came to the door, the

HE DID NOT AGAIN INTERRUPT THE DOCTOR'S VEHEMENT TALK

echo of the music on his still dreaming face.

"He's in the garden, sir, the master is, but if you'll kindly take a seat I'll step an' call him. He likes to take one look around before we go to bed. They say around here that he can't sleep unless he's tucked the plants up and given them a pat like."

Dr. Farquhar sat down and crossed his legs. The hanging foot jerked nervously. It was extremely quiet there on the side road. He could hear the distant murmur of the boy's voice and the man's answer. He could count every step of their return as though they were the beats of his own heart—across the soft ground of the field, the dusty road, the hard-beaten path.

The big, roughly dressed man stood there before him, looking up at him with a quiet smile.

"Were you wanting to see me, Doctor?" said the gardener.

The doctor rose, breathing quickly, facing the other's kindly, patient eyes with some nervous irritation.

"Yes, yes—I have a great deal to say to you, Mr.—" He hesitated, balked over the name, used his hesitation as a desperately seized opening, and said, impatiently, "Of course you know that your name is not really O'Donovan."

The gardener turned to the slim figure loitering at the gate and called, "Tim, 'tis time you were in bed." The lad moved obediently up the path, humming under his breath the slow melody he had been playing on his violin.

"All right, Uncle," he said, good-humoredly, and disappeared.

The gardener sat down on the edge of the tiny porch. "I take it it is something very particular you have to say, Doctor?" he asked, not without a touch of apprehension in his voice.

The doctor nodded and began to speak rapidly, violently. He had not gone far before the gardener stood up in evident agitation. He shook his head, frowning, and motioned the other to silence.

"I'm all right as I am," he said, curtly. "What is the good of prying into what's long past and nobody knows about, anyhow. Such things oughtn't to be stirred up—they only—" The doctor beginning to talk again, he raised his voice to cry angrily: "I don't want to hear any more such talk! 'Tis better to take things as they are. Nobody is the better for prying into secrets that—"

Dr. Farquhar flew at him in a passion of intensity which beat down his opposition. "Will you listen to me!" he commanded in a voice of fury. "Just listen to what I have to say! Almost your life and death are at stake. You *shall* listen!"

The gardener gave a gesture of impatience, but he sat down and did not again interrupt the doctor's vehement monologue. Occasionally he rubbed his big palms on his knees stiffly. The crickets sang loudly. From up-stairs Tim's window threw a square of yellow light on the flower-beds in the front yard. His clear alto dropped down to them in snatches of his slowly moving adagio. The stars came out, one by one, and then in clusters, until an innumerable radiant company shone down on the two figures on the porch. The doctor's harangue drew to a close.

"I have followed your case from the beginning; and although one can never be absolutely sure of the results of so grave an operation, I am *so* certain that I cannot but insist that you place yourself in my hands. When you have come to yourself and realize your lost identity, you will fully understand and share the intensity of my feeling on this point—" He stopped to draw breath, leaning forward toward the man he was addressing, his brows drawn together as he tried to read the other man's expression. The faint light of the stars allowed him to see that the other's face showed emotion. It seemed a good moment for a pause.

The light went out in the room above them. The crickets had stopped chirping. It was in an intense silence that the man in the rough clothes turned his head and looked strangely at the doctor. He drew a long breath and said, gravely, "Why, Jim, my memory came back more than eight years ago."

TALKING OF PRESENTIMENTS
by W.D. Howells

OVER our coffee in the Turkish room Minver was usually a censor of our several foibles rather than a sharer in our philosophic speculations and metaphysical conjectures. He liked to disable me as one professionally vowed to the fabulous, and he had unfailing fun with the romantic sentimentality of Rulledge, which was in fact so little in keeping with the gross superabundance of his person, his habitual gluttony and his ridiculous indolence. Minver knew very well that Rulledge was a good fellow withal, and would willingly do any kind action that did not seriously interfere with his comfort, or make too heavy a draft upon his pocket. His self-indulgence, which was quite blameless, unless surfeit is a fault, was the basis of an interest in occult themes, which was the means of even higher diversion to Minver. He liked to have Rulledge approach Wanhope from this side, in the invincible persuasion that the psychologist would be interested in these themes by the law of his science, though he had been assured again and again that in spite of its misleading name psychology did not deal with the soul as Rulledge supposed the soul; and Minver's eyes lighted up with a prescience of uncommon pleasure when, late one night, after we had vainly tried to hit it off in talk, now of this, now of that, Rulledge asked Wanhope, abruptly as if it followed from something before:

"Wasn't there a great deal more said about presentiments thirty or forty years ago than there is now?"

Wanhope had been lapsing deeper and deeper into the hollow of his chair; but he now pulled himself up, and turned quickly toward Rulledge. "What made you think of that?" he asked.

"I don't know. Why?"

"Because I was thinking of it myself."

He glanced at me, and I shook my head. "Well," Minver said, "if it will leave Acton out in the cold, I'll own that I was thinking of it, too. I was going back in my mind, for no reason that I know of, to my childhood, when I first heard of such a thing as a presentiment, and when I was afraid of having one. I had the notion that presentiments ran in the family."

"Why had you that notion?" Rulledge demanded.

"I don't know that I proposed telling," the painter said, giving himself to his pipe.

"Perhaps you didn't have it," Rulledge retaliated.

"Perhaps," Minver assented.

Wanhope turned from the personal aspect of the matter. "It's rather curious that we should all three have had the same thing in mind just now; or, rather, it is not very curious. Such coincidences are really very common. Something must have been said at dinner which suggested it to all of us."

"All but Acton," Minver demurred.

"I mightn't have heard what was said," I explained. "I suppose the passing of all that sort of sub-beliefs must date from the general lapse of faith in personal immortality."

"Yes, no doubt," Wanhope assented. "It is very striking how sudden the lapse was. Every one who experienced it in himself could date it to a year, if not to a day. The agnosticism of the scientific men was of course all the time undermining the fabric of faith, and then it fell in abruptly, reaching one believer after another as fast as the ground was taken wholly or partly from under his feet. I can remember how people once disputed whether there were such beings as guardian spirits or not. That minor question was disposed of when it was decided that there were no spirits at all."

"Naturally," Minver said. "And the decay of the presentiment must have been hastened by the failure of so many presentiments to make good."

" The great majority of them have failed to make good, from the beginning of time," Wanhope replied.

" There are two kinds of presentiments," Rulledge suggested, with a philosophic air. " The true and the untrue."

" Like mushrooms," Minver said. " Only the true presentiment kills, and the true mushroom nourishes. Talking of mushrooms, they have a way in Switzerland of preserving them in walnut oil, and they fill you with the darkest forebodings, after you've filled yourself with the mushrooms. There's some occult relation between the two. Think it out, Rulledge!"

Rulledge ignored him in turning to Wanhope. " The trouble is how to distinguish the true from the untrue presentiment."

" It would be interesting," Wanhope began, but Minver broke in upon him maliciously.

" To know how much the dyspepsia of our predecessors had to do with the prevalence of presentimentalism? I agree with you, that a better diet has a good deal to do with the decline of the dark foreboding among us. What I can't understand is, how a gross and reckless feeder, like Rulledge here, doesn't go about like ancestral voices prophesying all sorts of dreadful things."

" That's rather cheap talk, even for you, Minver," Rulledge said. " Why did you think presentiments ran in *your* family?"

" Well, there you have me, Rulledge. That's where my theory fails. I can remember," Minver continued soberly, " the talk there used to be about them among my people. They were serious people in an unreligious way, or rather an unecclesiastical way. They were never spiritualists, but I don't think there was one of them who doubted that he should live hereafter; he might doubt that he was living here, but there was no question of the other thing. I must say it gave a dignity to their conversation, which when they met, as they were apt to do at each others' houses on Sunday nights, was not of common things. One of my uncles was a merchant, another a

doctor; my father was a portrait-painter by profession, and a sign-painter by practice. I suppose that's where I got my knack, such as it is. The merchant was an invalid, rather, though he kept about his business, and our people merely recognized him as being out of health. He was what we could call, for that day and region—the Middle West of the early fifties—a man of unusual refinement. I suppose this was temperamental with him largely; but he had cultivated tastes, too. I remember him as a peculiarly gentle person, with a pensive cast of face, and the melancholy accomplishment of playing the flute."

" I wonder why nobody plays the flute nowadays," I mused aloud.

" Yes, it's quite obsolete," Minver said. " They only play the flute in the orchestras now. I always look at the man who plays it and think of my uncle. He used to be very nice to me as a child; and he was very fond of my father, in a sort of filial way; my father was so much older. I can remember my young aunt; and how pretty she was as she sat at the piano, and sang and played to his fluting. When she looked forward at the music, her curls fell into her neck; they wore curls then, grown-up women; and though I don't think curls are beautiful, my aunt's beauty would have been less without them; in fact, I can't think of her without them.

" She was delicate, too; they were really a pair of invalids; but she had none of his melancholy. They had had several children, who died, one after another, and there was only one left at the time I am speaking of. I rather wonder, now, that the thought of those poor little ghost-cousins didn't make me uncomfortable. I was a very superstitious boy, but I seem not to have thought of them. I played with the little girl who was left, and I liked going to my uncle's better than anywhere else. I preferred going in the daytime and in the summer-time. Then my cousin and I sat in a nook of the garden and fought violets, as we called it; hooked the wry necks of the flowers together and twitched to see which blossom would come off first. She was a sunny little thing, like her mother, and she had curls, like her. I can't express the feeling I had for my aunt; she seemed the embodiment of a world that was at once very proud and very good. I suppose she dressed fashionably, as things went then and there; and her style as well as her beauty fascinated me. I would have done anything to please her, far more than to please my cousin. With her I used to squabble, and sometimes sent her crying to her mother. Then I always ran off home, but when I sneaked back, or was sent for to come and play with my cousin, I was not scolded for my wickedness.

"My uncle was more prosperous than his brothers; he lived in a much better house than ours, and I used to be quite awe-struck by its magnificence. He went East, as we said, twice a year to buy goods, and he had things sent back for his house such as we never saw elsewhere; those cask-shaped seats of blue china for the verandas, and bamboo chairs. There were cane-bottom chairs in the sitting-room, such as we had in our best room; in the parlor the large pieces were of mahogany veneer, upholstered in black hair-cloth; they held me in awe. The piano filled half the place; the windows came down to the ground, and had Venetian blinds and lace curtains.

"We all went in there after the Sunday night supper, and then the fathers and mothers were apt to begin talking of those occult things that gave me the creeps. It was after the Rochester Knockings, as they were called, had been exposed, and so had spread like an infection everywhere. It was as if people were waiting to have the fraud shown up in order to believe in it."

"That sort of thing happens," Wanhope agreed. "It's as if the seeds of the ventilated imposture were carried atmospherically into the human mind broadcast and a universal crop of self-delusion sprang up."

"At any rate," Minver resumed, "instead of the gift being confined to a few persons—a small sisterhood with detonating knee-joints—there were rappings in every well-regulated household; all the tables tipped; people went to sleep to the soft patter of raps on the headboards of their beds; and girls who could not spell were occupied in delivering messages from Socrates, Ben Franklin

and Shakespeare. Besides the physical demonstrations, there were all sorts of psychical intimations from the world which we've now abolished."

"Not permanently, perhaps," I suggested.

"Well, that remains to be seen," Minver said. "It was this sort of thing which my people valued above the other. Perhaps they were exclusive in their tastes, and did not care for an occultism which the crowd could share with them; though this is a conjecture too long after the fact to have much value. As far as I can now remember, they used to talk of the double presence of living persons, like their being where they greatly wished to be as well as where they really were; of clairvoyance; of what we call mind-transference, now; of weird coincidences of all kinds; of strange experiences of their own and of others; of the participation of animals in these experiences, like the testimony of cats and dogs to the presence of invisible spirits; of dreams that came true, or came near coming true; and, above everything, of forebodings and presentiments.

"I dare say they didn't always talk of such things, and I'm giving possibly a general impression from a single instance; everything remembered of childhood is as if from large and repeated occurrence. But it must have happened more than once, for I recall that when it came to presentiments my aunt broke it up, perhaps once only. My cousin used to get very sleepy on the rug before the fire, and her mother would carry her off to bed, very cross and impatient of being kissed good night by her aunts, while I was left to the brunt of the occult alone. I could not go with my aunt and cousin, and I folded myself in my mother's skirt, where I sat at her feet, and listened in an anguish of drowsy terror. The talk would pass into my dreams, and the dreams would return into the talk; and I would suffer a sort of double nightmare, waking and sleeping."

"Poor little devil!" Rulledge broke out. "It's astonishing how people will go on before children, and never think of the misery they're making for them."

"I believe my mother thought of it," Minver returned, "but when that sort of talk began, the witchery of it was probably too strong for her. 'It held her like a two years' child'; I was eight that winter. I don't know how long my suffering had gone on, when my aunt came back and seemed to break up the talk. It had got to presentiments, and whether they knew that this was forbidden ground with her, or whether she now actually said something about it, they turned to talk of other things. I'm not telling you all this from my own memory, which deals with only a point or two. My father and mother used to recur to it when I was older, and I am piecing out my story from their memories.

"My uncle, with all his temperamental pensiveness, was my aunt's stay and cheer in the fits of depression which she paid with for her usual gayety. But these fits always began with some uncommon depression of his—some effect of the forebodings he was subject to. Her opposition to that kind of thing was purely unselfish, but certainly she dreaded it for him as well as herself. I suppose there was a sort of conscious silence in the others which betrayed them to her. 'Well,' she said, laughing, 'have you been at it again? That poor child looks frightened out of his wits.'

"They all laughed then, and my father said, hypocritically, 'I was just going to ask Felix whether he expected to start East this week or next.'

"My uncle tried to make light of what was always a heavy matter with him. 'Well, yesterday,' he answered, 'I should have said next week; but it's this week, now. I'm going on Wednesday.'

"'By stage or packet?' my father asked.

"'Oh, I shall take the canal to the lake, and get the boat for Buffalo there,' my uncle said.

"They went on to speak of the trip to New York, and how much easier it was then than it used to be when you had to go by stage over the mountains to Philadelphia and on by stage again. Now, it seemed, you got the Erie Canal packet at Buffalo and the Hudson River steamboat at Albany, and reached New York in four or five days, in great comfort without the least fatigue. They had all risen and my aunt had gone out with her sisters-in-law to help them get their wraps. When they returned, it seemed that they had been talking of the journey too, for she said to my mother, laughing again, 'Well, Richard may think it's easy; but somehow Felix never expects to get home alive.'

"I don't think I ever heard my uncle laugh, but I can remember how he smiled at my aunt's laughing, as he put his hand on her shoulder; I thought it was somehow a very sad smile. On Wednesday I was allowed to go with my aunt and cousin to see him off on the packet, which came up from Cincinnati early in the morning: I had lain awake most of the night, and then nearly overslept myself, and then was at the canal in time. We made a gay parting for him, but when the boat started, and I was gloating on the three horses making up the tow-path at a spanking trot, under the snaky spirals of the driver's smacking whip-lash, I caught sight of my uncle standing on the deck, and smiling that sad smile of his. My aunt was waving her handkerchief, but when she turned away she put it to her eyes.

"The rest of the story, such as it is, I know, almost to the very end, from what I heard my father and mother say from my uncle's report afterwards. He told them that, when the boat started, the stress to stay was so strong upon him that if he had not been ashamed he would have jumped ashore and followed us home. He said that he could not analyze his feeling; it was not yet any definite foreboding, but simply a depression that seemed to crush him so that all his movements were leaden, when he turned at last, and went down to breakfast in the cabin below. The stress did not lighten with the little changes and chances of the voyage to the lake. He was never much given to making acquaintance with people, but now he found himself so absent-minded that he was aware of being sometimes spoken to by friendly strangers without replying until it was too late even to apologize. He was not only steeped in this gloom, but he had the constant distress of the effort he involuntarily made to trace it back to some cause or follow it forward to some consequence. He kept trying at this, with a mind so tensely bent to the mere horror, that he could not for a moment strain away from it. He would very willingly have occupied himself with other things, but the anguish which the double action of his mind gave him was such that he could not bear the effort; all he could do was to abandon himself to his obsession. This would ease him only for a while, though, and then he would suffer the misery of trying in vain to escape from it.

" He thought he must be going mad, but insanity implied some definite delusion or hallucination, and so far as he could make out, he had none. He was simply crushed by a nameless foreboding. Something dreadful was to happen, but this was all he felt; knowledge had no part in his condition. He could not say whether he slept during the two nights that passed before he reached Toledo, where he was to take the lake steamer for Buffalo. He wished to turn back again, but the relentless pressure which had kept him from turning back at the start was as strong as ever with him. He tried to give his presentiment direction by talking with the other passengers about a recent accident to a lake steamer, in which several hundred lives were lost; there had been a collision in rough weather, and one of the boats had gone down in a few minutes. There was a sort of relief in that, but the double action of the mind brought the same intolerable anguish again, and he settled back for refuge under the shadow of his impenetrable doom. This did not lift till he was well on his way from Albany to New York by the Hudson River. The canalboat voyage from Buffalo to Albany had been as eventless as that to Toledo, and his lake steamer had reached Buffalo in safety, for which it had seemed as if those lost in the recent disaster had paid.

" He tried to pierce his heavy cloud by argument from the security in which he had travelled so far, but the very security had its hopelessness. If something had happened—some slight accident—to interrupt it, his reason, or his unreason, might have taken it for a sign that the obscure doom, whatever it was, had been averted.

" Up to this time he had not been able to connect his foreboding with anything definite, and he was not afraid for himself. He was simply without the formless hope that helps us on at every step,

through good and bad, and it was a mortal peril, which he came through safely while scores of others were lost, that gave his presentiment direction. He had taken the day boat from Albany, and about the middle of the afternoon the boat, making way under a head-wind, took fire. The pilot immediately ran her ashore, and her passengers, those that had the courage for it, ran aft, and began jumping from the stern, but a great many women and children were burnt up. My uncle was one of the first of those who jumped, and he stood in the water, trying to save those who came after from drowning; it was not very deep. Some of the women lost courage for the leap, and some turned back into the flames, remembering children they had left behind. One poor creature stood hesitating wildly, and he called up to her to jump. At last she did so, almost into his arms, and then she clung about him as he helped her ashore. ' Oh,' she cried out between her sobs, ' if you have a wife and children at home, God will take you safe back to them; you have saved my life for my husband and little ones.' ' No,' he was conscious of saying, ' I shall never see my wife again,' and now his foreboding had the direction that it had wanted before.

" From that on he simply knew that he should not get home alive, and he waited resignedly for the time and form of his disaster. He had a sort of peace in that. He went about his business intelligently, and from habit carefully, but it was with a mechanical action of the mind, something, he imagined, like the mechanical action of his body in those organs which do their part without bidding from the will. He was only a few days in New York, but in the course of them he got several letters from his wife telling him that all was going well with her and their daughter. It was before the times when you can ask and answer questions by telegraph, and he started back, necessarily without having heard the latest news from home.

" He made the return trip in a sort of daze, talking, reading, eating and sleeping in the calm certainty of doom, and only wondering how it would be fulfilled, and what hour of the night and day. But it is no use my eking this out; I heard it, as I say, when I was a child, and I am afraid that if I should try to give it with the full detail, I should take to inventing particulars. But there was one thing that impressed itself indelibly on my memory, perhaps because it coincided with a frequent experience of my own. My uncle got back perfectly safe and well."

"Oh!" Rulledge snorted in rude dissatisfaction.

"What was it impressed itself on your memory?" Wanhope asked, with scientific detachment from the story as a story.

"Why, you know that sort of instant change which takes place in you sometimes in coming back to a familiar place which you have somehow got to the north of you when it was really to the south, or to the east when it was really to the west; and all at once, while you have been keeping your eyes on it, has shifted round subjectively and is visibly in the right place."

"What has that got to do with it?" Rulledge asked.

"My uncle," Minver continued to address Wanhope, without regarding Rulledge, "told my father that some such change took place within him as 'he came in sight of his house, but it was a change that concerned his spiritual orientation—"

"Yes," Wanhope consented.

"And not anything physical. He had driven down from the canal packet in the old omnibus which used to meet passengers and distribute them at their destinations in town. All the way to his house he was still under the doom as regarded himself, but bewildered that he should be getting home safe and well, and he was refusing his escape, as it were, and then suddenly, at the sight of the familiar house, the points of the compass within him shifted. He looked out of the omnibus window and saw a group of neighbors at his gate. As he got out of the omnibus, my father took him by the hand, as if to hold him back a moment. Then he said to my father, very quietly, 'You needn't tell me: my wife is dead.'"

There was an appreciable pause, in which we were all silent, and then Rulledge demanded, greedily, "And was she?"

"Really, Rulledge!" I could not help saying.

Minver asked him, almost compassionately, and with unwonted gentleness, as from the mood in which his reminiscence had left him, "You suspected a hoax? She had died suddenly the night before while she and my cousin were getting things ready to welcome my uncle home in the morning. I'm sorry you're disappointed," he added, getting back to his irony.

"Whatever," Rulledge pursued, "became of the little girl?"

"She died rather young; a great many years ago; and my uncle soon after her."

Rulledge went out without saying anything, but presently returned with the sandwich which he had apparently gone for, while Wanhope was remarking: "That want of definition in the presentiment at first, and then its determination in the wrong direction by chance—it is all very curious. Possibly we shall some day discover a law in such matters."

Rulledge said: "How was it your boyhood was passed in the Middle West, Minver? I always thought you were a Bostonian."

"I was an adoptive Bostonian for a good while, until I decided to become a native New-Yorker, so that I could always be near you, Rulledge. You can never know what a delicate satisfaction you are."

Minver laughed, and we were severally restored to the wonted relations which his story had interrupted.

JULIA BRIDE
(PART 1)
by Henry James

A STORY IN TWO PARTS

SHE had walked with her friend to the top of the wide steps of the Museum, those that descended from the galleries of painting, and then, after the young man had left her, smiling, looking back, waving all gayly and expressively his hat and stick, had watched him, smiling too, but with a different intensity—had kept him in sight till he passed out of the great door. She might have been waiting to see if he would turn there for a last demonstration; which was exactly what he did, renewing his cordial gesture and with his look of glad devotion, the radiance of his young face, reaching her across the great space, as she felt, in undiminished truth. Yes, so she could feel, and she remained a minute even after he was gone; she gazed at the empty air as if he had filled it still, asking herself what more she wanted and what, if it didn't signify glad devotion, his whole air could have represented.

She was at present so anxious that she could wonder if he stepped and smiled like that for mere relief at separation; yet if he wanted, in that degree, to break the spell and escape the danger why did he keep coming back to her, and why, for that matter, had she felt safe a moment before in letting him go? She felt safe, felt almost reckless—that was the proof—so long as he was with her; but the chill came as soon as he had gone, when she took the measure, instantly, of

all she yet missed. She might now have been taking it afresh, by the testimony of her charming clouded eyes and of the rigor that had already replaced her beautiful play of expression. Her radiance, for the minute, had "carried" as far as his, travelling on the light wings of her brilliant prettiness—he, on his side, not being facially handsome, but only sensitive, clean and eager. Then, with its extinction, the sustaining wings dropped and hung.

She wheeled about, however, full of a purpose; she passed back through the pictured rooms, for it pleased her, this idea of a talk with Mr. Pitman—as much, that is, as anything could please a young person so troubled. It happened indeed that when she saw him rise at sight of her from the settee where he had told her five minutes before that she would find him, it was just with her nervousness that his presence seemed, as through an odd suggestion of help, to connect itself. Nothing truly would be quite so odd for her case as aid proceeding from Mr. Pitman; unless perhaps the oddity would be even greater for himself—the oddity of her having taken into her head an appeal to him.

She had had to feel alone with a vengeance — inwardly alone and miserably alarmed—to be ready to "meet," that way, at the first sign from him, the successor to her dim father in her dim father's lifetime, the second of her mother's two divorced husbands. It made a queer relation for her; a relation that struck her at this moment as less edifying, less natural and graceful than it would have been even for her remarkable mother—and still in spite of this parent's third marriage, her union with Mr. Connery, from whom she was informally separated. It was at the back of Julia's head as she approached Mr. Pitman, or it was at least somewhere deep within her soul, that if this last of Mrs. Connery's withdrawals from the matrimonial yoke had received the sanction of the Court (Julia had always heard, from far back, so much about the " Court ") she herself, as after a fashion, in that event, a party to it, would not have had the cheek to make up—which was how she inwardly phrased what she was doing to the long, lean, loose, slightly cadaverous gentleman who was a memory, for her, of the period from her twelfth to her seventeenth year. She had got on with him, perversely, much better than her mother had, and the bulging misfit of his duck waistcoat, with his trick of swinging his eye-glass, at the end of an extraordinarily long string, far over the scene, came back to her as positive features of the image of her remoter youth. Her present age—for her later time had seen so many things happen—gave her a perspective.

Fifty things came up as she stood there before him, some of them floating in from the past, others hovering with freshness: how she used to dodge the rotary movement made by his pince-nez while he always awkwardly, and kindly, and often funnily, talked—it had once hit her rather badly in the eye; how she used to pull down and straighten his waistcoat, making it set a little better, a thing of a sort her mother never did; how friendly and familiar she must have been with him for that, or else a forward little minx; how she felt almost capable of doing it again now, just to sound the right note, and how sure she was of the way he would take it if she did; how much nicer he had clearly been, all the while, poor dear man, than his wife and the Court had made it possible for him publicly to appear; how much younger too he now looked, in spite of his rather melancholy, his mildly-jaundiced, hu-morously-determined sallowness and his careless assumption, everywhere, from his forehead to his exposed and relaxed blue socks, almost sky-blue, as in past days, of creases and folds and furrows that would have been perhaps tragic if they hadn't seemed rather to show, like his whimsical black eyebrows, the vague interrogative arch.

Of course he wasn't wretched if he wasn't more sure of his wretchedness than that! Julia Bride would have been sure—had she been through what she supposed *he* had! With his thick, loose black hair, in any case, untouched by a thread of gray, and his kept gift of a certain big-boyish awkwardness — that of his taking their encounter, for instance, so amusedly, so crudely, though, as she was not unaware, so eagerly too—he could by no means have been so little his wife's junior as it had been that lady's habit, after the divorce, to represent him. Julia had remembered him as old, since she had so constantly thought of her mother as old; which Mrs. Connery was indeed now, for her daughter, with her dozen years of actual seniority to Mr. Pitman and her exquisite hair, the densest, the finest tangle of arranged silver tendrils that had ever enhanced the effect of a preserved complexion.

Something in the girl's vision of her quondam stepfather as still comparatively young—with the confusion, the immense element of rectification, not to say of rank disproof, that it introduced into Mrs. Connery's favorite picture of her own injured past—all this worked, even at the moment, to quicken once more the clearness and harshness of judgment, the retrospective disgust, as she might have called it, that had of late grown up in her, the sense of all the folly and vanity and vulgarity, the lies, the perversities, the falsification of all life in the interest of who could say what wretched frivolity, what preposterous policy, amid which she had been condemned so ignorantly, so pitifully to sit, to walk, to grope, to flounder, from the very dawn of her consciousness. Didn't poor Mr. Pitman just touch the sensitive nerve of it when, taking her in with his facetious, cautious eyes, he spoke to her, right out, of the old, old story, the everlasting little wonder of her beauty?

Drawn by W. T. Smedley

THE YOUNG MAN HAD LEFT HER, SMILING, LOOKING BACK

"Why, you know, you've grown up so lovely—you're the prettiest girl I've ever seen!" Of course she was the prettiest girl he had ever seen; she was the prettiest girl people much more privileged than he had ever seen; since when hadn't she been passing for the prettiest girl any one had ever seen? She had lived in that, from far back, from year to year, from day to day and from hour to hour she had lived for it and literally *by* it, as who should say; but Mr. Pitman was somehow more illuminating than he knew, with the present lurid light that he cast upon old dates, old pleas, old values and old mysteries, not to call them old abysses: it had rolled over her in a swift wave, with the very sight of him, that her mother couldn't possibly have been right about him—as about what in the world had she ever been right?—so that in fact he was simply offered her there as one more of Mrs. Connery's lies. She might have thought she knew them all by this time; but he represented for her, coming in just as he did, a fresh discovery, and it was this contribution of freshness that made her somehow feel she liked him. It was she herself who, for so long, with her retained impression, had been right about him; and the rectification he represented had *all* shone out of him, ten minutes before, on his catching her eye while she moved through the room with Mr. French. She had never doubted of his probable faults—which her mother had vividly depicted as the basest of vices; since some of them, and the most obvious (not the vices, but the faults) were written on him as he stood there: notably, for instance, the exasperating "business slackness" of which Mrs. Connery had, before the tribunal, made so pathetically much. It might have been, for that matter, the very business slackness that affected Julia as presenting its friendly breast, in the form of a cool loose sociability, to her own actual tension; though it was also true for her, after they had exchanged fifty words, that he had as well his inward fever and that, if he was perhaps wondering what was so particularly the matter with her, she could make out not less that something was the matter with *him*. It had been vague, yet it had been intense, the

mute reflection, "Yes, I'm going to like him, and he's going somehow to help me!" that had directed her steps so straight to him. She was sure even then of this, that he wouldn't put to her a query about his former wife, that he took to-day no grain of interest in Mrs. Connery; that his interest, such as it was—and he couldn't look *quite* like that, to Julia Bride's expert perception, without something in the nature of a new one—would be a thousand times different.

It was as a value of *disproof* that his worth meanwhile so rapidly grew: the good sight of him, the good sound and sense of him, such as they were, demolished at a stroke so blessedly much of the horrid inconvenience of the past that she thought of him, she clutched at him, for a *general* saving use, an application as sanative, as redemptive, as some universal healing wash, precious even to the point of perjury if perjury should be required. That was the terrible thing, that had been the inward pang with which she watched Basil French recede: perjury would have to come in somehow and somewhere—oh so quite certainly!—before the so strange, so rare young man, truly smitten though she believed him, could be made to rise to the occasion, before her measureless prize could be assured. It was present to her, it had been present a hundred times, that if there had only been some one to (as it were) "deny everything" the situation might yet be saved. She so needed some one to lie for her—ah she so needed some one to lie! Her mother's version of everything, her mother's version of anything, had been at the best, as they said, discounted; and she herself could but show of course for an interested party, however much she might claim to be none the less a decent girl—to whatever point, that is, after all that had both remotely and recently happened, presumptions of anything to be called decency could come in.

After what had recently happened—the two or three indirect but so worrying questions Mr. French had put to her—it would only be some thoroughly detached friend or witness who might effectively testify. An odd form of detachment certainly would reside, for Mr. Pitman's evidential character, in her mother's hav-

ing so publicly and so brilliantly—
though, thank the powers, all off in North
Dakota!—severed their connection with
him; and yet mightn't it do *her* some
good, even if the harm it might do her
mother were so little ambiguous? The
more her mother had got divorced—with
her dreadful cheap-and-easy second performance in that line and her present
extremity of alienation from Mr. Connery, which enfolded beyond doubt the
germ of a third petition on one side or
the other—the more her mother had distinguished herself in the field of folly the
worse for her own prospect with the
Frenches, whose minds she had guessed
to be accessible, and with such an effect
of dissimulated suddenness, to some insidious poison.

It was very unmistakable, in other
words, that the more dismissed and detached Mr. Pitman should have come to
appear, the more as divorced, or at least
as divorcing, his before-time wife would
by the same stroke figure—so that it was
here poor Julia could but lose herself.
The crazy divorces only, or the half-
dozen successive and still crazier engagements only—gathered fruit, bitter fruit,
of her own incredibly allowed, her own
insanely fostered frivolity—either of
these two groups of skeletons at the banquet might singly be dealt with; but the
combination, the fact of each party's having been so mixed-up with whatever was
least presentable for the other, the fact
of their having so shockingly amused
themselves together, made all present
steering resemble the classic middle
course between Scylla and Charybdis.

It was not, however, that she felt wholly
a fool in having obeyed this impulse to
pick up again her kind old friend. *She*
at least had never divorced him, and her
horrid little filial evidence in Court had
been but the chatter of a parrakeet, of
precocious plumage and croak, repeating
words earnestly taught her and that she
could scarce even pronounce. Therefore,
as far as steering went, he *must* for the
hour take a hand. She might actually
have wished in fact that he shouldn't
now have seemed so tremendously struck
with her; since it was an extraordinary
situation for a girl, this crisis of her fortune, this positive wrong that the flagran-
cy, what she would have been ready to

call the very vulgarity, of her good looks
might do her at a moment when it was
vital she should hang as straight as a
picture on the wall. Had it ever yet befallen any young woman in the world to
wish with secret intensity that she might
have been, for her convenience, a shade
less inordinately pretty? She had come
to that, to this view of the bane, the
primal curse, of their lavish physical outfit, which had included everything and
as to which she lumped herself resentfully with her mother. The only thing
was that her mother was, thank goodness,
still so much prettier, still so assertively,
so publicly, so trashily, so ruinously
pretty. Wonderful the small grimness
with which Julia Bride put off on this
parent the middle-aged maximum of their
case and the responsibility of their defect.
It cost her so little to recognize in Mrs.
Connery at forty-seven, and in spite, or
perhaps indeed just by reason, of the arranged silver tendrils which were so like
some rare bird's-nest in a morning frost,
a facile supremacy for the dazzling effect
—it cost her so little that her view even
rather exaggerated the lustre of the different maternal items. She would have
put it *all* off if possible, all off on other
shoulders and on other graces and other
morals than her own, the burden of physical charm that had made so easy a
ground, such a native favoring air, for
the aberrations which, apparently inevitable and without far consequences at
the time, had yet at this juncture so
much better not have been.

She could have worked it out at her
leisure, to the last link of the chain, the
way their prettiness had set them trap
after trap, all along—had foredoomed
them to awful ineptitude. When you
were as pretty as that you could, by the
whole idiotic consensus, be nothing *but*
pretty; and when you were nothing
"but" pretty you could get into nothing
but tight places, out of which you could
then scramble by nothing but masses of
fibs. And there was no one, all the while,
who wasn't eager to egg you on, eager to
make you pay to the last cent the price
of your beauty. What creature would
ever for a moment help you to behave as
if something that dragged in its wake a
bit less of a lumbering train would, on
the whole, have been better for you? The

consequences of being plain were only negative—you failed of this and that; but the consequences of being as *they* were, what were these but endless? though indeed, as far as failing went, your beauty too could let you in for enough of it. Who, at all events, would ever for a moment credit you, in the luxuriance of that beauty, with the study, on your own side, of such truths as these? Julia Bride could, at the point she had reached, positively ask herself this even while lucidly conscious of the inimitable, the triumphant and attested projection, all round her, of her exquisite image. It was only Basil French who had at last, in his doubtless dry, but all distinguished way—the way, surely as it was borne in upon her, of all the blood of all the Frenches—stepped out of the vulgar rank. It was only he who, by the trouble she discerned in him, had made her see certain things. It was only for him— and not a bit ridiculously, but just beautifully, almost sublimely—that their being "nice," her mother and she between them, had *not* seemed to profit by their being so furiously handsome.

This had, ever so grossly and ever so tiresomely, satisfied every one else; since every one had thrust upon them, had imposed upon them, as by a great cruel conspiracy, their silliest possibilities; fencing them in to these, and so not only shutting them out from others, but mounting guard at the fence, walking round and round outside it, to see they didn't escape, and admiring them, talking to them, through the rails, in mere terms of chaff, terms of chucked cakes and apples—as if they had been antelopes or zebras, or even some superior sort of performing, of dancing, bear. It had been reserved for Basil French to strike her as willing to let go, so to speak, a pound or two of this fatal treasure if he might only have got in exchange for it an ounce or so more of their so much less obvious and less published personal history. Yes, it described him to say that, in addition to all the rest of him, and of *his* personal history, and of his family, and of theirs, in addition to their social posture, as that of a serried phalanx, and to their notoriously enormous wealth and crushing respectability, she might have been ever so much less lovely for him if she

had been only—well, a little prepared to answer questions. And it wasn't as if, quiet, cultivated, earnest, public-spirited, brought up in Germany, infinitely travelled, awfully like a high-caste Englishman, and all the other pleasant things, it wasn't as if he didn't love to be with her, to look at her, just as she was; for he loved it exactly as much, so far as that footing simply went, as any free and foolish youth who had ever made the last demonstration of it. It was that marriage was, for him—and for them all, the serried Frenches—a great matter, a goal to which a man of intelligence, a real shy, beautiful man of the world, didn't hop on one foot, didn't skip and jump, as if he were playing an urchins' game, but toward which he proceeded with a deep and anxious, a noble and highly just deliberation.

For it was one thing to stare at a girl till she was bored with it, it was one thing to take her to the Horse Show and the Opera, and to send her flowers by the stack, and chocolates by the ton, and "great" novels, the very latest and greatest, by the dozen; but something quite other to hold open for her, with eyes attached to eyes, the gate, moving on such stiff silver hinges, of the grand square forecourt of the palace of wedlock. The state of being "engaged" represented to him the introduction to this precinct of some young woman with whom his outside parley would have had the duration, distinctly, of his own convenience. That might be cold-blooded if one chose to think so; but nothing of another sort would equal the high ceremony and dignity and decency, above all the grand gallantry and finality, of their then passing in. Poor Julia could have blushed red, before that view, with the memory of the way the forecourt, as she now imagined it, had been dishonored by her younger romps. She had tumbled over the wall with this, that and the other raw playmate, and had played "tag" and leap-frog, as she might say, from corner to corner. That would be the "history" with which, in case of definite demand, she should be able to supply Mr. French: that she had already, again and again, any occasion offering, chattered and scuffled over ground provided, according to his idea, for walking the gravest of minuets. If that then had been all their *kind* of history, hers and her mother's, at least there was plenty of it: it was the superstructure raised on the other group of facts, those of the order of their having been always so perfectly pink and white, so perfectly possessed of clothes, so perfectly splendid, so perfectly idiotic. These things had been the "points" of antelope and zebra; putting Mrs. Connery for the zebra, as the more remarkably striped or spotted. Such were the *data* Basil French's inquiry would elicit: her own six engagements and her mother's three nullified marriages—nine nice distinct little horrors in all. What on earth was to be done about them?

It was notable, she was afterwards to recognize, that there had been nothing of the famous business slackness in the positive pounce with which Mr. Pitman put it to her that, as soon as he had made her out "for sure," identified her there as old Julia grown-up and gallivanting with a new admirer, a smarter young fellow than ever yet, he had had the inspiration of her being exactly the good girl to help him. She certainly found him strike the hour again, with these vulgarities of tone—forms of speech that her mother had anciently described as by themselves, once he had opened the whole battery, sufficient ground for putting him away. Full, however, of the use she should have for him, she wasn't going to mind trifles. What she really gasped at was that, so oddly, he was ahead of her at the start. "Yes, I want something of you, Julia, and I want it right now: you can do me a turn, and I'm blest if my luck—which has once or twice been pretty good, you know—hasn't sent you to me." She knew the luck he meant—that of her mother's having so enabled him to get rid of her; but it was the nearest allusion of the merely invidious kind that he would make. It had thus come to our young woman on the spot and by divination: the service he desired of her matched with remarkable closeness what she had so promptly taken into her head to name to himself—to name in her own interest, though deterred as yet from having brought it right out. She had been prevented by his speaking, the first thing, in that way, as if he had known

Mr. French—which surprised her till he explained that every one in New York knew by appearance a young man of his so quoted wealth ("What did she take them all in New York then *for?*") and of whose marked attention to her he had moreover, for himself, round at clubs and places, lately heard. This had accompanied the inevitable free question "Was she engaged to *him* now?"—which she had in fact almost welcomed as holding out to her the perch of opportunity. She was waiting to deal with it properly, but meanwhile he had gone on, and to such effect that it took them but three minutes to turn out, on either side, like a pair of pickpockets comparing, under shelter, their day's booty, the treasures of design concealed about their persons.

"I want you to tell the truth for me—as you only can. I want you to say that I was really all right—as right as you know; and that I simply acted like an angel in a story-book, gave myself away to have it over."

"Why, my dear man," Julia cried, "you take the wind straight out of my sails! What I'm here to ask of *you* is that you'll confess to having been even a worse fiend than you were shown up for; to having made it impossible mother should *not* take proceedings." There!—she had brought it out, and with the sense of their situation turning to high excitement for her in the teeth of his droll stare, his strange grin, his characteristic "Lordy, lordy! What good will that do you?'" She was prepared with her clear statement of reasons for her appeal, and feared so he might have better ones for his own that all her story came in a flash. "Well, Mr. Pitman, I want to get married this time, by way of a change; but you see we've been such fools that, when something really good at last comes up, it's too dreadfully awkward. The fools we were capable of being—well, you know better than any one: unless perhaps not quite so well as Mr. Connery. It has got to be denied," said Julia ardently—"it has got to be denied flat. But I can't get hold of Mr. Connery—Mr. Connery has gone to China. Besides, if he were here," she had ruefully to confess, "he'd be no good—on the contrary. He wouldn't deny anything—he'd only tell more. So thank heaven he's away—

there's *that* amount of good! I'm not engaged yet," she went on—but he had already taken her up.

"You're not engaged to Mr. French?" It was all, clearly, a wondrous show for him, but his immediate surprise, oddly, might have been greatest for that.

"No, not to any one—for the seventh time!" She spoke as with her head held well up both over the shame and the pride. "Yes, the next time I'm engaged I want something to happen. But he's afraid; he's afraid of what may be told him. He's dying to find out, and yet he'd die if he did! He wants to be talked to, but he has got to be talked to right. You could talk to him right, Mr. Pitman—if you only *would!* He can't get over mother—that I feel: he loathes and scorns divorces, and we've had first and last too many. So if he could hear from you that you just made her life a hell—why," Julia concluded, "it would be too lovely. If she *had* to go in for another—after having already, when I was little, divorced father — it would 'sort of' make, don't you see? one less. You'd do the high-toned thing by her: you'd say what a wretch you then were, and that she had had to save her life. In that way he mayn't mind it. Don't you see, you sweet man?" poor Julia pleaded. "Oh," she wound up as if his fancy lagged or his scruple looked out, "of course I want you to *lie* for me!"

It did indeed sufficiently stagger him. "It's a lovely idea for the moment when I was just saying to myself—as soon as I saw you—that you'd speak the truth for *me!*"

"Ah, what's the matter with 'you'?" Julia sighed with an impatience not sensibly less sharp for her having so quickly scented some lion in her path.

"Why, do you think there's no one in the world but you who has seen the cup of promised affection, of something really to be depended on, only, at the last moment, by the horrid jostle of your elbow, spilled all over you? I want to provide for my future too as it happens; and my good friend who's to help me to that—the most charming of women this time—disapproves of divorce quite as much as Mr. French. Don't you see," Mr. Pitman candidly asked, "what that by itself must have done toward attaching me to her?

She has got to be talked to—to be told how little I could help it."

"Oh, lordy, lordy!" the girl emulously groaned. It was such a relieving cry. "Well, *I* won't talk to her!" she declared.

"You *won't,* Julia?" he pitifully echoed. "And yet you ask of *me—!*"

His pang, she felt, was sincere, and even more than she had guessed, for the previous quarter of an hour, he had been building up his hope, building it with her aid for a foundation. Yet was he going to see how their testimony, on each side, would, if offered, *have* to conflict? If he was to prove himself for her sake—or, more queerly still, for that of Basil French's high conservatism — a person whom there had been no other way of dealing with, how could she prove him, in this other and so different interest, a mere gentle sacrifice to his wife's perversity? She had, before him there, on the instant, all acutely, a sense of rising sickness—a wan glimmer of foresight as to the end of the fond dream. Everything else was against her, everything in her dreadful past—just as if she had been a person represented by some "emotional actress," some desperate erring lady "hunted down" in a play; but was that going to be the case too with her own very decency, the fierce little residuum deep within her, for which she was counting, when she came to think, on so little glory or even credit? Was this also going to turn against her and trip her up—just to show she was really, under the touch and the test, as decent as any one; and with no one but herself the wiser for it meanwhile, and no proof to show but that, as a consequence, she should be unmarried to the end? She put it to Mr. Pitman quite with resentment: "Do you mean to say you're going to be married—?"

"Oh, my dear, I too must get engaged first!"—he spoke with his inimitable grin. "But that, you see, is where you come in. I've told her about you. She wants awfully to meet you. The way it happens is too lovely—that I find you just in this place. She's coming," said Mr. Pitman—and as in all the good faith of his eagerness now; "she's coming in about three minutes."

"Coming here?"

"Yes, Julia—right here. It's where

we usually meet;" and he was wreathed again, this time as if for life, in his large slow smile. "She loves this place—she's awfully keen on art. Like *you*, Julia, if you haven't changed—I remember how you did love art." He looked at her quite tenderly, as to keep her up to it. "You must still of course—from the way you're here. Just let her *feel* that," the poor man fantastically urged. And then with his kind eyes on her and his good ugly mouth stretched as for delicate emphasis from ear to ear: "Every little helps!"

He made her wonder for him, ask herself, and with a certain intensity, questions she yet hated the trouble of; as whether he were still as moneyless as in the other time—which was certain indeed, for any fortune he ever would have made. His slackness, on that ground, stuck out of him almost as much as if he had been of rusty or "seedy" aspect —which, luckily for him, he wasn't at all: he looked, in his way, like some pleasant eccentric, ridiculous, but real gentleman, whose taste might be of the queerest, but his credit with his tailor none the less of the best. She wouldn't have been the least ashamed, had their connection lasted, of going about with him: so that what a fool, again, her mother had been—since Mr. Connery, sorry as one might be for him, was irrepressibly vulgar. Julia's quickness was, for the minute, charged with all this; but she had none the less her feeling of the right thing to say and the right way to say it. If he was after a future financially assured, even as she herself so frantically was, she wouldn't cast the stone. But if he had talked about her to strange women she couldn't be less than a little majestic. "Who then is the person in question for you—?"

"Why, such a dear thing, Julia—Mrs. David E. Drack. Have you heard of her?" he almost fluted.

New York was vast, and she had not had that advantage. "She's a widow—?"

"Oh yes: she's not—!" He caught himself up in time. "She's a real one." It was as near as he came. But it was as if he had been looking at her now so pathetically hard. "Julia, she has millions."

Hard, at any rate—whether pathetic or not—was the look she gave him back.

"Well, so has—or so *will* have—Basil French. And more of them than Mrs. Drack, I guess," Julia quavered.

"Oh, I know what *they've* got!" He took it from her—with the effect of a vague stir, in his long person, of unwelcome embarrassment. But was she going to give up because he was embarrassed? He should know at least what he was costing her. It came home to her own spirit more than ever; but meanwhile he had found his footing. "I don't see how your mother matters. It isn't a question of his marrying *her*."

"No; but, constantly together as we've always been, it's a question of there being so disgustingly much to get over. If we had, for people like them, but the one ugly spot and the one weak side; if we had made, between us, but the one vulgar *kind* of mistake: well, I don't say!" She reflected with a wistfulness of note that was in itself a touching eloquence. "To have our reward in this world we've had too sweet a time. We've had it all right down here!" said Julia Bride. "I should have taken the precaution to have about a dozen fewer lovers."

"Ah, my dear, 'lovers'—!" He ever so comically attenuated.

"Well they *were*!" She quite flared up. "When you've had a ring from each (three diamonds, two pearls and a rather bad sapphire: I've kept them all, and they tell my story!) what are you to call them?"

"Oh, rings—!" Mr. Pitman didn't call rings anything. "I've given Mrs. Drack a ring."

Julia stared. "Then aren't you her lover?"

"That, dear child," he humorously wailed, "is what I want you to find out! But I'll handle your rings all right," he more lucidly added.

"You'll 'handle' them?"

"I'll fix your lovers. I'll lie about them, if that's all you want."

"Oh, about 'them'—!" She turned away with a sombre drop, seeing so little in it. "That wouldn't count — from *you!*" She saw the great shining room, with its mockery of art and "style" and security, all the things she was vainly after, and its few scattered visitors who had left them, Mr. Pitman and herself, in their ample corner, so conveniently at ease. There was only a lady in one of the far doorways, of whom she took vague note and who seemed to be looking at them. "They'd have to lie for themselves!"

"Do you mean he's capable of putting it to them?"

Mr. Pitman's tone threw discredit on that possibility, but she knew perfectly well what she meant. "Not of getting at them directly, not, as mother says, of nosing round himself; but of listening— and small blame to him!—to the horrible things other people say of me."

"But what other people?"

"Why, Mrs. George Maule, to begin with—who intensely loathes us, and who talks to his sisters, so that they may talk to *him*: which they do, all the while, I'm morally sure (hating me as they also must). But it's she who's the real reason—I mean of his holding off. She poisons the air he breathes."

"Oh well," said Mr. Pitman with easy optimism, "if Mrs. George Maule's a cat—!"

"If she's a cat she has kittens—four little spotlessly white ones, among whom she'd give her head that Mr. French should make his pick. He could do it with his eyes shut—you can't tell them apart. But she has every name, every date, as you may say, for my dark 'record'—as of course they all call it: she'll be able to give him, if he brings himself to ask her, every fact in its order. And all the while, don't you see? there's no one to speak *for* me."

It would have touched a harder heart than her loose friend's to note the final flush of clairvoyance witnessing this assertion and under which her eyes shone as with the rush of quick tears. He stared at her, and at what this did for the deep charm of her prettiness, as in almost witless admiration. "But can't you—lovely as you are, you beautiful thing!—speak for yourself?"

"Do you mean can't I tell the lies? No then, I can't—and I wouldn't if I could. I don't lie myself, you know— as it happens; and it could represent to him then about the only thing, the only bad one, I don't do. I *did*—'lovely as I am'!—have my regular time; I wasn't so

hideous that I couldn't! Besides, do you imagine he'd come and ask me?"

"Gad, I wish he would, Julia!" said Mr. Pitman with his kind eyes on her.

"Well then, I'd tell him!" And she held her head again high. "But he won't."

It fairly distressed her companion. "Doesn't he want then to know—?"

"He wants *not* to know. He wants to be told without asking—told, I mean, that each of the stories, those that have come to him, is a fraud and a libel. *Qui s'excuse s'accuse*, don't they say?— so that do you see me breaking out to him, unprovoked, with four or five what-do-you-call-'ems, the things mother used to have to prove in Court, a set of neat little 'alibis' in a row? How can I get hold of so *many* precious gentlemen, to turn them on? How can *they* want everything fished up?"

She had paused for her climax, in the intensity of these considerations; which gave Mr. Pitman a chance to express his honest faith. "Why, my sweet child, they'd be just glad—!"

It determined in her loveliness almost a sudden glare. "Glad to swear they never had anything to do with such a creature? Then *I'd* be glad to swear they had lots!"

His persuasive smile, though confessing to bewilderment, insisted. "Why, my love, they've got to swear either one thing or the other."

"They've got to keep out of the way— that's *their* view of it, I guess," said Julia. "Where *are* they, please—now that they *may* be wanted? If you'd like to hunt them up for me you're very welcome." With which, for the moment, over the difficult case, they faced each other helplessly enough. And she added to it now the sharpest ache of her despair. "He knows about Murray Brush. The others"—and her pretty white-gloved hands and charming pink shoulders gave them up—"may go hang!"

"Murray Brush—?" It had opened Mr. Pitman's eyes.

"Yes—yes; I do mind *him*."

"Then what's the matter with his at least rallying—?"

"The matter is that, being ashamed of himself, as he well might, he left the country as soon as he could and has stayed away. The matter is that he's in

Paris or somewhere, and that if you expect him to come home for me—!" She had already dropped, however, as at Mr. Pitman's look.

"Why, you foolish thing, Murray Brush is in New York!" It had quite brightened him up.

"He has come back—?"

"Why, sure! I saw him—when was it? Tuesday!—on the Jersey boat." Mr. Pitman rejoiced in his news. "*He's* your man!"

Julia too had been affected by it; it had brought, in a rich wave, her hot color back. But she gave the strangest dim smile. "He *was!*"

"Then get hold of him, and—if he's a gentleman—he'll prove for you, to the hilt, that he wasn't."

It lighted in her face, the kindled train of this particular sudden suggestion, a glow, a sharpness of interest, that had deepened the next moment, while she gave a slow and sad head-shake, to a greater strangeness yet. "He isn't a gentleman."

"Ah, lordy, lordy!" Mr. Pitman again sighed. He struggled out of it but only into the vague. "Oh then, if he's a pig—!"

"You see there are only a few gentlemen—not enough to go round—and that makes them count so!" It had thrust the girl herself, for that matter, into depths; but whether most of memory or of roused purpose he had no time to judge—aware as he suddenly was of a shadow (since he mightn't perhaps too quickly call it a light) across the heaving surface of their question. It fell upon Julia's face, fell with the sound of the voice he so well knew, but which could only be odd to her for all it immediately assumed.

"There are indeed very few—and one mustn't try *them* too much!" Mrs. Drack, who had supervened while they talked, stood, in monstrous magnitude—at least to Julia's reimpressed eyes—between them: she was the lady our young woman had descried across the room, and she had drawn near while the interest of their issue so held them. We have seen the act of observation and that of reflection alike swift in Julia—once her subject was within range—and she had now, with all her perceptions at the

acutest, taken in, by a single stare, the strange presence to a happy connection with which Mr. Pitman aspired and which had thus sailed, with placid majesty, into their troubled waters. She was clearly not shy, Mrs. David E. Drack, yet neither was she ominously bold; she was bland and "good," Julia made sure at a glance, and of a large complacency, as the good and the bland are apt to be—a large complacency, a large sentimentality, a large innocent, elephantine archness: she fairly rioted in that dimension of size. Habited in an extraordinary quantity of stiff and lustrous black brocade, with enhancements, of every description, that twinkled and tinkled, that rustled and rumbled with her least movement, she presented a huge, hideous, pleasant face, a featureless desert in a remote quarter of which the disproportionately small eyes might have figured a pair of rash adventurers all but buried in the sand. They reduced themselves when she smiled to barely discernible points — a couple of mere tiny emergent heads — though the foreground of the scene, as if to make up for it, gaped with a vast benevolence. In a word Julia saw—and as if she had needed nothing more; saw Mr. Pitman's opportunity, saw her own, saw the exact nature both of Mrs. Drack's circumspection and of Mrs. Drack's sensibility, saw even, glittering there in letters of gold and as a part of the whole metallic coruscation, the large figure of her income, largest of all her attributes, and (though perhaps a little more as a luminous blur beside all this) the mingled ecstasy and agony of Mr. Pitman's hope and Mr. Pitman's fear.

He was introducing them, with his pathetic belief in the virtue for every occasion, in the solvent for every trouble, of an extravagant, genial, professional humor; he was naming her to Mrs. Drack as the charming young friend he had told her so much about and who had been as an angel to him in a weary time; he was saying that the loveliest chance in the world, this accident of a meeting in those promiscuous halls, had placed within his reach the pleasure of bringing them together. It didn't indeed matter, Julia felt, what he was saying: he conveyed everything, as far as she was concerned, by a moral pressure as unmistakable as if, for a symbol of it, he had thrown himself on her neck. Above all, meanwhile, this high consciousness prevailed—that the good lady herself, however huge she loomed, had entered, by the end of a minute, into a condition as of suspended weight and arrested mass, stilled to artless awe by the effect of her vision. Julia had practised almost to lassitude the art of tracing in the people who looked at her the impression promptly sequent; but it was a singular fact that if, in irritation, in depression, she felt that the lighted eyes of men, stupid at their clearest, had given her pretty well all she should ever care for, she could still gather a freshness from the tribute of her own sex, still care to see her reflection in the faces of women. Never, probably, never would that sweet be tasteless—with such a straight grim spoon was it mostly administered, and so flavored and strengthened by the competence of their eyes. Women knew so much best *how* a woman surpassed—how and where and why, with no touch or torment of it lost on them; so that as it produced mainly and primarily the instinct of aversion, the sense of extracting the recognition, of gouging out the homage, was on the whole the highest crown one's felicity could wear. Once in a way, however, the grimness beautifully dropped, the jealousy failed: the admiration was all there and the poor plain sister handsomely paid it. It had never been so paid, she was presently certain, as by this great generous object of Mr. Pitman's flame, who without optical aid, it well might have seemed, nevertheless entirely grasped her — might in fact, all benevolently, have been groping her over as by some huge mild proboscis. She gave Mrs. Drack pleasure in short; and who could say of what other pleasures the poor lady hadn't been cheated?

It was somehow a muddled world in which one of her conceivable joys, at this time of day, would be to marry Mr. Pitman—to say nothing of a state of things in which this gentleman's own fancy could invest such a union with rapture. That, however, was their own mystery, and Julia, with each instant, was more and more clear about hers: so

remarkably primed in fact, at the end of three minutes, that though her friend, and though *his* friend, were both saying things, many things and perhaps quite wonderful things, she had no free attention for them and was only rising and soaring. She was rising to her value, she was soaring *with* it—the value Mr. Pitman almost convulsively imputed to her, the value that consisted for her of being so unmistakably the most dazzling image Mrs. Drack had ever beheld. These were the uses, for Julia, in fine, of adversity; the range of Mrs. Drack's experience might have been as small as the measure of her presence was large: Julia was at any rate herself in face of the occasion of her life and, after all her late repudiations and reactions, had perhaps never yet known the quality of this moment's success. She hadn't an idea of what, on either side, had been uttered —beyond Mr. Pitman's allusion to her having befriended him of old: she simply held his companion with her radiance and knew she might be, for her effect, as irrelevant as she chose. It was relevant to do what he wanted—it was relevant to dish herself. She did it now with a kind of passion, to say nothing of her knowing, with it, that every word of it added to her beauty. She gave him away in short, up to the hilt, for any use of her own, and should have nothing to clutch at now but the possibility of Murray Brush.

" He says I was good to him, Mrs. Drack; and I'm sure I hope I was, since I should be ashamed to be anything else. If I could be good to him now I should be glad—that's just what, a while ago, I rushed up to him here, after so long, to give myself the pleasure of saying. I saw him years ago very particularly, very miserably tried—and I saw the way he took it. I did see it, you dear man," she sublimely went on—" I saw it for all you may protest, for all you may hate me to talk about you! I saw you behave like a gentleman — since Mrs. Drack agrees with me, so charmingly, that there are not many to be met. I don't know whether you care, Mrs. Drack " she abounded, she revelled in the name— " but I've always remembered it of him: that under the most extraordinary provocation he was decent and patient and

"HE SAYS I WAS GOOD TO HIM, MRS. DRACK"

brave. No appearance of anything different matters, for I speak of what I *know*. Of course I'm nothing and nobody; I'm only a poor frivolous girl, but I was very close to him at the time. That's all my little story—if it *should* interest you at all." She measured every beat of her wing, she knew how high she was going and paused only when it was quite vertiginous. Here she hung a moment as in the glare of the upper blue; which was but the glare—what else could it be?—of the vast and magnificent attention of both her auditors, hushed, on their side, in the splendor she emitted. She had at last to steady herself and she scarce knew afterwards at what rate or in what way she had still inimitably come down—her own eyes fixed all the while on the very figure of her achievement. She had sacrificed her mother on the altar—proclaimed her as false and cruel; and if that didn't "fix" Mr. Pitman, as he would have said—well, it was all she could do. But the cost of her action already somehow came back to her with increase; the dear gaunt man fairly wavered, to her sight, in the glory of it, as if signalling at her, with wild gleeful arms, from some mount of safety, while the massive lady just spread and spread like a rich fluid a bit helplessly spilt. It was really the outflow of the poor woman's honest response, into which she seemed to melt, and Julia scarce distinguished the two apart even for her taking gracious leave of each. "Goodby, Mrs. Drack; I'm awfully happy to have met you"—like as not it was for this she had grasped Mr. Pitman's hand. And then to him or to her, it didn't matter which, "Good-by, dear good Mr. Pitman—hasn't it been nice after so long?"

[TO BE CONCLUDED.]

JULIA BRIDE
(PART 2)
by Henry James

A STORY IN TWO PARTS

II

JULIA floated even to her own sense swanlike away—she left in her wake their fairly stupefied submission: it was as if she had, by an exquisite authority, now *placed* them, each for each, and they would have nothing to do but be happy together. Never had she so exulted as on this ridiculous occasion in the noted items of her beauty. *Le compte y était,* as they used to say in Paris—every one of them, for her immediate employment, was there; and there was something in it after all. It didn't necessarily, this sum of thumping little figures, imply charm—especially for "refined" people: nobody knew better than Julia that inexpressible charm and quotable "charms" (quotable like prices, rates, shares, or whatever, the things they dealt in downtown) are two distinct categories; the safest thing for the latter being, on the whole, that it might include the former, and the great strength of the former being that it might perfectly dispense with the latter. Mrs. Drack was not refined, not the least little bit; but what would be the case with Murray Brush now—after his three years of Europe? He had done so what he liked with her—which had seemed so then just the meaning, hadn't it? of their being "engaged"—that he had made her not see, while the absurdity lasted (the absurdity of their pretending to believe they could marry without a cent) how little he was of metal without alloy: this had come up for her, remarkably, but afterwards—come up for her as she looked back. Then she had drawn her conclusion, which was one of the many that Basil French had made her draw. It was a queer service Basil was going to have rendered her, this having made everything she had ever done impossible, if he wasn't going to give her a new chance.

If he was it was doubtless right enough. On the other hand Murray might have improved, if such a quantity of alloy, as she called it, *were,* in any man, reducible, and if Paris were the place all happily to reduce it. She had her doubts —anxious and aching on the spot, and had expressed them to Mr. Pitman: certainly, of old, he had been more open to the quotable than to the inexpressible, to charms than to charm. If she could try the quotable, however, and with such a grand result, on Mrs. Drack, she couldn't now on Murray—in respect to whom everything had changed. So that if he hadn't a sense for the subtler appeal, the appeal appreciable by people *not* vulgar, on which alone she could depend, what on earth would become of her? She could but yearningly hope, at any rate, as she made up her mind to write to him immediately at his club. It was a question of the right sensibility in him. Perhaps he would have acquired it in Europe.

Two days later indeed—for he had promptly and charmingly replied, keeping with alacrity the appointment she had judged best to propose for a morning hour in a sequestered alley of the Park—two days later she was to be struck well-nigh to alarm by everything he had acquired: so much it seemed to make that it threatened somehow a complication, and her plan, so far as she had arrived at one, dwelt in the desire above all to simplify. She wanted no grain more of extravagance or excess of anything—risking as she had done, none the less, a recall of ancient license in proposing to Murray such a place of meeting. She had her reasons—she wished intensely to discriminate: Basil French had several times waited on her at her mother's habitation, their horrible flat which was so much too far up and too near the East side; he had dined there and lunched there and gone with her thence to other places, notably to see pictures, and had in particular adjourned with her twice to the Metropolitan Museum, in which he took a great interest, in which she professed a delight, and their second visit to which had wound up in her encounter with Mr. Pitman, after her companion had yielded, at her urgent instance, to an exceptional need of keeping a business engagement. She mightn't, in delicacy, in decency, entertain Murray Brush where she had entertained Mr. French— she was given over now to these exquisite perceptions and proprieties and bent on devoutly observing them; and Mr. French, by good luck, had never been with her in the Park: partly because he had never pressed it, and partly because she would have held off if he had, so haunted were those devious paths and favoring shades by the general echo of her untrammelled past. If he had never suggested their taking a turn there this was because, quite divinably, he held it would commit him further than he had yet gone; and if she on her side had practised a like reserve it was because the place reeked for her, as she inwardly said, with old associations. It reeked with nothing so much perhaps as with the memories evoked by the young man who now awaited her in the nook she had been so competent to indicate; but in what corner of the town, should she look for them, wouldn't those footsteps creak back into muffled life, and to what expedient would she be reduced should she attempt to avoid all such tracks? The Museum was full of tracks, tracks by the hundred—the way really she had knocked about!—but she had to see people somewhere, and she couldn't pretend to dodge every ghost.

All she could do was not to make confusion, make mixtures, of the living; though she asked herself enough what mixture she mightn't find herself to have prepared if Mr. French should, not so very impossibly, for a restless, roaming man—*her* effect on him!—happen to pass while she sat there with the mustachioed personage round whose name Mrs. Maule would probably have caused detrimental anecdote most thickly to cluster. There existed, she was sure, a mass of luxuriant

legend about the "lengths" her engagement with Murray Brush had gone; she could herself fairly feel them in the air, these streamers of evil, black flags flown as in warning, the vast redundancy of so cheap and so dingy social bunting, in fine, that flapped over the stations she had successively moved away from and which were empty now, for such an ado, even to grotesqueness. The vivacity of that conviction was what had at present determined her, while it was the way he listened after she had quickly broken ground, while it was the special character of the interested look in his handsome face, handsomer than ever yet, that represented for her the civilization he had somehow taken on. Just so it was the quantity of that gain, in its turn, that had at the end of ten minutes begun to affect her as holding up a light to the wide reach of her step. "There was never anything the least serious, between us, not a sign or a scrap, do you mind? of anything beyond the merest pleasant friendly acquaintance; and if you're not ready to go to the stake on it for me you may as well know in time what it is you'll probably cost me."

She had immediately plunged, measuring her effect and having thought it well over; and what corresponded to her question of his having become a better person to appeal to was the appearance of interest she had so easily created in him. She felt on the spot the difference that made—it was indeed his form of being more civilized: it was the sense in which Europe in general and Paris in particular had made him develop. By every calculation—and her calculations, based on the intimacy of her knowledge, had been many and deep—he would help her the better the more intelligent he should have become; yet she was to recognize later on that the first chill of foreseen disaster had been caught by her as, at a given moment, this greater refinement of his attention seemed to exhale it. It was just what she had wanted —"if I can only get him interested—!" so that, this proving quite vividly possible, why did the light it lifted strike her as lurid? Was it partly by reason of his inordinate romantic good looks, those of a gallant, genial conqueror, but which, involving so glossy a brownness of eye, so manly a crispness of curl, so red-lipped a radiance of smile, so natural a bravery of port, prescribed to any response he might facially, might expressively make a sort of florid, disproportionate amplitude? The explanation, in any case, didn't matter; he was going to mean well—that she could feel, and also that he had meant better in the past, presumably, than he had managed to convince her of his doing at the time: the oddity she hadn't now reckoned with was this fact that from the moment he did advertise an interest it should show almost as what she would have called weird. It made a change in him that didn't go with the rest—as if he had broken his nose or put on spectacles, lost his handsome hair or sacrificed his splendid mustache: her conception, her necessity, as she saw, had been that something should be added to him for her use, but nothing for his own alteration.

He had affirmed himself, and his character, and his temper, and his health, and his appetite, and his ignorance, and his obstinacy, and his whole charming, coarse, heartless personality, during their engagement, by twenty forms of natural emphasis, but never by emphasis of interest. How in fact could you feel interest unless you should know, within you, some dim stir of imagination? There was nothing in the world of which Murray Brush was less capable than of such a dim stir, because you only began to imagine when you felt some approach to a need to understand. *He* had never felt it; for hadn't he been born, to his personal vision, with that perfect intuition of everything which reduces all the suggested preliminaries of judgment to the impertinence—when it's a question of your entering your house— of a dumpage of bricks at your door? He had had, in short, neither to imagine nor to perceive, because he had, from the first pulse of his intelligence, simply and supremely known: so that, at this hour, face to face with him, it came over her that she had, in their old relation, dispensed with any such convenience of comprehension on her part even to a degree she had not measured at the time. What therefore must he not have seemed to her as a form of life, a form of avidity and activity, blatantly successful in

its own conceit, that he could have dazzled her so against the interest of her very faculties and functions? Strangely and richly historic all that backward mystery, and only leaving for her mind the wonder of such a mixture of possession and detachment as they would clearly to-day both know. For each to be so little at last to the other when, during months together, the idea of all abundance, all quantity, had been, for each, drawn from the other and addressed to the other—what was it monstrously like but some fantastic act of getting rid of a person by going to lock yourself up in the *sanctum sanctorum* of that person's house, amid every evidence of that person's habits and nature? What was going to happen, at any rate, was that Murray would show himself as beautifully and consciously understanding—and it would be prodigious that Europe should have inoculated him with that delicacy. Yes, he wouldn't claim to know now till she had told him—an aid to performance he had surely never before waited for, or been indebted to, from any one; and then, so knowing, he would charmingly endeavor to "meet," to oblige and to gratify. He would find it, her case, ever so worthy of his benevolence, and would be literally inspired to reflect that he must hear about it first.

She let him hear then everything, in spite of feeling herself slip, while she did so, to some doom as yet incalculable; she went on very much as she had done for Mr. Pitman and Mrs. Drack, with the rage of desperation and, as she was afterwards to call it to herself, the fascination of the abyss. She didn't know, couldn't have said at the time, *why* his projected benevolence should have had most so the virtue to scare her: he would patronize her, as an effect of her vividness, if not of her charm, and would do this with all high intention, finding her case, or rather *their* case, their funny old case, taking on of a sudden such refreshing and edifying life, to the last degree curious and even important; but there were gaps of connection between this and the intensity of the perception here overtaking her that she shouldn't be able to move in *any* direction without dishing herself. That she couldn't afford it where she had got to—couldn't afford the deplorable vulgarity of having been so many times informally affianced and contracted (putting it only at that, at its being by the new lights and fashions so unpardonably vulgar): he took this from her without turning, as she might have said, a hair; except just to indicate, with his new superiority, that he felt the distinguished appeal and notably the pathos of it. He still took it from her that she hoped nothing, as it were, from any other *alibi*—the people to drag into court being too many and too scattered; but that, as it was with him, Murray Brush, she had been *most* vulgar, most everything she had better not have been, so she depended on him for the innocence it was actually vital she should establish. He flushed or frowned or winced no more at that than he did when she once more fairly emptied her satchel and, quite as if they had been Nancy and the Artful Dodger, or some nefarious pair of that sort, talking things over in the manner of " Oliver Twist," revealed to him the fondness of her view that, could she but have produced a cleaner slate, she might by this time have pulled it off with Mr. French. Yes, he let her in that way sacrifice her honorable connection with him—all the more honorable for being so completely at an end—to the crudity of her plan for not missing another connection, so much more brilliant than what he offered, and for bringing another man, with whom she so invidiously and unflatteringly compared him, into her greedy life.

There was only a moment during which, by a particular lustrous look she had never had from him before, he just made her wonder which turn he was going to take; she felt, however, as safe as was consistent with her sense of having probably but added to her danger, when he brought out, the next instant: " Don't you seem to take the ground that we were guilty — that *you* were ever guilty—of something we shouldn't have been? What did we ever do that was secret, or underhand, or any way not to be acknowledged? What did we do but exchange our young vows with the best faith in the world — publicly, rejoicingly, with the full assent of every one connected with us? I mean of course,"

he said with his grave kind smile, " till we broke off so completely because we found that—practically, financially, on the hard worldly basis—we couldn't work it. What harm, in the sight of God or man, Julia," he asked in his fine rich way. " did we ever do?"

She gave him back his look, turning pale. " Am I talking of *that*? Am I talking of what *we* know? I'm talking of what others feel—of what they *have* to feel; of what it's just enough for them to know not to be able to get over it, once they do really know it. How do they know what *didn't* pass between us, with all the opportunities we had? That's none of their business—if we were idiots enough, on the top of everything! What you may or mayn't have done doesn't count, for *you;* but there are people for whom it's loathsome that a girl should have gone on like that from one person to another and still pretend to be—well, all that a nice girl is supposed to be. It's as if we had but just waked up, mother and I, to such a remarkable prejudice; and now we have it —when we could do so well without it!— staring us in the face. That mother should have insanely *let* me, should so vulgarly have taken it for my natural, my social career—*that's* the disgusting, humiliating thing: with the lovely account it gives of both of us! But mother's view of a delicacy in things!" she went on with scathing grimness; " mother's measure of anything, with her grand ' gained cases' (there'll be another yet, she finds them so easy!) of which she's so publicly proud! You see I've no margin," said Julia; letting him take it from her flushed face as much as he would that her mother hadn't left her an inch. It was that he should make use of the spade with her for the restoration of a bit of a margin just wide enough to perch on till the tide of peril should have ebbed a little, it was that he should give her *that* lift—!

Well, it was all there from him after these last words; it was before her that he really took hold. " Oh, my dear child, I can see! Of course there are people— ideas change in our society so fast!— who are not in sympathy with the old American freedom and who read, I dare say, all sorts of uncanny things into it.

Naturally you must take them as they are—from the moment," said Murray Brush, who had lighted, by her leave, a cigarette, "your life-path does, for weal or for woe, cross with theirs." He had every now and then such an elegant phrase. "Awfully interesting, certainly, your case. It's enough for me that it *is* yours—I make it my own. I put myself absolutely in your place; you'll understand from me, without professions, won't you? that I do. Command me in every way! What I do like is the sympathy with which you've inspired *him*. I don't, I'm sorry to say, happen to know him personally"—he smoked away, looking off; "but of course one knows all about him generally, and I'm sure he's right for you, I'm sure it would be charming, if you yourself think so. Therefore trust me and even—what shall I say?—leave it to me a little, won't you?" He had been watching, as in his fumes, the fine growth of his possibilities; and with this he turned on her the large warmth of his charity. It was like a subscription of a half-a-million. "I'll take care of you."

She found herself for a moment looking up at him from as far below as the point from which the school-child, with round eyes raised to the wall, gazes at the particolored map of the world. Yes, it was a warmth, it was a special benignity, that had never yet dropped on her from any one; and she wouldn't for the first few moments have known how to describe it or even quite what to do with it. Then, as it still rested, his fine improved expression aiding, the sense of what had happened came over her with a rush. She was being, yes, patronized; and that was really as new to her—the freeborn American girl who might, if she had wished, have got engaged and disengaged not six times but sixty—as it would have been to be crowned or crucified. The Frenches themselves didn't do it—the Frenches themselves didn't dare it. It was as strange as one would: she recognized it when it came, but anything might have come rather—and it was coming by (of all people in the world) Murray Brush! It overwhelmed her; still she could speak, with however faint a quaver and however sick a smile. "You'll lie for me like a gentleman?"

"As far as that goes till I'm black in the face!" And then while he glowed at her and she wondered if he would pointedly look his lies that way, and if, in fine, his florid, gallant, knowing, almost winking intelligence, *common* as she had never seen the common vivified, would represent his notion of "blackness": "See here, Julia; I'll do more."

"'More'—?"

"Everything. I'll take it right in hand. I'll fling over you—"

"Fling over me—?" she continued to echo as he fascinatingly fixed her.

"Well, the biggest *kind* of rose colored mantle!" And this time, oh, he did wink: it *would* be the way he was going to wink (and in the grandest good faith in the world) when indignantly denying, under inquisition, that there had been "a sign or a scrap" between them. But there was more to come; he decided she should have it all. "Julia, you've got to know now." He hung fire but an instant more. "Julia, I'm going to be married." His "Julias" were somehow death to her; she could feel that even *through* all the rest. "Julia, I announce my engagement."

"Oh, lordy, lordy!" she wailed: it might have been addressed to Mr. Pitman.

The force of it had brought her to her feet, but he sat there smiling up as at the natural tribute of her interest. "I tell you before any one else; it's not to be 'out' for a day or two yet. But we want you to know; *she* said that as soon as I mentioned to her that I had heard from you. I mention to her everything, you see!"—and he almost simpered while, still in his seat, he held the end of his cigarette, all delicately and as for a form of gentle emphasis, with the tips of his fine fingers. "You've not met her, Mary Lindeck, I think: she tells me she hasn't the pleasure of knowing you, but she desires it so much—particularly longs for it. She'll take an interest too," he went on; "you must let me immediately bring her to you. She has heard so much about you and she really wants to see you."

"Oh mercy me!" poor Julia gasped again—so strangely did history repeat itself and so did this appear the echo, on Murray Brush's lips, and quite to drollery, of that sympathetic curiosity of

Mrs. Drack's which Mr. Pitman, as they said, voiced. Well, there had played before her the vision of a ledge of safety in face of a rising tide; but this deepened quickly to a sense more forlorn, the cold swish of waters already up to her waist and that would soon be up to her chin. It came really but from the air of her friend, from the perfect benevolence and high unconsciousness with which he kept his posture—as if to show he could patronize her from below upward quite as well as from above down. And as she took it all in, as it spread to a flood, with the great lumps and masses of truth it was floating, she knew inevitable submission, not to say submersion, as she had never known it in her life; going down and down before it, not even putting out her hands to resist or cling by the way, only reading into the young man's very face an immense fatality and, for all his bright nobleness, his absence of rancor or of protesting pride, the great gray blankness of her doom. It was as if the earnest Miss Lindeck, tall and mild, high and lean, with eye-glasses and a big nose, but "marked" in a noticeable way, elegant and distinguished and refined, as you could see from a mile off, and as graceful, for common despair of imitation, as the curves of the "copy" set of old by one writing-master—it was as if this stately well-wisher, whom indeed she had never exchanged a word with, but whom she had recognized and placed and winced at as soon as he spoke of her, figured there beside him now as also in portentous charge of her case.

He had ushered her into it in that way, as if his mere right word sufficed; and Julia could see them throne together, beautifully at one in all the interests they now shared, and regard her as an object of almost tender solicitude. It was positively as if they had become engaged for her good—in such a happy light as it shed. That was the way people you had known, known a bit intimately, looked at you as soon as they took on the high matrimonial propriety that sponged over the more or less wild past to which you belonged and of which, all of a sudden, they were aware only through some suggestion it made them for reminding you definitely that you still had a place. On her having had a day or two before to

meet Mrs. Drack and to rise to her expectation she had seen and felt herself act, had above all admired herself, and had at any rate known what she said, even though losing, at her altitude, any distinctness in the others. She could have repeated afterwards the detail of her performance—if she hadn't preferred to keep it with her as a mere locked-up, a mere unhandled treasure. At present, however, as everything was for her at first deadened and vague, true to the general effect of sounds and motions in water, she couldn't have said afterwards what words she spoke, what face she showed, what impression she made—at least till she had pulled herself round to precautions. She only knew she had turned away, and that this movement must have sooner or later determined his rising to join her, his deciding to accept it, gracefully and condoningly—condoningly in respect to her natural emotion, her inevitable little pang—for an intimation that they would be better on their feet.

They trod then afresh their ancient paths; and though it pressed upon her hatefully that he must have taken her abruptness for a smothered shock, the flare-up of her old feeling at the breath of his news, she had still to see herself condemned to allow him this, condemned really to encourage him in the mistake of believing her suspicious of feminine spite and doubtful of Miss Lindeck's zeal. She was so far from doubtful that she was but too appalled at it and at the officious mass in which it loomed, and this instinct of dread, before their walk was over, before she had guided him round to one of the smaller gates, there to slip off again by herself, was positively to find on the bosom of her flood a plank by the aid of which she kept in a manner and for the time afloat. She took ten minutes to pant, to blow gently, to paddle disguisedly, to accommodate herself, in a word, to the elements she had let loose; but as a reward of her effort at least she then saw how her determined vision accounted for everything. Beside her friend on the bench she had truly felt all his cables cut, truly swallowed down the fact that if he still perceived she was pretty—and how pretty!—it had ceased appreciably to matter to him. It

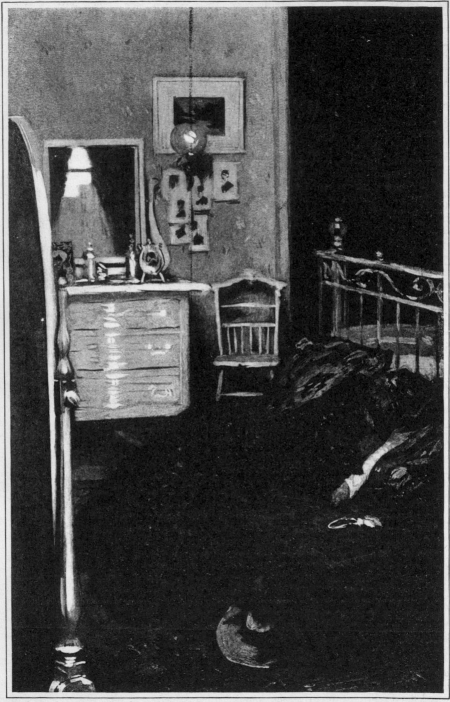

Drawn by W. T. Smedley

SHE YIELDED TO THE BITTERNESS

had lighted the folly of her preliminary fear, the fear of his even yet, to some effect of confusion or other inconvenience for her, proving more alive to the quotable in her, as she had called it, than to the inexpressible. She had reckoned with the awkwardness of that possible failure of his measure of her charm, by which his renewed apprehension of her grosser ornaments, those with which he had most affinity, might too much profit; but she need have concerned herself as little for his sensibility on one head as on the other. She had ceased personally, ceased materially—in respect, as who should say, to any optical or tactile advantage—to exist for him, and the whole office of his manner had been the more piously and gallantly to dress the dead presence with flowers. This was all to his credit and his honor, but what it clearly certified was that their case was at last not even one of spirit reaching out to spirit. *He* had plenty of spirit—had all the spirit required for his having engaged himself to Miss Lindeck; into which result, once she had got her head well up again, she read, as they proceeded, one sharp meaning after another. It was therefore toward the subtler essence of that mature young woman alone that he was occupied in stretching; what was definite to him about Julia Bride being merely, being entirely—which was indeed thereby quite enough—that she *might* end by scaling her worldly height. They would push, they would shove, they would "boost," they would arch both their straight backs as pedestals for her tiptoe; and at the same time, by some sweet prodigy of mechanics, she would pull them up and up with her.

Wondrous things hovered before her in the course of this walk; her consciousness had become, by an extraordinary turn, a music-box in which, its lid well down, the most remarkable tunes were sounding. It played for her car alone, and the lid, as she might have figured, was her firm plan of holding out till she got home, of not betraying—to her companion at least—the extent to which she was demoralized. To see him think her demoralized by mistrust of the sincerity of the service to be meddlesomely rendered her by his future wife—she would have hurled herself publicly into the lake there at their side, would have splashed, in her beautiful clothes, among the frightened swans, rather than invite him to that ineptitude. Oh, her sincerity, Mary Lindeck's—she would be drenched with her sincerity, and she would be drenched, yes, with *his;* so that, from inward convulsion to convulsion, she had, before they reached their gate, pulled up in the path. There was something her head had been full of these three or four minutes, the intensest little tune of the music-box, and it had made its way to her lips now; belonging—for all the good it could do her!—to the two or three sorts of solicitude she might properly express.

"I hope *she* has a fortune, if you don't mind my speaking of it: I mean some of the money we didn't in *our* time have —and that we missed, after all, in our poor way and for what we then wanted of it, so quite dreadfully."

She had been able to wreathe it in a grace quite equal to any he himself had employed; and it was to be said for him also that he kept up, on this, the standard. "Oh, she's not, thank goodness, at all badly off, poor dear. We shall do very well. How sweet of you to have thought of it! May I tell her that too?" he splendidly glared. Yes, he glared—how couldn't he, with what his mind was really full of? But, all the same, he came just here, by her vision, nearer than at any other point to being a gentleman. He came quite within an ace of it—with his taking from her thus the prescription of humility of service, his consenting to act in the interest of her avidity, his letting her mount that way, on his bowed shoulders, to the success in which he could suppose she still believed. He couldn't know, he would never know, that she had then and there ceased to believe in it—that she saw as clear as the sun in the sky the exact manner in which, between them, before they had done, the Murray Brushes, all zeal and sincerity, all interest in her interesting case, would dish, would ruin, would utterly destroy her. He wouldn't have needed to go on, for the force and truth of this; but he did go on—he was as crashingly consistent as a motor-car without a brake. He was visibly in love with the idea of what they might do for her and of the rare "social" opportunity that they would, by the same stroke, embrace. How he had been offhand with it, how he had made it parenthetic, that he didn't happen "personally" to know Basil French—as if it would have been at all likely he *should* know him, even *im*personally, and as if he could conceal from her the fact that, since she had made him her overture, this gentleman's name supremely baited her hook! Oh, they would help Julia Bride if they could—they would do their remarkable best; but they would at any rate have made his acquaintance over it, and she might indeed leave the rest to their thoroughness. He would already have known, he would already have heard; her appeal, she was more and more sure, wouldn't have come to him as a revelation. He had already talked it over with *her,* with Miss Lindeck, to whom the Frenches, in their fortress, had never been accessible, and his whole attitude bristled, to Julia's eyes, with the betrayal of her hand, her voice, her pressure, her calculation. His tone in fact, as he talked, fairly thrust these things into her face. "But you must see her for yourself. You'll judge her. You'll love her. My dear child" —he brought it all out, and if he spoke of children he might, in his candor, have been himself infantine — "my dear child, she's the person to do it for you. Make it over to her; but," he laughed, "of course see her first! Couldn't you," he wound up—for they were now near their gate, where she was to leave him— "couldn't you just simply make us meet him, at tea say, informally; just *us* alone, as pleasant old friends of whom you'd have so naturally and frankly spoken to him: and then see what we'd *make* of that?"

It was all in his expression; he couldn't keep it out of that, and his shining good looks couldn't: ah he was so fatally much too handsome for her! So the gap showed just there, in his admirable mask and his admirable eagerness; the yawning little chasm showed where the gentleman fell short. But she took this in, she took everything in, she felt herself do it, she heard herself say, while they paused before separation, that she quite saw the point of the meeting, as he suggested, at her tea. She would propose it to Mr. French and would let them know; and he must assuredly bring Miss Lindeck, bring her "right away," bring her soon, bring *them,* his *fiancée* and her, together somehow, and as quickly as possible—so that they *should* be old friends before the tea. She would propose it to Mr. French, propose it to Mr. French: that hummed in her ears as she went—after she had really got away; hummed as if she were repeating it over, giving it out to the passers, to the pavement, to the sky, and all as in wild discord with the intense little concert of her music-box. The extraordinary thing too was that she quite believed she should do it, and fully meant to; desperately, fantastically passive—since she almost reeled with it as she proceeded—she was capable of proposing anything to any one: capable too of thinking it likely Mr. French would come, for he had never on her previous proposals declined anything. Yes, she would keep it up to the end, this pretence of owing them salvation, and might even live to take comfort in having done for them what they wanted. What they wanted *couldn't* but be to get at the Frenches, and what Miss Lindeck above all wanted, baffled of it otherwise, with so many others of the baffled, was to get at Mr. French—for all Mr. French would want of either of them!—still more than Murray did. It was not till after she had got home, got straight into her own room and flung herself on her face, that she yielded to the full taste of the bitterness of missing a connection, missing the man himself, with power to create such a social appetite, such a grab at what might be gained by them. He could make people, even people like these two and whom there were still other people to envy, he could make them push and snatch and scramble like that—and then remain as incapable of taking her from the hands of such patrons as of receiving her straight, say, from those of Mrs. Drack. It was a high note, too, of Julia's wonderful composition that, even in the long, lonely moan of her conviction of her now certain ruin, all this grim lucidity, the perfect clearance of passion, but made her supremely proud of him.

[THE END.]

LITTLE BIG HORN MEDICINE
by Owen Wister

SOMETHING new was happening among the Crow Indians. A young pretender had appeared in the tribe. What this might lead to was unknown alike to white man and to red; but the old Crow chiefs discussed it in their councils, and the soldiers at Fort Custer, and the civilians at the agency twelve miles up the river, and all the white settlers in the valley, discussed it also. Lieutenants Stirling and Haines, of the First Cavalry, were speculating upon it as they rode one afternoon.

"Can't tell about Indians," said Stirling. "But I think the Crows are too reasonable to go on the war-path."

"Reasonable!" said Haines. He was young, and new to Indians.

"Just so. Until you come to his superstitions, the Indian can reason as straight as you or I. He's perfectly logical."

"Logical!" echoed Haines again. He held the regulation Eastern view that the Indian knows nothing but the three blind appetites.

"You'd know better," remarked Stirling, "if you'd been fighting 'em for fifteen years. They're as shrewd as Æsop's fables."

Just then two Indians appeared round a bluff—one old and shabby, the other young and very gaudy—riding side by side.

"That's Cheschapah," said Stirling. "That's the agitator in all his feathers. His father, you see, dresses more conservatively."

The feathered dandy now did a singular thing. He galloped towards the two officers almost as if to bear them down, and steering much too close, flashed by yelling, amid a clatter of gravel.

"Nice manners," commented Haines. "Seems to have a chip on his shoulder."

But Stirling looked thoughtful. "Yes," he muttered, "he has a chip."

Meanwhile the shabby father was approaching. His face was mild and sad, and he might be seventy. He made a gesture of greeting. "How!" he said, pleasantly, and ambled on his way.

"Now there you have an object-lesson," said Stirling. "Old Pounded Meat has no chip. The question is, are the fathers or the sons going to run the Crow Nation?"

"Why did the young chap have a dog on his saddle?" inquired Haines.

"I didn't notice it. For his supper, probably—probably he's getting up a dance. He is scheming to be a chief. Says he is a medicine-man, and can make water boil without fire; but the big men of the tribe take no stock in him—not yet. They've seen soda-water before. But I'm told this water-boiling astonishes the young."

"You say the old chiefs take no stock in him yet?"

"Ah, that's the puzzle. I told you just now Indians could reason."

"And I was amused."

"Because you're an Eastern man. I tell you, Haines, if it wasn't my business to shoot them I'd study them."

"You're a crank," said Haines.

But Stirling was not a crank. He knew that so far from being a mere animal, the Indian is of a subtlety more ancient than the Sphinx. In his primal brain—nearer nature than our own—the directness of a child mingles with the profoundest cunning. He believes easily in powers of light and darkness, yet is a sceptic all the while. Stirling knew this; but he could not know just when, if ever, the young charlatan Cheschapah would succeed in cheating the older chiefs; just when, if ever, he would strike the chord of their superstition. Till then they would reason that the white man was more comfortable as a friend than as a foe, that rations and gifts of clothes and farming implements were better than battles and prisons. Once their superstition was set alight, these three thousand Crows might suddenly follow Cheschapah to burn and kill and destroy.

"How does he manage his soda-water, do you suppose?" inquired Haines.

"That's mysterious. He has never been known to buy drugs, and he's careful where he does his trick. He's still a little afraid of his father. All Indians are. It's queer where he was going with that dog."

Hard galloping sounded behind them, and a courier from the Indian agency overtook and passed them, hurrying to Fort Custer. The officers hurried too, and arriving, received news and orders. Forty Sioux were reported up the river coming to visit the Crows. It was peaceable, but untimely. The Sioux agent over at Pine Ridge had given these forty permission to go, without first finding out if it would be convenient to the Crow agent to have them come. It is a rule of the Indian Bureau that if one tribe desire to visit another, the agents of both must consent. Now, most of the Crows were farming and quiet, and it was not wise that a visit from the Sioux and a season of feasting should tempt their hearts and minds away from the tilling of the soil. The visitors must be taken charge of and sent home.

"Very awkward, though," said Stirling to Haines. He had been ordered to take two troops and arrest the unoffending visitors on their way. "The Sioux will be mad, and the Crows will be madder. What a bungle! and how like the way we manage Indian affairs!" And so they started.

Thirty miles away, by a stream towards which Stirling with his command was steadily marching through the night, the visitors were gathered. There was a cookfire and a pot, and a stewing dog leaped in the froth. Old men in blankets and feathers sat near it, listening to young Cheschapah's talk in the flighty lustre of the flames. An old squaw acted as interpreter between Crow and Sioux. Round about, at a certain distance, the figures of the crowd lounged at the edge of the darkness. Two grizzled squaws stirred the pot, spreading a clawed fist to their eyes against the red heat of the coals, while young Cheschapah harangued the older chiefs.

"And more than that I, Cheschapah, can do," said he, boasting in Indian fashion. "I know how to make the white man's heart soft so he cannot fight." He paused for effect, but his hearers seemed uninterested. "You have come pretty

"BOASTING IN INDIAN FASHION."

far to see us," resumed the orator, "and I, and my friend Two Whistles, and my father, Pounded Meat, have come a day to meet you and bring you to our place. I have brought you a fat dog. I say it is good the Crow and the Sioux shall be friends. All the Crow chiefs are glad. Pretty Eagle is a big chief, and he will tell you what I tell you. But I am bigger than Pretty Eagle. I am a medicine-man."

He paused again; but the grim old chiefs were looking at the fire, and not at him. He got a friendly glance from his henchman, Two Whistles, but he heard his father give a grunt.

That enraged him. "I am a medicine-man," he repeated, defiantly. "I have been in the big hole in the mountains where the river goes, and spoken there with the old man who makes the thunder. I talked with him as one chief to another. I am going to kill all the white men."

At this old Pounded Meat looked at his son angrily, but the son was not afraid of his father just then. "I can make medicine to bring the rain," he continued. "I can make water boil when it is cold. With this I can strike the white man blind when he is so far that his eyes do not show in his face."

He swept out from his blanket an old cavalry sabre painted scarlet. Young Two Whistles made a movement of awe, but Pounded Meat said, "My son's tongue has grown longer than his sword."

Laughter sounded among the old chiefs. Cheschapah turned his impudent yet somewhat visionary face upon his father. "What do you know of medicine?" said he. "Two sorts of Indians are among the Crows to-day," he continued to the chiefs. "One sort are the fathers, and the sons are the other. The young warriors are not afraid of the white man. The old plant corn with the squaws. Is this the way with the Sioux?"

"With the Sioux," remarked a grim visitor, "no one fears the white man. But the young warriors do not talk much in council."

Pounded Meat put out his hand gently, as if in remonstrance. Other people must not chide his son.

"You say you can make water boil with no fire?" pursued the Sioux, who was named Young-man-afraid-of-his-horses, and had been young once.

Pounded Meat came between. "My

son is a good man," said he. "These words of his are not made in the heart, but are head words you need not count. Cheschapah does not like peace. He has heard us sing our wars and the enemies we have killed, and he remembers that he has no deeds, being young. When he thinks of this sometimes he talks words without sense. But my son is a good man."

The father again extended his hand, which trembled a little. The Sioux had listened, looking at him with respect, and forgetful of Cheschapah, who now stood before them with a cup of cold water.

"You shall see," he said, "who it is that talks words without sense."

Two Whistles and the young bucks crowded to watch, but the old men sat where they were. As Cheschapah stood relishing his audience, Pounded Meat stepped up suddenly and upset the cup. He went to the stream and refilled it himself. "Now make it boil," said he.

Cheschapah smiled, and as he spread his hand quickly over the cup, the water foamed up.

"Huh!" said Two Whistles, startled.

The medicine-man quickly seized his moment. "What does Pounded Meat know of my medicine?" said he. "The dog is cooked. Let the dance begin."

The drums set up their dull blunt beating, and the crowd of young and less important bucks came from the outer circle nearer to the council. Cheschapah set the pot in the midst of the flat camp, to be the centre of the dance. None of the old chiefs said more to him, but sat apart with the empty cup, having words among themselves. The flame reared high into the dark, and showed the rock wall towering close, and at its feet the light lay red on the streaming water. The young Sioux stripped naked of their blankets, hanging them in a screen against the wind from the jaws of the cañon, with more constant shouts as the drumming beat louder, and strokes of echo fell from the black cliffs. The figures twinkled across each other in the glare, drifting and alert, till the dog-dance shaped itself into twelve dancers with a united sway of body and arms, one and another singing his song against the lifted sound of the drums. The twelve sank crouching in simulated hunt for an enemy back and forth over the same space, swinging together.

Presently they sprang with a shout

upon their feet, for they had taken the enemy. Cheschapah, leading the line closer to the central pot, began a new figure, dancing the pursuit of the bear. This went faster; and after the bear was taken, followed the elk-hunt, and a new sway and crouch of the twelve gesturing bodies. The thudding drums were ceaseless; and as the dance went always faster and always nearer the dog-pot, the steady blows of sound inflamed the dancers; their chests heaved, and their arms and bodies swung alike as the excited crew filed and circled closer to the pot, following Cheschapah, and shouting uncontrollably. They came to firing pistols and slashing the air with knives, when suddenly Cheschapah caught up a piece of steaming dog from the pot, gave it to his best friend, and the dance was done. The dripping figures sat quietly, shining and smooth with sweat, eating their dog-flesh in the ardent light of the fire and the cold splendor of the moon. By-and-by they lay in their blankets to sleep at ease.

The elder chiefs had looked with distrust at Cheschapah as he led the dance; now that the entertainment was over, they rose with gravity to go to their beds. "It is good for the Sioux and the Crows to be friends," said Pounded Meat to Young-man-afraid-of-his-horses. "But we want no war with the white man. It is a few young men who say that war is good now."

"We have not come for war," replied the Sioux. "We have come to eat much meat together, and remember that day when war was good on the Little Horn, and our warriors killed Yellow Hair and all his soldiers."

Pounded Meat came to where he and Cheschapah had their blankets.

"We shall have war," said the confident son to his father. "My medicine is good."

"Peace is also pretty good," said Pounded Meat. "Get new thoughts. My son, do you not care any more for my words?"

Cheschapah did not reply.

"I have lived a long while. Yet one man may be wrong. But all cannot be. The other chiefs say what I say. The white men are too strong."

"They would not be too strong if the old men were not cowards."

"Have done," said the father, sternly. "If you are a medicine-man, do not talk like a light fool."

The Indian has an "honor thy father" deep in his religion too, and Cheschapah was silent. But after he was asleep, Pounded Meat lay brooding. He felt himself dishonored, and his son to be an evil in the tribe. With these sore notions keeping him awake, he saw the night wane into gray, and then he heard the distant snort of a horse. He looked, and started from his blankets, for the soldiers had come, and he ran to wake the sleeping Indians. Frightened, and ignorant why they should be surrounded, the Sioux leaped to their feet; and Stirling, from where he sat on his horse, saw their rushing, frantic figures.

"Go quick, Kinney," he said to the interpreter, "and tell them it's peace, or they'll be firing on us."

Kinney rode forward alone, with one hand raised; and seeing that sign, they paused, and crept nearer like crafty rabbits, while the sun rose and turned the place pink. And then came the parley, and the long explanation; and Stirling thanked his stars to see they were going to allow themselves to be peaceably arrested. Bullets you get used to; but after the firing's done, you must justify it to important personages who live comfortably in Eastern towns and have never seen an Indian in their lives, and are rancid with philanthropy and ignorance. Stirling would sooner have faced Sioux than sentimentalists, and he was fervently grateful to these savages for coming with him quietly without obliging him to shoot them. Cheschapah was not behaving so nicely; and recognizing him, Stirling understood about the dog. The medicine-man, with his faithful Two Whistles, was endeavoring to excite the prisoners as they were marched down the river to the Crow Agency.

Stirling sent for Kinney. "Send that rascal away," he said. "I'll not have him bothering here."

The interpreter obeyed, but with a singular smile to himself. When he had ordered Cheschapah away, he rode so as to overhear Stirling and Haines talking. When they speculated about the soda-water, Kinney smiled again. He was a quiet sort of man. The people in the valley admired his business head. He supplied grain and steers to Fort Custer, and used to say that business was always slow in time of peace.

By evening Stirling had brought his

prisoners to the agency, and there was the lieutenant of Indian police of the Sioux come over from Pine Ridge to bring them home. There was restlessness in the air as night fell round the prisoners and their guard. It was Cheschapah's hour, and the young Crows listened while he declaimed against the white man for thwarting their hospitality. The strong chain of sentinels was kept busy preventing these hosts from breaking through to fraternize with their guests. Cheschapah did not care that the old Crow chiefs would not listen. When Pretty Eagle remarked laconically that peace was good, the agitator laughed; he was gaining a faction, and the faction was feeling its oats. Accordingly, next morning, though the prisoners were meek on being started home by Stirling with twenty soldiers, and the majority of the Crows were meek at seeing them thus started, this was not all. Cheschapah, with a yelling swarm of his young friends, began to buzz about the column as it marched up the river. All had rifles.

"It's an interesting state of affairs," said Stirling to Haines. "There are at least fifty of these devils at our heels now, and more coming. We've got twenty men. Haines, your Indian experiences may begin quite early in your career."

"Yes, especially if our prisoners take to kicking."

"Well, to compensate for spoiling their dinner party, the agent gave them some rations and his parting blessing. It may suffice."

The line of march had been taken up by ten men in advance, followed in the usual straggling fashion by the prisoners, and the rear-guard was composed of the other ten soldiers under Stirling and Haines. With them rode the chief of the Crow police and the lieutenant of the Sioux. This little band was, of course, far separated from the advance-guard, and it listened to the young Crow bucks yelling at its heels. They yelled in English. Every Indian knows at least two English words; they are pungent, and far from complimentary.

"It's got to stop here," said Stirling, as they came to a ford known as Reno's Crossing. "They've got to be kept on this side."

"Can it be done without gunpowder?" Haines asked.

"If a shot is fired now, my friend, it's war, and a court of inquiry in Washington for you and me, if we're not buried here. Sergeant, you will take five men and see the column is kept moving. The rest remain with me. The prisoners must be got across and away from their friends."

The fording began, and the two officers went over to the east bank to see that the instructions were carried out.

"See that?" observed Stirling. As the last of the rear-guard stepped into the stream, the shore they were leaving filled instantly with the Crows. "Every man jack of them is armed. And here's an interesting development," he continued.

It was Cheschapah riding out into the water, and with him Two Whistles. The rear-guard passed up the trail, and the little knot of men with the officers stood halted on the bank. They were nine — the two Indian police, the two lieutenants, and five long muscular boys of K troop of the First Cavalry. They remained on the bank, looking at the thick painted swarm that yelled across the ford.

"Bet you there's a hundred," remarked Haines.

"You forget I never gamble," murmured Stirling. Two of the five long boys overheard this and grinned at each other, which Stirling noted; and he loved them. It was curious to mark the two shores; the feathered multitude and its yells and its fifty yards of rifles that fronted a small spot of white men sitting easily in the saddle; and the clear, pleasant water speeding between. Cheschapah and Two Whistles came tauntingly towards this spot, and the mass of Crows on the other side drew forward a little.

"You tell them," said Stirling to the chief of the Crow police, "that they must go back."

Cheschapah came nearer, by way of obedience.

"Take them over, then," the officer ordered.

The chief of Crow police rode to Cheschapah, speaking and pointing. His horse drew close, shoving the horse of the medicine-man, who now launched an insult that with Indians calls for blood. He struck the man's horse with his whip, and at that a volume of yells chorussed from the other bank.

"Looks like the court of inquiry," re-

"HIS HORSE DREW CLOSE, SHOVING THE HORSE OF THE MEDICINE-MAN."

marked Stirling. "Don't shoot, boys," he commanded aloud.

The amazed Sioux policeman gasped. "You not shoot?" he said. "But he hit that man's horse, all the same hit your horse, all the same hit you."

"Right. Quite right," growled Stirling. "All the same hit Uncle Sam. But we soldier devils have orders to temporize." His eye rested hard and serious on the party in the water as he went on speaking with jocular unconcern. "Tom po-rize, Johnny," said he. "You savvy temporize?"

"Ump! Me no savvy."

"Bully for you, Johnny. Too many syllables. Well, now! he's hit that horse again. One more for the court of inquiry. Steady, boys! There's Two Whistles switching now. They ought to call that lad Young Dog Tray. And there's a chap in paint fooling with his gun. If any more do that—it's very catching— Yes, we're going to have a circus. Attention! Now what's that, do you suppose?"

An apparition, an old chief, came suddenly on the other bank, pushing through the crowd, grizzled and little and lean, among the smooth, full-limbed young blood. They turned and saw him, and slunk from the tones of his voice and the light in his ancient eye. They swerved and melted among the cottonwoods, so the ford's edge grew bare of dusky bodies and looked sandy and green again. Cheschapah saw the wrinkled figure coming, and his face sank tame. He stood uncertain in the stream, seeing his banded companions gone and the few white soldiers firm on the bank. The old chief rode to him through the water, his face brightened with a last flare of command.

"Make your medicine!" he said. "Why are the white men not blind? Is the medicine bad to-day?" And he whipped his son's horse to the right, and to the left he slashed the horse of Two Whistles, and whirling the leather quirt, drove them cowed before him and out of the stream, with never a look or word to the white men. He crossed the sandy margin, and as a man drives steers to the corral, striking spurs to his horse and following the frightened animals close when they would twist aside, so did old Pounded Meat herd his son down the valley.

"Useful old man," remarked Stirling;

"and brings up his children carefully. Let's get these prisoners along."

"How rural the river looks now!" Haines said, as they left the deserted banks.

So the Sioux went home in peace, the lieutenants, with their command of twenty, returned to the post, and all white people felt much obliged to Pounded Meat for his act of timely parental discipline— all except one white person.

Sol Kinney sauntered into the agency store one evening. "I want ten pounds of sugar," said he, "and navy plug as usual. And say, I'll take another bottle of them Seltzer fizz salts. Since I quit whiskey," he explained, "my liver's poorly."

He returned with his purchase to his cabin, and set a lamp in the window. Presently the door opened noiselessly, and Cheschapah came in.

"Maybe you got that now?" he said, in English.

The interpreter fumbled among bottles of liniment and vaseline, and from among these household remedies brought the blue one he had just bought. Cheschapah watched him like a child, following his steps round the cabin. Kinney tore a half-page from an old Sunday *World*, and poured a little heap of the salts into it. The Indian touched the heap timidly with his finger. "Maybe no good," he suggested.

"Heap good!" said the interpreter, throwing a pinch into a glass. When Cheschapah saw the water effervesce, he folded his newspaper with the salt into a tight lump, stuck the talisman into his clothes, and departed, leaving Mr. Kinney well content. He was doing his best to nourish the sinews of war, for business in the country was discouragingly slack.

Now the Crows were a tribe that had never warred with us, but only with other tribes; they had been valiant enough to steal our cattle, but sufficiently discreet to stop there; and Kinney realized that he had uphill work before him. His dearest hopes hung upon Cheschapah, in whom he thought he saw a development. From being a mere humbug, the young Indian seemed to be getting a belief in himself as something genuinely out of the common. His success in creating a party had greatly increased his conceit, and he walked with a strut, and his face was more unsettled and visionary than ever.

One clear sign of his mental change was that he no longer respected his father at all, though the lonely old man looked at him often with what in one of our race would have been tenderness. Cheschapah had been secretly maturing a plot ever since his humiliation at the crossing, and now he was ready. With his lump of newspaper carefully treasured, he came to Two Whistles.

"Now we go," he said. "We shall fight with the Piegans. I will make big medicine, so that we shall get many of their horses and women. Then Pretty Eagle will be afraid to go against me in the council. Pounded Meat whipped my horse. Pounded Meat can cut his hay without Cheschapah, since he is so strong."

But little Two Whistles wavered. "I will stay here," he ventured to say to the prophet.

"Does Two Whistles think I cannot do what I say?"

"I think you make good medicine."

"You are afraid of the Piegans."

"No, I am not afraid. I have hay the white man will pay me for. If I go, he will not pay me. If I had a father, I would not leave him." He spoke pleadingly, and his prophet bore him down by ridicule. Two Whistles believed, but he did not want to lose the money the agent was to pay for his hay. And so, not so much because he believed as because he was afraid, he resigned his personal desires.

The next morning the whole band had disappeared with Cheschapah. The agent was taken aback at this marked challenge to his authority—of course they had gone without permission—and even the old Crow chiefs held a council.

Pretty Eagle resorted to sarcasm. "He has taken his friends to the old man who makes the thunder," he said. But others did not feel sarcastic, and one observed, "Cheschapah knows more than we know."

"Let him make rain, then," said Pretty Eagle. "Let him make the white man's heart soft."

The situation was assisted by a step of the careful Kinney. He took a private journey to Junction City, through which place he expected Cheschapah to return, and there he made arrangements to have as much whiskey furnished to the Indian and his friends as they should ask for. It was certainly a good stroke of business.

The victorious raiders did return that way, and Junction City was most hospitable to their thirst. The valley of the Big Horn was resonant with their homeward yells. They swept up the river, and the agent heard them coming, and he locked his door immediately. He listened to their descent upon his fold, and he peeped out and saw them ride round the tightly shut buildings in their war-paint and the pride of utter success. They had taken booty from the Piegans, and now, knocking at the store, they demanded ammunition, proclaiming at the same time in English that Cheschapah was a big man, and knew a "big heap medicine." The agent told them from inside that they could not have any ammunition. He also informed them that he knew who they were, and that they were under arrest. This touched their primitive sense of the incongruous. On the buoyancy of the whiskey they rode round and round the store containing the agent, and then rushed away, firing shots at the buildings and shots in the air, and so gloriously home among their tribe, while the agent sent a courier packing to Fort Custer.

The young bucks who had not gone on the raid to the Piegans thronged to hear the story, and the warriors told it here and there, walking in their feathers among a knot of friends, who listened with gay exclamations of pleasure and envy. Great was Cheschapah, who had done all this! And one and another told exactly and at length how he had seen the cold water rise into foam beneath the medicine-man's hand; it could not be told too often; not every companion of Cheschapah's had been accorded the privilege of witnessing this miracle, and each narrator in his circle became a wonder himself to the bold boyish faces that surrounded him. And after the miracle he told how the Piegans had been like a flock of birds before the medicine-man. Cheschapah himself passed among the groups, alone and aloof; he spoke to none, and he looked at none, and he noted how their voices fell to whispers as he passed; his ear caught the magic words of praise and awe; he felt the gaze of admiration follow him away, and a mist rose like incense in his brain. He wandered among the scattered tepees, and turning came along the same paths again that he might once more overhear his worshippers. Great was Cheschapah!

His heart beat, a throb of power passed through his body, and "Great is Cheschapah!" said he, aloud; for the fumes of hallucination wherewith he had drugged others had begun to make him drunk also. He sought a tepee where the wife of another chief was alone, and at his light call she stood at the entrance and heard him longer than she had ever listened to him before. But she withstood the temptation that was strong in the young chief's looks and words. She did not speak much, but laughed unsteadily, and shaking her head with averted eyes, left him, and went where several women were together, and sat among them.

Cheschapah told his victory to the council, with many sentences about himself, and how his medicine had fended all hurt from the Crows. The elder chiefs sat cold.

"Ump!" said one at the close of the oration, and "Heh!" remarked another. The sounds were of assent without surprise.

"It is good," said Pretty Eagle. His voice seemed to enrage Cheschapah.

"Heh! it is always pretty good!" remarked Spotted Horse.

"I have done this too," said Pounded Meat to his son, simply. "Once, twice, three times. The Crows have always been better warriors than the Piegans."

"Have you made water boil like me?" Cheschapah said.

"I am not a medicine-man," replied his father. "But I have taken horses and squaws from the Piegans. You make good medicine, maybe; but a cup of water will not kill many white men. Can you make the river boil? Let Cheschapah make bigger medicine, so the white man shall fear him as well as the Piegans, whose hearts are well known to us."

Cheschapah scowled. "Pounded Meat shall have this," said he. "I will make medicine to-morrow, old fool!"

"Drive him from the council!" said Pretty Eagle.

"Let him stay," said Pounded Meat. "His bad talk was not to the council, but to me, and I do not count it."

But the medicine-man left the presence of the chiefs, and came to the cabin of Kinney.

"Hello!" said the white man. "Sit down."

"You got that?" said the Indian, standing.

"More water medicine? I guess so. Take a seat."

"No, not boil any more. You got that other?"

"That other, eh? Well, now, you're not going to blind them yet? What's your hurry?"

"Yes. Make blind to-morrow. Me great chief!"

A slight uneasiness passed across the bantering face of Kinney. His Seltzer salts performed what he promised, but he had mentioned another miracle, and he did not want his dupe to find him out until a war was thoroughly set agoing. He looked at the young Indian, noticing his eyes.

"What's the matter with you, anyway, Cheschapah?"

"Me great chief!" The raised voice trembled with unearthly conviction.

"Well, I guess you are. I guess you've got pretty far along," said the frontier cynic. He tilted his chair back and smiled at the child whose primitive brain he had tampered with so easily. The child stood looking at him with intent black eyes. "Better wait, Cheschapah. Come again. Medicine heap better after a while."

The Indian's quick ear caught the insincerity without understanding it. "You give me that quick!" he said, suddenly terrible.

"Oh, all right, Cheschapah. You know more medicine than me."

"Yes, I know more."

The white man brought a pot of scarlet paint, and the Indian's staring eyes contracted. Kinney took the battered cavalry sabre in his hand, and set its point in the earth floor of the cabin. "Stand back," he said, in mysterious tones, and Cheschapah shrank from the impending sorcery. Now Kinney had been to school once, in his Eastern childhood, and there had committed to memory portions of Shakespeare, Mrs. Hemans, and other poets out of a Reader. He had never forgotten a single word of any of them, and it now occurred to him that for the purposes of an incantation it would be both entertaining for himself and impressive to Cheschapah if he should recite "The Battle of Hohenlinden." He was drawing squares and circles with the point of the sabre. "No," he said to himself, "that piece won't do. He knows too much English.

Some of them words might strike him as bein' too usual, and he'd start to kill me, and spoil the whole thing. 'Munich' and 'chivalry' are snortin', but 'sun was low' ain't worth a d——. I guess—"

He stopped guessing, for the noon recess at school came in his mind, like a picture, and with it certain old-time preliminaries to the game of tag.

"'Eeny, meeny, money, my,'"

said Kinney, tapping himself, the sabre, the paint-pot, and Cheschapah in turn, one for each word. The incantation was begun. He held the sabre solemnly upright, while Cheschapah tried to control his excited breathing where he stood flattened against the wall.

"'Butter, leather, boney, stry;
Hare-bit, frost-neck,
Harrico, barrico, whee, why, whoa, whack!'

You're it, Cheschapah." After that the weapon was given its fresh coat of paint, and Cheschapah went away with his new miracle in the dark.

"He is it," mused Kinney, grave, but inwardly lively. He was one of those sincere artists who need no popular commendation. "And whoever he does catch, it won't be me," he concluded. He felt pretty sure there would be war now.

Dawn showed the summoned troops near the agency at the corral, standing to horse. Cheschapah gathered his hostiles along the brow of the ridge in the rear of the agency buildings, and the two forces watched each other across the intervening four hundred yards.

"There they are," said the agent, jumping about. "Shoot them, colonel; shoot them!"

"You can't do that, you know," said the officer, "without an order from the President, or an overt act from the Indians."

So nothing happened, and Cheschapah told his friends the white men were already afraid of him. He saw more troops arrive, water their horses in the river, form line outside the corral, and dismount. He made ready at this movement, and all Indian on-lookers scattered from the expected fight. Yet the white man staid quiet. It was issue day, but no families remained after drawing their rations. They had had no dance the night before, as was usual, and they did not linger a moment now, but came and departed with their beef and flour at once.

"I have done all this," said Cheschapah to Two Whistles.

"Cheschapah is a great man," assented the friend and follower. He had gone at once to his hay-field on his return from the Piegans, but some one had broken the little Indian's fence, and cattle were wandering in what remained of his crop.

"Our nation knows I will make a war, and therefore they do not stay here," said the medicine-man, caring nothing what Two Whistles might have suffered. "And now they will see that the white soldiers dare not fight with Cheschapah. The sun is high now, but they have not moved because I have stopped them. Do you not see it is my medicine?"

"We see it." It was the voice of the people.

But a chief spoke. "Maybe they wait for us to come."

Cheschapah answered. "Their eyes shall be made sick. I will ride among them, but they will not know it." He galloped away alone, and lifted his red sword as he sped along the ridge of the hills, showing against the sky. Below at the corral the white soldiers waited ready, and heard him chanting his war-song through the silence of the day. He turned in a long curve, and came in near the watching troops and through the agency, and then, made bolder by their motionless figures and guns held idle, he turned again and flew singing along close to the line, so they saw his eyes; and a few that had been talking low as they stood side by side fell silent at the spectacle. They could not shoot until some Indian should shoot. They watched him and the gray pony pass and return to the hostiles on the hill. Then they saw the hostiles melt away like magic. Their prophet had told them to go to their tepees and wait for the great rain he would now bring. It was noon, and the sky utterly blue over the bright valley. The sun rode a space nearer the west, and thick black clouds assembled in the mountains and descended; their shadow flooded the valley with a lake of slatish blue, and presently the sudden torrents sluiced down with flashes and the ample thunder of Montana. Thus not alone the law against our soldiers' firing the first shot in an Indian excitement, but now also the elements coincided to help the medicine-man's destiny.

Cheschapah sat in a tepee with his

father, and as the rain splashed heavily on the earth the old man gazed at the young one.

"Why do you tremble, my son? You have made the white soldier's heart soft," said Pounded Meat. "You are indeed a great man, my son."

Cheschapah rose. "Do not call me your son," said he. "That is a lie." He went out into the fury of the rain, lifting his face against the drops, and exultingly calling out at each glare of the lightning. He went to Pretty Eagle's young squaw, who held off from him no longer, but got on a horse, and the two rode into the mountains. Before the sun had set, the sky was again utterly blue, and a cool scent rose everywhere in the shining valley.

The Crows came out of their tepees, and there were the white soldiers obeying orders and going away. They watched the column slowly move across the flat land below the bluffs, where the road led down the river twelve miles to the post.

"They are afraid," said new converts. "Cheschapah's rain has made their hearts soft."

"They have not all gone," said Pretty Eagle. "Maybe he did not make enough rain." But even Pretty Eagle began to be shaken, and he heard several of his brother chiefs during the next few days openly declare for the medicine-man. Cheschapah with his woman came from the mountains, and Pretty Eagle did not dare to harm him. Then another coincidence followed that was certainly most reassuring to the war party. Some of them had no meat, and told Cheschapah they were hungry. With consummate audacity he informed them he would give them plenty at once. On the same day another timely electric storm occurred up the river, and six steers were struck by lightning.

When the officers at Fort Custer heard of this they became serious.

"If this was not the nineteenth century," said Haines, "I should begin to think the elements were deliberately against us."

"It's very careless of the weather," said Stirling. "Very inconsiderate, at such a juncture."

Yet nothing more dangerous than red-tape happened for a while. There was a beautiful quantity of investigation from Washington, and this gave the hostiles

time to increase both in faith and numbers.

Among the excited Crows only a few wise old men held out. As for Cheschapah himself, ambition and success had brought him to the weird enthusiasm of a fanatic. He was still a charlatan, but a charlatan who believed utterly in his star. He moved among his people with growing mystery, and his hapless adjutant, Two Whistles, rode with him, slaved for him, abandoned the plans he had for making himself a farm, and desiring peace in his heart, weakly cast his lot with war. Then one day there came an order from the agent to all the Indians: they were to come in by a certain fixed day. The department commander had assembled six hundred troops at the post, and these moved up the river and went into camp. The usually empty ridges, and the bottom where the road ran, filled with white and red men. Half a mile to the north of the buildings, on the first rise from the river, lay the cavalry, and some infantry above them with a howitzer, while across the level, three hundred yards opposite, along the river-bank, was the main Indian camp. Even the hostiles had obeyed the agent's order, and come in close to the troops, totally unlike hostiles in general; for Cheschapah had told them he would protect them with his medicine, and they shouted and sang all through this last night. The women joined with harsh cries and shriekings, and a scalp-dance went on, besides lesser commotions and gatherings, with the throbbing of drums everywhere. Through the sleepless din ran the barking of a hundred dogs, that herded and hurried in crowds of twenty at a time, meeting, crossing from fire to fire among the tepees. Their yelps rose to the high bench of land, summoning a horde of coyotes. These cringing nomads gathered from the desert in a tramp army, and skulking down the bluffs, sat in their outer darkness and ceaselessly howled their long shrill greeting to the dogs that sat in the circle of light. The general sent scouts to find the nature of the dance and hubbub, and these brought word it was peaceful; and in the morning another scout summoned the elder chiefs to a talk with the friend who had come from the Great Father at Washington to see them and find if their hearts were good.

"Our hearts are good," said Pretty

Eagle. "We do not want war. If you want Cheschapah, we will drive him out from the Crows to you."

"There are other young chiefs with bad hearts," said the commissioner, naming the ringleaders that were known. He made a speech, but Pretty Eagle grew sullen. "It is well," said the commissioner; "you will not help me to make things smooth, and now I step aside and the war chief will talk."

"If you want any other chiefs," said Pretty Eagle, "come and take them."

"Pretty Eagle shall have an hour and a half to think on my words," said the general. "I have plenty of men behind me to make my words good. You must send me all those Indians who fired at the agency."

The Crow chiefs returned to the council, which was apart from the war party's camp; and Cheschapah walked in among them, and after him, slowly, old Pounded Meat, to learn how the conference had gone.

"You have made a long talk with the white man," said Cheschapah. "Talk is pretty good for old men. I and the young chiefs will fight now and kill our enemies."

"Cheschapah," said Pounded Meat, "if your medicine is good, it may be the young chiefs will kill our enemies to-day. But there are other days to come, and after them still others; there are many, many days. My son, the years are a long road. The life of one man is not long, but enough to learn this thing truly: the white man will always return. There was a day on this river when the dead soldiers of Yellow Hair lay in hills, and the squaws of the Sioux warriors climbed among them with their knives. What do the Sioux warriors do now when they meet the white man on this river? Their hearts are on the ground, and they go home like children when the white man says, 'You shall not visit your friends.' My son, I thought war was good once. I have kept you from the arrows of our enemies on many trails when you were so little that my blankets were enough for both. Your mother was not here any more, and the chiefs laughed because I carried you. Oh, my son, I have seen the hearts of the Sioux broken by the white man, and I do not think war is good."

"The talk of Pounded Meat is very good," said Pretty Eagle. "If Chescha-

pah were wise like his father, this trouble would not have come to the Crows. But we could not give the white chief so many of our chiefs that he asked for to-day."

Cheschapah laughed. "Did he ask for so many? He wanted only Cheschapah, who is not wise like Pounded Meat."

"You would have been given to him," said Pretty Eagle.

"Did Pretty Eagle tell the white chief that? Did he say he would give Cheschapah? How would he give me? In one hand or two? Or would the old warrior take me to the white man's camp on the horse his young squaw left?"

Pretty Eagle raised his rifle, and Pounded Meat, quick as a boy, seized the barrel and pointed it up among the poles of the tepee, where the quiet black fire smoke was oozing out into the air. "Have you lived so long," said Pounded Meat to his ancient comrade, "and do this in the council?" His wrinkled head and hands shook, the sudden strength left him, and the rifle fell free.

"Let Pretty Eagle shoot," said Cheschapah, looking at the council. He stood calm, and the seated chiefs turned their grim eyes upon him. Certainty was in his face, and doubt in theirs. "Let him send his bullet five times—ten times. Then I will go and let the white soldiers shoot at me until they all lie dead."

"It is heavy for me," began Pounded Meat, "that my friend should be the enemy of my son."

"Tell that lie no more," said Cheschapah. "You are not my father. I have made the white man blind, and I have softened his heart with the rain. I will call the rain to-day." He raised his red sword, and there was a movement among the sitting figures. "The clouds will come from my father's place, where I have talked with him as one chief to another. My mother went into the mountains to gather berries. She was young, and the thunder-maker saw her face. He brought the black clouds, so her feet turned from home, and she walked where the river goes into the great walls of the mountain, and that day she was stricken fruitful by the lightning. You are not the father of Cheschapah." He dealt Pounded Meat a blow, and the old man fell. But the council sat still until the sound of Cheschapah's galloping horse died away. They were ready now to risk everything. Their scepticism was conquered.

"THE HEAD LAY IN THE WATER."

The medicine-man galloped to his camp of hostiles, and seeing him, they yelled and quickly finished plaiting their horses' tails. Cheschapah had accomplished his wish; he had become the prophet of all the Crows, and he led the armies of the faithful. Each man stripped his blanket off and painted his body for the fight. The forms slipped in and out of the brush, buckling their cartridge-belts, bringing their ponies, while many families struck their tepees and moved up nearer the agency. The spare horses were run across the river into the hills, and through the yelling that shifted and swept like flames along the wind the hostiles made ready and gathered, their crowds quivering with motion, and changing place and shape as more mounted riders appeared.

"Are the holes dug deep as I marked them on the earth?" said Cheschapah to Two Whistles. "That is good. We shall soon have to go into them from the great rain I will bring. Make these strong, to stay as we ride. They are good medicine, and with them the white soldiers will not see you any more than they saw me when I rode among them that day."

He had strips and capes of red flannel, and he and Two Whistles fastened them to their painted bodies.

"You will let me go with you?" said Two Whistles.

"You are my best friend," said Cheschapah, "and to-day I will take you. You shall see my great medicine when I make the white man's eyes grow sick."

The two rode forward, and one hundred and fifty followed them, bursting from their tepees like an explosion, and rushing along quickly in skirmish-line. Two Whistles rode beside his speeding prophet, and saw the red sword waving near his face, and the sun in the great still sky, and the swimming, fleeting earth. His superstition and the fierce ride put him in a sort of trance.

"The medicine is beginning," shouted Cheschapah; and at that Two Whistles saw the day grow large with terrible shining, and heard his own voice calling and could not stop it. They left the hundred and fifty behind, he knew not where or when. He saw the line of troops ahead change to separate waiting shapes of men, and their legs and arms become plain; then all the guns took clear form in lines of steady glitter. He seemed suddenly

alone far ahead of the band, but the voice of Cheschapah spoke close by his ear through the singing wind, and he repeated each word without understanding; he was watching the ground rush by, lest it might rise against his face, and all the while he felt his horse's motion under him, smooth and perpetual. Something weighed against his leg, and there was Cheschapah he had forgotten, always there at his side, veering him round somewhere. But there was no red sword waving. Then the white men must be blind already, wherever they were, and Cheschapah, the only thing he could see, sat leaning one hand on his horse's rump firing a pistol. The ground came swimming towards his eyes always, smooth and wide like a gray flood, but Two Whistles knew that Cheschapah would not let it sweep him away. He saw a horse without a rider floated out of blue smoke, and floated in again with a cracking noise; white soldiers moved in a row across his eyes, very small and clear, and broke into a blurred eddy of shapes which the flood swept away clean and empty. Then a dead white man came by on the quick flood. Two Whistles saw the yellow stripe on his sleeve; but he was gone, and there was nothing but sky and blaze, with Cheschapah's head-dress in the middle. The horse's even motion continued beneath him, when suddenly the head-dress fell out of Two Whistles' sight, and the earth returned. They were in brush, with his horse standing and breathing, and a dead horse on the ground with Cheschapah, and smoke and moving people everywhere outside. He saw Cheschapah run from the dead horse and jump on a gray pony and go. Somehow he was on the ground too, looking at a red sword lying beside his face. He stared at it a long while, then took it in his hand, still staring; all at once he rose and broke it savagely, and fell again. His faith was shivered to pieces like glass. But he got on his horse, and the horse moved away. He was looking at the blood running on his body. The horse moved always, and Two Whistles followed with his eye a little deeper gush of blood along a crease in his painted skin, noticed the flannel, and remembering the lie of his prophet, instantly began tearing the red rags from his body, and flinging them to the ground with cries of scorn. Presently he heard some voices, and soon one voice much nearer, and saw he had come to a new place, where there were white soldiers looking at him quietly. One was riding up and telling him to give up his pistol. Two Whistles got off and stood behind his horse, looking at the pistol. The white soldier came quite near, and at his voice Two Whistles moved slowly out from behind the horse, and listened to the cool words as the soldier repeated his command. The Indian was pointing his pistol uncertainly, and he looked at the soldier's coat and buttons, and the straps on the shoulders, and the bright steel sabre, and the white man's blue eyes; then Two Whistles looked at his own naked, clotted body, and turning the pistol against himself, fired it into his breast.

Far away up the river, on the right of the line, a lieutenant with two men was wading across after some hostiles that had been skirmishing with his troop. The hostiles had fallen back after some hot shooting, and had dispersed among the brush and tepees on the further shore, picking up their dead, as Indians do. It was interesting work this splashing breast-high through a river into a concealed hornets'-nest, and the lieutenant thought a little on his unfinished plans and duties in life; he noted one dead Indian left on the shore, and went steadfastly in among the half-seen tepees, rummaging and beating in the thick brush to be sure no hornets remained. Finding them gone, and their dead spirited away, he came back on the bank to the one dead Indian, who had a fine head-dress, and was still ribanded with gay red streamers of flannel, and was worth all the rest of the dead put together, and much more. The head lay in the water, and one hand held the rope of the gray pony, who stood quiet and uninterested over his fallen rider. They began carrying the prize across to the other bank, where many had now collected, among others Kinney, and the lieutenant's captain, who subsequently said, "I found the body of Cheschapah"; and,

indeed, it was a very good thing to be able to say.

"This busts the war," said Kinney to the captain, as the body was being lifted over the Little Horn. "They know he's killed, and they've all quit. I was up by the tepees near the agency just now, and I could see the hostiles jamming back home for dear life. They was chucking their rifles to the squaws, and jumping in the river—ha! ha!—to wash off their war-paint, and each son of a —— would crawl out and sit innercint in the family blanket his squaw had ready. If you was to go there now, cap'n, you'd find just a lot of harmless Injuns eatin' supper like all the year round. Let me help you, boys with that carcass."

Kinney gave a hand to the lieutenant and boys of G troop, First United States Cavalry, and they lifted Cheschapah up the bank. In the tilted position of the body the cartridge-belt slid a little, and a lump of newspaper fell into the stream. Kinney watched it open and float away with a momentary effervescence. The dead medicine-man was laid between the white and red camps, that all might see he could be killed like other people; and this wholesome discovery brought the Crows to terms at once. Pretty Eagle had displayed a flag of truce, and now he surrendered the guilty chiefs whose hearts had been bad. Every one came where the dead prophet lay to get a look at him. For a space of hours Pretty Eagle and the many other Crows he had deceived rode by in single file, striking him with their whips; after them came a young squaw, and she also lashed the upturned face.

This night was untroubled at the agency, and both camps and the valley lay quiet in the peaceful dark. Only Pounded Meat, alone on the top of a hill, mourned for his son; and his wailing voice sounded through the silence until the new day came. Then the general had him stopped and brought in, for it might be that the old man's noise would unsettle the Crows again.

THE HOUSEWIFE
by James Branch Cabell

HERE we have to do with the fifth tale of the Dizain of Queens. I abridge, at discretion, since the scantiness of our leisure is balanced by the prolixity of our author; the result is that to the Norman cleric appertains whatever the tale may have of merit, whereas what you find distasteful in it you must impute to my delinquencies in skill rather than in volition.

One August day in the year of grace 1346 (here you overtake Nicolas midcourse) Master John Copeland, secretary to the Queen, brought his mistress the unhandsome news that David Bruce had invaded her realm with forty thousand Scots to back him. He found the Queen in company with the kingdom's arbitress,—Dame Catherine de Salisbury, whom King Edward, third of that name to reign in Britain and now warring in France, very notoriously adored and obeyed. These two heard him out. Already Northumberland, Westmoreland, and Durham were the broken meats of King David.

The countess then exclaimed: "Let me pass, sir. My place is not here."

Philippa said, half hopefully, "Do you forsake Sire Edward, Catherine?"

"Madame and Queen," the countess answered, "in this world every man must scratch his own back. My lord has entrusted to me his castle of Wark, his fiefs in Northumberland. These, I hear, are being laid waste. Were there a thousand men-at-arms left in England I would say fight. As it is, our men are yonder in France and the island is defenceless. Accordingly I ride for the north to make what terms I may with the King of Scots."

Now you might have seen the Queen's eyes flame. "Undoubtedly," said she, "in her lord's absence it is the wife's part to defend his belongings. And my lord's fief is England. I bid you Godspeed, Catherine." And when the countess was gone, Philippa turned, her round face all flushed. "She betrays him! she compounds with the Scot! Mother of Christ, let me not fail!"

"A ship must be despatched to bid Sire Edward return," said the secretary. "Otherwise all England is lost."

"Not so, John Copeland! Let Sire Edward conquer in France, if such be the Trinity's will. Always he has dreamed of that, and if I bade him return now he would be vexed."

"The disappointment of the King," John Copeland considered, "is a lesser evil than allowing all of us to be butchered."

"Not to me, John Copeland," the Queen said.

Now came many lords into the chamber, seeking Madame Philippa. "We must make peace with the Scottish rascal!— England is lost! A ship must be sent entreating succor of Sire Edward!" So they shouted.

"Messieurs," said Queen Philippa, "who commands here? Am I, then, some woman of the town?"

Ensued a sudden silence. Now the Marquis of Falmouth stepped from the throng. "Pardon, highness. But the occasion is urgent."

"The occasion is very urgent, my lord," the Queen assented. "Therefore it is my will that to-morrow one and all your men be mustered at Blackheath. We will take the field without delay against the King of Scots."

The riot began anew. "Madness!" they shouted; "lunar madness! We can do nothing until the King return with our army!"

"In his absence," the Queen said, "I command here."

"You are not Regent," the marquis said. Then he cried, "This is the Regent's affair!"

"Let the Regent be fetched," Dame

Philippa said, very quietly. Presently they brought in her son Lionel, now a boy of eight years, and Regent, in name at least, of England.

Both the Queen and the marquis held papers. "Highness," Falmouth began, "for reasons of state, which I need not here explain, this document requires your signature. It is an order that a ship be despatched in pursuit of the King. Your highness may remember the pony you admired yesterday?" The marquis smiled ingratiatingly. "Just here, your highness—a cross-mark."

"The dappled one?" said the Regent; "and all for making a little mark?" The boy jumped for the pen.

"Lionel," said the Queen, "you are Regent of England, but you are also my son. If you sign that paper, you will beyond doubt get the pony, but you will not, I think, care to ride him. You will not care to sit down at all, Lionel."

The Regent considered. "Thank you very much, my lord," he said, in the ultimate, "but I do not like ponies any more. Do I sign here, mother?"

Philippa handed the marquis a subscribed order to muster the English forces at Blackheath; then another, closing the English ports. "My lords," the Queen said, "this boy is the King's vicar. In defying him you defy the King. Yes, Lionel, you have fairly earned a pot of jam for supper."

Then Falmouth went away without speaking. That night assembled at his lodgings, by appointment, Viscount Heringaud, Adam Frere, the Marquis of Orme, Lord Stourton, the Earls of Ufford and Gage, and Sir John Biddulph. These seven found a long table there littered with pens and parchment; to the rear of it, a lackey behind him, sat the Marquis of Falmouth, meditative over a cup of Bordeaux.

Presently Falmouth said: "My friends, in creating our womankind the Eternal Father was beyond doubt actuated by laudable and cogent reasons, so that I can merely lament my inability to fathom these reasons. I shall obey the Queen faithfully, since if I did otherwise Sire Edward would have my head off within a day of his return. In consequence I do not consider it convenient to oppose his vicar. To-morrow I shall assemble the tatters of troops which remain to us, and to-morrow we march northward to inevitable defeat. To-night I am sending a courier into Northumberland. He is an obliging person and would convey—to cite an instance—eight letters quite as blithely as one."

Each man glanced furtively about him. England was in a panic by this and knew itself to lie before the Bruce defenceless. The all-powerful Countess of Salisbury had compounded with King David; now Falmouth, their generalissimo, compounded. What the devil! loyalty was a sonorous word, and so was patriotism, but, after all, one had estates in the north.

The seven wrote in silence. When they had ended, I must tell you that Falmouth gathered the letters into a heap, and without glancing at the superscriptures, handed them to the attendant lackey. "For the courier," he said.

The fellow left the apartment. Presently there was a clatter of hoofs without, and Falmouth rose. He was a gaunt, terrible old man, gray-bearded, and having high eyebrows that twitched and jerked.

"We have saved our precious skins," said he. "Hey, you—you Falmouths! I commend your common sense, messieurs, and request you to withdraw. Even a damned rogue such as I has need of a cleaner atmosphere when he would breathe." The seven went away without further speech.

They narrate that next day the troops marched for Durham, where the Queen took up her quarters. The Bruce had pillaged and burned his way to a place called Beaurepair, within three miles of the city. He sent word to the Queen that if her men were willing to come forth from the town he would abide and give them battle.

She replied that she accepted his offer, and that her barons would gladly risk their lives for the realm of their lord the King. The Bruce grinned and kept silence, since he had in his pocket letters from nine-tenths of them protesting they would do nothing of the sort.

There is comedy here. On one side you have a horde of half-naked savages, a shrewd master holding them in leash till the moment be auspicious, on the other, a housewife at the head of a tiny force lieutenanted by perjurers, by men already purchased. God knows the dreams she had of impossible victories, what time her barons trafficked in secret with the Bruce. On the Saturday before Michaelmas, when the opposing armies marshalled in the Bishop's Park, at Auckland, it is recorded that not a captain on either side believed the day to be pregnant with battle. There would be a decent counterfeit of resistance; afterward the little English army would vanish pellmell, and the Bruce would be master of the island. The farce was prearranged, the actors therein were letter-perfect.

That morning at daybreak John Copeland came to the Queen's tent, and informed her quite frankly how matters stood. He had been drinking overnight with Adam Frere and the Earl of Gage, and after the third bottle had found them candid. "Madame and Queen, we are betrayed. The Marquis of Falmouth, our commander, is inexplicably smitten with a fever. He will not fight to-day. Not one of your lords will fight to-day." He laid bare such part of the scheme as yesterday's conviviality had made familiar. "Therefore I counsel retreat. Let the King be summoned out of France."

But Queen Philippa shook her head, as she cut up squares of toast and dipped them in milk for the Regent's breakfast. "Sire Edward would be vexed. He has always intended to conquer France. I shall visit the Marquis as soon as Lionel is fed—do you know, John Copeland, I am anxious about Lionel; he is irritable and coughed five times during the night—and I will arrange this affair."

She found the marquis in bed, groaning, the coverlet pulled up to his chin. "Pardon, highness," said Falmouth, "but I am an ill man. I cannot rise from this couch."

"I do not question the gravity of your disorder," the Queen retorted, "since it is well known that the same illness brought about the death of Iscariot. Nevertheless, I bid you get up and lead our troops against the Scot."

Now the hand of the marquis veiled his countenance. But "I am an ill man," he muttered, doggedly. "I cannot rise from this couch."

There was a silence.

"My lord," the Queen presently began, "without is an army prepared—ay, and

able—to defend our England. The one requirement of this army is a leader. Afford them that, my lord—ah, I know that our peers are sold to the Bruce, yet our yeomen at least are honest. Give them, then, a leader, and they cannot but conquer, since God also is honest and incorruptible. Pardieu! a woman might lead these men, and lead them to victory!"

Falmouth answered: "I am an ill man. I cannot rise from this couch."

You saw that Philippa was not beautiful. You perceived that to the contrary she was superb, saw the soul of the woman aglow, gilding the mediocrities of color and curve as a conflagration does a hovel.

"There is no man left in England," said the Queen, "since Sire Edward went into France. Praise God, I am his wife." And she was gone without flurry.

Through the tent-flap Falmouth beheld all which followed. The English force was marshalled in four divisions, each commanded by a bishop and a baron. You could see the men fidgeting, puzzled by the delay; as a wind goes about a cornfield, vague rumors were going about those wavering spears. Toward them rode Philippa, upon a white palfrey, alone and quite tranquil. Her eight lieutenants were now gathered about her in voluble protestation, and she heard them out. Afterward she spoke, without any particular violence, as one might order a strange cur from his room. Then the Queen rode on, as though these eight muttering persons had ceased to be of interest, and reined up before her standard-bearer, and took the standard in her hand. She began again to speak, and immediately the army was in an uproar; the barons were clustering behind her, in stealthy groups of two or three whisperers each; all were in the greatest amazement and knew not what to do; but the army was shouting the Queen's name.

"Now is England shamed," said Falmouth, "since a woman alone dares to encounter the Scot. She will lead them into battle,—and by God! there is no braver person under heaven than yonder Dutch Frau! Friend David, I perceive that your venture is lost, for those men would within the moment follow her to storm hell if she desired it."

He meditated and more lately shrugged. "And so would I," said Falmouth.

A little afterward a gaunt and haggard old man, bareheaded and very hastily dressed, reined his horse by the Queen's side. "Madame and Queen," said Falmouth, "I rejoice that my recent illness is departed. I shall, by God's grace, on this day drive the Bruce from England."

Philippa was not given to verbiage. Doubtless she had her emotions now, but none were visible upon the honest face; yet one hand had fallen into the big-veined hand of Falmouth. "I welcome back the gallant gentleman of yesterday. I was about to lead your army, my friend, since there was no one else to do it, but I was hideously afraid. At bottom every woman is a coward."

"You were afraid to do it," said the marquis, "but you were going to do it, because there was no one else to do it! Ho! madame, had I an army of such cowards I would drive the Scot not past the Border but to the Orkneys."

The Queen then said, "But you are unarmed."

"Highness," he replied, "it is surely apparent that I, who have played the traitor to two monarchs within the same day, cannot with either decency or comfort survive that day." He turned upon the lords and bishops twittering about his horse's tail. "You merchandise, get back to your stations, and if there was ever an honest woman in any of your families, the which I doubt, contrive to get yourselves killed this day, as I mean to do, in the cause of the honestest and bravest woman our time has known." Presently the English forces marched toward Neville's Cross.

Philippa returned to her pavilion and inquired for John Copeland. He had ridden off, she was informed, armed, in company with five of her immediate retainers. She considered this strange, but made no comment.

You picture her, perhaps, as spending the morning in prayer, in beatings upon her breast, and in lamentations. Philippa did nothing of the sort. As you have heard, she considered her cause to be so clamantly just that to expatiate to the Holy Father upon its merits were an impertinence; it was not conceivable that He would fail her; and in any event, she had in hand a deal of sewing that required immediate attention. Accordingly she set-

tled down to her needlework, while the Regent of England leaned his head against her knee, and his mother told him that agelong tale of Lord Huon, who in a wood near Babylon encountered the King of Faëry, and subsequently stripped the atrocious Emir of both beard and daughter. All this the industrious woman narrated in a low and pleasant voice, while the wide-eyed Regent attended and at the proper intervals gulped his cough-mixture.

You must know that about noon Master John Copeland came into the tent. "We have conquered," he said. "Ho! Madame Philippa, there was never a victory more complete. The Scottish army is not beaten but demolished."

"I rejoice," the Queen said, looking up from her sewing, "that we have conquered, though in nature I expected nothing else. Oh, horrible!" She sprang to her feet with a cry of anguish: and here in little you have the entire woman; the victory of her armament was to her a thing of course, since her cause was just, whereas the loss of two front teeth by John Copeland was a genuine calamity.

He drew her toward the tent-flap, which he opened. Without was a mounted knight, in full panoply, his arms bound behind him, surrounded by the Queen's five retainers. "In the rout I took him," said John Copeland; "though, as my mouth witnesses, I did not find David Bruce a tractable prisoner."

"Is that, then, the King of Scots?" Philippa demanded, as she mixed salt and water for a mouth-wash; and presently: "Sire Edward should be pleased, I think. Will he not love me a little now, John Copeland?"

John Copeland lifted either plump hand toward his lips. "He could not choose," John Copeland said,—"madame, he could no more choose but love you than I could choose."

Philippa sighed. Afterward she bade John Copeland rinse his gums and then take his prisoner to Falmouth. He told her the marquis was dead, slain by the Knight of Liddesdale. "That is a pity," the Queen said; and more lately: "There is left alive in England but one man to whom I dare entrust the keeping of the King of Scots. My barons are sold to him; if I retain David by me, one or another lord will engineer his escape within the week, and Sire Edward will be vexed. Yet listen, John—" She unfolded her plan.

"I have long known," he said, when she had done, "that in all the world there was no lady more lovable. Twenty years I have loved you, my Queen, and yet it is but to-day I perceive that in all the world there is no lady more wise than you."

Philippa touched his cheek, maternally. "Foolish boy! You tell me the King of Scots has an arrow-wound in his nose? I think a bread-poultice would be best." . . . . So then he left the tent and presently rode away with his company.

Philippa saw that the Regent had his dinner, and afterward mounted her white palfrey and set out for the battle-field. There the Earl of Ufford, as second in command, received her with great courtesy. God had shown to her Majesty's servants most singular favor: despite the calculations of reasonable men—to which, she might remember, he had that morning taken the liberty to assent—some fifteen thousand Scots were slain. True, her gallant general was no longer extant, though this was scarcely astounding when one considered the fact that he had voluntarily entered the mêlée quite unarmed. A touch of age, perhaps; Falmouth was always an eccentric man; and in any event, as epilogue, he congratulated the Queen that—by blind luck, he was forced to concede—her worthy secretary had made a prisoner of the Scottish King. Doubtless, Master Copeland was an estimable scribe, and yet— Ah, yes, he quite followed her Majesty—beyond doubt, the wardage of a king was an honor not lightly to be conferred. Oh yes, he understood; her Majesty desired that the office should be given some person of rank. And pardie! her Majesty was in the right. Eh? said the Earl of Ufford.

Intently gazing into the man's shallow eyes, Philippa assented. Master Copeland had acted unwarrantably in riding off with his captive. Let him be sought at once. She dictated a letter to Ufford's secretary, which informed John Copeland that he had done what was not agreeable in purloining her prisoner without leave. Let him sans delay deliver the King to her good friend the Earl of Ufford.

To Ufford this was satisfactory, since he intended that once in his possession David Bruce should escape forthwith. The letter, I repeat, suited him in its tiniest syllable, and the single difficulty was to convey it to John Copeland, for as to his whereabouts neither Ufford nor any one else had the least notion.

This was immaterial, however, for they narrate that next day a letter signed with John Copeland's name was found pinned to the front of Ufford's tent. I cite a passage therefrom: "I will not give up my royal prisoner to a woman or a child, but only to my own lord, Sire Edward, for to him I have sworn allegiance, and not to any woman. Yet you may tell the Queen she may depend on my taking excellent care of King David. I have poulticed his nose, as she directed."

Here was a nonplus, not perhaps without its comical side. Two great realms had met in battle, and the king of one of them had vanished like a soap-bubble. Philippa was in a rage,—you could see that both by her demeanor and by the indignant letters she dictated; true, they could not be delivered, since they were all addressed to John Copeland. Meanwhile, Scotland was in despair, whereas the English barons now within that realm were in a frenzy, because, however willing you may be, you cannot well betray a kingdom to an unlocateable enemy. The circumstances were unique and they remained unchanged for three feverish weeks.

We will now return to affairs in France, where on the day of the Nativity, as night gathered about Calais, John Copeland came unheralded to the quarters of King Edward, then besieging that city. Master Copeland entreated audience, and got it readily enough, since there was no man alive whom Edward more cordially desired to lay his fingers upon.

Within he found the King, a stupendous person, blond and incredibly big. With him were a smirking Italian, that Almerigo di Pavia who afterward betrayed him, and a lean soldier whom Master Copeland recognized as John Chandos. These three were drawing up an account of the recent victory at Créçi, to be forwarded to all mayors and sheriffs in England, with a cogent postscript as to the King's incidental and immediate need of money.

Now King Edward sat leaning far back in his chair, a hand on either hip, and his eyes narrowing as he regarded Master Copeland. Had the Brabanter flinched, the King would probably have hanged him within the next ten minutes; finding his gaze unwavering, the King was pleased. Here was a novelty; most people blinked quite genuinely under the scrutiny of those fierce big eyes, which were blue and cold and of an astounding lustre, gemlike as the March sea.

The King rose with a jerk and took John Copeland's hand. "Ha!" he grunted, "I welcome the squire who by his valor has captured the King of Scots. And now, my man, what have you done with Davie?"

John Copeland answered: "Highness, you may find him at your convenience safely locked in Bamborough Castle. Meanwhile, I entreat you, sire, do not take it amiss if I did not surrender King David to the orders of my lady Queen, for I hold my lands of you, and not of her, and my oath is to you, and not to her, unless indeed by choice."

"John," the King sternly replied, "the loyal service you have done us is considerable, whereas your excuse for kidnapping Davie is a farce. Hey, Almerigo, do you and Chandos avoid the chamber! I have something in private with this fellow." When they had gone, the King sat down and composedly said, "Now tell me the truth, John Copeland."

"Sire," he began, "it is necessary you first understand I bear a letter from Madame Philippa—"

"Then read it," said the King. "Heart of God! have I an eternity to waste on you Brabanters!"

John Copeland read aloud, while the King trifled with a pen, half negligent, and in part attendant. Read, John Copeland:

"MY DEAR LORD,—I recommend me to your lordship with soul and body and all my poor might, and with all this I thank you, as my dear lord, dearest and best beloved of all earthly lords I protest to me, and thank you, my dear lord, with all this as I say before. Your comfortable letter came to me on St. Gregory's day, and I was never so glad as when I heard by your letter that ye were strong enough

in Ponthieu by the grace of God for to keep you from your enemies. Among them I estimate Madame Catherine of Salisbury, who would have betrayed you to the Scot. And, dear lord, if it be pleasing to your high lordship that as soon as ye may that I might hear of your gracious speed, which may God Almighty continue and increase, I shall be glad, and also if ye do each night chafe your feet with a rag of woollen stuff. And, my dear lord, if it like you for to know of my fare, John Copeland will acquaint you concerning the Bruce his capture, and the syrup he brings for our son Lord Edward's cough, and the great malice-workers in these shires which would have so despitefully wrought to you, and of the manner of taking it after each meal. I am lately informed that Madame Catherine is now at Stirling with Robert Stewart and has lost all her good looks. God is invariably gracious to His servants. Farewell, my dear lord, and may the Holy Trinity keep you from your adversaries and ever send me comfortable tidings of you. Written at York, in the Castle, on St. Gregory's day last past, by your own poor

PHILIPPA.

"To my true lord."

"H'm!" said the King; "and now give me the entire story."

John Copeland obeyed. I must tell you that early in the narrative Edward arose and, with a sob, strode toward a window. "Catherine!" he said. He remained motionless what time Master Copeland went on without any manifest emotion. When he had ended, King Edward said, "And where is Madame de Salisbury now?"

At this the Brabanter went mad. As a leopard springs he leapt upon the King, and grasping him by either shoulder, shook him as one punishing a child.

"Now by the splendor of God—!" King Edward began, very terrible in his wrath. He saw that John Copeland held a dagger to his breast, and shrugged. "Well, my man, you perceive I am defenceless. Therefore make an end, you dog."

"First you will hear me out," John Copeland said.

"It would appear," the King retorted, "that I have little choice."

At this time John Copeland began:

" Sire, you are the greatest monarch our race has known. England is yours, France is yours, conquered Scotland lies prostrate at your feet. To-day there is no man in all the world who possesses a tithe of your glory; yet twenty years ago Madame Philippa first beheld you and loved you, an outcast, an exiled, empty-pocketed prince. Twenty years ago the love of Madame Philippa, great Count William's daughter, got for you the armament wherewith England was regained. Twenty years ago, but for Madame Philippa you had died naked in some ditch."

" Go on," the King said, presently.

" And afterward you took a fancy to reign in France. You learned then that we Brabanters are a frugal people : Madame Philippa was wealthy when she married you, and twenty years had but quadrupled her fortune. She gave you every penny of it that you might fit out this expedition; now her very crown is in pawn at Ghent. In fine, the love of Madame Philippa gave you France as lightly as one might bestow a toy upon a child who whined for it."

The King fiercely said, " Go on."

" Eh, sire, I intend to. You left England undefended that you might posture a little in the eyes of Europe. And meanwhile a woman preserves England, a woman gives you all Scotland as a gift, and in return demands nothing—God ha' mercy on us !—save that you nightly chafe your feet with a bit of woollen. You hear of it—and ask, ' Where is Madame de Salisbury?' Here beyond doubt is the cock of Æsop's fable," snarled John Copeland, " who unearthed a gem and grumbled that his diamond was not a grain of corn."

" You will be hanged ere dawn," the King replied, and yet by this one hand had screened his face. " Meanwhile spit out your venom."

" I say to you, then," John Copeland continued, " that to-day you are the master of Europe. That but for this woman whom for twenty years you have neglected you would to-day be mouldering in some pauper's grave. Eh, without question, you most magnanimously loved that shrew of Salisbury ! because you fancied the color of her eyes, Sire Edward, and admired the angle between her nose and her forehead. I say to you,"—now the man's rage was monstrous,—" I say to you go home to your wife, the source of all your glory ! sit at her feet ! and let her teach you what love is !" He flung away the dagger. " There you have the truth. Now summon your attendants and have me hanged."

The King gave no movement. " You have been bold," he said at last.

" You have been far bolder, sire. For twenty years you have dared to flout that love which is God made manifest as His one heritage to His children."

King Edward sat in meditation for a long while. He rose, and flung back his big head as a lion might. " John, the loyal service you have done us and our esteem for your valor are so great that they may well serve you as an excuse. May shame fall on those who bear you any ill-will ! You will now return home, and take your prisoner, the King of Scotland, and deliver him to my wife, to do with as she may elect. You will convey to her my entreaty—not my orders, John—that she come to me here at Calais. As remuneration for this evening's insolence, I assign lands as near your house as you can choose them to the value of £500 a year for you and for your heirs."

You must know that John Copeland fell upon his knees before King Edward. " Sire—" he stammered.

But the King raised him. " Nay," he said, " you are the better man. Were there any equity in Fate, John Copeland, she would have loved you, not me. As it is, I shall strive to prove not altogether unworthy of my fortune. Go, then, John Copeland—go, my squire, and bring me back my Queen."

Presently he heard John Copeland singing without. And through that instant was youth returned to Edward Plantagenet, and all the scents and shadows and faint sounds of Valenciennes on that ancient night when a tall girl came to him, running, stumbling in her haste to bring him kingship. Now at last he understood the heart of Philippa.

" Let me live !" the King prayed; " O Eternal Father, let me live a little while that I may make atonement !" And meantime John Copeland sang without and the Brabanter's heart was big with joy.